ESSENTIALS OF
SOCIOLOGY

fifth edition

Recent Sociology Titles
from W. W. Norton

To learn more about Norton Sociology, please visit wwnorton.com/soc.

ESSENTIALS OF
SOCIOLOGY

fifth edition

Anthony Giddens

LONDON SCHOOL OF ECONOMICS

Mitchell Duneier

CITY UNIVERSITY OF NEW YORK
GRADUATE CENTER

PRINCETON UNIVERSITY

Richard P. Appelbaum

UNIVERSITY OF CALIFORNIA,
SANTA BARBARA

Deborah Carr

RUTGERS UNIVERSITY

W. W. NORTON & COMPANY, INC.

New York • London

W. W. NORTON & COMPANY has been independent since its founding in 1923, when Wiliam Warder Norton and Mary D. Herter Norton first published lectures delivered at the People's Institute, the adult education division of New York City's Cooper Union. The firm soon expanded its program beyond the Institute, publishing books by celebrated academics from America and abroad. By midcentury, the two major pillars of Norton's publishing program—trade books and college texts—were firmly established. In the 1950s, the Norton family transferred control of the company to its employees, and today—with a staff of four hundred and a comparable number of trade, college, and professional titles published each year—W. W. Norton & Company stands as the largest and oldest publishing house owned wholly by its employees.

Editor: Sasha Levitt
Associate Editor: Nicole Sawa
Assistant Editor: Thea Goodrich
Project Editor: Diane Cipollone
Managing Editor, College: Marian Johnson
Managing Editor, College Digital Media: Kim Yi
Production Manager: Vanessa Nuttry
Media Editor: Eileen Connell
Associate Media Editor: Laura Musich
Marketing Manager: Julia Hall
Design Director: Hope Miller Goodell
Photo Editor: Stephanie Romeo
Permissions Manager: Megan Jackson
Information Graphics Design: Kiss Me I'm Polish LLC, New York
Composition: Graphic World
Manufacturing: Courier-Kendallville

The text of this book is composed in Sentinel with the display set in Gotham.

Library of Congress Cataloging-in-Publication Data

Giddens, Anthony.
    Essentials of sociology / Anthony Giddens, Mitchell Duneier, Richard P. Appelbaum, Deborah Carr. -- Fifth edition.
        pages cm
    Revised edition of: Essentials of sociology / Anthony Giddens ... [et al.]. 4th ed.
    Includes bibliographical references and index.
    ISBN 978-0-393-93745-9 (pbk. : alk. paper)
    1. Sociology. I. Title.
    HM585.G52 2015
    301--dc23

                    2014027695

W. W. Norton & Company, Inc., 500 Fifth Avenue, New York, N.Y. 10110
W. W. Norton & Company, Ltd., Castle House, 75/76 Wells Street, London W1T 3QT
wwnorton.com

1 2 3 4 5 6 7 8 9 0

contents

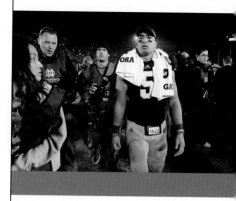

Contents   vii

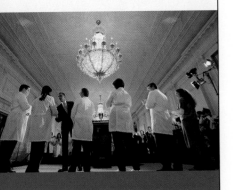

CHAPTER 14 The Sociology of the Body: Health, Illness, and Sexuality 430

CHAPTER 15 Urbanization, Population, and the Environment 464

CHAPTER 16 Globalization in a Changing World 500

preface

We believe that sociology plays an essential role in modern intellectual culture and occupies a central place within the social sciences. We have aimed to write a book that merges classic sociological theories with up-to-the-minute social issues that interest sociologists today. We also believe that sociologists must use rigorous research methods in order to study and understand human behavior. We highlight findings from ethnographic studies to document the hows and whys of social behavior, and also present current statistical data to document important social trends. We aim to present material in a "fair and balanced" way. Although each of the authors has his or her own perspective on social theories, methods, and social policy, we have worked hard to ensure that our treatment is unbiased and non-partisan. We strive to present the most complete picture of sociology possible. Given the vast array of topics encompassed by sociology, however, we made difficult choices about what the most essential topics in sociology are today. We hope readers are engaged, intrigued, and occasionally inspired by the ideas presented in this book.

ABOUT THE ESSENTIALS EDITION

The Fifth Edition of *Essentials of Sociology* is based on the Ninth Edition of our best-selling text, *Introduction to Sociology*. We created the Essentials Edition for instructors and students who are looking for a briefer book that can fit into a compressed academic schedule. We have reduced the length of the book by roughly one-third, and we reduced the number of chapters from twenty to sixteen. We cut selected topics to focus the chapters on the core ideas of sociology, while still retaining the themes that have made the text a successful teaching tool.

MAJOR THEMES

The book is constructed around four basic themes that provide its character. The newest theme is applying sociology to everyday life. Sociological thinking enables self-understanding, which in turn can be focused back on an improved understanding of the social world. Studying sociology can be a liberating experience: It expands our sympathies and imagination, opens up new perspectives on the sources of our own behavior, and creates an awareness of cultural settings different from our own. Sociological ideas challenge dogma, teach appreciation of cultural variety, and allow us insight into the working of social institutions. At a more practical level, the text shows how sociological concepts are used every day by American workers ("Making Sociology Work" boxes), how technology affects our daily experiences (new "Digital Life" sections), and how societal trends vary from place to place ("Globalization by the Numbers" full-page infographics).

Our second theme is inequalities. Throughout the text, we highlight that important resources—whether education, health, income, or social support—are not fairly or evenly distributed to all individuals. We highlight the ways that gender, race, social class, and age shape our daily life in the United States. We also pay keen attention to global inequalities, and reveal how differences in economic and even natural resources throughout the world powerfully influence even very personal experiences—including health, religion, and relationships.

A third theme of the book is that of social and historical context. Sociology was born of the transformations that wrenched the industrializing social order of the West away from the lifestyles characteristic of earlier societies. The pace of social change has continued to accelerate, and it is possible that we now stand on the threshold of transitions as significant as those that occurred in the late eighteenth and nineteenth centuries. Sociology has the prime responsibility for charting the transformations of our past and for grasping the major lines of development taking place today. Our understanding of the past also contributes to our understanding of institutions in the present and future.

The fourth fundamental theme of the book is globalization. For far too long, sociology has been dominated by the view that societies can be studied as independent entities. But even in the past, societies never really existed in isolation. Today we can see a clear acceleration in processes of global integration. This is obvious, for example, in the expansion of international trade across the world. The emphasis on globalization also connects closely with the weight given to the interdependence of the industrialized and developing worlds today.

Despite these interconnections, however, societies have their own distinctive attributes, traditions, and experiences. Sociology cannot be taught solely by understanding the institutions of any one particular society. While we have slanted our discussion toward the United States, we have also balanced it with a rich variety of materials drawn from other regions—especially those undergoing rapid social change, such as the Middle East, Asia, Africa, and Eastern Europe. The book also includes much more material on developing countries than has been usual in introductory texts.

All of the chapters in the book have been updated and revised to reflect the most recent available data. Each chapter opens with a contemporary news event or social trend—ranging from the most local and seemingly trivial (like a young boy's choice of Halloween costume) to the most global and profound (such as the catastrophic earthquakes in Haiti and Japan). These events are used to motivate and explain the key sociological concepts, themes, and studies that are elaborated throughout the text. Other substantive changes include:

Chapter 1 (Sociology: Theory and Method) opens by recounting the recent suicides of middle-schooler Devin Brown and fifteen-year-old Audrie Pott, both victims of bullying, some of which took place online. These timely and tragic deaths are used to illustrate key principles of sociological theory and research methods. Data on college students' goals and values are revised to reflect the most recent studies, and the discussion of bullying focuses more on its growing cyber side. The Digital Life box "Bullying Goes Viral" speaks to cyberbullying, apps like Ugly Meter and Back Off Bully, and the "It Gets Better" project.

Chapter 2 (Culture and Society) begins with a discussion of the plight of Pussy Riot, the masked punk rock protest band that has gained an international following for its condemnation of Russia's stances on issues of LGBT and women's rights and its challenges to the Russian Orthodox Church. This segues into musing on how the Internet has helped foster such acts of revolution prompted by clashes of cultural values. The chapter also includes updated data on Internet usage throughout the world and a brief look at *biological determinism*, a new key term. The Digital Life box "The Secret Power of Cultural Norms and Values" talks about the highly popular PostSecret website, which showcases secrets sent anonymously on one side of a postcard by people from all walks of life. The infographic about global Internet connectivity has been re-designed and its data updated.

Chapter 3 (Socialization, the Life Course, and Aging) now includes a discussion of fitness video games' effect on kids and the story of two parents who decided, to the anger of many, not to reveal their baby's sex. It outlines five benchmarks of adulthood and shows that such a transition from adolescence has been delayed in recent years, and how definitions of "middle-aged" are changing as well. New data in this chapter involves the spousal situations of older men and women. The Digital Life box "Projecting Your Future" looks at apps like AgingBooth, Aging Album, and Age My Face, which allow users to see what old age has in store for them. To better compare life course transitions among different cultures, the new Globalization by the Numbers infographic compares the mean age of first sexual experience, first marriage, and first childbirth in ten countries.

Chapter 4 (Social Interaction and Everyday Life in the Age of the Internet) demonstrates, through the story of "catfished" football star Manti Te'o and his faked online girlfriend, the ways that social networking sites have drastically changed social interaction. The concepts of microsociology and agency are examined and the actions of impression management and eye contact are studied more in-depth. Highly relevant additions to this chapter are new discussions of WikiLeaks and street harassment. The Digital Life box "Dating and Mating Online" discusses online dating apps and websites like Tinder and Skout, and the pros and cons thereof. An all-new Globalization by the Numbers infographic highlights cell phone usage across the world.

Chapter 5 (Groups, Networks, and Organizations) begins with an account of the lethal hazing of drum major Robert Champion by fellow members of the marching band of Florida A&M University. This story introduces the sociological concept of "group," which the band's actions clearly demonstrate. Similarly, this chapter points out the groupthink involved in the Penn State sexual abuse case. The new policies of Yahoo CEO Marissa Mayer are touched on to show that women in the corporate world are still on the outside of the male network, and the company culture of Google is described to show its focus on innovation and teamwork. Statistics on Internet usage and telecommuting have been updated, along with data on citizens' trust in the government following the NSA revelations of 2013. The Digital Life box "Fund-Raising Goes Online" details the success of crowdfunding apps and websites like Kickstarter and Watsi. The new infographic for this chapter highlights nonprofit work and rates of volunteering in selected countries.

Chapter 6 (Conformity, Deviance, and Crime) opens with the tragic story of the lethal shooting of Trayvon Martin in February 2012 by George Zimmerman. A racially charged event, Martin's death and Zimmerman's subsequent trial and acquittal quickly became the center of a reinvigorated discussion of race relations and the "stand your ground" self-defense statute in America. This illuminates current issues of crime and deviance, including what deviant behavior is, why people commit crimes, and what the statistical profiles of criminals and crime victims look like. Also added is more context about gun ownership and hate crimes in the United States, plus a deeper look at the gender gap and age range of American criminals. The chapter refines its treatment of the concepts of values and self-perception. Additionally, it updates statistics on imprisonment in the United States and throughout the world, as well as the rates of violent crime, crime reporting, victimization, and death penalty usage in the United States. The section on corporate crime now highlights the devastation collapse of Rana Plaza. The Digital Life box "The New War on Crime" talks about crime detection and reporting apps that can let users report crimes, submit tips to police, or even determine the location of registered sex offenders. Data for the "Incarceration Rates" infographic has also been updated.

Chapter 7 (Stratification, Class, and Inequality) opens with a discussion of Liz Murray's autobiography *Breaking Night* (2010), which recounts how Liz went from being a young homeless girl in the Bronx to a Harvard-educated graduate student. Her story is used to convey the concepts and patterns of social mobility in the United States and elsewhere. This fifth edition incorporates more attention to issues of inequality as manifested in the growing gap between America's rich and poor, illustrated by rates of college attendance and subprime home loans, the Occupy Wall Street movement, and the demographics of the middle class and working poor. New key terms defined here to expand students' sociological vocabulary include *bourgeoisie* and *proletariat*, *cultural capital*, and *blue- and pink-collar jobs*. Other chapter features include updated statistics on education, income, occupations, and assets in the United States (with an emphasis on racial disparities), and poverty rates throughout the world. The Digital Life box "A Class-Free Virtual Society?" discusses social networking apps like The Right Stuff and Good Part of Town that provide search results based on class lines, and the advantages or disadvantages of such engines. The new Globalization by the Numbers infographic for this chapter sheds light on income inequality throughout the world and within the United States.

Chapter 8 (Global Inequality) begins with a summary of two devastating recent events: the earthquakes in Haiti and Japan. Despite the tragedy of these natural disasters, Haiti received far more charitable donations from Americans than did Japan, illustrating the magnitude and impact of global inequalities. Alongside examples of struggling people in places like Bangladesh and Zambia, the chapter provides the most current data on economic inequalities throughout the world, such as malnourishment and the HIV/AIDS epidemic, and on the impact of these inequalities for people's health and well-being. The discussion of the four theories of global inequality has also been deepened here. The Digital Life box "Can Apps Heal Global

Inequalities?" looks at how smartphones are being transformed into tools in the battle against HIV/AIDS in Africa. Statistics for the infographic on global inequality now reflect the most recent findings.

Chapter 9 (Gender Inequality) opens with a summary of two recent court cases brought against the brokerage firm Merrill Lynch, each by three female former employees who alleged they were treated differently than their male colleagues. These lawsuits reveal the ways that gender shapes one's experiences in the workplace, including one's pay, status, and interactions with coworkers. The chapter also includes new examples of gendered (or non-gendered) societies throughout the world, an added discussion of the gender divide in and after college, an explanation of the "he-cession," and more emphasis on the *glass ceiling* and balancing paid work with the *second shift*. It pays increased attention to hegemonic masculinity, intersex infants, and sexual harassment and assault. Statistics and legislation on the gender pay gap, work-family strategies, sex segregation in the workplace, gender inequalities in politics in and outside of the United States, violence against women, and global gender inequalities have been updated. The Digital Life box "'His' and 'Hers' Apps?" explores the gender divide of app and website users, like male-dominated Reddit versus female-dominated Pinterest. To highlight gender inequality clearly throughout the globe, the infographic for this chapter has been re-designed and its data updated.

Chapter 10 (Ethnicity and Race) opens with a summary of a recent Cheerios commercial featuring a mixed-race family that garnered a swift racist backlash. The ad, and the acknowledgment that Americans of multiracial identity are more populous than ever, provides a springboard for understanding the ways that race is socially constructed, and the ways that race shapes everyday experiences, such as in the New York stop-and-frisk policy, the death of Trayvon Martin, and the conflict over education for undocumented immigrants. New key terms include *theory of racial formation*, *scientific racism*, and *refugee*. Additional updates include new data from the Pew Research Center on racial identity in the United States and updated statistics on racial differences in a range of areas, including health, education, income, residential patterns, and political representation. The Digital Life box "What *Are* You, Anyway?" speaks to issues involved with the Guess My Race smartphone app. The infographic for this chapter, now re-imagined and made global in scope, shows the racial and ethnic populations of several different countries.

Chapter 11 (Families and Intimate Relationships) starts with the story of Edith Windsor's historic Supreme Court fight to repeal the Defense of Marriage Act and thus allow same-sex married couples to have all the legal and financial federal benefits that heterosexual ones do. This opener launches a discussion of the changing attitudes toward personal relationships, such as gay couples' marriage and adoption, single-parent families, divorce's effect on children, and China's one-child policy. The chapter also newly outlines five trends related to marriage in Western industrialized countries in the last thirty years. The data for statistics like fertility rates and American family structure have also been updated. The Digital Life box "Divorce—There's an App for That" details apps like iDivorce and Parenting Apart that help ease the logistical difficulty of spousal and parental splits. The new Globalization by the Numbers infographic compares maternity leave benefits given to new mothers in the workplace in eleven different countries.

Chapter 12 (Education and Religion) begins by recounting the bravery of Malala Yousafzai, the young Pakistani woman who was shot in the head at age fifteen for protesting the Taliban's restrictions on female education. This example reveals the principles and characteristics of the social institutions of both education and religion, which have profound effects on individuals' lives throughout the world. With an expanded discussion of Jonathan Kozol's study of American schools, of the No Child Left Behind Act, and of the privatization of school services and administration, this chapter raises important questions about the state of education in the United States. It also includes summaries about religious nationalism being globally on the rise while religious participation is simultaneously declining across the country and yet growing ever more visible in American politics. All statistics, such as the number of Jews and Muslims living in the United States, have been updated to reflect the most recent available data. The Digital Life box "From Pulpits to iPads?" shows ways in which technology provides easier access to aspects of religion, such as apps that allow users to download scripture, live-stream services, and present virtual prayer offerings. The new Globalization by the Numbers infographic compares levels of educational attainment in ten different countries.

Chapter 13 (Politics and Economic Life) opens with a recounting of the December 2013 strikes by fast-food workers across the United States. These protests over low hourly pay and a lack of health benefits reveal the complex interplay between government and the economy, as legislators begin to discuss raising the national minimum wage and allowing low-wage workers to unionize. The chapter has also been updated to include the most recent data on earnings, occupational structure, voter turnouts, and the demographic composition of U.S. elected officials. The consideration of Communism, minority political parties, and American labor unions has been expanded and new material has been added on the Knowledge Economy Index and how health care reform would apply to immigrants. The Digital Life box "Job Searches Go High Tech" details some of the apps available to job hunters. The new Globalization by the Numbers infographic depicts unemployment levels in eleven different countries, with a detailed look at unemployment in the United States.

Chapter 14 (The Sociology of the Body: Health, Illness, and Sexuality) introduces the Affordable Care Act signed into law by President Obama that increases Americans' access to health care through controversial provisions like the individual mandate and low-income subsidies. This opening section on "Obamacare" provides the foundation for a discussion of the *social class gradient in health*. The social factors surrounding the sick role, current stigmas of illness, the various causes of changes in mental health, and homophobia have all been detailed further. New studies exploring the racial differences in mental health and the gender gap in life expectancy are also discussed. All health statistics, including data related to the HIV/AIDS epidemic and sexual experiences, have been updated to reflect the most current available data. The five-year results of the 2005 President's Malaria Initiative are included as well. The Digital Life box "Can Your Smartphone Keep You Healthy?" lists health-related apps—like nutritional databases and diaries, drug information records, and fitness and sleep trackers—that make people more aware of their daily state of being and their good or bad habits. The new Globalization by the Numbers infographic provides a global picture of sexual habits.

Chapter 15 (Urbanization, Population, and Environment) begins by highlighting the challenges that China now faces: Its large population is threatening the nation's economic and environmental well-being. The case of China clearly demonstrates issues at the core of population and environment. In this revision, more information has been added to the discussions of suburbanization and rural America, and the terms *exurban county* and *informal economy* are introduced. The plight of Detroit, the recent slackening of China's one-child policy, and a discussion of the current trend toward "child quality" versus "child quantity" has been added. The section on *created environment* and restructured space has also been expanded. Statistics on population growth, birthrates, death rates, urbanization, suburbanization, and global warming have been updated. The Digital Life box "What's Your Carbon Footprint?" talks about apps that track individuals' carbon emissions—whether via vehicular usage or normal daily routines—with an aim toward reducing them through raised awareness. This chapter's Globalization by the Numbers infographic depicts the quickly growing rates of urbanization in areas all across the globe.

Chapter 16 (Globalization in a Changing World) begins by describing the Arab Spring protests and how subsequent protests emerged, powered by youth and making full use of social media, from Yemen to the Ukraine (a political hotbed that is focused on here). The Arab Spring protests reveal how globalization may forge and facilitate social change. With new references to elements of American life like bitcoin, the Lehman Brothers bankruptcy, Hurricane Sandy, and the Tea Party, this chapter helps put the United States in global perspective. Additionally, statistics on transnational corporations, Internet usage, egregious global economic inequalities, and global farm subsidies have been updated. The Digital Life box "Online Activism Trends Upward" describes the use of social media sites like Twitter and Facebook in recent protest movements. The Globalization by the Numbers Infographic "The Widening Gap" has been updated to include data from 2012.

ORGANIZATION

There is very little abstract discussion of basic sociological concepts at the beginning of this book. Instead, concepts are explained when they are introduced in the relevant chapters, and we have sought throughout to illustrate them by means of concrete examples. While these are usually taken from sociological research, we have also used material from other sources (such as newspaper or popular magazine articles). We have tried to keep the writing style as simple and direct as possible, while endeavoring to make the book lively and full of surprises.

The chapters follow a sequence designed to help achieve a progressive mastery of the different fields of sociology, but we have taken care to ensure that the book can be used flexibly and is easy to adapt to the needs of individual courses. Chapters can be skipped or studied in a different order without much loss. Each has been written as a fairly autonomous unit, with cross-referencing to other chapters at relevant points.

STUDY AIDS

In the Fifth Edition of *Essentials of Sociology*, we have expanded the pedagogical program. Each chapter features:

- **New "Digital Life" boxes** in every chapter get students thinking critically about how the Internet and smartphones are transforming the way we date, manage our health, and even practice religion.
- **New "Globalization by the Numbers" infographics** transform raw numbers into visually interesting displays that put the United States in a global context. Interactive versions in the ebook make the data dynamic and include integrated assignments that engage students with the data.
- **"Big Picture" Concept Maps** at the end of every chapter, which integrate the "Big Questions," key terms, and "Concept Checks" into a handy and visually interesting study tool, serve as both a pre-reading guide to the chapter as well as a post-reading review.
- **"Concept Checks"** throughout the chapter help students assess their understanding of the major topics in the chapter. Each "Concept Check" has at least three questions that range from reading comprehension to more advanced critical thinking skills.
- **Learning Goals** are outlined at the start of the chapter and then recur throughout the chapter in marginal notations at the beginning of the relevant sections to promote active learning.
- **"Making Sociology Work" features** provide students with scenarios from the working world and ask them to apply sociological concepts to each situation.

ACKNOWLEDGMENTS

Many individuals offered us helpful comments and advice on particular chapters, and, in some cases, large parts of the text. They helped us see issues in a different light, clarified some difficult points, and allowed us to take advantage of their specialist knowledge in their respective fields. We are deeply indebted to them. Special thanks go to Jason Phillips, who worked assiduously to help us update data in all chapters and contributed significantly to editing as well; and Dmitry Khodyakov, who wrote thought-provoking Concept Check questions for each chapter.

We would like to thank the many readers of the text who have written with comments, criticisms, and suggestions for improvements. We have adopted many of their recommendations in this new edition.

Adalberto Aguirre, University of California, Riverside
Colleen Avedikian, University of Massachusetts Dartmouth
Debbie Bishop, Lansing Community College
Kim Brackett, Auburn University
Edith Brotman, Towson University
Caroline Calogero, Brookdale Community College
Paul Calarco, Hudson Valley Community College
Karen Coleman, Winona State University
Dawn Conley, Gloucester County College
Raymonda Dennis, Delgado Community College
Matthew Flynn, University of Texas at Austin

Nicole Hotchkiss, Washington College
Howard Housen, Broward College
Annie Hubbard, Northwest Vista College
Onoso Imoagene, University of Pennsylvania
Ryan Kelty, Washington College
Kalyna Lesyna, Palomar College
Danilo Levi, Delgado Community College
Ke Liang, Baruch College
Jayne Mooney, John Jay College of Criminal Justice
Kendra Murphy, University of Memphis
Rafael Narvaez, Winona State University
Carolyn Pevey, Germanna Community College
Robert Pullen, Troy University
Fernando Rivera, University of Central Florida
Susan Cody-Rydzewski, Georgia Perimeter College
Rachel Stehle, Cuyahoga Community College
Larry Stern, Collin College
Daniel Steward, University of Illinois at Urbana-Champaign
Richard Sweeney, Modesto Junior College
Kristi Williams, Ohio State University
Annice Yarber, Auburn University

We have many others to thank as well. Nina Hnatov did a marvelous job of co-
pyediting the new edition. We are also extremely grateful to project editor Diane
Cipollone, who managed the countless details involved in creating the book. Assistant editor Thea Goodrich skillfully tracked all the moving parts that go into
publishing this complicated project. Production manager Vanessa Nuttry did impressive work guiding the book through production, so that it came out on time and
in beautiful shape. We also thank Eileen Connell, our e-media editor, and Laura
Musich, our associate e-media editor, for developing all of the useful supplements
that accompany the book. Agnieszka Gasparska and the entire team of designers at
Kiss Me I'm Polish managed to digest a huge amount of data to create the "Globalization by the Numbers" infographics throughout *Essentials of Sociology*. Finally, Hope
Miller Goodell earns our special thanks for creating the elegant design.

We are also grateful to our editors at Norton—Steve Dunn, Melea Seward, Karl
Bakeman, and Sasha Levitt—who have made important substantive and creative
contributions to the book's chapters and have ensured that we have referenced the
very latest research. We also would like to register our thanks to a number of current and former graduate students—many of whom are now tenured professors at
prestigious universities—whose contributions over the years have proved invaluable:
Wendy Carter, Audrey Devin-Eller, Neha Gondal, Neil Gross, Black Hawk Hancock,
Paul LePore, Alair MacLean, Ann Meier, Susan Munkres, Josh Rossol, Sharmila
Rudrappa, Christopher Wildeman, David Yamane, and Katherina Zippel.

Anthony Giddens
Mitchell Duneier
Richard Appelbaum
Deborah Carr

ESSENTIALS OF
SOCIOLOGY

fifth edition

1

Sociology: Theory and Method

THE BIG QUESTIONS

WHAT IS THE "SOCIOLOGICAL IMAGINATION"?

Learn what sociology covers as a field and how everyday topics like love and romance are shaped by social and historical forces. Recognize that sociology involves developing a sociological imagination and a global perspective, and understanding social change.

WHAT THEORIES DO SOCIOLOGISTS USE?

Learn about the development of sociology as a field. Be able to name some of the leading social theorists and the concepts they contributed to sociology. Learn the different theoretical approaches modern sociologists bring to the field.

WHAT KINDS OF QUESTIONS CAN SOCIOLOGISTS ANSWER?

Be able to describe the different types of questions sociologists address in their research.

WHAT ARE THE SEVEN STEPS OF THE RESEARCH PROCESS?

Learn the steps of the research process and be able to complete the process yourself.

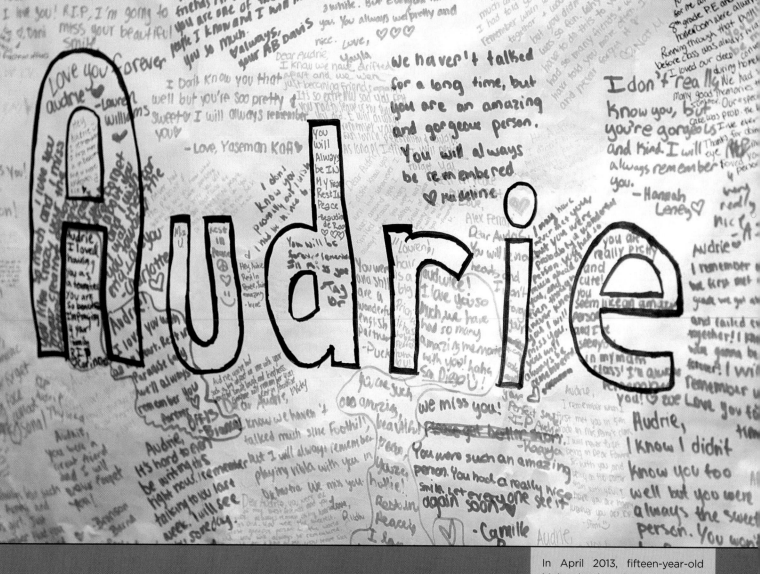

WHAT RESEARCH METHODS DO SOCIOLOGISTS USE?

Familiarize yourself with the methods available to sociological researchers, and know the advantages and disadvantages of each. See how researchers use multiple methods in a real study.

WHAT ETHICAL DILEMMAS DO SOCIOLOGISTS FACE?

Recognize the ethical problems researchers may face and identify possible solutions to these dilemmas.

HOW DOES THE SOCIOLOGICAL IMAGINATION AFFECT YOUR LIFE?

Understand how adopting a sociological perspective allows us to develop a richer understanding of ourselves, our significant others, and the world.

In April 2013, fifteen-year-old high school student Audrie Pott was sexually assaulted by three sixteen-year-old boys at a classmate's house party. The boys took cell phone photos of Audrie while she was unconscious, later sharing them with other students. Eight days later, Audrie hanged herself.

sociology • The study of human groups and societies, giving particular emphasis to analysis of the industrialized world. Sociology is one of a group of social sciences, which include anthropology, economics, political science, and human geography. The divisions among the various social sciences are not clear-cut, and all share a certain range of common interests, concepts, and methods.

Sociology is the scientific study of human social life, groups, and societies. It is a dazzling and compelling enterprise, as its subject matter is our own behavior as social beings. The scope of sociological study is extremely wide, ranging from the analysis of how people establish social connections with one another in interactions to the investigation of global social processes such as the rise of Islamic fundamentalism.

Sociology teaches us that what we regard as natural, inevitable, good, or true may not be such, and that the "givens" of our life—including things we assume to be genetic or biological—are strongly influenced by historical and social forces. Understanding the subtle yet complex and profound ways in which our individual lives reflect the contexts of our social experience is basic to the sociological outlook. A brief example will provide a taste of the nature and objectives of sociology.

Anyone who has attended middle school or high school knows that bullying is a common occurrence. Through much of history, teachers, principals, and parents turned a blind eye, often believing that "boys will be boys." This cavalier attitude toward bullying has been called into question by students, teachers, and policymakers alike in recent years. A recent spate of suicides by teenagers subjected to merciless bullying has raised awareness that bullying is no longer "kid stuff," and in nearly all states is grounds for suspension, expulsion, or even more serious punishment. Over the past five years, bullying-related tragedies have been documented throughout the United States, involving teenagers of all backgrounds—male and female, black and white, Asian and Latino, gay and straight, rich and poor, rural and suburban.

For Devin Brown, the bullying began shortly after he started at Rothschild Middle School. Things escalated after he reported another student for carrying a knife and threatening a teacher. Rather than being regarded as a hero by his classmates, he was derided as a "snitch" and was regularly threatened and beaten up at school. In April 2013, after months of relentless harassment, Brown hanged himself at home in his closet.

That same month, fifteen-year-old high school student Audrie Pott hanged herself in her San Jose, California, home. Eight days earlier, Pott had been sexually assaulted at a classmate's house party by three sixteen-year-old boys. She woke up to find her clothes pulled off and her body covered in lewd markings. The trauma didn't end there, though. The boys took pictures of Pott while she was unconscious and shared them with other students. Just days before she took her life, a devastated Pott posted messages on Facebook that read, "My life is over" and "The whole school knows."

Brown and Pott are just two of hundreds of teenagers who have committed suicide after being bullied and humiliated by their classmates. Today, anti-bullying laws exist in forty-nine of the fifty United States; Montana is the one state yet to pass such legislation (Sacco et al. 2013). In 2011, New Jersey passed the nation's toughest anti-bullying legislation, triggered in part by the high-profile suicide of Tyler Clementi. In 2010, the eighteen-year-old Rutgers University freshman committed suicide by jumping off the George Washington Bridge, just two weeks after he started his first semester in college. The suicide came days after his sexual encounter with a man in his dorm room was video streamed over the Internet without Clementi's knowledge by his roommate and a fellow hallmate.

personal troubles • Difficulties that are located in individual biographies and their immediate milieu, a seemingly private experience.

public issues • Difficulties or problems that are linked to the institutional and historical possibilities of social structure.

Sociology helps us to understand and analyze scientifically social phenomena like bullying and suicide. American sociologist C. Wright Mills (1959) observed that social sciences enable people to "translate private troubles into public issues." What Mills meant is that individuals often believe that the problems that they (and others) face are personal, perhaps resulting from one's own traits or decisions. But social scientists recognize that these seemingly "**personal**" **troubles**, if occurring in patterned ways, to large numbers of individuals, reflect important "**public issues**," or consequences of social structures.

For example, Devin Brown, Audrie Pott, and Tyler Clementi all committed suicide shortly after being tormented by their peers. Some observers might think that the suicides are an isolated problem, perhaps the reaction of three teens who were depressed or emotionally unstable. However, a sociologist would look at the social context and try to understand just how common such events are and to understand whether some subgroups are particularly vulnerable to such problems.

They might consult data from national surveys, such as the 2011 Pew Internet and American Life Project, which found that one in three teenagers who use the Internet say he or she has been the target of annoying and potentially menacing online activities. Nearly four in ten teens who use social networking sites say that they've been cyberbullied. The study also detected strong gender differences, with girls (like Audrie Pott) reporting more online victimization than boys; 38 percent of girls but only 26 percent of boys who use the Internet report harassment (Lenhart 2007). However, recent research suggests that the gender gap is largest among young teenagers; one-third of young teenage girls (ages twelve to thirteen), yet just 9 percent of young teenage boys, report unkind interactions online. As teens age, the gender gap narrows. By ages fourteen to seventeen, roughly equal numbers of teenage girls (20 percent) and boys (18 percent) report harassment or mistreatment online (Jones, Mitchell, and Finkelhor 2012; Lenhart et al. 2011).

Other sociologists have studied bullying "off-line" and found that gay and lesbian teens are far more likely than their straight peers to be harassed at school. One survey of more than 7,500 high school students found that nearly 44 percent of gay male and 40 percent of lesbian teens said they had been bullied in the previous year, compared with just 26 and 15 percent of heterosexual boys and girls, respectively (Berlan et al. 2010). Studies such as these help us recognize that the anguish experienced by Clementi, Pott, and Brown is hardly an isolated incident and instead reflects pervasive social problems that require far-reaching solutions. Sociology can help us understand the questions of what, why, and how public issues and personal troubles arise.

WHAT IS THE "SOCIOLOGICAL IMAGINATION"?

Learn what sociology covers as a field and how everyday topics like love and romance are shaped by social and historical forces. Recognize that sociology involves developing a sociological imagination and a global perspective, and understanding social change.

When we learn to think sociologically, we can also better understand the most personal aspects of our own lives. For instance, have you ever been in love? Almost certainly you have. Most people who are in their teens or older know what being in love is like. Love and romance provide some of the most intense feelings we ever experience. Why do people fall in love? The answer may seem obvious: Love expresses a mutual physical and personal attachment between two individuals. These days, we might not all think that love is "forever," but falling in love, we may agree, is an experience arising from universal human emotions. It seems natural for a couple in love to want personal and sexual fulfillment in their relationship, perhaps through marriage.

Yet this pattern whereby love leads to marriage is in fact very unusual. Romantic love is not an experience all people across the world have—and where it does happen, it is rarely connected to marriage. The idea of romantic love did not become widespread until fairly recently in our society, and it has never even existed in many other cultures.

Only in modern times have love and sexuality become closely connected. In the Middle Ages and for centuries afterward, men and women married mainly to keep

What is the origin of romantic love? Originally, romantic love was limited to affairs for medieval aristocrats such as Tristan and Isolde, the subjects of a thirteenth-century court romance who inspired poems, operas, and films.

sociological imagination • The application of imaginative thought to the asking and answering of sociological questions. Someone using the sociological imagination "thinks himself away" from the familiar routines of daily life.

property in the hands of the family or to raise children to work the family farm—or, in the case of royalty, to seal political alliances. Spouses may have become close companions after marriage, but not before. People sometimes had sexual affairs outside marriage, but these inspired few of the emotions we associate with love today. Romantic love was regarded as a weakness at best and a kind of sickness at worst.

Romantic love developed in courtly circles as a characteristic of extramarital sexual adventures by members of the aristocracy. Until about two centuries ago, it was confined to such circles and kept separate from marriage. Relations between husband and wife among aristocratic groups were often cool and distant. Each spouse had his or her own bedroom and servants; they may rarely have seen each other in private. Sexual compatibility was not considered relevant to marriage. Among both rich and poor, the decision of whom to marry was made by one's immediate and extended family; the individuals concerned had little or no say in the matter.

This remains true in many non-Western countries today. (Social scientists typically define "Western" countries as economically rich nations, including most in North America and Europe, as well as Japan and Australia.) For example, in Afghanistan under the rule of the Taliban, men were prohibited from speaking to women they were not related or married to, and marriages were arranged by parents. If a girl and boy were seen by authorities to be speaking with each other, they would be whipped and left seriously injured, if not dead. The Taliban government saw romantic love as so offensive that it outlawed all nonreligious music and films. Like many in the non-Western world, the Taliban believed Afghanistan was being inundated by Hollywood movies and American pop music and videos, which are filled with sexual images.

Neither romantic love, then, nor its association with marriage can be understood as a natural or universal feature of human life. Rather, such love has been shaped by social and historical influences. These are the influences sociologists study.

Most of us see the world in terms of the familiar features of our own lives. Sociology demonstrates the need for a much broader view of our nature and our actions. It teaches that what we regard as "natural" in our lives is strongly influenced by historical and social forces. Understanding the subtle yet profoundly complex ways in which our individual lives reflect the contexts of our social experience is basic to the sociological outlook.

Learning to think sociologically means cultivating the **sociological imagination**. As sociologists, we need to imagine, for example, what the experience of sex and marriage is like for people who consider the ideals of romantic love to be alien or absurd. Sociology is not just a routine process of acquiring knowledge; it requires breaking free from the immediacy of personal circumstances and putting things in a wider context. It requires what sociologist C. Wright Mills (1959), in a famous phrase, called the sociological imagination.

The sociological imagination requires us, above all, to "think ourselves away" from our daily routines in order to look at them anew. Consider the simple act of drinking a cup of coffee. What might the sociological point of view illuminate about such apparently uninteresting behavior? An enormous amount. First, coffee possesses symbolic value as part of our daily social activities. Often the ritual associated with coffee drinking is much more important than the act itself. Two people who arrange to meet for coffee are probably more interested in getting together and chatting than in what they actually drink. Drinking and eating in all societies, in fact, promote social interaction and the enactment of rituals—rich subject matter for sociological study.

Second, coffee contains caffeine, a drug that stimulates the brain. In Western culture, coffee addicts are not regarded as drug users. Like alcohol, coffee is a socially acceptable drug, whereas cocaine and opium, for instance, are not. Yet some societies tolerate the recreational use of opium or even cocaine but frown on coffee and alcohol. Sociologists are interested in why these contrasts exist.

Third, an individual who drinks a cup of coffee is participating in a complicated set of social and economic relationships stretching across the world. The production and distribution of coffee require continuous transactions among people who may be thousands of miles away from the coffee drinker. Studying such global transactions is an important task of sociology because many aspects of our lives are now affected by worldwide social influences and communications.

Finally, the act of sipping a cup of coffee presumes a process of past social and economic development. Widespread consumption of coffee—along with other now-familiar items of Western diets like tea, bananas, potatoes, and white sugar—began only in the late 1800s under Western colonial expansion. Virtually all the coffee we drink today comes from areas (South America and Africa) that were colonized by Europeans; it is in no sense a "natural" part of the Western diet.

STUDYING SOCIOLOGY

The sociological imagination allows us to see that many behaviors or feelings that we view as private and individualized actually reflect larger social issues. Try applying this sort of outlook to your own life. Consider, for instance, why you are attending college right now. You may think that you worked hard in high school, or that you have decided to go to college so that you have the academic credential required to find a good job, yet other, larger social forces also may have played a role. Many students who work hard in high school cannot attend college because their parents cannot afford to send them. Others have their schooling interrupted by large-scale events like wars or economic depressions. The notion that we need college to find a good job is also shaped by social context. In past eras, when most people worked in agricultural rather than professional jobs, college attendance was rare—rather than an expected rite of passage.

Although we are all influenced by the social contexts in which we find ourselves, none of us is simply determined in his or her behavior by those contexts. We possess and create our own individuality. It is the goal of sociology to investigate the connections between what society makes of us and what we make of ourselves. Our activities structure—give shape to—the social world around us and at the same time are structured by that social world.

Social structure is an important concept in sociology. It refers to the fact that the social contexts of our lives do not just consist of random assortments of events or actions; they are structured, or patterned, in distinct ways. There are regularities in the ways we behave and in the relationships we have with one another. But social structure is not like a physical structure, such as a building, which exists independently of human actions. Human societies are always in the process of **structuration**. They are reconstructed at every moment by the very "building blocks" that compose them—human beings like you.

structuration • The two-way process by which we shape our social world through our individual actions and by which we are reshaped by society.

DEVELOPING A GLOBAL PERSPECTIVE

As we just saw in our discussion of the sociological dimensions of drinking a cup of coffee, all our local actions—the ways in which we relate to one another in face-to-face contexts—form part of larger social settings that extend around the globe. These connections between the local and the global are quite new in human history. They have accelerated over the past thirty or forty years as a result of dramatic advances in communications, information technology, and transportation. The development of jet planes; large, speedy container ships; and other means of rapid travel has meant that people and goods can be continuously transported across the world. And our worldwide system of satellite communication, established only some thirty years ago, has made it possible for people to get in touch with one another instantaneously.

American society is influenced every moment of the day by globalization, the growth of world interdependence—a social phenomenon that will be discussed throughout this book. Globalization should not be thought of simply as the development of worldwide networks—social and economic systems that are remote from our individual concerns. It is a local phenomenon, too. For example, in the 1950s and 1960s, most Americans had few culinary choices when they dined out at restaurants. In many U.S. towns and cities today, a single street may feature Italian, Mexican, Japanese, Thai, Ethiopian, and other types of restaurants next door to one another. In turn, the dietary decisions we make are consequential for food producers who may live on the other side of the world.

Do college students today have a global perspective? By at least one measure, the answer is yes. According to an annual survey of 192,912 first-year college students in 2012, nearly one-third (30.7 percent) reported that they had discussed politics "frequently" in the last year. This proportion fell slightly from the 33.1 percent in 2009 who reported the same. Slightly more than one-third (34.5 percent) of students also reported that keeping up with political issues is "very important" or "essential" (versus 39.5 percent in 2009; Higher Education Research Institute 2009, 2012). Concern with these issues reflects an awareness that globalization has a direct effect on our daily, private lives.

A global perspective not only allows us to become more aware of the ways that we are connected to people in other societies, it also makes us more aware of the many problems the world faces at the beginning of the twenty-first century. The global perspective opens our eyes to the fact that our interdependence with other societies means that our actions have consequences for others, and that the world's problems have consequences for us.

UNDERSTANDING SOCIAL CHANGE

The changes in human ways of life in the last two hundred years, such as globalization, have been far-reaching. We have become accustomed, for example, to the fact that most of the population lives in towns and cities rather than in small agricultural communities. But this was never the case until the middle of the nineteenth century. For most of human history, the vast majority of people had to produce their own food and shelter and lived in tiny groups or in small village communities. Even at the height of the most developed traditional civilizations—such as ancient Rome or pre-industrial China—less than 10 percent of the population lived in urban areas; everyone else was engaged in food production in a rural setting. Today, in most industrialized societies, these proportions have become almost completely reversed. By 2050, nearly 70 percent of the world population is expected to live in urban areas. In more developed regions, including Europe, North America, Australia, New Zealand, and Japan, an estimated 86 percent will live in urban areas (United Nations 2012).

These sweeping social transformations have radically altered, and continue to alter, the most personal and intimate side of our daily existence. To extend a previous example, the spread of ideals of romantic love was strongly conditioned by the transition from a rural to an urban, industrialized society. As people moved into urban areas and began to work in industrial production, marriage was no longer prompted mainly by economic motives—by the need to control the inheritance of land and to work the land as a family unit. "Arranged" marriages—fixed through the negotiations of parents and relatives—became less and less common. Individuals began to initiate marriage relationships on the bases of emotional attraction and personal fulfillment. The idea of "falling in love" as a precondition for marriage was formed in this context.

Sociology was founded by thinkers who sought to understand the initial impact of transformations that accompanied industrialization in the West. Although our world today is radically different from that of former ages, the original goal of sociologists remains: to understand our world and what future it is likely to hold for us. ✓

CONCEPT CHECKS ✓

1. How does sociology help us understand the causes of bullying?

2. Contrast public issues and personal troubles.

3. What is the sociological imagination, according to C. Wright Mills?

4. How does the concept of social structure help sociologists better understand social phenomena?

5. What is globalization? How might it affect the lives of college students today?

WHAT THEORIES DO SOCIOLOGISTS USE?

Sociologists do more than collect facts; they also want to know why things happen. For instance, we know that industrialization has had a major influence on the emergence of modern societies. But what are the origins and preconditions of industrialization? Why is industrialization associated with changes in ways of criminal punishment or in family and marriage systems? To respond to such questions, we must construct explanatory theories.

Learn about the development of sociology as a field. Be able to name some of the leading social theorists and the concepts they contributed to sociology. Learn the different theoretical approaches modern sociologists bring to the field.

THEORIES AND THEORETICAL APPROACHES

Theories involve constructing abstract interpretations that can be used to explain a wide variety of situations. Of course, factual research and theories can never completely be separated. Sociologists aiming to document facts must begin their studies with a theory that they will evaluate. Theory helps researchers identify and frame a factual question, yet facts are needed to evaluate the strength of a theory. Conversely, once facts have been obtained, sociologists must use theory to interpret and make sense of these facts.

Theoretical thinking also must respond to general problems posed by the study of human social life, including issues that are philosophical in nature. For example, based on their theoretical and methodological orientations, sociologists hold very different beliefs about whether sociology should be modeled on the natural sciences.

EARLY THEORISTS

Humans have always been curious about why we behave as we do, but for thousands of years our attempts to understand ourselves relied on ways of thinking passed down from generation to generation, often expressed in religious rather than

Bullying Goes Viral

Bullying has been around as long as there have been schools. Our great-grandparents may recount tales of mean-spirited classmates who dipped girls' braids into their desk inkwells, while our parents and grandparents can recall friends being called names or pushed into their lockers. Those bullies were often caught right away; classmates, teachers, or hall monitors could witness the bad behavior with their own eyes and reprimand the offender on the spot. Further, the victimization was often private, witnessed only by those who were in immediate proximity to the event.

Not so in the twenty-first century. For you and your college classmates, bullying often occurs online. Social life in the twenty-first century has "gone digital"—for both good and bad. As we saw earlier in this chapter, teens like Audrie Pott and Tyler Clementi were tormented by tech-savvy classmates who shared images and videos of their victims with untold numbers of people. How did this happen? How did these incidents, which happened behind closed doors, "go viral" for all to see?

Countless websites and apps facilitate cyberbullying, or the use of the Internet, cell phones, or other electronic devices to embarrass or hurt another person (Sagan 2013). Take Ugly Meter, for example. The app takes your picture and then rates your looks on a scale of 1 to 10. These ratings are accompanied by corresponding comments that are just plain cruel: "You're so ugly, you could make a glass eye cry." Just months after the app debuted in 2010, Ugly Meter skyrocketed in popularity, attracting more than 5 million users and joining Angry Birds as one of the most popular apps. Ugly Meter provides bullies with an easy way to share unflattering photos of their victims and invite millions of other mean-spirited people to participate in the bullying and berating (Black and Goldwert 2010).

Yet even technologies that serve positive purposes, like Facebook, are used by cyberbullies. While Facebook allows people to connect with friends from around the world, it can also be used in hurtful ways. Teenagers can create a "page" for their victim, posting unflattering photos and insulting remarks and inviting others to harass the defenseless target online. Because the bullying victim did not create the page, he or she has no way of removing unkind or untrue remarks. Given the anonymous nature of the Internet, teens who would never dream of bullying a classmate face-to-face may get lured into the cruel behavior online (Hoffman 2010).

Yet the Internet also has the potential to promote positive social action. In response to hurtful and senseless apps like Ugly Meter, dozens of apps have been developed to combat online bullying. For example, Stop Bullies allows users to record videos and take photos to send to campus police or school authorities, while Back Off Bully lets students book appointments with their school counselors. The "It Gets Better" project, created by columnist Dan Savage and his partner, has inspired more than 50,000 user-created videos that convey a message of hope to lesbian, gay, bisexual, and transgender (LGBT) youth facing bullying.

Does the explosion of cyberbullying indicate that today's youth are cruel and insensitive to others' vulnerabilities? Or is there something about the current cyber culture that promotes cruelty and insensitivity?

Jill Brown of Generation Text, an organization that partners with schools to create a safe environment for students, talks to parents at Ben Franklin Middle School about cyberbullying.

Revising Mills's notions of "personal troubles" and "public issues," how might you explain cyberbullying? Do you think anti-bullying apps will work, or are larger social changes needed?

scientific terms. The systematic scientific study of human behavior is a relatively recent development, dating back to the late 1700s and early 1800s. The sweeping changes ushered in by the French Revolution of 1789 and the emergence of the Industrial Revolution in Europe formed the backdrop for the development of sociology. These major historical events shattered traditional ways of life and forced thinkers to develop new understandings of both the social and natural worlds.

A key development was the use of science instead of religion to understand the world. The types of questions these nineteenth-century thinkers sought to answer are the very same questions sociologists try to answer today. What is human nature? How and why do societies change?

AUGUSTE COMTE

Auguste Comte (1798–1857)

Many scholars contributed to early sociological thinking, yet particular credit is given to the French philosopher Auguste Comte (1798–1857), if only because he invented the word *sociology*. Comte originally used the term *social physics*, but some of his intellectual rivals at the time were also making use of that term. Comte wanted to distinguish his own views from theirs, so he introduced sociology to describe the subject he wished to establish.

Comte believed that this new field could produce a knowledge of society based on scientific evidence. He regarded sociology as the last science to be developed—following physics, chemistry, and biology—but as the most significant and complex of all the sciences. Sociology, he believed, should contribute to the welfare of humanity by using science to understand, predict, and control human behavior. Late in his career, Comte drew up ambitious plans for the reconstruction of both French society in particular and human societies in general, based on scientific knowledge.

ÉMILE DURKHEIM

Émile Durkheim (1858–1917)

Another French scholar, Émile Durkheim (1858–1917), has had a much more lasting effect on modern sociology than Comte. Although he drew on aspects of Comte's work, Durkheim thought that many of his predecessor's ideas were too speculative and vague and that Comte had not successfully established a scientific basis for studying human behavior. To become a science, according to Durkheim, sociology must study **social facts**, aspects of social life that shape our actions as individuals, such as the state of the economy or the influence of religion. Durkheim believed that we must study social life with the same objectivity as scientists who study the natural world. In fact, he viewed sociology as "the science of social facts." His famous first principle of sociology was "Study social facts as things!" By this he meant that social life can be analyzed as rigorously as objects or events in nature. The key task of the sociologist, according to Durkheim, was to search for correlations among social facts in order to reveal laws of social structure.

Like a biologist studying the human body, Durkheim saw society as a set of independent parts, each of which could be studied separately. A body consists of specialized parts, each of which contributes to sustaining the continuing life of the organism. These necessarily work in harmony with one another; if they do not, the life of the organism is under threat. So it is, according to Durkheim, with society. For a society to function and persist over time, its specialized institutions (such as the political system, religion, the family, and the educational system) must work in harmony with one another and function as an integrated whole. Durkheim referred to this social cohesion as **"organic solidarity."** He argued that the continuation of a society thus depends on cooperation, which in turn presumes a consensus, or agreement, among its members over basic values and customs.

social facts • According to Émile Durkheim, the aspects of social life that shape our actions as individuals. Durkheim believed that social facts could be studied scientifically.

organic solidarity • According to Émile Durkheim, the social cohesion that results from the various parts of a society functioning as an integrated whole.

social constraint • The conditioning influence on our behavior by the groups and societies of which we are members. Social constraint was regarded by Émile Durkheim as one of the distinctive properties of social facts.

anomie • A concept first brought into wide usage in sociology by Durkheim, referring to a situation in which social norms lose their hold over individual behavior.

materialist conception of history • The view developed by Marx, according to which material, or economic, factors have a prime role in determining historical change.

capitalism • An economic system based on the private ownership of wealth, which is invested and reinvested in order to produce profit.

Karl Marx (1818–1883)

Another major theme pursued by Durkheim, and by many others since, is that the society exerts **social constraint** over the actions of its members. Durkheim argued that society is far more than the sum of individual acts; when we analyze social structures, we are studying characteristics that have "solidity" comparable to structures in the physical world. Social structure, according to Durkheim, constrains our activities in a parallel way, setting limits on what we can do as individuals. It is "external" to us, just as the walls of the room are.

One of Durkheim's most influential studies was concerned with the analysis of suicide (Durkheim 1966, orig. 1897). Suicide may appear to be a purely personal act, the outcome of extreme personal unhappiness. Durkheim showed, however, that social factors exert a fundamental influence on suicidal behavior—**anomie**, a feeling of aimlessness or despair provoked by modern social life, being one of these influences. Suicide rates show regular patterns from year to year, he argued, and these patterns must be explained sociologically. According to Durkheim, changes in the modern world are so rapid and intense that they give rise to major social difficulties, which he linked to anomie. Traditional moral controls and standards, which were supplied by religion in earlier times, are largely broken down by modern social development; this leaves individuals in many societies feeling that their daily lives lack meaning. Many critiques of Durkheim's study can be raised, but it remains a classic work that is relevant to sociology today.

KARL MARX

The ideas of the German philosopher Karl Marx (1818–1883) contrast sharply with those of Comte and Durkheim, but like them, he sought to explain the societal changes that took place during the Industrial Revolution. When Marx was a young man, his political activities brought him into conflict with the German authorities; after a brief stay in France, he settled permanently in exile in Great Britain. Marx's viewpoint was founded on what he called the **materialist conception of history**. According to this view, it is not the ideas or values human beings hold that are the main sources of social change, as Durkheim claimed. Rather, social change is prompted primarily by economic influences. The conflicts between classes—the rich versus the poor—provide the motivation for historical development. In Marx's words, "All human history thus far is the history of class struggles."

Though he wrote about many historical periods, Marx concentrated on change in modern times. For him, the most important changes were bound up with the development of **capitalism**. Capitalism is a system of production that contrasts radically with previous economic systems in history. It involves the production of goods and services sold to a wide range of consumers. Those who own capital, or factories, machines, and large sums of money, form a ruling class. The mass of the population make up the working class, or wage workers who do not own the means of their livelihood but must find employment provided by the owners of capital. Capitalism is thus a class system in which conflict between classes is a common occurrence because it is in the interests of the ruling class to exploit the working class and in the interests of the workers to seek to overcome that exploitation.

Marx predicted that in the future capitalism will be supplanted by a society in which there are no classes—no divisions between rich and poor. He didn't mean that all inequalities would disappear; rather, societies will no longer be split into a small class that monopolizes economic and political power and the large mass of people who benefit little from the wealth their work creates. The economic system will come under communal ownership, and a more equal society than we know at present will be established.

Marx's work had a far-reaching effect in the twentieth century. Through most of the century, until the fall of Soviet communism in the early 1990s, more than a third of the world population lived in societies whose governments claimed to derive their inspiration from Marx's ideas. In addition, many sociologists have been influenced by Marx's ideas about class inequalities.

MAX WEBER

Like Marx, Max Weber (pronounced "VAY-ber"; 1864–1920) cannot be labeled simply a sociologist; his interests and concerns ranged across many areas. Born in Germany, where he spent most of his academic career, Weber was educated in a range of fields. Like other thinkers of his time, Weber sought to understand social change. He was influenced by Marx but was also strongly critical of some of Marx's views. He rejected the materialist conception of history and saw class conflict as less significant than did Marx. In Weber's view, economic factors are important, but ideas and values have just as much effect on social change.

Max Weber (1864–1920)

Some of Weber's most influential writings compared the leading religious systems in China and India with those of the West. Weber concluded that certain aspects of Christian beliefs strongly influenced the rise of capitalism. He argued that the capitalist outlook of Western societies did not emerge only from economic changes, as Marx had argued. In Weber's view, cultural ideas and values help shape society and affect our individual actions.

One of the most influential aspects of Weber's work was his study of bureaucracy. A bureaucracy is a large organization that is divided into jobs based on specific functions and staffed by officials ranked according to a hierarchy. Industrial firms, government organizations, hospitals, and schools are examples of bureaucracies. Bureaucracy makes it possible for these large organizations to run efficiently, but at the same time it poses problems for effective democratic participation in modern societies. Bureaucracy involves the rule of experts, whose decisions are made without much consultation with those whose lives are affected by those decisions.

Weber's contributions range over many other areas, including the study of the development of cities, systems of law, types of economy, and the nature of classes. He also wrote about the overall character of sociology itself. According to Weber, humans are thinking, reasoning beings; we attach meaning and significance to most of what we do; and any discipline that deals with human behavior must acknowledge this.

Table 1.1 | Interpreting Modern Development

DURKHEIM	**1.** The main dynamic of modern development is the **division of labor** as a basis for social cohesion and **organic solidarity**.
	2. Durkheim believed that sociology must study **social facts** as things, just as science would analyze the natural world. His study of suicide led him to stress the important influence of social factors, qualities of a society external to the individual, on a person's actions. Durkheim argued that society exerts **social constraint** over our actions.
MARX	**1.** The main dynamic of modern development is the expansion of **capitalism**. Rather than being cohesive, society is divided by class differences.
	2. Marx believed that we must study the divisions within a society that are derived from the economic inequalities of capitalism.
WEBER	**1.** The main dynamic of modern development is the **rationalization** of social and economic life.
	2. Weber focused on why Western societies developed so differently from other societies. He also emphasized the importance of cultural ideas and values on social change.

NEGLECTED FOUNDERS

Durkheim, Marx, and Weber are widely acknowledged as foundational figures in sociology, yet other important thinkers from the same period also made valuable contributions to sociological thought. Very few women or members of racial minorities were given the opportunity to become professional sociologists during the "classical" period of the late nineteenth and early twentieth centuries. Their contributions deserve the attention of sociologists today.

HARRIET MARTINEAU

Harriet Martineau (1802–1876)

Harriet Martineau (1802–1876) was born and educated in England. She was the author of more than fifty books and numerous essays. Martineau is now credited with introducing sociology to England through her translation of Comte's founding treatise of the field, *Positive Philosophy* (Rossi 1973). She also conducted a firsthand systematic study of American society during her extensive travels throughout the United States in the 1830s, which is the subject of her book *Society in America*. Martineau is significant to sociologists today for several reasons. First, she argued that when one studies a society, one must focus on all its aspects, including key political, religious, and social institutions. Second, she insisted that an analysis of a society must include an understanding of women's lives. Third, she was the first to turn a sociological eye on previously ignored issues such as marriage, children, domestic and religious life, and race relations. As she wrote, "The nursery, the boudoir, and the kitchen are all excellent schools in which to learn the morals and manners of a people" (2009, orig. 1837). Finally, she argued that sociologists should do more than just observe; they should also act in ways to benefit a society. Martineau herself was an active proponent of women's rights and the emancipation of slaves.

W. E. B. DU BOIS

W. E. B. Du Bois (1868–1963)

W. E. B. Du Bois (1868–1963) was the first African American to earn a doctorate at Harvard University. Du Bois made many contributions to sociology. Perhaps most important is the concept of "double consciousness," which is a way of talking about identity through the lens of the particular experiences of African Americans. He argued that American society lets African Americans see themselves only through the eyes of others: "It is a particular sensation, this double consciousness, this sense of always measuring one's soul by the tape of a world that looks on in amused contempt and pity. One ever feels his two-ness—an American, a Negro, two souls, two thoughts, two unreconciled strivings, two warring ideals in one dark body, whose dogged strength alone keeps it from being torn asunder" (1903). Du Bois made a persuasive claim that one's sense of self and one's identity are greatly influenced by historical experiences and social circumstances—in the case of African Americans, the effect of slavery and, after emancipation, segregation and prejudice. Throughout his career, Du Bois focused on race relations in the United States. As he said in an often-repeated quote, "The problem of the twentieth century is the problem of the color line." His influence on sociology today is evidenced by continued interest in the questions that he raised, particularly his concern that sociology must explain "the contact of diverse races of men." Du Bois was also the first social researcher to trace the problems faced by African Americans to their social and economic underpinnings, a connection that most sociologists now widely accept. Finally,

Du Bois became known for connecting social analysis to social reform. He was one of the founding members of the National Association for the Advancement of Colored People (NAACP) and a longtime advocate for the collective struggle of African Americans. Later in his life, Du Bois became disenchanted by the lack of progress in American race relations. He moved to the African nation of Ghana in 1961 when he was invited by the nation's president, Kwame Nkrumah, to direct the *Encyclopedia Africana*, a government publication that Du Bois had long been interested in. He died in Ghana in 1963.

MODERN THEORETICAL APPROACHES

The origins of sociology were mainly European, yet the subject is now firmly established worldwide—with some of the most important developments having taken place in the United States.

SYMBOLIC INTERACTIONISM

The work of George Herbert Mead (1863–1931), a philosopher teaching at the University of Chicago, had an important influence on the development of sociological thought, in particular through a perspective called **symbolic interactionism**. Mead placed great importance on the study of language in analyzing the social world. He reasoned that language allows us to become self-conscious beings—aware of our own individuality. The key element in this process is the **symbol**, something that stands for something else. For example, the word *tree* is a symbol that represents the object tree. Once we have mastered such a concept, Mead argued, we can think of a tree even if none is visible; we have learned to think of the object symbolically. Symbolic thought frees us from being limited in our experience to what we actually see, hear, or feel.

Unlike animals, according to Mead, human beings live in a richly symbolic universe. This applies even to our very sense of self. Each of us is a self-conscious being because we learn to look at ourselves as if from the outside—we see ourselves as others see us. When a child begins to use "I" to refer to that object (herself) whom others call "you," she is exhibiting the beginnings of self-consciousness.

Virtually all interactions between individuals involve an exchange of symbols, according to symbolic interactionists. When we interact with others, we constantly look for clues to what type of behavior is appropriate in the context and how to interpret what others are doing and saying. Symbolic interactionism directs our attention to the detail of interpersonal interaction and how that detail is used to make sense of what others say and do. For instance, suppose two people are out on a date for the first time. Each is likely to spend a good part of the evening sizing the other up and assessing how the relationship is likely to develop, if at all. Both individuals are careful about their own behavior, making every effort to present themselves in a favorable light; but, knowing this, both are likely to be looking for aspects of the other's behavior that would reveal his or her true beliefs and traits. A complex and subtle process of symbolic interpretation shapes the interaction between the two.

FUNCTIONALISM

Symbolic interactionism is open to the criticism that it concentrates too much on things that are small in scope. Symbolic interactionists have found difficulty in

symbolic interactionism • A theoretical approach in sociology developed by George Herbert Mead that emphasizes the role of symbols and language as core elements of all human interaction.

symbol • One item used to stand for or represent another—as in the case of a flag, which symbolizes a nation.

functionalism • A theoretical perspective based on the notion that social events can best be explained in terms of the functions they perform—that is, the contributions they make to the continuity of a society.

dealing with larger-scale structures and processes—the very thing that a rival tradition of thought, **functionalism**, tends to emphasize. Functionalist thinking in sociology was originally pioneered by Comte, who saw it as closely bound up with his overall view of the field.

To study the function of a social activity is to analyze the contribution that the activity makes to the continuation of the society as a whole. The best way to understand this idea is by analogy to the human body, a comparison Comte, Durkheim, and other functionalist authors made. To study an organ such as the heart, we need to show how it relates to other parts of the body. When we learn how the heart pumps blood around the body, we then understand that the heart plays a vital role in the continuation of the life of the organism. Similarly, analyzing the function of some aspect of society, such as religion, means showing the part it plays in the continued existence and health of a society. Functionalism emphasizes the importance of moral consensus in maintaining order and stability in society. Moral consensus exists when most people in a society share the same values. Functionalists regard order and balance as the normal state of society—this social equilibrium is grounded in the existence of a moral consensus among the members of society.

Functionalism became prominent in sociology in the mid-twentieth century through the writings of Talcott Parsons and Robert K. Merton, each of whom saw functionalist analysis as providing the key to the development of sociological theory and research. Merton's version of functionalism has been particularly influential.

manifest functions • The functions of a particular social activity that are known to and intended by the individuals involved in the activity.

latent functions • Functional consequences that are not intended or recognized by the members of a social system in which they occur.

Merton distinguished between manifest and latent functions. **Manifest functions** are those known to, and intended by, the participants in a specific type of social activity. **Latent functions** are consequences of that activity of which participants are unaware. To illustrate this distinction, Merton used the example of a rain dance performed by the Hopi tribe of Arizona and New Mexico. The Hopi believe that the ceremony will bring the rain they need for their crops (manifest function). This is why they organize and participate in it. But using Durkheim's theory of religion, Merton argued that the rain dance also has the effect of promoting the cohesion of the Hopi society (latent function). A major part of sociological explanation, according to Merton, consists in uncovering the latent functions of social activities and institutions.

For much of the twentieth century, functionalist thought was considered the leading theoretical tradition in sociology, particularly in the United States. In recent years, its popularity has declined as its limitations have become apparent. While this was not true of Merton, many functionalist thinkers (Talcott Parsons is an example) unduly stressed factors leading to social cohesion at the expense of those producing division and conflict. In addition, many critics argue that functional analysis attributes to societies qualities they do not have. Functionalists often wrote as though societies have "needs" and "purposes," even though these concepts make sense only when applied to individual human beings.

MARXISM AND CLASS CONFLICT

Marxism • A body of thought deriving its main elements from Karl Marx's ideas.

A third influential approach is **Marxism**. Marxists, of course, trace their views back to the writings of Karl Marx. But numerous interpretations of Marx's major ideas are possible, and today there are schools of Marxist thought that take very different theoretical positions.

In all of its versions, Marxism differs from non-Marxist perspectives in that its adherents see it as a combination of sociological analysis and political reform.

KEY WORKS IN SOCIOLOGY

Sociology is the scientific study of human social life, groups, and societies. As the titles of the works below indicate, the scope of sociological study is extremely wide.

1837
HARRIET MARTINEAU
Society in America

1838
AUGUSTE COMTE
Cours de Philosophie Positive

1848
KARL MARX & FRIEDRICH ENGELS
Communist Manifesto

1897
ÉMILE DURKHEIM
Suicide

1893
ÉMILE DURKHEIM
The Division of Labor in Society

1867
KARL MARX
Das Kapital

1902
CHARLES COOLEY
Human Nature and the Social Order

1903
W.E.B. DU BOIS
The Souls of Black Folk

1904
MAX WEBER
The Protestant Ethic and the Spirit of Capitalism

1934
GEORGE HERBERT MEAD
Mind, Self, and Society

1922
MAX WEBER
Economy and Society

1912
ÉMILE DURKHEIM
The Elementary Forms of the Religious Life

1937
TALCOTT PARSONS
The Structure of Social Action

1949
ROBERT MERTON
Social Theory and Social Structure

1956
C. WRIGHT MILLS
The Power Elite

1967
PETER M. BLAU & OTIS DUDLEY DUNCAN
The American Occupational Structure

1959
C. WRIGHT MILLS
The Sociological Imagination

1959
ERVING GOFFMAN
The Presentation of Self in Everyday Life

1973
DANIEL BELL
The Coming of Post-Industrial Society

1974
IMMANUEL WALLERSTEIN
The Modern-World System

1978
WILLIAM JULIUS WILSON
The Declining Significance of Race

1996
MANUEL CASTELLS
The Information Age: Economy, Society and Culture

1991
SASKIA SASSEN
The Global City

1984
PIERRE BOURDIEU
Distinction

power • The ability of individuals or the members of a group to achieve aims or further the interests they hold. Power is a pervasive element in all human relationships. Many conflicts in society are struggles over power, because how much power an individual or group is able to obtain governs how far they are able to put their wishes into practice.

ideology • Shared ideas or beliefs that serve to justify the interests of dominant groups. Ideologies are found in all societies in which there are systematic and ingrained inequalities among groups. The concept of ideology connects closely with that of power, since ideological systems serve to legitimize the power that groups hold.

feminist theory • A sociological perspective that emphasizes the centrality of gender in analyzing the social world and particularly the experiences of women. There are many strands of feminist theory, but they all share the intention to explain gender inequalities in society and to work to overcome them.

feminism • Advocacy of the rights of women to be equal with men in all spheres of life. Feminism dates from the late eighteenth century in Europe, and feminist movements exist in most countries today.

postmodernism • The belief that society is no longer governed by history or progress. Postmodern society is highly pluralistic and diverse, with no "grand narrative" guiding its development.

Marxism is supposed to generate a program of radical political change. Moreover, Marxists lay more emphasis on conflict, class divisions, power, and ideology than many non-Marxist sociologists, especially those influenced by functionalism. The concept of **power** and a closely associated notion, **ideology**, are of great importance to Marxist sociologists and to sociology in general. Power refers to the ability of individuals or groups to make their own concerns or interests count, even when others resist. Power sometimes involves the direct use of force but is almost always accompanied by the development of ideas (ideologies), which are used to justify the actions of the powerful. Power, ideology, and conflict are always closely connected. Many conflicts are about power, because of the rewards it can bring. Those who hold the most power may depend mainly on the influence of ideology to retain their dominance but are usually also able to use force if necessary.

FEMINISM AND FEMINIST THEORY

Feminist theory is one of the most prominent areas of contemporary sociology. This is a notable development because issues of gender are nearly absent in the work of the major figures who established the discipline. The success of feminism's entry into sociology required a fundamental—and often contested—shift in the discipline's approach.

Many feminist theorists brought their experiences in the women's movement of the 1960s and 1970s to their work as sociologists. Like Marxism, **feminism** makes a link between sociological theory and political reform. Feminist sociologists often have been advocates for political and social action to remedy the inequalities between women and men in both the public and private spheres.

Feminist sociologists argue that women's lives and experiences are central to the study of society. Historically, sociology, like most academic disciplines, has presumed a male point of view. Driven by a concern with women's subordination in American society, feminist sociologists highlight gender relations and gender inequality as important determinants of social life in terms of both social interaction and social institutions such as the family, the workplace, and the educational system. Feminist theory emphasizes that gender differences are not natural but socially constructed.

Today, feminist sociology often encompasses a focus on the intersection of gender, race, and class. A feminist approach to the study of inequality has influenced new academic fields, like gay and lesbian studies.

POSTMODERN THEORY

Postmodernists claim that the very foundation upon which classic social thought is based has collapsed. Early thinkers were inspired by the idea that history unfolds sequentially and leads to progress. Adherents of **postmodernism** counter that there are no longer any "grand narratives," or metanarratives—overall conceptions of history or society—that make any sense (Lyotard 1985). Some go so far as to argue there is no such thing as history. The postmodern world is not destined, as Marx hoped, to be a socialist one. Instead, it is one dominated by the new media, which "take us out" of our past. Postmodern society is highly pluralistic and diverse. In countless films, videos, TV programs, and websites, images circulate around the world. We are exposed to many ideas and values, but these have little connection with the history of places where we live, or with our own personal histories. The world is constantly in flux.

One of the important theorists of postmodernism is the French philosopher and sociologist Jean Baudrillard, who believes that the electronic media have

New York City's Times Square serves as the backdrop for live television programs such as ESPN's *SportsCenter* and movies like *Midnight Cowboy* and *Captain America*. Covered with advertisements and constantly in flux, it epitomizes Baudrillard's theories of postmodern society.

destroyed our relationship to our past and created a chaotic, empty world. Baudrillard was strongly influenced by Marxism in his early years. However, he argues that the spread of electronic communication and the mass media have reversed the Marxist theorem that economic forces shape society. Rather, social life is influenced above all by signs and images.

In a media-dominated age, Baudrillard says, meaning is created by the flow of images, as in TV programs. Much of our world has become a sort of make-believe universe in which we are responding to media images rather than to real persons or places. Is "reality" television a portrayal of social "reality," or does it feature televised people who are perceived to be "real"? Do housewives in New Jersey really look and act like the *Real Housewives of New Jersey*, and do the tough guys in *Amish Mafia* resemble the peaceful Amish who live and work in Lancaster County, Pennsylvania? Baudrillard would say no and would describe such images as "the dissolution of life into TV."

THEORETICAL THINKING IN SOCIOLOGY

We have described five theoretical approaches, which refer to broad orientations to the subject matter of sociology. Yet theoretical approaches are distinct from theories. Theories are more narrowly focused and represent attempts to explain particular social conditions or events. They are usually formed as part of the research process and in turn suggest problems to be investigated by researchers. An example would be Durkheim's theory of suicide, referred to earlier in this chapter.

Sometimes theories are set out very precisely and are even occasionally expressed in mathematical form—although this is more common in other social sciences (especially economics) than in sociology. Some theories, by contrast, have a much broader scope. Sociologists do not share a unified position on whether theories should be specific, wide-ranging, or somewhere in between. Robert K. Merton (1957), for example, argues forcefully that sociologists should concentrate their attention on what he calls middle-range theories. Middle-range theories are specific enough to be tested directly by empirical research, yet are sufficiently general to cover a range of different phenomena.

Relative deprivation theory is an example of a middle-range theory. It holds that how people evaluate their circumstances depends on whom they compare themselves with. Feelings of deprivation do not necessarily correspond to the absolute level of material deprivation one experiences. A family living in a small home in a poor area where everyone is in more or less similar circumstances is likely to feel less deprived than a family living in a similar house in a neighborhood where the majority of the other homes are much larger and neighbors are wealthier.

Assessing theories, and especially theoretical approaches, in sociology is a challenging and formidable task. The fact that there is not a single theoretical approach that dominates the field of sociology might be viewed as a limitation. But this is not the case at all: The jostling of rival theoretical approaches and theories reveals the vitality of the sociological enterprise. This variety rescues us from dogma or narrow-mindedness. Human behavior is complex, and no single theoretical perspective could adequately cover all of its aspects. Diversity in theoretical thinking provides a rich source of ideas that can be drawn on in research, and stimulates the imaginative capacities so essential to progress in sociological work.

LEVELS OF ANALYSIS: MICROSOCIOLOGY AND MACROSOCIOLOGY

One important distinction among the different theoretical perspectives we have discussed in this chapter involves the level of analysis at which each is directed. The study of everyday behavior in situations of face-to-face interaction is usually called **microsociology**. **Macrosociology**, by contrast, is the analysis of large-scale social systems, like the political system or the economy. It also includes the analysis of long-term processes of change, such as the development of industrialization. At first glance, it may seem as though micro and macro perspectives are distinct from each other. In fact, the two are closely connected (Giddens 1984; Knorr-Cetina and Cicourel 1981).

microsociology • The study of human behavior in contexts of face-to-face interaction.

macrosociology • The study of large-scale groups, organizations, or social systems.

Macro analysis is essential if we are to understand the institutional background of daily life. The ways in which people live their everyday lives are shaped by the broader institutional framework. For example, because of societal-level technological developments, we have many ways of maintaining friendships today. We may choose to call, send an e-mail or text message, or communicate via Facebook or Skype, yet we may also choose to fly thousands of miles to spend the weekend with a friend.

Micro studies, in turn, are necessary for illuminating broad institutional patterns. Face-to-face interaction is clearly the main basis of all forms of social organization, no matter how large scale. Suppose we are interested in understanding how business corporations function. We could analyze the face-to-face interactions of directors in the boardroom, staff working in their offices, or workers on the factory floor. We would not build up a picture of the whole corporation in this way, since some of its business is transacted through printed materials, letters, the telephone, and computers. Yet we would certainly gain a good understanding of how the organization works.

In later chapters, we will explore further examples of how interaction in micro contexts affects larger social processes, and how macro systems in turn influence more confined settings of social life. ✓

CONCEPT CHECKS

1. What role does theory play in sociological research?

2. According to Émile Durkheim, what makes sociology a social science? Why?

3. According to Karl Marx, what are the differences between the classes that make up a capitalist society?

4. What are the differences between symbolic interactionist and functionalist approaches to the analysis of society?

5. How are macro and micro analyses of society connected?

WHAT KINDS OF QUESTIONS CAN SOCIOLOGISTS ANSWER?

Be able to describe the different types of questions sociologists address in their research.

Can we really study human social life in a scientific way? To answer this question, we must first define the word *science*.

Science is the use of systematic methods of **empirical investigation**, the analysis of data, theoretical thinking, and the logical assessment of arguments, to develop a body of knowledge about a particular subject matter. Sociology is a scientific endeavor, according to this definition. It involves systematic methods of empirical investigation, the analysis of data, and the assessment of theories in the light of evidence and logical argument.

High-quality sociological research goes beyond surface-level descriptions of ordinary life; rather, it helps us understand our social lives in a new way. Sociologists are interested in the same questions that other people worry about and debate: Why do racism and sexism exist? How can mass starvation exist in a world that is far wealthier than it has ever been before? How does the Internet affect our lives? However, sociologists often develop answers that run counter to our commonsense beliefs—and that generate further questions.

Good sociological work also tries to make the questions as precise as possible and seeks to gather factual evidence before coming to conclusions. Some of the questions that sociologists ask in their research studies are largely **factual**, or empirical, **questions**.

Factual information about one society, of course, will not always tell us whether we are dealing with an unusual case or a general set of influences. For this reason, sociologists often want to ask **comparative questions**, relating one social context within a society to another or contrasting examples drawn from different societies. A typical comparative question might be, How much do patterns of criminal behavior and law enforcement vary between the United States and Canada? Similarly, **developmental questions** ask whether patterns in a given society have shifted over time: How is the past different from the present?

Yet sociologists are interested in more than just answering factual questions, however important and interesting they may be. To obtain an understanding of

science • The disciplined marshaling of empirical data, combined with theoretical approaches and theories that illuminate or explain those data. Scientific activity combines the creation of new modes of thought with the careful testing of hypotheses and ideas. One major feature that helps distinguish science from other idea systems (such as religion) is the assumption that all scientific ideas are open to criticism and revision.

empirical investigation • Factual inquiry carried out in any area of sociological study.

factual questions • Questions that raise issues concerning matters of fact (rather than theoretical or moral issues).

comparative questions • Questions concerned with drawing comparisons among different human societies for the purposes of sociological theory or research.

developmental questions • Questions that sociologists pose when looking at the origins and path of development of social institutions from the past to the present.

theoretical questions • Questions posed by sociologists when seeking to explain a particular range of observed events. The asking of theoretical questions is crucial to allowing us to generalize about the nature of social life.

human behavior, sociologists also pose broader **theoretical questions** that encompass a wide array of specific phenomena (Table 1.2). For example, a factual question may ask: To what extent do expected earnings affect one's choice of an occupation? By contrast, a theoretical question may ask: To what extent does the maximization of rewards affect human decision making?

Sociologists do not strive to attain theoretical or factual knowledge simply for its own sake, however. Social scientists agree that personal values should not be permitted to bias conclusions, but at the same time research should pose questions that are relevant to real-world concerns. In this chapter, we look further into such issues by asking whether it is possible to produce objective knowledge. First, we examine the steps involved in sociological research. We then compare the most widely used research methods as we consider some actual investigations. As we shall see, there are often significant differences between the way research should ideally be carried out and real-world studies. ✓

CONCEPT CHECKS ✓

1. Why is sociology considered to be science?
2. What are the differences between comparative and developmental questions?

Learn the steps of the research process and be able to complete the process yourself.

WHAT ARE THE SEVEN STEPS OF THE RESEARCH PROCESS?

The research process begins with the definition of a research question, and ends with the dissemination of the study findings (Figure 1.1). Although researchers do not necessarily follow all seven steps in the order set forth here, these steps serve as a model for how to conduct a sociological study. Conducting research is a bit like cooking. New researchers, like novice cooks, may follow the "recipe" to a tee. Experienced cooks often don't work from recipes at all, yet they might cook better than those who do—relying on the skills and insights they've acquired through years of hands-on experience.

Table 1.2 | A Sociologist's Line of Questioning

FACTUAL QUESTION	What happened?	During the 2010s, there was an increase in the proportion of women in their forties bearing children for the first time.
COMPARATIVE QUESTION	Did this happen everywhere?	Was this a global phenomenon or did it occur just in the United States or only in a certain region of the United States?
DEVELOPMENTAL QUESTION	Has this happened over time?	What have been the patterns of childbearing over time?
THEORETICAL QUESTION	What underlies this phenomenon?	Why are more women now waiting until their thirties and older to bear children? What factors would we look at to explain this change?

1. DEFINE THE RESEARCH PROBLEM

All research starts from a research problem. Often, researchers strive to uncover a fact: What proportion of the population attends weekly religious services? Are people today really disaffected with big government? How far does the economic position of women lag behind that of men? Do gay and straight teens differ in their levels of self-esteem?

The best sociological research, however, begins with problems that are also puzzles. A puzzle is not just a lack of information but a gap in our understanding. The most intriguing and influential sociological research correctly identifies and solves important puzzles.

Rather than simply answering the question "What is happening?" skilled researchers contribute to our understanding by asking "Why is this phenomenon happening?" We might ask, for example, "What accounts for the decline in the proportion of the population voting in presidential elections throughout the twentieth century?" "Why are women underrepresented in science and technology jobs?" or "What are the characteristics of high schools with high levels of bullying?"

Research does not take place in a vacuum. A sociologist may discover puzzles by reading the work of other researchers in books and professional journals or by being aware of emerging trends in society. For example, over recent years, an increasing number of public health programs have sought to treat the mentally ill while they continue to live in the community rather than confining them in asylums. Sociologists might be prompted to ask "What has given rise to this shift in attitudes toward the mentally ill?" and "What are the likely consequences both for the patients themselves and for the rest of the community?"

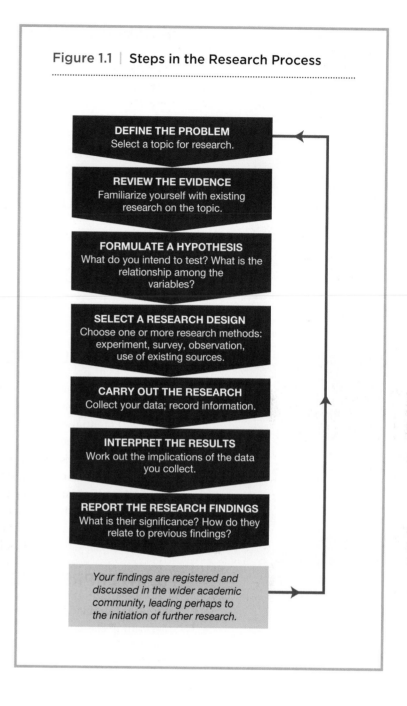

Figure 1.1 | Steps in the Research Process

DEFINE THE PROBLEM
Select a topic for research.

REVIEW THE EVIDENCE
Familiarize yourself with existing research on the topic.

FORMULATE A HYPOTHESIS
What do you intend to test? What is the relationship among the variables?

SELECT A RESEARCH DESIGN
Choose one or more research methods: experiment, survey, observation, use of existing sources.

CARRY OUT THE RESEARCH
Collect your data; record information.

INTERPRET THE RESULTS
Work out the implications of the data you collect.

REPORT THE RESEARCH FINDINGS
What is their significance? How do they relate to previous findings?

Your findings are registered and discussed in the wider academic community, leading perhaps to the initiation of further research.

2. REVIEW THE EVIDENCE

Once a research problem is identified, the next step is to review the available evidence; it's possible that other researchers have already satisfactorily clarified the problem. If not, the sociologist will need to sift through whatever related research does exist to see how useful it is for his or her purposes. What have others found? If their findings conflict with one another, what accounts for the conflict? What aspects of the problem has their research left unanalyzed? Have they looked only at small segments of the population, such as one age group, gender, or region? Drawing on others' ideas helps the sociologist clarify the issues that may be raised and the methods that could be used in the research.

3. MAKE THE PROBLEM PRECISE

A third stage involves working out a clear formulation of the research problem. If relevant literature already exists, the researcher may have a good idea of how to approach the problem. Hunches about the nature of the problem can sometimes be turned into definite **hypotheses**—educated guesses about what is going on—at this stage. A hypothesis must be formulated in such a way that the factual material gathered will provide evidence either supporting or disproving it.

hypothesis • An idea or a guess about a given state of affairs, put forward as a basis for empirical testing.

4. WORK OUT A DESIGN

The researcher must then decide how to collect the research material, or **data**. Many different research methods exist, and researchers should choose the method (or methods) that are best suited to the study's overall objectives and topic. For some purposes, a survey (in which questionnaires are normally used) might be suitable. In other circumstances, interviews or an observational study may be appropriate.

data • Factual information used as a basis for reasoning, discussion, or calculation. Social science data often refer to individuals' responses to survey questions.

5. CARRY OUT THE RESEARCH

Researchers then proceed to carry out the plan developed in step 4. However, practical difficulties may arise, forcing the researcher to rethink his or her initial strategy. Potential subjects may not agree to answer questionnaires or participate in interviews. A business firm may not give a researcher access to its records. Yet omitting such persons or institutions from the study could bias the results, creating an inaccurate or incomplete picture of social reality. For example, it would be difficult for a researcher to answer questions about how corporations have complied with affirmative action programs if companies that have not complied do not want to be studied.

6. INTERPRET THE RESULTS

Once the information has been gathered, the researcher's work is not over—it is just beginning! The data must be analyzed, trends tracked, and hypotheses tested. Most important, researchers must interpret their results in such a way that they tell a clear story and that they directly address the research puzzle outlined in step 1.

7. REPORT THE FINDINGS

The research report, usually published as a book or an article in a scholarly journal, provides an account of the research question, methods, findings, and the implications of the findings for social theory, public policy, or practice. This is a final stage only in terms of addressing the original research puzzle. In their written reports, most social scientists pose questions that remain unanswered and suggest new questions that might be explored in future studies. Each individual study contributes to the larger, collective process of understanding the human condition. ✓

CONCEPT CHECKS ✓

1. What are the seven steps of the research process?

2. What is a hypothesis?

In looking at this painting by Brueghel, we can observe the number of people, what each is doing, the style of the buildings, and the colors the painter chose. But without the title, *Netherlandish Proverbs* (1559), these facts tell us nothing about the picture's meaning. In the same way, sociologists need theory as a context for their observations.

WHAT RESEARCH METHODS DO SOCIOLOGISTS USE?

Familiarize yourself with the methods available to sociological researchers, and know the advantages and disadvantages of each. See how researchers use multiple methods in a real study.

ETHNOGRAPHY

An investigator using **ethnography** (firsthand studies of people using **participant observation** or interviews) socializes or works or lives with members of a group, organization, or community and perhaps participates directly in its activities. An ethnographer cannot secretly infiltrate the groups she studies, but must explain and justify her presence to its members. She must gain the cooperation of the community and sustain it over a period of time if any worthwhile results are to be achieved.

For a long while, research reports based on participant observation usually omitted any account of the hazards or problems that the researcher had to overcome, but more recently the published reminiscences and diaries of field-workers have been more honest and open. The researcher may be frustrated because the

ethnography • The firsthand study of people using participant observation or interviewing.

participant observation • A method of research widely used in sociology and anthropology in which the researcher takes part in the activities of the group or community being studied. Also called *fieldwork*.

Sociologist Mitchell Duneier worked as a street vendor in New York's Greenwich Village as part of his ethnographic research for his book *Sidewalk*.

members of the group refuse to talk frankly about themselves; direct queries may be welcomed in some contexts but met with a chilly silence in others. Some types of fieldwork may be emotionally isolating or even physically dangerous; for instance, a researcher studying a street gang might be seen as a police informer or might become unwittingly embroiled in conflicts with rival gangs.

In traditional works of ethnography, accounts were presented without very much information about the observer. It was believed that ethnographers could present "objective" observations of the things they studied. More recently, ethnographers have been willing to talk and write about themselves and the nature of their connection to the people under study. For example, a researcher might discuss how her race, class, gender, or sexual orientation affected the work, or how the status differences between observer and observed distorted the dialogue between them.

ADVANTAGES AND LIMITATIONS OF FIELDWORK

Where it is successful, ethnography provides rich information on the behavior of people in real-world settings. We may develop a better understanding not only of the group but of social processes that transcend the situation under study.

But fieldwork also has serious limitations. Only fairly small groups or communities can be studied. And much depends on the skill of the researcher in gaining the confidence of the individuals involved; without this skill, the research is unlikely to get off the ground at all. The reverse is also possible. A researcher may begin to identify so closely with the group that she loses the perspective of an objective observer. Or she may reach conclusions that are more about her own effects on the situation than she or her readers ever realize. Finally, the findings of field studies are seldom generalizable, meaning that researchers' conclusions may not hold true for other groups or settings.

SURVEYS

When conducting a **survey**, researchers ask subjects to provide answers to structured questionnaires. The researcher may administer the survey in person or mail it to a study participant who will then return the survey by mail. Survey results—especially those based on random samples of the larger population—often can be generalized to the population at large, yet this method provides less in-depth information than the highly descriptive, nuanced slices of life obtained in fieldwork.

survey • A method of sociological research in which questionnaires are administered to the population being studied.

"How would you like me to answer that question? As a member of my ethnic group, educational class, income group, or religious category?"

STANDARDIZED AND OPEN-ENDED QUESTIONS

Two types of questions are used in surveys. Some contain a standardized, or fixed-choice, set of questions, to which only a fixed range of responses is possible—for instance, Yes/No/Don't know or Very likely/Likely/Unlikely/Very unlikely. Such questions have the advantage that responses are easy to compare and count up because only a small number of categories are involved. However, the information they yield is limited because they do not allow for subtleties of opinion or verbal expression. For example, in a national survey of high school and middle school students' experiences with bullying, study participants answered yes/no questions such as "Has someone ever sent you a threatening or aggressive email, instant message, or text message?" but this question does not tell how severe the threat was or how upset a student was by this event (Lenhart 2007; Lenhart et al. 2011).

Table 1.3 | Three of the Main Methods Used in Sociological Research

RESEARCH METHOD	STRENGTHS	LIMITATIONS
Ethnography	Usually generates richer and more in-depth information than other methods.	Can be used to study only relatively small groups or communities.
	Provides a broader understanding of social processes.	Findings might apply only to groups or communities studied; not easy to generalize on the basis of a single fieldwork study.
Surveys	Make possible the efficient collection of data on large numbers of individuals.	Material gathered may be superficial; if questionnaire is highly standardized, important differences among respondents' viewpoints may be glossed over.
	Allow for precise comparisons to be made among the answers of respondents.	Responses may be what people profess to believe rather than what they actually believe.
Experiments	Influence of specific variables can be controlled by the investigator.	Many aspects of social life cannot be brought into the laboratory.
	Are usually easier for subsequent researchers to repeat.	Responses of those studied may be affected by the experimental situation.

Making Sociology Work
POLITICAL POLLSTER

On the night of the 2000 presidential election, each of the major television networks trumpeted that Al Gore had won Florida, and that he would be the forty-third president of the United States. When George W. Bush was officially declared the victor hours later, Dan Rather sheepishly acknowledged, "We were wrong to call it as early as we did" (Penenberg 2004). What went wrong? The television networks were relying heavily on data from exit polls; exit poll workers wait outside polling places on election night and ask people face-to-face, as they exit the building, how they voted. As a sociologist trained in survey research, would you recommend the use of exit poll data for projecting the results of presidential elections? What are the advantages of using a random sampling technique as a way to measure the views and political positions of American voters?

Open-ended questions, by contrast, typically provide more detailed information because respondents may express their views in their own words. The researcher can probe more deeply into what the respondent thinks. However, the lack of standardization means that answers may be difficult to compare across respondents. For example, the national study of Internet bullying supplemented its survey with open-ended interviews. These data allowed researchers to understand more fully what bullying entailed. One middle school girl told researchers, "I have this one friend and he's gay and his [e-mail] account got hacked and someone put all these [sic] really homophobic stuff on there and posted like a mass bulletin of some guy with his head smashed open like run over by a car. It was really gruesome and disgusting." This intensity could hardly be captured in a simple yes/no question (Lenhart 2007).

In surveys, all the items must be readily understandable to interviewers and interviewees alike. Questions are usually asked in a set order. Large national surveys are conducted regularly by government agencies and research organizations, with interviews carried out more or less simultaneously across the whole country. Those who conduct the interviews and those who analyze the data could not do their work effectively if they constantly had to be checking with one another about ambiguities in the questions or answers.

Survey researchers take care to ensure that respondents can easily understand both the questions and the response categories posed. For instance, a seemingly simple question like "What is your relationship status?" might baffle some people. It would be more appropriate to ask "Are you single, married, separated, divorced, or widowed?" Many survey questions are tried-and-true measures that have been used successfully in numerous prior studies. Researchers developing new survey questions often conduct a pilot study to test out new items. A **pilot study** is a trial run in which a questionnaire is completed by a small number of people, and problematic questions are identified and revised.

pilot study • A trial run in survey research.

SAMPLING

Often sociologists are interested in the characteristics of large numbers of individuals—for example, the political attitudes of the American population as a whole. It would be impossible to study all these people directly, so researchers' solution is to use **sampling**—they concentrate on a **sample**, or small proportion, of the overall group. One can usually be confident that results from a population sample can be generalized to the total population, as long as the sample was properly chosen. Studies of only two or three thousand voters, for instance, can give a very accurate indication of the attitudes and voting intentions of the entire population. But to achieve such accuracy, a sample must be **representative**: The group of individuals studied must be typical of the population as a whole.

A single best procedure for ensuring that a sample is representative is **random sampling**, in which a sample is chosen so that every member of the population has an equal probability of being included. The most sophisticated way of obtaining a

sampling • Studying a proportion of individuals or cases from a larger population as representative of that population as a whole.

sample • A small proportion of a larger population.

representative sample • A sample from a larger population that is statistically typical of that population.

random sampling • Sampling method in which a sample is chosen so that every member of the population has the same probability of being included.

random sample is to assign each member of the population a number and then use a computer to generate a random numbers list from which the sample is derived—for instance, by picking every tenth number.

EXPERIMENTS

An **experiment** enables a researcher to test a hypothesis under highly controlled conditions established by the researcher. Experiments are often used in the natural sciences and psychology, as they are considered the best method for ascertaining causality, or the influence of a particular factor on the study's outcome. In an experimental situation, the researcher directly controls the circumstances being studied. Because most experiments occur in laboratories, however, the scope of topics explored is quite restricted. We can bring only small groups of individuals into a laboratory setting, and in such experiments, people know that they are being studied and may behave unnaturally. Experiments also neglect the macrosocial context, such as historical or political influences.

Nevertheless, several experimental studies have made important contributions to sociological knowledge. One example is the ingenious experiment carried out by Philip Zimbardo (1972), who set up a make-believe prison, randomly assigning some student volunteers to the role of prison guards and others to the role of prisoners. His aim was to see how one's social role shaped one's attitudes and behavior. The results shocked the investigators. Students who played at being guards quickly assumed an authoritarian manner; they displayed genuine hostility toward the prisoners, ordering them around and verbally abusing and bullying them. The prisoners, by contrast, showed a mixture of apathy and rebelliousness—a response often noted among inmates in real prisons. These effects were so marked and the level of tension so high that the experiment had to be called off at an early stage. Zimbardo concluded that behavior in prisons is influenced more by the nature of the prison situation itself than by the individual characteristics of those involved.

experiment • A research method in which variables can be analyzed in a controlled and systematic way, either in an artificial situation constructed by the researcher or in naturally occurring settings.

comparative research • Research that compares one set of findings on one society with the same type of findings on other societies.

COMPARATIVE RESEARCH

Comparative research is of central importance in sociology because it enables researchers to document whether social behavior varies across time and place and by one's social group memberships. For example, divorce rates rose rapidly in the United States after World War II, reaching a peak in the early 1980s, then declining slightly and leveling off in recent years. As many as one in three couples marrying today will divorce (National Center for Family and Marriage Research 2013)—a statistic that expresses profound changes taking place in the area of sexual relations and family life. Do these changes reflect specific features of American society? We can find out by comparing divorce rates in the United States with those in other countries. Although the U.S. rate is higher than the rate in most other Western societies, the overall trends are similar. Virtually all Western countries have experienced steadily climbing divorce rates over the past half-century.

In Philip Zimbardo's make-believe jail, tension between students playing guards and students playing prisoners became dangerously real.

STATISTICAL TERMS

Research in sociology often makes use of statistical techniques in the analysis of findings. Some are highly sophisticated and complex, but those most often used are easy to understand. The most common are **measures of central tendency** (ways of calculating averages) and **correlation coefficients** (measures of the degree to which one variable relates consistently to another). There are three methods of calculating averages, each of which has certain advantages and shortcomings. Take as an example the amount of personal wealth (including all assets such as houses, cars, bank accounts, and investments) owned by thirteen individuals. Suppose the thirteen own the following amounts:

1. $0
2. $5,000
3. $10,000
4. $20,000
5. $40,000
6. $40,000
7. $40,000
8. $80,000
9. $100,000
10. $150,000
11. $200,000
12. $400,000
13. $10,000,000

The **mean** corresponds to the average, arrived at by adding together the personal wealth of all thirteen people and dividing the result by thirteen. The total is $11,085,000; dividing this by thirteen, we reach a mean of $852,692.31. This mean is often a useful calculation because it is based on the whole range of data provided. However, it can be misleading where one or a small number of cases are very different from the majority. In the above example, the mean is not in fact an appropriate measure of central tendency, because the presence of one very large figure, $10,000,000, skews the picture. One might get the impression when using the mean to summarize these data that most of the people own far more than they actually do. In such instances, one of two other measures may be used.

The **mode** is the figure that occurs most frequently in a given set of data. In our example, it is $40,000.

The problem with the mode is that it doesn't take into account the overall distribution of the data—that is, the range of figures covered. The most frequently occurring case in a set of figures is not necessarily representative of their distribution as a whole and thus may not be a useful average. In this case, $40,000 is too close to the lower end of the figures.

The third measure is the **median**, which is the middle of any set of figures; here, this would be the seventh figure, again $40,000. Our example gives an odd number of figures, thirteen. If there had been an even number—for instance, twelve—the median would be calculated by taking the mean of the two middle cases, figures 6 and 7. Like the mode, the median gives no idea of the actual range of the data measured.

Sometimes a researcher will use more than one measure of central tendency to avoid giving a deceptive picture of the average. More often, he or she will calculate the **standard deviation** for the data in question. This is a way of calculating the **degree of dispersal**, or the range, of a set of figures—which in this case goes from $0 to $10,000,000.

Correlation coefficients offer a useful way of expressing how closely connected two (or more) variables are. Where two variables correlate completely, we can speak of a perfect positive correlation, expressed as 1.0. Where no relation is found between two variables—they have no consistent connection at all—the coefficient is 0. A perfect negative correlation, expressed as -1.0, exists when two variables are in a completely inverse relation to each other. Perfect correlations are never found in the social sciences. Correlations of the order of 0.6 or more, whether positive or negative, are usually regarded as indicating a strong degree of connection between whatever variables are being analyzed. Positive correlations on this level might be found between, say, social class background and voting behavior.

HISTORICAL ANALYSIS

A key aspect of the sociological imagination is considering ways that historical context shapes individual lives. As such, we frequently need a time perspective to make sense of the material we collect about a particular problem.

Sociologists commonly want to investigate past events directly. Some periods of history can be studied retrospectively, when potential study participants or reporters are still alive—such as in the case of the 1960s civil rights movement in the United States. Research in **oral history** means interviewing people about events they witnessed at some point earlier in their lives. This kind of research can stretch back in time at the most only some sixty or seventy years. For historical research on an earlier period, sociologists depend on the use of documents and written records, often held in special collections at libraries or the National Archives.

An interesting example of the use of historical documents is sociologist Anthony Ashworth's (1980) study of trench warfare during World War I. Ashworth was interested in the lives of men who had to endure being under constant fire, crammed in close proximity for weeks on end. He used a range of documentary sources: official histories of the war, including those written about different military divisions and battalions; official publications of the time; the notes and records kept informally by individual soldiers; and personal accounts of war experiences. He discovered that most soldiers formed their own ideas about how often they intended to engage in combat with the enemy and often effectively ignored the commands of their officers. For example, on Christmas Day, German and Allied soldiers suspended hostilities, and in one place the two sides even staged an informal soccer match. These insights were gleaned from a rich and diverse array of sources.

Despite the distinctive strengths of ethnography, surveys, experiments, comparative research, and historical analysis, each method has limitations. Sociologists often combine several methods in a single piece of research, using each method to supplement and check on the others. This process is known as **triangulation**. Laud Humphreys's classic *Tearoom Trade* (1970) study is an example of how researchers may use multiple methods to develop a deep understanding of social behavior. *Tearoom Trade* is an exploration of the phenomenon within the gay community involving the pursuit of impersonal homosexual sex in public restrooms. This study used surveys and observation to obtain fascinating glimpses into the secret lives of gay men. Yet, as we will see in the next section, it also revealed the important ethical challenges faced by sociologists. ✓

measures of central tendency • The ways of calculating averages.

correlation coefficient • A measure of the degree of correlation between variables.

mean • A statistical measure of central tendency, or average, based on dividing a total by the number of individual cases.

mode • The number that appears most often in a given set of data.

median • The number that falls halfway in a range of numbers—a way of calculating central tendency.

standard deviation • A way of calculating the spread of a group of figures.

degree of dispersal • The range or distribution of a set of figures.

oral history • Interviews with people about events they witnessed earlier in their lives.

triangulation • The use of multiple research methods as a way of producing more reliable empirical data than are available from any single method.

CONCEPT CHECKS ✓

1. What are the main advantages and limitations of ethnography as a research method?

2. Contrast the two types of questions commonly used in surveys.

3. What is a random sample?

4. Discuss the main strengths of experiments.

5. What are the similarities and differences between comparative and historical research?

6. Why is it important to use triangulation in social research?

WHAT ETHICAL DILEMMAS DO SOCIOLOGISTS FACE?

Recognize the ethical problems researchers may face and identify possible solutions to these dilemmas.

In his groundbreaking *Tearoom Trade* study (1970), Humphreys investigated "tearooms," or public restrooms where men would go to have sex with other men—often hiding their "secret" lives from their wives, children, and coworkers. Humphreys's study cast a new light on the struggles of men who were forced to keep their sexual

READING A TABLE

You will often come across tables when reading sociological literature. They sometimes look complex but are easy to decipher if you follow a few basic steps, listed here; with practice, these will become automatic. (See Table 1.4 as an example.) Do not succumb to the temptation to skip over tables; they contain information in concentrated form, which can be read more quickly than would be possible if the same material were expressed in words. By becoming skilled in the interpretation of tables, you will also be able to check how justified the conclusions a writer draws actually seem.

1. Read the title in full. Tables frequently have longish titles that represent an attempt by the researcher to state accurately the nature of the information conveyed. The title of Table 1.4 gives first the subject of the data, second the fact that the table provides material for comparison, and third the fact that data are given only for a limited number of countries.

2. Look for explanatory comments, or notes, about the data. A note at the foot of Table 1.4 linked to the main column heading indicates that the data cover only licensed cars. This is important because in some countries the proportion of vehicles properly licensed may be lower than in others. Notes may say how the material was collected or why it is displayed in a particular way. If the data have not been gathered by the researcher but are based on findings originally reported elsewhere, a source will be included. The source sometimes gives you some insight into how reliable the information is likely to be, as well as showing where to find the original data. In our table, the source note makes clear that the data have been taken from more than one source.

3. Read the headings along the top and left-hand side of the table. (Sometimes tables are arranged with "headings" at the foot rather than the top.) These tell you what type of information is contained in each row and column. In reading the table, keep in mind each set of headings as you scan the figures. In our example, the headings on the left give the countries involved, whereas those at the top refer to the levels of car ownership and the years for which they are given.

4. Identify the units used; the figures in the body of the table may represent cases, percentages, averages, or other measures. Sometimes it may be helpful to convert the figures to a form more useful to you: If percentages are not provided, for example, it may be worth calculating them.

5. Consider the conclusions that might be reached from the information in the table. Most tables are discussed by the author, and what he or she has to say should of course be borne in mind. But you should also ask what further issues or questions could be suggested by the data.

proclivities secret. His book led to a deeper understanding of the consequences of the social stigma and legal persecution associated with gay lifestyles. His work is just as timely as ever, given recent incidents like the harassment of Rutgers University student Tyler Clementi, who committed suicide shortly after being "outed" by his freshman-year roommate.

Despite the value and impact of Humphreys's work, it also is held up as a cautionary example of the ethical dilemmas that researchers face. The key ethical questions that sociologists must ask are (1) Does the research pose risks to the subjects that are greater than the risks they face in their everyday lives? (2) Do the scientific gains or "benefits" of the research balance out the "risks" to the subjects? These questions do not have easy answers, as Humphreys's work reveals.

Table 1.4 | Automobile Ownership: Comparisons of Several Selected Countries

Several interesting trends can be seen from the figures in this table. First, the level of car ownership varies considerably among different countries. The number of cars per 1,000 people is more than six times greater in the United States than in Brazil, for example. Second, there is a clear connection between car ownership ratios as a rough indicator of differences in prosperity. Third, in all the countries represented, the rate of car ownership increased between 1971 and 2002, but in some the rate of increase was higher than others— probably indicating differences in the degree to which countries have successfully generated economic growth or are catching up.

NUMBER OF CARS PER 1,000 OF THE ADULT POPULATION[a]

COUNTRY	1971	1981	1984	1989	1993	1996	2001	2002	2008	2010
Brazil	12	78	84	98	96	79	95	116	158[e]	178[f]
Chile	19	45	56	67	94	110	133	NA	109	184
China	NA	NA	NA	5[c]	6	8	12[d]	16	27	58
France	261	348	360	574	503	524	584	592	495	580
Greece	30	94	116	150	271	312	428	450	443	624
Ireland	141	202	226	228	290	307	442	445	451	434[f]
Italy	210	322	359	424	586	674	638	655	596	679
Japan	100	209	207	286	506	552	577	581	319	591
Sweden	291	348	445	445	445	450	497	500	464	520
United Kingdom	224	317	343	366	386	399	554	551	462	519
United States	448	536	540	607	747	767	785	789	451	797
West Germany[b]	247	385	312	479	470	528	583	588	502	572

[a] Includes all licensed cars.
[b] Germany as a whole after 1989.
[c] Data for 1990.
[d] Data for 2000.
[e] Data for 2007.
[f] Data for 2009.
NA, not applicable.

SOURCES: Baltic 21 Secretariat 2006; International Monetary Fund 2005; International Road Federation 1987, p. 68; Organization for Economic Co-operation and Development [OECD] 2005a; Statistical Office of the European Communities 1991; *The Economist* 1996; Toyota Corporation 2003; United Nations Economic Commission for Europe 2003; World Bank 1999, 2005, 2013e.

Humphreys set out to understand what kinds of men came to the tearooms. In order to answer this question, he took on the role of a "lookout"—a person who loitered in the tearoom and would let the others know if an intruder, such as a police officer, was nearby. This allowed him to observe the gay men's activity. He could not easily ask questions or talk to the men in the tearoom, however, because of the norm of silence that prevailed. Humphreys also could not ask personal questions of men who wanted to remain anonymous.

Given his desire to learn more than his observations would allow, Humphreys's solution was to learn about the men in the tearooms by using survey methods. He would write down the license plate numbers of men who drove into the parking lot and who then went into the restrooms for the purpose of engaging in sexual relations.

Humphreys then gave those license plate numbers to a friend who worked at the Department of Motor Vehicles, securing the addresses of the men.

Months later, Washington University in St. Louis was conducting a door-to-door survey of sexual habits. Humphreys asked the principal investigators in that survey if he could add the names and addresses of his sample of tearoom participants. Humphreys then disguised himself as one of the investigators and went to interview these men at their homes, supposedly just to ask the survey questions but actually also to learn more about their social backgrounds and lives. He found that most of these men were married and led very conventional lives.

Humphreys later acknowledged that he was less than truthful to those whose behavior he was studying. He didn't reveal his identity as a sociologist when observing the tearoom activities. People who came into the tearoom assumed he was there for the same reasons they were and that his presence could be accepted at face value. While he did not tell any direct lies while observing the tearoom, he also did not reveal the real reason for his presence there.

Was his behavior ethical? The study had many benefits, including moving forward scientific knowledge about gay men during a period when their behaviors were highly stigmatized. If Humphreys had been completely frank at every stage of the research, his study might not have gotten as far as it did. At the same time, however, the costs to the research subjects were potentially high.

The observational part of his study posed only modest risk: Humphreys did not collect information about the participants that would have identified them. What he knew about them was similar to what all the other people in the tearoom knew. His presence did not expose them to any more risk than they already encountered in their everyday lives.

The more problematic aspect of Humphreys's study was that he wrote down the license plate numbers of the people who came into the tearooms, obtained their home addresses from the Department of Motor Vehicles, and visited their homes under the guise of conducting a survey for Washington University. Even though Humphreys did not reveal to the men's families anything about the activities he observed in the tearooms, and even though he took great pains to keep the data confidential, the knowledge he gained could have been damaging. Because the activity he was documenting was illegal at the time, police officers might have demanded that he release information about the men's identities. A less skilled investigator might have slipped up when interviewing the subjects' families. Humphreys could have lost his notes, which could then have been found later by someone else.

Humphreys was one of the first sociologists to study the lives of gay men. (However, researchers today still face challenges in studying the lives of gays and lesbians.) Humphreys's account was a humane treatment that went well beyond what little was known about gay men at that time. Although none of his research subjects suffered as a result of his book, Humphreys himself later said that if he were to do the study again, he would not trace license plates or go to people's homes. Instead, after gathering his data in the public tearooms, he might try to get to know a subset of the people well enough to inform them of his goals for the study.

It is unlikely that Humphreys's tactics will be repeated in the future. In recent years, the federal government has become increasingly strict with universities that make use of government grant money for research purposes. The National Science Foundation and the National Institutes of Health have strict requirements outlining how human subjects must be treated. In response to these requirements, American universities now have Institutional Review Boards (IRBs) that routinely review all research involving human subjects.

The result of these review procedures has been both positive and negative. On the positive side, researchers are more aware of ethical considerations than ever before. On the negative side, however, many sociologists are finding it increasingly difficult to get their work done when IRBs require them to secure informed consent from their research subjects before they are able to establish a rapport with the subjects. **Informed consent** means that study participants are given a broad description of the study prior to agreeing to participate. After reading this summary, they are free to opt out of the research. Another safeguard used to protect subjects is **debriefing**; after the research study ends, the investigator discusses any concerns the subjects may have, and acknowledges whether strategies such as deception were used. Despite these safeguards, there will likely never be easy solutions to vexing problems posed by research ethics. ✓

CONCEPT CHECKS ✓

1. What ethical dilemmas did Humphreys's *Tearoom Trade* study pose?

2. Contrast informed consent and debriefing.

HOW DOES THE SOCIOLOGICAL IMAGINATION AFFECT YOUR LIFE?

Understand how adopting a sociological perspective allows us to develop a richer understanding of ourselves, our significant others, and the world.

When we observe the world through the prism of the sociological imagination, we are affected in several important ways. First, we develop a greater awareness and understanding of cultural differences. For example, a high school guidance counselor won't easily gain the confidence of his or her students who are the targets of bullying without being sensitive to the ways that gender and sexual orientation shape students' experiences at school.

Second, we are better able to assess the results of public policy initiatives. For instance, while forty-nine states have anti-bullying laws, we will not be able to understand how effective they are unless we systematically obtain data on the levels of bullying before and after the implementation of these policies.

Third, we may become more self-enlightened and may develop wise insights into our own behaviors. Have you ever bullied or picked on a classmate at school? Have you ever harassed a classmate online? If yes, why did you pick on that particular student? Were you encouraged to do so by your classmates? Did the anonymous nature of the Internet make you feel like you wouldn't get "caught"? Sociology helps us understand why we act as we do, and helps us recognize that social context—such as our peers or school dynamics—also may shape our behaviors.

Fourth, developing a sociological eye toward social problems and developing rigorous research skills opens many career doors—as industrial consultants, urban planners, social workers, and personnel managers, among other jobs. An understanding of society also serves those working in law, journalism, business, and medicine.

In sum, sociology is a discipline in which we often set aside our personal views and biases to explore the influences that shape our lives and those of others. Sociology emerged as an intellectual endeavor along with the development of modern societies, and the study of such societies remains its principal concern. Sociology has major practical implications for people's lives. Learning to become a sociologist is an exciting academic pursuit! The best way to make sure it is exciting is to approach the subject in an imaginative way and to relate sociological ideas and findings to your own life. ✓

informed consent • The process whereby the study investigator informs potential participants about the risks and benefits involved in the research study. Informed consent must be obtained before an individual participates in a study.

debriefing • Following a research study, the investigator will inform study participants about the true purpose of the study, and will reveal any deception that happened during the study.

CONCEPT CHECKS ✓

1. Describe four ways that sociology can help us in our lives.

2. What skills and perspectives do sociologists bring to their work?

EXERCISES:
Thinking Sociologically

1. Healthy older Americans often encounter discriminatory treatment when younger people assume that they are feebleminded and thus overlook them for jobs they are fully capable of doing. How would each of the popular theoretical perspectives—functionalism, class conflict theory, and symbolic interactionism—explain the dynamics of prejudice against the elderly?

2. Explain in some detail the advantages and disadvantages of doing comparative or historical research. What will it yield that will be better than experimentation, surveys, and ethnographic fieldwork? What are its limitations compared with those approaches?

3. Let's suppose the dropout rate in your local high school increased dramatically. Faced with such a serious problem, the school board offers you a $500,000 grant to do a study to explain the sudden increase. Following the recommended study procedures outlined in your text, explain how you would go about doing your research. What might be some of the hypotheses to test in your study? How would you prove or disprove them?

Chapter 1

Sociology: Theory and Method

p.5 — What Is the "Sociological Imagination"?

Learn what sociology covers as a field and how everyday topics like love and romance are shaped by social and historical forces. Recognize that sociology involves developing a sociological imagination and a global perspective, and understanding social change.

p.9 — What Theories Do Sociologists Use?

Learn about the development of sociology as a field. Be able to name some of the leading social theorists and the concepts they contributed to sociology. Learn the different theoretical approaches modern sociologists bring to the field.

p.21 — What Kinds of Questions Can Sociologists Answer?

Be able to describe the different types of questions sociologists address in their research.

p.22 — What Are the Seven Steps of the Research Process?

Learn the steps of the research process and be able to complete the process yourself.

p.25 — What Research Methods Do Sociologists Use?

Familiarize yourself with the methods available to sociological researchers, and know the advantages and disadvantages of each. See how researchers use multiple methods in a real study.

p.31 — What Ethical Dilemmas Do Sociologists Face?

Recognize the ethical problems researchers may face and identify possible solutions to these dilemmas.

p.35 — How Does the Sociological Imagination Affect Your Life?

Understand how adopting a sociological perspective allows us to develop a richer understanding of ourselves, our significant others, and the world.

TERMS TO KNOW	CONCEPT CHECKS

sociology • personal troubles • public issues

sociological imagination • structuration

1. How does sociology help us understand the causes of bullying?
2. Contrast public issues and personal troubles.
3. What is the sociological imagination, according to C. Wright Mills?
4. How does the concept of social structure help sociologists better understand social phenomena?
5. What is globalization? How might it affect the lives of college students today?

social facts • organic solidarity • social constraint • anomie • materialist conception of history • capitalism • symbolic interaction-ism • symbol • functionalism • manifest functions • latent functions • Marxism • power • ideology • feminist theory • feminism • postmodernism • microsociology • macrosociology

1. What role does theory play in sociological research?
2. According to Émile Durkheim, what makes sociology a social science? Why?
3. According to Karl Marx, what are the differences between the classes that make up a capitalist society?
4. What are the differences between symbolic interactionist and functionalist approaches to the analysis of society?
5. How are macro and micro analyses of society connected?

science • empirical investigation • factual questions • comparative questions • developmental questions • theoretical questions

1. Why is sociology considered to be science?
2. What are the differences between comparative and developmental questions?

hypothesis • data

1. What are the seven steps of the research process?
2. What is a hypothesis?

ethnography • participant observation • survey • pilot study • sampling • sample • representative sample • random sampling • experiment • comparative research • measures of central tendency • correlation coefficient • mean • mode • median • standard deviation • degree of dispersal • oral history • triangulation

1. What are the main advantages and limitations of ethnography as a research method?
2. Contrast the two types of questions commonly used in surveys.
3. What is a random sample?
4. Discuss the main strengths of experiments.
5. What are the similarities and differences between comparative and historical research?
6. Why is it important to use triangulation in social research?

informed consent • debriefing

1. What ethical dilemmas did Humphreys's *Tearoom Trade* study pose?
2. Contrast informed consent and debriefing.

1. Describe four ways that sociology can help us in our lives.
2. What skills and perspectives do sociologists bring to their work?

Culture and Society

THE BIG QUESTIONS

WHAT IS CULTURE?

Know what culture consists of, and recognize how it differs from society.

HOW DOES HUMAN CULTURE DEVELOP?

Begin to understand how both biological and cultural factors influence our behavior. Learn the ideas of sociobiology and how others have tried to refute these ideas by emphasizing cultural differences.

WHAT HAPPENED TO PREMODERN SOCIETIES?

Learn how societies have changed over time.

HOW HAS INDUSTRIALIZATION SHAPED MODERN SOCIETY?

Recognize the factors that transformed premodern societies, particularly how industrialization and colonialism influenced global development. Know the differences among industrialized societies, emerging economies, and developing societies, and how these differences developed.

HOW DOES GLOBALIZATION AFFECT CONTEMPORARY CULTURE?

Recognize the effect of globalization on your life and the lives of people around the world. Think about the effect of a growing global culture.

Members of feminist punk rock protest group Pussy Riot perform in Moscow's Red Square. The politically charged performances have attracted praise from proponents of free speech, yet led to criminal charges against the band members in their home country of Russia. What do these divergent reactions tell us about cultural norms and values?

T o many young people and creative artists throughout the world, Pussy Riot is a cultural icon—an edgy, angry Russian feminist punk rock protest group and YouTube sensation. Influential musicians like Madonna and Sting have embraced Pussy Riot, celebrating their radical politics and feminist messages and supporting their right to freedom of speech. But in the eyes of the Russian Orthodox Church, and local authorities in Pussy Riot's hometown of Moscow, Russia, the approximately eleven members of the all-female punk band are criminals.

How did the members of Pussy Riot, heroines of the punk rock community, become heretics in the eyes of the "old guard" members of Russian society? Formed in August 2011, days after Russian president Vladimir Putin announced his plans to run for re-election, Pussy Riot began staging miniature flash protests in public places like the Moscow Metro and store windows. Wearing brightly colored ski masks to protect their identities, the women of Pussy Riot performed short, fast, politically charged punk songs critical of Putin's government, especially its restrictive positions on women's and LGBT issues. These performances were recorded and then posted on the Internet for the entire world to see.

As Pussy Riot's popularity and following grew, they chose larger and more politically charged spaces for their performances. In late 2011, they staged a concert from the roof of a detention center where an anti-Putin protest leader and blogger was being held in police custody. In January 2012, in what has been called the group's "breakthrough performance," Pussy Riot performed a song titled "Putin Zassal" (which loosely translates to "Putin Is Wetting Himself"). The lyrics called for a popular revolt against the Russian government and an occupation of Russia's main square. During the performance they ignited a smoke bomb that led to their arrest and detainment for a misdemeanor. Two members were found guilty and each had to pay a fine of 500 rubles (roughly $15).

Their troubles escalated the next month when five group members entered a mostly empty Cathedral of Christ the Savior of the Russian Orthodox Church in Moscow to perform their song "Punk Prayer." Protesting the re-election of Putin, the women played for less than a minute before being escorted out of the church by guards. Church leaders demanded that the women be charged with the crime of blasphemy, while the local law enforcement agencies argued for a charge of hooliganism, which could carry a punishment of up to eight years in prison. The government also ordered local Cossack groups to patrol churches to ensure that similar events didn't happen elsewhere. On August 17, 2012, after long and intricate legal proceedings, three members of the band were convicted of hooliganism motivated by religious hatred and sentenced to two years in a penal colony (Freed 2012).

Almost instantly after the sentence was announced, protests erupted in the group's native Russia and throughout the world. Amnesty International declared August 17, 2012, "Pussy Riot Global Day." Actors and performance artists such as Karen Finley gathered in New York to read aloud statements by the convicted band members. In Bulgaria, activists placed Pussy Riot–style ski masks on Soviet sculptures. Countless protests, both in person and online, continue in support of Pussy Riot.

In December 2013, the women were released from prison after surviving twenty-one months of their sentences. Their saga, however, is far from over. The remaining members of the group still perform, and controversy and legal troubles will no doubt continue to dog them. In February 2014, Russian security forces beat six members of the group with horse whips as they tried to perform a song in Sochi, site of the Winter Olympics. A few days later, Pussy Riot released a new music video with clips of the attack—titled "Putin Will Teach You to Love the Motherland"—slamming Putin and Russia's handling of the Winter Games.

The church and local government's attack on members of Pussy Riot—and the outcry of support from international artists, politicians, and musicians—raises important questions about values and culture in our increasingly diverse and global society. How do values and culture shape our everyday lives? And given rapid levels of social change throughout the world, how do individuals balance the cultural and religious practices of today with those of earlier times? Or the values of their own homelands with the values of other nations that they observe and embrace via the Internet? How do societies help to ensure that individuals are able to maintain their own subcultures while also adopting some practices and values of the "mainstream" culture? These are some of the questions we explore in this chapter.

First, however, we look at what culture is and its role in encouraging conformity to shared ways of thinking and acting. We then consider the early development of human culture, emphasizing features that distinguish human behavior from that of other species. After assessing the role of biology in shaping human behavior, we examine the different aspects of culture that are essential for human society. This leads to a discussion of cultural diversity, examining the cultural variations not only across different societies but also within a single society such as the United States.

Cultural variations among human beings are linked to differing types of society, and we will compare and contrast the main forms of society found in history. The point of doing this is to tie together closely the two aspects of human social existence—the different cultural values and products that human beings have developed and the contrasting types of society in which such cultural development has occurred. Too often, culture is discussed separately from society as though the two were disconnected, whereas in fact, as we've already emphasized, they are closely intertwined. Throughout the chapter, we concentrate on how social change has affected cultural development. One instance of this is the effect of technology and globalization on the many cultures of the world; for example, would Pussy Riot have received support from artists throughout the world without technology to help them spread their message? We explore this topic in the conclusion to this chapter.

WHAT IS CULTURE?

Know what culture consists of, and recognize how it differs from society.

The sociological study of **culture** began with Émile Durkheim in the nineteenth century and soon became the basis of anthropology, a social science specifically focused on the study of cultural differences and similarities among the world's peoples. Early social scientists assumed that "primitive" cultures were inferior, lagging far behind modern European "civilization." However, sociologists and anthropologists now recognize that different cultures each have their own distinctive characteristics. The task of social science is to understand this cultural diversity, which is best done by avoiding value judgments.

DEFINING "CULTURE"

Culture consists of the values held by members of a particular group, the languages they speak, the symbols they revere, the norms they follow, and the material goods they create, from tools to clothing. Some elements of culture, especially the beliefs and expectations people have about one another and the world they inhabit, are a component of all social relations. **Values** are abstract ideals. For example, monogamy—being faithful to one's sole romantic partner—is a prominent value in most Western societies. In other cultures, on the other hand, a person may be permitted to have several wives or husbands simultaneously. Likewise, freedom of expression is a cherished value in the United States and many other nations. The Pussy Riot case vividly reveals an instance when the competing values of freedom of expression and silent obedience to political and religious authority came into conflict with each other. **Norms** are widely agreed-upon principles or rules people are expected to observe; they represent the dos and don'ts of social life. Norms of behavior in marriage include, for example, how husbands and wives are supposed to behave toward their in-laws. In some societies, they are expected to develop a close relationship; in others, they keep a clear distance from each other.

culture • The values, norms, and material goods characteristic of a given group. Like the concept of society, the notion of culture is widely used in sociology and the other social sciences (particularly anthropology). Culture is one of the most distinctive properties of human social association.

values • Ideas held by individuals or groups about what is desirable, proper, good, and bad. What individuals value is strongly influenced by the specific culture in which they happen to live.

norms • Rules of conduct that specify appropriate behavior in a given range of social situations. A norm either prescribes a given type of behavior or forbids it. All human groups follow definite norms, which are always backed by sanctions of one kind or another—varying from informal disapproval to physical punishment.

Norms, like the values they reflect, vary widely both across and within cultures. Among most Americans, for example, one norm calls for direct eye contact between persons engaged in conversation; completely averting one's eyes is usually interpreted as a sign of weakness or rudeness. Yet, among the Navajo, a cultural norm calls for averting one's eyes as a sign of respect. Direct eye contact, particularly between strangers, is considered rude because it violates a norm of politeness. When a Navajo and a Western tourist encounter each other for the first time, the Navajo's cultural norm calls for averting the eyes, while the tourist's cultural norm calls for direct eye contact. The result is likely to be a misunderstanding: The Navajo may see the tourist as impolite and vulgar, while the tourist may see the Navajo as disrespectful or deceptive. Such cultural misunderstandings may lead to unfair generalizations and stereotypes and even promote outright hostility. Values and norms work together to shape how members of a culture behave within their surroundings.

Even within a single culture, the norms of conduct differ by age, gender, and other important social subgroups. Gender norms are particularly powerful; women are expected to be more docile, caring, and even more moral than men. Some feminist writers argue that one reason why the members of Pussy Riot were so vilified by the Russian government is that they defied norms about "typical" female behavior. In fact, two members are mothers of young children; performing in costume with a punk rock ensemble and spewing expletives may be viewed as a violation of both gender and parenting norms (Douglas and Michaels 2005).

material goods • The physical objects that a society creates; these influence the ways in which people live.

Finally, **material goods** refer to the physical objects that individuals in society create. These objects, in turn, influence how we live. They include the food we eat, the clothes we wear, the cars we drive to the houses we live in; the tools and technologies we use to make those goods, from sewing machines to computerized factories; and the towns and cities that we build as places in which to live and work. As we saw in the case of Pussy Riot, material goods such as clothing can communicate very powerful social meaning. While a brightly colored ski mask might not be noticed on the snowy ski slopes of Colorado, the same article of clothing carries a highly politically charged message when worn in sacred public places. What people wear may reveal what they believe, how they live, and what norms and values they abide by.

Today, material culture is rapidly becoming globalized, thanks in large part to modern information technology such as the computer, smartphone, and Internet. As noted at the beginning of this chapter, the United States has been in the forefront of this technological revolution, although most other industrial countries are rapidly catching up. In fact, it no longer makes sense to speak of an exclusively "U.S. technology" any more than it makes sense to speak of a U.S. car. The "world car," with parts manufactured across the planet in a global assembly line, embodies technology developed in Japan, the United States, and Europe.

When we use the term *culture* in daily conversation, we often think of "high culture"—like fine art, literature, classical music, ballet. For a sociological perspective, the concept includes these activities, but also many more. Culture refers to the ways of life of the individual members or groups within a society: their apparel, marriage customs and family life, patterns of work, religious ceremonies, and leisure pursuits. The concept also covers the goods they create and the goods that become meaningful for them—bows and arrows, plows, factories and machines, computers, books, dwellings. We should think of culture as a "design for living" or "tool kit" of practices, knowledge, and symbols acquired—as we shall see later—through learning rather than by **instinct** (Kluckhohn 1949; Swidler 1986).

Is it possible to describe an "American" culture? Although the United States is culturally diverse, we can identify several characteristics of a uniquely American culture. First, it reflects a particular range of values shared by many, if not all, Americans—such as the belief in the merits of individual achievement or in equality of opportunity. Second, these values are connected to specific norms: For example, it is usually expected that people will work hard to achieve occupational success (Bellah et al. 1985; Parsons 1964). Third, it involves the use of material artifacts created mostly through modern industrial technology, such as cars, mass-produced food, clothing, and so forth.

Values and norms vary enormously across and even within cultures. Some cultures value individualism highly, whereas others place great emphasis on collectivism. A simple example makes this clear. Most pupils in the United States would be outraged to find another student cheating on an examination. In the United States, copying from someone else's paper goes against core values of individual achievement, equality of opportunity, hard work, and respect for the rules. Russian students, however, might be puzzled by this sense of outrage among their American peers. Helping one another pass an examination reflects the value Russians place on equality and on collective problem solving in the face of authority. Think of your own reaction to this example. What does it say about the values of your society?

Within a single society or community, values also may conflict: As we saw with the Pussy Riot controversy, some groups or individuals may value traditional religious beliefs, whereas others may favor freedom of expression, individual rights, and gender-based equality. Some people may prefer material comfort and success, whereas others may favor simplicity and a quiet life. In our changing age—filled with the global movement of people, ideas, goods, and information—it is not surprising that we encounter instances of cultural values in conflict.

Norms, like the values they reflect, also change over time. For example, beginning in 1964, with the U.S. surgeon general's report "Smoking and Health," which presented definitive medical evidence linking smoking with a large number of serious health problems, the U.S. government waged a highly effective campaign to discourage people from smoking. A social norm favoring smoking—once associated with independence, sex appeal, and glamour—has given way to an equally strong antismoking social norm that depicts smoking as unhealthful, unattractive, and selfish. Today, the percentage of American adults who smoke is 19 percent, less than half the rate in 1964, when the surgeon general's report was issued (Centers for Disease Control and Prevention 2012d).

instinct • A fixed pattern of behavior that has genetic origins and that appears in all normal animals within a given species.

Smoking was portrayed as sophisticated and elegant in the 1950s. Today, smokers are vilified for harming themselves and their children. What has contributed to these drastic changes in our perceptions of smokers?

Many of our everyday behaviors and habits are grounded in cultural norms. Movements, gestures, and expressions are strongly influenced by cultural factors. A clear example of this can be seen in the way people smile—particularly in public contexts—across different cultures.

Among the Inuit (Eskimos) of Greenland, for example, one does not find the strong tradition of public smiling that exists in many areas of western Europe and North America. This does not mean that the Inuit are cold or unfriendly; it is simply not their common practice to smile at or exchange pleasantries with strangers. As the service industry has expanded in Greenland in recent years, however, some employers have made efforts to instill smiling as a cultural value in the belief that smiling and expressing "polite" attitudes toward customers are essential to competitive business practices. Clients who are met with smiles and told "Have a nice day" are more likely to become repeat customers. In many supermarkets in Greenland, shop assistants are now shown training videos on friendly service techniques; the staff at some have even been sent abroad on training courses. Initially these requirements were met with discomfort by some staff, who found the style insincere and artificial. Over time, however, the idea of public smiling—at least in the workplace—has become more accepted.

CULTURE AND SOCIETY

society • A group of people who live in a particular territory, are subject to a common system of political authority, and are aware of having a distinct identity from other groups. Some societies, like hunting and gathering societies, are small, numbering no more than a few dozen people. Others are large, numbering millions—modern Chinese society, for instance, has a population of more than a billion people.

"Culture" can be distinguished from "society," but these notions are closely connected. A **society** is a system of interrelationships that connects individuals together. No culture could exist without a society; equally, no society could exist without culture. Without culture, we would not be human at all, in the sense in which we usually understand that term. We would have no language in which to express ourselves, we would have no sense of self-consciousness, and our ability to think or reason would be severely limited.

Culture also serves as a society's glue because culture is an important source of conformity, providing its members with ready-made ways of thinking and acting. For example, when you say that you subscribe to a particular value, such as formal learning, you are probably voicing the beliefs that conform to those of your family members, friends, teachers, or others who are significant in your life.

Cultures differ, however, in how much they value conformity. Research based on surveys of more than 100,000 adults in over sixty countries shows that Japanese culture lies at one extreme in terms of valuing conformity (Hofstede 1997), while at the other extreme lies American culture, one of the least conformist, ranking among the world's highest in cherishing individualism (Hamamura 2012).

American high school and college students often see themselves as especially nonconformist. The hipsters of today, like the hippies of the 1960s and the punks of the 1980s, sport distinctive clothing styles, haircuts, and other forms of bodily adornment. Yet how individualistic are they? Are young people with nose rings or studs in their tongues or tattoos really acting independently? Or are their styles perhaps as much the "uniforms" of their group as are navy blue suits among middle-aged business people? There is an aspect of conformity to their behavior—conformity to their own group.

Since some degree of conformity to norms is necessary for any society to exist, one of the key challenges for all cultures is to instill in people a willingness to conform. This is accomplished in two ways (Parsons 1964). First, individuals learn the norms of their culture. While this occurs throughout one's life, the most crucial learning occurs during childhood, and parents play a key role. When learning is

In the photo on the left, members of a 1960s commune pose for a group portrait. On the right, Harajuku girls stroll down a street in Tokyo, Japan. Though their distinctive styles set them apart from mainstream society, these people are not as nonconformist as they may think they are. Both subcultures conform to the norms of their respective social groups.

successful, the norms are so thoroughly internalized that they become unquestioned ways of thinking and acting; they come to appear "normal." (Note the similarity between the words *norm* and *normal*.)

When a person fails to learn and adequately conform to a culture's norms, a second way of instilling cultural conformity comes into play: social control. Social control often involves the punishment of rule-breaking. Administration of punishment includes such informal behavior as rebuking friends for minor breaches of etiquette, gossiping behind their backs, or ostracizing them from the group. Official, formal forms of discipline might range from parking tickets to imprisonment (Foucault 1979). Durkheim, one of the founders of sociology (introduced in Chapter 1), argued that punishment serves not only to help guarantee conformity among those who would violate a culture's norms and values but also to vividly remind others what the norms and values are. ✓

CONCEPT CHECKS ✓

1. Describe the main elements of culture.

2. What role does culture play in society?

HOW DOES HUMAN CULTURE DEVELOP?

Begin to understand how both biological and cultural factors influence our behavior. Learn the ideas of sociobiology and how others have tried to refute these ideas by emphasizing cultural differences.

Human culture and human biology are closely intertwined. Understanding how culture is related to the physical evolution of the human species can help us better understand the central role that culture plays in shaping our lives.

The Secret Power of Cultural Norms and Values

Norms are widely agreed-upon principles or rules that people are expected to observe; they represent the dos and don'ts of social life. One way to illustrate the power of a social norm is to examine reactions to norm violations. Those who violate norms are often subject to the overt or subtle disapproval of others. Common reactions might include being scolded or mocked by friends for minor breaches of etiquette, being gossiped about behind our backs, or being ostracized from the social group. Yet norms are so powerful that violators often feel shame or self-criticism even in the absence of others' words or actions.

A vivid display of the power of norms is PostSecret, an ongoing community art project where people mail in their secrets anonymously on one side of a homemade postcard. The postcards are then posted online for others to view or comment on. What does it tell us about social norms when a young woman confesses, "He found my vomit in the sink…. I said I was fine. I LIED"? In American society, eating disorders like bulimia violate a social norm that says we shouldn't hurt ourselves. Yet it also subtly conveys another norm: Young women are expected to be thin in order to live up to our cultural ideals of "beauty." Using means other than the socially approved strategies of healthy diet and exercise, however, is a source of shame.

Other postcards make claims like "I've been stealing $$$ from the piggy banks of the kids I babysit to buy groceries and weed." This postcard reveals the violations of several important norms and values (and laws): that we should not steal (especially from children), that we should not do drugs, and that poverty is a stigmatized status—and one that people are often ashamed of.

A simple scroll through the postcards on the PostSecret website reveals the many social norms at play in our culture, and the deep shame or fear of reprisal that comes from violating these behavioral expectations. Yet the fact that people throughout the world are willing to anonymously share their transgressions with others shows just how common norm violations are. It also shows just how powerful and even oppressive norms can be, given how many seek refuge by silently and anonymously "confessing" their wrongs on PostSecret.

A quick look at the site also reveals that the vast majority of participants are women. As we noted earlier in the chapter, some scholars have argued that norms regarding women's behavior are more rigid than those guiding men's behavior. Can you think of secrets that men may post, and how they might differ from those posted by women? How might sites like PostSecret reinforce or challenge social norms, especially gender norms? Do you think a forum like PostSecret would work in a venue other than the anonymous world of the Internet?

Our secrets powerfully reveal the social norms that govern our behavior. Postcards submitted to PostSecret, an ongoing community art project, highlight how certain behaviors like theft, eating disorders, and infidelity are stigmatized.

EARLY HUMAN CULTURE: ADAPTATION TO PHYSICAL ENVIRONMENT

Scientists believe that the first humans evolved from apelike creatures on the African continent some 4 million years ago. Their conclusion is based on archaeological evidence and knowledge of the close similarities in blood chemistry and genetics between chimpanzees and humans. The first evidence of humanlike culture dates back only two million years. In these early cultures, humans fashioned stone tools, derived sustenance by hunting animals and gathering nuts and berries, harnessed the use of fire, and established a highly cooperative way of life. Because early humans planned their hunts, they must also have had some ability for abstract thought.

Culture enabled early humans to compensate for their physical limitations, such as lack of claws, sharp teeth, and running speed, relative to other animals (Deacon 1998). Culture freed humans from dependence on the instinctual and genetically determined set of responses to the environment characteristic of other species. The larger, more complex human brain permitted a greater degree of adaptive learning in dealing with major environmental changes such as the Ice Age. For example, humans figured out how to build fires and sew clothing for warmth. Through greater flexibility, humans were able to survive unpredictable challenges in their surroundings and shape the world with their ideas and their tools.

Yet early humans were closely tied to their physical environment, since they still lacked the technological ability to modify their immediate surroundings significantly (Bennett 1976; Harris 1975, 1978, 1980). Their ability to secure food and make clothing and shelter depended largely on the physical resources that were close at hand. Cultures in different environments varied widely as a result of adaptations by which people fashioned their cultures to be suitable to specific geographic and climatic conditions. For example, the cultures developed by desert dwellers, where water and food were scarce, differed significantly from the cultures that developed in rain forests, where such natural resources abounded. Human inventiveness spawned a rich tapestry of cultures around the world. As you will see at the conclusion of this chapter, however, modern technology and other forces of globalization pose both challenges and opportunities for future global cultural diversity.

NATURE OR NURTURE?

Because humans evolved as a part of the world of nature, it would seem logical to assume that human thinking and behavior are the result of biology and evolution. In fact, one of the oldest and most enduring controversies in the social sciences is the "nature/nurture" debate: Are we shaped by our biology or are we products of learning through life's experiences—that is, of nurture? Biologists and some psychologists emphasize biological factors in explaining human thinking and behavior. Sociologists, not surprisingly, stress the role of learning and culture. They are also likely to argue that because human beings are capable of making conscious choices, neither biology nor culture wholly determines human behavior.

The nature/nurture debate has raged for more than a century. In the 1930s and 1940s, many social scientists focused on biological factors, with some researchers seeking (unsuccessfully), for example, to prove that a person's physique determined his or her personality. In the 1960s and 1970s, scholars in different fields emphasized culture. For example, social psychologists argued that even the most severe forms of mental illness were the result of the labels that society attaches to unusual behavior rather than of biochemical processes (Scheff 1966). Today, partly because of new understandings in genetics and brain neurophysiology, the pendulum is again swinging toward the side of biology.

The resurgence of biological explanations for human behavior began in the 1970s, when the evolutionary biologist Edward O. Wilson published *Sociobiology: The New Synthesis* (1975). The term **sociobiology** refers to the application of biological principles to explain the social activities of animals, including human beings. Using studies of insects and other social creatures, Wilson argued that genes influence not only physical traits but behavior as well. In most species, for example, males are larger and more aggressive than females and tend to dominate the "weaker sex." Some suggest that genetic factors explain why, in all human societies that we know of, men tend to hold positions of greater authority than women.

sociobiology • An approach that attempts to explain the behavior of both animals and human beings in terms of biological principles.

One way in which sociobiologists have tried to illuminate the relations between the sexes is by means of the idea of "reproductive strategy." A reproductive strategy is a pattern of behavior, arrived at through evolutionary selection, that favors the chances of survival of offspring. The female body has a larger investment in its reproductive cells than the male—a fertilized egg takes nine months to develop. Thus, according to sociobiologists, women will not squander that investment and are not driven to have sexual relations with many partners; their overriding aim is the care and protection of children. Men, on the other hand, tend toward promiscuity. Their wish to have sex with many partners is sound strategy from the point of view of the species; to carry out their mission, which is to maximize the possibility of impregnation, they move from one partner to the next. In this way, it has been suggested, we can explain differences in sexual behavior and attitudes between men and women.

Sociobiologists do not argue that our genes determine 100 percent of our behavior. For example, they note that depending on the circumstances, men can choose to act in nonaggressive ways. Yet even though this argument would seem to open up the field of sociobiology to culture as an additional explanatory factor in describing human behavior, social scientists have roundly condemned sociobiology for claiming that a propensity for particular behaviors, such as violence, is somehow "genetically programmed" into our brains (Seville Statement on Violence 1990).

HOW NATURE AND NURTURE INTERACT

Most sociologists today would acknowledge a role for nature in determining attitudes and behavior, but with strong qualifications. For example, babies are born with the ability to recognize faces: Babies a few minutes old turn their heads in response to patterns that resemble human faces but not in response to other patterns (Cosmides and Tooby 1997; Johnson and Morton 1991). But it is a large leap to conclude that because babies are born with basic reflexes, the behavior of adults is governed by instincts: inborn, biologically fixed patterns of action found in all cultures. Sociologists tend to argue strongly against **biological determinism**, or the belief that differences we observe between groups of people, such as men and women, are explained wholly by biological (rather than social) causes.

biological determinism • The belief that differences we observe between groups of people, such as men and women, are explained wholly by biological causes

Sociologists no longer pose the question as one of nature or nurture. Instead, they ask how nature and nurture interact to produce human behavior. But their main concern is with how our different ways of thinking and acting are learned through interactions with family, friends, schools, television, and every other facet of the social environment. For example, sociologists argue that it's not an inborn biological disposition that makes American heterosexual males feel romantically attracted to a particular type of woman. Rather, it is the exposure they've had throughout their lives to tens of thousands of magazine ads, TV commercials, and film stars that emphasize specific cultural standards of female beauty.

Early child rearing is especially relevant to this kind of learning. Human babies have a large brain, requiring birth relatively early in their fetal development, before their heads have grown too large to pass through the birth canal. As a result, human babies are totally unequipped for survival on their own, compared with the young of other species, and must spend a number of years in the care of adults. This need, in turn, fosters a lengthy period of learning, during which the child is taught his or her society's culture.

Because humans think and act in so many different ways, sociologists do not believe that "biology is destiny." If biology were all-important, we would expect all cultures to be highly similar, if not identical. Yet this is hardly the case. For example, pork is forbidden to religious Jews and Muslims, but it is a dietary staple in China. This is not to say that human cultures have nothing in common. Surveys of thousands of different cultures have concluded that all known human cultures have such common characteristics as language, forms of emotional expression, rules that tell adults how to raise children or engage in sexual behavior, and even standards of beauty (Brown 1991). But there is enormous variety in exactly how these common characteristics play themselves out.

All cultures provide for childhood socialization, but what and how children are taught varies greatly from culture to culture. An American child learns the multiplication tables from a classroom teacher, while a child born in the forests of Borneo learns to hunt with older members of the tribe. All cultures have standards of beauty and ornamentation, but what is regarded as beautiful in one culture may be seen as ugly in another (Elias 1987; Elias and Dunning 1987; Foucault 1988). However, some feminist scholars have argued that with global access to Western images of beauty on the Internet, cultural definitions of beauty throughout the world are growing narrower and increasingly emphasize the slender physique that is so cherished in many Western cultures (Sepulveda and Calado 2012).

CULTURAL DIVERSITY

The study of cultural differences highlights the importance of cultural learning as an influence on our behavior. Human behavior and practices—as well as beliefs—also vary widely from culture to culture and often contrast radically with what people from Western societies consider normal. For example, in the modern West, we regard the deliberate killing of infants or young children as one of the worst of all crimes. Yet in traditional Chinese culture, female children were sometimes strangled at birth because a daughter was regarded as a liability rather than an asset to the family. In the West, we eat oysters but we do not eat kittens or puppies, both of which are regarded as delicacies in some parts of the world. Westerners regard kissing as a normal part of sexual behavior, but in other cultures the practice is either unknown or regarded as disgusting. All these different kinds of behavior are aspects of broad cultural differences that distinguish societies from one another.

SUBCULTURES

subculture • Values and norms distinct from those of the majority, held by a group within a wider society.

Small societies tend to be culturally uniform, but industrialized societies are themselves culturally diverse or multicultural, involving numerous different **subcultures**. As you will discover in the discussion of global migration in Chapter 10, practices and social processes such as slavery, colonialism, war, migration, and contemporary globalization have led to populations dispersing across borders and settling in new areas. This, in turn, has led to the emergence of societies that are cultural composites, meaning that the population is made up of a number of groups from diverse cultural and linguistic backgrounds. In modern cities, many subcultural communities live side by side. For example, over ninety different cultural groups can be found in New York City today. Some experts have estimated that as many as eight hundred different languages are regularly spoken by residents of New York City and its surrounding boroughs (Roberts 2010).

Most major European cities have become increasingly diverse in the past two decades, as large numbers of persons from North Africa have arrived. As transnational migration has increased, many European societies have struggled with how to integrate persons who bring with them distinct cultural and religious backgrounds. For example, in 2011, the French government made it a punishable offense for Muslim women to wear full-face veils in public spaces (except for houses of worship and private cars). France is a country based on the values of "liberty and equality" for all, and the *niqab*, a veil that covers a woman's hair and face, leaving only the eyes clearly visible, is viewed as a cultural practice that oppresses women and deprives them of their freedoms (Erlanger 2011). This controversy over Muslim women's veils vividly portrays the challenges when different subcultural communities live side by side.

Subculture does not refer only to people from different cultural backgrounds, or who speak different languages, within a larger society. It can also refer to any segment of the population that is distinguishable from the rest of society by its cultural patterns. Examples might include Goths, computer hackers, hipsters,

The tension between subgroup values and national values came to a head in 2011 when the French government banned Muslim women from wearing full-face veils in public. French policymakers believed that the *niqab* oppressed women and violated the nation's values of liberty and equality.

Rastafarians, and fans of hip-hop. Some people might identify themselves clearly with a particular subculture, whereas others may move fluidly among a number of different ones.

Culture plays an important role in perpetuating the values and norms of a society, yet it also offers important opportunities for creativity and change. Subcultures and countercultures—groups that largely reject the prevailing values and norms of society—can promote views that represent alternatives to the dominant culture. Social movements or groups of people sharing common lifestyles are powerful forces of change within societies. In this way, subcultures give people the freedom to express and act on their opinions, hopes, and beliefs.

U.S. schoolchildren are frequently taught that the United States is a vast melting pot into which various subcultures are assimilated. **Assimilation** is the process by which different cultures are absorbed into a single mainstream culture. Although it is true that virtually all peoples living in the United States take on many common cultural characteristics, many groups strive to retain some subcultural identity. In fact, identification based on race or country of origin in the United States persists today and is particularly strong among African Americans and immigrants from Asia, Mexico, and Latin America (Totti 1987).

Given the immense cultural diversity and number of subcultures in the United States, a more appropriate metaphor than the assimilationist "melting pot" might be the culturally diverse "salad bowl," in which all the various ingredients, though mixed together, retain some of their original flavor and integrity, contributing to the richness of the salad as a whole. This viewpoint, termed **multiculturalism**, calls for respecting cultural diversity and promoting equality of different cultures. Adherents to multiculturalism acknowledge that certain central cultural values are shared by most people in a society but also that certain important differences deserve to be preserved (Anzaldua 1990).

assimilation • The acceptance of a minority group by a majority population, in which the new group takes on the values and norms of the dominant culture.

multiculturalism • The viewpoint according to which ethnic groups can exist separately and share equally in economic and political life.

CULTURAL IDENTITY AND ETHNOCENTRISM

Every culture displays its own unique patterns of behavior, which seem alien to people from other cultural backgrounds. If you have traveled abroad, you are probably familiar with the sensation that can result when you find yourself in a new culture. Everyday habits, customs, and behaviors that you take for granted in your own culture may not be part of everyday life in other parts of the world—even in countries that share the same language. The expression "culture shock" is an apt one! Often people feel disoriented when they become immersed in a new culture. This is because they have lost the familiar reference points that help them understand the world around them and have not yet learned how to navigate the new culture.

A culture must be studied in terms of its own meanings and values—a key presupposition of sociology. Sociologists endeavor as far as possible to avoid **ethnocentrism**, or judging other cultures in terms of the standards of one's own. Because human cultures vary so widely, it is not surprising that people belonging to one culture frequently find it difficult to understand the ideas or behavior of people from a different culture. In studying and practicing sociology, we must remove our own cultural blinders in order to see the ways of life of different peoples in an unbiased light. The practice of judging a society by its own standards is called **cultural relativism**.

Applying cultural relativism—that is, suspending your own deeply held cultural beliefs and examining a situation according to the standards of another

ethnocentrism • The tendency to look at other cultures through the eyes of one's own culture, and thereby misrepresent them.

cultural relativism • The practice of judging a society by its own standards.

culture—can be fraught with uncertainty and challenge. Not only can it be hard to see things from a completely different point of view but cultural relativism sometimes raises troubling issues. Consider, for example, the ritual acts of what opponents have called "genital mutilation" practiced in some societies. Young girls in certain African, Asian, and Middle Eastern cultures may undergo clitoridectomies. This is a painful cultural ritual in which the clitoris and sometimes all or part of the vaginal labia of young girls are removed with a knife or a sharpened stone and the two sides of the vulva are partly sewn together as a means of controlling the young woman's sexual activity and increasing the sexual pleasure of her male partner.

In cultures where clitoridectomies have been practiced for generations, they are regarded as a normal, even expected, practice. A study of two thousand men and women in two Nigerian communities found that nine out of ten women interviewed had undergone clitoridectomies in childhood and that the large majority favored the procedure for their own daughters, primarily for cultural reasons; they would be viewed as social outcasts if they did not have the procedure. Yet a significant minority believed that the practice should be stopped (Ebomoyi 1987). Clitoridectomies are regarded with abhorrence by most people from other cultures and by a growing number of women in the cultures where they are practiced (El Dareer 1982; Johnson-Odim 1991; Lightfoot-Klein 1989).

These differences in views can result in a clash of cultural values, especially when people from cultures where clitoridectomies are common migrate to countries where the practice is actually illegal. In France, many mothers in the North African immigrant community arrange for traditional clitoridectomies to be performed on their daughters. Some of these women have been tried and convicted under French law for mutilating their daughters. These African mothers have argued that they were only engaging in the same cultural practice that their own mothers had performed on them, that their grandmothers had performed on their mothers, and so on. They complain that the French are ethnocentric, judging traditional African rituals by French customs. Feminists from Africa and the Middle East, while themselves strongly opposed to clitoridectomies, have been critical of Europeans and Americans who sensationalize the practice by calling it backward or primitive without seeking any understanding of the cultural and economic circumstances that sustain it (Accad 1991; Johnson-Odim 1991; Mohanty 1991). In this instance, globalization has led to a fundamental clash of cultural norms and values that has forced members of both cultures to confront some of their most deeply held beliefs. The role of the sociologist is to avoid knee-jerk responses and to examine complex questions carefully from as many different angles as possible.

cultural universals • Values or modes of behavior shared by all human cultures.

language • The primary vehicle of meaning and communication in a society, language is a system of symbols that represent objects and abstract thoughts.

marriage • A socially approved sexual relationship between two individuals. Marriage normally forms the basis of a family of procreation—that is, it is expected that the married couple will produce and raise children.

CULTURAL UNIVERSALS

Amid the diversity of human behavior, several **cultural universals** prevail. For example, there is no known culture without a grammatically complex **language**. All cultures possess some recognizable form of family system, in which there are values and norms associated with the care of children. The institution of **marriage** is a cultural universal, as are religious rituals and property rights. All cultures also practice some form of incest prohibition—the banning of sexual relations between close relatives, such as father and daughter, mother and son, and brother and sister. A variety of other cultural universals have been identified by anthropologists, including art, dancing, bodily adornment, games, gift giving, joking, and rules of hygiene.

Papua New Guinean men in traditional clothing and face paint at the annual Mt. Hagan Cultural Show. Beginning in 1964, tribes on the island gathered in Mt. Hagen City to compete with one another through singing and dancing. The event, called a sing-sing, provides an important opportunity to celebrate cultural traditions.

Yet there are variations within each category. Consider, for example, the prohibition against incest. Incest is typically defined as sexual relations between members of the immediate family, but in some cultures "the family" has been expanded to include cousins and others bearing the same family name. There have also been societies in which a small proportion of the population has been permitted to engage in incestuous practices. Within the ruling class of ancient Egypt, for instance, brothers and sisters were permitted to have sex with each other.

Among the cultural characteristics shared by all societies, two stand out in particular. All cultures incorporate ways of communicating and expressing meaning. All cultures also depend on material objects in daily life. In all cultures, language is the primary vehicle of meaning and communication. It is not the only such vehicle, however. We will now explore how material culture itself carries meaning.

LANGUAGE

Language is one of the best examples for demonstrating both the unity and the diversity of human culture because there are no cultures without language, yet there are thousands of different languages spoken in the world. Anyone who has visited a foreign country armed with only a dictionary knows how difficult it is either to understand anything or to be understood. Although languages that have similar origins have words in common with one another—as do, for example, German and English—most of the world's major language groups have no words in common at all.

Language is involved in virtually all of our activities. In the form of ordinary talk or speech, it is the means by which we organize most of what we do. (We discuss the importance of talk and conversation in social life at some length in Chapter 4.) However, language is involved not just in mundane, everyday activities, but also in ceremony, religion, poetry, and many other spheres. One of the most distinctive features of human language is that it allows us to vastly extend the scope of our thought and experience. Using language, we can convey information about events remote in time or space and can discuss things we have never seen. We can develop abstract concepts, tell stories, make jokes, and express sarcasm.

In the 1930s, the anthropological linguist Edward Sapir and his student Benjamin Lee Whorf advanced the **linguistic relativity hypothesis**, which argues that the language we use influences our perceptions of the world. That is because we are much more likely to be aware of things in the world if we have words for them (Haugen 1977; Malotki 1983; Witkowski and Brown 1982). Expert skiers or snowboarders, for example, use terms such as *black ice, corn, powder*, and *packed powder* to describe different snow and ice conditions. Such terms enable them to more readily perceive potentially life-threatening situations that would escape the notice of a novice. In a sense, then, experienced winter athletes have a different perception of the world—or at least, a different perception of the alpine slopes—than do novices.

linguistic relativity hypothesis • A hypothesis, based on the theories of Edward Sapir and Benjamin Lee Whorf, that perceptions are relative to language.

Language also helps give permanence to a culture and an identity to a people. Language outlives any particular speaker or writer, affording a sense of history and cultural continuity, a feeling of "who we are." One of the central paradoxes of our time is that despite the globalization of the English language through the Internet and other forms of global media, local attachments to language persist, often out of cultural pride. For example, the French-speaking residents of the Canadian province of Quebec are so passionate about their linguistic heritage that they often refuse to speak English, the dominant language of Canada, and periodically seek political independence from the rest of Canada.

Languages—indeed, all symbols—are representations of reality. The symbols we use may signify things we imagine, such as mathematical formulas or fictitious creatures, or they may represent (that is, "re-present," or make present again in our minds) things initially experienced through our senses. Symbols even represent emotions, as the common emoticons of :) (happy) and ;) (good-natured winking) reveal. Human behavior is oriented toward the symbols we use to represent reality, rather than to the reality itself—and these symbols are determined within a particular culture. Because symbols are representations, their cultural meanings must be interpreted when they are used. When you see

Making Sociology Work
HEALTH-CARE PROVIDER

Health-care providers are well trained in anatomy and human physiology. They know how the human body functions and how to detect and treat illnesses. But more than ever, physicians, nurses, and physicians' assistants need a thorough understanding of culture if they hope to effectively treat their patients. For example, practitioners should be trained to assess patients' facial expressions for cues to their pain as well as their receptiveness toward the practitioners' advice. In some cultures, patients will not tell doctors or nurses anything they think might disappoint them. Many Asian patients don't like to answer no, so they may answer yes to everything. And in some cultures, people are taught to respect doctors, nurses, and people in authority, so they won't complain to them, even if they're in pain. In other cultures, still, women are raised to be modest and may be uncomfortable having a male doctor give her a physical exam, and might expect a female care provider to be in the exam room at the same time. What are other ways that knowledge of cultural diversity may help health-care providers effectively care for their patients?

a four-footed furry animal, for example, you must determine which cultural symbol to attach to it. Do you decide to call it a dog, a wolf, or something else? If you determine it is a dog, what cultural meaning does that convey? In American culture, dogs are typically regarded as household pets and lavished with affection. Among the Akha of northern Thailand, dogs are seen as food and treated accordingly. The diversity of cultural meanings attached to the word *dog* thus requires an act of interpretation. In this way, we are freed, in a sense, from being directly tied to the physical world around us.

SPEECH AND WRITING

All societies use speech as a vehicle of language. However, there are other ways of "carrying," or expressing, language—most notably, writing. The invention of writing marked a major transition in human history. Writing first began as the drawing up of lists. Marks would be made on wood, clay, or stone to keep records about significant events, objects, or people. For example, a mark, or sometimes a picture, might be drawn to represent each tract of land possessed by a particular family or set of families (Gelb 1952). Writing began as a means of storing information and as such was closely linked to the administrative needs of early civilizations. A society that possesses writing can locate itself in time and space. Documents can be accumulated that record the past, and information can be gathered about present-day events and activities.

Writing is not just the transfer of speech to paper or some other durable material. It is a phenomenon of interest in its own right. Written documents or texts have qualities in some ways quite distinct from the spoken word. The impact of speech is always by definition limited to the particular contexts in which words are uttered. Ideas and experiences can be passed down through generations in cultures without writing, but only if they are regularly repeated and passed on by word of mouth. Written texts, on the other hand, can endure for thousands of years, and through them people from past ages can in a certain sense address us directly. This is, of course, why documentary research is so important to historians. By interpreting the texts that are left behind by past generations, historians can reconstruct what their lives were like.

MATERIAL CULTURE

The symbols expressed in speech and writing are the chief ways in which cultural meanings are formed and expressed. But they are not the only ways. As we saw earlier in this chapter, both material objects and aspects of behavior can be used to generate meanings. A **signifier** is any vehicle of meaning—any set of elements used to communicate. The sounds made in speech are signifiers, as are the marks made on paper or other materials in writing. Other signifiers, however, include dress, pictures or visual signs, modes of eating, forms of building or architecture, and many other material features of culture (Hawkes 1977). Styles of dress, for example, normally help signify differences between the sexes. In our culture, at least until relatively recently, women have worn skirts and men pants, although in other societies the reverse is true (Leach 1976). Even colors can signify important aspects of culture. In contemporary society, young girls are typically dressed in pink while boys are dressed in blue—but this wasn't always the case (Paoletti 2012). In the nineteenth century, both boys and girls wore frilly white clothing. A June 1918 article in *Ladies' Home Journal* stated, "The generally accepted rule is pink for the boys, and blue for the girls. The reason is that pink, being a more decided and stronger color, is more suitable for the boy, while blue, which is more delicate and dainty, is prettier for the girl" (Paoletti 2012).

signifier • Any vehicle of meaning and communication.

This paper doll set of "Polly Pratt's Sister and Brother," from an issue of *Good Housekeeping* published in 1920, blurs modern gender boundaries in terms of color and clothing style.

Material culture is not simply symbolic; it is also vital for catering to physical needs—in the tools or technology used to acquire food, make weaponry, construct dwellings, manufacture our clothing, and so forth. We have to study both the practical and the symbolic aspects of material culture in order to understand it completely.

CULTURE AND SOCIAL DEVELOPMENT

Cultural traits are closely related to overall patterns in the development of society. The level of material culture reached in a given society influences, although by no means completely determines, other aspects of cultural development. This is easy to see, for example, in the level of technology. Many aspects of culture characteristic of our lives today—cars, cell phones, tablet computers, Wi-Fi, running water, electric light—depend on technological innovations that have been made only very recently in human history.

The same is true at earlier phases of social development. Before the invention of the smelting of metal, for example, goods had to be made of organic or naturally occurring materials like wood or stone—a basic limitation on the artifacts that could be constructed. Variations in material culture provide the main means of distinguishing different forms of human society, but other factors are also influential. Writing is an example. As has been mentioned, not all human cultures have possessed writing—in fact, for most of human history, writing was unknown. The development of writing altered the scope of human cultural potentialities, making possible different forms of social organization than those that had previously existed. Yet writing continues to evolve even today. Think about the language you use when you send texts to your friends. If you sent your grandparents a text with abbreviations like LOL, OMG, and ROFL, would they understand what you were saying?

We now turn to analyzing the main types of society that existed in the past and that are still found in the world. In the present day, we are accustomed to societies that contain millions of people, many of them living crowded together in urban areas. But for most of human history, the earth was much less densely populated than it is now, and it is only over the past hundred years or so that any societies have existed in which the majority of the population were city dwellers. To understand the forms of society that existed before modern industrialism, we have to call on the historical dimension of the sociological imagination. ✓

CONCEPT CHECKS ✓

1. Explain the nature/nurture debate.

2. Why do sociologists disagree with the claim that biology is destiny?

3. Give examples of subcultures that are typical of American society.

4. What is the difference between cultural ethnocentrism and cultural relativism?

5. Why is language considered to be a cultural universal?

6. What is the linguistic relativity hypothesis?

WHAT HAPPENED TO PREMODERN SOCIETIES?

Learn how societies have changed over time.

Premodern societies can actually be grouped into three main categories: hunters and gatherers, larger agrarian or pastoral societies (involving agriculture or the tending of domesticated animals), and nonindustrial civilizations or traditional states. We shall look at the main characteristics of these societies in turn.

THE EARLIEST SOCIETIES: HUNTERS AND GATHERERS

For all but a tiny part of our existence on this planet, human beings have lived in hunting and gathering societies, small groups or tribes often numbering no more than thirty or forty people. Hunters and gatherers gain their livelihood from hunting, fishing, and gathering edible plants growing in the wild. Hunting and gathering cultures continue to exist in some parts of the world, such as in a few arid parts of Africa and the jungles of Brazil and New Guinea. Most such cultures, however, have been destroyed or absorbed by the spread of Western culture, and those that remain are unlikely to stay intact for much longer. Currently, fewer than a quarter of a million people in the world support themselves through hunting and gathering—only 0.004 percent of the world's population.

Compared with larger societies—particularly modern societies such as the United States—most hunting and gathering groups were egalitarian. Thus there was little difference among members of the society in the number or kinds of material possessions; there were no divisions of rich and poor. The material goods they needed were limited to weapons for hunting, tools for digging and building, traps, and cooking utensils. Differences of position or rank tended to be limited to age and gender; men were almost always the hunters, while women gathered wild crops, cooked, and brought up the children.

The elders—the oldest and most experienced men in the community—usually had an important say in major decisions affecting the group. But just as there was little variation in wealth among members, power was more equally shared than in larger types of society. Hunting and gathering societies were usually participatory rather than competitive: All adult male members tended to assemble together when important decisions were to be made or crises were faced.

Hunters and gatherers moved about a good deal, but not in a completely erratic way. They had fixed territories, around which they migrated regularly from year to year. Because they were without animal or mechanical means of transport, they could only take a few goods or possessions with them. Many hunting and gathering communities did not have a stable membership; people often moved among different camps, or groups split up and joined others within the same overall territory.

Hunters and gatherers had little interest in developing material wealth beyond what was needed for their basic needs. Their main concerns were with religious values and ritual activities. Members participated regularly in elaborate ceremonials and often spent a great deal of time preparing the dress, masks, paintings, or other sacred objects used in such rituals.

Hunters and gatherers are not merely primitive peoples whose ways of life no longer hold any interest for us. Studying their cultures allows us to see more clearly that some of our institutions are far from being natural features of human life. While we shouldn't idealize the circumstances in which hunters and gatherers lived, the lack of major inequalities of wealth and power and the emphasis on cooperation rather than competition are instructive reminders that the world created by modern industrial civilization is not necessarily to be equated with progress.

PASTORAL AND AGRARIAN SOCIETIES

About 15,000 years ago, some hunting and gathering groups turned to the raising of domesticated animals and the cultivation of fixed plots of land as their means of livelihood. **Pastoral societies** relied mainly on domesticated livestock, while **agrarian societies** grew crops (practiced agriculture). Some societies had mixed pastoral and agrarian economies.

Depending on the environment in which they lived, pastoralists reared animals such as cattle, sheep, goats, camels, or horses. Some pastoral societies still exist in the modern world, concentrated especially in areas of Africa, the Middle East, and Central Asia. They are usually found in regions of dense grasslands or in deserts or mountains, which are too poor in arable land for agriculture to be profitable.

At some point, hunting and gathering groups began to sow their own crops rather than simply collect those growing in the wild. This practice first developed as what is usually called horticulture, in which small gardens were cultivated by the use of simple hoes or digging instruments. Like pastoralism, horticulture provided for a more reliable supply of food than was possible from hunting and gathering and therefore could support larger communities. Because they were not on the move, people whose livelihood was horticulture could develop larger stocks of material possessions than people in either hunting and gathering or pastoral communities. Some peoples in the world still rely primarily on horticulture for their livelihood.

pastoral societies • Societies whose subsistence derives from the rearing of domesticated animals.

agrarian societies • Societies whose means of subsistence are based on agricultural production (crop growing).

A Bedouin woman accompanies her goats across a road in the Negev Desert in Israel. Pastoral societies, which rely on domesticated livestock as their means of livelihood, still exist in certain areas of Africa, the Middle East, and Central Asia.

TRADITIONAL SOCIETIES OR CIVILIZATIONS

From about 6000 BCE onward, we find evidence of societies larger than any that existed before and that contrast in distinct ways with earlier types. These societies were based on the development of cities, led to pronounced inequalities of wealth and power, and were ruled by kings or emperors. Because writing was used and science and art flourished, these societies are often called "civilizations."

The earliest civilizations developed in the Middle East, usually in fertile river areas. The Chinese Empire originated in about 1800 BCE, at which time powerful states were also in existence in what are now India and Pakistan.

Most traditional (premodern) civilizations were also empires: They achieved their size through the conquest and incorporation of other peoples (Kautsky 1982). This was true, for instance, of traditional Rome and China. At its height, in the first century CE, the Roman Empire stretched from Britain in northwest Europe to beyond the Middle East. The Chinese Empire, which lasted for more than two thousand years, up to the threshold of the twentieth century, covered most of the massive region of eastern Asia now occupied by modern China. ✓

industrialization • The emergence of machine production, based on the use of inanimate power resources (such as steam or electricity).

> ### CONCEPT CHECKS ✓
> 1. Compare the two main types of premodern societies.
> 2. Contrast pastoral and agrarian societies.

HOW HAS INDUSTRIALIZATION SHAPED MODERN SOCIETY?

Recognize the factors that transformed premodern societies, particularly how industrialization and colonialism influenced global development. Know the differences among industrialized societies, emerging economies, and developing societies, and how these differences developed.

What happened to destroy the forms of society that dominated the whole of history up to two centuries ago? The answer, in a word, is **industrialization**—the emergence of machine production, based on the use of inanimate power resources (such as steam or electricity). The industrialized, or modern, societies differ in several key respects from any previous type of social order, and their development has had consequences stretching far beyond their European origins.

THE INDUSTRIALIZED SOCIETIES

industrialized societies •
Highly developed nation-states in which the majority of the population work in factories or offices rather than in agriculture, and most people live in urban areas.

Industrialization originated in eighteenth-century Britain as a result of the Industrial Revolution, a complex set of technological changes that affected the means by which people gained their livelihood. These changes included the invention of new machines (such as the spinning jenny for weaving yarn), the harnessing of power resources (especially water and steam) for production, and the use of science to improve production methods. Because discoveries and inventions in one field lead to more in others, the pace of technological innovation in **industrialized societies** is extremely rapid compared with that of traditional social systems.

In even the most advanced of traditional civilizations, the majority of people were engaged in working on the land. The relatively low level of technological development did not permit more than a small minority to be freed from the chores of agricultural production. By contrast, a prime feature of industrialized societies today is that the large majority of the employed population work in factories, offices, or shops rather than in agriculture. And over 90 percent of people live in towns and cities, where most jobs are to be found and new job opportunities created. The largest cities are vastly greater in size than the urban settlements found in traditional civilizations. In the cities, social life becomes more impersonal and anonymous than before, and many of our day-to-day encounters are with strangers rather than with individuals known to us. Large-scale organizations, such as business corporations or government agencies, come to influence the lives of virtually everyone.

People crowd the streets of Tokyo's entertainment district. Japan is an exemplar of an industrialized society. It is the third-largest economy, measured by GDP, lagging behind only the United States and China.

A further feature of modern societies concerns their political systems, which are more developed and intensive than forms of government in traditional states. In traditional civilizations, the political authorities (monarchs and emperors) had little direct influence on the customs and habits of most of their subjects, who lived in fairly self-contained local villages. With industrialization, transportation and communications became much more rapid, making for a more integrated "national" community.

The industrialized societies were the first **nation-states** to come into existence. Nation-states are political communities with clearly delimited borders dividing them from one another, rather than the vague frontier areas that used to separate traditional states. Nation-state governments have extensive powers over many aspects of citizens' lives, framing laws that apply to all those living within their borders. The United States is a nation-state, as are virtually all other societies in the world today.

nation-state • A particular type of state, characteristic of the modern world, in which a government has sovereign power within a defined territorial area, and the population are citizens who know themselves to be part of a single nation.

The application of industrial technology has been by no means limited to peaceful processes of economic development. From the earliest phases of industrialization, modern production processes have been put to military use, and this has radically altered ways of waging war, creating weaponry and modes of military organization much more advanced than those of nonindustrial cultures. Together, superior economic strength, political cohesion, and military superiority account for the seemingly irresistible spread of Western ways of life across the world over the past two centuries.

GLOBAL DEVELOPMENT

From the seventeenth to the early twentieth century, the Western countries established colonies in numerous areas previously occupied by traditional societies, using their superior military strength where necessary. Although virtually all these colonies have now attained their independence, **colonialism** was central to shaping the social map of the globe as we know it today. In some regions, such as North America, Australia, and New Zealand, which were only thinly populated by hunting and gathering or pastoral communities, Europeans became the majority population. In other areas, including much of Asia, Africa, and South America, the local populations remained in the majority.

colonialism • The process whereby Western nations established their rule in parts of the world away from their home territories.

Societies of the first of these two types, including the United States, have become industrialized. Those in the second category are mostly at a much lower level of industrial development and are often referred to as less-developed societies, or the **developing world**. Such societies include China, India, most African countries (such as Nigeria, Ghana, and Algeria), and those in South America (such as Brazil, Peru, and Venezuela). Because many of these societies are situated south of the United States and Europe, they are sometimes referred to collectively as the South, and contrasted to the wealthier, industrialized North.

developing world • The less-developed societies, in which industrial production is either virtually nonexistent or only developed to a limited degree. The majority of the world's population live in less-developed countries.

THE DEVELOPING WORLD

The large majority of less-developed societies are in areas that underwent colonial rule in Asia, Africa, and South America. A few colonized areas gained independence early, such as Haiti, which became the first autonomous black republic in January 1804. The Spanish colonies in South America acquired their freedom in 1810; Brazil broke away from Portuguese rule in 1822.

Women wait in line for food in Calcutta, India. Why does poverty disproportionately affect women around the world?

Some countries that were never ruled from Europe were nonetheless strongly influenced by colonial relationships, the most notable example being China. By force of arms, China was compelled from the seventeenth century on to enter into trading agreements with European powers, by which the Europeans were allocated the government of certain areas, including major seaports. Hong Kong was the last of these. Most nations in the developing world have become independent states only since World War II—often following bloody anticolonial struggles. Examples include India, which shortly after achieving self-rule split into India and Pakistan; a range of other Asian countries (like Myanmar, Malaysia, and Singapore); and countries in Africa (including Kenya, Nigeria, the Democratic Republic of Congo, Tanzania, and Algeria).

Although they may include peoples living in traditional fashion, developing countries are very different from earlier forms of traditional society. Their political systems are modeled on systems first established in the societies of the West—that is to say, they are nation-states. Most of the population still live in rural areas, but many of these societies are experiencing a rapid process of city development. Although agriculture remains the main economic activity, crops are now often produced for sale in world markets rather than for local consumption. Developing countries are not merely societies that have "lagged behind" the more industrialized areas. They have in large part been created by contact with Western industrialism, which has undermined the earlier, more traditional systems that were in place.

There are nearly 1.29 billion people living on less than $1.25 per day, and an additional 1.18 billion people live on less than $2 per day (World Bank 2012c). Together, nearly 40 percent of the world's population face the reality of extreme poverty on a daily basis. In China, progress has been erratic. While the number of people living in poverty has been reduced by three-fourths since 1981, 173 million people in China still live on less than $1.25 per day (World Bank 2012c). Forty-seven percent of the population in sub-Saharan Africa live on less than $1.25 a day, down slightly from 51 percent in 1981 (World Bank 2012c). A substantial proportion of those in extreme poverty, however, live on the doorstep of the United States—in Central and South America.

Once more, the existence of global poverty shouldn't be seen as remote from the concerns of Americans. Whereas in previous generations the majority of immigrants into the United States came from Europe, most now come from poor, developing societies. Recent years have seen waves of Hispanic immigrants, nearly all from Latin America. Some U.S. cities near the entry points of much of this immigration, such as Los Angeles and Miami, are bursting with new immigrants and also maintain trading connections with developing countries.

In most developing societies, poverty tends to be at its worst in rural areas. Malnutrition, lack of education, low life expectancy, and substandard housing are generally most severe in the countryside. Many of the poor are to be found in areas where arable land is scarce, agricultural productivity low, and drought or floods common. Women are usually more disadvantaged than men. They encounter cultural, social, and economic problems that even the most underprivileged men do not. For instance, they often work longer hours and, when they are paid at all, earn lower wages. (See Chapter 9 for a lengthier discussion of gender inequality.)

The poor in developing countries live in conditions almost unimaginable to Americans. Many have no permanent dwellings apart from shelters made of cartons or loose pieces of wood. Most have no running water, sewer systems, or electricity. Nonetheless, millions of poor people also live in the United States, and there are connections between poverty in America and global poverty. Almost half of the people living in poverty in the United States immigrated from the global South. This is true of the descendants of the black slaves brought over by force centuries ago, and it is true of more recent, and willing, immigrants who have arrived from Latin America, Asia, and elsewhere.

THE EMERGING ECONOMIES

Although the majority of developing countries lag well behind societies of the West, some have now successfully embarked on a process of industrialization. These **emerging economies**, which were previously referred to as newly industrializing economies (NIEs), include Brazil, Mexico, Hong Kong, South Korea, Singapore, and Taiwan. Emerging economies are characterized by a great deal of industry and/or international trade. The rates of economic growth of the most successful emerging economies, such as those in East Asia, are several times those of the Western industrial economies. No developing country figured among the top thirty exporters in the world in 1968, but today South Korea is ranked seventh (Central Intelligence Agency [CIA] 2013d).

The emerging economies of East Asia have shown the most sustained levels of economic prosperity. They are investing abroad as well as promoting growth at home. South Korea's production of steel has doubled in the last decade, and its shipbuilding

emerging economies • Developing countries that over the past two or three decades have begun to develop a strong industrial base, such as Singapore and Hong Kong.

CONCEPT CHECKS ✓

1. What does the concept of industrialization mean?

2. How has industrialization hurt traditional social systems?

3. Why are many African and South American societies classified as part of the developing world?

and electronics industries are among the world's leaders. Singapore is becoming the major financial and commercial center of Southeast Asia. Taiwan is an important player in the manufacturing and electronics industries. All these changes in the emerging economies have directly affected the United States, whose share of global steel production, for example, has dropped significantly since the 1970s. ✓

Recognize the effect of globalization on your life and the lives of people around the world. Think about the effect of a growing global culture.

HOW DOES GLOBALIZATION AFFECT CONTEMPORARY CULTURE?

In Chapter 1 we noted that the chief focus of sociology historically has been the study of industrialized societies. As sociologists, can we thus safely ignore the developing world, leaving this as the domain of anthropology? We certainly cannot. The industrialized and the developing societies have developed in interconnection with one another and are today more closely related than ever before. Those of us living in industrialized societies depend on many raw materials and manufactured products coming from developing countries to sustain our lives. Conversely, the economies of most developing states depend on trading networks that bind them to industrialized countries. We can fully understand the industrialized order only against the backdrop of societies in the developing world—in which, in fact, by far the greater proportion of the world's population lives.

As the world rapidly moves toward a single, unified economy, businesses and people move about the globe in increasing numbers in search of new markets and economic opportunities. As a result, the cultural map of the world changes: Networks of peoples span national borders and even continents, providing cultural connections between their birthplaces and their adoptive countries (Appadurai 1986). A handful of languages come to dominate, and in some cases replace, the thousands of different languages that were once spoken on the planet.

It is increasingly impossible for cultures to exist as islands. There are few, if any, places on earth so remote as to escape radio, television, air travel—and the throngs of tourists this technology brings—or the computer. A generation ago, there were still tribes whose way of life was completely untouched by the rest of the world. Today, these peoples use machetes and other tools made in the United States or Japan, wear T-shirts and shorts manufactured in garment factories in the Dominican Republic or Guatemala, and take medicine manufactured in Germany or Switzerland to combat diseases contracted through contact with outsiders. These people also have their stories broadcast to people around the world through satellite television and the Internet. Within a generation or two at the most, all the world's once-isolated cultures will be touched and transformed by global culture, despite their persistent efforts to preserve their age-old ways of life.

The forces that produce a global culture are discussed throughout this book. These include:

- Television, which brings U.S. culture (through networks such as MTV and shows such as *The Big Bang Theory*) into homes throughout the world daily

- The emergence of a unified global economy, with businesses whose factories, management structures, and markets often span continents and countries
- "Global citizens," such as managers of large corporations, who may spend as much time crisscrossing the globe as they do at home, identifying with a global, cosmopolitan culture rather than with their own nation's
- A host of international organizations, including United Nations agencies, regional trade and mutual defense associations, multinational banks and other global financial institutions, international labor and health organizations, and global tariff and trade agreements, that are creating a global political, legal, and military framework
- Electronic communications (via cell phone, Skype, fax, e-mail, text message, Facebook, Twitter, and other communications on the Internet), which make instantaneous communication with almost any part of the planet an integral part of daily life in the business world

DOES THE INTERNET PROMOTE A GLOBAL CULTURE?

Many believe that the rapid growth of the Internet around the world will hasten the spread of a global culture—one resembling the cultures of Europe and North America, currently home to nearly three-quarters of all Internet users. Although the Internet is a truly global space, several languages prevail among Internet users. For example, 27 percent of Internet users speak English as their main language, compared with 24 percent who speak Chinese and 8 percent who speak Spanish. In fact, ten languages alone account for fully 82 percent of all Internet users (Internet World Stats 2012a).

Given the dominance of the English language and Western values on the Internet, belief in such values as equality between men and women, the right to speak freely, democratic participation in government, and the pursuit of pleasure through consumption may be readily diffused throughout the world over the Internet. Moreover, Internet technology itself would seem to foster such values: Global communication, seemingly unlimited (and uncensored) information, and instant gratification are all characteristics of the new technology. Yet it may be premature to conclude that the Internet will sweep aside traditional cultures, replacing them with radically new cultural values. Cyberspace is becomingly increasingly global. In 2000, nearly half of all Internet users worldwide were Americans (Nua.com 2000). By 2012, just over 10 percent of world Internet users were American (Internet World Stats 2012a). The Chinese are also going online in increasingly large numbers, with almost 538 million Internet users in 2012—over 2,020 percent more than in 2000 (Internet World Stats 2012a).

As the Internet spreads around the world, scholars continue to debate whether it will be used to perpetuate traditional cultural values or forge new cultural and political pathways. Consider, for example, the Middle Eastern country of Kuwait, a traditional Islamic culture that has recently experienced strong American and European influences. Kuwait, an oil-rich country on the Persian Gulf, has one of the highest average per-person incomes in the world (UNESCWA 2011). The government provides free public education through the university level, resulting in high rates of literacy and education for both men and women. Kuwaiti television frequently carries NFL football and other U.S. programming, although broadcasts are regularly interrupted for the traditional Muslim calls to prayer. Half of

Kuwait's approximately 2.7 million people are under thirty years old, and like their youthful counterparts in Europe and North America, many surf the Internet for new ideas, information, and consumer products.

Although Kuwait is in many respects a modern country, Kuwaiti law treats men and women differently. Legally, women have equal access to education and employment, yet they are barred from voting or running for political office. Cultural norms treating men and women differently have just as powerful an influence on daily life as formal laws. Women are generally expected to wear traditional clothing that leaves only the face and hands visible and are forbidden to leave home at night or be seen in public at any time with a man who is not a spouse or relative.

Deborah Wheeler and her colleagues (2006) have investigated the effect of the Internet on Kuwaiti culture. Although the Internet is highly popular in Kuwait, Wheeler found that Kuwaitis were extremely reluctant to voice strong opinions or political views online. With the exception of discussing conservative Islamic religious beliefs, which are freely disseminated over the Internet, Kuwaitis were remarkably inhibited online.

Wheeler concluded that Kuwaiti culture, which is hundreds of years old, is not likely to be easily transformed by simple exposure to different beliefs and values on the Internet. Did Wheeler's predictions prove true? Not necessarily, as the events of the Arab Spring reveal. Some scholars say that the political protests that

Protesters recharge their cell phones and computers at a charging center in Tahrir Square during the Arab Spring protests. Technology helped the movement take off and enabled participants to organize and communicate effectively.

INTERNET CONNECTIVITY

While cyberspace is becomingly increasingly global, there remains a digital divide between individuals with access to the Internet and those without. While 78.1 percent of the U.S. population is using the Internet, only 15.6 percent of the population of Africa is online.

% OF WORLD INTERNET USERS

AFRICA	7.0%
ASIA	44.8%
EUROPE	21.6%
MIDDLE EAST	3.7%
NORTH AMERICA	11.4%
LATIN AMERICA/CARIBBEAN	10.6%
OCEANIA/AUSTRALIA	1.0%

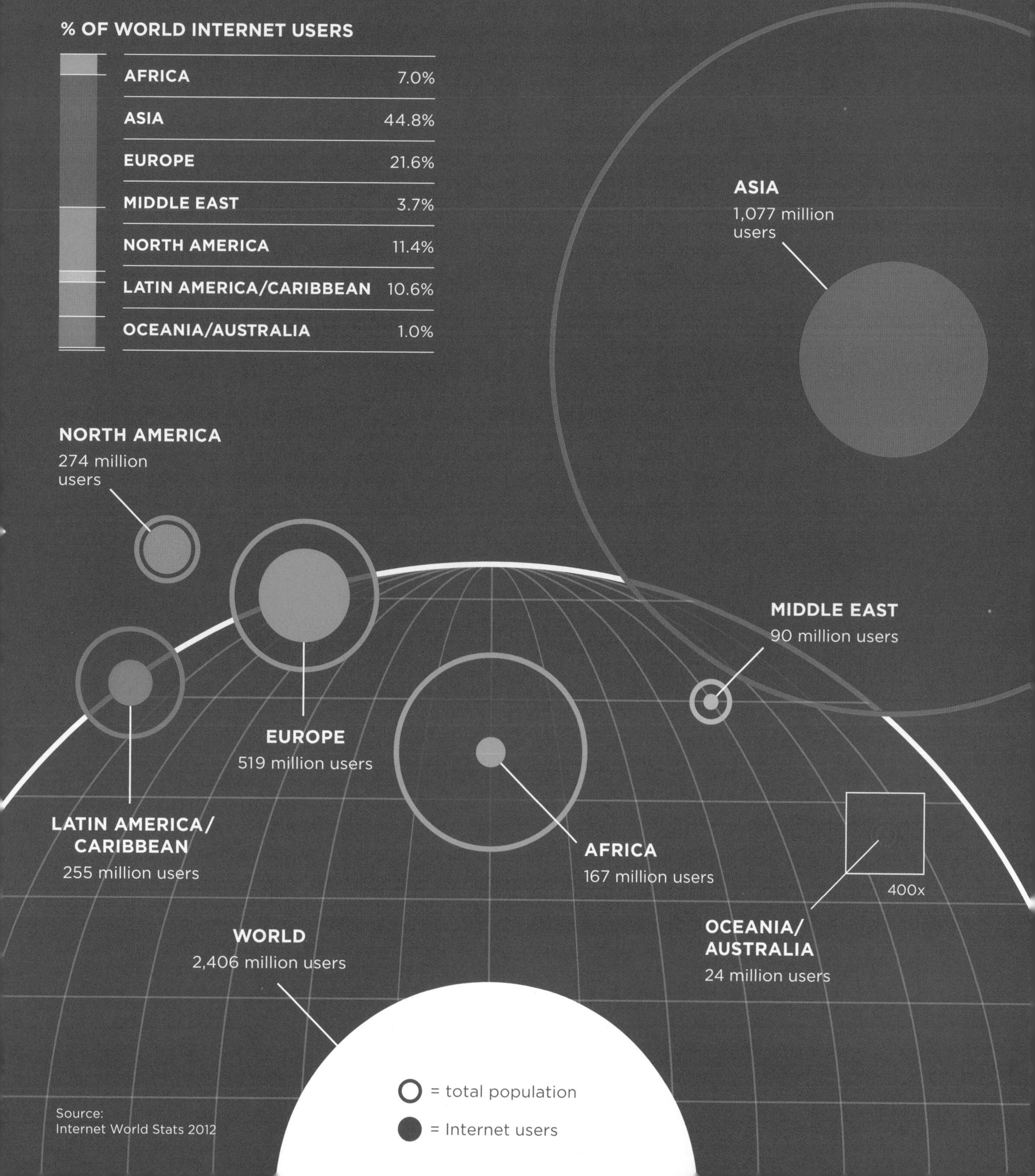

ASIA
1,077 million users

NORTH AMERICA
274 million users

MIDDLE EAST
90 million users

EUROPE
519 million users

**LATIN AMERICA/
CARIBBEAN**
255 million users

AFRICA
167 million users

400x

**OCEANIA/
AUSTRALIA**
24 million users

WORLD
2,406 million users

○ = total population

● = Internet users

Source:
Internet World Stats 2012

erupted throughout major urban centers of North Africa and the Middle East during the spring of 2011 were fueled, in part, by communication on the Internet, including Facebook postings, chat room communications, and tweets (Howard 2011). According to Howard (2011), one activist who participated in the Cairo, Egypt, protests boasted, "We use Facebook to schedule the protests, Twitter to coordinate, and YouTube to tell the world."

Although the protests in Kuwait were smaller and shorter-lived than those in Egypt, Tunisia, and Bahrain, young people's use of the Internet played an important role (Al-Haqhaq 2011). However, young people may still feel constrained by their traditional culture, and thus find protection behind the anonymous nature of the Internet. As Kuwaiti technology expert Mustapha Said pointed out, "The feature of social media that allows you to become anonymous has encouraged many people to use them and become actively involved" (Al-Haqhaq 2011).

GLOBALIZATION AND LOCAL CULTURES

The world has become a single social system as a result of the growing interdependence, both social and economic, that now affects virtually everyone. But it would be a mistake to think of this increasing interdependence, or globalization, of the world's societies simply as the growth of world unity. The globalizing of social relations should be understood primarily as the reordering of time and distance in social life. Our lives, in other words, are increasingly and quickly influenced by events happening far away from our everyday activities.

Globalizing processes have brought many benefits to Americans: A much greater variety of goods and foodstuffs is available than ever before. At the same time, the fact that we are all now caught up in a much wider world has helped create some of the most serious problems American society faces, such as the threat of terrorism.

The influence of a growing global culture has provoked numerous reactions at the local level. Many local cultures remain strong or are experiencing rejuvenation, partly as a response to the diffusion of global culture. Such a response grows out of the concern that a global culture, dominated by North American and European cultural values, will corrupt the local culture. For example, the Taliban, an Islamic movement that controlled most of Afghanistan until 2001, historically has sought to impose traditional, tribal values throughout the country. Through its governmental "Ministry for Ordering What Is Right and Forbidding What Is Wrong," the Taliban banned music, closed movie theaters, prohibited the consumption of alcohol, and required men to grow full beards. Women were ordered to cover their entire bodies with *burkas*, tentlike garments with a woven screen over the eyes; they were forbidden to work outside their homes or even be seen in public with men who were not their spouses or relations. Violations of these rules resulted in severe punishment, sometimes death. The rise of the Taliban can be understood at least partly as a rejection of the spread of Western culture.

The resurgence of local cultures is sometimes seen throughout the world in the rise of **nationalism**, a sense of identification with one's people that is expressed through a common set of strongly held beliefs. Sometimes these include the belief that the people of a particular nation have historical or God-given rights that supersede those of other people. Nationalism can be strongly political, involving attempts to assert the power of a nation based on a shared ethnic or

nationalism • A set of beliefs and symbols expressing identification with a national community.

racial identity over people of a different ethnicity or race. The world of the twenty-first century may well witness responses to globalization that celebrate ethnocentric nationalist beliefs, promoting intolerance and hatred rather than celebrating diversity.

HOW GLOBALIZATION AND CULTURE AFFECT YOU

New nationalisms, cultural identities, and religious practices are constantly being forged throughout the world. When you socialize with students from the same cultural background or celebrate traditional holidays with your friends and family, you are sustaining your culture. The very technology that helps foster globalization also supports local cultures: The Internet enables you to communicate with others who share your cultural identity, even when they are dispersed around the world. Those who share a passion for a particular type of music might spend hours playing Song-Pop on their smartphone with competitors (whom they've never met in person) from around the globe. You might have even learned about Pussy Riot on the Internet and watched their videos on YouTube. A casual search reveals thousands of websites and apps devoted to different cultures and subcultures.

Although sociologists do not yet fully understand these processes, they often conclude that despite the powerful forces of globalization operating in the world today, local cultures remain strong and indeed flourish. Yet as the cautionary tale of Pussy Riot reveals, local cultural and social movements can thrive and flourish only if they are allowed to do so. Given the rapid social changes in recent decades, it is still too soon to tell whether and how globalization will transform our world, whether it will result in the homogenization of the world's diverse cultures, the flourishing of many individual cultures, or both. ✓

CONCEPT CHECKS ✓

1. How does global culture influence local cultures?

2. What is nationalism?

EXERCISES:
Thinking Sociologically

1. Mention at least two cultural traits that you would claim are universals; mention two others you would claim are culturally specific traits. Locate and use case study materials from different societies you are familiar with to show the differences between universal and specific cultural traits. Are the cultural universals you have discussed derivatives of human instincts? Explain your answer fully.

2. What does it mean to be ethnocentric? How is ethnocentrism dangerous in conducting social research? How is ethnocentrism problematic among nonresearchers in their everyday lives?

3. Think about a favorite article of clothing of yours. What values does it convey, and what messages about you or your subculture does it tell to others?

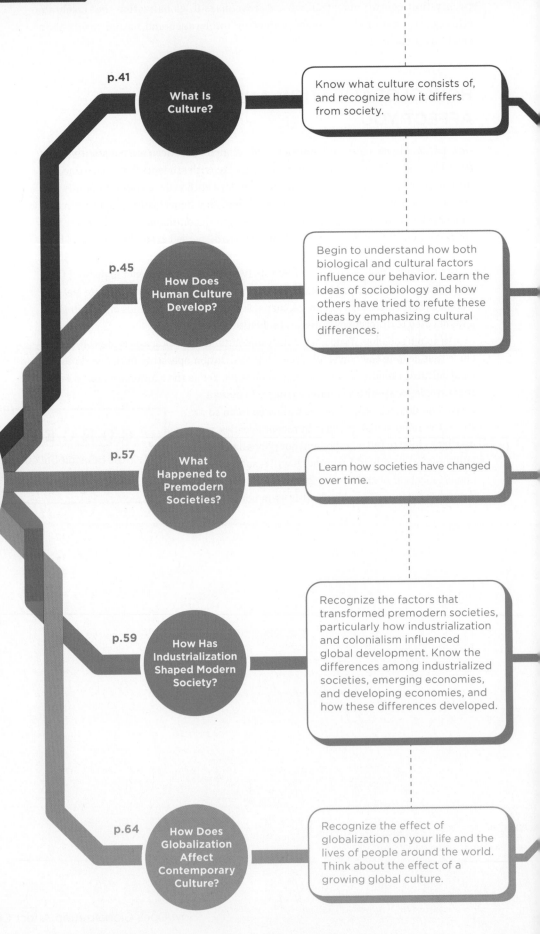

Chapter 2

Culture and Society

p.41 **What Is Culture?**

Know what culture consists of, and recognize how it differs from society.

p.45 **How Does Human Culture Develop?**

Begin to understand how both biological and cultural factors influence our behavior. Learn the ideas of sociobiology and how others have tried to refute these ideas by emphasizing cultural differences.

p.57 **What Happened to Premodern Societies?**

Learn how societies have changed over time.

p.59 **How Has Industrialization Shaped Modern Society?**

Recognize the factors that transformed premodern societies, particularly how industrialization and colonialism influenced global development. Know the differences among industrialized societies, emerging economies, and developing economies, and how these differences developed.

p.64 **How Does Globalization Affect Contemporary Culture?**

Recognize the effect of globalization on your life and the lives of people around the world. Think about the effect of a growing global culture.

culture • values • norms • material goods • instinct • society

1. Describe the main elements of culture.
2. What role does culture play in society?

sociobiology • biological determinism • subculture • assimilation • multiculturalism • ethnocentrism • cultural relativism • cultural universals • language • marriage • linguistic relativity hypothesis • signifier

1. Explain the nature/nurture debate.
2. Why do sociologists disagree with the claim that biology is destiny?
3. Give examples of subcultures that are typical of American society.
4. What is the difference between cultural ethnocentrism and cultural relativism?
5. Why is language considered to be a cultural universal?
6. What is the linguistic relativity hypothesis?

pastoral societies • agrarian societies

1. Compare the two main types of premodern societies.
2. Contrast pastorial and agrarian societies.

industrialization • industrialized societies • nation-state • colonialism • developing world • emerging economies

1. What does the concept of industrialization mean?
2. How has industrialization hurt traditional social systems?
3. Why are many African and South American societies classified as part of the developing world?

1. How does global culture influence local cultures?
2. What is nationalism?

nationalism

3

Socialization, the Life Course, and Aging

THE BIG QUESTIONS

HOW ARE CHILDREN SOCIALIZED?
Learn about socialization (including gender socialization), and know the most important agents of socialization.

WHAT ARE THE FIVE MAJOR STAGES OF THE LIFE COURSE?
Learn the various stages of the life course, and see the similarities and differences among different cultures.

HOW DO PEOPLE AGE?
Understand that aging is a combination of biological, psychological, and social processes. Consider key theories of aging, particularly those that focus on how society shapes the social roles of older people and that emphasize aspects of age stratification.

WHAT ARE THE CHALLENGES OF AGING IN THE UNITED STATES?
Evaluate the experience of growing old in the United States. Identify the physical, emotional, and financial challenges faced by older adults.

Five-year-old Boo dressed up as his favorite character, Daphne from *Scooby-Doo*, for Halloween. This simple act triggered a national conversation about "appropriate" behavior for boys and girls.

A child's Halloween costume is seldom the topic of national debate—but that changed in October 2010. A Kansas City, Missouri, mother and blogger named Sarah allowed her five-year-old son Boo to attend his preschool Halloween party dressed up as his favorite cartoon character—Daphne, a red-haired young woman from *Scooby-Doo*. Boo asked his mother if he could dress up as Daphne for the school party, and Sarah happily obliged. She bought him the costume, which included a bright orange wig and a pink velvet dress. Boo and his best friend, a girl, both decided to wear the same costume to the party. As Sarah recounted, "Halloween is a night to dress up. You get to be something you are not. He loves *Scooby-Doo*" (Parker-Pope 2010).

When she arrived at his preschool on the day of the party, Sarah observed that "two mothers went wide-eyed and made faces as if they smelled" a foul odor. "Did he ask to be that?!" one asked. Another woman said she was shocked that a mother would let her son dress up as a girl. Sarah recalled, "They continued with their nosy, probing questions . . . [while another mom] mostly just stood there in shock and dismay." Still another mother said Sarah "never should have allowed it. . . . She continued on and on about how cruel children could be and how he would be ridiculed. My response to that: The only people that seem to have a problem with it [are] their mothers" (Nerdy Apple Bottom 2010).

Hurt and puzzled by the strong reaction to her son's colorful costume, Sarah posted on her blog a photo of Boo (in costume) along with her rationale for letting him dress as he wished for Halloween. Her blog post attracted more than 45,000 comments. Sarah and her son were subsequently invited to appear on nearly every major national news program, from the *Today Show* to *CNN American Morning*. Angry opponents accused Sarah of everything from "turning" her child gay to "inviting" abuse and teasing by dressing her son as a "sissy boy" and "wussifying" him. Supporters praised Sarah for giving her son the freedom to play and dress up as he liked. What did Sarah say to her detractors, when interviewed on the *Today Show*?

> "If you think that me allowing my son to be a female character for Halloween is somehow going to 'make' him gay then [you are wrong]. Secondly, if my son is gay, OK. I will love him no less. Thirdly, I am not worried that your son will grow up to be an actual ninja so back off."

The tale of Boo, his Halloween costume, the heated reactions from his class-mates' parents, and his mom's impassioned rebuttal illustrate the importance of socialization to everyday life. Sociologists are interested in the processes through which a young child learns to become a member of society, complying with (or reject-ing) society's expectations for how one acts, thinks, feels, and even dresses. Social institutions and social actors encourage conformity through praise and discourage nonconformity through punishment and disapproval.

socialization • The social processes through which we develop an awareness of social norms and values and achieve a distinct sense of self.

Socialization is the process whereby an innocent child becomes a self-aware, knowledgeable person, skilled in the ways of the culture into which he or she was born. Socialization among the young allows for the more general phenomenon of **social reproduction**—the process whereby societies have structural continuity over time. During the course of socialization, especially in the early years of life, chil-dren learn the ways of their elders, thereby carrying on their values, norms, and social practices. All societies have characteristics that endure over long stretches of time, even though their members change as individuals are born and die. But at the same time, some old norms and customs die out as members of the older generation pass away, and are replaced with new "rules" to live by. For instance, while older genera-tions of parents might have reprimanded their girls for roughhousing and acting like "tomboys," newer generations of parents may encourage their daughters to give their all on the soccer field. Yet some customs are slower to change, as we have seen with the outcry over Boo's Halloween costume.

social reproduction • The process whereby societies have structural continuity over time. Social reproduction is an important pathway through which parents transmit or produce values, norms, and social practices among their children.

resocialization • The process of learning new norms, values, and behaviors when one joins a new group or takes on a new social role, or when life circumstances change dramatically.

Yet socialization is not limited to childhood. Throughout the life course, individuals may experience **resocialization** when their life circumstances and social roles change. Resocialization involves either learning new skills and norms appropriate to one's new roles and contexts, or unlearning those skills and norms that may no longer be relevant. For example, upon retirement one must learn to take on a new social role that is different from the role of worker, and upon release from prison, ex-convicts must re-learn how to be a member of mainstream society.

Socialization connects the different generations to one another (Turnbull 1983). The birth of a child alters the lives of those who are responsible for his or her upbringing—who themselves therefore undergo new learning experiences. Parent-ing usually ties the activities of adults to children for the remainder of their lives. Older people still remain parents when they become grandparents, thus forging another set of relationships that bond the generations. Although the process of cultural learning is much more intense in infancy and early childhood than later, learning and adjustment go on through the whole life course.

In the sections to follow, we continue the theme of "nature interacting with nurture," introduced in the previous chapter. We first describe the process of human development from infancy to early childhood. We compare different theoretical interpretations of how and why children develop as they do, and how gender identities develop. We move on to discuss the main groups and social contexts that influence socialization throughout the life course. Finally, we focus on one distinctive stage of the life course: old age. We discuss the unique problems faced by older adults, who now make up the most rapidly growing age group in the United States and the developed world.

HOW ARE CHILDREN SOCIALIZED?

Learn about socialization (including gender socialization), and know the most important agents of socialization.

THEORIES OF CHILD DEVELOPMENT

One of the most distinctive features of human beings, compared with other animals, is self-awareness—the awareness that one has an identity distinct and separate from others. During the first months of life, an infant possesses little or no understanding of differences between human beings and material objects in the environment, and has no awareness of self. Children begin to use concepts such as "I," "me," and "you" around age two or after. They gradually come to understand that others have distinct identities, consciousness, and needs separate from their own.

The problem of the emergence of self is much debated, in part, because the most prominent theories about child development emphasize different aspects of socialization. The American philosopher and sociologist George Herbert Mead gives attention mainly to how children learn to use the concepts of "I" and "me." Jean Piaget, the Swiss student of child behavior, focused on **cognition**—the ways in which children learn to think about themselves and their environment.

cognition • Human thought processes involving perception, reasoning, and remembering.

G. H. MEAD AND THE DEVELOPMENT OF SELF

Because Mead's ideas form the basis of a general tradition of theoretical thinking, symbolic interactionism, they have had a very broad impact in sociology. Symbolic interactionism emphasizes that interaction between human beings takes place through symbols and the interpretation of meanings (see Chapter 1). Mead's work also provides an account of the main phases of child development, giving particular attention to the emergence of a sense of self.

According to Mead, infants and young children develop as social beings by imitating the actions of those around them. Play is one way in which this takes place; small children often imitate what adults do. A small child will make mud pies, having seen an adult cooking, or dig in the dirt with a spoon, having observed someone gardening. Children's play evolves from simple imitation to more complicated games in which a child of four or five years old will act out an adult role. Mead called this "taking the role of the other"—learning what it is like to be in the shoes of another person. At this stage, children acquire a developed sense of self; that is, they develop an understanding of themselves as separate agents—as a "me"—by seeing themselves through the eyes of others.

We achieve self-awareness, according to Mead, when we learn to distinguish the "me" from the "I." The "I" is the unsocialized infant, a bundle of spontaneous

social self • The basis of self-consciousness in human individuals, according to the theory of George Herbert Mead. The social self is the identity conferred upon an individual by the reactions of others. A person achieves self-consciousness by becoming aware of this social identity.

self-consciousness • Awareness of one's distinct social identity as a person separate from others. Human beings are not born with self-consciousness but acquire an awareness of self as a result of early socialization.

generalized other • A concept in the theory of George Herbert Mead, according to which the individual takes over the general values of a given group or society during the socialization process.

sensorimotor stage • According to Jean Piaget, a stage of human cognitive development in which the child's awareness of his or her environment is dominated by perception and touch.

preoperational stage • According to Jean Piaget, a stage of human cognitive development in which the child has advanced sufficiently to master basic modes of logical thought.

egocentric • According to Jean Piaget, the characteristic quality of a child during the early years of his or her life. Egocentric thinking involves understanding objects and events in the environment solely in terms of the child's own position.

concrete operational stage • A stage of human cognitive development, as formulated by Jean Piaget, in which the child's thinking is based primarily on physical perception of the world. In this phase, the child is not yet capable of dealing with abstract concepts or hypothetical situations.

wants and desires. The "me," as Mead used the term, is the **social self**. Individuals develop **self-consciousness**, Mead argued, by coming to see themselves as others see them. A further stage of child development, according to Mead, occurs when the child is about eight or nine years old. This is the age at which children tend to take part in organized games, rather than unsystematic play. It is at this period that children begin to understand the overall values and morality that guide human behavior. To learn organized games, children must understand the rules of play and notions of fairness and equal participation. Children at this stage learn to grasp what Mead termed the **generalized other**—the general values and moral rules of the culture in which they are developing.

JEAN PIAGET AND THE STAGES OF COGNITIVE DEVELOPMENT

Piaget emphasized the child's active capability to make sense of the world. Children do not passively soak up information, but instead select and interpret what they see, hear, and feel in the world around them. Piaget described several distinct stages of cognitive development during which children learn to think about themselves and their environment. Each stage involves the acquisition of new skills and depends on the successful completion of the preceding one.

Piaget called the first stage, which lasts from birth up to about age two, the **sensorimotor stage** because infants learn mainly by touching objects, manipulating them, and physically exploring their environment. Until about age four months, infants cannot differentiate themselves from their environment. Objects are not differentiated from persons, and the infant is unaware that anything exists outside his or her range of vision. Infants gradually learn to distinguish people from objects, coming to see that both have an existence independent of their immediate perceptions. By the end of the sensorimotor stage, children understand that their environment has distinct and stable properties.

The next phase, called the **preoperational stage**, is the one to which Piaget devoted the bulk of his research. This stage lasts from age two to seven. Children acquire a mastery of language and an ability to use words to represent objects and images in a symbolic fashion. A four-year-old might use a sweeping hand, for example, to represent the concept "airplane." Piaget termed the stage "preoperational" because children are not yet able to use their developing mental capabilities systematically. Children in this stage are **egocentric**. As Piaget used it, this concept does not refer to selfishness, but to the tendency of the child to interpret the world exclusively in terms of his or her own position. A child during this period does not understand, for instance, that others see objects from a different perspective from his or her own. Holding a book upright, the child may ask about a picture in it, not realizing that the other person sitting opposite can only see the back of the book.

Children at the preoperational stage cannot hold connected conversations with others. In egocentric speech, what the child says is more or less unrelated to what the other speaker said. Children talk together but not to one another in the same sense that adults do. During this phase of development, children have no general understanding of categories of thought that adults tend to take for granted: concepts such as causality, speed, weight, or number.

A third period, the **concrete operational stage**, lasts from age seven to eleven. During this phase, children can master logical but not abstract notions. They are able to handle ideas such as causality without much difficulty. They become capable of carrying out the mathematical operations of multiplication, division, and subtraction. Children by this stage are much less egocentric. In the preoperational stage, if a girl is asked "How many sisters do you have?" she may correctly answer one. But if asked "How many sisters does your sister have?" she will probably answer none because she cannot see herself from the point of view of her sister. The concrete operational child is able to answer such a question with ease.

The years from eleven to fifteen cover what Piaget called the **formal operational stage**. During adolescence, the developing child becomes able to grasp highly abstract and hypothetical ideas. When faced with a problem, children at this stage are able to review all the possible ways of solving it and go through them theoretically in order to reach a solution.

According to Piaget, the first three stages of development are universal, but not all adults reach the formal operational stage. The development of formal operational thought depends in part on processes of schooling. Adults of limited educational attainment tend to continue to think in more concrete terms and retain large traces of egocentrism.

formal operational stage • According to Jean Piaget, a stage of human cognitive development at which the growing child becomes capable of handling abstract concepts and hypothetical situations.

AGENTS OF SOCIALIZATION

Agents of socialization are groups or social contexts in which significant processes of socialization occur. Primary socialization occurs in infancy and childhood and is the most intense period of cultural learning. It is the time when children learn language and basic behavioral patterns that form the foundation for later learning. The family is the main agent of socialization during this phase. Secondary socialization takes place later in childhood and into maturity. In this phase, schools, peer groups, social organizations (such as sports teams), the media, and eventually the workplace become socializing forces for individuals. Social interactions in these contexts help people learn the values, norms, and beliefs that make up the patterns of their culture.

agents of socialization • Groups or social contexts within which processes of socialization take place.

nuclear family • A family group consisting of an adult or adult couple and their dependent children.

The family is a key site of social reproduction. Children model the behavior of their parents. In this way, values and behaviors are reproduced across generations.

THE FAMILY

Since family systems vary widely, the range of family contacts that the infant experiences is by no means standard across cultures. The mother is commonly the most important individual in the child's early life, but the nature of the relationships established between mothers and their children is influenced by the form and regularity of their contact.

In modern societies, most early socialization occurs within a small-scale or **nuclear family** context. Most American children spend their early years within a domestic unit containing mother, father, and perhaps one or two other children, although the proportion growing up in two-parent households is certainly lower than it was in prior decades (U.S. Bureau of the Census 2012p). In many other cultures, by contrast, aunts, uncles, and grandparents are often part of a single household and serve as caretakers even for very young infants. Yet even within American society, family contexts vary widely. Some children are brought up in single-parent households; some are cared for by one biological and one non-biological parent figure (for example, a divorced parent and a stepparent, or parents in a same-sex relationship). The majority of mothers are now employed outside the home and return to their paid work relatively soon after the births of their children. In spite of these variations, the family typically remains the major agent of socialization from infancy to adolescence and beyond—in a sequence of development connecting the generations.

In most traditional societies, the family into which a person was born largely determined the individual's social position for the rest of his or her life. In modern societies, social position is not inherited at birth in this way, yet the region and social class of the family into which an individual is born affect patterns of socialization. Children pick up ways of behaving from their parents or others in their neighborhood or community. Patterns of child rearing and discipline, together with contrasting values and expectations, are found in different sectors of large-scale societies. It is easy to understand the influence of different types of family background if we think of what life is like, say, for a child growing up in a poor single-parent family living in a disadvantaged urban neighborhood compared with one born into an affluent two-parent family living in a posh suburb (Kohn 1977).

Of course, few, if any, children simply take over unquestioningly the outlook of their parents. This is especially true in the modern world, in which change is so pervasive. Moreover, the very existence of a range of socializing agents in modern societies leads to many divergences between the outlooks of children, adolescents, and the parental generation. For example, while young Boo's mother supported her son's desire to dress however he wished, Boo's classmates' parents and teachers at preschool held very different views that emphasized conformity to traditional gender norms rather than freedom of expression.

SCHOOLS

Another important socializing agent is the school. Schooling is a formal process: Students pursue a definite curriculum of subjects. Yet schools are agents of socialization in more subtle respects. Students are expected to be punctual, to be quiet in class, to obey their teachers, and to observe rules of school discipline. How teachers react to their students, in turn, affects the students' views and expectations of themselves. These expectations also become linked to later job experience when students leave school. Peer groups are often formed at school, and the system of keeping children in classes according to age reinforces their impact.

PEER RELATIONSHIPS

peer group • A friendship group composed of individuals of similar age and social status.

age-grades • The system found in small traditional cultures by which people belonging to a similar age group are categorized together and hold similar rights and obligations.

Another socializing agency is the **peer group**. Peer groups consist of individuals of a similar age. In some cultures, particularly small traditional societies, peer groups are formalized as **age-grades** (normally confined to males). There are often specific ceremonies or rites that mark the transition of men from one age-grade to another. A typical set of age-grades consists of childhood, junior warriorhood, senior warriorhood, junior elderhood, and senior elderhood. Men move through these grades not as individuals but as whole groups.

The family's importance in socialization is obvious because the experience of the infant and young child is shaped more or less exclusively within it. It is less apparent, especially to those of us living in Western societies, how significant peer groups are. Yet even without formal age-grades, children over four or five usually spend a great deal of time in the company of friends the same age. Given the high proportion of women now in the workforce whose young children play together in day-care centers and preschool, peer relations are more important than ever before (Corsaro 1997; Harris 1998).

Peer relations are likely to have a significant effect beyond childhood and adolescence. Informal groups of people of similar ages, at work and in other situations, are usually of enduring importance in shaping individuals' attitudes and behavior. Peer groups also play an important role in changing norms. While the mothers of Boo's classmates promoted gender conformity, Boo and his young friends may grow up to hold and encourage in one another much more open-minded views about gender and gender roles.

THE MASS MEDIA

Newspapers and periodicals flourished in the West from the early 1800s onward, but they were confined to a fairly small readership. It was not until a century later that such printed materials became part of the daily experience of millions of people, influencing their attitudes and opinions. The spread of mass media involving printed documents was soon accompanied by electronic communication—radio, television, records, and videos. In 2009, American children between the ages of eight and eighteen averaged four hours and twenty-nine minutes of TV watching a day, up from three hours and forty-seven minutes per day in 1999 (Kaiser Family Foundation 2010).

Much research has been done to assess the effects of the media, especially television programs, on the audiences they reach, particularly children. Children and adolescents often model the gender roles and practices that they see on their favorite television shows. Media, including fashion magazines and music videos, are also cited as powerful influences on girls' body image, or their beliefs about the "ideal" body weight and physique (Grabe, Ward, and Hyde 2008). The most commonly researched topic, however, is the impact of television on propensities to crime and violence.

The most extensive studies are those carried out by George Gerbner (2002) and his collaborators. In 1967, Gerbner founded the Cultural Indicators Project to study the effects of television violence on society. His research team has analyzed samples of prime-time and weekend daytime TV for all major American networks every year since 1967. Violence is defined as physical force directed against the self or others in which physical harm or death occurs. A recent study investigating the depiction of violence during prime time on six major networks in the United States found the season beginning in fall 2006 to be one of the most violent in recent history. Between 2000 and 2007, violent content in the "family hour" slot, defined as a start time between 7 and 9 PM (EST), has increased by 52.4 percent. During this period, the FOX network experienced the largest increase of 426 percent. Nearly half of all programs (46.2 percent) contained violence. On average, prime-time TV contains 4.2 violent

Video games have become a key part of the culture and experience of childhood today.

episodes per hour (Parents Television Council 2007). In addition, violent scenes increasingly include a sexual element. Children's programs show even higher levels of violence, although killing is less commonly portrayed. Cartoons depict the highest number of violent acts and episodes of any type of television program.

In recent years researchers have become interested in studying the ways that video games (especially violent video games) affect children. There are currently some 134 million Nintendo, Microsoft, and Sony games in the United States, and many more in other countries (NPD 2009). According to one recent study, 64 percent of all Americans played a computer game in the past week; by contrast, just 55 percent went out to see a movie (NPD 2009). A sizeable proportion of all video game devices are owned and operated by children. According to Eugene Provenzo, author of *Video Kids* (1991), such games have become a key part of the culture and experience of childhood and adolescence today. But is this a potentially harmful trend?

It is doubtful that a child's involvement with most video games harms his or her achievement at school. While at times increased video game use and decreased school performance go hand in hand, it is unlikely that video games cause a decline in school performance. For example, where strong pressures deflect students from an interest in their schoolwork, absorption with TV or video pursuits will tend to reinforce these attitudes. Video games and TV can then become a refuge from a disliked school environment.

It is also possible that video games can help youth to develop skills that might be relevant both to formal education and to wider participation in a society that depends increasingly on electronic communication. Patricia Greenfield (1993) has argued that "video games are the first example of a computer technology that is having a socializing effect on the next generation on a mass scale, and even on a world-wide basis." However, experts also find that some video games fail to carry the benefits for children that we might expect. For example, a recent study found that children who played fitness-related games like *Wii Sports* or *Dance Dance Revolution* were no more fit and got no more exercise than children who played with sedentary games such as *Super Mario Galaxy* (Baranowski et al. 2012). The researchers speculated that children either play the fitness games with little effort, or else they exercise less during the rest of the day.

WORK

Across all cultures, work is an important setting within which socialization processes operate, although it is only in industrial societies that large numbers of people go out to work—that is, go each day to places of work separate from the home. In traditional communities, many people farmed the land close to where they lived or had workshops in their dwellings. "Work" in such communities was not as clearly distinct from other activities as it is for most members of the workforce in the modern West. In the industrialized countries, joining the workforce ordinarily marks a much greater transition in an individual's life than beginning work in traditional societies. The work environment often poses unfamiliar demands, perhaps calling for major adjustments in the person's outlook or behavior.

SOCIAL ROLES

social roles • Socially defined expectations of an individual in a given status, or occupying a particular social position. In every society, individuals play a number of social roles, such as teenager, parent, worker, or political leader.

Through the process of socialization, individuals learn about **social roles**—socially defined expectations that a person in a given social position follows. The social role of doctor, for example, encompasses a set of behaviors that should be enacted by all individual doctors, regardless of their personal opinions or outlooks. Because all doctors share this role, it is possible to speak in general terms about the professional behavior of doctors, regardless of the specific individuals who occupy that position.

Some sociologists, particularly those associated with the functionalist school, regard social roles as fixed and relatively unchanging parts of a society's culture. According to this view, individuals learn the expectations that surround social positions in their particular culture and perform those roles largely as they have been defined. Social roles do not involve negotiation or creativity. Rather, they prescribe, contain, and direct an individual's behavior. Through socialization, individuals internalize social roles and learn how to carry them out.

This view, however, is mistaken. It suggests that individuals simply take on roles, rather than creating or negotiating them. Socialization is a process in which humans can exercise agency; we are not simply passive subjects waiting to be instructed or programmed. Individuals come to understand and assume social roles through an ongoing process of social interaction.

IDENTITY

The cultural settings in which we are born and mature to adulthood influence our behavior, but that does not mean that humans are robbed of individuality or free will. Some sociologists do tend to write about socialization as though this were the case. But such a view is fundamentally flawed—socialization is also at the origin of our very individuality and freedom. In the course of socialization, each of us develops a sense of identity and the capacity for independent thought and action.

Identity is a multifaceted concept—it relates to the understandings people hold about who they are and what is meaningful to them. Some of the main sources of identity include gender, sexual orientation, nationality or ethnicity, and social class. Sociologists typically speak of two types of identity: social identity and self-identity (or personal identity). These concepts are analytically distinct but are closely related to each other. Social identity refers to the characteristics that other people attribute to an individual. These can be seen as markers that indicate who the individual is. At the same time, they place that individual in relation to other individuals who share the same attributes. Examples of social identities include student, mother, lawyer, Catholic, homeless, Asian, dyslexic, married, and so forth. Nearly all individuals have social identities comprising more than one attribute. A person could simultaneously be a mother, an engineer, a Muslim, and a city council member. Multiple social identities reflect the

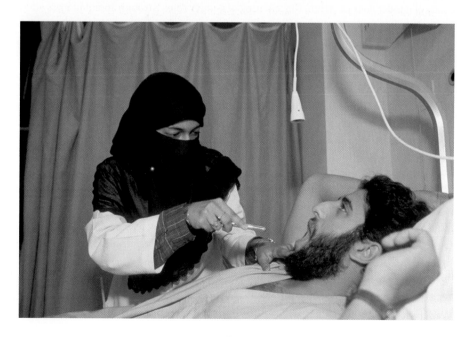

People often exhibit multiple social identities simultaneously, sometimes seemingly conflicting ones.

self-identity • The ongoing process of self-development and definition of our personal identity through which we formulate a unique sense of ourselves and our relationship to the world around us.

many dimensions of people's lives. Although this plurality of social identities can be a potential source of conflict for people, most individuals organize meaning and experience in their lives around a primary identity that is fairly continuous across time and place.

If social identities mark ways in which individuals are the same as others, self-identity (or personal identity) sets us apart as distinct individuals. **Self-identity** refers to the process of self-development through which we formulate a unique sense of ourselves and our relationship to the world around us. The notion of self-identity draws heavily on the work of symbolic interactionists. The individual's constant negotiation with the outside world helps create and shape his or her sense of self. Though the cultural and social environments are factors in shaping self-identity, individual agency and choice are of central importance.

If at one time people's identities were largely informed by their membership in broad social groups, bound by class or nationality, they are now more multifaceted and less stable. Individuals have become more socially and geographically mobile due to processes such as urban growth and industrialization. This has freed people from the tightly knit, relatively homogeneous communities of the past in which patterns were passed down in a fixed way across generations. It has created the space for other sources of personal meaning, such as gender and sexual orientation, to play a greater role in people's sense of identity.

In today's world, we have unprecedented opportunities to create our own identities. We are our own best resources in defining who we are, where we come from, and where we are going. Now that the traditional signposts of identity have become less essential, the social world confronts us with a dizzying array of choices about who to be, how to live, and what to do, without offering much guidance about which selections to make. The decisions we make in our everyday lives—about what to wear, how to behave, and how to spend our time—help make us who we are. Through our capacity as self-conscious, self-aware human beings, we constantly create and re-create our identities.

GENDER SOCIALIZATION

As we learned in the case of Boo, gender shapes every aspect of daily life, yet exactly how one "should" behave as a boy or girl must be, in part, learned. Agents of socialization play an important role in how children learn gender roles. Let's now turn to the study of gender socialization, the learning of gender roles through social factors such as the family and the media.

REACTIONS OF PARENTS AND ADULTS

Many studies have been carried out on the degree to which gender differences are the result of social influences. Studies of mother–infant interaction show differences in the treatment of boys and girls even when parents believe their reactions to both are the same. Adults asked to assess the personality of a baby give different answers according to whether they believe the child to be a girl or a boy. In one experiment, five young mothers were observed while interacting with a six-month-old named Beth. They tended to smile at her often and offer her dolls to play with. She was seen as "sweet," having a "soft cry." The reaction of a second group of mothers to a child the same age, named Adam, was noticeably different. The baby was likely to be offered a train or other "male" toys to play with. Beth and Adam were actually the same child, dressed in different clothes (Will and Datan 1976).

The case of baby Storm Stocker vividly reveals how powerfully we adhere to subtle expectations about gender differences, even for infants. Storm's parents, Kathy Witterick and David Stocker, decided to keep their baby's gender a secret, informing

In her "Pink & Blue" project, photographer JeongMee Yoon records girls' obsession with the color pink. What are the implications of the gender-typed packaging and color coding that we see in children's toys and clothing?

only their midwives and two older sons of four-month-old Storm's sex. They dressed Storm in gender-neutral clothing and refused to use gender-specific pronouns like *he* or *she* when describing their baby. They wanted to make sure that others did not treat their child in stereotypically gendered ways, such as those experienced by babies Beth and Adam (Will and Datan 1976). When announcing Storm's birth, Kathy and David sent out an announcement proclaiming, "We decided not to share Storm's sex for now—a tribute to freedom and choice in place of limitation, a standup to what the world could become in Storm's lifetime." This simple act was met by a firestorm of angry reactions from bloggers, media commentators, and even family and friends. The hostility directed toward Kathy and David shows just how deeply entrenched gender and gender socialization are even in the twenty-first century (Davis and James 2011).

GENDER LEARNING

Gender learning by infants is almost certainly unconscious. Before a child can accurately label itself as either a boy or a girl, it receives a range of preverbal cues. For instance, male and female adults usually handle infants differently. The cosmetics women use contain scents different from those the baby might learn to associate with males. Systematic differences in dress, hairstyle, and so on provide visual cues for the infant in the learning process. By age two, children have a partial understanding of what gender is. They know whether they are boys or girls, and they can usually categorize others accurately. Not until five or six, however, does a child know that everyone has gender, and that sex differences between girls and boys are anatomically based.

The toys, picture books, and television programs with which young children come into contact all tend to emphasize differences between male and female attributes. Toy stores and mail-order catalogs usually categorize their products by gender. Even toys that seem neutral in terms of gender are not always so in practice. For example, toy kittens and rabbits are recommended for girls, whereas lions and tigers are seen as more appropriate for boys. Similarly, boys are expected to dress up like ninjas or superheroes for Halloween, whereas girls are expected to dress up like princesses or other highly "feminine" characters.

Vanda Lucia Zammuner (1986) studied the toy preferences of boys and girls between the ages of seven and ten in Italy and Holland. On average, the Italian children chose gender-differentiated (versus gender-neutral) toys to play with more often than the Dutch children—a finding that conformed to expectations because Italian culture tends to hold a more traditional view of gender divisions than does Dutch society. As in other studies, girls from both societies chose gender-neutral or boys' toys to play with far more often than boys chose girls' toys.

STORYBOOKS AND TELEVISION

Children's books and television shows teach important, though subtle, lessons about gender. However, scholarly analyses of children's books and TV shows find that girls are highly underrepresented. A recent study by McCabe and colleagues (2011) examined nearly 6,000 books published from 1900 to 2000. They found that males are central characters in 57 percent of children's books published per year, whereas only 31 percent have female central characters. Although male characters (including male animal characters) were found in each and every book, only one-third of children's books published in any given year featured central characters that were female. On average, 36.5 percent of books in each year studied include a male in the title, compared with 17.5 percent that include a female.

Other studies have found that the activities of males and females in children's books also differ. A classic study by Lenore Weitzman and colleagues (1972) found that male characters in picture books engaged in adventurous pursuits and outdoor activities demanding independence and strength. When girls did appear, they were portrayed as passive and confined mostly to indoor activities. Girls cooked and cleaned for the males or awaited their return. Much the same was true of the adult men and women represented in the storybooks. Women who were not wives and mothers were imaginary creatures like witches or fairy godmothers. There was not a single woman in all the books analyzed who held an occupation outside the home. By contrast, the men were depicted as fighters, policemen, judges, and kings.

More recent research suggests that things have changed somewhat but that the large bulk of children's literature remains much the same (Davies 1991). Fairy tales, for example, reflect traditional attitudes toward gender and the sorts of aims and ambitions girls and boys are expected to have. "Someday my prince will come," in versions of fairy tales from several centuries ago, usually implied that a girl from a poor family might dream of wealth and fortune. Today, its meaning has become more closely tied to the ideals of romantic love. Even the popular *Twilight* series enchanted teenage girls with the romantic tale of high school student Bella Swan meeting her soul mate (and vampire) Edward Cullen.

Although there are some notable exceptions, analyses of television programs designed for children conform to the findings about children's books. Studies of the most frequently watched cartoons show that most of the leading figures are male and that males dominate the active pursuits. Similar images are found in the commercials that appear throughout the programs. Gender socialization is very powerful, and gender-typed expectations are fulfilled and reproduced in everyday life (Bourdieu 1990; Lorber 1994). ✓

CONCEPT CHECKS ✓

1. What is social reproduction? What are some specific ways that the four main agents of socialization contribute to social reproduction?

2. According to Mead, how does a child develop a social self?

3. What are the four stages of cognitive development according to Piaget?

4. Compare and contrast social roles and social identities.

5. How do the media contribute to gender role socialization?

WHAT ARE THE FIVE MAJOR STAGES OF THE LIFE COURSE?

Learn the various stages of the life course, and see the similarities and differences among different cultures.

The transitions that individuals pass through during their lives seem at first glance to be biologically fixed—from childhood to adulthood and eventually to death. But the stages of the human **life course** are social as well as biological in nature. They are influenced by culture and by the material circumstances of people's lives. For example, in the modern West, death is usually thought of in relation to old age because most people enjoy a life span of seventy-five years or more. In traditional societies of the past, however, more people died at younger ages than survived to old age.

life course • The various transitions and stages people experience during their lives.

CHILDHOOD

To people living in modern societies, childhood is a clear and distinct stage of life. Children are different from babies or toddlers; childhood is the stage between infancy and adolescence. Yet the concept of childhood, like so many other aspects of social life today, has come into being only over the past two or three centuries. In earlier societies, the young moved directly from a lengthy infancy into working roles within the community. French historian Philippe Ariès (1965) argued that "childhood," conceived of

This *Madonna and Child*, painted in the thirteenth century by Duccio da Buoninsegna, depicts the infant Jesus with a mature face. Until recently, children in Western society were viewed as little adults.

as a separate phase of development, did not exist in medieval times. In the paintings of medieval Europe, children are portrayed as little adults, with mature faces and the same style of dress as their elders. Children took part in the same work and play activities as adults, rather than in the childhood games we now take for granted.

Until the early twentieth century, in the United States and most other Western countries, children were put to work at what now seems a very young age. There are countries in the world today, in fact, where young children are engaged in full-time work, sometimes in physically demanding circumstances (for example, in coal mines). The ideas that children have distinctive rights and that the use of child labor is morally wrong are quite recent developments.

Because of the prolonged period of childhood that we recognize today, modern societies are in some respects more child centered than traditional ones. Parents are viewed as the sole protectors of their children, and parents who behave in ways that may be considered hurtful to their children are judged harshly. For instance, blogger and mother Sarah, whom we met earlier, was maligned by bloggers, Internet trolls, and TV viewers as a selfish mother. Her decision to allow her son to dress like a girl (and worse yet, her decision to post photos of him, in costume, on the Internet) was judged harshly and viewed as putting her child in harm's way.

Of course, many other observers believe that Sarah is a fine parent and argue that attacks against her detract attention from the much more harsh forms of abuse that take place in society. Not all children experience love and care from parents or other adults. The physical and sexual abuse of children is a not uncommon feature of family life in present-day society, although the full extent of such abuse has only recently come to light. Although it is difficult to obtain accurate counts, some researchers estimate that 15 to 25 percent of women and 5 to 15 percent of men were the victims of child sexual abuse (including inappropriate touching), with more than one-third of the abuse perpetuated by family members (U.S. Department of Health and Human Services 2012a).

It seems possible that as a result of changes currently occurring in modern societies, the separate character of childhood is diminishing once more. Some observers have suggested that children now grow up too fast. Even small children may watch the same television programs as adults, thereby becoming much more familiar early on with the adult world than did preceding generations.

THE TEENAGER

The idea of the "teenager," so familiar to us today, also didn't exist until recently. The biological changes involved in puberty (the point at which a person becomes capable of adult sexual activity and reproduction) are universal. Yet in many cultures, these physical changes do not produce the degree of emotional turmoil and uncertainty often found among teens in modern societies. In cultures that celebrate "rites of passage," or distinct ceremonies that signal a person's transition to adulthood, the process of psychosexual development generally seems easier to negotiate. Adolescents in such societies have less to "unlearn" because the pace of change is slower. There is a time when children in Western societies are required to be children no longer: to put away their toys and break with childish pursuits. In traditional cultures, where children are already working alongside adults, this process of unlearning is normally much less jarring.

In Western societies, teenagers are betwixt and between: Pop culture promotes sexy clothing among teens, yet frowns upon teenage sexual activity. Teens may wish to go to work and earn money as adults do, but are legally required to stay in school. Teenagers in the West live in between childhood and adulthood, growing up in a society subject to continuous change.

LIFE COURSE TRANSITIONS

Individuals pass through a number of key transitions during the course of their lives. The transition to adulthood, often indicated by benchmarks such as getting married and having a child, is being delayed today, particularly in high-income countries. In many northern and western European nations, many young adults have their first child before marriage while in cohabiting relationships.

First sexual experience   First marriage*   Birth of first child*

MEAN AGE (IN YEARS)

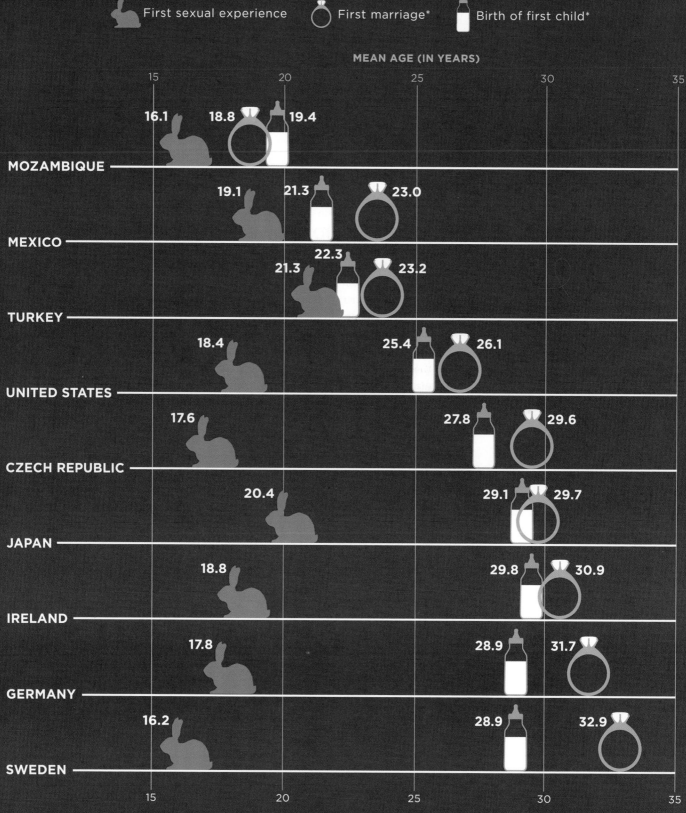

MOZAMBIQUE — 16.1 · 18.8 · 19.4

MEXICO — 19.1 · 21.3 · 23.0

TURKEY — 21.3 · 22.3 · 23.2

UNITED STATES — 18.4 · 25.4 · 26.1

CZECH REPUBLIC — 17.6 · 27.8 · 29.6

JAPAN — 20.4 · 29.1 · 29.7

IRELAND — 18.8 · 29.8 · 30.9

GERMANY — 17.8 · 28.9 · 31.7

SWEDEN — 16.2 · 28.9 · 32.9

*Mean age of women

Sources: Durex 2012; OECD 2009; UNECE 2011; World Bank 2010, 2011

YOUNG ADULTHOOD

Young adulthood is a stage of exploration, often before one settles on a permanent job, spouse, or home. This stage of personal and sexual development is unique to modern societies (Furstenburg et al. 2004). Particularly among more affluent groups, people in their early twenties are taking the time to travel; to explore sexual, political, and religious affiliations; to try out different careers; and to date and live with several romantic partners before eventually marrying. The importance of this postponement of the responsibilities of full adulthood is likely to increase, given the extended period of education many people now undergo.

Although it is difficult to pinpoint precisely when one makes the "transition to adulthood," one team of researchers identified five benchmarks of adulthood: leaving one's parents' home, finishing school, getting married, having a child, and achieving financial independence. In 1960, fully 65 percent of men and 77 percent of women had achieved all five benchmarks by age thirty. By contrast, only 25 percent of men and 39 percent of women had done so in 2010 (Furstenburg and Kennedy 2013; Furstenburg et al. 2004). These statistics clearly show that the transition to adulthood is being delayed today, and that some benchmarks historically considered a signifier of adulthood, such as becoming a parent, may be less central to one's identity as an adult in the twenty-first century.

MIDLIFE OR "MIDDLE AGE"

Most young adults in the West today can look forward to a life stretching right through to old age. In premodern times, few could anticipate such a future with much confidence. Death through sickness or injury was much more frequent among all age groups than it is today. Given these advances in life expectancy, a "new" life course stage has been recognized in the twentieth century: midlife, or middle age (Cohen 2012). Midlife, the stage between young adulthood and old age, is generally described as the years between ages forty-five and sixty-five.

Midlife is distinct from other life course stages in that there is not an "official" or legal age of entry. For example, American youth become a legal adult at age eighteen, whereas age sixty-five is generally believed to signify the transition to old age and the receipt of retirement benefits. One's entry to midlife, by contrast, tends to be signified by the social roles one adopts (or relinquishes). While some scholars believe that menopause, or the loss of reproductive potential, signals women's transition to midlife, others believe that for both men and women, midlife is marked by transitions such as the "empty-nest" stage (when children leave the family home).

Midlife is also a psychological turning point where men and women may assess their past choices and accomplishments and make new choices that prepare them for the second half of life. Keeping a forward-looking outlook in middle age has taken on a particular importance in modern societies. Most people do not expect to be doing the same thing their whole lives, as was the case for the majority in traditional cultures. For example, women who spent their early adulthood raising a family and whose children have left home may feel free to pursue new personal goals, whereas men who stayed at financially stable jobs while supporting their young families may choose to pursue their earlier career dreams (Lachman 2001).

LATER LIFE OR "OLD AGE"

In traditional societies, older people were normally accorded a great deal of respect. Among cultures that included age-grades, the elders usually had a say over

Figure 3.1 | Growth of the Elderly Population in the U.S. by Age Group, 1900–2050

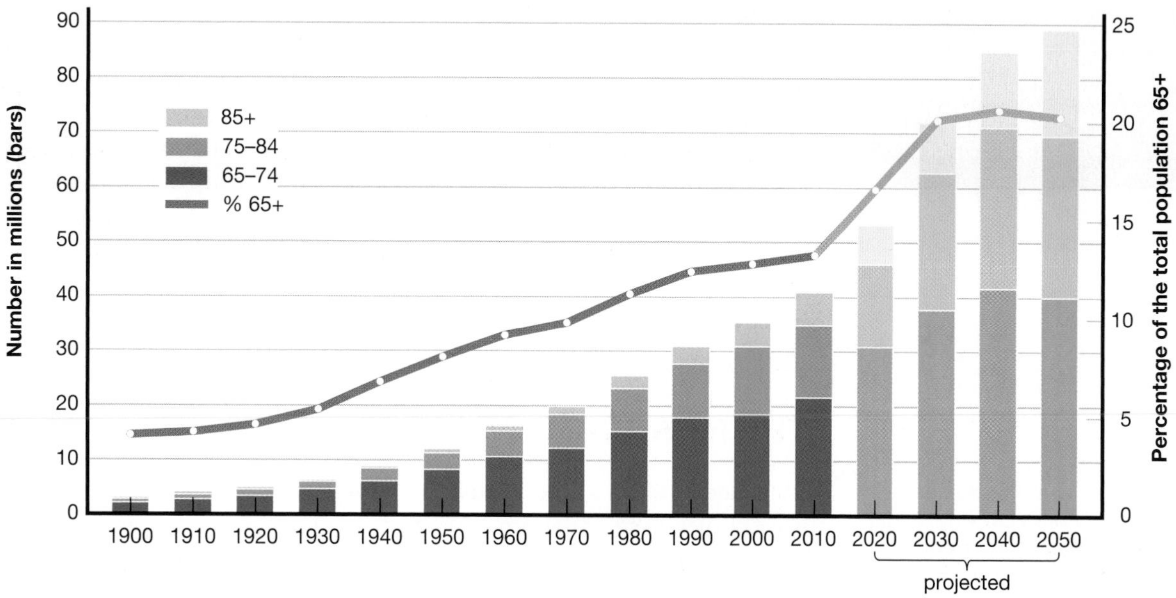
85+
75–84
65–74
% 65+
Number in millions (bars)
Percentage of the total population 65+
0
10
20
30
40
50
60
70
80
90
5
15
25
1900 1910 1920 1930 1940 1950 1960 1970 1980 1990 2000 2010 2020 2030 2040 2050
projected

SOURCE: U.S. Bureau of the Census 2010e

matters of importance to the community. Within families, the authority of both men and women typically increased with age. In industrialized societies, by contrast, older people tend to lack authority within both the family and the wider social community. Having retired from the labor force, they may be poorer than ever before in their lives. At the same time, there has been a great increase in the proportion of the population over age sixty-five. In 1900, only one in thirty people in the United States was over sixty-five. Today, more than one in eight is over sixty-five, and this proportion is projected to rise to one in five by the year 2030 (U.S. Bureau of the Census 2010e). The same trend is found in all industrially advanced countries.

Surviving until the life course stage of "elder" in a traditional culture often marked the pinnacle of the status an individual could achieve. In modern societies, retirement tends to bring the opposite consequences. No longer living with their children and often having retired from paid work, some older people find it difficult to make the final period of their life rewarding. It used to be thought that those who successfully cope with old age do so by turning to their inner resources, becoming less interested in the material rewards that social life has to offer. Although this may often be true, it seems likely that in a society in which many are physically healthy in old age, an outward-looking view will become more and more prevalent. Those in retirement might find renewal in what has been called the "third age," in which a new phase of education begins. ✓

CONCEPT CHECKS ✓

1. What is meant by the term *life course*?
2. What are the five stages of the life course, and what are some defining features of each stage?

HOW DO PEOPLE AGE?

Understand that aging is a combination of biological, psychological, and social processes. Consider key theories of aging, particularly those that focus on how society shapes the social roles of older people and that emphasize aspects of age stratification.

Of all the life course stages that sociologists study, older adults are the group of greatest interest to policymakers. Why? Older adults, or individuals age sixty-five and older, are the most rapidly growing segment of the U.S. population; as such, they will create new challenges for American society. In 2012, 43.1 million Americans were sixty-five or older, including 5.9 million over eighty-five years old (Federal Interagency Forum on Aging-Related Statistics 2013). Growing old can be a fulfilling and rewarding experience, or it can be filled with physical distress and social isolation. For most older Americans, the experience of aging lies somewhere in between.

In this section, we delve into the meaning of being old and look at the ways in which people adapt to growing old, at least in the eyes of sociologists.

THE MEANINGS OF "AGE"

aging • The combination of biological, psychological, and social processes that affect people as they grow older.

What does it mean to age? **Aging** can be defined as the combination of biological, psychological, and social processes that affect people as they grow older (Abeles and Riley 1987; Atchley 2000; Riley et al. 1988). These three processes suggest the metaphor of three different, although interrelated, developmental "clocks": (1) a biological one, which refers to the physical body; (2) a psychological one, which refers to the mind and mental capabilities; and (3) a social one, which refers to cultural norms, values, and role expectations having to do with age. Our notions about the meaning of age are rapidly changing, both because recent research is dispelling many myths about aging and because advances in nutrition and health have enabled many people to live longer, healthier lives than ever before.

GROWING OLD: TRENDS AND COMPETING SOCIOLOGICAL EXPLANATIONS

social gerontologists • Social scientists who study aging and the elderly.

Social gerontologists, or social scientists who study aging, have offered a number of theories regarding the nature of aging in U.S. society. Some of the earliest theories emphasized individual adaptation to changing social roles as a person grows older. Later theories focused on how society shapes the social roles of older adults, often in inequitable ways. The most recent theories have been more multifaceted, focusing on the ways in which older persons actively create their lives within specific institutional contexts (Hendricks 1992).

THE FIRST GENERATION OF THEORIES: FUNCTIONALISM

The earliest theories of aging reflected the functionalist approach that was dominant in sociology during the 1950s and 1960s. They emphasized how individuals adjusted to changing social roles as they aged and how those roles were useful to society. The earliest theories often assumed that aging brings with it physical and psychological decline and that changing social roles have to take this decline into account (Hendricks 1992).

Talcott Parsons, one of the most influential functionalist theorists of the 1950s, argued that U.S. society needs to find roles for older persons consistent with advanced age. He expressed concern that the United States, with its emphasis on youth and its avoidance of death, had failed to provide roles that adequately drew on the potential wisdom and maturity of its older citizens. Moreover, given the graying of U.S. society that was evident even in Parsons's time, he argued that this failure could well lead to older people becoming discouraged and alienated from society. To achieve a "healthy maturity," Parsons (1960) argued, older adults need to adjust psychologically to their changed circumstances, while society needs to redefine the social roles of older persons. Their former roles (such as work) have to be abandoned, while new forms of productive activity (such as volunteer service) need to be identified.

Parsons's ideas set the foundation for **disengagement theory**, the notion that it is functional for society to remove people from their traditional roles when they become older, thereby freeing up those roles for others (Cumming and Henry 1961; Estes et al. 1992). According to this perspective, given the increasing frailty, illness, and dependency of older people, it becomes increasingly dysfunctional for them to occupy traditional social roles they are no longer capable of adequately fulfilling. Older adults, therefore, should retire from their jobs, pull back from civic life, and eventually withdraw from other activities as well. Disengagement is assumed to be functional for the larger society because it opens up roles formerly filled by older individuals for younger people, who presumably will carry them out with fresh energy and new skills. Disengagement is also assumed to be functional for older persons because it enables them to take on less taxing roles consistent with their advancing age and declining health.

Although there is some intuitive appeal to disengagement theory, the idea that older people should completely disengage from the larger society is based on the outdated stereotype that old age involves frailty and dependence. As a result, no sooner did the theory appear than these very assumptions were challenged, often by some of the theory's original proponents (Cumming 1963, 1975; Hendricks 1992; Henry 1965; Hochschild 1975; Maddox 1965, 1970). These challenges gave rise to two distinct yet related functionalist theories of aging, which drew conclusions quite opposite to those of disengagement theory: activity and continuity theories.

According to **activity theory**, people who are busy leading fulfilling and productive lives can be functional for society. The guiding assumption is that an active individual is much more likely to remain healthy, alert, and socially useful. In this view, people should remain engaged in their work and other social roles as long as they are capable of doing so. If a time comes when a particular role becomes too difficult or taxing, then other roles can be sought—for example, volunteer work in the community.

Activity theory finds support in research showing that continued activity well into old age—whether volunteer work, paid employment, hobbies, or visits with friends and family—is associated with good mental and physical health (Birren and Bengston 1988; Rowe and Kahn 1987; Schaie 1983). Yet critics observe that not all activities are equally valuable, giving rise to **continuity theory**. This theory specifies that older adults fare best when they participate in activities that are consistent with their personality, preferences, and activities earlier in life (Atchley 1989). For instance, a retired elementary school teacher may find volunteering at a local elementary school to be much more satisfying than taking bus trips to Atlantic City or playing bingo at a local community center.

Most social gerontologists agree that older adults should remain engaged in their work and social roles for as long as they are able. Rewarding activities such as meaningful employment can enhance health and well-being in later life.

disengagement theory • A functionalist theory of aging that holds that it is functional for society to remove people from their traditional roles when they become elderly, thereby freeing up those roles for others.

activity theory • A functionalist theory of aging, which holds that busy, engaged people are more likely to lead fulfilling and productive lives.

continuity theory • Theoretical perspective on aging that specifies that older adults fare best when they participate in activities consistent with their personality, preferences, and activities earlier in life.

Projecting Your Future

When we think about old age, we might have a particular image of what "old" looks like. We might think an older person has graying or white hair, wrinkled skin, and less physical vigor or vitality than they did years earlier. Many of us wonder what we will look and feel like when we're in our seventies, eighties, or even older.

We no longer need to imagine the future. A number of online sites and apps such as AgingBooth, Aging Album, Age My Face, and Make Me Old allow us to upload a photo of ourselves, "age" it, and then share the image of a much more senior version of ourselves with our friends via social networking sites. Some apps even allow us to hear an older version of our own voices.

These popular apps capture a very narrow view of what "aging" means. As we learned earlier in the chapter, "biological aging" does involve changes to our physical body. As we grow older, facial lines, wrinkles, age spots, and graying hair may be inevitable. However, growing old encompasses far more than just physiological changes; it involves changes—as well as continuity—in our mental and emotional capacities and the social roles we hold. In fact, the numbers of older Americans who are remaining in the workforce well into their sixties and early seventies is on the rise (Pew Research Center 2014).

Older adults regularly say that they "feel" much younger than their physical appearance or chronological age. However, in daily social interaction, people may not take the time to understand older adults, instead relying on stereotypes of the traits, attitudes, and behaviors of a person whose face shows the passage of time.

Discrimination based on age—ageism—is fueled in part by stereotypes of older adults as senile and infirm. Have you "aged" yourself using a site like AgingBooth? How did you feel when you saw the "old" you? Can you imagine ways that your "social" and "psychological" age might be out of sync with this physical depiction of your future "biological" age?

We also can use a range of smartphone apps and websites to project other aspects of our future, such as our life expectancy. As we discussed earlier in the chapter, men and women are living longer than ever before, due in part to medical advances and healthy lifestyle choices. However, the length of our lives reflects our gender, social class, and the adversities and advantages we encounter over the life course. Apps like the Ignite Wellness Lifestyle Tracker calculate life expectancy based on one's daily decisions, from how much we eat and sleep to the amount of time we spend exercising. Dozens of websites, often maintained by life insurance companies, also allow us to project our life span.

Have you used an app to project your life expectancy? What surprised you? What factors did you identify as contributing to your projected life span? Some social gerontologists acknowledge that while life expectancy

While biological aging involves changes to our physical bodies, older adults maintain many important traits such as their personalities. Smartphone apps like AgingBooth focus solely on change, rather than continuity, in the aging process.

provides a good snapshot of how long one will likely live, it does not tell us whether those years will be filled with vigor and good health, or frailty and disability.

Critics of functionalist theories of aging argue that these theories emphasize the need for the elderly to adapt to existing conditions, either by disengaging from socially useful roles or by actively pursuing them, but that they do not question whether the circumstances faced by the elderly are just. In response to this critique, another group of theorists arose—those growing out of the social conflict tradition (Hendricks 1992).

THE SECOND GENERATION OF THEORIES: SOCIAL CONFLICT

Unlike their predecessors, who emphasized the ways that older adults could be integrated into the larger society, the second generation of theorists focused on sources of **social conflict** between the elderly and society (Hendricks 1992). Like other theorists who were studying social conflict in U.S. society during the 1970s and early 1980s, these theorists stressed the ways in which the larger social structure helped shape the opportunities available to the elderly; unequal opportunities were seen as creating the potential for conflict.

According to this view, many of the problems of aging—such as poverty, poor health, or inadequate health care—are systematically produced by the routine operation of social institutions. A capitalist society, the reasoning goes, favors those who are most economically powerful. While there are certainly some elderly people who have "made it" and are set for life, many have not—and these people must fight to get even a meager share of society's scarce resources. Among the elderly, those who fare worst tend to include women, low-income people, and ethnic minorities (Atchley 2000; Estes 1986, 1991; Hendricks 1992; Hendricks and Hendricks 1986). For example, poverty rates among older adults have plummeted over the past sixty years, with roughly 9 percent of older adults living in poverty today, compared with 35 percent in 1959 (U.S. Bureau of the Census 2012l). However, even today the poverty rate among older adults is as high as 40 percent among unmarried black and Hispanic older women (Carr 2010).

THE THIRD GENERATION OF THEORIES: LIFE COURSE PERSPECTIVES

Life course theorists reject what they regard as the one-sided emphases of both functionalism and conflict theories, where older adults are viewed either as merely adapting to the larger society (functionalism) or as victims of the stratification system (social conflict). Rather, **life course theorists** view older persons as playing an active role in determining their own physical and mental well-being, yet recognize the constraints imposed by social structural factors.

Making Sociology Work

EMPLOYMENT POLICY SPECIALIST

Helmut Panke, the former chief executive of BMW, was widely regarded as one of the most successful auto chief executives in Europe. In just four years with the company, he expanded the German automaker into China, earned record profits, and diversified the product line with sharp new vehicles that appealed to younger car buyers. So why, given this stellar record, was Panke forced to step down in 2006? BMW company policy mandated that its workers retire at age sixty to open up jobs for younger workers. Some advocates of mandatory retirement say that older workers simply can't keep up with new technology and that car buyers are drawn by the new and modern. Others—Panke included—view the policy as ageist and based on dated assumptions about older adults. How could sociological theories and research on aging inform the corporate policymakers at BMW? How might knowledge of disengagement, activity, continuity, and life course theories shape employment policy?

social conflict theories of aging • Arguments that emphasize the ways in which the larger social structure helps to shape the opportunities available to the elderly. Unequal opportunities are seen as creating the potential for conflict.

life course theory • A perspective based on the assumptions that the aging process is shaped by historical time and place; individuals make choices that reflect both opportunities and constraints; aging is a lifelong process; and the relationships, events, and experiences of early life have consequences for later life.

1. What factors or processes should we keep in mind when studying aging or the meaning of being old? Why?

2. Summarize the three theoretical frameworks used to describe the nature of aging in U.S. society.

3. What are the main criticisms of functionalism and conflict theory?

According to life course theory, the aging process is shaped by historical time and place; factors such as wars, economic shifts, or the development of new technologies shape how people age. Yet this perspective also emphasizes agency, where individuals make choices that reflect both the opportunities and constraints facing them. Yet the most important theme of the life course perspective is that aging is a lifelong process; relationships, events, and experiences of early life have consequences for later life. ✓

Evaluate the experience of growing old in the United States. Identify the physical, emotional, and financial challenges faced by older adults.

WHAT ARE THE CHALLENGES OF AGING IN THE UNITED STATES?

Older individuals make up a highly diverse category about whom few broad generalizations can be made. For one thing, the aged population reflects the diversity of U.S. society that we've made note of elsewhere in this textbook: They are rich, poor, and in between; they belong to all racial and ethnic groups; they live alone and in families of various sorts; they vary in their political values and preferences; and they are gay and lesbian as well as heterosexual. Furthermore, like other Americans, they are diverse with respect to health: Although some suffer from mental and physical disabilities, most lead active, independent lives.

Race has a powerful influence on the lives of older persons. Whites, on average, live five years longer than African Americans, largely because blacks have much greater odds of dying in infancy, childhood, and young adulthood. Blacks also have much higher rates of poverty and, therefore, are more likely to suffer from inadequate health care compared with whites. As a result, a much higher percentage of whites have survived past age sixty-five compared with other racial groups. The combined effect of race and sex is substantial. White women live, on average, twelve years longer than black men (Federal Interagency Forum on Aging-Related Statistics 2013).

Currently, 4.5 million or 12 percent of the age 65+ population in the United States are foreign born (U.S. Bureau of the Census 2012a). In California, New York, Hawaii, and other states that receive large numbers of immigrants, as many as one-fifth of the population ages sixty-five and older were born outside the United States (Federal Interagency Forum on Aging-Related Statistics 2013). Most older immigrants either do not speak English well or do not speak it at all.

Integrating older immigrants into U.S. society poses special challenges: Some are highly educated, but most are not. Most lack a retirement income, so they must depend on their families or public assistance for support. Among those who arrived in the United States during the first decade of the twenty-first century, 22 percent were living beneath the poverty line in 2008, over twice the rate of older people born in this country (U.S. Bureau of the Census 2009). In 2011, 791,000 foreign-born elders (15.9 percent) were living below the poverty line in the United States (U.S. Bureau of the Census 2012o).

Finally, as people live to increasingly older ages, they are diverse in terms of age itself. It is useful to distinguish among different age categories of the 65+ population, such as the **young old** (ages sixty-five to seventy-four), the **old old** (ages seventy-five to eighty-four), and the **oldest old** (age eighty-five and older). The young old are most likely to be economically independent, healthy, active, and engaged; the oldest old—the fastest-growing segment of the age 65+ population—are most likely to encounter difficulties such as poor health, financial insecurity, isolation, and loneliness (U.S. Bureau of the Census 2011f). Not only are these differences due to the effects of aging, they also reflect cohort differences. The young old came of age during the post–World War II period of strong economic growth and benefited as a result: They are more likely to be educated; to have acquired wealth in the form of a home, savings, or investments; and to have had many years of stable employment. These advantages are much less likely to be enjoyed by the oldest old, partly because their education and careers began at an earlier time, when economic conditions were not so favorable (Treas 1995).

What is the experience of growing old in the United States? Although older persons do face some special challenges, most older people lead relatively healthy, satisfying lives. Still, one national survey found a substantial discrepancy between what most Americans under sixty-five thought life would be like when they passed that milestone and the actual experiences of those who had. We will next examine some of the common problems that older adults confront (see Chapter 7 for a discussion of poverty among older Americans) and identify the factors that put older persons at risk for these problems.

HEALTH PROBLEMS

The prevalence of chronic disabilities among the older population has declined in recent years, and most older adults rate their health as reasonably good and free of major disabilities (Federal Interagency Forum on Aging-Related Statistics 2013). Still, older people suffer from more health problems than most younger people, and health difficulties often increase with advancing age. In 2010, more than half of all noninstitutionalized persons age sixty-five and older reported having at least some problems with hypertension, slightly more than half reported suffering from arthritis, about 30 percent have heart disease, and 24 percent have experienced some type of cancer (Federal Interagency Forum on Aging-Related Statistics 2013).

In 2010, more than three-quarters of noninstitutionalized people over sixty-five considered their health to be "good," "very good," or "excellent"; slightly more than two out of three persons age eighty-five or older reported the same (Federal Interagency Forum on Aging-Related Statistics 2013). It is not surprising that the percentage of people needing help with daily activities increases with age: Only one in ten persons between the ages of sixty-five and seventy-five report needing daily assistance, yet this figure rises to one in five for people between seventy-five and seventy-nine and to one in three for people between eighty and eighty-four. Half of all people over eighty-five require assistance (Federal Interagency Forum on Aging-Related Statistics 2013).

Paradoxically, there is some evidence that the fastest-growing group of the aged population, the oldest old (those eighty-five and older), tend to enjoy relative robustness, which partially accounts for their having reached their advanced age. This is possibly one of the reasons that health-care costs for a person who dies at ninety are about a third of those for a person who dies at seventy (Angier 1995). Unlike many other Americans, persons age sixty-five and older are fortunate in having access to public health insurance (Medicare) and, therefore, medical services. The United States,

young old • Sociological term for persons between the ages of sixty-five and seventy-four.

old old • Sociological term for persons between the ages of seventy-five and eighty-four.

oldest old • Sociological term for persons age eighty-five and older.

however, stands virtually alone among the industrialized nations in failing to provide adequately for the complete health care of its most senior citizens, as well as younger persons (Hendricks and Hatch 1993).

Although nearly 48 million Americans lacked health insurance in 2012 (15.4 percent of the population), less than 2 percent of older adults lacked coverage (U.S. Bureau of the Census 2013k). About 93 percent of the 65+ population are covered to some extent by Medicare. But because this program covers about half of the total health-care expenses of individuals age sixty-five and older, nearly 60 percent of older people supplement Medicare with their own private insurance (U.S. Bureau of the Census 2013k). The rising costs of private insurance, unfortunately, have made this option impossible for a growing number of older adults. Between 1977 and 2009, the number of older adults with out-of-pocket health care expenses increased from roughly 83 to over 94 percent. Despite Medicare, older persons today still spend on average about one-fifth of their income on health care (Federal Interagency Forum on Aging-Related Statistics 2013).

When older adults become physically unable to care for themselves, they may move into assisted-living facilities, long-term care facilities, or nursing homes. Only about 1 percent of people between age sixty-four and seventy-four are in a nursing home, a figure that rises to about 7 percent among people seventy-five to eighty-four, and to almost 22 percent for those over eighty-five (Federal Interagency Forum on Aging-Related Statistics 2013). Medicaid, the government program that provides health insurance for the poor, covers long-term supervision and nursing costs, although only when most of one's assets (except for one's home) have been used up. About 7 percent of older people in nursing homes receive assistance from Medicaid (Federal Interagency Forum on Aging-Related Statistics 2010). Because the average (median) cost of a nursing home is now over $77,000 a year (Genworth 2011), the nonpoor older people who require such institutionalization may find that their lifetime savings will be quickly depleted. Nursing homes have long had a reputation for austerity and loneliness. However, the quality of most has improved in recent years, both because federal programs such as Medicaid help cover the cost of care and because of federal quality regulations. Still, living for many years in a nursing home or assisted-living facility was cited as a concern about growing old by over half of respondents, according to a recent national survey.

More than three-quarters of non-institutionalized older adults rate their health as "good" or better. Experts urge persons age sixty-five and older to "use it or lose it" when it comes to physical fitness.

Even if the problems of social isolation, prejudice, physical abuse, and health declines affect only a relatively small proportion of all older persons, the raw numbers of people facing these challenges will increase as the large baby boom cohort enters into old age. The baby boom cohort refers to the 75 million people born between 1946 and 1964 in the United States; the oldest boomers turned sixty-five in 2011. This large population will provide unforeseen challenges for government-funded programs such as Social Security and Medicare, while reinventing the very meaning of old age. The baby boom cohort is more educated than any generation that has come before it; American society will no doubt benefit by incorporating rather than isolating future cohorts of older adults, by drawing on their considerable reserves of experience and talents.

ELDER ABUSE

Mistreatment and abuse of older adults may take many forms, including physical, sexual, emotional, or financial abuse; neglect; or abandonment (National Center on Elder Abuse [NCEA] 1999). Elder mistreatment is very difficult to measure and document. Older adults who are embarrassed, ashamed, or fearful of retaliation by their abusers may be reluctant to report such experiences. As a result, official prevalence rates are low. Worldwide, it is estimated that between 4 and 6 percent of the elderly experience some form of abuse at home.

The National Social Life, Health and Aging Project (NSHAP) is the first nationally representative population-based survey to ask older adults about their recent experiences of mistreatment. Laumann and colleagues (2008) found that 9 percent of older adults reported verbal mistreatment, 3.5 percent reported financial mistreatment, and less than 1 percent reported physical mistreatment by a family member. Women and persons with physical disabilities were most likely to report abuse.

It is widely believed that abuse results from the anger and resentment that adult children feel when confronted with the need to care for their infirm parents (King 1984; Steinmetz 1983). Most studies have found this to be a false stereotype, however. In the NSHAP study, most mistreatment was perpetrated by someone other than a member of the elder's immediate family. Of those who reported verbal mistreatment, 26 percent named their spouse or romantic partner as the perpetrator; 15 percent named their child; and 57 percent named someone other than a spouse, parent, or child. Similarly, 56 percent of elders who reported financial mistreatment said that someone other than a family member was responsible; of family members, though, children were mentioned most often, and spouses were rarely named. Other studies show that when a child abused an aged parent, it was found that he or she was more likely to be financially dependent on the parent. The child may feel resentment about being dependent, whereas the parent may be unwilling to terminate the abusive relationship because he or she feels obligated to help the child (Pillemer 1985).

SOCIAL ISOLATION

One common stereotype about older adults is that they are socially isolated. This is not true of the majority of older people, however: Four out of five older persons have living children, and the vast majority of them can rely on their children for support if necessary (Federal Interagency Forum on Aging-Related Statistics 2012). More than nine out of ten adult children believe that maintaining parental contact is important to them, including the provision of financial support if it is needed (Finley et al. 1988). The reverse is also true: Many studies have found that older parents continue to provide support for their adult children, particularly during times of difficulty such as divorce. Being geographically distant from family members does not seem to be a problem either. Among older adults who do not live with their child, approximately three-quarters live within a thirty-five-minute drive of at least one child (Lin and Rogerson 1995). This arrangement is exactly what most older adults want; studies repeatedly show that they prefer to remain independent and reside in their own homes (albeit near their children). In other words, they want "intimacy at a distance" (Gans and Silverstein 2006).

Future generations may suffer more from social isolation than do older people today. Changing patterns of family structure, including increases in divorce and a decline in remarriage, may mean that an increasing proportion of older people will live alone (Goldscheider 1990). In 2010, 37 percent of older women and 19 percent of men lived alone (Federal Interagency Forum on Aging-Related Statistics 2013). Women are more likely than men to live alone because they are more likely to outlive their spouse; they are also less likely than men to remarry following widowhood or divorce. Only 56 percent of all women between the ages of sixty-five and seventy-four are married, compared with 76 percent of men in that age range. Among those eighty-five and over, only 18 percent of all women are married; the rate for men is 56 percent. Women are also more likely than men to be widowed. In 2012, 24 percent of women and only 7 percent of men age fifty-five and over were widowed (U.S. Bureau of the Census 2012p).

Part of the reason why older women are less likely than men to remarry is the highly skewed sex ratio among older adults. Among people over fifty-five, there are only eighty-four men for every 100 women; for those eighty-five or older, the number of men per 100 women drops to fifty-seven (U.S. Bureau of the Census 2011b).

The fact that women outlive men means that older women are more likely to experience problems of isolation and loneliness. These problems are compounded by cultural values that make growing old gracefully easier for men than for women. In U.S. culture, youth and beauty are viewed as especially desirable qualities for women. Older men, on the other hand, are more likely to be valued for their material success: Graying at the temples is a sign of distinction for a man, rather than a call for a visit to the hair salon. As a result, older divorced or widowed men are much more likely to find a mate than older women who are living alone because the pool of eligible mates for older men is more likely to include potential partners who are many years younger.

The mere presence of social relationships does not ward off loneliness, however. An estimated 29 percent of older married persons report some symptoms of loneliness; this pattern is particularly common among persons whose spouses are ill, have a dissatisfying (or nonexistent) sexual relationship, or have infrequent or conflicted conversations (AARP 2012; de Jong Gierveld et al. 2009). As de Jong Gierveld and Havens (2004) noted, loneliness depends on one's "standards as to what constitutes an optimal network of relationships." That is, it's getting less support than we want rather than the objective number of social ties that matters when it comes to loneliness.

PREJUDICE

ageism • Discrimination or prejudice against a person on the grounds of age.

Discrimination on the basis of age, or **ageism**, is now against federal law. The Age Discrimination in Employment Act of 1967 (ADEA) protects job applicants and employees forty years of age and older from discrimination on the basis of age in hiring, firing, promotion, and pay. Nonetheless, prejudices based on false stereotypes are common. Older adults are frequently seen as perpetually lonely, sad, infirm, forgetful, dependent, senile, old-fashioned, inflexible, and embittered.

There are a number of reasons for such prejudice. The American obsession with youthfulness, reflected in popular entertainment and advertising, leads many younger people to disparage their elders, frequently dismissing them as irrelevant. The new information technology culture undoubtedly reinforces these prejudices because youthfulness and computer abilities seem to go hand in hand. In the fast-paced world of Twitter and dot-com businesses that seem to flourish and perish overnight, young people may come to view the elderly as anachronistic.

These stereotypes are harmful, especially if they translate into discriminatory or ageist treatment. However, the actions of the aging baby boom cohort may help to chip away at outdated and inaccurate notions of what old age is. Consider that Gloria Estefan graced the cover of *AARP* magazine in 2013, the year she turned fifty-six. Just four years earlier, in 2009, Bruce Springsteen was featured on the cover; that same year, Springsteen and the E Street Band had the second-highest-grossing concert tour—topped only by the then-fifty-year-old Bono and his bandmates in U2.

Just as older adults are a vital part of popular culture, they are becoming an increasingly large presence online. About 53 percent of Americans ages sixty-five and older go online, according to a 2012 Pew Internet and American Life Project survey, and older adults—especially women ages fifty-five and older—make up the fastest-growing group of Facebook users, increasing by 35 percent in the first six months of 2010 alone (Pew Internet and American Life Project 2012). Experts agree that baby boomers may play a critical role in further helping to dissolve stereotypes of the frail, senile older adult.

In many ways, older adults face some of the same problems experienced by Sarah and Boo, whom we met at the beginning of the chapter. Young boys are stereotyped as being strong and tough—not "sissies." Girls, but not boys, are believed to like pink, wear skirts, and behave in a feminine way. Boo, a young boy who decided to wear a girl's costume on Halloween, was then stereotyped as being a "wuss" and not "really" a boy. Likewise, older adults are stereotyped as being old-fashioned and out of it. Even though these two examples are very different—one involving the youngest stage of the life course, and the other involving the oldest—they both reveal the power of social expectations. However, social expectations can change over time, and as old "cohorts" or generations die out and are replaced with younger generations holding more contemporary beliefs, we might expect that stereotypes—whether based on age or gender—may slowly fade away. ✓

The social meaning of age shifts over time. Gloria Estefan was fifty-six when she appeared on the cover of *AARP* magazine, an age now considered mid-life.

CONCEPT CHECKS ✓

1. Contrast the young old, old old, and oldest old.

2. Describe at least three common problems that older Americans often confront.

3. What characteristics differentiate those older adults who are emotionally and physically well from those who face great distress in later life?

EXERCISES:
Thinking Sociologically

1. Concisely review how an individual becomes a social person according to each of the two leading theorists discussed in this chapter: George Herbert Mead and Jean Piaget. Which of these two theories seems most appropriate and correct to you? Explain why.

2. Conforming to gender-typed expectations regarding clothing, hair, and other aspects of personal appearance is one of many things we do as a result of socialization. Suggest how the family, peers, schools, and mass media help establish the desire to conform with (or reject) typically "male" versus "female" expectations for appearance. Of the preceding, which force is the most persuasive? Explain.

Chapter 3

Socialization, the Life Course, and Aging

p.75 **How Are Children Socialized?**

Learn about socialization (including gender socialization), and know the most important agents of socialization.

p.85 **What Are the Five Major Stages of the Life Course?**

Learn the various stages of the life course, and see the similarities and differences among different cultures.

p.90 **How Do People Age?**

Understand that aging is a combination of biological, psychological, and social processes. Consider key theories of aging, particularly those that focus on how society shapes the social roles of older people and that emphasize aspects of age stratification.

p.94 **What Are the Challenges of Aging in the United States?**

Evaluate the experience of growing old in the United States. Identify the physical, emotional, and financial challenges faced by older adults.

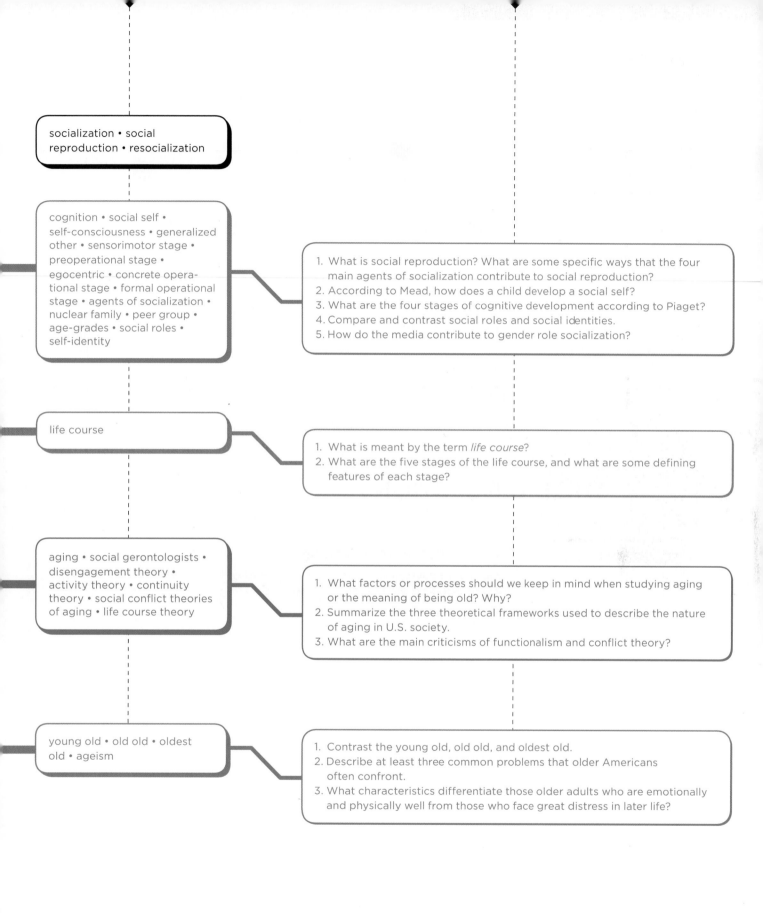

socialization • social reproduction • resocialization

cognition • social self • self-consciousness • generalized other • sensorimotor stage • preoperational stage • egocentric • concrete operational stage • formal operational stage • agents of socialization • nuclear family • peer group • age-grades • social roles • self-identity

1. What is social reproduction? What are some specific ways that the four main agents of socialization contribute to social reproduction?
2. According to Mead, how does a child develop a social self?
3. What are the four stages of cognitive development according to Piaget?
4. Compare and contrast social roles and social identities.
5. How do the media contribute to gender role socialization?

life course

1. What is meant by the term *life course*?
2. What are the five stages of the life course, and what are some defining features of each stage?

aging • social gerontologists • disengagement theory • activity theory • continuity theory • social conflict theories of aging • life course theory

1. What factors or processes should we keep in mind when studying aging or the meaning of being old? Why?
2. Summarize the three theoretical frameworks used to describe the nature of aging in U.S. society.
3. What are the main criticisms of functionalism and conflict theory?

young old • old old • oldest old • ageism

1. Contrast the young old, old old, and oldest old.
2. Describe at least three common problems that older Americans often confront.
3. What characteristics differentiate those older adults who are emotionally and physically well from those who face great distress in later life?

Social Interaction and Everyday Life in the Age of the Internet

THE BIG QUESTIONS

WHAT IS SOCIAL INTERACTION?

Familiarize yourself with the study of everyday life. Know the various forms of nonverbal communication.

HOW DO WE MANAGE IMPRESSIONS IN DAILY LIFE?

Learn about the ways you carefully choose to present yourself to others in daily interactions—both face-to-face and virtually.

WHAT RULES GUIDE HOW WE COMMUNICATE WITH OTHERS?

Learn the research process of ethnomethodology, the study of our conversations, and how we make sense of one another.

HOW DO TIME AND SPACE AFFECT OUR INTERACTIONS?

Understand that interaction is situated, that it occurs in a particular place and for a particular length of time. See that the way we organize our social actions is not unique by learning how other cultures organize their social lives.

HOW DO THE RULES OF SOCIAL INTERACTION AFFECT YOUR LIFE?

See how face-to-face interactions reflect broader social factors such as social hierarchies.

Notre Dame football star Manti Te'o was widely ridiculed when news broke that Lennay Kekua, his girlfriend of nearly a year, never existed. Kekua, constructed as part of an elaborate "catfishing" hoax by an acquaintance of Te'o, existed only on social media.

For most college students, romantic relationships are just as important as their schoolwork. In the 1950s and 1960s, coeds might have met for the first time at a formal "mixer" and written long heartfelt letters to each other during their summer months spent apart. In the 1980s and 1990s, a couple might have met while standing in line at a keg party and kept in touch over late-night phone calls during winter and summer breaks.

Today, many college students first meet their boyfriend or girlfriend in their dorm or through a mutual friend, but many also meet (and keep in touch) online, whether through meet-up websites and smartphone apps or social networking sites like Facebook. But is it possible to maintain a meaningful romantic relationship with no face-to-face contact and only virtual exchanges with one's partner? Manti Te'o thought so.

Seemingly overnight, Manti Te'o was transformed from a national sports star to a national joke. In 2012, Te'o was a star football player for Notre Dame. An All-American and finalist for the Heisman Trophy, Te'o was a highly decorated college football player. But Te'o was more than a football star; he became a hometown hero when he led his team to victory on the same day in September 2012 that he learned of the deaths of both his grandmother and girlfriend. Despite his heartbreak, Te'o did not miss a single football game that season, telling reporters and teammates that he had promised his girlfriend, Lennay Kekua, that he would play regardless of what happened to her. Kekua, a Stanford University student, had been battling leukemia.

In January 2013, Te'o made headlines again. The sports blog Deadspin broke the shocking news that Te'o's girlfriend, Lennay Kekua, hadn't died. In fact, she had never existed at all. Kekua was entirely fictional, constructed as part of an elaborate Internet hoax by a distant acquaintance of Te'o.

How was it possible that Te'o had maintained a nearly yearlong "relationship" with a fictional young woman? In a public statement, Te'o explained, "This is incredibly embarrassing to talk about, but over an extended period of time, I developed an emotional relationship with a woman I met online. We maintained what I thought to be an authentic relationship by communicating frequently online and on the phone, and I grew to care deeply about her" (ESPN 2013b). Te'o had previously lied to his family, teammates, and the press about meeting Kekua in person, afraid they would think he was "crazy." Was Te'o crazy or was he simply trying to maintain a long-distance online relationship while also juggling his busy schedule as a student athlete? Is an exclusively online relationship really a form of social interaction?

Throughout most of human history, people have communicated mainly face-to-face. The U.S. Postal Service was established in the late eighteenth century, making it easier than ever to communicate through writing. Then, in the nineteenth century, the advent of the telephone revolutionized how Americans interacted with one another. In the last two decades, e-mail, SMS, and social networking sites have once again revolutionized the way humans communicate. In this chapter, we will explore how each of these forms of communication—along with subtle, nonverbal aspects of communication—constitutes social interaction and carries important messages about how our society functions.

social interaction • The process by which we act and react to those around us.

microsociology • The study of human behavior in contexts of face-to-face interaction.

WHAT IS SOCIAL INTERACTION?

Erving Goffman was a highly influential sociologist who created a new field of study focused on **social interaction**. In the 1950s and 1960s, Goffman wrote that sociologists needed to concern themselves with seemingly trivial aspects of everyday social behavior. His work on social interaction is just one example of the broader sociological subfield called **microsociology**. This term was conceived by sociologist Harold Garfinkel to describe a field of study that focused on individual interaction and communication within small groups; this subfield stood in contrast with earlier sociological work, which historically had examined large social groups and societal-level behaviors. Goffman, and eminent scholars such as George Herbert Mead and Herbert Blumer, examined seemingly small exchanges, such as conversation patterns and the ways that social actors develop a shared understanding of their social context.

The study of social interaction reveals important things about human social life. For instance, think about the last time you walked down the street and passed a stranger, or shared an elevator ride with a stranger. Did you subtly try to avoid eye contact? Goffman believed that such small gestures are meaningful and rich with messages about human interaction. When passersby—either strangers or intimates—quickly glance at each other and then look away again, they demonstrate what Goffman (1967, 1971) calls **civil inattention**. Civil inattention is not the same as merely ignoring another person. Each individual indicates recognition of the other

civil inattention • The process whereby individuals in the same physical setting demonstrate to each other that they are aware of the other's presence.

person's presence but avoids any gesture that might be taken as too intrusive. Goffman argued that the study of such apparently insignificant forms of social interaction is of major importance in sociology and, far from being uninteresting, is one of the most absorbing of all areas of sociological investigation. There are three reasons for this.

First, our ordinary routines give structure and form to what we do. We can learn a great deal about ourselves as social beings, and about social life itself, from studying them. Our lives are organized around the repetition of similar patterns of behavior from day to day, week to week, month to month, and year to year. Think of what you did yesterday, for example, and the day before that. If they were both weekdays, you probably woke up at about the same time each day (an important routine in itself). You may have gone to class fairly early in the morning, making a journey from home to school that you make virtually every weekday. You perhaps met some friends for lunch, returning to classes or private study in the afternoon. Later, you retraced your steps back home or to your dorm, possibly going out later in the evening with other friends.

Of course, the routines we follow are not identical from day to day, and our patterns of activity on weekends usually contrast with those on weekdays. If we make a major change in our life, like leaving college to take a full-time job, alterations in our daily routines are usually necessary, but then we establish a new and fairly regular set of habits again.

Second, the study of everyday life reveals to us how humans can act creatively to shape reality. Although social behavior is guided to some extent by forces such as roles, norms, and shared expectations, individuals also have **agency**, or the ability to act, think, and make choices independently (Emirbayer and Mische 1998). The ways that people perceive reality may vary widely based on their backgrounds, interests, and motivations. Because individuals are capable of creative action, they continuously shape reality through the decisions and actions they take. In other words, reality is not fixed or static—it is created through human interactions. However, as we shall see later in this chapter, even our most private or seemingly minor interactions are shaped by **structure**, or the recurrent patterned arrangements and hierarchies that influence or limit the choices and opportunities available to us.

Third, studying social interaction in everyday life sheds light on larger social structures, systems, and institutions. All large-scale social systems depend on the patterns of social interaction we engage in daily. This is easy to demonstrate. Let's reconsider the case of two strangers passing on the street. Such an event may seem to have little direct relevance to large-scale, more permanent forms of social structure. But when we take into account many such interactions, they are no longer irrelevant. In modern societies, most people live in towns and cities and constantly interact with people they do not know personally. Civil inattention is one of many mechanisms that give public life—with its bustling crowds and fleeting, impersonal contacts—its distinctive character.

When we published the first edition of this book more than twenty-five years ago, the study of face-to-face communication was a well-settled territory. Over the past decade or so, however, social interaction has been transformed due to the rise of the Internet. In this chapter, we review the traditional findings of the field, but we will also ask how these findings must be modified in light of the rise of e-mail, Twitter, iPhone apps, and social networking sites like Facebook. We will first learn about the nonverbal cues (facial expressions and bodily gestures) all of us use when interacting with one another. We then move on to analyze everyday speech—how we use language to communicate to others the meanings we wish to get across. Finally, we focus on the ways in which our lives are structured by daily routines, paying particular attention to how we coordinate our actions across space and time.

agency • The ability to think, act, and make choices independently.

structure • The recurrent patterned arrangements and hierarchies that influence or limit the choices and opportunities available to us.

NONVERBAL COMMUNICATION

nonverbal communication •
Communication between
individuals based on facial
expression or bodily gestures
rather than on language.

Social interaction requires many forms of **nonverbal communication**—the exchange of information and meaning through facial expressions, eye contact, gestures, and movements of the body. Nonverbal communication, sometimes referred to as "body language," often alters or expands on what is said with words. In some cases, our body language may convey a message that is discrepant with our words.

FACE, GESTURES, AND EMOTION

One major aspect of communication is the facial expression of emotion. Paul Ekman and his colleagues have developed what they call the Facial Action Coding System (FACS) for describing movements of the facial muscles that give rise to particular expressions (Ekman and Friesen 1978). By this means, they have tried to inject some precision into an area notoriously open to inconsistent or contradictory interpretations—for there is little agreement about how emotions are to be identified and classified. Charles Darwin, one of the originators of evolutionary theory, claimed that basic modes of emotional expression are the same in all human beings and across all cultures. Although some have disputed the claim, Ekman's research among people from widely different cultural backgrounds seems to confirm Darwin's view. Ekman and W. V. Friesen carried out a study of an isolated community in New Guinea, whose members previously had virtually no contact with outsiders. When they were shown pictures of facial expressions conveying six emotions, the New Guineans identified the same emotions (happiness, sadness, anger, disgust, fear, surprise) we would.

According to Ekman, the results of his own and similar studies of different peoples support the view that the facial expression of emotion and its interpretation are innate in human beings. He acknowledges that his evidence does not conclusively demonstrate this, and it's possible that widely shared cultural learning experiences are involved; however, his conclusions are supported by other types of research. Irenäus Eibl-Eibesfeldt (1972) studied six children born deaf and blind to determine to what extent their facial expressions were the same as those of sighted and hearing individuals in particular emotional situations. He found that the children smiled when engaged in obviously pleasurable activities, raised their eyebrows in surprise when sniffing at an object with an unaccustomed smell, and frowned when repeatedly offered a disliked object. Because the children could not have seen other people behaving in these ways, it seems that these responses must be innately determined.

By contrast, there are no gestures or bodily postures that are universally known and understood in all cultures. In some societies, for instance, people nod when they mean no, the opposite of Anglo-American practice. Gestures Americans tend to use a great deal, such as pointing, seem not to exist among certain peoples (Bull 1983). Similarly, a straightened forefinger placed in the center of the cheek and rotated is used in parts of Italy as a gesture of praise but appears to be unknown elsewhere (Donadio 2013).

Like facial expressions, gestures and bodily posture are continually used to fill out utterances as well as to convey meanings when nothing is actually said. All three can be used to joke, show irony, or indicate skepticism. The nonverbal impressions that we convey may inadvertently indicate that what we say is not quite what we really mean. Blushing is perhaps the most obvious example, but innumerable other subtle indicators can be picked up by other people. Genuine facial expressions tend to evaporate after four or five seconds. A smile that lasts longer could indicate deceit. An expression of surprise that lasts too long may indicate deliberate sarcasm—to show that the individual is not in fact surprised after all.

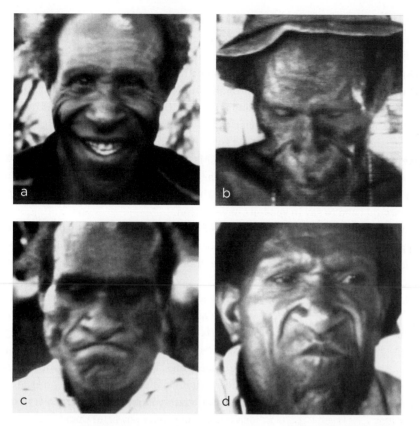

Paul Ekman's photographs of facial expressions from a tribesman in an isolated community in New Guinea helped to test the idea that basic modes of emotional expression are the same among all people. Here the instructions were to show how your face would look if you were a person in a story and (a) your friend had come and you were happy, (b) your child had died, (c) you were angry and about to fight, and (d) you saw a dead pig that had been lying there a long time.

On the Internet, it is very difficult to capture dimensions of emotion that are present only with facial expression. At first, the need that Internet users felt to approximate facial gestures resulted in at least two common faces:

:) or :-)

As time passed, a need for greater subtlety resulted in other widely understood variations, such as this winking smiley face:

;-)

E-mail may have once been devoid of facial expression, but today the average e-mail user may insert different emotions into a message. Strongly felt sentiments might be typed in all capitals, a gesture that is considered "shouting." The strong need human beings feel to communicate with their faces has also led to other innovations, like Skype and Facetime. But in general, people who communicate over e-mail or phone lack the benefit of seeing the faces of their conversational partners as they speak. If they could, then perhaps Manti Te'o would not have been duped into thinking that Lennay Kekua was a real woman, rather than a virtual creation. This is especially true of text messaging, which strips away both faces and voices

status • The social honor or prestige that a particular group is accorded by other members of a society. Status groups normally display distinct styles of life—patterns of behavior that the members of a group follow. Status privilege may be positive or negative.

and sometimes relies on cryptic abbreviations that may be unfamiliar to the other texter (especially when the other texter is from an older generation).

Why and how does this matter for human relationships and interactions? On the phone, whether it's a cell phone or landline, an individual will frequently talk for a longer stretch of time than he or she would in face-to-face conversation. Unable to see the face of a conversational partner, the speaker can't as readily adjust what he or she is saying in response to clues from the listener that he or she "gets it." Yet, the phone maintains at least some immediacy of feedback that e-mail and text messages, to a lesser extent, lack. This is why in e-mail disputes, people who are unable to make mutual adjustments in response to verbal or facial cues will end up saying much more—communicated in the form of long messages—than they would need to say in spoken conversation.

Which is best? Would you prefer to make your point via e-mail or text message, over the phone or Skype, or in person? Using sociological insights like these might make you prefer electronic communication at certain times and face-to-face communication at others. For example, if you are dealing with a powerful person and want to get your thoughts across, you may want to avoid a situation where he or she can signal with facial gestures that your idea is silly and thus inhibit you from making all your points. The power to signal with facial gestures is one of the things that people do to control the flow of a conversation. On the other hand, face-to-face communication gives you an opportunity to try out an idea on someone more powerful than yourself without going too far down the road if he or she is actually unreceptive. You probably would not want to have an important conversation via text message, instead limiting its use to minor or immediate issues. ✓

CONCEPT CHECKS ✓

1. What is microsociology?

2. What are three reasons why it is important to study daily social interaction?

3. What is nonverbal communication?

4. Describe several ways that individuals communicate their emotions to one another.

5. How do e-mail and in-person communication differ?

Learn about the ways you carefully choose to present yourself to others in daily interactions—both face-to-face and virtually.

HOW DO WE MANAGE IMPRESSIONS IN DAILY LIFE?

IMPRESSION MANAGEMENT

Goffman and other writers on social interaction often draw on imagery from drama and theater in their analyses. The concept of social role, which we learned about in Chapter 3, is an important component of social interaction. Roles are socially defined expectations that a person in a given **status** (or **social position**) follows. For example, most children are socialized to conform to gender-specific behavioral expectations that are consistent with their biological sex. Roles can also be much more specific; for example, the teacher's role involves acting in specified ways toward his or her pupils. Goffman sees social life as though played out by actors on a stage, or on many stages, because how we act depends on the roles we are playing at a particular time. People are sensitive to how they are seen by others (that is, their "audience") and use many forms of **impression management** to compel others to react to them in the ways they wish. Although we may sometimes do this in a calculated way, usually it is among the things we do without conscious attention. When going on a job interview,

social position • The social identity an individual has in a given group or society. Social positions may be general in nature (those associated with gender roles) or may be more specific (occupational positions).

impression management • Preparing for the presentation of one's social role.

a person will typically dress more formally and try to put his or her best foot forward; however, when going out with friends, he or she might dress down, use slang, and act in ways that may not impress a prospective employer.

A crucial observation of social interaction is that every human being possesses a self that is forever fragile and vulnerable to embarrassment or even humiliation. People are intensely attuned to what others think of them and how they are being viewed. That's part of the reason why we're so careful about what we post on Facebook and why we cringe if we're tagged by friends in unflattering or embarrassing photos. Seeking approval and respect, individuals want to "save face" at every turn. In social interactions, human beings tend to collaborate with others to make sure that the encounter ends without embarrassment for anyone. Social life, like a play, involves many players and they must collaborate to make each scene work.

Think of examples from your own life when you had a choice of whether to collaborate with another person. If you're at a party and someone approaches you whom you don't want to talk to, you will likely try to end the interaction in a way that spares the other person embarrassment. It is highly unlikely that you would simply tell the person "Get lost!" rather than help him or her save face. This is because there is a norm of collaboration by which human beings try to move through life without embarrassing or humiliating others. When this collaboration does not occur, the interaction is notable for the participants.

The "pose" or "front" that we adopt depends a great deal on our social role, but no specific role dictates any particular presentation of self. A person's demeanor can be different depending on the social context. For instance, as a "student" you have a certain status and are expected to act a certain way when you are around your professors. Some pupils will purposely present themselves as a dutiful student, whereas others will adopt an uncaring or apathetic pose. Some sociological studies suggest that in poor inner-city schools, some black students don't want to be accused of "acting white" and will adopt a personal style that is more "street" than studious. However, such an appearance may not give an accurate sense of how capable a student really is. A student who takes on the demeanor of the street may be studying just as hard as classmates who take on the demeanor of the mild-mannered scholar.

FOCUSED AND UNFOCUSED INTERACTION

In many social situations, we engage in what Goffman calls unfocused interaction with others. **Unfocused interaction** takes place whenever individuals exhibit mutual awareness of one another's presence but do not engage in direct communication or conversation. This is usually the case anywhere large numbers of people are assembled, as on a busy street, in a theater, or at a party. When people are in the presence of others, even if they do not directly talk to them, they continually communicate nonverbally through their posture and facial and physical gestures.

Focused interaction occurs when individuals directly attend to what others say or do. Except when someone is standing alone, say, at a party, all interaction involves both focused and unfocused exchanges. Goffman calls an instance of focused interaction an **encounter**, and much of our day-to-day life consists of encounters with other people—family, friends, colleagues—frequently occurring against the background of unfocused interaction with others present. Small talk, seminar discussions, games, and routine face-to-face interactions (with ticket clerks, waiters, shop assistants, and so forth) are all examples of encounters.

unfocused interaction •
Interaction occurring among people present in a particular setting but not engaged in direct face-to-face communication.

focused interaction •
Interaction between individuals engaged in a common activity or in direct conversation with each other.

encounter • A meeting between two or more people in a situation of face-to-face interaction. Our daily lives can be seen as a series of different encounters strung out across the course of the day. In modern societies, many of these encounters are with strangers rather than people we know.

Lunch at a crowded restaurant involves both unfocused interaction, when we acknowledge the presence of other diners, and focused interaction, when we place an order with a waiter.

Encounters always need "openings," which indicate that civil inattention is being discarded. When strangers meet and begin to talk at a party, the moment of ceasing civil inattention is always risky because misunderstandings can easily occur about the nature of the encounter being established (Goffman 1971). Hence, the making of eye contact may first be ambiguous and tentative. A person can then act as though he or she had made no direct move if the overture is not accepted. In focused interaction, each person communicates as much by facial expression and gesture as by the words actually exchanged.

Goffman distinguishes between the expressions individuals "give" and those they "give off." The first are the words and facial expressions people use to produce certain impressions on others. The second are the clues that others may spot to check their sincerity or truthfulness. For instance, a restaurant owner listens with a polite smile to the statements of customers about how much they enjoyed their meals. At the same time, he is noting how pleased they seemed to be while eating the food, whether a lot was left over, and the tone of voice they use to express their satisfaction.

Think about how Goffman's concepts of focused and unfocused interaction, developed mainly to explain face-to-face social encounters, would apply to our current age of Internet communication. Can you think of a way in which unfocused interaction occurs on Facebook and Twitter? In some small online communities, everyone can have a mutual awareness of who else is online, without being in direct contact with them. On sites like Twitter, people are constantly broadcasting status updates about what they're doing at that moment. These status updates make it possible for people in unfocused interaction to have even more control over how they are perceived than people who are merely in one another's presence. Instead of revealing their facial expressions or posture, which they may be unconscious of, people can carefully craft the message or tweet they wish to broadcast.

AUDIENCE SEGREGATION

Although people cooperate to help one another "save face," they also endeavor individually to preserve their own dignity, autonomy, and respect. One of the ways that people do this is by arranging for "audience segregation" in their lives. In each of their roles they act somewhat differently, and they endeavor to keep the roles both distinct and separate from one another. This means that they can have multiple selves. Frequently these selves are consistent, but sometimes they are not. People find it very stressful when boundaries break down, or when they cannot reconcile their role in one part of life with their role in another. For example, we may have two friends who do not like each other. Rather than choose between them, we will spend time with both friends, but never mention to either friend that we are close with the other. Similarly, some college freshmen try to distance themselves from former classmates in order to carve out a new "college" identity that won't be tainted by embarrassing stories from high school. Or, some people live very different lives at home and at work. For example, due to discrimination against gays and lesbians, someone who appears "straight" at work may live happily with a same-sex partner at home. Like all people who engage in audience segregation, they show a different face to different people.

Audience segregation implicitly encourages impression management. Some people maintain two different Facebook pages, one linked to family members or coworkers and another linked to friends and peers. Why might someone do this? Our Facebook pages are a strategy to "impression manage," or to carefully and selectively portray an image of ourselves to the outside world. On your "professional" page, you might try to convey an image of a respectable student and employee by carefully curating the information and images you post. By contrast, on your personal page, you might post photos that present a more fun and carefree version of yourself.

IMPRESSION MANAGEMENT IN THE INTERNET AGE

The concept of "audience segregation" helps us understand some of the dilemmas of electronic communication. Many people are very sensitive about having things sent to their business e-mail address that they don't want their coworkers or supervisors to know about. Thus, they maintain different addresses for home ("back region") and office ("front region"), a practice that is increasingly important because many companies have policies against sending personal e-mails from a company's computer.

For example, in 2012, Captain Jon Sprague, a firefighter in Spokane Valley, Washington, was dismissed for sending a Christian-themed e-mail to his fellow firefighters. A seventeen-year veteran on the force, Sprague had started a Christian Firefighter Fellowship and communicated with members via e-mail. However, rather than using his personal e-mail account, Sprague sent the faith-based messages from his taxpayer-funded work account, which violated department rules. The assumption is that people's religious lives should be lived out at home, not in the workplace (especially among government employees).

Or consider the social situation of a copied message. You write a message to a friend asking her whether she prefers to go to the early show or the late show. You also tell your friend that you have a new boyfriend whom you hope she will like. She replies and copies the other people who are thinking of going to the movie, many of whom you never intended to tell about the new romance. Suddenly, the audience segregation you had imagined has broken down.

In recent years, undergraduate students have posted pictures of themselves drinking at parties, or even naked, only to discover that future employers conducted web searches before making hiring decisions. Some students have even found themselves expelled from their colleges for posting inappropriate photos or comments on Facebook. For example, T. Hayden Barnes, who was then a Valdosta

State University sophomore, was expelled for criticizing his college president's policies, while nursing student Doyle Byrnes was forced to leave Johnson County Community College after she posted a photo on Facebook of her dangling a placenta. An even more devastating example of blurring audiences is the case of sexting; a high school student may send a revealing photo of herself to her boyfriend, only to have him forward it to the entire school—whether out of cruelty or by mistake. Personal catastrophes like these occur frequently in the age of e-mail and smartphones. ✓

CONCEPT CHECKS ✓

1. What is impression management?

2. Compare and contrast focused and unfocused interaction.

3. Why do we segregate our audiences in daily life?

Learn the research process of ethnomethodology, the study of our conversations, and how we make sense of one another.

WHAT RULES GUIDE HOW WE COMMUNICATE WITH OTHERS?

We can make sense of what is said in conversation only if we know the social context, which does not appear in the words themselves. Take the following conversation (Heritage 1985):

> A: I have a fourteen-year-old son.
> B: Well, that's all right.
> A: I also have a dog.
> B: Oh, I'm sorry.

What do you think is happening here? What is the relation between the speakers? What if you were told that this is a conversation between a prospective tenant and a landlord? The conversation then becomes sensible: Some landlords accept children but don't permit their tenants to keep pets. Yet if we don't know the social context, the responses of individual B seem to bear no relation to the statements of A. Part of the sense is in the words, and part is in the way in which the meaning emerges from the social context.

SHARED UNDERSTANDINGS

The most inconsequential forms of daily talk presume complicated, shared knowledge brought into play by those speaking. In fact, our small talk is so complex that it has so far proved impossible to program even the most sophisticated computers to converse with human beings. The words used in ordinary talk do not always have precise meanings, and we "fix" what we want to say through the unstated assumptions that back it up. If Maria asks Tom, "What did you do yesterday?" the words in the question themselves suggest no obvious answer. A day is a long time, and it would be logical for Tom to answer, "Well, at 7:16, I woke up. At 7:18, I got out of bed, went to the bathroom, and started to brush my teeth. At 7:19, I turned on the shower...." We understand the type of response the question calls for by knowing Maria, what sort of activities she and Tom consider relevant, and what Tom usually does on a particular day of the week, among other things.

CELL PHONE SUBSCRIPTIONS

Mobile phone subscriptions worldwide are approaching 7 billion, with the developing world accounting for more than three-quarters of the world's total. A 2013 study by the U.N. showed that more people on earth have access to cell phones than toilets.

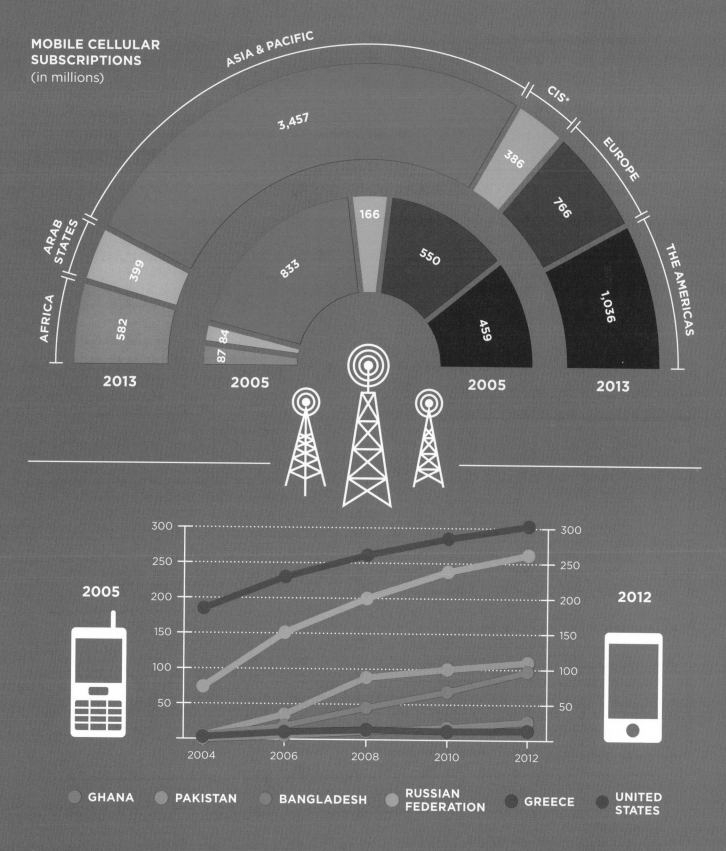

MOBILE CELLULAR SUBSCRIPTIONS
(in millions)

ASIA & PACIFIC

3,457

CIS*

386

EUROPE

766

ARAB STATES

399

AFRICA

582

833

166

550

459

THE AMERICAS

1,036

2013

2005

2005

2013

2005

2012

300 · 250 · 200 · 150 · 100 · 50

2004 · 2006 · 2008 · 2010 · 2012

GHANA · PAKISTAN · BANGLADESH · RUSSIAN FEDERATION · GREECE · UNITED STATES

Source: International Telecommunications Union 2014

*Commonwealth of Independent States

ETHNOMETHODOLOGY

ethnomethodology • The study of how people make sense of what others say and do in the course of day-to-day social interaction. Ethnomethodology is concerned with the "ethnomethods" by which people sustain meaningful exchanges with one another.

Ethnomethodology is the study of the "ethnomethods"—the folk, or lay, methods—people use to make sense of what others do and particularly of what they say. We all apply these methods, normally without having to give any conscious attention to them. This field was created by Harold Garfinkel, who, along with Goffman, was one of the most important figures in the study of micro interaction.

Garfinkel argued that in order to understand the way people use context to make sense of the world, sociologists need to study the "background expectancies" with which we organize ordinary conversations. He highlighted these in some experiments he undertook with student volunteers (1963). The students were asked to engage a friend or relative in conversation and to insist that casual remarks or general comments be actively pursued to make their meaning precise. If someone said, "Have a nice day," the student was to respond, "Nice in what sense, exactly?" "Which part of the day do you mean?" and so forth. One of the exchanges that resulted ran as follows. S is the friend; E, the student volunteer (Garfinkel 1963):

> S: How are you?
> E: How am I in regard to what? My health, my finances, my school work, my peace of mind, my . . . ?
> S: (red in the face and suddenly out of control) Look! I was just trying to be polite. Frankly, I don't give a damn how you are.

Why do people get so upset when apparently minor conventions of talk are not followed? The answer is that the stability and meaningfulness of our daily social lives depend on the sharing of unstated cultural assumptions about what is said and why. If we weren't able to take these for granted, meaningful communication would be impossible. Any question or contribution to a conversation would have to be followed by a massive "search procedure" of the sort Garfinkel's subjects were told to initiate, and interaction would simply break down. What seem at first sight to be unimportant conventions of talk, therefore, turn out to be fundamental to the very fabric of social life, which is why their breach is so serious.

SOCIAL RULES AND TALK

Although we routinely use nonverbal cues in our own behavior and in making sense of the behavior of others, much of our interaction is done through talk—casual verbal exchange—carried on in informal conversations with others. Sociologists have always accepted that language is fundamental to social life. However, an approach has been developed that is specifically concerned with how people use language in the ordinary contexts of everyday life.

Making Sociology Work
RESTAURATEUR

Restaurant owners know that food alone does not make for a five-star dining experience. Rather, customers are looking to enjoy a physical space and to interact with restaurant workers who make them feel good about themselves and their evening out. Whether it's the gregarious young waitstaff, mechanical jungle animals, and simulated rainstorm in the tree-filled Rainforest Cafe or the elegant European-style service at one of New York's venerable French restaurants, restaurateurs know that image is everything. But even the most beautiful setting and delicious meal can be ruined if diners are exposed to squabbles among restaurant workers or get a glimpse into an unsanitary kitchen. How might the writings of Erving Goffman guide the decisions made by the professionals who design, manage, and work at eating establishments? How can waitstaff and food-preparation workers ensure that diners enjoy their experience in the restaurant's front region?

INTERACTIONAL VANDALISM

We have already seen that conversations are one of the main ways in which our daily lives are maintained in a stable and coherent manner. We feel most comfortable when the tacit conventions of small talk are adhered to; when they are breached, we can feel threatened, confused, and insecure. In most everyday talk, conversants are carefully attuned to the cues they get from others—such as changes in intonation, slight pauses, or gestures—to facilitate conversation smoothly. By being mutually aware, conversants "cooperate" in opening and closing interactions and in taking turns to speak. Interactions in which one party is conversationally "uncooperative," however, can create tension.

Garfinkel's students created tense situations by intentionally undermining conversational rules as part of a sociological experiment. But what about situations in the real world in which people make trouble through their conversational practices? One study investigated verbal interchanges between pedestrians and street people in New York City to understand why such interactions are often seen as problematic by passersby. The researchers used a technique called **conversation analysis** to compare a selection of street interchanges with samples of everyday talk. Conversation analysis is a methodology that examines all facets of a conversation for meaning—from the smallest filler words (such as *um* and *ah*) to the precise timing of interchanges (including pauses, interruptions, and overlaps).

The study looked at interactions between black men—many of whom were homeless or addicted to drugs or alcohol—and white women who passed by them on the street. The men often try to initiate conversations with passing women by calling out to them, complimenting them, or asking them questions. But something "goes wrong" in these conversations because the women rarely respond as they would in a normal interaction. Even though the men's comments are rarely hostile in tone, the women tend to quicken their step and stare fixedly ahead (Duneier and Molotch 1999).

The term **interactional vandalism** describes cases like these in which a subordinate person breaks the tacit rules of everyday interaction that are of value to the more powerful. Men on the street often do conform to everyday forms of speech in their interactions with one another, local shopkeepers, the police, relatives, and acquaintances. But when they choose to, they subvert the tacit conventions for everyday talk in a way that leaves passersby disoriented. Even more than physical assaults or vulgar verbal abuse, interactional vandalism leaves victims unable to articulate what has happened.

This study of interactional vandalism provides another example of the two-way links between micro-level interactions and forces that operate on the macro level. To the men on the street, the white women who ignore their attempts at conversation appear distant, cold, and bereft of sympathy—legitimate targets for such interactions. The women, meanwhile, may often take the men's behavior as proof that they are indeed dangerous and best avoided. Interactional vandalism is closely tied up with overarching class, gender, and racial structures. The fear and anxiety generated by these mundane interactions help reinforce the outside statuses and forces that, in turn, influence the interactions themselves. Interactional vandalism is part of a self-reinforcing system of mutual suspicion and incivility.

How might interactional vandalism play out on the Internet? Can we think of ways in which less powerful people engaged in electronic communications undermine the taken-for-granted rules of interaction that are of value to the more

conversation analysis • The empirical study of conversations, employing techniques drawn from ethnomethodology. Conversation analysis examines details of naturally occurring conversations to reveal the organizational principles of talk and its role in the production and reproduction of social order.

interactional vandalism • The deliberate subversion of the tacit rules of conversation.

Julian Assange, cofounder of WikiLeaks, committed interactional vandalism by leaking classified documents, including reports about the war in Afghanistan.

powerful? The very existence of the Internet creates spaces in which less powerful people can hold their superiors accountable in ways they never were before. Think of all the blogs in which workers talk anonymously about their bosses or situations in which workers forward rude messages from their boss to other employees. Because of the Internet, powerful people are less able to segregate their audiences—treating some people poorly behind the scenes and treating others very nicely in public.

The actions of WikiLeaks—an international online organization that publishes secret information, news leaks, and classified media obtained from anonymous sources—are an extreme example of interactional vandalism. Between 2006 and 2012, the not-for-profit group released dozens of documents that later made headlines, including reports about expenditures and fatalities in the Afghanistan and Iraq wars and the treatment of prisoners at the Guantanamo Bay detention center. The goal of the organization, according to its website, is to "publish original source material alongside our news stories so readers and historians alike can see evidence of the truth." Another of their stated goals is to protect journalists and corporate or government whistleblowers. A high-security online drop box allows sources to leak information to the group anonymously and securely. Although many applaud the group's dedication to preserving the freedom of speech, the WikiLeaks website has been censored or blocked by many countries.

RESPONSE CRIES

response cries • Seemingly involuntary exclamations individuals make when, for example, being taken by surprise, dropping something inadvertently, or expressing pleasure.

Some kinds of utterances are not talk but consist of muttered exclamations, or what Goffman (1981) has called **response cries**. Consider Lucy, who exclaims, "Oops!" after knocking over a glass of water. "Oops!" seems to be merely an uninteresting reflex response to a mishap, rather like blinking your eye when a person moves a hand sharply toward your face. It is not a reflex, however, as shown by the fact that people do not usually make the exclamation when alone. "Oops!" is normally directed toward others present. The exclamation demonstrates to witnesses that the lapse is only minor and momentary, not something that should cast doubt on Lucy's command of her actions.

Phrases like "oops!" or "my bad" are used only in situations of minor failure, rather than in major accidents or calamities—which also demonstrates that the exclamation is part of our controlled management of the details of social life. This may all sound contrived and exaggerated. Why bother to analyze such an inconsequential utterance in this detail? Surely we don't pay as much attention to what we say as this example suggests? Of course we don't—on a conscious level. The crucial point, however, is that we take for granted an immensely complicated, continuous control of our appearance and actions. In situations of interaction, we are never expected just to be present on the scene. Others expect, as we expect of them, that we will display what Goffman calls "controlled alertness." A fundamental part of being human is continually demonstrating to others our competence in the routines of daily life.

PERSONAL SPACE

There are cultural differences in the definition of **personal space**. In Western culture, people usually maintain a distance of at least three feet when engaged in focused interaction with others; when standing side by side, they may stand closer together. In the Middle East, people often stand closer to each other than is thought acceptable in the West. Westerners visiting that part of the world might find themselves disconcerted by this unexpected physical proximity.

Edward T. Hall (1969, 1973), who has worked extensively on nonverbal communication, distinguishes four zones of personal space. Intimate distance, of up to one and a half feet, is reserved for very few social contacts. Only those involved in relationships in which regular bodily touching is permitted, such as lovers or parents and children, operate within this zone of private space. Personal distance, from one and a half to four feet, is the normal spacing for encounters with friends and close acquaintances. Some intimacy of contact is permitted, but this

personal space • The physical space individuals maintain between themselves and others.

Cultural norms frequently dictate the acceptable boundaries of personal space. In the Middle East, for example, people frequently stand closer to each other than is common in the West.

tends to be strictly limited. Social distance, from four to twelve feet, is the zone usually maintained in formal settings such as interviews. The fourth zone is that of public distance, beyond twelve feet, preserved by those who are performing to an audience.

In ordinary interaction, the most fraught zones are those of intimate and personal distance. If these zones are invaded, people try to recapture their space. We may stare at the intruder as if to say, "Move away!" or elbow him or her aside. When people are forced into proximity closer than they deem desirable, they might create a kind of physical boundary: A reader at a crowded library desk might physically demarcate a private space by stacking books around its edges (Hall 1969, 1973).

EYE CONTACT

Eye contact is yet another aspect of social interaction that illustrates important social norms and reveals (and perpetuates) power differentials. As we saw earlier in this chapter, we are guided by a powerful norm that strangers should not make eye contact. Strangers or chance acquaintances virtually never hold the gaze of another. To do so may be taken as an indication of hostile intent. It is only where two groups are strongly antagonistic to each other that strangers might indulge in such a practice—for example, when whites in the United States have been known to give a "hate stare" to blacks walking past.

Studies show that we tend to rate a person who makes eye contact as more likable, pleasant, intelligent, credible, and dominant as compared with a person exhibiting less or no eye contact. However, excessive eye contact may make an observer feel uncomfortable in certain situations. To look too intently might be taken as a sign of mistrust about, or at least failure to understand, what the other is saying. Eye contact also reveals power relations. Looking at a colleague when speaking conveys confidence and respect. Prolonged eye contact during a debate or disagreement can signal you're standing your ground. It also signifies your position in the hierarchy. People who are high status tend to look longer at people they're talking to, compared with others. Culture also guides how we look at each other. In many Eastern and some Caribbean cultures, meeting another's eyes is considered rude. Asians are more likely than persons from Europe or the United States to regard a person who makes eye contact as angry or unapproachable (Akashi et al. 2013). ✓

CONCEPT CHECKS ✓

1. What is interactional vandalism?
2. Give an example of a response cry.
3. What are the four zones of personal space?

Understand that interaction is situated, that it occurs in a particular place and for a particular length of time. See that the way we organize our social actions is not unique by learning how other cultures organize their social lives.

HOW DO TIME AND SPACE AFFECT OUR INTERACTIONS?

Understanding how activities are distributed in time and space is fundamental to analyzing encounters and to understanding social life in general. All interaction is situated—it occurs in a particular place and has a specific duration in time. Our actions over the course of a day tend to be "zoned" in time as well as in space. Thus, for example, most people spend a zone—say, from 9:00 AM to 5:00 PM—of their daily time working. Their weekly time is also zoned: They are likely to work on weekdays and spend weekends at home, altering the pattern of their activities on the weekend days. As we move through the temporal zones of the day, we are also often moving across space as well: To get to work, we may take a bus from one area of a city to another or perhaps commute in from the suburbs. When we analyze the contexts of social interaction, therefore, it is often useful to look at people's movements across **time-space**.

The concept of **regionalization** will help us understand how social life is zoned in time-space. Take the example of a private house. A modern house is regionalized into rooms, hallways, and floors (if there is more than one story). These spaces are not just physically separate areas but are zoned in time as well. The living rooms and kitchen are used most in the daylight hours, the bedrooms at night. The interaction that occurs in these regions is bound by both spatial and temporal divisions. Some areas of the house form back regions, such as the den or the basement, where people can be themselves without worrying about what other people think. For instance, some people may leave their old furniture and children's tattered toys in the den or family room and may be slightly less vigilant about "keeping up appearances" in rooms that guests seldom visit. By contrast, the living room may display lovely furniture, well-appointed decorations, and sophisticated coffee-table books, so that a family can convey to others that they are dignified and respectable. At times, the whole house can become a back region. Once again, this idea is beautifully captured by Goffman (1973):

> On a Sunday morning, a whole household can use the wall around its domestic establishment to conceal a relaxing slovenliness in dress and civil endeavor, extending to all rooms the informality that is usually restricted to the kitchen and bedrooms. So, too, in American middle-class neighborhoods, on afternoons the line between children's playground and home may be defined as backstage by mothers, who pass along it wearing jeans, loafers, and a minimum of make-up.

time-space • When and where events occur.

regionalization • The division of social life into different regional settings or zones.

CLOCK TIME

In modern societies, the zoning of our activities is strongly influenced by **clock time**. Without clocks and the precise timing of activities, and their resulting coordination across space, industrialized societies could not exist (Mumford 1973). Today the measuring of time by clocks is standardized across the globe, making possible the complex international transport systems and communications we now depend on. World standard time was first introduced in 1884 at a conference of nations held in Washington, D.C. The globe was then partitioned into twenty-four time zones, one hour apart, and an exact beginning of the universal day was fixed.

Today, virtually all social institutions schedule their activities precisely across the day and week. The greater the number of people and resources involved, the more precise the scheduling must be. Eviatar Zerubavel (1979, 1982) demonstrated this in his study of the temporal structure of a large modern hospital. A hospital must operate on a twenty-four-hour basis, and coordinating the staff and resources is a highly

clock time • Time as measured by the clock, in terms of hours, minutes, and seconds. Before the invention of clocks, time reckoning was based on events in the natural world, such as the rising and setting of the sun.

complex matter. For instance, the nurses work for one time period in Ward A, another time period in Ward B, and so on, and are also called on to alternate between day- and night-shift work. Nurses, doctors, and other staff, plus the resources they need, must be integrated both in time and in space.

SOCIAL LIFE AND THE ORDERING OF SPACE AND TIME

The Internet is another example of how closely forms of social life are bound up with our control of space and time. The Internet makes it possible for us to interact with people we never see or meet, in any corner of the world. Such technological change re-arranges space—we can interact with anyone without moving from our chair. It also alters our experience of time because communication on the electronic highway is almost immediate. We are so used to being able to watch our favorite TV show online or send an e-mail to a friend in another state, at any hour of the day, that it is hard for us to imagine what life would be like otherwise.

THE COMPULSION OF PROXIMITY

In modern societies, we are constantly interacting with others whom we may never see or meet. Almost all of our everyday transactions, such as buying groceries or making a bank deposit, bring us into contact—but indirect contact—with people who may live thousands of miles away. The banking system, for example, is international. Any money you deposit is a small part of the financial investments the bank makes worldwide.

Some people are concerned that the rapid advances in communications tech-nology such as e-mail, the Internet, and e-commerce will only increase this tenden-cy toward indirect interactions. Our society is becoming "devoiced," some claim, as the capabilities of technology grow ever greater. According to this view, as the pace of life accelerates, people are increasingly isolating themselves; we now interact more with our televisions and computers than with our neighbors or members of the community.

Now that e-mail, social networking sites, electronic discussion groups, and chat rooms have become facts of life for many people in industrialized countries, it is important to ask, What is the nature of these interactions and what new com-plexities are emerging from them? A recent study found that the percentage of adults online who use social networking sites has more than doubled since 2008 from 29 to 65 percent. Half of all adults use social networking sites (Pew Inter-net and American Life Project 2011). One study conducted at Stanford University found that about 20 percent of Internet users use the medium to communicate with people whom they do not know (Nie et al. 2004). Another study conducted on 170,000 school-age children found that 35 percent of fifth through twelfth graders said their parents would disapprove if they knew about all their Internet activities. Fifty-three percent said they would meet face-to-face with someone they first met online (National Assessment Center 2008).

The G8 summit, a face-to-face meeting of the heads of governments of eight leading industrialized countries, is an example of what Molotch and Boden call the compulsion of proximity. Individuals, including world leaders, prefer face-to-face interactions because they provide richer information about how people think and feel.

At the same time, the study found that Internet use cuts into the time we spend socializing with people face-to-face, watching TV, and sleeping. Some researchers conclude that the substitution of e-mail for face-to-face communication has led to a weakening of social ties and a disruption of techniques used in personal dialogue for avoiding conflict. Further, online communication seems to allow more room for misinterpretation, confusion, and abuse than more traditional forms of communication (Friedman and Currall 2003). Others counter, however, that social relations continue to thrive and might even be facilitated by frequent online communication (Hampton et al. 2011; Wellman 2008).

Many Internet enthusiasts disagree. They argue that online communication has many inherent advantages that cannot be claimed by more traditional forms of interaction such as the telephone and face-to-face meetings. The human voice, for example, may be far superior in terms of expressing emotion and subtleties of meaning, but it can also convey information about the speaker's age, gender, ethnicity, or social position—information that could be used to the speaker's disadvantage. Electronic communication, it is noted, masks all these identifying markers and ensures that attention focuses strictly on the content of the message. This can be a great advantage for women or other traditionally disadvantaged groups whose opinions are sometimes devalued in other settings (Pascoe 2000). Electronic interaction is often presented as liberating and empowering because people can create their own online identities and speak more freely than they would elsewhere.

Recent research shows that social networking may even enhance social integration and friendships (Hampton et al. 2011). A national survey conducted by the Pew Internet and American Life Project reports that persons who use social networking sites are more trusting, have more close relationships, receive more emotional and practical social support, and are more politically engaged than those who do not use such sites. For many people, online relationships are quite meaningful. Fully 40 percent of Facebook users say that they "friend" only those people whom they consider close confidants (Pew Internet and American Life Project 2013).

Dating and Mating Online

How did you meet your last romantic partner? Perhaps you met at a party or sat next to each other in your introduction to sociology course. Can you remember what it was that drew you to him or her? Was there something subtle that signaled to you there might be an attraction, like a tone of voice, a wink, or light touch to the shoulder? For many couples throughout the world, these initial face-to-face encounters are critical; they help us determine whether a new acquaintance will be a friend—or something more.

While popular music suggests that two strangers will lock eyes across a crowded room and true love will follow, in our current digital age, meetings can happen in a far less romantic way. Dozens of smartphone apps like MiuMeet, Skout, Tinder, Tingle, and Zoosk take face-to-face encounters out of the initial attraction stage. Rather, these apps allow people to search through dozens of photos of eligible partners and screen them based on personal preferences like age, height, gender, sexual orientation, and race. Users can then zip a text message to communicate their interest. These apps stand in stark contrast with more "traditional" online dating sites like Match, eHarmony, JDate, and Christian Mingle, where potential daters exchange carefully composed e-mail messages and tentative phone conversations before the "first date." Apps like Blendr and Tinder use GPS functionality to help users find like-minded people in their vicinity at any given time, allowing them to meet up on a moment's notice if both parties are available and willing (Wortham 2013).

Do these apps take the romance and intrigue out of dating? Defenders say that young people can shop for a date in exactly the same way they would shop for a new car; they can specify precisely what they want and search for potential partners who share those traits. Some apps help users find potential partners who share their own religion, beliefs, and hobbies, which is viewed as a particularly efficient way to date.

But how does a nervous, inexperienced dater know that he or she isn't meeting up with a creep, or worse yet, a criminal? The anonymity of such apps makes dating more dangerous than if you simply met someone at a dorm party. You could easily ask a classmate what he or she thought of your new crush in order to obtain important information. Some apps serve a similar function, yet also put potential daters' anonymity and privacy at risk.

Apps like Lulu were designed by and for women, ostensibly to protect them from potentially "bad" dates. Young women can post reports and ratings on the men they've dated, including very private details of their behind-closed-doors encounters. According to designers of the app, young women will "know what they're getting themselves into" before they start dating a particular young man. The app is anonymous, so the women raters don't have to worry about retribution from those men they've given bad reviews to. Not surprisingly, the app has riled up anger among some of the 2 million men rated on the site, so the entrepreneurial designers of Lulu have since started a LuluDude app, where men can share information about the women they've dated (ABC News 2013).

Thinking about sociological writings on the differences between face-to-face and online interaction, what do you see as the pros and cons of such apps? Do you think dating apps will be used in the future, or do you predict that young people will return to dating "the old-fashioned way"? Why or why not?

Smartphone apps like Blendr, Tinder, and Crazy Blind Date are re-inventing the way singles connect, removing the initial face-to-face interactions.

Further, people can communicate with those who don't share their geographic region; perhaps you have reconnected via Facebook with childhood friends who live hundreds of miles away.

Who is right in this debate? How far can electronic communication substitute for face-to-face interaction? Sociologists Deirdre Boden and Harvey Molotch (1994) argue that there is no substitute for face-to-face interaction. They argue further that humans have a true need for personal interaction, which they call the "**compulsion of proximity**." People put themselves out to attend meetings, Boden and Molotch suggest, because situations of co-presence provide much richer information about how other people think and feel, and about their sincerity, than any form of electronic communication. Only by actually being in the presence of people who make decisions affecting us in important ways do we feel able to learn what is going on and confident that we can impress them with our own views and our own sincerity. And as Manti Te'o learned, electronic communication in the absence of accompanying face-to-face communication may provide a platform for highly insincere and dishonest behavior. ✓

compulsion of proximity • People's need to interact with others in their presence.

CONCEPT CHECKS ✓

1. How does time structure human life?
2. Is face-to-face interaction, or co-presence, an important aspect of human action? Why or why not?

HOW DO THE RULES OF SOCIAL INTERACTION AFFECT YOUR LIFE?

See how face-to-face interactions reflect broader social factors such as social hierarchies.

As we saw in Chapter 1, microsociology, the study of everyday behavior in situations of face-to-face interaction, and macrosociology, the study of the broader features of society like race, class, or gender hierarchies, are closely connected. We now examine a social encounter that you may experience frequently—walking down a crowded city sidewalk—to illustrate this point. The ways that you may interact with others on the street are likely shaped by your gender and race.

WOMEN AND MEN IN PUBLIC

Take, for example, a situation that may seem micro on its face: A woman walking down the street is verbally harassed by a group of men. In a study published as *Passing By: Gender and Public Harassment*, Carol Brooks Gardner (1995) found that in various settings, most famously the edges of construction sites, these types of unwanted interaction occur as something women frequently experience as abusive.

Although the harassment of a single woman might be analyzed in microsociological terms by looking at a single interaction, it is not fruitful to view it that simply. Such harassment is typical of street talk involving men and women who are strangers (Gardner 1995). And these kinds of interactions cannot be understood without also looking at the larger background of gender hierarchy in the United States. In this way we can see how microanalysis and macroanalysis are connected. For example, Gardner linked the harassment of women by men to the larger system of gender inequality, represented by male privilege in public spaces, women's physical vulnerability, and the omnipresent threat of rape.

A recent controversy in Princeton, New Jersey, regarding a mall's billboard vividly displays that street harassment is more than just a micro exchange between one man (or a group of men) and one woman walking down the street. In 2012, MarketFair Mall was undergoing renovation, and a sign was erected that said, "We apologize for the whistling construction workers, but man you look good! So will we soon, please pardon our dust, dirt and other assorted inconveniences." A passerby, Elizabeth Harman, saw the billboard and took offense, posting an image of the sign on Facebook. The image went viral, spurring an online petition, a series of angry blogs, and the eventual removal of the sign. As Harman, a philosophy professor, explained, "The issue of street harassment is really normalized in our society. . . . I didn't want my daughter to think that was a normal way to think about men yelling at women" (Karas 2012).

Sociologist Gwen Sharp (2012) observed that street harassment (and the celebration of it through the MarketFair Mall sign) not only perpetuates the assumption that women are sexual objects to be admired but that working-class men such as construction workers are sexist, uncouth, and unable to restrain their lustful thoughts.

BLACKS AND WHITES IN PUBLIC

Have you ever crossed to the other side of the street when you felt threatened by someone behind you or someone coming toward you? In a case that captured national attention, George Zimmerman, claiming he acted in self-defense, shot and killed Trayvon Martin, a seventeen-year-old black high school student who was walking unarmed through a gated community in Sanford, Florida. The shooting elicited strong reactions from all sides, as we will see in later chapters. While many aspects of the case remain under dispute, the exchange that happened on the street between Zimmerman and Martin can be partly understood by the sociological work of Elijah Anderson. In his book *Streetwise: Race, Class, and Change in an Urban Community*, Anderson (1990) noted that studying everyday life sheds light on how social order is created by the individual building blocks of infinite microlevel interactions. He was particularly interested in understanding interactions when at least one party was viewed as threatening. Anderson showed that the ways many blacks and whites interact on the streets of a northern city had a great deal to do with the structure of racial stereotypes, which is itself linked to the economic structure of society. In this way, he showed the link between micro interactions and the larger macro structures of society.

Anderson began by recalling Erving Goffman's description of how social roles and statuses come into existence in particular contexts or locations: When an individual enters the presence of others, they commonly seek to acquire information about him or bring into play information already possessed. Information about the individual helps to define the situation, enabling others to know in advance what he will expect of them and they may expect of him (Anderson 1990).

Following Goffman's lead, Anderson asked, What types of behavioral cues and signs make up the vocabulary of public interaction? He concluded that the people most likely to pass inspection are those who do not fall into commonly accepted stereotypes of dangerous persons: "Children readily pass inspection, while women and white men do so more slowly, black women, black men, and black male teenagers most slowly of all." In showing that interactional tensions derive from outside statuses such as race, class, and gender, Anderson shows that we cannot develop a full understanding of the situation by looking at the micro interactions themselves. This is how he makes the link between micro interactions and macro processes.

Anderson argues that people are streetwise when they develop skills such as "the art of avoidance" to deal with the vulnerability they feel to violence and crime. According to Anderson, whites who are not streetwise do not recognize the difference between different kinds of black men (for example, middle-class youths versus gang members). They may also not know how to alter the number of paces to walk behind a suspicious person or how to bypass bad blocks at various times of day. In these ways, social science research can help you understand how a very ordinary behavior—navigating one's way through the city streets—reveals important lessons about the nature of social interaction today. It also helps us to partly understand extreme behaviors, such as the shooting of Trayvon Martin by George Zimmerman.

One of the great puzzles that social scientists will seek to resolve in the coming decades is whether "new" forms of social interaction, such as social networking sites, will alter gender relations and race relations. As we have seen throughout this chapter, virtual communication shares many of the same properties as face-to-face communication. For instance, we carefully impression manage in both venues. Yet we have also seen that online communication has started to chip away at hierarchies based on power and status, perhaps paving the way for a future where race and class will no longer matter as they did in the days when Anderson conducted his *Streetwise* research. ✓

CONCEPT CHECKS ✓

1. How would sociologists explain the street harassment that women often experience?

2. How would sociologist Elijah Anderson define *streetwise*?

EXERCISES:
Thinking Sociologically

1. Identify the elements important to the dramaturgical perspective. This chapter shows how the theory might be used to understand interactions between customers and service providers. How would you apply the theory to account for a plumber's visit to a client's home?

2. Smoking cigarettes is a pervasive habit found in many parts of the world and a habit that could be explained by both microsociological and macrosociological forces. Give an example of each that would be relevant to explain the proliferation of smoking. How might your suggested micro- and macro-level analyses be linked?

3. Think about the last photo you posted or the last status update you reported on Facebook. What impression were you trying to convey to others? How would Goffman characterize your impression-management goals?

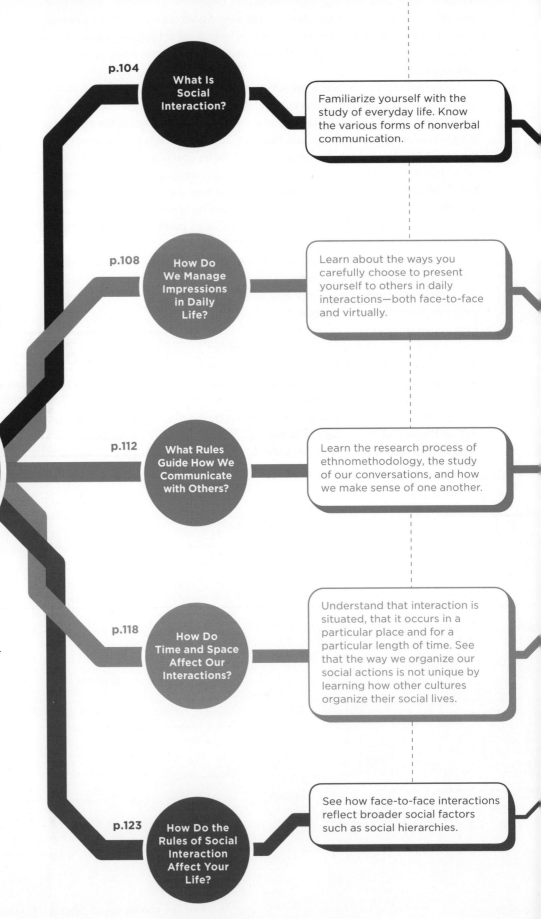

Chapter 4

Social Interaction and Everyday Life in the Age of the Internet

p.104 — **What Is Social Interaction?**

Familiarize yourself with the study of everyday life. Know the various forms of nonverbal communication.

p.108 — **How Do We Manage Impressions in Daily Life?**

Learn about the ways you carefully choose to present yourself to others in daily interactions—both face-to-face and virtually.

p.112 — **What Rules Guide How We Communicate with Others?**

Learn the research process of ethnomethodology, the study of our conversations, and how we make sense of one another.

p.118 — **How Do Time and Space Affect Our Interactions?**

Understand that interaction is situated, that it occurs in a particular place and for a particular length of time. See that the way we organize our social actions is not unique by learning how other cultures organize their social lives.

p.123 — **How Do the Rules of Social Interaction Affect Your Life?**

See how face-to-face interactions reflect broader social factors such as social hierarchies.

social interaction • micro-sociology • civil inattention • agency • structure • nonverbal communication

1. What is microsociology?
2. What are three reasons why it is important to study daily social interaction?
3. What is nonverbal communication?
4. Describe several ways that individuals communicate their emotions to one another.
5. How do e-mail and in-person communication differ?

status • social position • impression management • unfocused interaction • focused interaction • encounter

1. What is impression management?
2. Compare and contrast focused and unfocused interaction.
3. Why do we segregate our audiences in daily life?

ethnomethodology • conversation analysis • interactional vandalism • response cries • personal space

1. What is interactional vandalism?
2. Give an example of a response cry.
3. What are the four zones of personal space?

1. How does time structure human life?
2. Is face-to-face interaction, or co-presence, an important aspect of human action? Why or why not?

time-space • regionalization • clock time • compulsion of proximity

1. How would sociologists explain the street harassment that women often experience?
2. How would sociologist Elijah Anderson define *streetwise*?

5

Groups, Networks, and Organizations

THE BIG QUESTIONS

WHAT ARE SOCIAL GROUPS?

Learn the variety and characteristics of groups, as well as the effect of groups on an individual's behavior.

HOW DO WE BENEFIT FROM SOCIAL NETWORKS?

Understand the importance of social networks and the advantages they confer on some people.

HOW DO ORGANIZATIONS FUNCTION?

Know how to define an organization and understand how organizations developed over the last two centuries. Learn Max Weber's theory of organizations and view of bureaucracy.

IS BUREAUCRACY AN OUTDATED MODEL?

Familiarize yourself with some of the alternatives to bureaucracy that have developed in other societies or in recent times. Think about the influence of technology on how organizations operate.

HOW DO GROUPS AND ORGANIZATIONS AFFECT YOUR LIFE?

Learn how social capital enables people to accomplish their goals and expand their influence.

The Marching 100 was long a source of great pride at Florida A&M University (FAMU). Pride turned to shock and shame in 2011 when a hazing incident led to the brutal death of drum major Robert Champion. Hazing is rampant on many college campuses and shows the tremendous power of social groups.

H umans are social creatures. Most of us want to "belong" to some sort of group, and we cherish the friendships, feeling of acceptance, and even the perks that go along with being a member of a group. But what are we willing to do in order to belong? Would you be willing to be beaten up? What about beating up someone else? Would you drink an entire bottle of vodka? Or stand outdoors in the January cold after being doused with cold water? Or run around in the sweltering summer heat wearing layers of heavy clothing?

Although this sounds barbaric, these types of hazing activities occur all too often on college campuses today. Hazing—or the rituals and other activities, involving harassment, abuse, or humiliation, used as a way of initiating a person into a group—occurs at an estimated 55 percent of all college fraternities and sororities today. Although some blithely view hazing as "boys being boys" or a rite of passage, others consider hazing an illegal activity that must be banished from all college campuses (Nuwer 2013).

News stories are replete with horrific incidences of hazing. In 2011, marching band members from Florida A&M University (FAMU) attacked drum major Robert Champion on a bus after a performance, paddling and beating him with musical instruments in a hazing ritual known as Crossing Bus C. The assault was so brutal that Champion died within the hour from "hemmorhagic shock caused by blunt-force trauma" (Alvarez 2013). This senseless crime shocked the nation; the FAMU band—dubbed the Marching 100—had been one of the most celebrated in the nation. The Marching 100, like many college fraternities and sororities, had a history of hazing its members, with authorities turning a blind eye. In fact, ten years earlier, another band member was beaten so badly that he suffered renal failure. Champion's death, though, was the breaking point, and the university acted swiftly. Fifteen former band members were charged with manslaughter or felony hazing. The university president was forced out. The band, once the shining star of FAMU, was suspended for nearly two years, with new band members taking the field again in September 2013 (Alvarez 2013).

What would cause otherwise upstanding young men and women—many of whom are top students, star athletes, and accomplished musicians—to torture their classmates? And why doesn't one brave soul in the group stand up to stop the abuse? Why do "pledges," those young men and women striving to join a college fraternity or sorority, subject themselves to this mistreatment?

The answers are complex but illustrate important aspects of group behavior, including conformity, or going along with the actions of the group regardless of the personal costs. In this chapter we examine the ways in which all of us—not just frat brothers—are group animals. We will consider different kinds of groups, the ways group size affects our behavior in groups, and the nature of leadership. We will explore how group norms promote conformity, often to disastrous ends. We also examine the role played by organizations in American society, the major theories of modern organizations, and the ways in which organizations are changing in the modern world. The increased effect of technology on organizations and the prominence of the Internet in our group life are also explored. The chapter concludes by discussing the debate over declines in social capital and social engagement in the United States today.

Learn the variety and characteristics of groups, as well as the effect of groups on an individual's behavior.

WHAT ARE SOCIAL GROUPS?

social group • A collection of people who regularly interact with one another on the basis of shared expectations concerning behavior and who share a sense of common identity.

Nearly all our important interactions occur through some type of social group. You and your roommates make up a social group, as do the members of your introductory sociology class. A **social group** is a collection of people who share a common identity and regularly interact with one another on the basis of shared expectations concerning behavior. People who belong to the same social group identify with one another, expect one another to conform to certain ways of thinking and acting, and recognize the boundaries that separate them from other groups or people. Fraternities or sororities are examples of social groups, as are sports teams, musical groups, or even book groups.

GROUPS: VARIETY AND CHARACTERISTICS

Every day nearly all of us participate in groups and group activities. We hang out with groups of friends, study with classmates, eat dinner with family members, play team sports, and go online to meet people who share our interests (Aldrich and Marsden 1988).

However, just being in one another's company does not make a collection of individuals a social group. People milling around in crowds or strolling on a beach make up a social aggregate. A **social aggregate** is a simple collection of people who happen to be together in a particular place but do not significantly interact or identify with one another. People waiting together at a bus station, for example, may be conscious of one another's presence, but they are unlikely to think of themselves as a "we"—the group waiting for the next bus to Poughkeepsie or Des Moines. By the same token, people may constitute a **social category**, sharing a common characteristic (such as gender, occupation, religion, or ethnicity) without necessarily interacting or identifying with one another. The sense of belonging to a common social group is missing.

social aggregate • A collection of people who happen to be together in a particular place but do not significantly interact or identify with one another.

social category • People who share a common characteristic (such as gender or occupation) but do not necessarily interact or identify with one another.

IN-GROUPS AND OUT-GROUPS

In-groups are groups toward which one feels particular loyalty and respect—the groups that "we" belong to. **Out-groups**, on the other hand, are groups toward which one feels antagonism and contempt—"those people." The "sense of belonging" among members of the in-group is sometimes strengthened by the group's scorning the members of other groups (Sartre 1965, orig. 1948). Creating a sense of belonging in this way is especially true of racist groups, which promote their identity as "superior" by hating "inferior" groups. Jews, Catholics, African Americans, immigrants, and gay people historically—and Muslims more recently—have been the targets of such prejudice in the United States.

Most people occasionally use in-group–out-group imagery to trumpet what they believe to be their group's strengths vis-à-vis some other group's presumed weaknesses. For example, members of a fraternity or a sorority may bolster their feelings of superiority—in academics, sports, or campus image—by ridiculing the members of a different house. Similarly, a church may hold up its "truths" as the only ones, while native-born Americans may accuse immigrants—always outsiders upon arriving in a new country—as ruining the country for "real Americans."

in-group • A group toward which one feels particular loyalty and respect—the group to which "we" belong.

out-group • A group toward which one feels antagonism and contempt—"those people."

PRIMARY AND SECONDARY GROUPS

Our lives and personalities are molded by our earliest experiences in **primary groups**, namely, our families, our peers, and our friends. Primary groups are small groups characterized by face-to-face interaction, intimacy, and a strong, enduring sense of commitment. There is also often an experience of unity, a merging of the self with the group into one personal "we." Sociologist Charles Horton Cooley (1864–1929) termed such groups *primary* because he believed that they were the basic form of association, exerting a long-lasting influence on the development of our social selves (Cooley 1964, orig. 1902).

Secondary groups, by contrast, are large and impersonal and often involve fleeting relationships. Secondary groups seldom involve intense emotional ties, powerful commitments to the group itself, or a feeling of unity. We seldom feel we can "be ourselves" in a secondary group; rather, we are often playing a particular role, such as employee or student. Cooley argued that while people belong to primary groups mainly because such groups are inherently fulfilling, people join secondary groups to achieve some specific goal: to earn a living, get a college degree, or compete in sports. Examples of secondary groups include business organizations, schools, work groups, athletic clubs, and governmental bodies. Secondary groups may become primary groups for some of their members. For example, when coworkers begin to socialize after hours, they create bonds of friendship that constitute a primary group.

primary group • A group that is characterized by intense emotional ties, face-to-face interaction, intimacy, and a strong, enduring sense of commitment.

secondary group • A group characterized by its large size and by impersonal, fleeting relationships.

For most of human history, nearly all interactions took place within primary groups. This pattern began to change with the emergence of larger, agrarian societies, which included such secondary groups as those based on governmental roles or occupation. Some early sociologists, such as Cooley, worried about a loss of intimacy as more and more interactions revolved around large, impersonal organizations. However, what Cooley saw as the growing anonymity of modern life may also offer an increasing tolerance of individual differences. Primary groups, which often enforce strict conformity to group standards (Durkheim 1964, orig. 1893; Simmel 1955), can be stifling. Secondary groups, by contrast, are more likely than primary groups to be concerned with accomplishing a task, rather than with enforcing conformity to group standards of behavior. However, as we will see in the Digital Life box, web-based crowdfunding efforts allow loosely knit collections of people who don't even know one another to accomplish important tasks, like raising funds for a charity or creative project.

REFERENCE GROUPS

We often judge ourselves by how we think we appear to others, which Cooley termed the *looking-glass self.* Robert K. Merton (1968, orig. 1938) elaborated on Cooley's concept by discussing reference groups as a standard by which we evaluate ourselves. A **reference group** is a group that provides a standard for judging one's own attitudes or behaviors (see also Hyman and Singer 1968). Family, peers, classmates, and coworkers are crucial reference groups. However, you do not have to belong to a group for it to be your reference group. For example, young people living thousands of miles away from the bright lights of Hollywood may still compare their looks and fashion choices with their favorite celebrity. Although most of us seldom interact socially with such reference groups as the glitterati, we may take pride in identifying with them, and even imitate those people who do belong to them. This is why it is critical for children—minority children in particular, whose groups are often represented in the media using negative stereotypes—to be exposed to reference groups that will shape their lives for the better.

reference group • A group that provides a standard for judging one's attitudes or behaviors.

How do we know whether we are attractive, stylish, or financially successful? Most of us rely on others as a "reference group"— although Americans' reference groups are often unrealistic images of celebrities and unattainable wealth.

THE EFFECTS OF SIZE

Another significant way in which groups differ has to do with their size. Sociological interest in group size can be traced to the German sociologist Georg Simmel (1858–1918), who studied and theorized about the impact of small groups on people's behavior. Since Simmel's time, small-group researchers have conducted a number of laboratory experiments to examine the effects of size on both the quality of interaction in the group and the effectiveness of the group in accomplishing certain tasks (Bales 1953, 1970; Hare et al. 1965; Homans 1950; Mills 1967).

DYADS

The simplest group, which Simmel (1955) called a **dyad**, consists of two persons. Simmel reasoned that dyads, which involve both intimacy and conflict, are likely to be simultaneously intense and unstable. To survive, they require the full attention and cooperation of both parties. If one person withdraws from the dyad, it vanishes. Dyads are typically the source of our most elementary social bonds, often constituting the group in which we are most likely to share our deepest secrets. But dyads can be very fragile. That is why, Simmel believed, a variety of cultural and legal supports for marriage—an example of a dyad—are found in societies where marriage is regarded as an important source of social stability.

dyad • A group consisting of two persons.

TRIADS

Triads, or three-person groups, are more stable than dyads according to Simmel, since the third person relieves some of the pressure on the other two to always get along and energize the relationship. In a triad, one person can temporarily withdraw attention from the relationship without necessarily threatening it. In addition, if two of the members have a disagreement, the third can play the role of mediator, as when you try to patch up a falling-out between two of your friends. Yet triads are not without potential problems. Alliances (sometimes termed *coalitions*) may form between two members of a triad, enabling them to gang up on the third and thereby destabilize the group.

triad • A group consisting of three persons.

LARGER GROUPS

Simmel identified an important aspect of groups: As group size increases, their intensity decreases while their stability and exclusivity increase. Larger groups have less intense interactions, simply because a larger number of potential smaller group relationships exist as outlets for individuals who are not getting along with other members of the group. In a dyad, only a single relationship between two people is possible; in a triad, three different two-person relationships can occur. In a ten-person group, the number of possible two-person relationships explodes to forty-five. When one relationship doesn't work out to your liking, you can easily move on to another, as you probably often do at large parties.

Large groups also tend to be more stable than smaller ones because the withdrawal of some members usually does not threaten the group's survival. A marriage or romantic relationship falls apart if one person leaves, whereas a sports team or drama club routinely survives—though it may sometimes temporarily suffer from—the loss of its graduating seniors. Larger groups also tend to be more exclusive, since it is easier for their members to limit their social relationships to the group itself and avoid relationships with nonmembers.

Fund-Raising Goes Online

Imagine that a major symphony orchestra or prominent art museum is holding a fund-raiser. You are probably imagining wealthy men and women of a certain age, dressed in tuxedos and gowns, sipping champagne and making small talk about investments. Perhaps they vacation in the Hamptons together or their children were friends at prep school. These images are perhaps an over-the-top stereotype, but one component of this description is probably true: Many of the attendees likely know one another.

But how might middle- and working-class people raise money for their favorite causes—whether it's to provide relief for hurricane victims, help the homeless, or even launch one's own music group? Over the past five years, the Internet has exploded with crowdfunding sites. Crowdfunding refers to the collective effort of many people who pool their money to support another person or group's cause. Crowdfunding relies on many smaller donations rather than a few large ones like we might see at a museum fund-raiser attended by very wealthy people. For example, on Watsi—a global crowdfunding platform that allows people to directly fund low-cost medical care for people in developing nations—donors can give as little as $5 to help a patient in need (LaPorte 2013).

One of the most fascinating aspects of crowdfunding is that it allows people to raise money by relying primarily on their "weak ties," or friends of friends of friends. By spreading the word about a venture, sharing information about the weblink and the project, crowdfunding involves many participants from all walks of life. Often, these donors know one another through loose social ties; perhaps they learn about a particular charity because they belong to the same Facebook group. Other times, though, donors to a particular project may belong to quite different social networks. They come together through crowdfunding platforms like Kickstarter and IndieGoGo, which provide a point of entry for making donations to specific charities and projects.

According to the consulting firm Massolution, crowdfunding platforms raised roughly $2.7 billion in 2012 (Crowdsourcing 2013). Different platforms cater to different types of projects. For example, MedStartr—like Watsi—focuses on health-related projects and innovations. In 2013, sisters Kara Gorski and Kristin Gembala turned to MedStartr to raise money for their new company BraGGs, which designs bras for breast cancer patients. Both sisters had undergone mastectomies, and their mother had died of breast cancer. Through crowdfunding, they raised more than $10,000 and were able to begin manufacturing their product (Emerson 2013). Other times, crowdfunding projects are purely recreational. One of the most successful crowdfunded projects to date is *Star Citizen*, an online video game; as of September 2013, the game had raised a whopping $18 million (Luzar 2013).

The "crowds" that support these projects would hardly constitute a primary group, as most of the members are not close significant others. In most cases, they do not even consist of secondary groups because the crowd members may not even know one another. Do you think that the "crowd" that supports such projects constitutes a

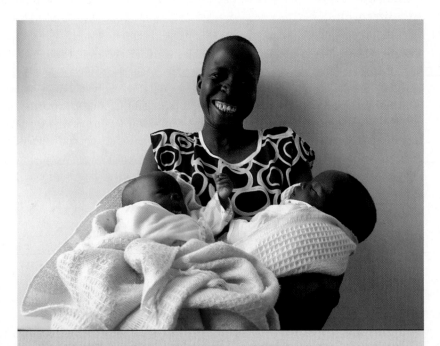

Crowdfunding platforms like Watsi and MedStartr help to raise money for maternal and child health programs in developing nations.

group? How might this type of group differ from the collection of people who attend fund-raising galas like the one described earlier? What makes crowdfunding successful? Have you ever used a crowdfunding site? What kind of people do you imagine might contribute to your project?

Beyond a certain size, perhaps a dozen people, groups tend to develop a formal structure. Formal leadership roles may arise, such as president or secretary, and official rules may be developed to govern what the group does. We discuss formal organizations later in this chapter.

TYPES OF LEADERSHIP

A **leader** is a person who is able to influence the behavior of other members of a group. All groups have leaders, even if the leader is not formally recognized as such. Some leaders are especially effective in motivating group members, inspiring them to achievements that might not ordinarily be accomplished. Such **transformational leaders** go beyond the merely routine, instilling in the members of their group a sense of mission or higher purpose and thereby changing the nature of the group itself (Burns 1978; Kanter 1983). They can also be a vital inspiration for social change in the world. For example, Nelson Mandela, the late South African leader who spent twenty-seven years in prison, successfully led his African National Congress (ANC) party into overthrowing South Africa's system of apartheid, or racial segregation. He was later elected president—leader—of the entire country. His leadership transcended national boundaries. After apartheid was abolished in 1990, Mandela and social rights activist Desmond Tutu established South Africa's Truth and Reconciliation Commission; created to explore the effects of apartheid, South Africa's Truth and Reconciliation Commission is recognized as a model for truth commissions worldwide, which are put in place to bring to light government misconduct in an effort to resolve past conflicts.

Most leaders are not as visionary as Mandela, however. Leaders who simply get the job done are termed **transactional leaders**. They are concerned with accomplishing the group's tasks, getting group members to do their jobs, and ensuring that the group achieves its goals. Transactional leadership is routine leadership. For example, the teacher who simply gets through the lesson plan each day—rather than making the classroom a place where students explore new ways of thinking and behaving—is exercising transactional leadership.

leader • A person who is able to influence the behavior of other members of a group.

transformational leader • A leader who is able to instill in the members of a group a sense of mission or higher purpose, thereby changing the nature of the group itself.

transactional leader • A leader who is concerned with accomplishing the group's tasks, getting group members to do their jobs, and making certain that the group achieves its goals.

CONFORMITY

Pressures to conform to the latest styles are especially strong among teenagers and young adults, for whom the need for group acceptance is often acute. While sporting tattoos or the latest fashion trend—or rigidly conforming to corporate workplace policies—may seem relatively harmless, conformity to group pressure can also lead to extremely destructive behavior, such as drug abuse, or even murder. For this reason, sociologists and social psychologists have long sought to understand why most people tend to go along with others, and under what circumstances they do not.

GOING ALONG WITH THE GROUP: ASCH'S RESEARCH

More than sixty years ago, psychologist Solomon Asch (1952) conducted some of the most influential studies of conformity to group pressures. In one of his classic experiments, Asch asked individual

Would you define Nelson Mandela as a transformational leader? Why?

subjects to decide which of three lines of different length most closely matched the length of a fourth line (Figure 5.1). The differences were obvious; subjects had no difficulty in making the correct match. Asch then arranged a version of the experiment in which the subjects were asked to make the matches in a group setting, with each person calling out the answer in turn. In this setting, all but one of the subjects were actually Asch's secret accomplices, and these accomplices all practiced a deception on that one true subject. Each accomplice picked a line as a match that was clearly unequal to the fourth line. The unwitting subject, one of the last to call out an answer, felt enormous group pressure to make the same error. Amazingly, at least half the time the experiment was conducted, one-third of these subjects gave the same wrong answer as the others in the group. They sometimes stammered and fidgeted when doing so, but they nonetheless yielded to the unspoken pressure to conform to the group's decision. Asch's experiments clearly showed that many people are willing to go along with the group consensus, even if they believe it is incorrect.

Although the Asch study was conducted decades ago, its findings provide some insight into why hazing happens. Just like the participants in Asch's study who bowed to group pressure, members of the FAMU marching band might have found it difficult to stop the abuse of their drum major when they perceived (perhaps incorrectly) that the majority was in strong agreement about the rites of initiation.

OBEDIENCE TO AUTHORITY: MILGRAM'S RESEARCH

Another classic study of conformity was conducted by Stanley Milgram (1963). Milgram wanted to see how far a person would go when ordered by a scientist to give another person increasingly powerful electric shocks. He did so by setting up an experiment that he told the subjects was about memorizing pairs of words. In reality, it was about obedience to authority.

The male subjects who volunteered for the study were supposedly randomly divided into "teachers" and "learners." In fact, the learners were actually Milgram's confederates. The teacher was told to read pairs of words from a list that the learner

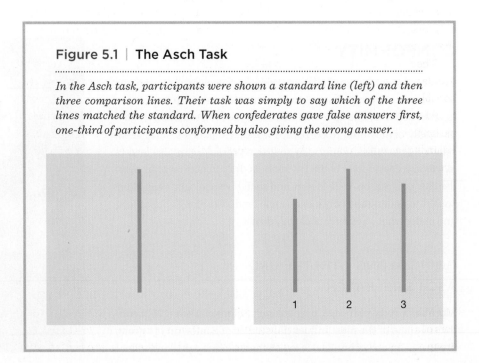

Figure 5.1 | The Asch Task

In the Asch task, participants were shown a standard line (left) and then three comparison lines. Their task was simply to say which of the three lines matched the standard. When confederates gave false answers first, one-third of participants conformed by also giving the wrong answer.

1 2 3

(a) The Milgram experiment required participants to "shock" the confederate learner (seated). The research participant (left) helped apply the electrodes that would be used to shock the learner. (b) An obedient participant shocks the learner in the "touch" condition. Fewer than one-third obeyed the experimenter in this condition. (c) After the experiment, all the participants were introduced to the confederate learner so they could see he was not actually harmed.

was to memorize. Whenever the learner made a mistake, the teacher was to give him an electric shock by flipping a switch on a fake but official-looking machine. The control board on the machine indicated shock levels ranging from "15 volts—slight shock" to "450 volts—danger, severe shock." For each mistake, the voltage of the shock was to be increased, until it eventually reached the highest level. As the experiment progressed, the learner began to scream out in pain for the teacher to stop delivering shocks. Milgram's assistant, who was administering the experiment, exercised his authority as a scientist and ordered the teacher to continue administering shocks if the teacher tried to quit. (In reality, the learner, who was usually carefully concealed from the teacher by a screen, never received any electric shocks, and his "screams" had actually been prerecorded on a tape.)

The teacher was confronted with a major moral decision: Should he obey the scientist and go along with the experiment, even if it meant injuring another human being? Much to Milgram's surprise, over half the subjects in the study kept on administering electric shocks. They continued even until the maximum voltage was reached and the learner's screams had subsided into an eerie silence as he presumably died of a heart attack. How could ordinary people so easily conform to orders that would turn them into possible accomplices to murder?

The answer, Milgram found, was deceptively simple: Ordinary citizens will conform to orders given by someone in a position of power or authority—even if those orders have horrible consequences. From this, we can learn something about Nazi atrocities during World War II, which were Milgram's original concern. Many ordinary Germans who participated in the mass execution of Jews in Nazi concentration camps did so on the grounds that they were "just following orders." Milgram's research has sobering implications for anyone who thinks that only "others" will bend to authority, but "not me" (Zimbardo et al. 1977).

GROUPTHINK AND GROUP PRESSURES TO CONFORM: JANIS'S RESEARCH

The pressure to conform to group opinions may occasionally lead to bad decisions, rather than creative new solutions to problems. Irving L. Janis (1972, 1989; Janis and Mann 1977) called this phenomenon **groupthink**, a process by which the members of a group ignore those ideas, suggestions, and plans of action that go against the group consensus. Groupthink may embarrass potential dissenters into conforming

groupthink • A process by which the members of a group ignore ways of thinking and plans of action that go against the group consensus.

and may also produce a shift in perceptions so that alternative possibilities are ruled out without being seriously considered. Groupthink may facilitate reaching a quick consensus, but the consensus may also be ill chosen. It may even be downright dangerous. Social scientists attribute a range of bad (and in some cases, catastrophic) decisions to groupthink, including the space shuttle *Challenger* disaster and the Bay of Pigs invasion (Haig 2011; Janis and Mann 1977). Some social analysts even partly attribute the Penn State sex-abuse scandal to groupthink; if powerful men like then-football coach Joe Paterno and then-Penn State president Graham Spanier wanted to protect Jerry Sandusky, it would be difficult, if not impossible, for other members of the university to dissent and blow the whistle on the cover-up (Schrock 2011).

Janis engaged in historical research to see if groupthink had characterized U.S. foreign policy decisions. He examined several critical decisions, including that behind the infamous Bay of Pigs invasion of Cuba in 1961. John F. Kennedy, then the newly elected president, inherited a plan from the previous administration to help Cuban exiles liberate Cuba from the Communist government of Fidel Castro. The plan called for U.S. supplies and air cover to assist an invasion by an ill-prepared army of exiles at Cuba's Bay of Pigs. Although a number of Kennedy's top advisers were certain that the plan was fatally flawed, they refrained from bucking the emerging consensus to carry it out. As history now shows, the invasion was a disaster. The army of exiles, after parachuting into a swamp nowhere near their intended drop zone, was immediately defeated, and Kennedy suffered a great deal of public embarrassment.

Kennedy's advisers were smart, strong willed, and well educated. How could they have failed to voice their concerns about the proposed invasion? Janis identified a number of possible reasons. First, the advisers were hesitant to disagree with the president lest they lose his favor. Second, they did not want to diminish group harmony in a crisis situation where teamwork was all-important. Third, they faced intense time pressures and had little opportunity to consult outside experts who might have offered radically different perspectives. All these circumstances contributed to a single-minded pursuit of the president's initial ideas, rather than an effort to generate effective alternatives. To avoid groupthink, the group must ensure the full and open expression of all opinions, even strong dissent. ✓

CONCEPT CHECKS ✓

1. What is the difference between social aggregates and social groups? Give examples that illustrate this difference.

2. Describe the main characteristics of primary and secondary groups.

3. When groups become large, why does their intensity decrease but their stability increase?

4. What is groupthink? How can it be used to explain why some decisions made by a group can lead to negative consequences?

Understand the importance of social networks and the advantages they confer on some people.

HOW DO WE BENEFIT FROM SOCIAL NETWORKS?

network • A set of informal and formal social ties that links people to one another.

"Whom you know is often as important as what you know." This adage expresses the value of having good connections. Sociologists refer to such connections as **networks**—all the direct and indirect connections that link a person or a group with other people or groups. Your personal networks thus include people you know directly (such as your friends) as well as people you know indirectly (such as your friends' friends). The groups and organizations you belong to also may be networked. For example, all the chapters of Gamma Phi Beta or Hillel are linked, as are alumni from your college or university, thus connecting members to like-minded individuals throughout the United States and the world.

Networks serve us in many ways. You are likely to rely on your networks for a broad range of contacts, from obtaining access to your congressperson or senator to scoring a summer internship. Sociologist Mark Granovetter (1973) demonstrated that there can be enormous strength in weak ties, particularly among higher socioeconomic groups. Upper-level professional and managerial employees are likely to hear about new jobs through connections such as distant relatives or remote acquaintances. Such weak ties can be of great benefit because relatives or acquaintances tend to have very different sets of connections from one's closer friends, whose social contacts are likely to be similar to one's own. Among lower socioeconomic groups, Granovetter argued, weak ties are not necessarily bridges to other networks and so do not really widen one's opportunities (see also Knoke 1990; Marsden and Lin 1982; Wellman et al. 1988). After graduation from college, you may rely on good grades and a strong résumé to find a job. But it may prove beneficial if it happens that your roommate's uncle went to school with a top person in the organization where you are seeking work.

Most people rely on their personal networks to gain advantages, but not everyone has equal access to powerful networks. In general, whites and men have more advantageous social networks than do ethnic minorities and women. Some sociologists argue, for example, that women's business, professional, and political networks are fewer and weaker than men's, so that women's power in these spheres is reduced (Brass 1985). Yet as more and more women move up into higher-level occupational and political positions, the resulting networks can foster further advancement. One study found that women are more likely to be hired or promoted into job levels that already have a high proportion of women (Cohen et al. 1998).

THE INTERNET AS SOCIAL NETWORK

Our opportunities to belong to and access social networks have skyrocketed in recent years due to the Internet. Until the early 1990s, when the World Wide Web was developed, there were few Internet users outside of university and scientific communities. By the middle of 2012, however, an estimated 274 million Americans were using the Internet (Internet World Stats 2012b), and on any given day in the United States, the average adult spends about 2.5 hours online (Television Bureau of Advertising 2010). With such rapid communication and global reach, it is now possible to radically extend one's personal networks. The Internet is especially useful for networking with like-minded people on specific issues such as politics, business, hobbies, or romance (Southwick 1996; Wellman et al. 1996). It also enables people who might otherwise lack contact with others to become part of global networks. For example, people too ill to leave their homes can join chat rooms to share common interests, people in small rural communities can now take online college courses (Lewin 2012), and long-lost high school friends can reconnect via Facebook.

The Internet fosters the creation of new relationships, often without the emotional and social baggage or constraints that go along with face-to-face encounters. In the absence of the usual physical and social cues, such as skin color or residential address, people can get together electronically on the basis of shared interests like gaming, rather than similar social characteristics. Factors such as social position, wealth, race, ethnicity, gender, and physical disability are less likely to cloud the social interaction (Coate 1994; Jones 1995; Kollock and Smith 1996). In fact, technologies like Twitter allow people from all walks of life to catch glimpses into the lives of celebrities (as well as noncelebs).

One limitation of Internet-based social networks is that not everyone has equal access to the Internet. Lower-income persons and ethnic minorities are less likely than wealthier persons and whites to have Internet access. For example, nearly all Americans (95 percent) who live in households earning $75,000 or more a year use the Internet at least occasionally compared with just over half (57 percent) of those who make less than $30,000 per year (Pew Internet and American Life Project 2010).

However, the "digital divide" has narrowed in recent years, and cyberspace is among the most egalitarian planes of social interaction (Nielsen Media Research 2001a, 2001b; Pew Internet and American Life Project 2005; U.S. Bureau of the Census 2011a). One recent study that tracked Internet use among different socioeconomic groups concluded, "The Internet was, at first, an elitist country club reserved only for individuals with select financial abilities and technical skills. . . . Now, nearly every socioeconomic group is aggressively adopting the Web" (Nielsen Media Research 2001b). This pattern is not limited to the United States; rates of Internet use are creeping up throughout the world, enabling individuals to connect with anyone in the world who shares their interests. ✓

CONCEPT CHECKS ✓

1. According to Granovetter, what are the benefits of weak ties? Why?

2. How do men's and women's weak ties differ?

Know how to define an organization and understand how organizations developed over the last two centuries. Learn Max Weber's theory of organizations and view of bureaucracy.

HOW DO ORGANIZATIONS FUNCTION?

organization • A large group of individuals with a definite set of authority relations. Many types of organizations exist in industrialized societies, influencing most aspects of our lives. While not all organizations are bureaucratic, there are close links between the development of organizations and bureaucratic tendencies.

formal organization • Means by which a group is rationally designed to achieve its objectives, often using explicit rules, regulations, and procedures.

People frequently band together to pursue activities that they could not otherwise accomplish by themselves. A principal means for accomplishing such cooperative actions—whether it's raising money for cancer research, winning a football game, or becoming a profitable corporation—is the **organization**, a group with an identifiable membership that engages in concerted collective actions to achieve a common purpose (Aldrich and Marsden 1988). An organization can be a small primary group, but it is more likely to be a larger, secondary one: Universities, religious bodies, and business corporations are all examples of organizations. Such organizations are a central feature of all societies, and their study is a core concern of sociology today.

Organizations tend to be highly formal in modern industrial and postindustrial societies. A **formal organization** is rationally designed to achieve its objectives, often by means of explicit rules, regulations, and procedures. As Max Weber (1979, orig. 1921) first recognized almost a century ago, there has been a long-term trend in Europe and North America toward formal organizations. This rise of formality in organizations is in part the result of the fact that formality is often a requirement for legal standing. For a college or university to be legally accredited, for example, it must satisfy explicit written standards governing everything from grading policy to faculty performance to fire safety. Today, formal organizations are the dominant form of organization throughout the entire world.

It is easy to see why organizations are so important to us today. In the premodern world, families, close relatives, and neighbors provided for most needs—food, the instruction of children, work, and leisure-time activities. In modern times, the majority of the population is much more interdependent than was ever the case before. Many of our requirements are supplied by people we never meet and who indeed might live many thousands of miles away. A substantial amount of coordination of activities

A visit to the DMV clearly shows the integral role that organizations such as the government—and their corresponding rules and regulations—play in our lives.

and resources—which organizations provide—is needed in such circumstances. A downside, however, is that organizations take things out of our own hands and put them under the control of officials or experts over whom we have little influence. For instance, we are all required to do certain things the government tells us to do—pay taxes, abide by laws, go off to fight wars—or face punishment.

THEORIES OF ORGANIZATIONS

Max Weber developed the first systematic interpretation of the rise of modern organizations. Organizations, he argued, are ways of coordinating the activities of human beings, or the goods they produce, in a stable manner across space and time. Weber emphasized that the development of organizations depends on the control of information, and he stressed the central importance of writing in this process: An organization needs written rules in order to function and files in which its "memory" is stored. Weber saw organizations as strongly hierarchical, with power tending to be concentrated at the top. Was Weber right? If he was, it matters a great deal to us all. For Weber detected a clash as well as a connection between modern organizations and democracy that he believed had far-reaching consequences for social life.

BUREAUCRACY

All large-scale organizations, according to Weber, tend to be bureaucratic in nature. The word *bureaucracy* was coined by Monsieur de Gournay in 1745, who combined the word *bureau,* meaning both an office and a writing table, with the suffix *cracy,* derived from the Greek verb meaning "to rule." **Bureaucracy** is thus the rule of officials. The term was first applied only to government officials, but it gradually was extended to refer to large organizations in general. Perceptions of "bureaucracy" range from highly negative—fraught with red tape, inefficiency, and wastefulness—to quite positive—a model of carefulness, precision, and effective administration.

bureaucracy • A type of organization marked by a clear hierarchy of authority and the existence of written rules of procedure and staffed by full-time, salaried officials.

Weber's account of bureaucracy steers between these two extremes. He argued that the expansion of bureaucracy is inevitable in modern societies; bureaucratic authority is the only way of coping with the administrative requirements of large-scale social systems. Yet he also conceded that bureaucracy exhibits a number of major failings that have important implications for the nature of modern social life.

To study the origins and nature of the expansion of bureaucratic organizations, Weber constructed an ideal type of bureaucracy. (*Ideal* here refers not to what is most desirable, but to a pure form of bureaucratic organization. An **ideal type** is an abstract description constructed by accentuating certain features of real cases in order to pinpoint their most essential characteristics.) Weber (1979, orig. 1921) listed several characteristics of the ideal type of bureaucracy:

1. **A clear-cut hierarchy of authority, such that tasks in the organization are distributed as "official duties."** Each higher office controls and supervises the one below it in the hierarchy, thus making coordinated decision making possible.

2. **Written rules govern the conduct of officials at all levels of the organization.** The higher the office, the more the rules tend to encompass a wide variety of cases and demand flexibility in their interpretation.

3. **Officials are full time and salaried.** Each job in the hierarchy has a definite and fixed salary attached to it. Promotion is possible on the basis of capability, seniority, or a mixture of the two.

4. **There is a separation between the tasks of an official within the organization and his or her life outside.**

5. **No members of the organization own the material resources with which they operate.** The development of bureaucracy, according to Weber, separates workers from the control of their means of production; officials do not own the offices they work in, the desks they sit at, or the office machinery they use.

Weber believed that the more an organization approaches the ideal type of bureaucracy, the more effective it will be in pursuing the objectives for which it was established. Yet he recognized that bureaucracy could be inefficient and accepted that many bureaucratic jobs are dull, offering little opportunity for the exercise of creative capabilities. While Weber feared that the bureaucratization of society could have negative consequences, he concluded that bureaucratic routine and the authority of officialdom over our lives are prices we pay for the technical effectiveness of bureaucratic organizations. Since Weber's time, the bureaucratization of society has become more widespread. Critics of this development who share Weber's initial concerns have questioned whether the efficiency of rational organizations comes at a price greater than Weber could have imagined. The most prominent of these critiques refers to "the McDonaldization of society," discussed later in this chapter.

FORMAL AND INFORMAL RELATIONS WITHIN BUREAUCRACIES

Weber's analysis of bureaucracy gave prime place to **formal relations** within organizations, or the relations between people as stated in the rules of the organization. Weber had little to say about the informal connections and small-group relations that may exist in all organizations. But in bureaucracies, informal ways of doing things often allow for a flexibility that couldn't otherwise be achieved.

Informal networks tend to develop at all levels of organizations. At the very top, personal ties and connections may be more important than the formal situations in

ideal type • A "pure type," constructed by emphasizing certain traits of a social item that do not necessarily exist in reality. An example is Max Weber's ideal type of bureaucratic organization.

formal relations • Relations that exist in groups and organizations, laid down by the norms, or rules, of the official system of authority.

informal networks • Relations that exist in groups and organizations developed on the basis of personal connections; ways of doing things that depart from formally recognized modes of procedure.

which decisions are supposed to be made. For example, meetings of boards of directors and shareholders supposedly determine the policies of business corporations. In practice, a few members of the board often really run the corporation, making their decisions informally and expecting the board to approve them. Informal networks of this sort can also stretch across different corporations. Business leaders from different firms frequently consult one another in an informal way and may belong to the same clubs and social circles.

John Meyer and Brian Rowan (1977) argue that formal rules and procedures in organizations are usually quite distant from the practices actually adopted by the organizations' members. Formal rules, in their view, are often "myths" that people profess to follow but that have little substance in reality. They serve to legitimize—to justify—ways in which tasks are carried out, even while these ways may diverge greatly from how things are supposed to be done, according to the rules.

Deciding how far informal procedures generally help or hinder the effectiveness of organizations is not a simple matter. Systems that resemble Weber's ideal type tend to give rise to a forest of unofficial ways of doing things. This is partly because the flexibility that is lacking ends up being achieved by unofficial tinkering with formal rules. For those in dull jobs, informal procedures often also help to create a more satisfying work environment. Informal connections between officials in higher positions may be effective in ways that aid the organization as a whole. On the other hand, these officials may be more concerned with advancing or protecting their own interests than furthering those of the overall organization.

BUREAUCRACY AND DEMOCRACY

The diminishing of democracy with the advance of modern forms of organization was another problem that worried Weber a great deal (see also Chapter 13). What especially disturbed him was the prospect of rule by faceless bureaucrats. How can democracy be anything other than a meaningless slogan in the face of the increasing power bureaucratic organizations are wielding over us? After all, Weber reasoned, bureaucracies are necessarily specialized and hierarchical. Those near the bottom of the organization inevitably find themselves reduced to carrying out mundane tasks and have no power over what they do; power passes to those at the top. Weber's student Robert Michels (1967, orig. 1911) invented a phrase to refer to this loss of power that has since become famous: In large-scale organizations, and more generally a society dominated by organizations, he argued, there is an "**iron law of oligarchy**." **Oligarchy** means rule by the few. According to Michels, the flow of power toward the top is simply an inevitable part of an increasingly bureaucratized world—hence the term *iron law*.

Was Michels right? It surely is correct to say that large-scale organizations involve the centralizing of power. Yet there is good reason to suppose that the iron law of oligarchy is not quite as hard-and-fast as Michels claimed. Unequal power is not just a function of size. In modest-sized groups there can be very marked differences of power. In a small business, for instance, where the activities of employees are directly visible to the directors, much tighter control might be exerted than in offices in larger organizations. Further, in many modern organizations, power is also quite often openly delegated downward from superiors to subordinates. In many large companies, corporate heads are so busy coordinating different departments, coping with crises, and analyzing budget and forecast figures that they have little time for original thinking. Many corporate leaders frankly admit that for the most part they simply accept the conclusions given to them.

iron law of oligarchy • A term coined by Weber's student Robert Michels meaning that large organizations tend toward centralization of power, making democracy difficult.

oligarchy • Rule by a small minority within an organization or society.

GENDER AND ORGANIZATIONS

Until some two decades ago, organizational studies did not devote very much attention to the question of gender. The rise of feminist scholarship in the 1970s, however, led to examinations of gender relations in all the main institutions in society, including organizations and bureaucracy. Feminist sociologists, most notably Rosabeth Moss Kanter in her classic book *Men and Women of the Corporation* (1977), focused on the imbalance of gender roles within organizations and the ways in which modern organizations themselves had developed in a specifically gendered way.

Feminists have argued that the emergence of the modern organization and the bureaucratic career depended on a particular gender configuration. They point to two main ways in which gender is embedded in the very structure of modern organizations. First, bureaucracies are characterized by occupational gender segregation. As women began to enter the labor market in greater numbers, they tended to be segregated into categories of occupations that were low paying and involved routine work. These positions were subordinate to those occupied by men and did not provide opportunities for women to be promoted. Women were used as a source of cheap, reliable labor but were not granted the same opportunities as men to build careers.

Second, the idea of a bureaucratic career was in fact a male career in which women played a crucial supporting role. In the workplace, women performed the routine tasks—as clerks, secretaries, and office managers—thereby freeing up men to advance their careers. Men could concentrate on obtaining promotions or landing big accounts because the female support staff handled much of the busywork. In the domestic sphere, women also supported the bureaucratic career by caring for the home, the children, and the man's day-to-day well-being. Women allowed male bureaucrats to work long hours, travel, and focus solely on their work without concern about personal or domestic issues.

As a result of these two tendencies, early feminist writers argued, modern organizations have developed as male-dominated preserves in which women are excluded from power, denied opportunities to advance their careers, and victimized on the basis of their gender through sexual harassment and discrimination.

Women have made tremendous strides in politics, work, education, and most other domains since the 1970s. However, concerns about unequal pay, discrimination, and the male hold on power persist today. Further, women in corporate power may not necessarily implement policies that help other women

Marissa Mayer, president and CEO of Yahoo, was named one of the fifty most powerful women in business by *Fortune* magazine in 2013. As women climb the corporate ladder, will they change the methods as well as the face of management?

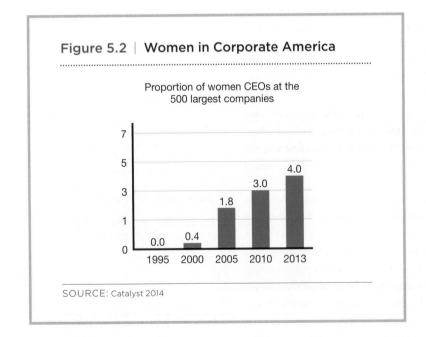

Figure 5.2 | Women in Corporate America

Proportion of women CEOs at the 500 largest companies

Year	Value
1995	0.0
2000	0.4
2005	1.8
2010	3.0
2013	4.0

SOURCE: Catalyst 2014

up the corporate ladder. For example, in February 2013, Marissa Mayer, newly appointed president and CEO of Yahoo, banned telecommuting in an effort to boost collaboration and productivity. This highly controversial policy change was criticized for making life harder for working mothers. Just a few months later, however, in April 2013, Yahoo changed its parental leave policy, increasing paid leave for both moms and dads and providing new parents with cash bonuses. This new parental leave policy may help ensure that working women (and especially mothers) can remain in and ultimately ascend the ranks at their corporate employers. ✓

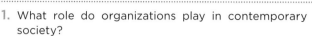

CONCEPT CHECKS ✓

1. What role do organizations play in contemporary society?

2. What does the term *bureaucracy* mean?

3. Describe five characteristics of an ideal type of bureaucracy.

4. Explain how modern organizations have developed in a gendered way.

IS BUREAUCRACY AN OUTDATED MODEL?

Familiarize yourself with some of the alternatives to bureaucracy that have developed in other societies or in recent times. Think about the influence of technology on how organizations operate.

For quite a long while in the development of Western societies, Weber's model held well. In government, hospital administration, universities, and business organizations, bureaucracy seemed to be dominant. Although informal social groups always develop in bureaucratic settings and tend to function effectively in the workplace, it seemed as though the future might be just what Weber had anticipated: constantly increasing bureaucratization.

Bureaucracies still exist aplenty in the West, but Weber's idea that a clear hierarchy of authority, with power and knowledge concentrated at the top, is the only way to run a large organization is starting to look archaic. Numerous organizations are overhauling themselves to become less, rather than more, hierarchical. Traditional bureaucratic structures are now believed to stifle innovation and creativity in cutting-edge industries. Departing from rigid vertical command structures, many organizations are turning to "horizontal," collaborative models in order to become more flexible and responsive to fluctuating markets. In this section we examine some of the main forces behind these shifts, including globalization and the growth of information technology, and consider some of the ways in which modern organizations are reinventing themselves in light of changing circumstances.

THE TRANSFORMATION OF MANAGEMENT

Traditional Western forms of management are hierarchical and authoritarian, whereas corporations in Japan, for example, typically focus on management-worker relations and try to ensure that employees at all levels feel a personal attachment to the company. The Japanese emphasis on teamwork, consensus-building approaches, and broad-based employee participation has been demonstrated to yield more productive and competitive workers. As a result, in the 1980s, many Western organizations began to introduce new management techniques in order to rival the productivity and competitiveness of their Japanese counterparts.

Two popular branches of management theory—human resource management and the corporate culture approach—have since been adopted by Western organizations. **Human resource management** is a style of management that regards a company's workforce as vital to its economic competitiveness: If the employees are not completely dedicated to the firm and its product, the firm will never be a leader in its field. To generate employee enthusiasm and commitment, the entire organizational culture must be retooled so that workers feel they have an investment in the workplace and in the work process.

The second management trend—creating a distinctive **corporate culture**—is closely related to human resource management. To promote loyalty to the company and pride in its work, the company's management works with employees to build an organizational culture involving rituals, events, or traditions unique to that company. These cultural activities are designed to draw all members of the firm—from the most senior managers to the newest employee—together in order to strengthen group solidarity. Company picnics, casual Fridays, and company-sponsored community service projects are examples of techniques for building a corporate culture.

Google, for example, has a distinctive corporate culture that is designed to help foster creativity and collaboration. The company encourages employees to design their own desks to fit their personal work styles. Scooters are kept on hand in the office so employees can zoom quickly to the other side of the building for a quick conversation with coworkers. Employees can take breaks at Lego play stations or grab a bite at gourmet cafeterias that serve free breakfast, lunch, and dinner. These quirky perks help Google to define and uphold its own unique culture. "The philosophy is very simple," said Google engineering director Craig Neville-Manning. "Google's success depends on innovation and collaboration. Everything we did was geared toward making it easy to talk" (Stewart 2013).

human resource management • A style of management that regards a company's workforce as vital to its economic competitiveness.

corporate culture • An organizational culture involving rituals, events, or traditions that are unique to a specific company.

For many, the word *corporation* conjures up images of a boring gray office. Yet, firms like Google are creating their own corporate cultures, encouraging play, creativity, and innovation in the workplace.

TECHNOLOGY AND MODERN ORGANIZATIONS

The development of **information technology**—computers and electronic communication media such as the Internet—is another factor currently influencing organizational structures (Attaran 2004; Bresnahan et al. 2002; Castells 2000, 2001; Kanter 1991; Kobrin 1997; Zuboff 1988). Since data can be processed instantaneously in any part of the world linked to a computer-based communications system, there is no need for physical proximity between those involved. As a result, the introduction of new technology has allowed many companies to reengineer their organizational structure.

As we discussed earlier in the chapter, Marissa Mayer was roundly criticized for banning telecommuting at Yahoo. Telecommuting is an example of how large organizations have become more decentralized as the more routine tasks disappear, reinforcing the tendency toward smaller, more flexible types of enterprises (Burris 1998). A good deal of office work, for instance, can be carried out by telecommuters who use the Internet and smartphones to do their work at home or somewhere other than their employer's primary office. One poll of workers in twenty-four countries found that 18 percent of workers frequently telecommuted (Ipsos 2011). Many who telecommute are "contract commuters" who work on contract, are self-employed, or are business owners, and the remaining were "employee telecommuters" who work from home for their employers. Of the estimated 26.2 million who telecommuted to work in 2010, 10 million telecommuted at least one day a week—and nearly 12 million telecommuted every day. Sixty-three percent of this work was performed at home. Telecommuters in the United States are typically males around forty years old who have college or advanced degrees and work in professional or managerial positions (WorldatWork 2011).

Telecommuting poses both advantages and disadvantages for workers and their employers. One rationale for why telecommuting increases productivity is that it eliminates time spent by workers commuting to and from the office, permitting greater concentration of energy on work-related tasks (Hartig et al. 2003). WorldatWork also found that 28 percent of employees considered working from home to be a benefit or a reward. However, these flexible new work arrangements have repercussions. First, the employees lose the human side of work; computer terminals are not an attractive substitute for face-to-face interaction with colleagues and friends at work. The flexibility of telework creates new types of stress stemming from isolation, distraction, and conflicting demands of work and home responsibilities (Ammons and Markham 2004; Raghuram and Wiesenfeld 2004). Nearly 59 percent of telecommuters say that they work longer hours because they are working at home, though employers view this increased productivity as a primary benefit of telecommuting (International Telework Association and Council [ITAC] 2004). On the other hand, management cannot easily monitor the activities of employees not under direct supervision (Dimitrova 2003; Kling 1996). While this may create problems for employers, it allows employees greater flexibility in managing their nonwork roles, thus contributing to increased worker satisfaction (Davis and Polonko 2001). Telecommuting also creates new possibilities for older workers and those with physical limitations to remain independent, productive, and socially connected (Bouma et al. 2004; Bricout 2004).

The growth of telecommuting is sparking profound changes in many social realms. It is restructuring business management practices and authority hierarchies within businesses (Illegems and Verbeke 2004; Spinks and Wood 1996), as well as contributing to new trends in housing and residential development that prioritize spatial and technological requirements for telework in homes, which are built at increasing distances from city centers (Hartig et al. 2003).

The experiences of telecommuters clearly show how organizational adaptations to new technologies can have both positive and negative consequences for

information technology •
Forms of technology based on information processing and requiring microelectronic circuitry.

More than 200 million people shop at Wal-Mart stores across the globe, but that does not mean that the chain store has been an instant success in all locations. In July 2006, Wal-Mart announced that it was pulling out of Germany, having lost hundreds of millions of dollars there since 1998. The giant retailer has also had a mixed record in its attempts to gain market share in recent years in locations throughout Asia and Latin America. The Wal-Mart model of shopping—where consumers drive to large, suburban stores, value one-stop shopping, seek quantity over quality, and aim for the lowest possible price—simply doesn't hold up throughout the world. In other nations, shoppers often do not own cars and cannot trek to large Wal-Marts on the outskirts of town. Those who take public transportation can't lug jumbo-size bottles of shampoo home from the store, nor can they fit them in the small cabinets of their houses. Many shoppers throughout the world are accustomed to making daily visits to the butcher, baker, and greengrocer and prefer fresh food to packaged foods. In some cases, Wal-Mart stocked products that simply were unfamiliar to shoppers, such as ice skates in Mexico. Wal-Mart spokespersons also noted that several of the regular practices at American stores alienated customers elsewhere, such as having clerks smile at customers (this was frowned upon as flirtatious in some areas). According to sociologist George Ritzer, the McDonaldization of corporate culture should lead to greater efficiency. If you were a corporate strategist at Wal-Mart, would you strive for uniformity in store practices throughout the world? Why or why not?

workers. While computerization has resulted in a reduction in hierarchy, it has created a two-tiered occupational structure composed of technical "experts" and less-skilled production or clerical workers. In these restructured organizations, jobs are redefined based more on technical skill than rank or position. For expert professionals, traditional bureaucratic constraints are relaxed to allow for creativity and flexibility, but other workers have limited autonomy (Burris 1993). Although professionals benefit more from this expanded autonomy, computerization makes production and service workers more visible and vulnerable to supervision (Wellman et al. 1996; Zuboff 1988).

Granted, the computerization of the workplace does have some positive effects. It has made some mundane tasks associated with clerical jobs more interesting and flexible. And, as in the case of telecommuting, computerization can contribute to greater flexibility for workers to manage both their personal and professional lives.

THE "MCDONALDIZATION" OF SOCIETY

Not everyone agrees that our society and its organizations are moving away from the Weberian view of rigid, orderly bureaucracies. The idea that we are witnessing a process of debureaucratization, they argue, is overstated.

In a contribution to the debate over debureaucratization, George Ritzer (1993) has developed a vivid metaphor to express his view of the transformations taking place in industrialized societies. He argues that although some tendencies toward debureaucratization have indeed emerged, on the whole what we are witnessing is the "McDonaldization" of society.

According to Ritzer, McDonaldization is "the process by which the principles of the fast-food restaurants are coming to dominate more and more sectors of American society as well as the rest of the world." Ritzer uses the four guiding principles for McDonald's restaurants—efficiency, calculability, uniformity, and control through automation—to show that our society is becoming ever more rationalized with time.

If you have ever visited McDonald's restaurants in two different locations, you will have noticed that there are very few differences between them. The interior decoration may vary slightly and the language spoken will most likely differ from country to country, but the layout, the menu, the procedure for ordering, the staff uniforms, the tables, the packaging, and the "service with a smile" are virtually identical. The McDonald's system is deliberately constructed to maximize efficiency and minimize human responsibility and involvement in the process. Except

What is McDonaldization? What are the consequences of highly standardized experiences?

for certain key tasks such as taking orders and pushing the start and stop buttons on cooking equipment, the restaurants' functions are highly automated and largely run themselves.

Ritzer argues that society as a whole is moving toward this highly standardized and regulated model for getting things done. Ritzer, like Weber before him, is fearful of the harmful effects of bureaucratization on the human spirit and creativity. He argues that McDonaldization is making social life more homogeneous, more rigid, and less personal. ✓

CONCEPT CHECKS ✓

1. How has the Japanese model influenced the Western approach to management?

2. Explain how the development of information technology has changed the ways people live and work.

3. According to George Ritzer, what are the four guiding principles used in McDonald's restaurants?

HOW DO GROUPS AND ORGANIZATIONS AFFECT YOUR LIFE?

Learn how social capital enables people to accomplish their goals and expand their influence.

SOCIAL CAPITAL: THE TIES THAT BIND

Most people join organizations to gain connections and increase their influence. The time and energy invested in an organization can yield valuable rewards. Parents who belong to the PTA, for example, are more likely to be able to influence school policy than those who do not belong. The members know whom to call, what to say, and how to exert pressure on school officials.

Sociologists call these benefits of organizational membership **social capital**, the social knowledge and connections that enable people to accomplish their goals and extend their influence (Coleman 1988, 1990; Loury 1987; Putnam 1993, 1995, 2000). Social capital is a broad concept and encompasses useful social networks, a sense of mutual obligation and trustworthiness, an understanding of the norms that govern effective behavior, and other social resources that enable people to act effectively. College students often become active in student government or the campus newspaper partly because they hope to learn social skills and make connections that will pay off when they graduate. They may, for example, get to interact with professors, administrators, or even successful alumni, who will then hopefully go to bat for them when they are looking for a job or applying to graduate school.

Differences in social capital mirror larger social inequalities. In general, men have more capital than women, whites more than nonwhites, the wealthy more than the poor. Differences in social capital can also be found among countries. According to the World Bank (2001), countries with high levels of social capital like the Netherlands and Finland, where businesspeople can effectively develop the "networks of trust" that foster healthy economies, are more likely to experience economic growth.

Robert Putnam (2000), a political scientist and author of the famous book *Bowling Alone*, distinguishes two types of social capital: bridging, which is outward looking and inclusive, and bonding, which is inward looking and exclusive. Bridging social capital unifies people across social cleavages, as exemplified by interfaith religious organizations or the civil rights movement, which brought blacks and whites together in the struggle for racial equality. Bonding social capital reinforces exclusive identities and homogeneous groups; it can be found in ethnic fraternal organizations, church-based women's reading groups, and elite country clubs.

People who actively belong to organizations are more likely to feel connected; they feel engaged, able to somehow make a difference. Democracy flourishes when social capital is strong. Historically, declines in organizational membership, neighborliness, and trust in organizations and corporations have been paralleled by a decline in democratic participation and trust in the government.

Although scholars have bemoaned the fact that political involvement, club membership, and other forms of social and civic engagement that bind Americans to one another eroded significantly in the late twentieth and early twenty-first centuries, the high levels of voter turnout, especially among young voters, in the presidential elections of 2008 and 2012 provide a glimmer of optimism. In the 2008 and 2012 elections, 62 and 59 percent of eligible voters went to the polls, respectively. Both figures represent high levels of participation relative to presidential elections conducted over the last forty-four years. Even more telling, however, is the stark increase in the turnout of youthful voters. Fifty-two percent of persons between the ages of eighteen and twenty-nine voted in the 2008 presidential election and 50 percent voted in 2012. Contrast those proportions with turnout rates of youthful voters of just 37 percent in 1996, 41 percent in 2000, and 48 percent in 2004 (Nonprofit Voter Engagement Network 2013).

Other indicators of social participation do not tell such an encouraging story. Attendance at public meetings concerning education or civic affairs has dropped

NONPROFIT & VOLUNTEER SECTOR

The nonprofit sector plays a key economic role worldwide. In countries such as the U.S., Israel, and Australia, the nonprofit workforce—including paid workers and volunteers—accounts for more than 10 percent of the total workforce, making it one of the largest employers of any industry.

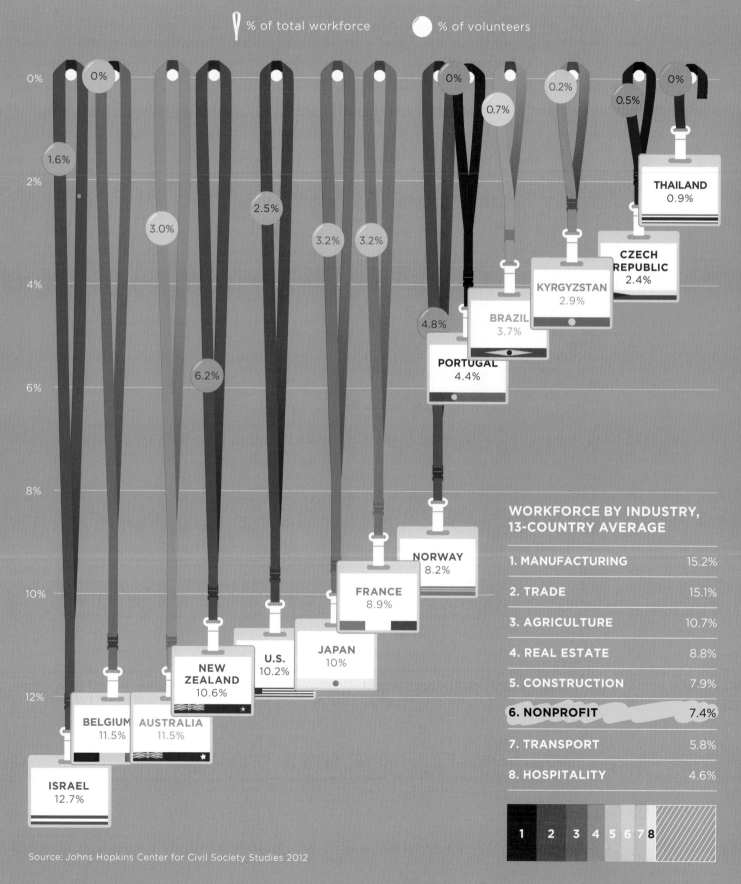

⚲ % of total workforce ⬤ % of volunteers

ISRAEL 12.7%
BELGIUM 11.5%
AUSTRALIA 11.5%
NEW ZEALAND 10.6%
U.S. 10.2%
JAPAN 10%
FRANCE 8.9%
NORWAY 8.2%
PORTUGAL 4.4%
BRAZIL 3.7%
KYRGYZSTAN 2.9%
CZECH REPUBLIC 2.4%
THAILAND 0.9%

Volunteer percentages: 1.6%, 0%, 3.0%, 6.2%, 2.5%, 3.2%, 3.2%, 4.8%, 0%, 0.7%, 0.2%, 0.5%, 0%

WORKFORCE BY INDUSTRY, 13-COUNTRY AVERAGE

Industry	%
1. MANUFACTURING	15.2%
2. TRADE	15.1%
3. AGRICULTURE	10.7%
4. REAL ESTATE	8.8%
5. CONSTRUCTION	7.9%
6. NONPROFIT	7.4%
7. TRANSPORT	5.8%
8. HOSPITALITY	4.6%

1 2 3 4 5 6 7 8

Source: Johns Hopkins Center for Civil Society Studies 2012

sharply since the 1970s. Confidence in the U.S. government has also waned, especially upon the public's discovery in June 2013 that the National Security Agency was collecting and monitoring private citizens' telephone records and Internet use. Polls in July 2013 showed that more than half of Americans believe that the federal government's monitoring program is too much of an intrusion into their privacy. Even more pessimistic are recent surveys asking Americans "How much of the time do you think you can trust the government in Washington to do what is right?" In May 2013, one national poll found that just 3 percent said "almost all the time," 12 percent said "most of the time," 47 percent indicated "some of the time," and a stunning 36 percent said "hardly ever" (Pew Research Center for the People and the Press 2013c).

However, trust in the U.S. government ebbs and flows as the world around us changes. For instance, following the terrorist attacks of September 11, 2001, researchers witnessed a resurgence of trust, with those saying that they trust the government some of the time doubling to nearly 60 percent (Pew Research Center for the People and the Press 2002). In times of crisis, Americans tend to pull together and social cohesion increases—even if just temporarily.

Some sociologists believe that another indicator of the weakening social ties in the United States is membership in clubs and social organizations. Research on declining membership in organizations such as the Sierra Club and the National Organization for Women is even more discouraging. The vast majority of these organizations' members simply pay their annual dues and receive a newsletter. Very few members actively participate, failing to develop the social capital Putnam regards as an important underpinning of democracy. Many of the most popular organizations today, such as twelve-step programs or weight loss groups, emphasize personal growth and health rather than collective goals to benefit society as a whole.

There are undoubtedly many reasons for these declines. For one, women, who were traditionally active in voluntary organizations, are more likely to hold a job than ever before. Furthermore, the commuting that results from flight to the suburbs uses up time and energy that might have been available for civic activities. But the principal source of declining civic participation, according to Putnam, is simple: television. The many hours Americans spend at home alone watching TV have replaced social engagement in the community.

However, there are reasons to speculate that voluntarism and social participation may increase in the coming decade. In 2009, President Barack Obama signed the Edward M. Kennedy Serve America Act, which authorized a significant expansion of national service programs such as AmeriCorps. Sociologists have also speculated that the economic recession has contributed to a spirit of community-mindedness, especially among young people. Empirical data provide some support for this prediction. For example, Teach for America, a program that places new teachers in poor inner-city and rural schools, saw their cohort of incoming new teachers rise from 4,000 in 2009 to 5,800 in 2012 (Teach for America 2012). Yet other service organizations, such as the Peace Corps, saw their applications fall by more than one-third between 2009 and 2012 (Vocativ 2013). The difference may reflect the fact that in tough economic times, young people want to both "do good" and obtain a salary at the same time. As such, socially minded work that pays a salary (like Teach for America) may be more appealing than service work that does not. ✓

CONCEPT CHECKS ✓

1. What is social capital?

2. Describe the difference between bridging social capital and bonding social capital.

National service programs like AmeriCorps attract young people eager to help their communities.

CONCLUSION

The primary groups of your earliest years were crucial in shaping your sense of self—a sense that changed very slowly thereafter. Throughout life, groups also instill in their members norms and values that enable and enrich social life. You may have found that close-knit, democratic groups with fair-minded leaders are better equipped to achieve their goals than less close-knit groups or those with dictatorial or narrow-minded leaders.

Although groups remain central in our lives, group affiliation in the United States is rapidly changing. As you have seen in this chapter, conventional groups appear to be losing ground in our daily life. For example, today's college students are less likely to join civic groups and organizations than were their parents, a decline that may well signal a weaker commitment to their communities. Some sociologists worry that this signals a weakening of society itself, which could bring about social instability. Yet others argue that group life has been redefined, as young people belong to virtual groups and communities via social networking websites like Facebook and LinkedIn.

The global economy and information technology are also redefining group life in many diverse ways. For instance, your parents are likely to spend much of their careers in a handful of long-lasting, bureaucratic organizations; you are much more likely to be part of a larger number of networked, "flexible" ones. As we just noted, many of your group affiliations probably are created through the Internet; in the future, your social ties may be created through other forms of communication that today can barely be envisioned. It will become increasingly easy to connect with like-minded people anywhere, creating geographically dispersed groups that span the planet—and whose members may never meet one another face-to-face.

How will these trends affect the quality of your social relationships? For nearly all of human history, most people interacted exclusively with others who were close at hand. The Industrial Revolution, which facilitated the rise of large, impersonal bureaucracies where people knew one another only casually if at all, changed social interaction. Today, the information revolution is once again changing human interaction. Tomorrow's groups and organizations could provide a renewed sense of communication and social intimacy—or they could spell further isolation and social distance.

EXERCISES:
Thinking Sociologically

1. According to Georg Simmel, what are the primary differences between dyads and triads? Explain, according to his theory, how the addition of a child would alter the relationship between spouses. Does the theory fit this situation?

2. The advent of computers and the computerization of the workplace may change our organizations and relationships with coworkers. Explain how you see modern organizations changing with the adaptation of newer information technologies.

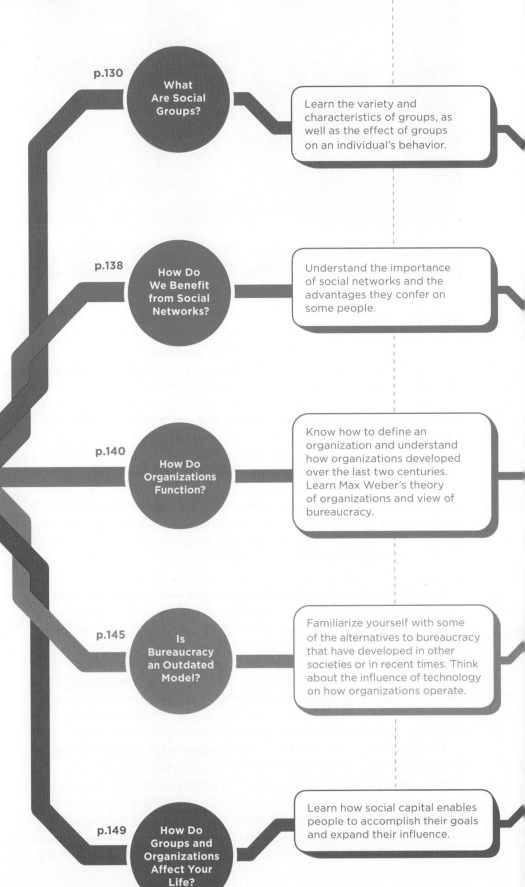

Chapter 5

Groups, Networks, and Organizations

p.130 **What Are Social Groups?**

Learn the variety and characteristics of groups, as well as the effect of groups on an individual's behavior.

p.138 **How Do We Benefit from Social Networks?**

Understand the importance of social networks and the advantages they confer on some people.

p.140 **How Do Organizations Function?**

Know how to define an organization and understand how organizations developed over the last two centuries. Learn Max Weber's theory of organizations and view of bureaucracy.

p.145 **Is Bureaucracy an Outdated Model?**

Familiarize yourself with some of the alternatives to bureaucracy that have developed in other societies or in recent times. Think about the influence of technology on how organizations operate.

p.149 **How Do Groups and Organizations Affect Your Life?**

Learn how social capital enables people to accomplish their goals and expand their influence.

social group • social aggregate • social category • in-group • out-group • primary group • secondary group • reference group • dyad • triad • leader • transformational leader • transactional leader • groupthink

1. What is the difference between social aggregates and social groups? Give examples that illustrate this difference.
2. Describe the main characteristics of primary and secondary groups.
3. When groups become large, why does their intensity decrease but their stability increase?
4. What is groupthink? How can it be used to explain why some decisions made by a group can lead to negative consequences?

network

1. According to Granovetter, what are the benefits of weak ties? Why?
2. How do men's and women's weak ties differ?

organization • formal organization • bureaucracy • ideal type • formal relations • informal networks • iron law of oligarchy • oligarchy

1. What role do organizations play in contemporary society?
2. What does the term *bureaucracy* mean?
3. Describe five characteristics of an ideal type of bureaucracy.
4. Explain how modern organizations have developed in a gendered way.

1. How has the Japanese model influenced the Western approach to management?
2. Explain how the development of information technology has changed the ways people live and work.
3. According to George Ritzer, what are the four guiding principles used in McDonald's restaurants?

human resource management • corporate culture • information technology

1. What is social capital?
2. Describe the difference between bridging social capital and bonding social capital.

social capital

6

Conformity, Deviance, and Crime

THE BIG QUESTIONS

WHAT IS DEVIANT BEHAVIOR?

Learn how sociologists define deviance and how it is closely related to social power and social class. See the ways in which conformity is encouraged.

WHY DO PEOPLE COMMIT DEVIANT ACTS?

Know the leading sociological, psychological, and biological theories of deviance and how each is useful in understanding crime.

HOW DO WE DOCUMENT CRIME?

Recognize the usefulness and limitations of crime statistics. Learn some important differences between men and women related to crime. Familiarize yourself with some of the varieties of crime.

WHOSE LIVES ARE AFFECTED BY CRIME?

Understand why members of some social groups are more likely to commit or be the victims of crime.

HOW CAN CRIME BE REDUCED?

Consider the ways in which individuals and governments can address crime.

HOW DO CRIME AND DEVIANCE AFFECT YOUR LIFE?

Understand the costs and functions of crime and deviance.

Protesters in the "Million Hoodie" March in March 2012 show their solidarity with Trayvon Martin, shot and killed the month prior by George Zimmerman, who claimed self-defense under Florida's stand-your-ground statute. Do you think the criminal justice system treats all people equally?

One of the most controversial and divisive events of the past decade was the fatal shooting of Trayvon Martin, and the subsequent acquittal of his killer, George Zimmerman. On February 26, 2012, Trayvon Martin, a seventeen-year-old high school junior, was shot and killed while walking through the multi-ethnic gated community in Sanford, Florida, where his father's fiancée lived. George Zimmerman, who resided in the community and served as a neighborhood watch volunteer, claimed he acted in self-defense when he shot Martin during an altercation. However, Martin was found to be unarmed, carrying only a pack of Skittles and an Arizona juice drink.

In June 2013, Zimmerman was put on trial for second-degree murder, but a Florida jury ultimately found him not guilty of all charges. The jury ruled that Zimmerman was justified in his use of deadly force against Martin. They determined that Zimmerman believed that shooting Martin was "necessary to prevent imminent death or great bodily harm" to himself—Florida's definition of self-defense (Alvarez and Buckley 2013). The controversial acquittal sparked protests and a nationwide debate over racial profiling and whether Zimmerman deliberately pursued Martin—a young black man wearing a hooded sweatshirt—because of his race.

The Trayvon Martin case raises countless questions for sociologists, including questions about crime, deviance, and violence. Does the criminal justice system treat all equally? How do cultural factors contribute to the perpetuation and acceptance of violence? Can we ever say that murder is "justifiable?" Sociologists are not the only ones who are captivated by such important questions. Americans are simultaneously fascinated and horrified by crime, and often search long and hard for answers to the question, "Why would someone do such a thing?" The popularity of true crime shows like *America's Most Wanted, Snapped, 48 Hours,* and *Cold Case Files* reveals our fascination with criminals and their victims. While savage crimes grab national headlines, more mundane crimes like car theft and vandalism are far more common, as we will learn later in this chapter.

Crime and punishment are tightly woven into the fabric of life in the United States. The U.S. rate of incarceration is five to eight times higher than those of Canada and the countries of Western Europe (OECD 2010). The United States is home to less than 5 percent of the world's population but almost a quarter of the world's prisoners (Walmsley 2009). The high rate of imprisonment in the United States in recent decades is due in part to "three strikes" laws, which became very popular in the 1990s. These laws require state courts to hand down mandatory and often lengthy prison sentences to persons who have been convicted of a serious criminal offense three or more times. Yet as we will see later in this chapter, not all people who commit a criminal offense are treated the same by agents of the criminal justice and legal systems.

In 2011, the number of prisoners held in federal and state facilities was just under 1.6 million (U.S. Bureau of Justice Statistics 2012b). Blacks and Latinos are overrepresented among the incarcerated. According to the U.S. Bureau of Justice Statistics, blacks accounted for 37.8 percent of the total prison and jail population yet just 13.1 percent of the overall U.S. population at the end of 2011. Hispanics made up just 16.7 percent of the U.S. population but 22.8 percent of the total jail and prison populations (U.S. Bureau of Justice Statistics 2012b).

Rates of imprisonment, in turn, have a profound impact on U.S. society. When individuals are in prison, they are not part of the labor force, and thus are not counted in the rates of unemployment reported by the government. As a result, estimates of unemployment among some subgroups, such as African American men, may be understated. At the same time, incarceration increases the long-term chances of unemployment even after someone is released from prison (Western and Beckett 1999).

The study of crime is one of the most important in sociology. But criminal behavior—whether dealing drugs or committing murder—is just one category of a much larger field of study called "deviance" or "deviant behavior." Deviants are those individuals who do not live by the rules that the majority of us follow. Some do so by choice; others are incapable of following the rules because they lack the resources to do so. Sometimes they're violent criminals, drug addicts, or down-and-outs who don't fit in with what most people would define as normal standards of acceptability. These are the cases that seem easy to identify. Yet things are not quite as they appear—a lesson sociology often teaches us, for it encourages us to look beyond the obvious. The notion of the deviant, as we shall see, is actually not an easy one to define.

We have learned in previous chapters that social life is governed by rules or norms. **Norms**, which we discussed in Chapter 2, are clearly defined and established principles or rules people are expected to observe; they represent the dos and don'ts of society. However, some norms are more powerful and important than others. Early twentieth-century sociologist William Graham Sumner identified two types of norms. **Mores** (pronounced "morays") are norms that are widely adhered to and have great social and moral significance. **Folkways**, by contrast, are the norms that

norms • Rules of conduct that specify appropriate behavior in a given range of social situations. A norm either prescribes a given type of behavior or forbids it. All human groups follow norms, which are always backed by sanctions of one kind or another—varying from informal disapproval to physical punishment.

mores • A subtype of norm; they are widely adhered to and have great moral or social significance. Violations are generally sanctioned strongly.

folkways • A subtype of norm; they guide our casual or everyday interactions. Violations are sanctioned subtly or not at all.

guide our everyday actions. For example, cutting in front of someone in line at a coffee shop would be the violation of a folkway, whereas harassing the hardworking barista would be the violation of a more.

Norms affect every aspect of our lives. Orderly behavior on the highway, for example, would be impossible if drivers didn't observe the rule of driving on the right. No deviants here, you might think, except perhaps for the drunken or reckless driver. If you did think this, you would be incorrect. When we drive, most of us are not merely deviants but criminals. Most of us regularly drive at well above the legal speed limit, and some of us even text while driving—assuming there isn't a police car in sight. In such cases, breaking the law is normal behavior!

We are all rule breakers as well as conformists. We are all also rule creators. Most American drivers may break the law on the freeway, but in fact they've evolved informal rules that are superimposed on the legal rules. When the legal speed limit on the highway is 65 miles per hour, most drivers don't go above 75 or so, and they drive slower when passing through urban areas.

When we begin the study of deviant behavior, we must consider which rules people are observing and which they are breaking. Nobody breaks all rules, just as no one conforms to all rules. As we shall see throughout this chapter, understanding who is or is not deviant, and why, is a fascinating question at the core of sociology.

WHAT IS DEVIANT BEHAVIOR?

The study of deviant behavior is one of the most intriguing yet complex areas of sociology. It teaches us that none of us is quite as normal as we might like to think. It also helps us see that people whose behavior might appear incomprehensible or odd can be seen as rational beings when we understand why they act as they do.

The study of deviance, like other fields of sociology, directs our attention to social power, which encompasses gender, race, and social class. When we look at deviance from or conformity to social rules or norms, we always have to bear in mind the question, "Whose rules?" As we shall see, social norms are strongly influenced by divisions of power and class.

Learn how sociologists define deviance and how it is closely related to social power and social class. See the ways in which conformity is encouraged.

deviance • Modes of action that do not conform to the norms or values held by most members of a group or society. What is regarded as deviant is as variable as the norms and values that distinguish different cultures and subcultures from one another.

WHAT IS DEVIANCE?

Deviance may be defined as nonconformity to a given set of norms that are accepted by a significant number of people in a community or society. No society can be divided up in a simple way between those who deviate from norms and those who conform to them. Most of us on some occasions violate generally accepted rules of behavior. Although a large share of all deviant behavior (such as committing assault or murder) is also criminal and violates the law, many deviant behaviors—ranging from bizarre fashion choices to joining a religious cult—are not criminal. By the same token, many behaviors that are technically "crimes," such as underage drinking or exceeding the speed limit, are not considered deviant because they are quite normative (see Figure 6.1). Sociologists

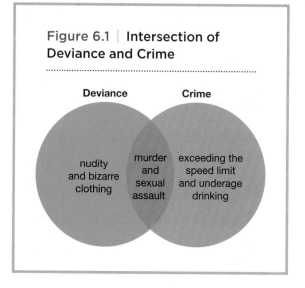

Figure 6.1 | Intersection of Deviance and Crime

Deviance — nudity and bizarre clothing

murder and sexual assault

Crime — exceeding the speed limit and underage drinking

Computer hacker Kevin Mitnick was arrested in 1995 and later convicted of stealing millions of dollars worth of software from a number of technology companies. His release from prison in 2000 was conditioned on the understanding that he would refrain from using computers or speaking publicly about technology issues.

deviant subculture • A subculture whose members hold values that differ substantially from those of the majority.

tend to focus much of their research on behaviors that are both criminal and deviant as such behaviors have importance for the safety and well-being of our nation.

Although most of us associate the word *deviant* with behaviors that we view as dangerous or unsavory, assessments of deviance are truly in the eye of the beholder, as our next example will illustrate. Kevin Mitnick has been described as the "world's most celebrated computer hacker." To computer hackers everywhere, Mitnick is a path-breaking genius whose five-year imprisonment in a U.S. penitentiary was unjust and unwarranted—proof of how misunderstood computer hacking has become with the spread of information technology. To U.S. authorities and high-tech corporations, Mitnick is one of the world's most dangerous men. A recent study estimates that hackers are responsible for 40 percent of all data breaches (Symantec Corporation 2013). Mitnick was captured by the FBI in 1995 and later convicted of downloading source code and stealing software allegedly worth millions of dollars from companies such as Motorola and Sun Microsystems. As a condition of his release from prison in January 2000, Mitnick was barred from using any communications technology other than a landline telephone. He successfully fought this legal decision and gained access to the Internet. He now is a consultant and best-selling author who teaches others about computer security (Mitnick and Simon 2011).

Over the past decade or so, hackers have been gradually transformed from a little-noticed population of computer enthusiasts to a much-reviled group of deviants who are believed to threaten the very stability of the information age. Yet, according to Mitnick and others in the hacker community, such depictions could not be further from the truth. Hackers are quick to point out that most of their activities are not criminal. Rather, they are primarily interested in exploring the edges of computer technology, trying to uncover loopholes and discover how far it is possible to penetrate other computer systems. Once flaws have been discovered, the "hacker ethic" demands that the information be shared publicly. Many hackers have even served as consultants for large corporations and government agencies, helping them defend their systems against outside intrusion.

Deviance does not refer only to individual behavior; it concerns the activities of groups as well. Heaven's Gate was a religious group whose beliefs and practices were different from those of the majority of Americans. The cult was established in the early 1970s when Marshall Herff Applewhite made his way around the West and Midwest of the United States preaching his beliefs, ultimately advertising on the Internet his belief that civilization was doomed and that the only way people could be saved was to kill themselves so their souls could be rescued by a UFO. On March 26, 1997, thirty-nine members of the cult followed his advice in a mass suicide at a wealthy estate in Rancho Santa Fe, California.

The Heaven's Gate cult represents an example of a **deviant subculture**. Its members were able to survive fairly easily within the wider society, supporting themselves by running a website business and recruiting new members by sending e-mail messages to people they thought might be interested in their beliefs. They had plenty of money and lived together in an expensive home in a wealthy California suburb.

NORMS AND SANCTIONS

We most often follow social norms because, as a result of socialization, we are accustomed to doing so. Individuals become committed to social norms through interactions with people who obey the law and mainstream values. Through these interactions, we learn self-control. The more numerous and frequent our interactions, the fewer opportunities we have to deviate from conventional norms. And, over time, the longer that we interact in ways that are conventional, the more we have to lose by not conforming (Gottfredson and Hirschi 1990).

All social norms are accompanied by sanctions that promote conformity and protect against nonconformity. A **sanction** is any reaction from others to the behavior of an individual or group that is meant to ensure that the person or group complies with a given norm. Sanctions may be positive (the offering of rewards for conformity) or negative (punishment for behavior that does not conform). They can also be formal or informal. Formal sanctions are applied by a specific body of people or an agency to ensure that a particular set of norms is followed, such as a speeding ticket or expulsion from school for cheating. Informal sanctions are less organized and more spontaneous reactions to nonconformity, such as when a student is teasingly accused by friends of being a nerd for deciding to stay home and study rather than go to a party.

The main types of formal sanctions in modern societies are those represented by the courts and prisons. The police, of course, are the agency charged with bringing offenders to trial and possible imprisonment. **Laws** are norms defined by governments as principles that their citizens must follow; sanctions are used against people who do not conform to them. Where there are laws, there are also **crimes**, since crime can most simply be defined as any type of behavior that breaks a law. ✓

sanction • A mode of reward or punishment that reinforces socially expected forms of behavior.

law • A rule of behavior established by a political authority and backed by state power.

crime • Any action that contravenes the laws established by a political authority.

CONCEPT CHECKS

1. How do sociologists define deviance?

2. Is all crime deviant? Is all deviance criminal? Why?

3. Contrast positive and negative sanctions.

WHY DO PEOPLE COMMIT DEVIANT ACTS?

Know the leading sociological, psychological, and biological theories of deviance and how each is useful in understanding crime.

One of the most vexing puzzles asked by social scientists and lay people alike is "Why are people deviant?" Part of the morbid allure of shows like *Snapped* is that we are truly puzzled and seek answers when we learn about the vicious beatings of innocent victims. Answers to the question vary widely, however, depending on one's academic discipline and even, within sociology, one's theoretical approach. We will briefly review biological and psychological explanations for deviance and will then turn to the four sociological approaches that have been developed to interpret and analyze deviance: functionalist theories, reinforcement theories, conflict theories, and interactionist theories.

THE BIOLOGICAL VIEW OF DEVIANCE

Some of the first attempts to explain crime emphasized biological factors. The Italian criminologist Cesare Lombroso, working in the 1870s, believed that criminal types could be identified by the shape of the skull. He accepted that social learning could influence the development of criminal behavior, but he regarded most criminals as biologically degenerate or defective. Lombroso's ideas were later thoroughly discredited, but similar views have repeatedly been suggested.

Another theory distinguished three main types of human physique and claimed that one type was directly associated with delinquency. Muscular, active types (mesomorphs) were considered more likely to become delinquent than those of thin physique (ectomorphs) or more fleshy people (endomorphs) (Glueck and Glueck 1956; Sheldon et al. 1949).

Most biological theories have been widely criticized on methodological grounds. Even if there were a correlation between body type and delinquency, this would not necessarily reveal that one's body type "causes" criminal behavior. For instance, people who engage in criminal activities may need to develop more muscular physiques in order to protect themselves on the streets. Moreover, nearly all studies in this field have been restricted to delinquents in reform schools, and it may be that the tougher, athletic-looking delinquents are more liable to be sent to such schools than fragile-looking, skinny ones.

More recent, methodologically rigorous research has sought to rekindle the argument that deviance has a biological or genetic basis. In a study of New Zealand children, researchers investigated whether a child's propensity for aggressive behavior was linked to biological factors present at birth (Moffitt 1996). Rather than viewing biology as deterministic, this new breed of research emphasizes that biological factors, when combined with certain social factors such as one's home environment, could lead to social situations involving crime. This perspective, which emphasizes gene-environment interaction, reasons that one's genes may "select" or draw a person into a particular behavior, such as aggression. Yet at the same time, the social environment may strengthen or weaken the link between genetics and deviant behavior. For instance, even if a baby was born with a genetic predisposition for alcoholism, that baby would not likely become a problem drinker if his or her social environment provided few opportunities to drink.

THE PSYCHOLOGICAL VIEW OF DEVIANCE

Like biological interpretations, psychological theories of crime associate criminality with particular types of personality. Some have suggested that in a minority of individuals, an amoral, or psychopathic, personality develops. **Psychopaths** are withdrawn, emotionless characters who delight in violence for its own sake.

psychopath • A specific personality type; such individuals lack the moral sense and concern for others held by most normal people.

Individuals with psychopathic traits do sometimes commit violent crimes, but there are major problems with the concept of the psychopath. It isn't at all clear that psychopathic traits are inevitably criminal. Nearly all studies of people said to possess these characteristics have been of convicted prisoners, and their personalities inevitably tend to be presented negatively. If we describe the same traits positively, the personality type sounds quite different, and there seems no reason why people of this sort should be inherently criminal. Should we be looking for psychopathic individuals for a research study, we might place the following ad (Widom and Newman 1985):

> ARE YOU ADVENTUROUS?
> Researcher wishes to contact adventurous, carefree people who've led exciting, impulsive lives. If you're the kind of person who'd do almost anything for a dare, call 337-XXXX anytime.

Such people might be explorers, spies, gamblers, or just bored with the routines of day-to-day life. They might be prepared to contemplate criminal adventures but could be just as likely to look for challenges in socially respectable ways.

Psychological theories of criminality can at best explain only some aspects of crime. While some criminals may possess personality characteristics distinct from characteristics of the remainder of the population, it is highly improbable that the majority of criminals do. There are all kinds of crimes, and it is implausible that those who commit them share some specific psychological characteristics. Some crimes are carried out by lone individuals, whereas others are the work of organized groups. It is not likely that the psychological makeup of people who are loners will have much in common with that of the members of a close-knit gang. Observational studies also can't discount the possibility that becoming involved with criminal groups influences people's outlooks, rather than that the outlooks actually produce criminal behavior in the first place.

Both biological and psychological approaches to criminality presume that deviance is a sign of something "wrong" with the individual rather than with society. They see crime and deviance as caused by factors outside an individual's control, embedded either in the body or in the mind. Often, scholars working in this tradition consider deviance to be caused by biological factors that require treatment, such as mental illness or a genetic tendency toward violence. These early approaches to criminology came under great criticism from later generations of scholars, who argued that any satisfactory account of the nature of crime must be sociological, for what crime is depends on the social institutions of a society.

SOCIOLOGICAL PERSPECTIVES ON DEVIANCE

Contemporary sociological thinking about crime emphasizes that definitions of conformity and deviance vary based on one's social context. Modern societies contain many different subcultures, and behavior that conforms to the norms of one particular subculture may be regarded as deviant outside it; for instance, there may be strong pressure on a gang member to prove himself or herself by stealing a car. Moreover, there are wide divergences of wealth and power in society that greatly influence opportunities open to different groups. Theft and burglary, not surprisingly, are carried out mainly by people from the poorer segments of the population; embezzling and tax evasion are by definition limited to persons in positions of some affluence.

FUNCTIONALIST THEORIES

Functionalist theories see crime and deviance resulting from structural tensions and a lack of moral regulation within society. If the aspirations held by individuals and groups in society do not coincide with available rewards, this disparity between desires and fulfillment will lead to deviant behavior.

CRIME AND ANOMIE: DURKHEIM AND MERTON

As we saw in Chapter 1, the notion of **anomie** was first introduced by Émile Durkheim, who suggested that in modern societies, social norms may lose their hold over individual behavior. Anomie exists when there are no clear standards to guide behavior in a given area of social life. Under such circumstances, Durkheim believed, people feel disoriented and anxious; anomie is therefore one of the social factors influencing dispositions to suicide.

anomie • A concept first brought into wide usage in sociology by Durkheim, referring to a situation in which social norms lose their hold over individual behavior.

Durkheim saw crime and deviance as social facts; he believed both of them to be inevitable and necessary elements in modern societies. According to Durkheim, people in the modern age are less constrained by social expectations than they were in traditional societies. Because there is more room for individual choice in the modern world, nonconformity is inevitable. Durkheim recognized that no society would ever be in complete consensus about the norms and values that govern it.

Deviance is also necessary for society, according to Durkheim; it fulfills two important functions. First, deviance has an adaptive function. By introducing new ideas and challenges into society, deviance is an innovative force. It brings about change. Second, deviance promotes boundary maintenance between "good" and "bad" behaviors in society. A criminal act can ultimately enhance group solidarity and clarify social norms. Deviance can also contribute to the stability of society. In his classic essay on prostitution, functionalist theorist Kingsley Davis (1937) wrote that prostitution may be illegal, yet it is functional for society because it allows married men to fulfill their sexual urges with a new partner without threatening their marriages. By contrast, a married man who forms an emotional attachment with a woman with whom he is having a "legal" though clandestine relationship can threaten both his and her marriages. Prostitution, Davis argued, indirectly contributes to the stability of the family.

Early functionalist perspectives on crime and deviance were influential in shifting attention from individual explanations to social forces. Durkheim's notion of anomie was drawn on by American sociologist Robert K. Merton (1957), who constructed a highly influential theory of deviance that located the source of crime within the very structure of American society.

Merton modified the concept of anomie to refer to the strain put on individuals' behavior when accepted norms conflict with social reality. In American society—and to some degree in other industrial societies—generally held values emphasize material success, and the means of achieving success are supposed to be self-discipline and hard work. Accordingly, it is believed that people who work hard can succeed no matter what their starting point in life. This idea is not in fact valid because most of the disadvantaged have very few conventional opportunities for advancement, such as high-quality education. Yet those who do not "succeed" find themselves condemned for their apparent inability to make material progress. In this situation, there is great pressure to try to get ahead by any means, legitimate or illegitimate. According to Merton, then, deviance is a by-product of economic inequalities.

Merton identifies five possible reactions to the tensions between socially endorsed values and the limited means of achieving them (see Figure 6.2). Conformists accept both societal values and the conventional means of realizing them regardless of whether they meet with success. The majority of the population falls into this category. Innovators accept socially approved values but use illegitimate or illegal means to follow them. Criminals who acquire wealth through illegal activities exemplify this type.

Ritualists conform to socially accepted standards although they have lost sight of the values behind these standards. They follow

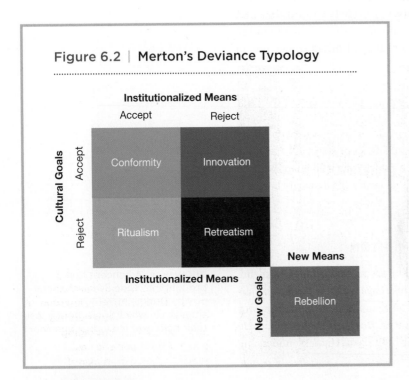

Figure 6.2 | Merton's Deviance Typology

rules for their own sake without a broader end in view, in a compulsive way. A ritualist might remain in a boring job even though it has no career prospects and provides few rewards. Retreatists have abandoned the competitive outlook altogether, thus rejecting both the dominant values and the approved means of achieving them. An example would be the members of a self-supporting commune. Finally, rebels reject both the existing values and the means of pursuing them but wish actively to substitute new values and reconstruct the social system. The members of radical political and religious groups, such as the Heaven's Gate cult, fall into this category.

Merton's writings addressed one of the main puzzles in the study of criminology: At a time when society as a whole is becoming more affluent, why do crime rates continue to rise? By emphasizing the contrast between rising aspirations and persistent inequalities, Merton points to a sense of **relative deprivation**, or the recognition that one has less than his or her peers, as an important element in deviant behavior.

relative deprivation • The recognition that one has less than his or her peers.

SUBCULTURAL EXPLANATIONS

Later researchers located deviance in terms of subcultural groups that adopt norms that encourage or reward criminal behavior. Like Merton, Albert Cohen saw the contradictions within American society as the main cause of crime. However, Cohen saw the responses occurring collectively, through subcultures, while Merton emphasized individual responses. In *Delinquent Boys* (1955), Cohen argued that boys in the lower working class who are frustrated with their positions in life often join together in delinquent subcultures, such as gangs. These subcultures reject middle-class values and replace them with norms that celebrate defiance, such as delinquency and other acts of nonconformity.

Richard A. Cloward and Lloyd E. Ohlin (1960) argued further that such gangs arise in subcultural communities where the chances of achieving success legitimately are slim, such as among deprived ethnic minorities. Recent research by sociologists has examined the validity of claims that immediate material deprivation and lack of opportunity can lead people to commit crimes. A survey of homeless youth in Canada, for instance, shows a strong correlation between hunger, lack of shelter, and

The Playboys Gang, to which these women belong, is an example of a subcultural group that has adopted norms encouraging criminal behavior, such as arms- and drug-trafficking.

unemployment, on the one hand, and theft, prostitution, and even violent crime on the other (Hagan and McCarthy 1992).

Functionalist theories rightly emphasize connections between conformity and deviance in different social contexts. We should be cautious, however, about the idea that people in poorer communities aspire to the same level of success as more affluent people. Most tend to adjust their aspirations to what they see as the reality of their situation. Merton, Cohen, and Cloward and Ohlin can all be criticized for presuming that middle-class values have been accepted throughout society. It would also be wrong to suppose that a mismatch of aspirations and opportunities is confined to the less privileged. There are pressures toward criminal activity among other groups, too, as indicated by the so-called white-collar crimes of embezzlement, fraud, and tax evasion.

REINFORCEMENT THEORIES

Sociologists studying crime and deviance in the reinforcement tradition focus on deviance as a behavior that we learn, just as we learn conventional behavior. Reinforcement theories are based on the assumption that individuals learn through rewards and punishments; we engage in behaviors that we find rewarding and either avoid or stop performing a behavior that is punished. The more we're rewarded for a behavior, the more likely we are to incorporate that behavior into our repertoire. "Rewards" and "punishments" are far-ranging and may be financial (such as a speeding ticket) or social (such as being rejected by one's friends and family). Opportunity costs, the benefits we lose or forgo by seizing another opportunity, also matter. For instance, a young person who chooses to commit a petty crime may risk being expelled from school; that is, the opportunity to get a high school diploma may be lost if one commits crimes. Opportunity costs vary widely based on one's social class, though, and persons with the lowest opportunity costs have the least to lose by committing a deviant act. A high school senior who has been accepted to a prestigious college has much more to lose upon expulsion than would a classmate who has no clear-cut plans for what to do after high school graduation.

The rewards and costs associated with committing deviant acts may also be social—such as the "reward" of acceptance by peers, or the "cost" of being shunned by one's social group. Differential association and control theory emphasize social relationships as an influence on deviant behavior. Differential association holds that we learn deviant behaviors from those significant others with whom we spend the greatest amount of time, while control theory proposes that deviance occurs when an individual's bonds to conventional society are inadequate.

LEARNED DEVIANCE: DIFFERENTIAL ASSOCIATION

One of the earliest writers to suggest that deviance is learned through interaction with others was Edwin H. Sutherland. In 1949, Sutherland advanced a notion that influenced much of the later interactionist work: He linked crime to what he called **differential association**. Differential association theory argues that we learn deviant behavior in precisely the same way we learn about conventional behavior: from our contacts with primary groups such as peers, family members, and coworkers. The term *differential* refers to the ratio of deviant to conventional social contacts. We become deviant when exposed to a higher level of deviant persons and influences, compared with conventional influences. In a society that contains a variety of subcultures, some individuals have greater exposure to social environments that encourage illegal activities.

differential association • An interpretation of the development of criminal behavior proposed by Edwin H. Sutherland, according to whom criminal behavior is learned through association with others who regularly engage in crime.

Control theory posits that crime occurs as a result of an imbalance between impulses toward criminal activity and the social or physical controls that deter it. Core assumptions are that people act rationally and that, given the opportunity, everyone would engage in deviant acts. Many types of crime, it is argued, are a result of "situational decisions"—a person sees an opportunity and is motivated to act.

One of the best-known control theorists, Travis Hirschi, has argued that humans are fundamentally rational beings who make calculated decisions about whether to engage in criminal activity by weighing the potential benefits and risks of doing so. In *Causes of Delinquency* (1969), Hirschi claimed that there are four types of bonds that link people to society and law-abiding behavior: attachment, commitment, involvement, and belief.

Attachment refers to emotional and social ties to persons who accept conventional norms, such as a peer group of students who value good grades and hard work. Commitment refers to the rewards obtained by participating in conventional activities and pursuits. For example, a high school dropout has little to lose by being arrested, whereas a dedicated student may lose his or her chance of going to college. Involvement refers to one's participation in conventional activities such as paid employment, school, or community activities. The time spent in conventional activities means time not spent in deviant activities. Finally, beliefs involve upholding morals and values that are consistent with conventional tenets of society. For example, if one believes that honesty and hard work are the keys to success, they may be less likely to resort to theft to get ahead in the world.

When sufficiently strong, these four elements help to maintain social control and conformity by rendering people unfree to break rules. If these bonds with society are weak, however, delinquency and deviance may result. Hirschi's approach suggests that delinquents are often individuals whose low levels of self-control are a result of inadequate socialization at home or at school (Gottfredson and Hirschi 1990).

control theory • A theory that views crime as the outcome of an imbalance between impulses toward criminal activity and controls that deter it. Control theorists hold that criminals are rational beings who will act to maximize their own reward unless they are rendered unable to do so through either social or physical controls.

CONFLICT THEORY

Like reinforcement theorists, adherents to **conflict theory** seek to identify why people commit crime. Conflict theorists draw on elements of Marxist thought to argue that deviance is deliberately chosen and often political in nature. Conflict theorists reject the idea that deviance is "determined" by factors such as biology, personality, anomie, social disorganization, or labels. Rather, individuals purposively engage in deviant behavior in response to the inequalities of the capitalist system. For example, many of the protesters who were arrested at Occupy Wall Street rallies were engaging in political acts that challenge the social order.

Theorists of the **new criminology** frame their analysis of crime and deviance in terms of the structure of society and the preservation of power among the ruling class. For example, they argue that laws are tools used by the powerful to maintain their own privileged positions. They reject the idea that laws are neutral and are applied evenly across the population. Instead, they claim that as inequalities increase between the ruling class and the working class, law becomes an ever-more-important instrument for the powerful to maintain order. This dynamic can be seen in the workings of the criminal justice system, which has become increasingly oppressive toward working-class "offenders," or in tax legislation that disproportionately favors the wealthy. This power imbalance is not restricted to the creation of laws, however. The powerful also

conflict theory • Argument that deviance is deliberately chosen and often political in nature.

new criminology • A branch of criminological thought, prominent in Great Britain in the 1970s, that regarded deviance as deliberately chosen and often political in nature. The new criminologists argued that crime and deviance could be understood only in the context of power and inequality within society.

break laws, but they are rarely caught. These crimes on the whole are much more significant than the everyday crime and delinquency that attract the most attention. But fearful of the implications of pursuing white-collar criminals, law enforcement instead focuses its efforts on less powerful members of society such as prostitutes, drug users, and petty thieves (Chambliss 1988; Pearce 1976).

Studies by Chambliss, Pearce, and others associated with the new criminology have played an important role in widening the debate about crime and deviance to include questions of social justice, power, and politics. They emphasize that crime occurs at all levels of society and must be understood in the context of inequalities and competing interests between social groups.

SYMBOLIC INTERACTIONIST APPROACHES

LABELING THEORY

labeling theory • An approach to the study of deviance that suggests that people become "deviant" because certain labels are attached to their behavior by political authorities and others.

Symbolic interactionists have made important contributions to our understanding of criminality, exemplified by their development of **labeling theory**. One of the earliest works based on labeling theory is Howard S. Becker's (1963) study of marijuana smokers. In the early 1960s, marijuana use was a marginal activity carried on by subcultures rather than the lifestyle choice—that is, an activity accepted by many in the mainstream of society—it is today (Hathaway 1997). Becker found that becoming a marijuana smoker depended on one's acceptance into the subculture, close association with experienced users, and one's attitudes toward nonusers. Labeling theorists like Becker interpret deviance not as a set of characteristics of individuals or groups but as a process of interaction between deviants and nondeviants. In other words, it is not the act of marijuana smoking that makes one a deviant but the way others react to marijuana smoking. While other sociological perspectives are focused on why people are deviant, labeling theorists seek to understand why some people become tagged with a deviant label.

In short, persons with the greatest social and economic power tend to place labels on those with less social power. Further, the labels that create categories of deviance thus express the power structure of society. The rules in terms of which deviance is

According to interactionists, it's not the act of smoking marijuana that makes one a deviant, but the way others react to marijuana smoking.

defined are framed by the wealthy for the poor, by men for women, by older people for younger people, and by ethnic majorities for minority groups. For example, many children wander into other people's gardens, steal fruit, or play truant. In an affluent neighborhood, these might be regarded by parents, teachers, and police alike as relatively innocent pastimes of childhood. In poor areas, they might be seen as evidence of tendencies toward juvenile delinquency.

Once a child is labeled a delinquent, he or she is stigmatized as a deviant and is likely to be considered untrustworthy by teachers and prospective employers. He or she then relapses into further criminal behavior, widening the gulf with orthodox social conventions. Edwin Lemert (1972) called the initial act of rule breaking **primary deviance**. **Secondary deviance** occurs when the individual comes to accept the label and sees himself or herself as deviant. The "self-fulfilling prophecy" may occur, where the labeled person begins to behave in such a way that perpetuates the deviant behavior. Research has shown that how we think of ourselves and how we believe others perceive us influence our propensity for committing crime. One study of a random national sample of young men showed that such negative self-appraisals are strongly tied to levels of criminality; in other words, the perception that one is deviant may in fact motivate deviant behavior (Matsueda 1992).

Labeling theory is important because it begins from the assumption that no act is intrinsically deviant. Rather, to be "deviant," one must be labeled as such. In the case of criminal activity, definitions of criminality are established by the powerful through the formulation of laws and their interpretation by police, courts, and correctional institutions. Critics of labeling theory have sometimes argued that certain acts such as murder, rape, and robbery are consistently prohibited across virtually all cultures. This view is surely incorrect. Even within our own culture, killing is not always regarded as murder; in times of war, killing of the enemy is positively approved. And as we saw in the chapter introduction, George Zimmerman, who shot and killed Trayvon Martin, was ultimately found not guilty of murder by a Florida jury. The jury ruled that Zimmerman acted in self-defense and was therefore protected under the state's stand-your-ground law, which permits an individual to use deadly force when faced with the risk of great bodily harm.

We can more convincingly criticize labeling theory on other grounds. First, in emphasizing the active process of labeling, labeling theorists neglect the processes that lead to acts defined as deviant. Labeling certain activities as deviant is not completely arbitrary; differences in socialization, attitudes, and opportunities influence how far people engage in behavior likely to be labeled deviant. For instance, children from deprived backgrounds are on average more likely to steal from shops than are richer children. It is not the labeling that leads them to steal in the first place so much as the background from which they come.

Second, it is not clear whether labeling actually does have the effect of increasing deviant conduct. Delinquent behavior tends to increase following a conviction, but is this the result of the labeling itself? Other factors, including increased interaction with other delinquents or learning about new criminal opportunities, may be involved.

primary deviance • According to Edwin Lemert, the actions that cause others to label one as a deviant.

secondary deviance • According to Edwin Lemert, following the act of primary deviance, secondary deviation occurs when an individual accepts the label of deviant and acts accordingly.

THEORETICAL CONCLUSIONS

The contributions of the sociological theories of crime are twofold. First, these theories correctly emphasize that criminal and "respectable" behavior are not two discrete categories; rather, they are points along a continuum. The contexts in which

1. What are the main similarities and differences between biological and psychological views of deviance?

2. How do Merton's and Durkheim's definitions of anomie differ?

3. According to subcultural explanations, how does criminal behavior get transmitted from one group to another?

4. What is the core idea behind differential association theory?

5. What are two criticisms of labeling theory?

6. What are the root causes of crime, according to conflict theorists?

particular types of activity are seen as criminal and punishable by law vary widely. Second, all agree that context is important in criminal activities. Whether someone engages in a criminal act or comes to be regarded as a criminal is influenced fundamentally by social learning and social surroundings.

The way in which crime is understood directly affects the policies developed to combat it. For example, if crime is seen as the product of deprivation or social disorganization, policies might be aimed at reducing poverty and strengthening social services. If criminality is seen as voluntaristic, or freely chosen by individuals, attempts to counter it will take a different form. Now let's look directly at the nature of the criminal activities occurring in modern societies, paying particular attention to crime in the United States. ✓

Recognize the usefulness and limitations of crime statistics. Learn some important differences between men and women related to crime. Familiarize yourself with some of the varieties of crime.

HOW DO WE DOCUMENT CRIME?

How dangerous are our streets compared with those of yesteryear? Is American society more violent than other societies? You should be able to use the sociological skills you have already developed to answer these questions.

In Chapter 1, for example, we learned a little about how to interpret statistics. Crime statistics are a constant focus of attention in the media. Most TV and newspaper reporting is based on official statistics on crime, collected by the police and published by the government. Most of these reports are based on two sources: Uniform Crime Reports (UCR) and victimization studies. Each has its own limitations and offers only a partial portrait of crime in American life.

Uniform Crime Reports (UCR) • Documents that contain official data on crime that is reported to law enforcement agencies that then provide the data to the FBI.

Uniform Crime Reports (UCR) contain official data on crime that is reported to law enforcement agencies across the country that then provide the data to the FBI. UCR focus on "index crimes," which include serious crimes such as murder and non-negligent manslaughter, robbery, forcible rape, aggravated assault, burglary, larceny/theft, motor vehicle theft, and arson. Critics of UCR note that the reports do not accurately reflect crime rates because they include only those crimes reported to law enforcement agencies; they don't, for example, include crimes reported to other agencies such as the IRS. Further, the index crimes do not include less serious crimes. Some argue that by excluding crimes that are traditionally committed by middle-class persons, such as fraud and embezzlement, UCR reify the belief that crime is an activity of ethnic minorities and the poor.

Because the UCR program focuses narrowly on crimes reported to the police, criminologists also rely on self-reports, or reports provided by the crime victims themselves. This second source of data is essential, as some criminologists think that about half of all serious crimes, such as robbery with violence, go unreported. The proportion of less serious crimes, especially small thefts, that don't come to the attention of the police is even higher. Since 1973, the Bureau of the Census has been interviewing households across the country to find out how many members were the victims of particular crimes over the previous six months. This procedure, which is called the National Crime Victimization Survey, has confirmed that the overall rate of crime is higher than the reported crime index. Crimes where victims may feel stigmatized are most likely to go unreported. Likewise, particularly vulnerable victims, such as older adults, may be reluctant to report a crime for fear their assailant will seek retribution. For instance, in 2012, only 28 percent of rape or sexual assault victimizations were reported, compared with 56 percent of robberies. In 2012, only 34 percent of property crimes were reported, including 26 percent of thefts and 55 percent of burglaries. Auto theft is the crime most frequently reported to the police (79 percent) (U.S. Bureau of Justice Statistics 2013a).

Public concern in the United States tends to focus on crimes of violence—murder, assault, and rape—even though only about 11.9 percent of all crimes are violent (Federal Bureau of Investigation [FBI] 2013a). To put this in perspective, roughly 1.2 million violent crimes occurred in the United States in 2012 compared with nearly 9 million property offenses, including vandalism and home break-ins. In general, whether indexed by police statistics or by the National Crime Victimization Survey, violent crime, burglary,

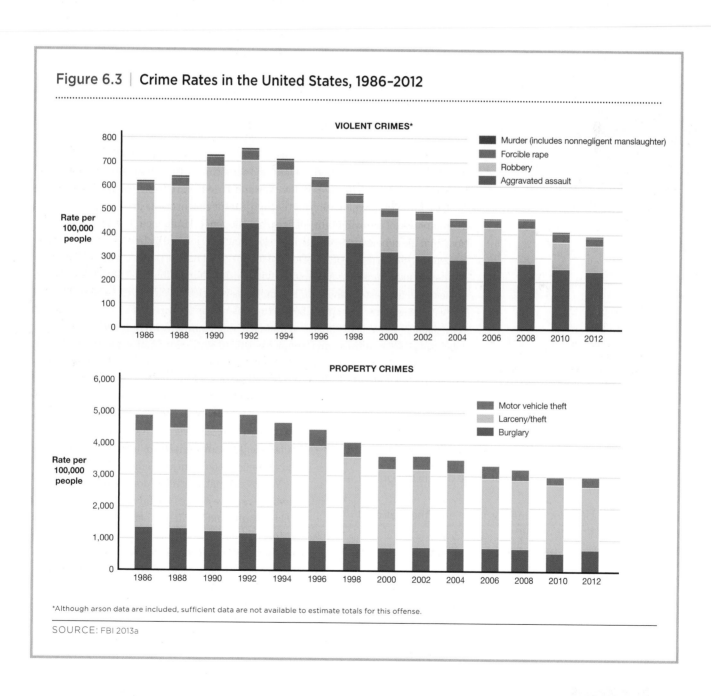

Figure 6.3 | Crime Rates in the United States, 1986–2012

*Although arson data are included, sufficient data are not available to estimate totals for this offense.

SOURCE: FBI 2013a

and car theft are more common in cities than in the suburbs surrounding them, and they are more common in the suburbs than in smaller towns.

In the 1990s, there was a drop in the overall crime rate throughout the United States to its lowest levels since 1973, when the victimization survey was first used. The steepest drops were recorded for violent crimes, including murder and robbery. After steady declines during the 1990s, rates declined slightly or leveled off in the first decade of the 2000s. There is no one prevailing explanation among sociologists for these declines, although many politicians would like to take credit for them. Aggressive efforts by local police to stop the use of guns certainly contributed to the decrease in homicides, but other social factors were also at work. Key among these were the declining market for crack cocaine and the stigmatization of crack among young urban dwellers and the booming economy of the 1990s, which provided job opportunities for those who may otherwise have been enticed to work in the drug trade (Levitt 2004).

One reason often given for the relatively high rates of violent crime in the United States is the widespread availability of handguns and other firearms. In the days following the deadly shooting of twenty children and six adult staff members at Sandy Hook Elementary School in Connecticut in 2012, President Obama spoke out strongly against easy access to handguns in the United States. However, just months later, the U.S. Senate defeated legislation to control access to guns. The belief that one has a personal right to "bear arms" is widespread in American culture.

But gun control laws alone would not be sufficient to tackle violent crime in the United States. Switzerland has very low rates of violent crime, yet firearms are easily accessible. All Swiss males are members of the citizen army and keep weapons in their homes, including rifles, revolvers, and sometimes other automatic weapons, plus ammunition; and gun licenses in Switzerland are easy to obtain (Bachmann 2012).

The most likely explanation for the high level of violent crime in the United States is a combination of the availability of firearms, the general influence of the "frontier tradition," and the subcultures of violence in large cities. Violence by frontiersmen and vigilantes is an honored part of American history; Daniel Boone, Davey Crockett, and other folk heroes are almost always depicted with a rifle in hand (Charles River Editors 2013). Some of the first established immigrant areas in cities developed their own informal modes of neighborhood control, backed by violence or the threat of violence. Similarly, young people in African American and Hispanic communities today have developed subcultures of manliness and honor associated with rituals of violence, and some belong to gangs whose everyday life is one of drug dealing, territory protection, and violence (Venkatesh 2008). Many states, including Florida, where George Zimmerman was arrested and tried, uphold a stand-your-ground law, which allows a person to use deadly force in self-defense without first attempting to retreat. This controversial law is believed by many social scientists to normalize or justify the use of guns and violence (Vedantam and Schultz 2013).

While dramatic crimes dominate the evening news, less severe crimes are far more commonplace. Most assaults and homicides bear little resemblance to the heinous, random acts of gunmen or the carefully planned homicides given most prominence in the media. Murders generally happen in the context of family and other interpersonal relationships; the victim usually knows his or her murderer. ✓

CONCEPT CHECKS ✓

1. What are the main sources of crime data in the United States?

2. Contrast Uniform Crime Reports and the National Crime Victimization Survey.

3. Describe crime trends in the 1970s through today.

4. How would sociologists explain the high rate of violent crime in the United States?

WHOSE LIVES ARE AFFECTED BY CRIME?

Are some individuals or groups more likely to commit crimes or to become the victims of crime? Criminologists say yes; research and crime statistics show that crime and victimization are not random occurrences across the population. Men, young persons, and African Americans are more likely than women, older persons, and whites to be both crime victims and perpetrators. Young African American men like Trayvon Martin face a triple disadvantage in the United States: Being young, black, and male are each associated with an elevated death rate due to murder (see Figure 6.4). For example, the rate of murder among black male teenagers is over six times the rate for their white counterparts, though this disparity has been declining in recent years.

Emerging evidence suggests that sexual minorities, including gays, lesbians, and transgendered persons, may also have a higher-than-average risk of crime victimization, including hate crimes. A **hate crime** is a criminal act motivated by some bias, such as racism, sexism, or homophobia. In 2012, 5,796 hate crimes were reported in the United States. Roughly half were racially motivated, 21 percent resulted from sexual orientation bias, 19 percent by religious bias, 20 percent stemmed from ethnicity/national origin bias, and 2 percent were prompted by disability bias (FBI 2013).

hate crime • A criminal act by an offender who is motivated by some bias, such as racism, sexism, or homophobia.

As of 2010, forty-five states have enacted laws criminalizing various types of bias-motivated violence or intimidation. While all of these laws cover bias on the basis of race, religion, and ethnicity, some states also cover other attributes such as sexual orientation or disability status. However, high-profile cases of homophobic attacks may spur states to widen their scope of protected groups (FBI 2012a). For instance, in late August 2013, twenty-one-year-old Islan Nettles was walking with a friend on a hot summer night in East Harlem. The two struck up a conversation with a group of young men. After the men discovered that Nettles and her friend were transgendered women, they started shouting homophobic insults and viciously beat Nettles into a coma. She died soon thereafter, raising public awareness of the victimization of young people on the basis of their sexuality.

The likelihood of someone becoming a victim of crime is not linked only to their personal characteristics. Rather, victimization rates also vary based on where a person lives. Areas suffering from greater material deprivation generally have higher crime rates. Individuals living in poor inner-city neighborhoods run a much greater risk of becoming victims of crime than do residents of more affluent suburban areas. That ethnic minorities are concentrated disproportionately in inner-city regions appears to be a significant factor in their higher rates of victimization.

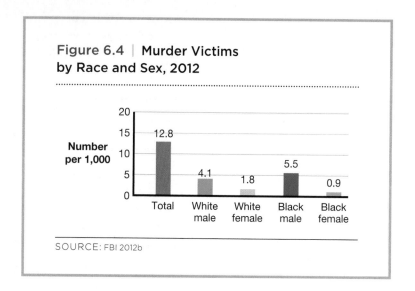

Figure 6.4 | Murder Victims by Race and Sex, 2012

Number per 1,000

	Total	White male	White female	Black male	Black female
	12.8	4.1	1.8	5.5	0.9

SOURCE: FBI 2012b

GENDER AND CRIME

If Americans are fascinated by true crime, they are perhaps even more spellbound by cases where women are charged with unthinkable crimes, such as the high-visibility cases of Casey Anthony and Amanda Knox, the American college student who was tried for the murder of her housemate Meredith Kercher when the two were studying abroad in Italy. Sociological studies of crime and deviance have traditionally ignored half the population. Feminists have been correct in criticizing criminology for being a male-dominated discipline in which women are largely invisible in both theoretical considerations and empirical studies. Since the 1970s, many important feminist works have drawn attention to the way in which criminal transgressions by women occur in different contexts from those by men and to how women's experiences with the criminal justice system are influenced by certain gendered assumptions about appropriate male and female roles. Feminists have also played a critical role in highlighting the prevalence of violence against women, both at home and in public.

MALE AND FEMALE CRIME RATES

The statistics on gender and crime are startling. In 2011, an overwhelming 93 percent of people in jail were men ages eighteen and older (U.S. Bureau of Justice Statistics 2012b). Men drastically outnumber women in prison, not only in the United States but in all industrialized countries. Women ages eighteen and older made up only 7 percent of the American prison population in 2011 and that number has dropped significantly in recent years according to a report prepared by the Sentencing Project (2013). Men and women also vary in the types of crimes they commit; women rarely engage in violent crime and instead tend to commit less serious offenses. Petty thefts like shoplifting and public order offenses such as public drunkenness and prostitution are typical female crimes.

Recent research by feminist scholars, however, reveals that violence is not exclusively a characteristic of male criminality. By studying girl gangs, female terrorists,

Amanda Knox, an American citizen charged with murdering her roommate while studying abroad in Perugia, is escorted to a court appearance by Italian police.

and women prisoners, scholars have demonstrated that women do in fact participate in violent crime (albeit less often than men). Moreover, men and women are often quite similar in their motivations for turning to criminal behavior.

One thing is clear, though: Female rates of criminality are consistently lower than those of men. A controversial argument set forth in the 1950s proposed that the gender gap in crime may be less vast than statistics suggest. Otto Pollak (1950) argued that women's crimes may go undetected or unreported, or may be treated more leniently by (male) police officers, who adopt a "chivalrous" attitude toward them. A number of empirical studies have been undertaken to test the chivalry thesis, but the results remain inconclusive.

There is some evidence, however, that female lawbreakers quite often escape coming before the courts because they are able to persuade the police or other authorities to see their actions in a particular light. They invoke what has been called the "gender contract"—the implicit contract between men and women whereby to be a woman is to be erratic and impulsive, on the one hand, and in need of protection on the other (Worrall 1990). Yet differential treatment could hardly account for the vast difference between male and female rates of crime.

The reasons are almost certainly the same as those that explain gender differences in other spheres. "Male crimes" remain "male" because of differences in socialization and because men's activities and involvements are still more nondomestic than those of most women. Further, control theory may also offer insights. Because women are usually the primary caregivers to their children and other relatives, they may have attachments and commitments that deter them from committing deviant acts. Imprisonment would have very high and undesirable costs both to women and to their kin.

As the boundaries between men's and women's social roles increasingly blur, however, criminologists have predicted that gender equality will reduce or eliminate the differences in criminality between men and women. Whether the variations between female and male crime rates will one day disappear we still cannot say with any certainty.

YOUTH AND CRIME

Popular fear about crime centers on offenses such as theft, burglary, assault, and rape—street crimes that are largely seen as the domain of young working-class males. Media coverage of rising crime rates often focuses on moral breakdown among young people and highlights such issues as vandalism, school truancy, and drug use to illustrate the increasing permissiveness in society. This equation of youth with criminal activity is not a new one, according to some sociologists. Young people are often taken as an indicator of the health and welfare of society itself.

Official crime statistics do reveal high rates of offense among young people; 28 percent of all offenders arrested for criminal offenses in 2012 were age twenty-one or younger (FBI 2013b). For both males and females, the share of arrests peaks around age eighteen or nineteen and declines thereafter (FBI 2013b). Control theory has been used to explain this pattern, called the age-crime curve. As young people gradually transition into adulthood, they acquire those social attachments and commitments that make "conventional" behavior rewarding. As they marry, have children, find jobs, and set up their own homes, the "cost" of deviance is high; rational actors would not want to risk losing their families and homes and thus avoid deviant acts.

Although criminologists have demonstrated persuasively that most youthful deviants go on to lead perfectly happy, healthy, law-abiding lives, widespread panic about youth criminality persists. Importantly, this panic may not accurately reflect social reality. An isolated event involving young people and crime can be transformed symbolically into a full-blown crisis of childhood, demanding tough law-and-order responses. The high-profile mass murders at Columbine High School, Virginia Tech University, Sandy Hook Elementary School, and a movie theater in Aurora, Colorado, are examples of how moral outrage can deflect attention from larger societal issues. Columbine was a watershed event in media portrayals of youth crime, and some have speculated that it led to "copycat" school killings in high schools in Arkansas, Kentucky, California, and elsewhere. Even though the number of murders committed on school and university grounds has been declining over the past half-century, attention to these mass murders has led many to think that all youth are potential violent threats. The perpetrators of these killings were labeled "monsters" and "animals"; less attention was paid to how easily they were able to obtain the weapons they used to commit these murders.

Similar caution can be expressed about the popular view of drug use by teenagers. Every year, the Department of Health and Human Services conducts the National Survey of Drug Use and Health about drug-use habits. In 2011 it surveyed more than 70,000 noninstitutionalized individuals over the age of twelve and found that 25.1 percent of respondents between the ages of twelve and twenty had reported drinking alcohol in the previous month, 15.8 percent had participated in binge drinking at least once in the prior month, 39.5 percent of young adults between the ages of eighteen and twenty-five are current tobacco users, and 21.4 percent had used an illicit drug in the last month (U.S. Department of Health and Human Services 2012c).

Trends in drug use have shifted away from hard drugs, such as heroin, and toward combinations of substances such as amphetamines, prescription drugs like Oxycontin, alcohol, and Ritalin and other stimulants. The war on drugs, some have argued, criminalizes large segments of the youth population who are generally law abiding (Muncie 1999).

Taking illegal drugs, like other forms of socially deviant behavior, is often defined in racial, class, and cultural terms; different drugs come to be associated with different groups and behaviors. When crack cocaine appeared in the 1980s, it was quickly defined by the media as the drug of choice for black inner-city kids who listened to hip-hop. Perhaps as a result, jail sentences for crack possession were set at higher levels than sentences for possession of cocaine, which was associated more with white and suburban users. Ecstasy has, until recently, had similar white and middle- or upper-class associations.

CRIMES OF THE POWERFUL

It is plain enough to see that there are connections between crime and poverty. But it would be a mistake to assume that crime is concentrated among the poor. Crimes carried out by people in positions of power and wealth can have farther-reaching consequences than the often petty crimes of the poor. One of the most devastating events of the early twenty-first century was the discovery that then-trusted investment adviser Bernie Madoff had defrauded his clients—many of them senior citizens and charitable organizations—robbing them of more than $18 billion. Madoff had run an elaborate Ponzi scheme, which left many of his investors destitute and nearly bankrupted charitable organizations such as the Elie Wiesel Foundation and Stony

One of the most high-profile white-collar criminals in recent memory is Bernie Madoff, a financier who choreographed a $50 million Ponzi scheme to defraud thousands of people and organizations.

Brook University Foundation (Creswell and Thomas 2009). This case revealed just how devastating the effects of white-collar crime can be.

The term **white-collar crime**, first introduced by Edwin Sutherland (1949), refers to crime typically carried out by people in the more affluent sectors of society. This category of criminal activity includes tax fraud, antitrust violations, illegal sales practices, securities and land fraud, embezzlement, the manufacture or sale of dangerous products, and illegal environmental pollution, as well as straightforward theft. The distribution of white-collar crimes is even harder to measure than that of other types of crime; most do not appear in the official statistics at all.

Efforts to detect white-collar crime are ordinarily limited, and it is only on rare occasions that those who are caught go to jail. Although the authorities regard white-collar crime in a more tolerant light than crimes of the less privileged, it has been calculated that the amount of money involved in white-collar crime in the United States is forty times greater than the amount involved in crimes against property, such as robberies, burglaries, larceny, forgeries, and car thefts (President's Commission on Organized Crime 1986). Some forms of white-collar crime, moreover, affect more people than lower-class criminality. An embezzler might rob thousands—or today, via computer fraud, millions—of people.

white-collar crime • Criminal activities carried out by those in white-collar, or professional, jobs.

CORPORATE CRIME

Corporate crime refers to criminal offenses committed by large corporations. Pollution, product mislabeling, and violations of health and safety regulations affect much larger numbers of people than does petty criminality. Both quantitative and qualitative studies of corporate crime have concluded that a large number of corporations do not adhere to the legal regulations that apply to them (Slapper and Tombs 1999). Corporate crime is not confined to a few bad apples but is instead pervasive and widespread. Studies have revealed six types of violations linked to large corporations: administrative (paperwork or noncompliance), environmental (pollution, permit violations), financial (tax violations, illegal payments), labor (working conditions, hiring practices), manufacturing (product safety, labeling), and unfair trade practices (anticompetition, false advertising).

Sometimes there are obvious victims, as in environmental disasters such as the 1984 spill at the Bhopal chemical plant in India and the health dangers posed to women

corporate crime • Offenses committed by large corporations in society, including pollution, false advertising, and violations of health and safety regulations.

by silicone breast implants. One of the most devastating examples in recent years was the collapse of an eight-story commercial building, Rana Plaza, in Bangladesh in April 2013. The death toll topped 1,100 with an additional 2,500 injured people rescued from the building. Rana Plaza housed several garment manufacturers. Although building inspectors had found cracks in the building days earlier and recommended that the building be evacuated and shut down, many of the garment workers were forced to return to work the following day. Their supervisors had declared the building to be "safe." Managers at some of the companies even threatened to withhold a month's pay from workers who refused to come to work (Manik and Yardley 2013).

As the Rana Plaza tragedy demonstrates, the hazards of corporate crime are all too real. But very often, victims of corporate crime do not see themselves as such. This is because in "traditional" crimes, the proximity between victim and offender is much closer; it is difficult not to realize that you have been mugged! In the case of corporate crime, greater distances in time and space mean that victims may not realize they have been victimized or may not know how to seek redress for the crime.

The effects of corporate crime are often experienced unevenly within society. Those who are disadvantaged by other types of socioeconomic inequalities tend to suffer disproportionately. For example, safety and health risks in the workplace tend to be concentrated most heavily in low-paying occupations. Many of the risks from health-care products and pharmaceuticals have had a greater impact on women than on men, as is the case with contraceptives or fertility treatments with harmful side effects (Slapper and Tombs 1999).

The collapse of Rana Plaza in Bangladesh, which killed at least 1,100 and injured another 2,500, is a tragic example of corporate crime.

An Afghan policeman sits near poppy bulbs confiscated during a raid on an opium farmer's field near Kandahar.

ORGANIZED CRIME

Organized crime refers to forms of activity that have some of the characteristics of orthodox business but that are illegal. Organized crime embraces illegal gambling, drug dealing, prostitution, large-scale theft, and protection rackets, among other activities. In *End of Millennium* (1998), Manuel Castells argues that the activities of organized crime groups are becoming increasingly international in scope. The coordination of criminal activities across borders—with the help of new information technologies—is becoming a central feature of the new global economy. Involved in activities ranging from the narcotics trade to counterfeiting to smuggling immigrants and human organs, organized crime groups are now operating in flexible international networks rather than within their own territorial realms.

According to Castells, criminal groups set up strategic alliances with one another. The international narcotics trade, weapons trafficking, the sale of nuclear material, and money laundering have all become linked across borders and crime groups. The flexible nature of this networked crime makes it relatively easy for crime groups to evade the reach of law-enforcement initiatives.

Despite numerous campaigns by the government and the police, the narcotics trade is one of the most rapidly expanding international criminal industries, with an annual growth rate of more than 10 percent in the 1980s and early 1990s and an extremely high level of profit. The United Nations Office on Drugs and Crime (2013) has estimated that the annual value of global trade in illegal drugs is higher than annual global trade in coffee, grains, or meat. Heroin networks stretch across Asia, particularly South Asia, and are also located in North Africa, the Middle East, and Latin America. Supply lines also pass through Vancouver and other parts of Canada; from those places, drugs are commonly supplied to the United States. ✓

organized crime • Criminal activities carried out by organizations established as businesses.

CONCEPT CHECKS ✓

1. Contrast the following two explanations for the gender gap in crime: behavioral differences and biases in reporting.

2. What is the age-crime curve, and what factors have contributed to this pattern?

3. What are some of the consequences of white-collar crime?

4. Give one example of an activity classified as organized crime.

HOW CAN CRIME BE REDUCED?

Despite the limitations of official crime statistics, they do provide laypersons with a snapshot of criminal activity in their neighborhoods. However, citizens often perceive themselves to be at greater risk of falling victim to crime than crime statistics would predict. Residents of inner-city areas have more reason to be concerned about crime than do people living in other settings. Regardless of whether these fears are accurate, both individuals and governments feel strongly that crime and victimization must be curtailed. In fact, one of the central tasks of social policy in modern states has been controlling crime and delinquency. Which policies and practices are most effective? And why?

ARE PRISONS THE ANSWER?

According to police statistics, rates of violent crime have declined since 1990. Ironically, however, many people in the United States continue to view crime as their most serious social concern (Lacayo 1994). Surveys show that Americans favor tougher prison sentences for all but relatively minor crimes. The price of imprisonment, however, is enormous: In 2011, it cost an average of $28,893 to keep a prisoner in the federal prison system for one year, an amount that was up from $25,985 in 2008 (U.S. Bureau of Prisons 2013; U.S. Courts 2008). Some argue that this is not money well spent: Even if the prison system were expanded, it wouldn't reduce the level of serious crime a great deal. Only about a fifth of all serious crimes result in an arrest—and this is of crimes known to the police, an underestimate of the true rate of crime. And no more than half of the arrests for serious crimes result in a conviction. Even so, America's prisons are so overcrowded (Figure 6.5) that the average convict serves only a third of his or her sentence.

The United States already locks up more people (nearly all men) per capita than any other country. Nearly 1.6 million people are presently incarcerated in American prisons (U.S. Bureau of Justice Statistics 2013b). More than one-quarter of African American men are either in prison or otherwise under the control of the penal system. Forty-eight percent of individuals imprisoned under federal jurisdiction are serving sentences for nonviolent drug-related crimes (U.S. Bureau of Justice Statistics 2012b).

Support for capital punishment, or the death penalty, is also high in the United States. In 2012, approximately 63 percent of adults surveyed said that they believed in capital punishment; 32 percent opposed it (Gallup Organization 2012). This represents a significant shift from 1965, when 38 percent of those surveyed supported the death penalty and 47 percent were opposed. However, given the choice between the death penalty and life imprisonment, the share of those supporting the death penalty falls to 48 percent (Quinnipiac University Poll 2013).

Just as Americans' acceptance of the death penalty has increased over time, the number of individuals awaiting execution has climbed since 1977, when the Supreme Court upheld state capital punishment laws. Since that time, there have been 1,340 executions in the United States (Death Penalty Information Center 2013). Nearly two-thirds (64 percent) of these executions have taken place in five states: Texas (502), Virginia (110), Oklahoma (105), Florida (77), and Missouri (68)

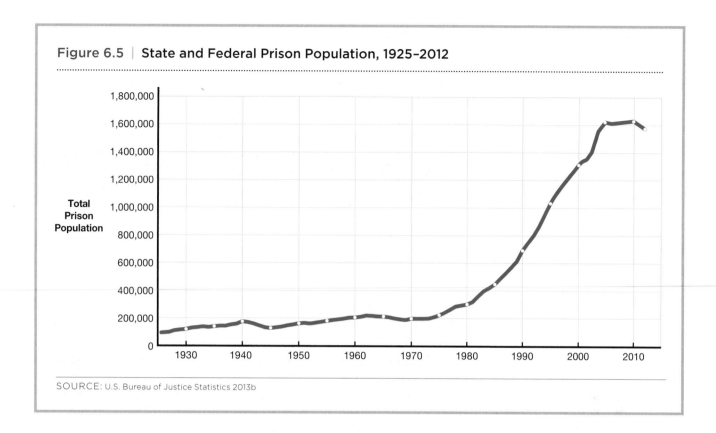

Figure 6.5 | State and Federal Prison Population, 1925–2012

SOURCE: U.S. Bureau of Justice Statistics 2013b

(Death Penalty Information Center 2013). In mid-2013, a total of 3,125 prisoners were held on death row. Blacks accounted for 42 percent of inmates on death row despite representing just 13 percent of the overall U.S. population. Nearly all (98 percent) were men. In 2012, a total of forty-three prisoners were executed in nine states.

While we might suppose that imprisoning large numbers of people or stiffening sentences would deter individuals from committing crimes, there is little evidence to support this. In fact, sociological studies have demonstrated that prisons can easily become schools for crime. Instead of preventing people from committing crimes, prisons often actually make them more hardened criminals. This pattern is consistent with the key theme of differential association theory, discussed earlier. Deviance is learned by deviant peers. The more harsh and oppressive prison conditions are, the more likely inmates are to be brutalized by the experience. Yet if prisons were made into attractive and pleasant places to live, would they have a deterrent effect?

Although prisons do keep some dangerous men (and a tiny minority of dangerous women) off the streets, evidence suggests that we need to find other means to deter crime. A sociological interpretation of crime makes clear that there are no quick fixes. The causes of crime, especially violent crimes, are bound up with structural conditions of American society, including widespread poverty, the condition of the inner cities, and the deteriorating life circumstances of many young men.

THE MARK OF A CRIMINAL RECORD

An experiment by sociologist Devah Pager (2003) showed the long-term consequences of prison on the lives of felons. Pager had pairs of young black and white men apply for real entry-level job openings throughout the city of Milwaukee. The applicant pairs were matched by appearance, by interpersonal style, and, most important, by all job-related characteristics such as education level and prior work experience. In addition to varying the race of the applicant pairs, Pager also had applicants alternate presenting themselves to employers as having criminal records. One member of each of the applicant pairs would check the box "yes" on the applicant form in answer to the question "Have you ever been convicted of a crime?" The pair alternated each week which young man would play the role of the ex-offender. The experimental design allowed Pager to make the applicant pairs identical on all job-relevant characteristics so that she could know for sure that any differences she saw were the result of discrimination against felons, rather than other qualifications or weaknesses of the applicant.

Pager's study revealed some striking findings. First, whites were much preferred over blacks, and nonoffenders were much preferred over ex-offenders. Whites with a felony conviction were half as likely to be considered by employers as equally qualified nonoffenders. For blacks the effects were even larger: Black ex-offenders were only one-third as likely to receive a call back compared with nonoffenders. Even more surprising was the comparison of these two effects: Blacks with no criminal history fared no better than did whites with a felony conviction. These results suggest that the experience of being a black male in America today is comparable with the experience of being a convicted white criminal, at least in the eyes of Milwaukee employers. For those who believe that race no longer represents a major barrier to opportunity, these results represent a powerful challenge. Being a black felon is a particularly tough obstacle to overcome.

POLICING

Some sociologists and criminologists have suggested that visible policing techniques, such as patrolling the streets, are reassuring for the public. Such activities are consistent with the perception that the police are actively engaged in controlling crime, investigating offenses, and supporting the criminal justice system. But sociologists also suggest that we need to reassess the role of policing in the early twenty-first century. Although maintaining law and order, interacting with citizens, and providing services are part of contemporary policing, they represent only a fraction of what the police actually do. Policing, sociologists argue, is now less about controlling crime and more about detecting and managing risks. Most of all, it is about communicating knowledge about risk to other institutions in society that demand that information (Ericson and Haggerty 1997).

According to this view, police are first and foremost "knowledge workers." As such, the vast majority of police time is spent on activities aimed at processing information, drafting reports, or communicating data. The "simple" case of an automobile accident in Ontario, Canada, illustrates this point. A police officer is called to the scene of an automobile accident involving two vehicles. No one has been killed, but there are minor injuries and one of the drivers is drunk. The investigation takes

INCARCERATION RATES

More than 10.2 million people are currently being held in penal institutions across the globe, with the U.S., Russia, and China accounting for nearly half of the worldwide prison population. The U.S. incarcerates more people per 100,000 residents than any country in the world.

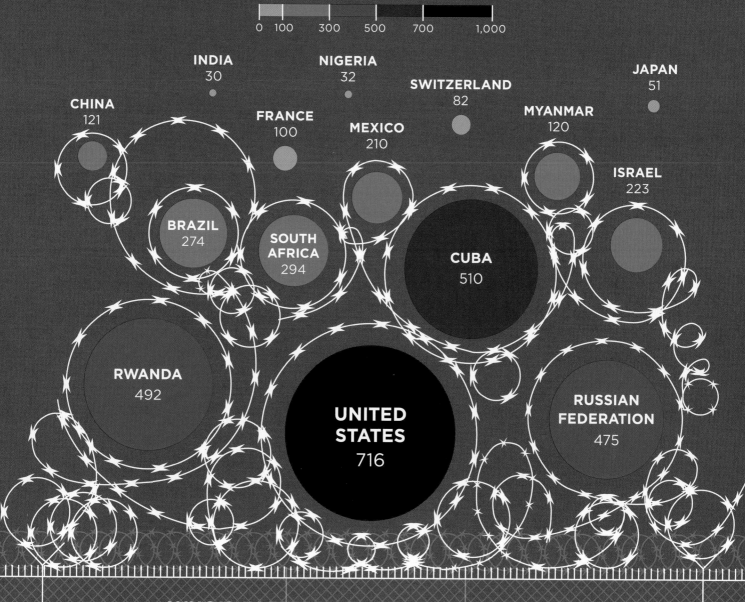

0   100   300   500   700   1,000

INDIA
30

NIGERIA
32

SWITZERLAND
82

JAPAN
51

CHINA
121

FRANCE
100

MEXICO
210

MYANMAR
120

ISRAEL
223

BRAZIL
274

SOUTH
AFRICA
294

CUBA
510

RWANDA
492

UNITED
STATES
716

RUSSIAN
FEDERATION
475

WHO'S IN PRISON IN THE UNITED STATES?

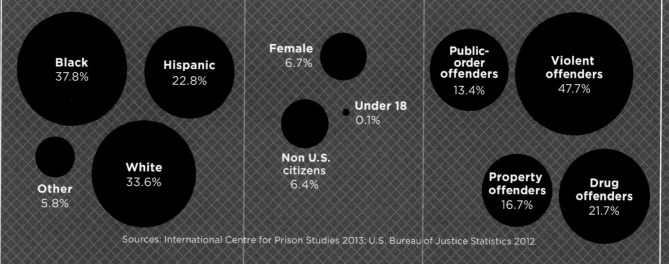

Black
37.8%

Hispanic
22.8%

Female
6.7%

Public-
order
offenders
13.4%

Violent
offenders
47.7%

Under 18
0.1%

Other
5.8%

White
33.6%

Non U.S.
citizens
6.4%

Property
offenders
16.7%

Drug
offenders
21.7%

Sources: International Centre for Prison Studies 2013; U.S. Bureau of Justice Statistics 2012

Nearly every day, the evening news recounts a story of a brutal crime committed by an offender who is out on parole. Among the most startling was the April 2006 murder of a Roman Catholic nun, Sister Karen Klimczak, age sixty-two. At the time of her murder, Klimczak had lived for sixteen years in a rectory that she had converted into Bissonette House, a halfway house for recently released convicts. Her upstate New York community was shocked when she was murdered by Craig Lunch, a convicted car thief who moved into Bissonette after being paroled from a medium-security prison. Such high-visibility stories draw attention away from the fact that many released convicts do resume law-abiding and successful lives after their release from jail. But reintegrating into society can be difficult, and ex-convicts' readjustment often depends on the assistance they receive from parole officers. Parole officers monitor the living arrangements, daily activities, and personal needs of ex-convicts and help them find and maintain jobs, and reestablish secure relationships with members of their family. However, parole officers often face uphill battles as they try to help their clients establish normal lives. The work of sociologist Devah Pager demonstrates just how difficult it is for parolees to find work. Drawing on the work of Pager and others, how would you try to assist your clients most effectively if you were a parole officer?

one hour; the drunk driver is charged with the impaired operation of a motor vehicle causing bodily harm and with operating a motor vehicle after drinking excess alcohol. The driver's license is automatically suspended for twelve hours.

Following this routine investigation, the officer spends three hours writing up sixteen separate reports documenting the incident. The officer is required to provide information for the provincial motor registry about the vehicle and people involved; the automobile industry must be informed about the vehicles involved in the accident; the insurance companies need information about the case; the public health system requires details on any injuries; the criminal courts require police information for the prosecution; and the police administration needs reports on the incident for internal records and national databases. This example reveals how the police are a key node in a complicated information circuit of institutions that are all in the business of risk management. With the help of new forms of technology, police work is increasingly about mapping and predicting risk within the population.

This emphasis on information collection and processing can be frustrating for police, especially those who entered the force because they wanted to interact with people—not paper files and computers. Many police officers see a vast distinction between "real" police work—such as investigating crimes—and the "donkey work" of reports and paper trails; they do not see the point of the extensive documentation that is required.

CRIME AND COMMUNITY

Preventing crime and reducing fear of crime are both important paths to rebuilding strong communities. One of the most significant innovations in criminology in recent years has been the discovery that the decay of day-to-day civility relates directly to criminality. Although sociologists and criminologists in earlier decades focused almost exclusively on serious crime—robbery, assault, and other violent crime—they have since discovered that minor crimes and public disorder have a powerful effect on neighborhoods. When asked to describe their problems, residents of troubled neighborhoods mention seemingly minor concerns such as abandoned cars, graffiti, youth gangs, and similar phenomena.

People act on their anxieties about these issues: They move out of these neighborhoods (if they can afford to), they buy heavy locks for their doors and bars for their windows, they abandon public places like parks, and they even avoid healthy behaviors like jogging and walking because of fear. As they withdraw physically, they also withdraw from roles of mutual support with fellow citizens, thereby relinquishing the social controls that formerly helped to maintain civility within the community.

The recognition that even seemingly small acts of crime and disorder can threaten a neighborhood is based on the **broken windows theory** (Wilson and Kelling 1982). This sociological theory evolved from an innovative study conducted by the social psychologist Philip Zimbardo. He abandoned cars without license plates and with their hoods up in two entirely different social settings: the wealthy community of Palo Alto, California, and a poor neighborhood in the Bronx, New York. In both places, the cars were vandalized once passersby, regardless of class or race, sensed that the cars were abandoned and that "no one cared" (Zimbardo 1969). Any sign of social disorder in a community, even one unrepaired broken window, is a sign that no one cares. Breaking more windows—that is, committing more serious crimes—is a rational response by criminals to this situation of social disorder. Minor acts of deviance can lead to a spiral of crime and social decay.

In the late 1980s and 1990s, the broken windows theory served as the basis for new policing strategies that aggressively focused on minor crimes such as traffic violations and drinking or using drugs in public. Studies have shown that proactive policing directed at maintaining public order can have a positive effect on reducing more serious crimes such as robbery (Sampson and Cohen 1988). However, one flaw of the broken windows theory is that the police are left to identify "social disorder" however they wish. Without a systematic definition of disorder, the police are authorized to see almost anything as a sign of disorder and anyone as a threat. In fact, as crime rates fell throughout the 1990s, the number of complaints of police abuse and harassment went up, particularly by young, urban, black men who fit the "profile" of a potential criminal. In response to these limitations, criminologists and policymakers have developed alternative strategies to crime prevention, including community policing, target hardening, and shaming.

COMMUNITY POLICING

One idea that has grown in popularity in recent years is that the police should work closely with citizens to improve local community standards and civil behavior, using education, persuasion, and counseling instead of incarceration.

Community policing implies not only drawing in citizens themselves but changing the characteristic outlook of police forces. A renewed emphasis on crime prevention rather than law enforcement can go hand in hand with the reintegration of policing with the community. The isolation of the police from those they are supposed to serve often produces a "siege mentality," since the police have little regular contact with ordinary citizens. The shooting and killing of Trayvon Martin by George Zimmerman, who served as a neighborhood watch coordinator, is an extreme example of such a siege mentality.

In order to work, partnerships among government agencies, the criminal justice system, local associations, and community organizations have to be inclusive; all economic and ethnic groups must be involved (Kelling and Coles 1997). Government and business can act together to help repair urban decay. One model is the creation of urban enterprise zones, which provide tax breaks for corporations that participate

broken windows theory • A theory proposing that even small acts of crime, disorder, and vandalism can threaten a neighborhood and render it unsafe.

community policing • A renewed emphasis on crime prevention rather than law enforcement to reintegrate policing within the community.

The New War on Crime

You don't have to be a sociologist to know that crime rates matter. Many people consider local crime rates when deciding where to buy a home. Vacationers may choose to avoid travel destinations where crime rates are high. You might have even been nervous to walk through a neighborhood that you were told had high crime rates. As you saw earlier in this chapter, the government generates many statistics, such as Uniform Crime Reports, to understand crime. But what if you want to simply find out how safe your neighborhood is? Or whether any crimes have been committed nearby? Or if there are criminals or ex-cons living close to you? And what if you witness a crime? How might you report it?

An explosion of "crime fighting" and "crime detection" apps are now available on smartphones, which allow users to both learn about local crimes and leave tips for local law-enforcement officials. The Santa Cruz, California, police department was one of the first police forces in the United States to adopt smartphone technology, unveiling a free mobile app in 2011 (Baxter 2011). The New York City police department followed shortly thereafter. Apps allow users to access the police departments' social media pages, receive important crime alerts, view neighborhood crime maps, leave tips of suspicious activities, and look at photos and videos (Sterbenz 2013).

In addition to apps created by local police departments, a number of commercial apps like iSpotACrime, TipSubmit, and iWitness allow users to upload photos and videos, add voice comments, and pinpoint their locations using GPS. Some have special features like a panic button for emergencies. Other apps allow users to specify where their "crime tips" are sent, such as a local school or federal and local law-enforcement agencies (Sterbenz 2013).

For people seeking—rather than offering—information on crime, there are apps like Offender Locater. Vigilant parents hoping to protect their children from so-called predators can use these apps to locate nearby registered sex offenders. The apps use the phone's built-in GPS to display a list of sex crime convicts in a given area. Some of the apps generate interactive maps that link users to more information and a picture of the convicted offender.

These crime-fighting and crime-detection apps have both fans and critics. Advocates say that they may help prevent and solve crimes because there are simply more eyes and ears on the street ready to report suspicious behavior to law-enforcement officials. For example, Boston Marathon spectators used their smartphones to provide photos to help police investigate the April 15, 2013, bombing (Loder and Deprez 2013).

Yet others say that these apps may create a false sense of security. Just because you're able to report or read about a local crime doesn't mean that you'll be any safer. Further, some apps may actually lead to increases in aggressive or menacing behavior. Apps that provide information on registered sex offenders could lead to vigilantism, where overzealous citizens attack or stalk those listed in the registries—some of whom pose little danger to the community.

An Amber Alert appears on a phone, alerting the user to be on the lookout for a car that may contain a kidnapped child. Systems like these can help involve citizens in reporting crime remotely.

What do you think? Have you ever used a crime-fighting or crime-detection app? If so, did it increase your feeling of security? Can you think of a time when it increased your actual security?

in strategic planning and invest in designated areas. To be successful, such schemes demand a long-term commitment to social objectives.

Emphasizing these strategies does not mean denying the links between unemployment, poverty, and crime. Rather, the struggle against these social problems should be coordinated with community-based approaches to crime prevention. These approaches can in fact contribute directly and indirectly to furthering social justice. Where social order has decayed along with public services, other opportunities, such as new jobs, decline as well. Improving the quality of life in a neighborhood can revive them.

TARGET HARDENING

Community policing is just one strategy that falls under a larger set of strategies that criminologists call **target hardening**. Consistent with the core notions of control theory, this practice makes it more difficult for criminals to commit crimes by minimizing their opportunities to do so. Rather than changing the criminal, the best policy is to take practical measures to control the criminal's ability to commit crime by promoting the use of crime-deterring technologies and practices like community policing, private security services, car alarms, house alarms, guard dogs, and even gated communities.

target hardening • Practical measures used to limit a criminal's ability to commit crime, such as community policing and use of house alarms.

Target-hardening techniques have gained favor among politicians in recent years and appear to have been successful in some contexts in curtailing crime. But criticisms of such an approach can also be made. These tactics do not address the underlying causes of crime but instead are aimed at protecting and defending certain elements of society from its reach. There is another unintended consequence of such policies: As popular crime targets are "hardened," patterns of crime may simply shift from one domain to another. Target-hardening approaches run the risk of displacing criminal offenses from better-protected areas to more vulnerable ones. Neighborhoods that are poor or lacking in social cohesion may well experience a growth in crime and delinquency as target hardening in affluent regions increases.

SHAMING AS PUNISHMENT

In recent years, **shaming**, a form of punishing criminal and deviant behavior that attempts to maintain the ties of the offender to the community, has grown in popularity as an alternative to incarceration. According to some criminologists, the fear of being shamed within one's community is an important deterrent to crime. As a result, the public's formal disapproval could achieve the same deterrent effect as incarceration without the high costs of building and maintaining prisons.

shaming • A way of punishing criminal and deviant behavior based on rituals of public disapproval rather than incarceration. The goal of shaming is to maintain the ties of the offender to the community.

Criminologist John Braithwaite (1996) has described two types of shaming: stigmatizing and reintegrative. Stigmatizing shaming is the process whereby a criminal is labeled as a threat to society and is treated as an outcast. The labeling process has potentially damaging consequences, as we learned earlier in this chapter. A negative label may trigger others' efforts to marginalize the individual, perhaps leading to future criminal behavior and higher crime rates. Reintegrative shaming, by contrast, involves rather than marginalizes the offender. People central to the criminal's immediate community—such as family members, employers and coworkers, and friends—are brought into court to state their condemnation of the offender's behavior. At the same time, these people accept responsibility for reintegrating the offender back into their community. The goal is to rebuild the social bonds of the individual to the community as a means of deterring future criminal conduct.

Japan, with one of the lowest crime rates in the world, has been quite successful in implementing this approach. The process is largely based on a voluntary network of over 500,000 local crime-prevention associations dedicated to facilitating reintegration into the community and on a criminal justice system that is encouraged to be lenient for this purpose. As a result, in Japan only 5 percent of persons convicted for a crime serve time in prison, as compared with 30 percent in the United States. Though reintegrative shaming is not a standard practice in the American criminal justice system, it is a familiar practice in other social institutions such as the family. A parent may express disapproval of a child's naughty behavior and try to make the child feel ashamed, but the parent may also reassure the child that he or she is a loved member of the family.

Could reintegrative shaming succeed in the United States? Skeptics say these tactics are soft on crime, that Americans are too individualistic to participate in community-based policing, and that high-crime areas are less community oriented. However, community networks have been successful in working with the police to prevent crime. These social bonds could also be fostered to increase the power of shame and reintegrate offenders into local networks of community involvement. ✓

CONCEPT CHECKS ✓

1. How does imprisonment affect the life chances of ex-cons?

2. Why has the U.S. prison population grown so steeply over the past three decades?

3. What are the primary tasks that police officers do each day?

4. Name at least two specific ways that community members can combat local crime.

Understand the costs and functions of crime and deviance.

HOW DO CRIME AND DEVIANCE AFFECT YOUR LIFE?

THE COSTS OF CRIME

Crime can take a toll on the financial and emotional well-being of even those people whose only contact with the criminal justice system is watching reruns of *Law and Order* or *CSI*. As we learned earlier in the chapter, corporate crime can affect everything from the quality of the food we eat to the safety of the cars we drive and the cleanliness of the air we breathe. Even those of us who live in safe and quiet neighborhoods may find our lives touched by the criminal acts of corporations, in the form of air pollution or tainted foods or medicines.

Our lives are also affected by the high fiscal costs of street crime. Maintaining local, state, and national criminal justice systems is costly—and growing costlier by the minute. As we learned earlier in this chapter, the number of people behind bars in the United States has climbed steadily in the past decade due in part to policies like the "three strikes" laws. State government is having a difficult time finding enough money to house, feed, and provide medical care to these growing numbers of inmates. Spending on corrections has risen dramatically over the past three decades. For example, spending has varied between 2.5 and 2.9 percent of state outlays over the last decade, with states spending $48.5 billion in 2010 as compared with $15 billion in 1982 (U.S. Bureau of Justice Statistics 2012c).

Lawmakers have few options for footing this large bill. Tax hikes are one option, but that would mean higher income taxes, property taxes, and sales taxes for everyone. In the absence of tax hikes, lawmakers may find themselves forced to cut back on other important social programs, including transportation, education, and health care (Pew Center on the States 2008). Corrections accounted for 3.1 percent of total state expenditures in 2011, and if this proportion increases, it could touch the lives of Americans using the many other state programs that compete for valuable tax dollars (National Association of State Budget Officers 2012).

THE FUNCTIONS OF DEVIANCE

The deviant acts of others also affect our personal behaviors in powerful ways. As noted earlier, deviants help us understand what is considered "right" and "wrong" among our peers, friends, and community members. Most of us try very hard to avoid the sanctions that result from doing "wrong," and we make our daily choices accordingly. For example, most of us don't want to be socially ostracized, so we may choose clothes, hobbies, romantic partners, and even our future career paths in order to fit in with peers. To be considered "deviant" often means being treated as a social outcast.

At a more serious level, though, most of us know what the punishments are for even minor violations such as speeding or running a red light. By learning about the fees and punishments levied on those who break the rules, most of us will behave in accordance with the law to avoid having our driver's license suspended or spending a night in jail. Public punishments—whether locking horse thieves into "stocks" in town squares and making an adulteress wear a scarlet letter *A* around her neck in the colonial United States, or publicizing the names and addresses of registered sex offenders and televising "perp walks" in the contemporary United States—are designed not only to punish the "guilty" but also to prevent others from behaving in a similar way. These public humiliations affect us because they make us rethink whether it's really worthwhile to try to get away with a crime.

EXERCISES:

Thinking Sociologically

1. Briefly summarize several leading theories explaining crime and deviance presented in this chapter: differential association, anomie, labeling, conflict, and control theories. Which theory appeals to you? Explain why.

2. Explain how differences in power and social influence can play a significant role in defining and sanctioning deviant behavior.

3. What do you consider the most harmful consequences of violent crimes? Of white-collar crimes? How do you think the "average" American views each of these different types of crimes?

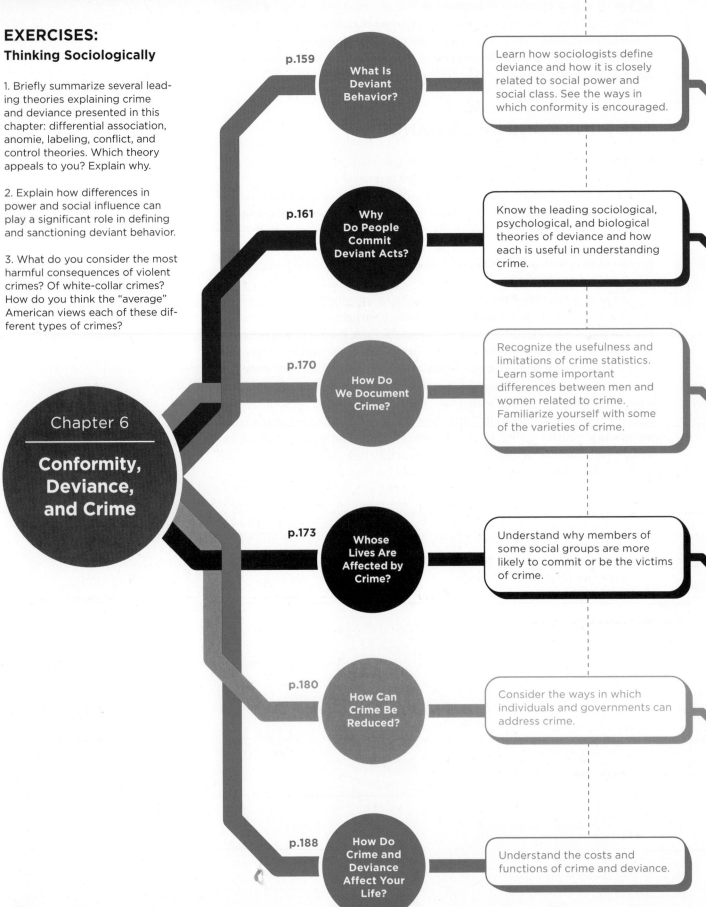

Chapter 6

Conformity, Deviance, and Crime

p.159 What Is Deviant Behavior?

Learn how sociologists define deviance and how it is closely related to social power and social class. See the ways in which conformity is encouraged.

p.161 Why Do People Commit Deviant Acts?

Know the leading sociological, psychological, and biological theories of deviance and how each is useful in understanding crime.

p.170 How Do We Document Crime?

Recognize the usefulness and limitations of crime statistics. Learn some important differences between men and women related to crime. Familiarize yourself with some of the varieties of crime.

p.173 Whose Lives Are Affected by Crime?

Understand why members of some social groups are more likely to commit or be the victims of crime.

p.180 How Can Crime Be Reduced?

Consider the ways in which individuals and governments can address crime.

p.188 How Do Crime and Deviance Affect Your Life?

Understand the costs and functions of crime and deviance.

TERMS TO KNOW	CONCEPT CHECKS

norms • mores • folkways

deviance • deviant subculture • sanction • law • crime

1. How do sociologists define deviance?
2. Is all crime deviant? Is all deviance criminal? Why?
3. Contrast positive and negative sanctions.

psychopath • anomie • relative deprivation • differential association • control theory • conflict theory • new criminology • labeling theory • primary deviance • secondary deviance

1. What are the main similarities and differences between biological and psychological views of deviance?
2. How do Merton's and Durkheim's definitions of anomie differ?
3. According to subcultural explanations, how does criminal behavior get transmitted from one group to another?
4. What is the core idea behind differential association theory?
5. What are two criticisms of labeling theory?
6. What are the root causes of crime, according to conflict theorists?

Uniform Crime Reports (UCR)

1. What are the main sources of crime data in the United States?
2. Contrast Uniform Crime Reports and the National Crime Victimization Survey.
3. Describe crime trends in the 1970s through today.
4. How would sociologists explain the high rate of violent crime in the United States?

hate crime • white-collar crime • corporate crime • organized crime

1. Contrast the following two explanations for the gender gap in crime: behavioral differences and biases in reporting.
2. What is the age-crime curve, and what factors have contributed to this pattern?
3. What are some of the consequences of white-collar crime?
4. Give one example of an activity classified as organized crime.

broken windows theory • community policing • target hardening • shaming

1. How does imprisonment affect the life chances of ex-cons?
2. Why has the U.S. prison population grown so steeply over the past three decades?
3. What are the primary tasks that police officers do each day?
4. Name at least two specific ways that community members can combat local crime.

191

7

Stratification, Class, and Inequality

THE BIG QUESTIONS

WHAT IS SOCIAL STRATIFICATION?
Learn about social stratification and how social background affects one's life chances. Become acquainted with the most influential theories of stratification.

HOW IS SOCIAL CLASS DEFINED IN THE UNITED STATES?
Understand the social causes and consequences of social class in U.S. society, as well as the complexities and challenges of defining class.

WHAT ARE THE CAUSES AND CONSEQUENCES OF SOCIAL INEQUALITY IN THE UNITED STATES?
Recognize why and how the gap between rich and poor has increased in recent decades. Understand social mobility, and think about your own mobility.

HOW DOES POVERTY AFFECT INDIVIDUALS?
Learn about poverty in the United States today, explanations for why it exists, and means for combating it. Learn how people become marginalized in a society and the forms that this marginalization takes.

HOW DOES SOCIAL INEQUALITY AFFECT YOUR LIFE?
Learn how changes in the American economy have led to growing inequalities since the 1970s.

Thanks to her own perseverance in the face of social and economic boundaries, Liz Murray (pictured here with her father) managed to overcome a difficult childhood spent on the streets of New York, leaving behind homeless shelters for Harvard University and a doctorate in clinical psychology. What does her story say about mobility in American society?

Liz Murray had a tumultuous adolescence, bouncing from one homeless shelter to the next, with an occasional night spent sleeping on the streets in the Bronx, New York. Born to poor, heroin-addicted parents who would later contract AIDS, Liz grew up with parents who tried to give her love and support but were incapable of providing the structure, nutrition, and stable home Liz needed. Her parents spent their monthly welfare checks within days of receiving it, with most of their money going to cocaine and heroin. Liz and her sister Lisa struggled to soothe their hunger pangs, subsisting on egg and mayonnaise sandwiches, and even toothpaste.

Liz was forced to grow up fast. At age six, she knew how to mainline drugs (although she never took drugs), and learned how to care for her drug-addicted parents. At age nine, she started bagging groceries and pumping gas to help support the family. Unlike other children, Liz found no solace in school, where she was taunted for her dirty clothing and lice-infested hair. She became homeless when she was just fifteen years old, shortly after her mother died of AIDS-related tuberculosis at age forty-two. Her father moved into a men's shelter, abandoning Liz. She survived by living on the streets, eating from trash cans, finding shelter on New York City's all-night subway routes, and occasionally staying at homeless shelters herself.

Miraculously, Liz managed to stay in school. She had very poor grades due to her sporadic attendance, but her life turned around when she was accepted by the Humanities Preparatory School, an alternative school in Greenwich Village, where she encountered teachers who truly cared about her welfare. Liz began to read literature and study physics but still had no stable place to stay. She did her homework in subway stations and stairwells. Because she started high school late (age seventeen), she doubled her course load and finished high school in two years. She eventually wrote an essay about her experiences that won her a *New York Times* College Scholarship for needy students. She was accepted to Harvard University, where she began classes in 2000 (Murray 2010).

Even after enrolling at Harvard, however, Liz couldn't escape her parents' troubles. Her education at Harvard was interrupted just one year later, when she returned to New York City to care for her father, who was dying of AIDS. Her father, a graduate school dropout, had been a voracious reader—yet his education didn't stop him from becoming a drug addict who illegally trafficked painkillers and other drugs. Steadfastly dedicated to receiving an education, Liz transferred to Columbia University in New York City. After her father's death in 2006, she returned to Harvard and earned her bachelor's degree in psychology in 2009. She has since enrolled in a doctoral program in clinical psychology, so that she can eventually help other young people whose childhoods are strained by poverty, disease, and parental drug use. Liz feels compelled to share her story with others and is now the founder and director of Manifest Living, an organization that provides workshops that empower adults to "create the extraordinary things in their lives." She is also the author of the autobiography *Breaking Night* (2010) and was the focus of a Lifetime movie, *Homeless to Harvard: The Liz Murray Story*.

For most Americans, one's socioeconomic background powerfully shapes one's future. Yet in Liz's case, early life poverty didn't stop her from earning an Ivy League degree and becoming a professionally and financially successful adult. How did she transcend her roots? How common are experiences like Liz's? In this chapter we examine the complex associations among social status, economic position, and inequality in society.

social stratification • The existence of structured inequalities between groups in society in terms of their access to material or symbolic rewards.

Sociologists speak of **social stratification** to describe inequalities among individuals and groups within human societies. Often we think of stratification in terms of wealth or property, but it can also occur on the basis of other attributes, such as gender, age, religious affiliation, or military rank. An important area of research in social stratification is social mobility, or one's movement up or down social class strata; an extreme example of this is Liz Murray. The three key aspects of social stratification are class, status, and power (Weber 1947). Although they frequently overlap, this is not always the case. The "rich and famous" often enjoy high status; their wealth often provides political influence and sometimes direct access to political power. Yet there are exceptions. Drug lords, for example, may be wealthy and powerful, yet they usually enjoy low status.

In this chapter, we focus on stratification in terms of inequalities based on wealth and income, status, and power. In later chapters, we will look at the ways in which gender (Chapter 9) and ethnicity and race (Chapter 10) all play a role in stratification.

WHAT IS SOCIAL STRATIFICATION?

Learn about social stratification and how social background affects one's life chances. Become acquainted with the most influential theories of stratification.

All socially stratified systems share three characteristics:

1. **The rankings apply to social categories of people who share a common characteristic such as gender or ethnicity.** Women may be ranked differently from men, wealthy people differently from the poor. This does not mean that individuals from a particular category cannot change their rank; however, it does mean that the category continues to exist even if individuals move out of it and into another category.

2. **People's life experiences and opportunities depend heavily on how their social category is ranked.** Being male or female, black or white, upper class or working class makes a big difference in terms of your life chances—often as big a difference as personal effort or good fortune.

3. **The ranks of different social categories tend to change very slowly over time.** In U.S. society, for example, only in the last forty-five years have women begun to achieve economic equality with men (see Chapter 9). Similarly, only since the 1970s have significant numbers of African Americans begun to obtain economic and political equality with whites—even though slavery was abolished nearly a century and a half ago and discrimination declared illegal in the 1950s and 1960s (see Chapter 10).

As you saw in Chapter 2, stratified societies have changed throughout human history. The earliest human societies, which were based on hunting and gathering, had very little social stratification—mainly because there were few resources to be divided up. The development of agriculture produced considerably more wealth and, as a result, a great increase in stratification. Social stratification in agricultural societies came to resemble a pyramid, with a large number of people at the bottom and a successively smaller number of people as one moves toward the top. Today, advanced industrial societies are extremely complex; their stratification is more likely to resemble a teardrop, with a large number of people in the middle and lower-middle ranks (the so-called middle class), a slightly smaller number of people at the bottom, and very few people as one moves toward the top.

But before turning to stratification in modern societies, let's first review the three basic systems of stratification: slavery, caste, and class.

SLAVERY

Slavery is an extreme form of inequality in which certain people are owned as property by others. Historically, sometimes slaves have been deprived of almost all rights by law, as was the case on Southern plantations in the United States. In other societies, their position was more akin to that of servants. For example, in the ancient Greek city-state of Athens, some slaves occupied positions of great responsibility. They were excluded from political positions and from the military but were accepted in most other types of occupations. Some were literate and worked as government administrators; many were trained in craft skills. For the less fortunate, however, their days began and ended in hard labor in the mines.

slavery • A form of social stratification in which some people are owned by others as their property.

Systems of slave labor have tended to be unstable because slaves have historically fought back against their subjection. Slavery also is not economically efficient, as it requires constant supervision and often involves severe punishment, which impedes worker productivity. Moreover, from about the eighteenth century on, many people in Europe and America came to see slavery as morally wrong. Today, slavery is illegal in every country of the world, but it still exists in some places. Recent research has documented that people are taken by force and held against their will—from enslaved brick makers in Pakistan to sex slaves in Thailand and domestic slaves in France. The United States is not immune to such travesties. News reports of teenage girls coerced into prostitution, maids locked up and forced to work by wealthy clients, and a recent case of immigrants forced to work at convenience stores underscore that marginalized persons who lack social power can still be exploited at the hands of cruel individuals (CNN 2013). For example, in June 2013, the owners and managers of fourteen 7-Eleven stores in the United States were charged with running what state prosecutors called a "modern-day plantation system." The store owners were forcing undocumented immigrants to work more than 100 hours a week at their stores, but paying them far less than minimum wage and forcing them to live in crowded and rundown group housing (Secret and Rashbaum 2013). Slavery remains a significant human rights violation in the world today (CNN 2013).

CASTE SYSTEMS

caste system • A social system in which one's social status is determined at birth and set for life.

A **caste system** is a social system in which one's social status is given for life. In **caste societies**, therefore, different social levels are closed so that all individuals must remain at the social level of their birth throughout life. In this system, social status is based on personal characteristics—such as perceived race or ethnicity (often based on such physical characteristics as skin color), parental religion, or parental caste—that are accidents of birth and are therefore believed to be unchangeable. Caste societies can be seen as a special type of class society—in which class position is ascribed at birth, rather than achieved through personal accomplishment. In caste systems, intimate contact with members of other castes is strongly discouraged. Such "purity" of a caste is often maintained by rules of **endogamy**, marriage within one's social group as required by custom or law.

caste society • A society in which different social levels are closed, so that all individuals must remain at the social level of their birth throughout life.

endogamy • The forbidding of marriage or sexual relations outside one's social group.

Before modern times, caste systems were found throughout the world. In modern times, caste systems have typically been found in agricultural societies that have not yet developed industrial capitalist economies, such as rural India or South Africa prior to the end of white rule in 1992. The Indian caste system, for example, reflects Hindu religious beliefs and is more than two thousand years old. According to Hindu beliefs, there are four major castes, each roughly associated with broad occupational groupings. Below the four castes are those known as the "untouchables" or Dalits (oppressed people), who—as their name suggests—are to be avoided at all costs. Untouchables are limited to the worst jobs in society, such as removing human waste, and they often resort to begging and searching in garbage for their food. India made it illegal to discriminate on the basis of caste in 1949, but aspects of the caste system remain in full force today, particularly in rural areas.

The few remaining caste systems in the world are being challenged further by globalization. For example, as India's modern capitalist economy brings people of different castes together, whether in the same workplace, airplane, or restaurant, it is increasingly difficult to maintain the rigid barriers required to sustain the caste system.

CLASS

The concept of **class** is most important for analyzing stratification in industrialized societies like the United States. Everyone has heard of class, but most people in everyday talk use the word in a vague way. As employed in sociology, it has some precision.

A social class is a large group of people who occupy a similar economic position in the wider society. The concept of life chances, introduced by Max Weber, is the best way to understand what class means. Your **life chances** are the opportunities you have for achieving economic prosperity. A person from a humble background, for example, has less chance of ending up wealthy than someone from a more prosperous one. And the best chance an individual has of being wealthy is to start off as wealthy in the first place.

The United States, it has been said, is the land of opportunity. For some, this is so. There are many examples of people who have risen from humble means to positions of great wealth and power. And yet there are many more cases of people who have not, including a disproportionate share of women and members of minority groups. The idea of life chances is important because it emphasizes that although class is an important influence on what happens in our lives, it is not completely determining. Class divisions affect which neighborhoods we live in, what lifestyles we follow, and even which romantic partners we choose (Mare 1991; Massey 1996). Yet they don't fix people for life in specific social positions, as the older systems of stratification did. A person born into a caste position has no opportunity of escaping from it; the same isn't true of class.

Class systems differ from slavery and castes in four main respects:

1. **Class systems are fluid.** Unlike the other types of strata, classes are not established by legal or religious provisions. The boundaries between classes are never clear-cut. There are no formal restrictions on intermarriage between people from different classes.

2. **Class positions are in some part achieved.** An individual's class is not simply assigned at birth, as is the case in the other types of stratification systems. Social mobility—movement upward and downward in the class structure—is relatively common.

3. **Class is economically based.** Classes depend on inequalities in the possession of material resources. In the other types of stratification systems, noneconomic factors (such as race in the former South African caste system) are generally most important.

4. **Class systems are large scale and impersonal.** In the other types of stratification systems, inequalities are expressed primarily in personal relationships of duty or obligation—between slave and master or lower- and higher-caste individuals. Class systems, by contrast, operate mainly through large-scale, impersonal associations such as pay or working conditions.

Women from the Dalit caste (also known as "untouchables") earn a living as sewage scavengers in the slums of Ranchi, India. They are paid between 30 and 100 rupees ($0.65–$2.25) per house per month for retrieving human waste from residential dry latrines and emptying the buckets into nearby gutters and streams.

class • Although it is one of the most frequently used concepts in sociology, there is no clear agreement about how the term should be defined. Most sociologists use the term to refer to socioeconomic variations among groups of individuals that create variations in their material prosperity and power.

life chances • A term introduced by Max Weber to signify a person's opportunities for achieving economic prosperity.

ARE CLASS BOUNDARIES WEAKENING?

The story of Liz Murray might lead us to believe that social class boundaries are permeable, where the daughter of drug-addicted, HIV-positive welfare recipients, who bounced from homeless shelter to homeless shelter, could ultimately graduate from an Ivy League university and become a respected author and motivational speaker. Although Murray's case is certainly inspiring, is it common? Is it unique to the United States and societies with fluid class strata? How much does social class mold our lives, and has its impact changed over time? Stratification scholars currently grapple with two important debates about the declining importance of social class. First, they ask whether caste systems will give way to class systems against the backdrop of globalization. Second, scholars question whether inequality is declining in class-based societies due in part to educational expansion and other social policies.

To address the first question, there is some evidence that globalization will hasten the end of legally sanctioned caste systems throughout the world. Most official caste systems have already given way to class-based ones in industrial capitalist societies. Modern industrial production requires that people move about freely, work at whatever jobs they are suited or able to do, and change jobs frequently according to economic conditions. The rigid restrictions found in caste systems interfere with this necessary freedom. Nonetheless, elements of caste systems persist even in advanced industrial societies. For example, some Indian immigrants to the United States seek to arrange traditional marriages for their children along caste lines, while the relatively small number of intermarriages between blacks and whites in the United States suggests the strength of racial barriers. For instance, of all marriages taking place between 2008 and 2010, only 1.7 percent were black-white unions (Pew Research Center 2012b).

To address the second question, some evidence suggests that at least until recently, mature capitalist societies have been increasingly open to movement between classes, thereby reducing the level of inequality. For example, studies of European countries, the United States, and Canada suggested that inequality peaked in these places before World War II, declined through the 1950s, and remained roughly the same through the 1970s (Berger 1986; Nielsen 1994). Lowered postwar inequality was due in part to economic expansion in industrial societies, which created opportunities for people at the bottom to move up, and because of government health insurance, welfare, and other programs aimed at reducing inequality. As you will see later in this chapter and in Chapter 13 (where we discuss the changing nature of the American economy), however, this trend has reversed in recent years: Inequality has actually been increasing in the United States since the 1970s.

THEORIES OF STRATIFICATION IN MODERN SOCIETIES

The most influential theoretical approaches to studying stratification are those developed by Karl Marx and Max Weber. Most subsequent theories of stratification are heavily indebted to their ideas.

MARX: MEANS OF PRODUCTION AND THE ANALYSIS OF CLASS

For Marx, the term *class* refers to people who stand in a common relationship to the **means of production**—the means by which they gain a livelihood. In modern societies, the two main classes are the bourgeoisie and proletariat. The **bourgeoisie**, or

means of production • The means whereby the production of material goods is carried on in a society, including not just technology but the social relations among producers.

bourgeoisie • People who own companies, land, or stocks (shares) and use these to generate economic returns, according to Marx.

capitalists, own the means of production. Members of the **proletariat**, or proleterians, by contrast, earn their living by selling their labor to the capitalists. The relationship between classes, according to Marx, is an exploitative one. In the course of the working day, Marx reasoned, workers produce more than is actually needed by employers to repay the cost of hiring them. This **surplus value** is the source of profit, which capitalists are able to put to their own use. A group of workers in a clothing factory, say, might be able to produce a hundred suits a day. Selling half the suits provides enough income for the manufacturer to pay the workers' wages. Income from the sale of the remainder of the garments is taken as profit.

Marx believed that the maturing of industrial capitalism would bring about an increasing gap between the wealth of the capitalist minority and the poverty of the large proletarian population. In his view, the wages of the working class could never rise far above subsistence level, while wealth would pile up in the hands of those owning capital. In addition, laborers would face work daily that is physically wearing and mentally tedious, as is the situation in many factories. At the lowest levels of society, particularly among those frequently or permanently unemployed, there would develop an "accumulation of misery, agony of labor, slavery, ignorance, brutality, moral degradation" (Marx 1977, orig. 1864).

Marx was right about the persistence of poverty in industrialized countries and in anticipating that large inequalities of wealth and income would continue. He was wrong in supposing that the income of most of the population would remain extremely low. Most people in Western countries today are much better off materially than were comparable groups in Marx's day.

WEBER: CLASS, STATUS, AND POWER

There are three main differences between Weber's theory and that of Marx. First, according to Weber, class divisions derive not only from control or lack of control of the means of production but from economic differences that have nothing directly to do with property. Such resources include especially people's skills and credentials, or qualifications. Those in managerial or professional occupations earn more and enjoy more favorable conditions at work, for example, than people in blue-collar jobs. The qualifications they possess—such as degrees, diplomas, and the skills they have acquired—make them more "marketable" than others without such qualifications.

Second, Weber distinguished another aspect of stratification besides class, which he called "status." According to Weber, **status** refers to differences among groups in the social honor, or prestige, they are accorded by others. Status distinctions can vary independent of class divisions. Social honor may be either positive or negative. For instance, doctors and lawyers have high prestige in American society. **Pariah groups**, on the other hand, are negatively privileged status groups subject to discrimination that prevents them from taking advantage of opportunities open to others. For example, members of the "untouchables" caste in India would be treated as pariahs; they are relegated to low-paying work and historically were barred from entering the homes of higher-caste persons. Possession of wealth normally tends to confer high status, but there are exceptions to this principle, such as Hollywood starlets who earn high salaries but lack the education or refinement typically associated with "status." Importantly, status depends on people's subjective evaluations of social differences, whereas class is an objective measure.

Third, Weber recognized that social classes also differ with respect to their **power**, or ability to enact change, command resources, or make decisions. Power is distinct from status and class, but these three dimensions often overlap. For

proletariat • People who sell their labor for wages, according to Marx.

surplus value • In Marxist theory, the value of a worker's labor power left over when an employer has repaid the cost of hiring the worker.

status • The social honor or prestige that a particular group is accorded by other members of a society. Status groups normally display distinct styles of life— patterns of behavior that the members of a group follow. Status privilege may be positive or negative.

pariah groups • Groups that suffer from negative status discrimination—they are looked down on by most other members of society. The Jews, for example, have been a pariah group throughout much of European history.

power • The ability of individuals or the members of a group to achieve aims or further the interests they hold. Power is a pervasive element in all human relationships. Many conflicts in society are struggles over power, because how much power an individual or group is able to obtain governs how far they are able to put their wishes into practice.

A Class-Free Virtual Society?

Some scholars have argued that digital life is a virtual "class-free" society. Social networking sites like Facebook allow people from all walks of life to share their photos, opinions, and hobbies with others. Any of us can follow the tweets of a celebrity or high-ranking political figure and feel, at least for a moment, that we are part of their rich social worlds. Yet researchers have also documented that a "digital divide" persists, where people with higher levels of education, higher incomes, and more financial assets are more likely to own computers and smartphones and thus spend more time online than people with fewer resources. The digital divide has narrowed over the past two decades, yet our virtual worlds are still not free of social class divides. Among the 15 percent of all Americans who say they don't go online, the most common reason given for staying offline is that it's too expensive (Zickuhr 2013). Further, while just 4 percent of college graduates say they don't go online, this figure reaches 41 percent among high school graduates.

Social class permeates our digital lives in other ways. Many websites and apps—ranging from crime-fighting to house-hunting to dating sites—subtly carry the message that we should "stick with our own kind." For example, the dating website The Right Stuff describes itself as an "international introduction network for single graduates and faculty of a select group of excellent universities and colleges. It is a civilized, manageable, and affordable way to meet well-educated members of the opposite sex" (The Right Stuff 2013). Those who want to find a mate on this site are required to provide proof that they attended an Ivy League college or other prestigious university.

The controversial app Ghetto Tracker provides an even more glaring example of the ways that social class divides us. This app, which featured a photo of a smiling, well-dressed white family in its advertisements, bills itself as a site that helps "professionals," "people on vacation," and "students" to identify good parts of town and avoid bad ones. Users can enter in a zip code and then learn whether the neighborhood is classified as "ghetto" based on perceptions of the neighborhood reported by users (Gayomali 2013). People can rate a neighborhood as safe, above average, average, below average, or unsafe. A public uproar regarding the app's racist and classist name quickly forced its inventors to change its name to Good Part of Town (O'Connor 2013).

Critics have lambasted Ghetto Tracker and Good Part of Town on the grounds that perceptions of a neighborhood as safe or unsafe typically have little to do with actual crime rates, and rather, reflect people's perceptions of whether a neighborhood is rich or poor, largely minority, or largely white (Gayomali 2013). Yet many websites (for example, city-data.com) and apps exist that do enable users to find neighborhoods based on characteristics like median household income, biggest houses, and best-educated people. Maybe you've used one of these sites to figure out where you might want to live after college graduation. Do you think that apps or websites that help us find homes (or romantic partners) on the basis of things like how rich the neighborhood is (or where one graduated college) are meeting an important and useful demand? Or do you think that they perpetuate class inequalities and the belief that some classes are "better" than others?

The NYC Housing Authority Digital Van—equipped with laptops, a printer, and wireless broadband—provides residents of public housing developments with access to computers and the Internet as part of a program designed to help close the digital divide.

Photograph courtesy of NYCHA/photographer: Pete Mikoleski

example, on most college campuses, the president or provost has much greater power to change campus policies than would a cafeteria worker. Weber's writings on stratification are important because they show that other dimensions of stratification besides class strongly influence people's lives. Most sociologists hold that Weber's scheme offers a more flexible and sophisticated basis for analyzing stratification than that provided by Marx.

DAVIS AND MOORE: THE FUNCTIONS OF STRATIFICATION

Kingsley Davis and Wilbert E. Moore (1945) provided a functionalist explanation of stratification, arguing that it has beneficial consequences for society. They claimed that certain positions or roles in society, such as brain surgeons, are functionally more important than others, and these positions require special skills for their performance. However, only a limited number of individuals in any society have the talents or experience appropriate to these positions. To attract the most qualified people, rewards need to be offered, such as money, power, and prestige. Davis and Moore determined that because the benefits of different positions in any society must be unequal, then all societies must be stratified. They concluded that social stratification and social inequality are functional for society because they ensure that the most qualified people, attracted by lucrative rewards, fill the roles that are most important to a smoothly functioning society.

Davis and Moore's theory suggests that a person's social position is based solely on his or her innate talents and efforts. Not surprisingly, their theory has been met with criticism by other sociologists. As we have seen, the United States is not entirely a meritocratic society. Those at the top tend to have unequal access to economic and cultural resources, such as the highest-quality education, which help the upper classes transmit their privileged status from one generation to the next. For those without access to these resources, even those with superior talents, social inequality serves as a barrier to reaching their full potential. ✓

CONCEPT CHECKS

1. What are the three shared characteristics of socially stratified systems?

2. What is one example of a caste system in the world today?

3. How is the concept of class different from that of caste?

4. According to Karl Marx, what are the two main classes and how do they relate to each other?

5. What are the three main differences between Max Weber's and Karl Marx's theories of social stratification?

6. How does social stratification contribute to the functioning of society? What is wrong with this argument?

HOW IS SOCIAL CLASS DEFINED IN THE UNITED STATES?

> Understand the social causes and consequences of social class in U.S. society, as well as the complexities and challenges of defining class.

Social class in the United States typically is defined by some combination of one's income, wealth, educational attainment, and occupational status. In this section, we describe each of these attributes and describe how they are distributed throughout the U.S. population. We also compare and contrast the five major social class groups in the United States. One's income, wealth, education, and occupational status also vary widely based on personal characteristics like ethnicity and race, as well as gender. We will delve further into gender stratification and race in Chapters 9 and 10, respectively. We will also show how inequalities vary starkly throughout the globe in Chapter 8.

INCOME

income • Payment, usually derived from wages, salaries, or investments.

Income refers to wages and salaries earned from paid occupations, plus unearned money (or interest) from investments. One of the most significant changes occurring in Western countries over the past century has been the rising real income of the majority of the working population. (Real income is income excluding increases owing to inflation, which provides a fixed standard of comparison from year to year.) The majority of the population today is vastly more affluent than any peoples have previously been in human history.

Even though real income has risen in the past century, these earnings have not been distributed evenly across all groups. In 2012, the top 5 percent of all households in the United States received 22.3 percent of total income, the top 20 percent obtained 51 percent, and the bottom 20 percent received only 3.2 percent. Furthermore, the share of aggregate income earned by the top 1 percent, top 5 percent, and top 20 percent of households in the United States are near their highest levels since 1917, while the share earned by the bottom 20 percent is near its lowest in the same period (U.S. Bureau of the Census 2012h; Saez 2013).

The growing gap between the top and bottom tiers of the U.S. class structure has grown dramatically between 1977 and 2012. The average household earnings (calculated at 2012 dollars), meaning the combined incomes of all persons living in a single household, of the bottom 20 percent of people in the United States was essentially unchanged from $11,510 in 1977 to $11,490 in 2012. During the same

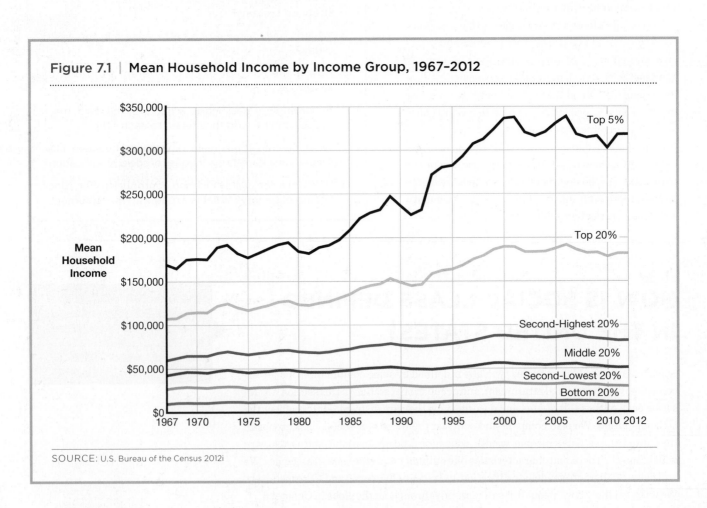

Figure 7.1 | Mean Household Income by Income Group, 1967–2012

SOURCE: U.S. Bureau of the Census 2012i

INCOME INEQUALITY

Income inequality refers to the unequal distribution of income across the population, or the gap between a country's richest and poorest citizens. One measure of income inequality is the income share held by the top 10 percent of the population. The greater the share, the higher the level of income inequality.

INCOME SHARE HELD BY THE TOP 10% OF THE POPULATION

SOUTH AFRICA
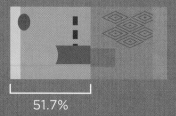
51.7%

BRAZIL

42.9%

MEXICO

38.7%

DOMINICAN REPUBLIC
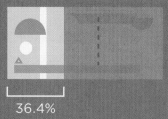
36.4%

CHINA
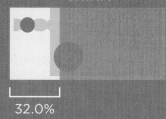
32.0%

RUSSIA

31.7%

UNITED STATES

29.9%

CANADA
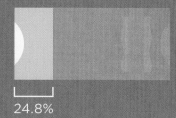
24.8%

SWEDEN
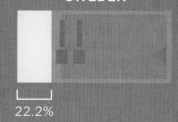
22.2%

DISTRIBUTION OF INCOME IN THE U.S. IN 2012

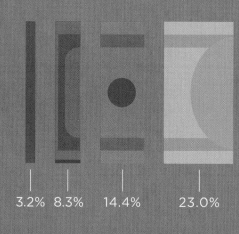
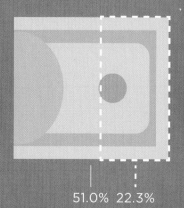

- BOTTOM 20%
- SECOND-LOWEST 20%
- MIDDLE 20%
- SECOND-HIGHEST 20%
- TOP 20%
- TOP 5%

3.2% 8.3% 14.4% 23.0% 51.0% 22.3%

Sources: World Bank 2013, U.S. Census Bureau 2012

period, the richest 20 percent saw their incomes grow by 48 percent, while for the richest 5 percent of the population, income rose by almost 70 percent (U.S. Bureau of the Census 2012i). Despite the growth of the economy and the creation of millions of new jobs, these trends continued throughout the 1990s and into the new century, leading some observers to deem the United States a "two-tiered society" (Freeman 1999).

WEALTH

wealth • Money and material possessions held by an individual or group.

Wealth refers to all assets individuals own: cash; savings and checking accounts; investments in stocks, bonds, and real estate properties; and so on. While most people earn their income from their work, the wealthy often derive the bulk of theirs from interest on their investments, some of them inherited. Some scholars argue that wealth—not income—is the real indicator of social class. While income can vary from year to year based on the number of hours one worked or whether one took leave or was temporarily laid off, wealth tends to be a more enduring measure that is less susceptible to annual fluctuations.

Net financial assets are far lower for minority groups than for whites (Oliver and Shapiro 1995). Between 1983 and 2007, the median net financial assets of white Americans rose from $19,900 to $170,400. Most African Americans began to accumulate net financial assets only in the 1990s; by 2000, the median net worth was $6,166. For Hispanic households, median net financial worth grew from effectively zero in 1998 to surpass that of African Americans, with a median net worth of $27,800 in 2007 (Survey of Consumer Finances 2009). However, since the start of the recession in 2007, the median net worth of all groups has decreased. This drop has been more profound for blacks and Latinos relative to whites; the U.S. Census estimates that between 2005 and 2010, the median net worth of whites dropped by 23 percent, whereas the wealth of blacks, Latinos, and Asians declined by 60 percent (U.S. Bureau of the Census 2011e).

What are some of the reasons for the racial disparity in wealth? Do blacks simply have less money with which to purchase assets? To some degree, the answer is yes. The old adage "It takes money to make money" is a fact of life for those who start with little or no wealth. Since whites historically have enjoyed higher incomes and levels of wealth than blacks, whites are able to accrue even more wealth, which they then are able to pass on to their children (Conley 1999). In fact, economists estimate that more than half the wealth that one accumulates in a lifetime can be traced to the person's progenitors.

But family advantages are not the only factors. Oliver and Shapiro (1995) argued that it is easier for whites to obtain assets even when they have fewer resources than blacks because discrimination plays a major role in the racial gap in home ownership. Blacks are rejected for mortgages 60 percent more often than whites, even when they have the same qualifications and creditworthiness. When blacks do receive mortgages, they are more likely to take subprime mortgage loans, which charge on average 2 percent more in interest. In 2006, of those who took out home loans, 30.3 percent of blacks took out subprime loans, compared with 24 percent of Hispanics and 17.7 percent of whites. Research shows that subprime loans are offered by only a few lenders, but those lenders focus on minority communities, whereas the prime lenders are unable or unwilling to lend in those communities (Avery and Canner 2005). Predatory lenders often step in, and they offer loans that carry unreasonably high fees, interest rates, and payment requirements (Rugh and

The recent subprime mortgage crisis left many Americans bankrupt. Blacks, Hispanics, and those living in the inner city were most likely to lose their homes.

Massey 2010). As a result of these high fees and monthly payments, those who take out subprime loans are much more likely to default on their loans and ultimately lose their homes.

These issues are particularly important because home ownership constitutes American families' primary means for accumulating wealth. The dangers of subprime lending became a painful reality during the financial crisis that began in 2008. Roughly one in five people who had taken out subprime loans had defaulted (i.e., they were two months behind in payment during the very first year of their loan), while less than 5 percent of people with prime mortgages had defaulted. In the process, many Americans lost their homes and were thrown into personal bankruptcy (Amromin and Paulson 2010). The effects of this crisis were far-reaching; as recently as 2011, one-third of all home sales were foreclosure sales, or the sale of homes purchased after the homeowners received a notice of default or that were repossessed by lenders (Kravitz 2011).

EDUCATION

Sociologists also believe that education, or the number of years of schooling a person has completed, is an important dimension of social stratification. As we will see later in this chapter, how much education one receives is often influenced by the social class of one's parents. Although Liz Murray, the daughter of unemployed drug addicts, went on to graduate from Harvard, her case is the exception to the rule.

Figure 7.2 | Mean Earnings by Educational Attainment, 1975–2012

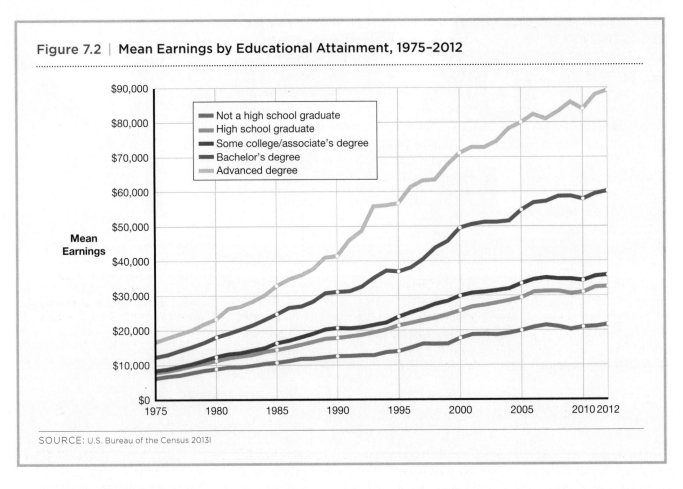

SOURCE: U.S. Bureau of the Census 2013l

The value of a college education has increased significantly in the past twenty years as a result of the increased demand for and wages paid to educated workers in the more technology- and information-based economy (Danziger and Gottschalk 1995). A recent Pew Social & Demographic Trends (2011) survey indicated that adults who graduated from college believe that, on average, they are earning $20,000 more a year as a result of having gotten that degree. Adults who did not attend college believe that, on average, they are earning $20,000 a year less as a result. This gap is remarkably close to the U.S. Census estimate that annual earnings of college graduates and nongraduates differed by roughly $19,550 in 2010. The survey also reports that, on average, a typical college graduate earns $650,000 more than a nongraduate over the course of a forty-year work life.

The economic benefits of education have increased over the past four decades (Figure 7.2). In 1979, college graduates eighteen years of age and older earned a mean wage that was 55 percent more than high school graduates. By 2012, the differential had grown to 85 percent (U.S. Bureau of the Census 2013l). Although this growing "wage premium" has encouraged more Americans to go to college—31.7 percent of Americans ages twenty-five and older had completed four or more years of college in 2013, compared with 16.4 percent in 1979 (U.S. Bureau of the Census 2013s)—it has also helped widen the gap between the wealthiest and the poorest workers.

Education is one of the strongest predictors of one's occupation, income, and wealth later in life. Yet, even college graduates are highly stratified with respect to their earnings potential. Persons whose undergraduate degrees required numerical competencies (like engineering and computers) tend to earn much more than other fields of study (like education and liberal arts) (Pew Social & Demographic Trends 2011). A recent study by the Center on Education and Workforce at Georgetown University compared 171 college majors and found that petroleum engineering had the highest median annual salary in 2009, $120,000, while counseling psychology majors earned the least, with a median of $29,000 per year (Carnevale et al. 2011).

Racial differences in levels of education persist, and this partly explains why racial differences in income and wealth also persist. In 2013, of those ages twenty-five and older, 88.6 percent of whites, 85.1 percent of blacks, and 90.1 percent of Asian Americans had completed high school, whereas only 66.2 percent of Latinos had completed high school (U.S. Bureau of the Census 2013f). We will delve more deeply into race and ethnic differences in educational attainment in Chapter 12.

OCCUPATION

Status refers to the prestige that goes along with one's social position. In the United States and other industrialized societies, occupation is an important indicator of one's social standing. Occupational status depends heavily on one's level of educational attainment. In fact, in studies where persons are asked to rate jobs in terms of how "prestigious" they are, the occupations that are ranked most highly are those requiring the most education (Treiman 1977). To read more about occupational prestige, see Table 7.1 on page 208.

upper class • A social class broadly composed of the more affluent members of society, especially those who have inherited wealth, own businesses, or hold large numbers of stocks (shares).

A PICTURE OF THE U.S. CLASS STRUCTURE

As we have seen so far, social class is a multifaceted concept, comprising how far we've gone in school, how much we earn, what we do for a living, and how many assets we possess. It is partly for this reason that it can be difficult to define precisely what social classes like upper, middle, and lower class mean in the United States. There can be wide differences in the lifestyles and personal characteristics of people even within a single social class group. Some scholars have gone so far as to argue that social class is a problematic concept because members of even a single social class "do not share distinct similar, life-defining experiences" (Kingston 2001). Despite this important critique, we can highlight some general characteristics that distinguish the major social strata. The purpose of the following discussion is to describe broad class differences in the United States. Bear in mind that there are no sharply defined boundaries between the classes.

THE UPPER CLASS

The **upper class** consists of the richest Americans—those households earning more than $311,000, or approximately 5 percent of all American households (U.S. Bureau of the Census 2012i). Most Americans in the upper class are wealthy but not superrich. They are likely to own a large suburban home as well as a town house or a vacation home, drive expensive automobiles, fly first class to vacations abroad, educate their children in private schools and colleges, and have their desires attended to by a staff of servants. Their wealth stems in large part from their substantial investments, including stocks and bonds and real estate, and the interest income derived from those investments. They are politically influential at the national, state, and local levels. The upper class includes people who acquired their wealth in a variety of ways: the heads of major corporations, people who have made large amounts of money through investments or

Two famous and wealthy philanthropists, Bill Gates of Microsoft and Bono of U2, meet with French President François Hollande. Like Bono and Gates, members of the upper class wield political power.

Table 7.1 | Relative Social Prestige of Selected U.S. Occupations

OCCUPATION	PRESTIGE SCORE	WHITE-COLLAR OCCUPATION	BLUE-COLLAR OCCUPATION
Physician	86	X	
Lawyer	75	X	
Architect	73	X	
Dentist	72	X	
Member of the clergy	69	X	
Registered nurse	66	X	
Secondary-school teacher	64	X	
Veterinarian	62	X	
Sociologist	61	X	
Police officer	60		X
Actor	58	X	
Aircraft mechanic	53		X
Firefighter	53		X
Realtor	49	X	
Machinist	47		X
Musician/composer	47	X	
Bank teller	43	X	
Welder	42		X
Farmer	40		X
Carpenter	39		X
Child-care worker	36		X
File clerk	36	X	
Bulldozer operator	34		X
Auto body repairperson	31		X
Retail apparel salesperson	30	X	
Truck driver	30		X
Cashier	29	X	
Taxi driver	28		X
Waiter/waitress	28		X
Bartender	25		X
Door-to-door salesperson	22		X
Janitor	22		X

SOURCE: National Opinion Research Center 2001

real estate, those fortunate enough to have inherited great wealth from their parents, a few highly successful celebrities and professional athletes, and a handful of others.

At the very top of this group are people who have accumulated vast fortunes that allow them to enjoy a lifestyle unimaginable to most Americans. The super-rich are highly self-conscious of their unique and privileged social class position; some give generously to such worthy causes as the fine arts, hospitals, and charities. Their homes are often lavish and sometimes filled with collections of fine art. Their common class identity is strengthened by such things as having attended the same exclusive private secondary schools (to which they also send their children). They sit on the same corporate boards of directors and belong to the same private clubs. They contribute large sums of money to their favorite politicians and may be on a first-name basis with members of Congress and perhaps even with the president (Domhoff 1998).

The turn of the twenty-first century saw extraordinary opportunities for the accumulation of such wealth. Globalization is one reason. Those entrepreneurs who are able to invest globally often prosper, both by selling products to foreign consumers and by making profits cheaply by using low-wage labor in developing countries. The information revolution is another reason for this accumulation of wealth. Before the dot-com bubble burst in 2012, young entrepreneurs with start-up high-tech companies such as Yahoo! or eBay made legendary fortunes. As a consequence, the number of superrich Americans has exploded in recent years. At the end of World War II, there were only $13,000 people worth a million dollars or more in the United States. In 2013, there were 9.63 million millionaire households in the United States (Spectrem Group 2014) and 492 billionaires (Forbes 2014), reflecting the continuing recovery from the sweeping global economic downturn that began in 2008 and had reduced these numbers in recent years. In 2008, there were 6.7 million millionaire households in the United States, the lowest level since 2003 (Spectrem Group 2009), as well as 371 billionaires (Forbes 2009).

Although the total number of millionaire households has dipped slightly, those at the top of the earnings ladder continue to hold vast amounts of resources. The 400 richest Americans are worth approximately just over $2 trillion—more than one-tenth of the gross domestic product of the United States and slightly more than the gross domestic product of Russia (Forbes 2013c). There are billionaires outside the United States as well. The collective net worth of the world's 1,645 billionaires was $6.4 trillion in 2014 (Forbes 2014), slightly less than 300 percent of the gross domestic product of India.

Unlike "old-money" families such as the Rockefellers or the Vanderbilts, who accumulated their wealth in earlier generations and thus are viewed as a sort of American aristocracy, this "new wealth" often consists of upstart entrepreneurs such as Facebook's Mark Zuckerberg, whose net worth was estimated by Forbes (2014) at $28.5 billion as of June 2014.

THE MIDDLE CLASS

When Americans are asked to identify their social class, the majority claim to be middle class. The reason is partly the American cultural belief that the United States is relatively free of class distinctions. Few people want to be identified as being too rich or too poor. Most Americans seem to think that others are not very different from their immediate family, friends, and coworkers (Kelley and Evans 1995; Simpson et al. 1988; Vanneman and Cannon 1987). Since people rarely interact with those outside of their social class, they tend to see themselves as like "most other people," whom they then regard as being "middle class" (Kelley and Evans 1995). A 2012 Gallup poll found that fully 40 percent of Americans describe themselves as "middle class," while another 13 percent identify as upper-middle class (Dugan 2012).

The **middle class** is a catchall for a diverse group of occupations, lifestyles, and people who earn stable and sometimes substantial incomes at primarily white-collar jobs. It grew throughout much of the first three-quarters of the twentieth century, then shrank during most of the last quarter-century. During the late 1990s, however, economic growth halted this decline. The incomes of middle-class Americans continued to stagnate for the next two decades due in large part to the recession. Currently, the middle class includes slightly more than half of all American households. While the middle class was once largely white, today it is increasingly diverse, both racially and culturally, including African Americans, Asian Americans, and Latinos.

The American middle class can be subdivided into two groups: the upper-middle class and the lower-middle class.

middle class • A social class composed broadly of those working in white-collar and lower managerial occupations.

THE UPPER-MIDDLE CLASS

The upper-middle class consists of highly educated professionals (for example, doctors, lawyers, engineers, and professors), mid-level corporate managers, people who own or manage small businesses and retail shops, and some large-farm owners. Household incomes range quite widely, from about $178,000 to perhaps $300,000. The lower end of the income category would include college professors, for example, while the higher end would include corporate managers and small business owners. The upper-middle class includes approximately 20 percent of all American households (U.S. Bureau of the Census 2012i). Its members are likely to be college educated (as are their children) with advanced degrees. Their jobs are secure and provide retirement and health benefits. They own comfortable homes, drive expensive late-model cars, have some savings and investments, and are often active in local politics and civic organizations. However, they tend not to enjoy the same high-end luxuries, social connections, or extravagancies as members of the upper class.

THE LOWER-MIDDLE CLASS

The lower-middle class consists of trained office workers (for example, secretaries and bookkeepers), elementary and high school teachers, nurses, salespeople, police officers, firefighters, and others who provide skilled services. This group, which includes about 40 percent of American households, is the most varied of the social class strata, and may include college-educated persons with relatively modest earnings, such as public elementary school teachers, as well as quite highly paid persons with high school diplomas only, such as skilled craftsmen (e.g., plumbers) and civil servants with many years of seniority. Household incomes in this group range from about $50,000 to $178,000 (U.S. Bureau of the Census 2012i). Members of the lower-middle class may own a modest house, although many live in rental units. Their automobiles may be late models, but not the more expensive ones. Almost all have a high school education, and some have college degrees. They want their children to attend college, although this usually requires work-study programs and student loans. They are rarely politically active beyond exercising their right to vote.

THE WORKING CLASS

The **working class**, about 20 percent of all American households, includes primarily **blue-collar** (for example, factory workers and mechanics) and **pink-collar** (for example, clerical aides and sales clerks) laborers. Household incomes range from about $29,204 to $49,842 (U.S. Bureau of the Census 2012i), and at least two household members work to make ends meet. Family income is just enough to pay the rent or the mortgage, put food on the table, and perhaps save for a summer vacation. The working class includes factory workers, mechanics, office workers, sales clerks, restaurant and hotel workers, and others who earn a modest weekly paycheck at a job that offers little control over the size of one's income or working conditions. As you will see later in this chapter, many blue-collar jobs in the United States are threatened by economic globalization, so members of the working class today are likely to feel insecure about their own and their family's future.

The working class is racially and ethnically diverse. While older members of the working class may own a home that was bought a number of years ago, younger members are likely to rent. The home or apartment is likely to be in a lower-income suburb or a city neighborhood. The household car, a lower-priced model, is unlikely to be new. Children who graduate from high school are unlikely to go to college and will attempt to get a job immediately instead. Most members of the working class are not likely to be politically active even in their own community, although they may vote in some elections.

working class • A social class broadly composed of people working in blue-collar, or manual, occupations.

blue- and pink-collar jobs • Jobs that typically pay low wages and often involve manual or low-skill labor. Blue-collar jobs typically are held by men (e.g., factory worker), whereas pink-collar jobs are typically held by women (e.g., clerical assistant).

THE LOWER CLASS

The **lower class**, roughly 15 percent of American households, includes those who work part time or not at all; household income is typically lower than $29,204 (U.S. Bureau of the Census 2012i). Most lower-class individuals are found in cities, although some live in rural areas and earn a little money as farmers or part-time workers. Some manage to find employment in semiskilled or unskilled manufacturing or service jobs, ranging from making clothing in sweatshops to cleaning houses. Their jobs, when they can find them, are dead-end jobs, meaning that years of work are unlikely to lead to promotion or substantially higher income. Their work is probably part time and highly unstable, without benefits such as medical insurance, disability, or Social Security. Even if they are fortunate enough to find a full-time job, there are no guarantees that it will be around next month or even next week. Many people in the lower class live in poverty. Very few own their own homes. Most of the lower class rent, and some are homeless. If they own a car at all, it is likely to be a used car. A higher percentage of the lower class is nonwhite than is true of other social classes. Its members do not participate in politics, and they seldom vote.

lower class • A social class composed of those who work part time or not at all and whose household income is typically low.

THE "UNDERCLASS"

In the lower class, some sociologists have identified a group that Swedish sociologist Gunnar Myrdal (1963) originally referred to as the **underclass** because they are "beneath" the class system, in that they lack access to the world of work and mainstream patterns of behavior. Located in the highest-poverty neighborhoods of the inner city, the underclass is sometimes called the "new urban poor."

The underclass includes many African Americans who have been trapped for more than one generation in a cycle of poverty from which there is little possibility of escape (Wacquant 1993, 1996; Wacquant and Wilson 1993; Wilson 1996). These

underclass • A class of individuals situated at the bottom of the class system, often composed of people from ethnic minority backgrounds.

CONCEPT CHECKS ✓

1. Name at least three components of social class. How do blacks and whites differ along these components?

2. What are the major social class groups in the United States today? Describe at least two ways (other than their income) that these groups differ from one another.

are the poorest of the poor. Their numbers have grown rapidly over the past quarter-century and today include unskilled and unemployed men, young single mothers and their children on welfare, teenagers from welfare-dependent families, and many homeless people. They live in poor neighborhoods troubled by drugs, gangs, and high levels of violence. They are the truly disadvantaged, people with extremely difficult lives who have little realistic hope of ever making it out of poverty. ✓

Recognize why and how the gap between rich and poor has increased in recent decades. Understand social mobility, and think about your own mobility.

WHAT ARE THE CAUSES AND CONSEQUENCES OF SOCIAL INEQUALITY IN THE UNITED STATES?

A GROWING GAP BETWEEN RICH AND POOR

The United States prides itself on being a nation of equals. But as we touched on earlier in the chapter, during the past quarter-century, the gap between the rich and the poor in the United States has started to grow. One statistical analysis of income and

The Occupy Wall Street protests of 2011 drew attention to rising income inequality in the United States.

poverty among industrial nations found that the United States had the most unequal distribution of household income among all twenty-one industrial countries studied (Sweden had the most equal) (Smeeding 2000).

Since the mid-twentieth century, the rich have gotten much, much richer. Middle-class incomes have stagnated, and the poor have grown in number. The current gap between the rich and the poor in the United States is the largest since the Census Bureau started measuring it in 1947 (U.S. Bureau of the Census 2000). Social movements like the Occupy Wall Street protests are a direct response to the realization among Americans that the divide between the very wealthy and everyone else is vast and growing. The rallying cry of the Occupy movement, "We are the 99 percent," refers in part to the fact that the very top 1 percent of the population holds more than one-third (34.5 percent) of the total net worth in the United States (Saez 2013).

ETHNIC MINORITIES VERSUS WHITE AMERICANS

There are substantial differences in income based on race and ethnicity, since minorities in the United States are more likely to hold the lowest-paying jobs. Black and Latino household income, for example, averages between two-thirds and three-quarters that of whites (Figure 7.3). For blacks, this is a slight improvement over previous years, as a growing number of blacks have gone to college and moved into middle-class occupations. For Latinos, however, the situation has worsened, as recent immigrants from rural areas in Mexico and Central America find themselves working at low-wage jobs (U.S. Bureau of the Census 2001). The situation has, however, worsened over the last decade. While the average income of whites has been rising consistently, that of blacks and Latinos has been declining (U.S. Bureau of the Census 2010c).

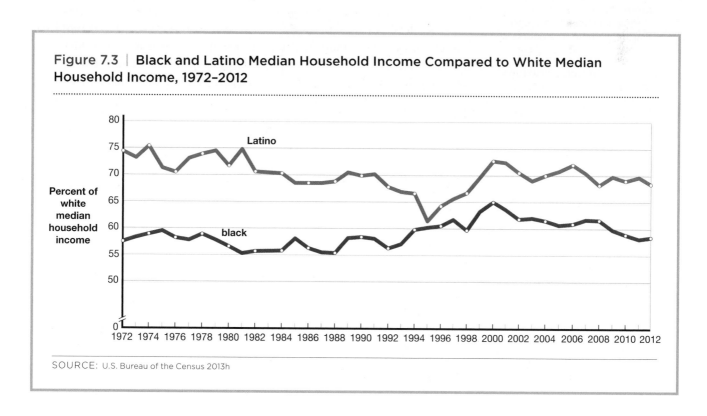

Figure 7.3 | Black and Latino Median Household Income Compared to White Median Household Income, 1972–2012

SOURCE: U.S. Bureau of the Census 2013h

Oliver and Shapiro (1995) found that the "wealth gap" between blacks and whites is even greater than the income gap. While blacks on average earned two-thirds as much as whites, their net worth was only one-tenth as much. More recent data show that the wealth gap has decreased only slightly. In 2010, white families had a median net worth of $130,600, compared with $20,400 for nonwhite or Hispanic families (Bricker et al. 2012). Oliver and Shapiro also found that when blacks attained educational or occupational levels comparable with that of whites, the wealth gap still did not disappear.

Oliver and Shapiro (1995) argued that blacks in the United States have encountered many barriers to acquiring wealth throughout history. After the Civil War ended slavery in 1865, legal discrimination (such as mandatory segregation in the South and separate schools) tied the vast majority of blacks to the lowest rungs of the economic ladder. Racial discrimination was made illegal by the Civil Rights Act of 1964; nonetheless, discrimination has remained, and although some blacks have moved into middle-class occupations, many have remained poor or in low-wage jobs where the opportunities for accumulating wealth are nonexistent. Less wealth means less social and cultural capital: fewer dollars to invest in schooling for one's children, a business, or the stock market—investments that in the long run would create greater wealth for future investments. We will further explore issues of racial inequality in Chapter 10.

SOCIAL MOBILITY

social mobility • Movement of individuals or groups among different social positions.

Social mobility refers to the upward or downward movement of individuals and groups among different class positions as a result of changes in occupation, wealth, or income. There are two ways of studying social mobility. First, we can look at people's own careers—how far they move up or down the socioeconomic scale in the course of their working lives. This is called **intragenerational mobility**. Alternatively, we can analyze where children are on the scale compared with their parents or grandparents. Mobility across the generations is called **intergenerational mobility**. Sociologists have long studied both types of mobility, with increasingly sophisticated methods. Unfortunately, with the exception of some recent studies, much of this research has been limited to male mobility, particularly of white males. We look at some of the research in this section.

intragenerational mobility • Movement up or down a social stratification hierarchy within the course of a personal career.

intergenerational mobility • Movement up or down a social stratification hierarchy from one generation to another.

OPPORTUNITIES FOR MOBILITY: WHO GETS AHEAD?

Is it possible for a young person from a working-class background to transcend class roots and become an upper-class professional? Is the case of Liz Murray a fairy tale or reality? If a reality, what factors contributed to her ascent up the social ladder? Sociologists have sought to answer this question by trying to understand which social factors are most influential in determining an individual's status or position in society. Most research shows that while the forces of social reproduction are very powerful, it is possible for people to transcend their roots; **social reproduction** refers to the processes whereby parents pass down to their children a range of resources, including both financial and cultural capital.

social reproduction • The process whereby societies have structural continuity over time. Social reproduction is an important pathway through which parents transmit or produce values, norms, and social practices among their children.

In a classic study of intergenerational mobility in the United States, sociologists Peter Blau and Otis Dudley Duncan (1967) found that long-range intergenerational mobility—that is, from working class to upper-middle class—was rare. Why? Blau

Chelsea Clinton has had successful careers as an NBC News correspondent and a management consultant. As the daughter of a former president and secretary of state, Chelsea's family background provided her with rich cultural capital.

and Duncan concluded that the key factor behind occupational status was educational attainment. A child's education is influenced by family social status; this, in turn, affects the child's social position later in life. Sociologists William Sewell and Robert Hauser (1980) later confirmed Blau and Duncan's conclusions. They added to the argument by claiming that the connection between family background and educational attainment occurs because parents, teachers, and friends influence the educational and career aspirations of the child and that these aspirations then become an important influence on the schooling and careers obtained throughout the child's life. In other words, aspirations are reproduced from generation to generation because parents and children share the social location and social ties that may shape one's aspirations.

French sociologist Pierre Bourdieu (1984, 1988) has also been a major figure in examining the importance of family background to social status, but his emphasis is on the cultural advantages that parents can provide to their children. Bourdieu argued that among the factors responsible for social status, the most important is the transmission of **cultural capital**, or the cultural advantages that coming from a "good home" confers. Wealthier families are able to afford to send their children to better schools, an economic advantage that benefits the children's social status as adults. Parents from the upper and middle classes are mostly highly educated themselves and tend to be more involved in their children's education—reading to them, helping with homework, purchasing books and learning materials, and encouraging their progress. Bourdieu noted that working-class parents are concerned about their children's education, but they lack the economic and cultural capital to make a difference.

Although Bourdieu focused on social status in France, the socioeconomic order in the United States is similar. Those who already hold positions of wealth and power can ensure their children have the best available education, and this will often lead them into the best jobs. Studies consistently show that the large majority of people who have "made money" did so on the basis of inheriting or being given at least a modest amount initially—which they then used to make

cultural capital • Noneconomic or cultural resources that parents pass down to their children, such as language or knowledge. These resources contribute to the process of social reproduction, according to Bourdieu.

downward mobility • Social mobility in which individuals' wealth, income, or status is lower than what they or their parents once had.

short-range downward mobility • Social mobility that occurs when an individual moves from one position in the class structure to another of nearly equal status.

more. In U.S. society, it's better to start at the top than at the bottom (Duncan et al. 1998; Jaher 1973; Rubinstein 1986); through social reproduction practices, those who start on the top are able to pass their economic and cultural resources down to their children.

DOWNWARD MOBILITY

Downward mobility is the process where one's own wealth, income, or occupational status is lower than what one's parents had. Downward mobility is less common than upward mobility; nevertheless, an estimated one-third of all Americans raised in the middle class—defined as households between the thirtieth and seventieth percentile of the income distribution—fall out of the middle class when they become adults (Acs 2011). A person with **short-range downward mobility** moves from one job to another that is similar in pay and prestige, for example, from a routine office job to semiskilled blue-collar work. Downward intragenerational mobility, also a common occurrence, is often associated with psychological problems and anxieties. Some people are simply unable to sustain the lifestyle into which they were born. But another source of downward mobility among individuals arises through no fault of their own. During the late 1980s and early 1990s, and again in the late 2000s, corporate America was flooded with instances in which middle-aged men lost their jobs because of company mergers, takeovers, or bankruptcies. These executives either had difficulty finding new jobs or could only find jobs that paid less than their previous jobs. ✓

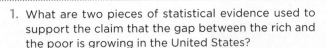

CONCEPT CHECKS ✓

1. What are two pieces of statistical evidence used to support the claim that the gap between the rich and the poor is growing in the United States?

2. How would you explain the wealth gap between blacks and whites in the United States today?

3. Contrast intragenerational and intergenerational mobility.

4. According to classic studies of mobility in the United States, how does family background affect one's social class in adulthood?

5. According to Pierre Bourdieu, how does the family contribute to the transmission of social class from generation to generation?

6. Describe at least two reasons for downward mobility.

Learn about poverty in the United States today, explanations for why it exists, and means for combating it. Learn how people become marginalized in a society and the forms that this marginalization takes.

HOW DOES POVERTY AFFECT INDIVIDUALS?

At the bottom of the class system in the United States are the millions of people who live in poverty. Many do not maintain a proper diet and live in miserable conditions; their average life expectancy is lower than that of the majority of the population. In addition, the number of individuals and families who have become homeless has increased greatly over the past twenty years.

In defining poverty, a distinction is usually made between absolute and relative poverty. **Absolute poverty** means that a person or family simply can't get enough to eat. People living in absolute poverty are undernourished and, in situations of famine, may actually starve to death. Absolute poverty is common in the poorer developing countries.

In the industrial countries, **relative poverty** is essentially a measure of inequality. It means being poor as compared with the standards of living of the majority. It is reasonable to call a person poor in the United States if he or she lacks

absolute poverty • The minimal requirements necessary to sustain a healthy existence.

relative poverty • Poverty defined according to the living standards of the majority in any given society.

the basic resources needed to maintain a decent standard of housing and healthy living conditions.

MEASURING POVERTY

When President Lyndon B. Johnson began his War on Poverty in 1964, around 36 million Americans lived in poverty. In 2012, this number sat at 46.5 million people, or roughly 15.0 percent of the population—the highest level recorded since 1993 when the poverty rate was 15.1 percent (National Poverty Center 2013; U.S. Bureau of the Census 2013k). The rate of child poverty is even worse: 21.8 percent of children live in a household with income levels beneath the poverty line. The official U.S. poverty rate is the highest among the major advanced industrial nations, more than three times that of such European countries as Sweden or Norway (Smeeding et al. 2000). The largest concentrations of poverty in the United States are found in the South and the Southwest, in inner cities, and in rural areas. Among the poor, 20.4 million Americans (or 6.6 percent of the U.S. population) live in extreme poverty: Their incomes are only half of the official poverty level, meaning that they live at near-starvation levels (DeNavas-Walt et al. 2010; U.S. Bureau of the Census 2013k).

What does it mean to be poor in the world's richest nation? The U.S. government calculates the **poverty line** as an income equal to three times the cost of a nutritionally adequate diet—a strict, no-frills budget that assumes a nutritionally adequate diet could be purchased in 1999 for only $3.86 per day for each member, along with about $7.72 on all other items (including rent and utilities, clothing, medical expenses, and transportation). For a family of four in 2013, that works out to an annual cash income of $23,550 (U.S. Department of Health and Human Services 2013).

poverty line • An official government measure to define those living in poverty in the United States.

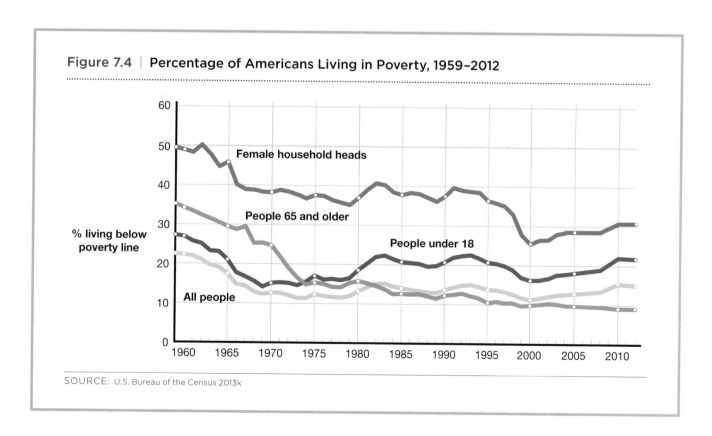

Figure 7.4 | Percentage of Americans Living in Poverty, 1959–2012

Female household heads

People 65 and older

People under 18

% living below poverty line

All people

SOURCE: U.S. Bureau of the Census 2013k

High school guidance counselors can play a pivotal role in helping teens formulate and work toward their future educational and career goals. But as much as guidance counselors would like to believe that every student can achieve his or her dreams, they also recognize that some students face particularly difficult obstacles. Students from poor families often have to work after school, giving up valuable after-school activities and study time. Other high school students are the first in their family to dream of going to college, and they're not sure of the best classes to take or whether to take the SAT. Guidance counselors at the largest inner-city schools face a further burden; they often can't make time for their many students. The American School Counselor Association recommends a ratio of one counselor for every 250 students; the national average in 2011, however, was 471:1 and was as high as 1,016:1 in California. Sociologists like Blau, Duncan, Hauser, Sewell, and Bourdieu have described the ways that social background and environment can shape one's future. Drawing on this sociological research, if you were a high school guidance counselor, what kind of advice would you offer to your students? Would you give different types of assistance and advice to students from upper-, middle-, working-, and lower-class and underclass backgrounds? Why?

How realistic is this formula? Some critics believe it overestimates the amount of poverty. They point out that the current standard fails to take into account noncash forms of income available to the poor such as food stamps, Medicare, Medicaid, and public housing subsidies, as well as under-the-table pay obtained from work at odd jobs that is concealed from the government. Other critics counter that the government's formula greatly underestimates the amount of poverty because it overemphasizes the proportion of a family budget spent on food and severely underestimates the share spent on housing. According to some estimates, poor families today may spend as much as three-quarters of their income on housing alone (Dolbeare 1995; Joint Center for Housing Studies of Harvard University 2005). Still others observe that this formula dramatically underestimates the proportion of older adults (age 65+) who live in poverty because they spend a relatively small proportion of their income on food yet are faced with high health-care costs (Carr 2010).

WHO ARE THE POOR?

Most Americans think of the poor as people who are unemployed or on welfare. Surveys repeatedly show that the majority of Americans regard the poor as responsible for their plight and are antagonistic to those who live on "government handouts." For example, a Gallup poll (Gallup Organization 1998) found that 55 percent of the public believed that lack of effort by the poor was the principal reason for poverty. More recently, attitudes toward the poor have become a bit more forgiving, perhaps due to the recession and the recognition that almost anyone can fall into poverty. In 2012, a Pew Research Center survey found that just 38 percent of Americans believed that a lack of effort on the part of the poor was responsible for poverty, whereas 46 percent cited circumstances beyond the control of the poor (Pew Research Center for the People and the Press 2012a).

Data on who the poor actually are show that blacks and Latinos are more likely than whites to live in poverty, but poverty strikes members of all ethnic and racial backgrounds. A recent report by the research organization Demos and Brandeis University estimated that a substantial segment of the middle class—one-fifth of white families, one-third of black families, and two-fifths of Latino families—will be in danger of downward social mobility, and ultimately, poverty, should the nation's recession continue (Wheary et al. 2010).

THE WORKING POOR

working poor • People who work but whose earnings are not enough to lift them above the poverty line.

Many Americans are the **working poor**—that is, people who work but whose earnings are not high enough to lift them above the poverty line. The federal minimum wage, the

Many fast food workers are counted among the working poor. Most earn minimum wage and many lack health benefits due to their part-time work schedules.

legal floor for wages in the United States, was first set in 1938 at $0.25 an hour. Set on July 24, 2009, the federal minimum wage is currently $7.25 per hour, although individual states can set higher minimum wages than the federal standard. Nineteen states and the District of Columbia have chosen to do so; the state of Washington currently has the highest minimum wage—$9.19 per hour (U.S. Department of Labor 2013). Although the federal minimum wage has increased over the years, since 1965 it has failed to keep up with inflation.

About one-fourth of those officially living in poverty are actually working. In 2011, there were an estimated 10.4 million working poor (3.4 percent of the population) (U.S. Bureau of Labor Statistics 2013i). Of those working poor, 4.9 million usually worked full-time and another 3.9 million usually worked part-time. Most poor people, contrary to popular belief, do not receive welfare payments because they earn too much to qualify. Only 5 percent of all low-income families with a full-time, full-year worker receive welfare benefits, and over half rely on public health insurance rather than employer-sponsored insurance. The working poor are disproportionately nonwhite and immigrant. Furthermore, 5.5 million of the individuals who comprised the working poor in 2011 were women and 4.9 million were men. Young workers are more likely to be classified as working poor than their older counterparts (Urban Institute 2005; U.S. Bureau of Labor Statistics 2013i). Qualitative research on low-wage fast-food workers further reveals that many working poor lack adequate education, do not have health insurance to cover medical costs, and are trying to support families on poverty-level wages (Newman 2000).

POVERTY, RACE, AND ETHNICITY

Poverty rates in the United States are much higher among most minority groups than among whites, even though more than two-thirds of the poor are white. As Figure 7.5 shows, blacks and Latinos continue to earn around two-thirds of what whites earn in the United States, while experiencing three times the poverty rate

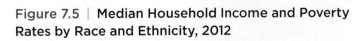

Figure 7.5 | Median Household Income and Poverty Rates by Race and Ethnicity, 2012

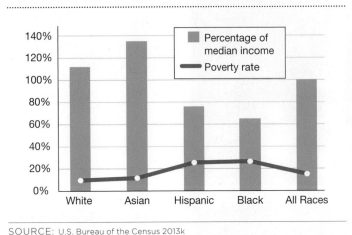

SOURCE: U.S. Bureau of the Census 2013k

that whites experience. This is because they often work at the lowest-paying jobs and because of racial discrimination. Asian Americans have the highest income of any group, but their poverty rate is slightly less than one and a half times that of whites, reflecting the recent influx of relatively poor Asian immigrant groups.

Latinos have somewhat higher incomes than blacks, although their poverty rate is comparable. Nonetheless, the number of blacks living in poverty has declined considerably in recent years. In 1959, 55.1 percent of blacks were living in poverty; by 2012, that figure had dropped to 27.2 percent. A similar pattern holds for Latinos: Poverty grew steadily between 1972 and 1994, peaking at 30.7 percent of the Latino population. By 2012, however, the poverty rate for Latinos had fallen to 25.6 percent (U.S. Bureau of the Census 2013k). This is mainly because the economic expansion of the 1990s created new job opportunities (DeNavas-Walt et al. 2005).

THE FEMINIZATION OF POVERTY

feminization of poverty • An increase in the proportion of the poor who are female.

Much of the growth in poverty is associated with the **feminization of poverty**, an increase in the proportion of the poor who are female. Growing rates of divorce, separation, and single-parent families have placed women at a particular disadvantage; it is extremely difficult for unskilled or semiskilled, low-income, poorly educated women to raise children by themselves while also holding down a job that pays enough to raise them out of poverty. As a result, in 2012, 30.9 percent of all single-parent families headed by women were poor, compared with only 6.3 percent of married couples with children (U.S. Bureau of the Census 2013k).

The feminization of poverty is particularly acute among families headed by Latino women. Although the rate declined by almost 30 percent since its peak in the mid-1980s (64 percent in 1985), 40.7 percent of all female-headed Latino families lived in poverty in 2012. Nearly 38 percent of female-headed African American families also live in poverty, both considerably higher than either white (27.8 percent) or Asian (19.2 percent) female-headed households (U.S. Bureau of the Census 2012n). A single woman attempting to raise children alone is caught in a vicious circle (Edin and Kefalas 2005). If she has a job, she must find someone to take care of her children because she cannot afford to hire a babysitter or pay for day care. From her standpoint, she will take in more money if she accepts welfare payments from the government and tries to find illegal part-time jobs that pay cash not reported to the government rather than find a regular full-time job paying minimum wage. Even though welfare will not get her out of poverty, if she finds a regular job, she will lose her welfare altogether, and she and her family may end up worse off economically. We will further explore the economic disadvantages facing women and mothers in Chapter 9.

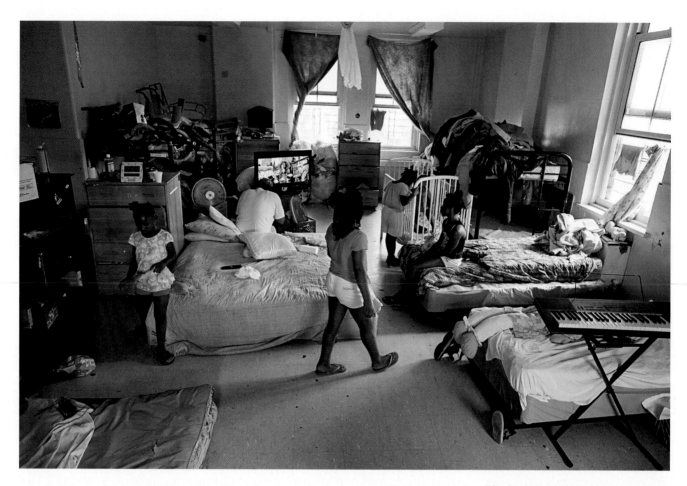

Blacks and Latinos are much more likely than whites to live in poverty. Many, like the family pictured above, live in overcrowded or substandard housing.

CHILDREN IN POVERTY

Given the high rates of poverty among families headed by single women, it follows that children are the principal victims of poverty in the United States. Child poverty rates (defined as poverty among people under eighteen) in the United States are by far the highest in the industrial world. Nonetheless, the child poverty rate has varied considerably over the last forty years, declining when the economy expands or the government increases spending on antipoverty programs and rising when the economy slows and government antipoverty spending falls. The child poverty rate declined from 27.3 percent of all children in 1959 to 14.4 percent in 1973—a period associated with both economic growth and the War on Poverty declared by the Johnson administration (1963–1969). During the late 1970s and 1980s, as economic growth slowed and cutbacks were made in government antipoverty programs, child poverty grew, exceeding 20 percent during much of the period. The economic expansion of the 1990s saw a drop in child poverty rates, and in 2002 the rate had fallen to 16.3 percent, a twenty-year low (U.S. Bureau of the Census 2003b).

However, these patterns have reversed in recent years, due in part to the current recession. A recent study by the Annie E. Casey Foundation found that child poverty surged in thirty-eight states during the past decade, erasing many of the gains in child well-being made in the last twenty years. In 2009, 15 million children lived in poor families, and another 31 million children lived in families where the loss of just two paychecks would result in economic catastrophe, according to the report. Taken together, this means that about 43 percent of the nation's

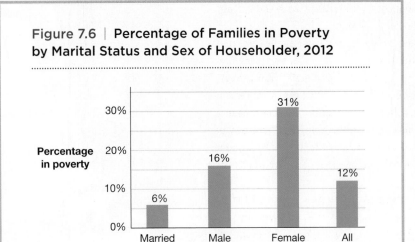

Figure 7.6 | Percentage of Families in Poverty by Marital Status and Sex of Householder, 2012

SOURCE: U.S. Bureau of the Census 2013k

children live in economically insecure households. The study also found that 4 percent of children had been directly affected by a foreclosure and 11 percent had at least one parent who lost his or her job since the recession began (Annie E. Casey Foundation 2011).

The economic well-being of racial minority children and children of single mothers is even more dire. In 2012, 17.9 percent of white children were poor compared with 37.5 percent of black children, 13.3 percent of Asian children, and 33.3 percent of Hispanic children; 42.6 percent of all racial minority children in 2011 lived in a single-mother household (U.S. Bureau of the Census 2012b, 2012m).

THE ELDERLY IN POVERTY

Although relatively few persons ages sixty-five and older live in poverty (8.37 percent), this aggregate statistic conceals vast gender, race, and marital status differences in the economic well-being of older adults. In 2011, elderly poverty rates ranged from just 3.9 percent among white married men to an astounding 32.2 percent for black women who live alone and 38.8 percent for Hispanic women living alone (U.S. Bureau of the Census 2012b; U.S. Department of Health and Human Services 2012b). As we noted earlier, these estimates may underestimate how widespread elderly poverty is because poverty rates fail to consider the high (and rising) costs of medical care, which disproportionately strike older adults (Carr 2010).

Because older people have for the most part retired from paid work, their income is based primarily on **Social Security** and private retirement programs. Social Security and **Medicare** have been especially important in lifting many elderly people out of poverty. Yet people who depend solely on these two programs for income and health-care coverage are likely to live modestly at best. Social Security accounts for only about 40 percent of the income of the typical retiree; most of the remainder comes from investments and private pension funds, and sometimes earnings. Low-income households are particularly likely to rely heavily on Social Security, which accounts for 94 percent of income for beneficiaries who live on less than $12,554 a year (Social Security Administration 2012). Yet even the combination of Social Security and private pensions results in modest retirement incomes for most people (Social Security Administration 2012).

Social Security • A government program that provides economic assistance to persons faced with unemployment, disability, or old age.

Medicare • A program under the U.S. Social Security Administration that reimburses hospitals and physicians for medical care provided to qualifying people over sixty-five years old.

EXPLAINING POVERTY: THE SOCIOLOGICAL DEBATE

Explanations of poverty can be grouped under two main headings: theories that see poor individuals as responsible for their status, and theories that view poverty as produced and reproduced by structural forces in society. These competing approaches are sometimes described as "blame the victim" and "blame the system" theories, respectively. We shall briefly examine each in turn.

There is a long history of attitudes that hold the poor responsible for their own disadvantaged positions. Early efforts to address the effects of poverty, such as the poorhouses of the nineteenth century, were grounded in a belief that poverty was the result of an inadequacy or pathology of individuals. The poor were seen as those who were unable—due to lack of skills, moral or physical weakness, absence of motivation, or below-average ability—to succeed in society. Social standing was taken as a reflection of a person's talent and effort; those who deserved to succeed did so, while others less capable were doomed to fail. The existence of winners and losers was regarded as a fact of life.

Such outlooks enjoyed a renaissance, beginning in the 1970s and 1980s, as the political emphasis on individual ambition rewarded those who "succeeded" in society and held those who did not responsible for the circumstances in which they found themselves. Often, explanations for poverty were sought in the lifestyles of poor people, along with the attitudes and outlooks they supposedly espoused. Oscar Lewis (1968) set forth one of the most influential of such theories, arguing that a **culture of poverty** exists among many poor people. According to Lewis, poverty is not a result of individual inadequacies but is a result of a larger social and cultural milieu into which poor children are socialized. The culture of poverty is transmitted across generations because young people from an early age see little point in aspiring to something more. Instead, they resign themselves fatalistically to a life of impoverishment.

The culture-of-poverty thesis has been taken further by American political scientist Charles Murray. According to Murray, individuals who are poor through "no fault of their own"—such as widows or widowers, orphans, or the disabled—fall into a different category from those who are part of the **dependency culture**. By this term, Murray refers to poor people who rely on government welfare provision rather than entering the labor market. He argues that the growth of the welfare state has created a subculture that undermines personal ambition and the capacity for self-help. Rather than orienting themselves toward the future and striving to achieve a better life, those dependent on welfare are content to accept handouts. Welfare, he argues, has eroded people's incentive to work (Murray 1984).

A second approach to explaining poverty emphasizes larger social processes that produce conditions of poverty that are difficult for individuals to overcome. According to such a view, structural forces within society—factors like class, gender, ethnicity, occupational position, education attainment, and so forth—shape the way in which resources are distributed (Wilson 1996). Writers who advocate structural explanations for poverty argue that the lack of ambition among the poor that is often taken for the dependency culture is in fact a consequence of their constrained situations, not a cause of it. Reducing poverty is not a matter of changing individual outlooks, they claim, but instead requires policy measures aimed at distributing income and resources more equally throughout society. Child-care subsidies, a minimum hourly wage, and guaranteed income levels for families are examples of policy measures that have sought to redress persistent social inequalities.

Both theories have enjoyed broad support, and social scientists consistently encourage variations of each view in public debates about poverty. Critics of the culture-of-poverty view accuse its advocates of "individualizing" poverty and blaming the poor for circumstances largely beyond their control. They see the poor as victims, not as freeloaders who are abusing the system. Yet we should be

culture of poverty • The thesis, popularized by Oscar Lewis, that poverty is not a result of individual inadequacies but is instead the outcome of a larger social and cultural atmosphere into which successive generations of children are socialized. The culture of poverty refers to the values, beliefs, lifestyles, habits, and traditions that are common among people living under conditions of material deprivation.

dependency culture • A term popularized by Charles Murray to describe individuals who rely on state welfare provision rather than entering the labor market. The dependency culture is seen as the outcome of the "paternalistic" welfare state that undermines individual ambition and people's capacity for self-help.

cautious about accepting uncritically the arguments of those who see the causes of poverty as lying exclusively in the structure of society itself. Such an approach implies that the poor simply passively accept the difficult situations in which they find themselves.

SOCIAL EXCLUSION

social exclusion • The outcome of multiple deprivations that prevent individuals or groups from participating fully in the economic, social, and political life of the society in which they live.

What are the social processes that lead to large numbers of people being marginalized in a society? The idea of **social exclusion** refers to new sources of inequality—ways in which individuals may become cut off from involvement in the wider society. It is a broader concept than that of the underclass and has the advantage that it emphasizes processes—mechanisms of exclusion. Social exclusion can take a number of forms. It may occur in isolated rural communities cut off from many services and opportunities or in inner-city neighborhoods marked by high crime rates and substandard housing. Exclusion and inclusion may be seen in economic terms, political terms, and social terms.

agency • The ability to think, act, and make choices independently.

The concept of social exclusion raises the question of agency. **Agency** refers to our ability to act independently and to use free will. When dealing with social exclusion, however, the word *exclusion* implies that someone or something is being shut out by another, and is beyond an individual's control. Certainly in some instances individuals are excluded through decisions that lie outside their own control. Insurance companies might reject an application for a policy on the basis of an applicant's personal history and background. An employee laid off later in life may be refused further jobs on the basis of his or her age.

But social exclusion can also result from people excluding themselves from aspects of mainstream society. Individuals can choose to drop out of education, to turn down a job opportunity and become economically inactive, or to abstain from voting in political elections. In considering the phenomenon of social exclusion, we must once again be conscious of the interaction between human agency and responsibility, on the one hand, and the role of social forces in shaping people's circumstances on the other hand.

HOMELESS PERSONS

No discussion of social exclusion is complete without reference to the people who are traditionally seen as at the very bottom of the social hierarchy: homeless persons. The growing problem of homelessness is one of the most distressing signs of changes in the American stratification system. Homeless people are a common sight in nearly every U.S. city and town and are increasingly found in rural areas as well. Two generations ago, homeless populations were mainly elderly, alcoholic men who were found on the skid rows of the largest metropolitan areas. Today they are primarily young single men, often of working age.

The fastest-growing group of homeless people, however, consists of families with children, who make up as much as a third of those currently homeless (National Coalition for the Homeless 2011). Approximately 42 percent of homeless children are under the age of six (National Center on Family Homelessness 2011). In 2011, the U.S. Department of Housing and Urban Development estimated that 72 percent of sheltered adult individuals were men and 28 percent were women.

Demand is so high at this young adult shelter in Seattle that staff members use a lottery system to determine who will get a bed. Today, 72 percent of homeless Americans are male.

Roughly equal shares of the homeless population are black (38.1 percent) and white (39.5 percent), while 8.9 percent are Hispanic and 4 percent are Native American (U.S. Department of Housing and Urban Development 2012). Only a small proportion of the homeless population are Latino or Asian American immigrants, possibly because these groups enjoy close-knit family and community ties that provide a measure of security against homelessness (Waxman and Hinderliter 1996). The National Coalition of Homeless Veterans estimates that there are nearly 107,000 homeless veterans on the streets on any given day (National Coalition of Homeless Veterans 2011). Much like other forms of poverty, veteran poverty, too, is race-based. Approximately 56 percent of all homeless veterans are African American or Hispanic, despite accounting for only 12.8 percent and 15.4 percent of the U.S. population, respectively (National Coalition of Homeless Veterans 2011).

It is extremely difficult to count people who do not have a stable residence (Appelbaum 1990), so estimates of the number of homeless vary widely. The most recent estimate is that there are 656,129 persons living in emergency shelters, transitional housing, and on the streets on any given night, while 112,076 are chronically homeless in the United States (National Alliance to End Homelessness 2011).

There are many reasons why people become homeless. A survey of twenty-five cities by the United States Conference of Mayors identified a lack of affordable housing, poverty, and unemployment as the leading causes of homelessness among families. For single, homeless individuals, substance abuse, a lack of affordable housing, and mental illness were identified as leading causes of homelessness (United States Conference of Mayors 2008). One reason for the widespread incidence of such problems among homeless people is that many public mental hospitals have closed their doors. The number of beds in state mental hospitals has declined by as many as half a million since the early 1960s, leaving many mentally ill people with no institutional alternative to a life on the streets or in homeless shelters. Such problems are compounded by the fact that many homeless people lack family, relatives, or other social networks to provide support.

CONCEPT CHECKS ✓

1. What is the poverty line, and how does the U.S. government calculate this statistic?

2. Describe the demographic characteristics of the poor in the United States.

3. Why are women and children at a high risk of becoming impoverished in the United States today?

4. Contrast the culture-of-poverty argument and structural explanations for poverty.

5. Describe the concept of social exclusion.

6. Describe the demographic characteristics of the homeless population in the United States today.

7. What are the main reasons people become homeless?

The rising cost of housing is another factor, particularly in light of the increased poverty noted elsewhere in this chapter. Declining incomes at the bottom, along with rising rents, create an affordability gap between the cost of housing and what poor people can pay in rents (Dreier and Appelbaum 1992). An estimated 50 percent of all renters today are spending more than 30 percent of their income on rent (Joint Center for Housing Studies of Harvard University 2011). The burden of paying rent is extremely difficult for low-income families whose heads work for minimum wage or slightly higher. Paying so much for rent leaves them barely a paycheck away from a missed rental payment and possible eviction (National Low Income Housing Coalition [NLIHC] 2000). ✓

Learn how changes in the American economy have led to growing inequalities since the 1970s.

HOW DOES SOCIAL INEQUALITY AFFECT YOUR LIFE?

Throughout this chapter, we have shown how changes in the American economy affect social stratification, emphasizing the importance of both globalization and changes in information technology. We have pointed out that the global spread of an industrial capitalist economy, driven in part by the information revolution, has helped to break down closed caste systems around the world and replace them with more open class systems. The degree to which this process will result in greater equality in countries undergoing capitalist development will be explored in the next chapter.

What do these changes hold in store for you? On the one hand, new jobs are opening up, particularly in high-technology fields that require special training and skills and pay high wages. A flood of new products are flowing into the United States, many made with cheap labor that has lowered their costs. This has enabled consumers such as yourselves to buy everything from computers to automobiles to athletic shoes at costs lower than you otherwise would have paid, thereby contributing to a rising standard of living.

But these benefits come with potentially significant costs. Given high levels of job loss in the recent recession and Americans' demands for low-cost products, you may find yourselves competing for jobs with workers in other countries who work for lower wages. This has already been the case for the manufacturing jobs that once provided the economic foundation for the working class and segments of the middle class. Companies that once produced in the United States—from automobiles to apparel to electronics—now use factories around the world, taking advantage of labor costs that are a fraction of those in the United States. Will the same hold true for other, more highly skilled jobs—jobs in the information economy itself? Many jobs that require the use of computers—from graphic design to software engineering—can be done by anyone with a high-speed computer connection, anywhere in the world. The global spread of tech companies will open up vastly expanded job opportunities for those with the necessary skills and training—but it will also open up equally expanded global competition for those jobs.

Partly as a result of these forces, inequality has increased in the United States since the early 1970s, resulting in a growing gap between the rich and the poor. The global economy has permitted the accumulation of vast fortunes at the same time that it has contributed to declining wages, economic hardship, and poverty in the United States. Although the working class is especially vulnerable to these changes, the middle class is not exempt: A growing number of middle-class households experienced downward mobility from the late 1970s through the mid-1990s, until a decade of economic growth benefited all segments of American society.

Yet the economic recession that began in 2008 has further contributed to the downward mobility of middle-class Americans and has left many recent college graduates with high levels of debt and few prospects for rewarding employment (Demos 2010). A recent Rutgers University study found that 12 percent of young adults who graduated from college between 2006 and 2011 are looking for full-time jobs because they either are unemployed or have only part-time jobs. Even those who do have full-time jobs have not necessarily found jobs that they consider their life's work. Just 22 percent of graduates described their first job as a "career," whereas 42 percent described their first position as a job they rely on "just to get by" (Stone, Van Horn, and Zukin 2012).

Although it is always hazardous to try to predict the future, global economic integration will likely continue to increase for the foreseeable future. How this will affect your jobs and careers—and stratification in the United States—is much more difficult to foresee. Although the rags-to-riches story of Liz Murray is uplifting and inspiring, fewer and fewer young adults will be able to transcend childhoods of disadvantage unless the economy rebounds, providing opportunities for education, gainful employment, and safe and secure housing. ✓

CONCEPT CHECKS ✓

1. How has globalization affected the life chances of young adults in the United States today?

2. How has the recent recession affected the life chances of young adults in the U.S. today?

EXERCISES:

Thinking Sociologically

1. If you were doing your own study of status differences in your community, how would you measure people's social class? Base your answer on the textbook's discussion of these matters to explain why you would take the particular measurement approach you've chosen. What would be its value(s) and shortcoming(s) compared with those of alternative measurement procedures?

2. Using occupation and occupational change as your mobility criteria, view the social mobility within your family for three generations. As you discuss the differences in jobs between your

paternal grandfather, your father, and yourself, apply all these terms correctly: *vertical* and *horizontal mobility*, *upward* and *downward mobility*, *intragenerational* and *intergenerational mobility*. Explain fully why you think people in your family have moved up, moved down, or remained at the same status level.

Chapter 7

Stratification, Class, and Inequality

p.195 What Is Social Stratification?

Learn about social stratification and how social background affects one's life chances. Become acquainted with the most influential theories of stratification.

p.201 How Is Social Class Defined in the United States?

Understand the social causes and consequences of social class in U.S. society, as well as the complexities and challenges of defining class.

p.212 What Are the Causes and Consequences of Social Inequality in the United States?

Recognize why and how the gap between rich and poor has increased in recent decades. Understand social mobility, and think about your own mobility.

p.216 How Does Poverty Affect Individuals?

Learn about poverty in the United States today, explanations for why it exists, and means for combating it. Learn how people become marginalized in a society and the forms that this marginalization takes.

p.226 How Does Social Inequality Affect Your Life?

Learn how changes in the American economy have led to growing inequalities since the 1970s.

social stratification

1. What are the three shared characteristics of socially stratified systems?
2. What is one example of a caste system in the world today?
3. How is the concept of class different from that of caste?
4. According to Karl Marx, what are the two main classes and how do they relate to each other?
5. What are the three main differences between Max Weber's and Karl Marx's theories of social stratification?
6. How does social stratification contribute to the functioning of society? What is wrong with this argument?

slavery • caste system • caste society • endogamy • class • life chances • means of production • bourgeoisie • proletariat • surplus value • status • pariah groups • power

1. Name at least three components of social class. How do blacks and whites differ along these components?
2. What are the major social class groups in the United States today? Describe at least two ways (other than their income) that these groups differ from one another.

income • wealth • upper class • middle class • working class • blue- and pink-collar jobs • lower class • underclass

1. What are two pieces of statistical evidence used to support the claim that the gap between the rich and the poor is growing in the United States?
2. How would you explain the wealth gap between blacks and whites in the United States today?
3. Contrast intragenerational and intergenerational mobility.
4. According to classic studies of mobility in the United States, how does family background affect one's social class in adulthood?
5. According to Pierre Bourdieu, how does the family contribute to the transmission of social class from generation to generation?
6. Describe at least two reasons for downward mobility.

social mobility • intragenerational mobility • intergenerational mobility • social reproduction • cultural capital • downward mobility • short-range downward mobility

1. What is the poverty line, and how does the U.S. government calculate this statistic?
2. Describe the demographic characteristics of the poor in the United States.
3. Why are women and children at a high risk of becoming impoverished in the United States today?
4. Contrast the culture-of-poverty argument and structural explanations for poverty.
5. Describe the concept of social exclusion.
6. Describe the demographic characteristics of the homeless population in the United States today.
7. What are the main reasons people become homeless?

absolute poverty • relative poverty • poverty line • working poor • feminization of poverty • Social Security • Medicare • culture of poverty • dependency culture • social exclusion • agency

1. How has globalization affected the life chances of young adults in the United States today?
2. How has the recent recession affected the life chances of young adults in the U.S. today?

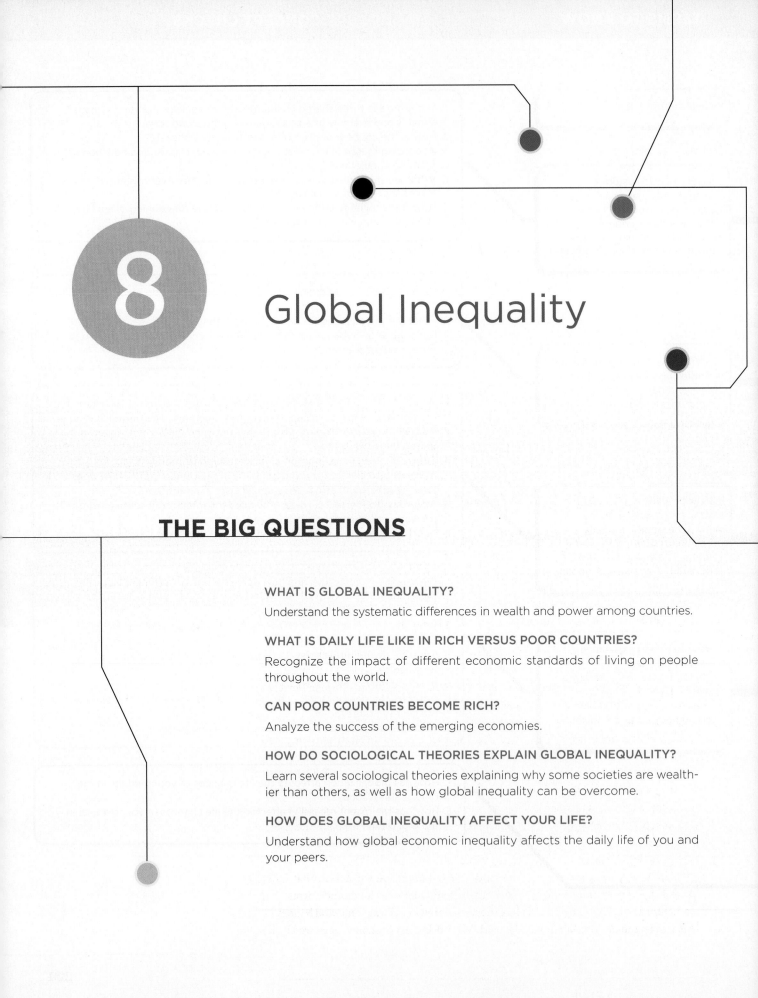

8

Global Inequality

THE BIG QUESTIONS

WHAT IS GLOBAL INEQUALITY?
Understand the systematic differences in wealth and power among countries.

WHAT IS DAILY LIFE LIKE IN RICH VERSUS POOR COUNTRIES?
Recognize the impact of different economic standards of living on people throughout the world.

CAN POOR COUNTRIES BECOME RICH?
Analyze the success of the emerging economies.

HOW DO SOCIOLOGICAL THEORIES EXPLAIN GLOBAL INEQUALITY?
Learn several sociological theories explaining why some societies are wealthier than others, as well as how global inequality can be overcome.

HOW DOES GLOBAL INEQUALITY AFFECT YOUR LIFE?
Understand how global economic inequality affects the daily life of you and your peers.

The nations of Haiti and Japan have little in common, at first glance. Haiti, an island in the Caribbean, is one of the world's poorest nations. Haiti ranked 161 of 187 countries in the 2012 United Nations Human Development Index and is ranked poorly on a range of quality of life indicators, including education, life expectancy at birth, sanitation, access to clean water, and quality of housing (United Nations 2013a). The average adult in Haiti has completed only 4.9 years of schooling, and life expectancy at birth is only 62.4 years. According to the United Nations, the island nation suffers from a shortage of skilled labor and widespread unemployment and underemployment, where more than two-thirds of the labor force do not have formal jobs. As recently as 2013, Haiti was described as the "poorest country in the Western Hemisphere, with 80 percent of the population living under the poverty line and 54 percent in abject poverty." Most Haitians live on $2 or less per day (Central Intelligence Agency [CIA] 2013b).

Japan, by contrast, is a wealthy and highly industrialized nation that most Americans recognize as a major producer of automobiles like Honda and Toyota, and computer and electronic products like those made by Sony, Panasonic, and Nintendo. Also an island nation, Japan has the world's third-largest economy measured by its gross domestic product (GDP) and fourth largest when considering its purchasing power parity. It is also the world's fifth-largest exporter and importer. In Japan, life expectancy at birth is 84.19 years—the third longest in the world behind only Monaco and Macau. Its infant mortality rate is the second lowest of any country in the world (CIA 2013c). More than half (57 percent) of Japanese persons ages twenty-five to thirty-four have achieved a postsecondary education. This percentage is the second highest among member nations of the Organization for Economic Co-operation and Development (OECD 2013).

Despite their vastly divergent fortunes, Haiti and Japan were unified in their grief in 2010 and 2011, respectively, when they were each devastated by unimaginable natural disasters. In January 2010, a powerful earthquake struck Haiti, killing an estimated 300,000 people and leaving more than 1 million persons homeless (CIA 2013b). Those not killed by the shock of the quake were at risk of illness and infection, especially given that so many were vulnerable even prior to the quake. Malnutrition is rampant in Haiti, more than 100,000 people are living with HIV or AIDS, and just half of the nation's children are vaccinated against basic diseases like diphtheria (UNAIDS 2013b).

Just thirteen months after the Haiti disaster, in March 2011, Japan was rocked by an earthquake and tsunami, which subsequently triggered a nuclear reactor meltdown. Much of northern Japan was leveled, leaving tens of thousands dead or missing and more than 100,000 buildings flattened. In the week following each disaster, the world responded in very different ways.

Charitable contributions to Japan were less than one-third the amount of the donations given to Haiti, according to Charity Navigator, an organization that tracks donations to charitable organizations. In the first week following the Japan disaster, the American Red Cross raised $47 million for the earthquake and tsunami victims. By contrast, in the week following the Haitian earthquake, the Red Cross raised a whopping $92 million. It's not just the Red Cross that witnessed such a large gap in donations. In the same time period, the Christian humanitarian aid group World Vision raised $3 million for Japan from American donors, compared with $15.8 million within the week after the Haiti earthquake. When Charity Navigator tallied up the total donations made by a dozen large U.S. charitable organizations, they found that

Musical artists Bono, Jay-Z, and Rihanna performed in the January 2010 "Hope for Haiti Now" benefit concert, which raised an estimated $60 million for the earthquake-ravaged nation.

$64 million had been raised for Japan in the first week after the disaster, compared with $210 million for Haiti (and $457 million after Hurricane Katrina devastated New Orleans and the southeastern United States) (Shaver 2011).

What can explain this vast gap in charitable giving? Officials who run philanthropic organizations say that Americans typically give money to other nations based on their sense of need and their familiarity with the country. Haiti, as we saw earlier, was impoverished even prior to the earthquake and is a neighbor of the United States. The nation's capital, Port-au-Prince, is just 710 miles from Miami, Florida. Japan, by contrast, is on the other side of the globe and is perceived by observers to be able to "fix it themselves" given their national wealth and high level of technological development (Shaver 2011). According to Daniel Borochoff, president of the American Institute of Philanthropy, in the eyes of potential U.S. donors, "Japan is not Haiti, and it's not Indonesia; it's a developed country with a GDP somewhat similar to our country. It's not what people typically think of as a country in need of wide-scale international aid." These sentiments were echoed by Caryl M. Stern, president and CEO of the U.S. Fund for the United Nations Children's Fund (UNICEF), in New York: "With Japan you have an industrialized country with a very strong, respected government with all of the structures and systems and the ability to take the lead" (Wallace 2011).

The stories of Japan and Haiti clearly illustrate the gross inequities in health, wealth, and well-being throughout the globe. **Globalization**—the increased economic, political, and social interconnectedness of the world—has produced opportunities for unthinkable wealth and technological development, as we have seen in Japan's recent history and in its efforts to rebuild and bounce back from disaster. Yet at the same time, globalization has produced widespread poverty and suffering, as we have seen in Haiti, as well as in countless nations throughout much of Asia, Africa, Latin America, and the Caribbean.

Consider Bina Khatun, a knitting operator at a Chinese-owned garment factory in Bangladesh. Khatun, along with thousands of other workers, puts in thirteen hours a day, six days a week, making sweaters for major European retailers. More experienced workers like Khatun make $0.22 an hour, which comes out to about $11 a week. When Khatun complained to factory management about being sexually harassed by her supervisor, she was beaten for speaking out (Kernaghan 2012). Millions of workers such as Khatun are being drawn into the global labor force, many working in oppressive conditions that would be unacceptable, if not unimaginable, under U.S. labor laws. And these are the fortunate ones: Those outside the global economy are frequently even worse off.

In the previous chapter we examined the American class structure, noting vast differences between individuals' income, wealth, jobs, and quality of life. The same is true in the world as a whole: Just as we can speak of rich or poor individuals within a country, we can also talk about rich or poor countries in the world system. A country's position in the global economy affects how its people live, work, and even die. In this chapter, we look closely at differences in wealth and power between countries in the late twentieth and early twenty-first centuries. We examine how differences in economic standards of living affect people throughout the world. We then turn to the emerging economies of the world to understand which countries are improving their fortunes and why. This will lead us to a discussion of different theories that attempt to explain why global inequality exists and what can be done about it. We conclude by speculating on the future of economic inequality in a global world.

globalization • The development of social and economic relationships stretching worldwide. In current times, we are all influenced by organizations and social networks located thousands of miles away. A key part of the study of globalization is the emergence of a world system—for some purposes, we need to regard the world as forming a single social order.

WHAT IS GLOBAL INEQUALITY?

global inequality • The systematic differences in wealth and power among countries.

Global inequality refers to the systematic differences in wealth and power that exist among countries. These differences exist alongside differences within countries: Even the wealthiest countries today have growing numbers of poor people, while less wealthy nations are producing many of the world's superrich. Sociology's challenge is not merely to identify all such differences but to explain why they occur—and how they might be overcome.

One simple way to classify countries in terms of global inequality is to compare the wealth produced by each country per average citizen. This approach measures the value of a country's yearly output of goods and services produced by its total population and then divides that total by the number of people in the country. The resulting measure is termed the *per person gross national income* (GNI), a measure of the country's yearly output of goods and services per person. The World Bank, an international lending organization that provides loans for development projects in poorer countries, uses this measure to classify countries as high income (an annual per person GNI of $12,616 or more, in 2012 dollars), upper-middle income ($4,086–$12,615), lower-middle income ($1,036–$4,085), or low income ($1,035 or less) (World Bank 2013a).

The infographic on the next page shows how the World Bank (2013a) divides 214 countries and economies (such as the West Bank and Gaza and Hong Kong), containing more than 7.1 billion people, into four economic classes. The infographic shows that while nearly 50 percent of the world's population live in low-income and low-middle-income countries, slightly more than 50 percent live in upper-middle- or high-income countries. Bear in mind that this classification is based on average income for each country; therefore, it masks income inequality within each country. Such differences can be significant, although we do not focus on them in this chapter. For example, the World Bank classifies India as a lower-middle-income country because its per person GNI in 2012 was only $1,340. Yet despite widespread poverty, India also boasts a large and growing middle class. China, on the other hand, was classified as upper-middle income because its GNI per capita in 2012 was $5,720, placing China in the world's upper-middle-income category; it nonetheless has hundreds of millions of people living in poverty (World Bank 2013a).

Comparing countries on the basis of economic output alone can also be misleading because GNI includes only goods and services that are produced for cash sale. Many people in low-income countries are farmers or herders who produce for their own families or for barter, involving noncash transactions. The value of their crops and animals is not taken into account in the statistics. Further, economic output is not the sole indicator of a country's worth: Poor countries are no less rich in history, culture, and traditions than their wealthier neighbors, but the lives of their people are much harsher.

HIGH-INCOME COUNTRIES

High-income countries are generally those that were the first to industrialize, a process that began in England some 250 years ago and then spread to Europe, the United States, and Canada. In the 1970s, Japan joined the ranks of high-income, industrialized nations, while Singapore, Hong Kong, and Taiwan moved into this category only within the last decade or so. The reasons for the success of these Asian latecomers to industrialization are much debated by sociologists and economists; we will look at them later in the chapter.

High-income countries are home to 18 percent of the world's population, or just more than 1.3 billion people, yet they lay claim to over 68 percent of the world's

GLOBAL INEQUALITY

Global inequality refers to the systematic differences in wealth and power that exist among countries. The World Bank uses per person gross national income (GNI) to classify countries into four economic classes: low income, lower-middle income, upper-middle income, and high income.

	LOW-INCOME COUNTRIES	LOWER-MIDDLE-INCOME COUNTRIES	UPPER-MIDDLE-INCOME COUNTRIES	HIGH-INCOME COUNTRIES
GROSS NATIONAL INCOME PER CAPITA (Current U.S. $)	$588	$1,913	$6,977	$38,182
TOTAL POPULATION	847 million	2,507 million	2,391 million	1,300 million
ANNUAL POPULATION GROWTH	+2.3%	+1.5%	+0.8%	+0.3%
LIFE EXPECTANCY AT BIRTH	62 / 62 years	66 / 66 years	74 / 74 years	79 / 79 years
FERTILITY RATE (Average # of births per woman)	4.1 births per woman	2.9 births per woman	1.9 births per woman	1.7 births per woman
INFANT MORTALITY RATE (# of infant deaths per 1,000 births)	56 per 1,000	46 per 1,000	16 per 1,000	5 per 1,000

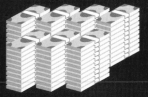

Note: World Bank 2012

annual output (derived from World Bank 2013d). High-income countries offer adequate housing and food, drinkable water, and other comforts unknown in many parts of the world. Although these countries often have large numbers of poor people, most of their inhabitants enjoy a standard of living unimaginable by the majority of the world's people.

MIDDLE-INCOME COUNTRIES

The middle-income countries (including lower- and upper-middle) are located primarily in East and Southeast Asia and include the oil-rich countries of the Middle East and North Africa, a few countries in the Americas (Mexico, Central America, Cuba, and other countries in the Caribbean, and South America), and the once-communist republics that formerly made up the Soviet Union and its Eastern European allies (Global Map 8.1). Most of these countries began to industrialize relatively late in the twentieth century and therefore are not yet as industrially developed (or as wealthy) as the high-income countries. The countries that once composed the Soviet Union, on the other hand, are highly industrialized, although their living standards have eroded during the past two decades as a result of the collapse of communism and the move to capitalist economies. In Russia, for example, the wages of ordinary people dropped by nearly a third between 1998 and 1999, while retirement pensions dropped by nearly half. Millions of people, many of them elderly, suddenly found themselves destitute (CIA 2000). Since then, the

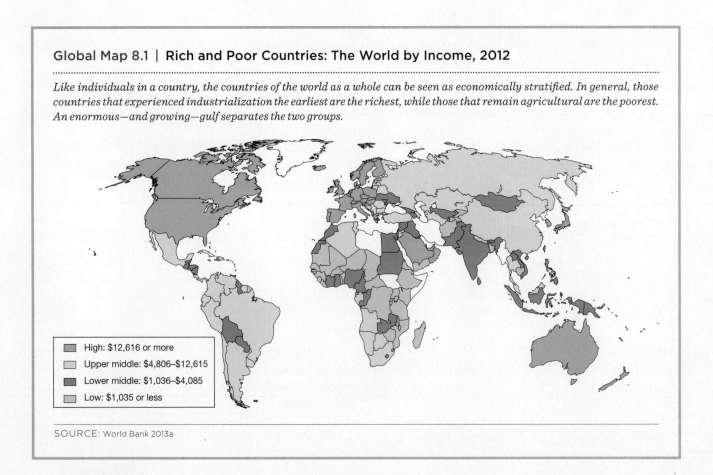

Global Map 8.1 | Rich and Poor Countries: The World by Income, 2012

Like individuals in a country, the countries of the world as a whole can be seen as economically stratified. In general, those countries that experienced industrialization the earliest are the richest, while those that remain agricultural are the poorest. An enormous—and growing—gulf separates the two groups.

■ High: $12,616 or more
□ Upper middle: $4,806–$12,615
■ Lower middle: $1,036–$4,085
□ Low: $1,035 or less

SOURCE: World Bank 2013a

Russian economy has recovered somewhat, with foreign investment gradually increasing and the energy market booming.

In 2012, middle-income countries were home to 69.5 percent of the world's population (4.9 billion people) but accounted for only 30.7 percent of the output produced in that year. Although many people in these countries are substantially better off than their neighbors in low-income countries, most do not enjoy anything resembling the standard of living common in high-income countries. The ranks of the world's middle-income countries expanded between 1999 and 2000, at least according to the World Bank's system of classification, when China—with 1.3 billion people (22 percent of the world's population)—was reclassified from low to middle income because of its economic growth. Today, China's per capita GNI is $5,720, which is just above the lower limit ($4,806) defined by the World Bank for upper-middle-income countries. Nonetheless, a majority of China's population is low income by World Bank standards.

LOW-INCOME COUNTRIES

Finally, the low-income countries include much of eastern, western, and sub-Saharan Africa; Cambodia and North Korea in East Asia; Nepal and Bangladesh in South Asia; and Haiti in the Caribbean. These countries have mostly agricultural economies and have only recently begun to industrialize. Scholars debate the reasons for their late industrialization and widespread poverty, as we will see later in this chapter.

In 2012, the low-income countries accounted for 12 percent of the world's population (846.5 million people) yet produced only 0.7 percent of the world's yearly output of wealth (World Bank 2013d). Moreover, this inequality is increasing. Fertility rates are much higher in low-income countries than elsewhere, with large families providing additional farm labor or otherwise contributing to family income. (In wealthy industrial societies, where children are more likely to be in school than on the farm, the economic benefit of large families declines, so people tend to have fewer children.) Because of this, the populations of low-income countries grew more than twice as fast as those of high-income countries between 1990 and 2005.

In many of these low-income countries, people struggle with poverty, malnutrition, and even starvation. Most people live in rural areas, although this is rapidly changing: Hundreds of millions of people are moving to huge, densely populated cities, where they live either in dilapidated housing or on the open streets (see Chapter 15).

GROWING GLOBAL INEQUALITY: THE RICH GET RICHER, THE POOR GET POORER

During the last thirty years, the overall standard of living in the world has risen slowly. The average global citizen is better off today than ever before. Illiteracy rates are down, infant mortality and malnutrition are less common, people are living longer, average income is higher, and poverty is down. Since these figures are overall averages, however, they hide the substantial differences among countries: Many of these gains have been in the high- and middle-income countries, while living standards in many of the poorest countries have declined.

Figure 8.1 | GNI per Person in Low-, Middle-, and High-Income Countries, 1984–2012

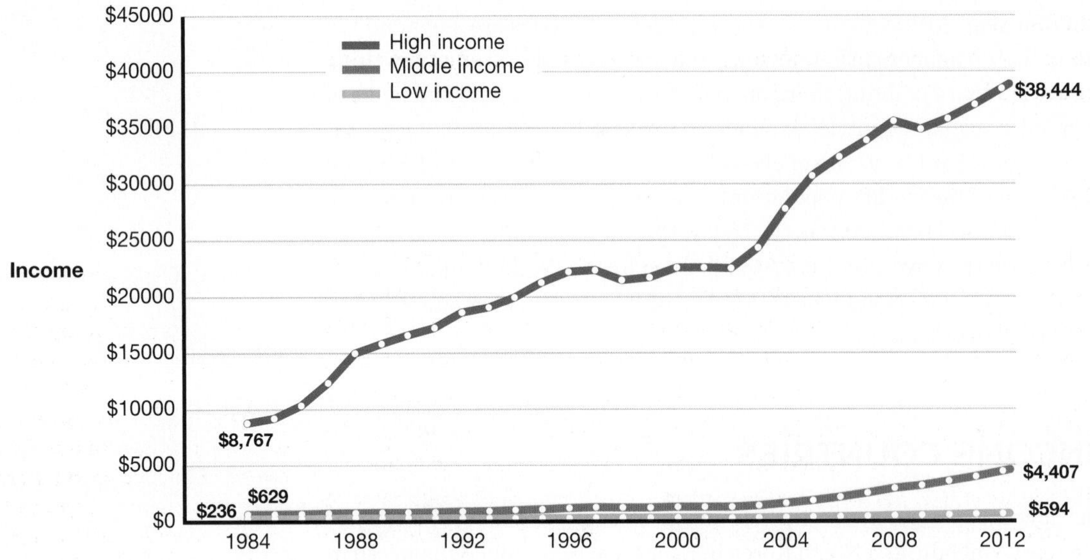

SOURCE: World Bank 2014b

Between 1984 and 2012, average per person GNI increased by 339 percent in high-income countries but only increased by 152 percent in low-income countries, widening the global gap between rich and poor (Figure 8.1). In 2012, the average person in a typical high-income country earned $38,444 (based on current U.S. dollars), nearly sixty-five times as much as the $594 earned by his or her counterpart in a low-income country (World Bank 2014b). In 2010, 2.4 billion people in the world were estimated to live on less than $2 a day (World Bank 2014c). ✓

CONCEPT CHECKS ✓

1. Explain how the World Bank measures global inequality, and discuss some of the problems associated with measuring global inequality.

2. Compare and contrast high-income, middle-income, and low-income countries.

Recognize the impact of different economic standards of living on people throughout the world.

WHAT IS DAILY LIFE LIKE IN RICH VERSUS POOR COUNTRIES?

An enormous gulf in living standards separates most people in rich countries from their counterparts in poor ones. Wealth and poverty make life different in a host of ways. For instance, about one-third of the world's poor are undernourished, and almost all are illiterate and lack access to even primary-school education. The world is no longer predominantly rural. A little more than half of the world's population now live in urban areas (World Bank 2013d). And by 2050, urban areas will house 70 percent of the world's population (United Nations 2007). More than

40 percent of all urban residents in developing countries live in slums (United Nations Food and Agriculture Organization [UN FAO] 2004). Many of the poor come from racial, ethnic, or religious groups that differ from the dominant groups of their countries, and their poverty is at least in part the result of discrimination (Narayan 1999).

Here we look at the differences among high- and low-income countries in terms of health and nutrition.

HEALTH

People in high-income countries are far healthier than their counterparts in low-income countries. Low-income countries generally suffer from inadequate health facilities, and their hospitals and clinics seldom serve the poorest people. People living in low-income countries also lack proper sanitation, drink polluted water, and run a much greater risk of contracting infectious diseases. They are more likely to suffer malnutrition, starvation, and famine. All of these factors contribute to physical weakness and poor health, making people in low-income countries susceptible to illness and disease. There is growing evidence that the high rates of HIV/AIDS infection found in many African countries and Haiti are due in part to the weakened health of impoverished people (Stillwagon 2001).

Because of poor health conditions, people in low-income countries are more likely to die in infancy and less likely to live to old age than people in high-income countries. Infants are thirteen times more likely to die at birth and—if they survive birth—are likely to live twenty years fewer. Children often die of illnesses, such as measles or diarrhea, that are readily treated in wealthier countries. In some parts of the world, such as sub-Saharan Africa, a child is more likely to die before the age of five than to enter secondary school (World Bank 2005). Still, conditions are improving somewhat. Between 1980 and 2012, for example, the infant mortality rate dropped from 97 (per 1,000 live births) to 56 in low-income countries and from 60 to 34 in middle-income countries (World Bank 2013d). However, AIDS and growing poverty have increased infant mortality in the poorest countries in recent years.

HUNGER, MALNUTRITION, AND FAMINE

Hunger, malnutrition, and famine are major global sources of poor health. As we saw in the case of Haiti, the impoverished population already suffered from hunger and malnutrition prior to the earthquake, which compromised the ability of many to survive the added tragedy of the natural disaster. Problems of inadequate food are nothing new. What seems to be new is their pervasiveness—the fact that so many people in the world today appear to be on the brink of starvation. A recent study by the United Nations (2013b) estimates that 870 million people go hungry every day, the vast majority of

Nkonge Mata (left), a ten-year-old displaced Congolese boy, sits in a clinic run by the medical charity Medecins Sans Frontieres (Doctors without Borders) in the remote town of Dubie in Congo's southeastern Katanga province. The world's greatest concentrations of hunger are in central and sub-Saharan Africa. The majority of deaths of children under the age of five are the result of starvation.

whom (852 million) live in developing countries. An earlier United Nations Food and Agriculture Organization (UN FAO 2011) report stated that two-thirds lived in just seven countries (Bangladesh, China, the Democratic Republic of the Congo, Ethiopia, India, Indonesia, and Pakistan) and over 40 percent lived in China and India alone. The program defines "hunger" as a diet of 1,800 or fewer calories a day—or 300 calories fewer than the 2,100 deemed sufficient for active adults.

According to the U.N. Children's Fund, in 2011 more than 100 million children under the age of five were underweight; 57 million of these children lived in Southern Asia, while 30 million lived in sub-Saharan Africa. The United Nations further estimates that more than a third of all deaths of children under the age of five are linked to malnutrition (United Nations Children's Fund [UNICEF] 2009). Yet, in some poor regions of the world, these troubles begin even before a baby is born. Close to 17 million babies are born with low birth weight stemming from the inadequate nutrition of their mothers (United Nations World Food Programme [UN WFP] 2004).

Most famine and hunger today are the result of a combination of natural and social forces. Drought alone affects an estimated 100 million people in the world today. In countries such as Sudan, Ethiopia, Eritrea, Indonesia, Afghanistan, Sierra Leone, Guinea, and Tajikistan, the combination of drought and internal warfare has wrecked food production, resulting in starvation and death for millions of people. The role of conflict and warfare in creating hunger is on the rise: Conflict and economic problems were cited as the main causes of 35 percent of food shortages between 1992 and 2003, compared with 15 percent in the period between 1986 and 1991 (UN FAO 2005). In Latin America and the Caribbean, 49 million people (8.3 percent of the population) are undernourished—and even higher numbers are undernourished in Asia (563 million, 13.9 percent) and sub-Saharan Africa (234 million, 26.8 percent) (UN FAO 2013a).

The AIDS epidemic has also contributed to the problem of food shortages and hunger, killing many working-age adults. One study by the United Nations predicts that HIV/AIDS–caused deaths in the ten African countries most afflicted by the epidemic will reduce the labor force by 26 percent by the year 2020 (United Nations 2004). Of the estimated 35 million people worldwide infected with HIV, the vast majority live in low- and middle-income countries. More than two-thirds (69 percent) of all people living with HIV/AIDS are in sub-Saharan Africa. In 2012, 1.6 million people died from AIDS-related causes and an estimated 36 million have died since the epidemic began (AIDS.gov 2013). According to the United Nations Food and Agriculture Organization (UN FAO 2001), the epidemic can be devastating to nutrition, food security, and agricultural production, affecting "the entire society's ability to maintain and reproduce itself."

Making Sociology Work

PROGRAM OFFICER FOR CHARITABLE FOUNDATION

In July 2006, Warren Buffett made the stunning announcement that he would give away most of his $40 billion fortune to the world's largest charitable organization, the Bill and Melinda Gates Foundation. Buffett is chairman and chief executive of Omaha, Nebraska–based Berkshire Hathaway Inc. and the third-richest man in the world. Buffett's gift, estimated at roughly $30 billion, could more than double the size of the Gates Foundation, which already commands a $29 billion endowment. Bill Gates (the only person other than Mexico's Carlos Slim Helú whose wealth outstrips Buffett's) and his wife, Melinda, have given nearly $26 billion to the foundation. The Gates Foundation, founded in 1994, has focused much of its efforts on global health, backing the development, testing, manufacturing, and delivery of vaccines for diseases such as malaria, tuberculosis, and acute diarrhea that kill millions of children in developing countries every year. As a program officer responsible for designing and implementing new initiatives at the Gates Foundation, how would you allocate the newly received funds? Drawing on sociological studies of health, hunger, malnutrition, and famine in low-income nations, what social problems would you earmark as high-priority initiatives? Why?

The countries affected by famine and starvation are for the most part too poor to pay for new technologies that would increase their food production. Nor can they afford to purchase sufficient food imports from elsewhere in the world. At the same time, paradoxically, as world hunger grows, food production continues to increase, often in the very countries experiencing hunger emergencies (UN FAO 2004). Between 1965 and 1999, for example, world production of grain doubled. Even allowing for the substantial world population increase over this period, the global production of grain per person was 15 percent higher in 1999 than it was thirty-four years earlier. This growth, however, is not evenly distributed around the world. In much of Africa, for example, food production per person declined in recent years. Surplus food produced in high-income countries such as the United States is seldom affordable to the countries that need it most. ✓

CONCEPT CHECKS ✓

1. Why do people who live in high-income countries have better health than those who live in low-income countries?

2. What factors contribute to famines?

CAN POOR COUNTRIES BECOME RICH?

Analyze the success of the emerging economies.

In the mid-1970s a number of low-income countries in East Asia were undergoing a process of industrialization that appeared to threaten the global economic dominance of the United States and Europe (Amsden 1989). This process began with Japan in the 1950s but quickly extended to the newly industrializing economies. Today the more widely used phrase is "**emerging economies**," or the rapidly growing economies of the world, particularly in East Asia but also in Latin America. The East Asian emerging economies included Hong Kong in the 1960s and Taiwan, South Korea, and Singapore in the 1970s and 1980s. Other Asian countries began to follow in the 1980s and the early 1990s, most notably China, but also Malaysia, Thailand, and Indonesia. Today, most are middle income, and some—such as Hong Kong, South Korea, Taiwan, and Singapore—have moved up to the high-income category.

emerging economies •
Developing countries that over the past two or three decades have begun to develop a strong industrial base, such as Singapore and Hong Kong.

China, the world's most populous country, has one of the most rapidly growing economies on the planet. According to projections by the International Monetary Fund, China ranks first in terms of GDP growth among all economies listed in the World Economic Outlook Projections (International Monetary Fund 2013). At an average annual growth rate of 10 percent between 1980 and 2010, the Chinese economy has more than doubled, and today is the world's second-largest economy behind the United States, having surpassed Japan in 2010. The low- and middle-income economies of East Asia as a whole averaged 7.7 percent growth per year during much of the 1980s and 1990s—a rate that is extraordinary by world standards (World Bank 2000–2001). By 1999, the GDP per person in Singapore was virtually the same as that in the United States.

Economic growth in East Asia has been accompanied by important social problems. These have included the sometimes violent repression of labor and civil rights, terrible factory conditions, the exploitation of an increasingly female workforce, the exploitation of immigrant workers from impoverished neighboring countries, and widespread environmental degradation. Many of these atrocities continue today;

Foxcon and Pegatron, two of Apple's biggest suppliers, have been found to badly mistreat workers in their Chinese factories (Neate 2013). Nonetheless, due to the sacrifices of past generations of workers, large numbers of people in these countries are prospering.

The economic success of the East Asian emerging economies can be attributed to a combination of factors. Some of these factors are historical, including those stemming from world political and economic shifts. Some are cultural. Still others have to do with the ways these countries pursued economic growth. Sociologists cite five main reasons for the recent economic advances of the East Asian emerging economies. First, most were part of colonial situations that, while imposing many hardships, also helped to pave the way for economic growth. For example, Hong Kong and Singapore were former British colonies; Britain encouraged industrial development, constructed roads and other transportation systems, built relatively efficient governmental bureaucracies, and actively developed both Hong Kong and Singapore as trading centers (Cumings 1987; Gold 1986).

Second, the East Asian region benefited from a long period of world economic growth. Between the 1950s and the mid-1970s, the growing economies of Europe and the United States provided a big market for the clothing, footwear, and electronics that were increasingly being made in East Asia, creating a window of opportunity for economic development (Henderson and Appelbaum 1992). Third, economic growth in this region took off at the high point of the Cold War, when the United States and its allies, in erecting a defense against communist China, provided generous economic aid that fueled investment in new technologies such as transistors, semiconductors, and

Hong Kong (pictured below), along with Taiwan, South Korea, and Singapore, have become some of the most rapidly growing economies on earth.

other electronics, contributing to the development of local industries (Mirza 1986; Cumings 1987, 1997; Deyo 1987; Evans 1987; Amsden 1989; Henderson 1989; Haggard 1990; Castells 1992). Fourth, many of the East Asian governments enacted strong policies that favored economic growth by keeping labor costs low, encouraging economic development through tax breaks and other economic policies, and offering free public education.

Finally, some argue that cultural traditions, including a shared Confucian philosophy, contributed to these economic advances. Scholars who view the rise of capitalism in Western Europe as a function of the Protestant belief in thrift, frugality, and hard work (Weber 1977, orig. 1904) have observed a similar process in Asian economic history. Confucianism, it is argued, inculcates respect for one's elders and superiors, education, hard work, and proven accomplishments as the key to advancement, as well as a willingness to sacrifice today to earn a greater reward tomorrow. As a result of these values, the Weberian argument goes, Asian workers and managers are highly loyal to their companies, submissive to authority, hardworking, and success oriented. Workers and capitalists alike are said to be frugal. Instead of living lavishly, they are likely to reinvest their wealth in further economic growth (Berger 1986; Wong 1986; Berger and Hsiao 1988; Redding 1990; Helm 1992).

Whether the growth of these economies will continue is unclear. In 1997 and 1998, a combination of poor investment decisions, corruption, and world economic conditions brought these countries' economic expansion to an abrupt halt. Their stock markets collapsed, their currencies fell, and the entire global economy was threatened. The experience of Hong Kong was typical: After thirty-seven years of continuous growth, the economy stalled and its stock market lost more than half its value. Yet the "Asian meltdown," as the newspapers called it in early 1998, turned out to have been merely a blip in the region's recent growth. China in particular has been growing at a high rate, as we learned earlier (World Bank 2012e).

Recent social and cultural changes may undermine the influence of traditional values on Asian economic development. For example, thrift, a central Confucian cultural value, appears to be on the decline in Japan and the East Asian emerging economies, as young people—raised in the booming prosperity of recent years—increasingly value conspicuous consumption over austerity and investment (Helm 1992). ✓

CONCEPT CHECKS ✓

1. What are the five factors that have facilitated the economic success of the East Asian emerging economies?

2. What are potential obstacles to the continued economic success of the emerging economies?

HOW DO SOCIOLOGICAL THEORIES EXPLAIN GLOBAL INEQUALITY?

Learn several sociological theories explaining why some societies are wealthier than others, as well as how global inequality can be overcome.

What causes global inequality? How can it be overcome? In this section we will examine four different theories that have been advanced over the years to explain global inequality: market-oriented, dependency, world-systems, and state-centered theories. These theories each have strengths and weaknesses. One shortcoming of all of them is that they frequently give short shrift to the role of women in economic development. By drawing on all four theories together, however, we should be able to answer a key question facing the 82 percent of the world's population living outside high-income countries: How can they move up in the world economy?

MARKET-ORIENTED THEORIES

market-oriented theories •
Theories about economic
development that assume that
the best possible economic
consequences will result if
individuals are free to make
their own economic decisions,
uninhibited by governmental
constraint.

Fifty years ago, the most influential theories of global inequality advanced by American economists and sociologists were **market-oriented theories**. These theories assume that the best possible economic consequences will result if individuals are free, uninhibited by any form of governmental constraint, to make their own economic decisions. Unrestricted capitalism, if allowed to develop fully, is said to be the avenue to economic growth. Government bureaucracy should not dictate which goods to produce, what prices to charge, or how much workers should be paid. According to market-oriented theorists, governmental direction of the economies of low-income countries results only in blockages to economic development (Rostow 1961; Warren 1980; Berger 1986; Ranis and Mahmood 1992; Ranis 1996).

Market-oriented theories inspired U.S. government foreign-aid programs that attempted to spur economic development in low-income countries by providing money, expert advisers, and technology, paving the way for U.S. corporations to make investments in these countries. One of the most influential early proponents of such theories was W. W. Rostow, an economic adviser to former U.S. president John F. Kennedy, whose ideas helped shape U.S. foreign policy toward Latin America during the 1960s. Rostow's explanation is one version of a market-oriented approach, termed *modernization theory*. **Modernization theory** argues that low-income societies can develop economically only if they give up their traditional ways and adopt modern economic institutions, technologies, and cultural values that emphasize savings and productive investment.

modernization theory • A
version of market-oriented
development theory that argues
that low-income societies develop
economically only if they give up
their traditional ways and adopt
modern economic institutions,
technologies, and cultural values
that emphasize savings and
productive investment.

According to Rostow (1961), the traditional cultural values and social institutions of low-income countries impede their economic effectiveness. For example, many people in low-income countries, in Rostow's view, would rather consume today than invest for the future. But to modernization theorists, the problems in low-income countries run even deeper. The cultures of such countries, according to the theory, tend to support "fatalism"—a value system that views hardship and suffering as the unavoidable plight of life. Acceptance of one's lot in life thus discourages people from working hard to overcome their fate. In this view, then, a country's poverty is due largely to the cultural failings of the people themselves. Such failings are reinforced by government policies that set wages and control prices and generally interfere in the operation of the economy. How can low-income countries escape poverty? Rostow viewed economic growth as going through several stages, which he likened to the journey of an airplane:

1. **Traditional stage.** This is the stage just described. It is characterized by low rates of savings, the supposed lack of a work ethic, and a fatalistic value system. The airplane is not yet off the ground.

2. **Takeoff to economic growth.** This stage occurs when poor countries begin to jettison their traditional values and institutions and start to save and invest money for the future. Wealthy countries, such as the United States, can facilitate this growth by financing birth-control programs or providing low-cost loans for electrification, road and airport construction, and the development of new industries.

3. **Drive to technological maturity.** According to Rostow, with the help of money and advice from high-income countries, the airplane of economic growth would taxi down the runway, pick up speed, and become airborne. The plane would slowly climb to cruising altitude, improving its technology, reinvesting its

recently acquired wealth in new industries, and adopting the institutions and values of the high-income countries.

4. **High mass consumption.** Finally, the country would reach the phase of high mass consumption. Now people are able to enjoy the fruits of their labor by achieving a high standard of living. The airplane (country) cruises along on automatic pilot, having entered the ranks of high-income countries.

Rostow's ideas remain influential. **Neoliberalism**, the prevailing view among economists today, argues that free-market forces, achieved by minimizing governmental restrictions on business, provide the only route to economic growth. Neoliberalism holds that global free trade will enable all countries of the world to prosper; eliminating governmental regulation is seen as necessary for economic growth to occur. Neoliberal economists therefore call for an end to restrictions on trade and often challenge minimum wage and other labor laws, as well as environmental restrictions on business.

Sociologists, on the other hand, question the extent to which moral, religious, and folk beliefs affect development (Davis 1987; So 1990). At the same time, they are interested in identifying local conditions that resist change, such as the belief in some cultures that business and trade lead to moral decay and social unrest.

neoliberalism • The economic belief that free-market forces, achieved by minimizing government restrictions on business, provide the only route to economic growth.

dependency theories • Marxist theories of economic development arguing that the poverty of low-income countries stems directly from their exploitation by wealthy countries and the multinational corporations that are based in wealthy countries.

colonialism • The process whereby Western nations established their rule in parts of the world away from their home territories.

DEPENDENCY THEORIES

During the 1960s, a number of theorists questioned market-oriented explanations of global inequality. Many of these critics were sociologists and economists from the low-income countries of Latin America and Africa who rejected the idea that their countries' economic underdevelopment was due to their own cultural or institutional failings. Instead, they built on the theories of Karl Marx, who argued that world capitalism would create a class of countries manipulated by more powerful countries just as capitalism within countries leads to the exploitation of workers. The **dependency theorists**, as they are called, argue that the poverty of low-income countries stems from their exploitation by wealthy countries and the multinational corporations that are based in wealthy countries. In their view, global capitalism locked their countries into a downward spiral of exploitation and poverty.

They argue that this exploitation began with **colonialism**, a political-economic system under which powerful countries establish, for their own profit, rule over weaker peoples or countries. Powerful nations have colonized other countries usually to procure the raw materials needed for their factories and to control markets for the products manufactured in those factories. Although colonialism typically involved European countries establishing colonies in North and South America, Africa, and Asia, some Asian countries (such as Japan) had colonies as well.

According to the United Nations International Labor Organization, nearly 153 million

Although Nigeria is the largest oil producer in Africa, the overwhelming majority of the profits generated in the energy trade go to oil companies and the military government, providing no benefit to the country's poverty-stricken inhabitants. These women are protesting Royal Dutch Shell's exploitation of Nigeria's oil and natural gas resources.

children between the ages of five and fourteen are working in the world today, almost one in every eight children in the world. Nearly 53 million of those children work under hazardous conditions. Child labor is found throughout the developing world—in Asia and the Pacific (14.8 percent of the children between five and fourteen are engaged in labor), sub-Saharan Africa (28.4 percent), and Latin America and the Caribbean (9.0 percent). They are forced to work because of a combination of family poverty, lack of education, and traditional indifference among some people in many countries to the plight of those who are poor or who are ethnic minorities (International Labor Organization [ILO] 2010). Two-thirds of working children labor in agriculture, with the rest in manufacturing, wholesale and retail trade, restaurants and hotels, and a variety of services, including working as servants in wealthy households. At best, these children work for long hours with little pay and are therefore unable to go to school and develop the skills that might eventually enable them to escape their lives of poverty. Many, however, work at hazardous and exploitative jobs under slavelike conditions, suffering a variety of illnesses and injuries.

Colonialism ended throughout most of the world after World War II, yet the exploitation did not: Transnational corporations continued to reap enormous profits from their branches in low-income countries. According to dependency theory, these global companies, often with the support of the powerful banks and governments of rich countries, established factories in poor countries, using cheap labor and raw materials to maximize production costs without governmental interference. In turn, the low prices set for labor and raw materials prevented poor countries from accumulating the profit necessary to industrialize themselves. Local businesses that might compete with foreign corporations were prevented from doing so. In this view, poor countries are forced to borrow from rich countries, thus increasing their economic dependency.

Low-income countries are thus seen not as underdeveloped but rather as misdeveloped (Emmanuel 1972; Amin 1974; Frank 1966, 1969a, 1969b, 1979; Prebisch 1967, 1971). Since dependency theorists believe that exploitation has kept their countries from achieving economic growth, they typically call for revolutionary changes that would push foreign corporations out of their countries altogether (Frank 1966, 1969a, 1969b).

In sub-Saharan Africa, an estimated 28 percent of children are forced to work, often for long hours with little pay in hazardous and exploitative jobs.

Dependency theorists regard the exercise of political and military power as central to enforcing unequal economic relationships. According to this theory, whenever local leaders question such unequal arrangements, their voices are quickly suppressed. When people elect a government opposing these policies, that government is likely to be overthrown by the country's military, often backed by the armed forces of the industrialized countries themselves. Dependency theorists point to many examples: the role of the CIA in overthrowing the Marxist governments of Guatemala in 1954 and Chile in 1973, and in undermining support for the leftist government in Nicaragua in the 1980s. In the view of dependency theory, global economic inequality is thus backed up by force.

WORLD-SYSTEMS THEORY

During the last quarter-century, sociologists have increasingly seen the world as a single (although often conflict-ridden) economic system. While dependency theories hold that individual countries are economically tied to one another, **world-systems theory** argues that the world capitalist economic system is not merely a collection of independent countries engaged in diplomatic and economic relations with one another but rather must be understood as a single unit. The world-systems approach is most closely identified with the work of Immanuel Wallerstein and his colleagues. Wallerstein showed that capitalism has long existed as a global economic system, beginning with the extension of markets and trade in Europe in the fifteenth and sixteenth centuries (Wallerstein 1974a, 1974b, 1979, 1990, 1996a, 1996b; Hopkins and Wallerstein 1996). The world system is seen as comprising four overlapping elements (Chase-Dunn 1989):

- a world market for goods and labor
- the division of the population into different economic classes, particularly capitalists and workers
- an international system of formal and informal political relations among the most powerful countries, whose competition with one another helps shape the world economy
- the carving up of the world into three unequal economic zones, with the wealthier zones exploiting the poorer ones

World-systems theorists term these three economic zones *core*, *periphery*, and *semiperiphery*. All countries in the world system are said to fall into one of the three categories. **Core countries** are the most advanced industrial countries, taking the lion's share of profits in the world economic system. These include Japan, the United States, and the countries of Western Europe. The **peripheral countries** comprise low-income, largely agricultural countries that are often manipulated by core countries for their own economic advantage. Examples of peripheral countries are found throughout Africa and to a lesser extent in Latin America and Asia. Natural resources, such as agricultural products, minerals, and other raw materials, flow from periphery to core—as do the profits. The core, in turn, sells finished goods to the periphery, also at a profit. World-systems theorists argue that core countries have made themselves wealthy with this unequal trade, while at the same time limiting the economic development of peripheral countries. Finally, the **semiperipheral countries** occupy an intermediate position: These are semi-industrialized, middle-income countries that extract profits from the more peripheral countries and in turn yield profits to the core countries. Examples of semiperipheral countries include Mexico in North America; Brazil, Argentina, and Chile in South America; and the

world-systems theory • Pioneered by Immanuel Wallerstein, this theory emphasizes the interconnections among countries based on the expansion of a capitalist world economy. This economy is made up of core countries, semiperipheral countries, and peripheral countries.

core countries • According to world-systems theory, the most advanced industrial countries, which take the lion's share of profits in the world economic system.

peripheral countries • Countries that have a marginal role in the world economy and are thus dependent on the core producing societies for their trading relationships.

semiperipheral countries • Countries that supply sources of labor and raw materials to the core industrial countries and the world economy but are not themselves fully industrialized societies.

Female workers make Barbie dolls at a toy factory in the Guangdong province of China.

emerging economies of East Asia. The semiperiphery, though to some degree controlled by the core, is thus also able to exploit the periphery. Moreover, the greater economic success of the semiperiphery holds out to the periphery the promise of similar development. Although the world system tends to change very slowly, once-powerful countries eventually lose their economic power and others take their place.

An important offshoot of the world-systems approach is a concept that emphasizes the global nature of economic activities. **Global commodity chains** are worldwide networks of labor and production processes yielding a finished product. These networks consist of all pivotal production activities that form a tightly interlocked "chain" extending from the raw materials needed to create the product to its final consumer (Gereffi 1995, 1996; Hopkins and Wallerstein 1996; Appelbaum and Christerson 1997).

The commodity-chain approach sees manufacturing as becoming increasingly globalized. Manufacturing accounted for approximately three-quarters of the world's total economic growth during the period from 1990 to 1998. The sharpest growth was among middle-income countries: Manufactured goods accounted for only 54 percent of these countries' exports in 1990, compared with 71 percent in 1998. In 2010, the export volume of manufactured goods increased by 18 percent—the highest growth in a decade (World Trade Organization [WTO] 2011). Between 2006 and 2010, there was a 19 percent increase in the number of companies exporting from the United States to other countries (Jackson 2013). China, which moved from the ranks of low-income countries to middle-income countries largely because of its role as an exporter of manufactured goods, partly accounts for this trend. Yet the most profitable activities in the commodity chain—engineering, design, and advertising—usually occur in core countries, whereas the least profitable activities, such as factory production, occur in peripheral countries.

Although manufacturing in the global commodity chain typically takes place in peripheral countries, an exception to this trend has developed. Low-wage, low-profit factories known as sweatshops are today reappearing in core countries, sometimes for the first time in half a century or more. A sweatshop is a small factory that has numerous violations of wage, health, and safety laws. In New York City and Los Angeles, for example, more than 100,000 workers labor in tiny garment factories that make many of the brands of clothing sold in major department stores. Many laborers work for less than minimum wage in buildings described by government officials as firetraps.

global commodity chain • A worldwide network of labor and production processes yielding a finished product.

STATE-CENTERED THEORIES

Some of the most recent explanations of successful economic development empha-size the role of state policy in promoting growth. Differing sharply from market-oriented theories, **state-centered theories** argue that appropriate government policies do not interfere with economic development but rather can play a key role in bringing it about. A large body of research now suggests that in some regions of the world, such as East Asia, successful economic development has been state led. Even the World Bank, long a strong proponent of free-market theories of development, has changed its thinking about the role of the state. In its 1997 report *The State in a Changing World*, the World Bank concluded that without an effective state, "sustain-able development, both economic and social, is impossible" (World Bank 1997).

Strong governments contributed in various ways to economic growth in the East Asian emerging economies during the 1980s and 1990s (Henderson and Appelbaum 1992; Amsden et al. 1994; Evans 1995; Cumings 1997; World Bank 1997):

state-centered theories •
Development theories that argue that appropriate government poli-cies do not interfere with economic development, but rather can play a key role in bringing it about.

1. **East Asian governments have sometimes aggressively acted to ensure politi-cal stability, while keeping labor costs low.** They have accomplished this by acts of repression, such as outlawing trade unions, banning strikes, jailing labor leaders, and, in general, silencing the voices of workers. The governments of Taiwan, South Korea, and Singapore in particular have engaged in such practices.

2. **East Asian governments have frequently sought to steer economic devel-opment in desired directions.** Some examples include state agencies providing cheap loans and tax breaks to businesses that invest in industries favored by the government and governments preventing businesses from investing their profits in other countries, forcing them to invest in economic growth at home.

3. **East Asian governments have often been heavily involved in social programs such as low-cost housing and universal education.** The world's largest public housing systems (outside of socialist or formerly socialist countries) have been in Hong Kong and Singapore, where government subsidies keep rents extremely low. As a result, workers don't require high wages to pay for their housing, so they can compete better with American and European workers in the emerging global labor market.

EVALUATING GLOBAL THEORIES OF INEQUALITY

Each of the four sets of theories of global inequality has strengths and weaknesses. Together, they enable us to better understand the causes of and cures for global inequality.

1. **Market-oriented theories** recommend the adoption of modern capitalist institu-tions to promote economic development. They further argue that countries can de-velop economically only if they open their borders to trade, and they cite evidence to support this argument. But market-oriented theories overlook economic ties between poor countries and wealthy ones—ties that can impede economic growth under some conditions and enhance it under others. They blame low-income coun-tries for their poverty rather than acknowledging outside factors, such as the busi-ness operations of more powerful nations. Market-oriented theories also ignore the ways government can work with the private sector to spur economic development.

Can Apps Heal Global Inequalities?

Think about how you use your smartphone. Maybe you check the latest news headlines or sports scores. Or maybe you like to post photos on Facebook. But can you think of ways that you might use your smartphone to improve the well-being of the millions of people living in poor nations? A number of app developers are doing just that. But these developers have their work cut out for them. Although an estimated 80 percent of the world's population today has mobile phones, only 20 percent have smartphones that can handle complex programs.

In Zambia, a nation particularly hard-hit by the AIDS crisis, a number of apps have been developed to educate people about their risk of HIV/AIDS and to deliver timely test results. A program called Zambia U-Report provides young people with individualized and real-time education and counseling services on HIV and other sexually transmitted diseases. Their privacy is guaranteed; they can sign up through SMS using a simple numerical code (Mwizabi 2013). Another app recently developed by the World Health Organization (WHO) helps give young mothers rapid results from their infants' HIV tests. In a rural nation like Zambia, mothers often have very long waits between the time their infants are tested, when the blood is assessed at a regional laboratory, and when the results are returned to their local health center. The new app uses SMS to transmit the test results well ahead of traditional paper copies, reducing the time between diagnosis and treatment (Seidenberg et al. 2012).

Smartphones are also emerging as a particularly effective way to diagnose eye disorders. According to the WHO, more than 280 million people around the world have vision problems or are blind; an estimated 90 percent of these sight-impaired people live in poor nations. However, many lack access to vision care. In response, a team of scientists at MIT created NETRA (Near Eye Tool for Refractive Assessment), which turns a smartphone into a mobile eye diagnostic device. After users download the app, they attach an inexpensive plastic eyepiece onto their smartphone. Looking into the eyepiece, users then use buttons on the phone to move images of two lines until they appear as one. Doctors can identify a user's vision problems based on the number of clicks it takes the user to line up the images. Those results can be forwarded along to an optician to make eye glasses. Similarly, another team of doctors is testing PEEK (Portable Eye Examination Kit) on more than 5,000 people in Kenya (Gallagher 2013); this app uses a phone's camera to scan people's eyes for cataracts.

Other entrepreneurs are developing apps to aid agricultural production in Africa. A competition called Apps4Africa encouraged young people to develop apps that address the impact of climate change on various communities. The Grainy Bunch, which was developed in Tanzania, features a national grain supply chain management system that monitors the purchase, storage, distribution, and consumption of grain across the entire nation. Similarly, Agro Universe, developed by a team from Uganda, creates a regional marketplace, helping communities prepare for pest- and drought-induced food shortages by linking communities to farmers with available produce (Fenner 2012).

PEEK (Portable Eye Examination Kit), which uses a phone's camera to scan people's eyes for cataracts, is being tested in Kenya. Smartphone apps like PEEK and NETRA are bringing eye exams and eye glasses to poor, remote communities in Africa.

Do you believe that apps can play an effective role in solving some of the problems of global inequality? Why or why not? Can you think of an app that would help to solve some of the problems of global inequality that you read about in this chapter?

Finally, they fail to explain why some countries take off economically while others remain grounded in poverty and underdevelopment.

2. **Dependency theories** emphasize how wealthy nations have exploited poor ones. However, although these theories account for much of the economic backwardness in Latin America and Africa, they cannot explain the occasional success stories such as Brazil, Argentina, and Mexico or the rapidly expanding economies of China and East Asia. In fact, some formerly low-income countries have risen economically despite the presence of multinational corporations. Even some former colonies, such as Hong Kong and Singapore, are among the success stories.

3. **World-systems theory** analyzes the world economy as a whole, looking at the complex global web of political and economic relationships that influence development and inequality in poor and rich nations alike. It is thus well suited to understanding the global economy at a time when businesses are increasingly free to set up operations anywhere, acquiring an economic importance rivaling that of many countries. One challenge faced by world-systems theory lies in the difficulty of modeling a complex and interdependent world economy. It also has been criticized for emphasizing economic and political forces at the expense of cultural ones, such as the combination of nationalism and religious belief that is currently reshaping the Middle East. Finally, world-systems theory has been said to place too much emphasis on the role of nation-states in a world economy increasingly shaped by transnational corporations that operate independently of national borders (Robinson 2004; Sklair 2002b).

4. **State-centered theories** stress the governmental role in fostering economic growth. They thus offer a useful alternative to both the prevailing market-oriented theories, with their emphasis on states as economic hindrances, and dependency theories, which view states as allies of global business elites in exploiting poor countries. When combined with the other theories—particularly world-systems theory—state-centered theories can explain the radical changes now transforming the world economy. ✓

> ## CONCEPT CHECKS ✓
>
> 1. Describe the main assumptions of market-oriented theories of global inequality.
> 2. Why are dependency theories of global inequalities often criticized?
> 3. Compare and contrast core, peripheral, and semiperipheral nations.
> 4. How have strong governments of some East Asian nations contributed to the economic development of that region?

HOW DOES GLOBAL INEQUALITY AFFECT YOUR LIFE?

Understand how global economic inequality affects the daily life of you and your peers.

Today the social and economic forces leading to a single global capitalist economy appear to be irreversible. What does rapid globalization mean for the future of global inequality? No sociologist knows for certain, but many possible scenarios exist. In one, our world might be dominated by large, global corporations, with workers everywhere competing with one another at a global wage. Such a scenario might predict falling wages for large numbers of people in today's high-income countries and rising wages for a few in low-income countries. There might be a general leveling out of average income around the world, although at a level much lower than that currently enjoyed in the United States and other industrialized nations. In this scenario,

The lack of modern technology in poor nations prevents residents from developing the skills needed to transcend poverty. A girl from a poor family in Montevideo, Uruguay, uses a laptop given to her as part of a new educational policy aimed at closing the technology gap.

the polarization between the haves and the have nots would grow, as the whole world would be increasingly divided into those who benefit from the global economy and those who do not. Such polarization could fuel conflict between ethnic groups and even nations, as those suffering from economic globalization would blame others for their plight (Hirst and Thompson 1992; Wagar 1992).

On the other hand, a global economy could mean greater opportunity for everyone, as the benefits of modern technology stimulate worldwide economic growth. According to this more optimistic scenario, the more successful East Asian emerging economies, such as Hong Kong, Taiwan, South Korea, and Singapore, are only a sign of things to come. Other emerging economies such as Malaysia and Thailand will soon follow, along with China, Indonesia, Vietnam, and other Asian countries. India, the world's second most populous country, already boasted a middle class of around 300 million people in 2007, about a third of its total population (David 2007; Deutsche Bank Research 2010).

A countervailing trend, however, is the technology gap that divides rich and poor countries, which today appears to be widening, making it even more difficult for poor countries to catch up. This gap is a result of the disparity in wealth between nations, but it also reinforces those disparities. Poor countries cannot easily afford modern technology—yet, in the absence of modern technology, they face major barriers to overcoming poverty. They are caught in a vicious downward spiral from which it is difficult to escape.

Jeffrey Sachs, director of the Earth Institute and Quetelet professor of sustainable development and professor of health policy and management at Columbia University, and a prominent adviser to many Eastern European and developing countries, claims that the world is divided into three classes: technology innovators, technology adopters, and the technologically disconnected (Sachs 2000).

Technology innovators are those regions that provide nearly all of the world's technological inventions; they account for no more than 15 percent of the world's population. Technology adopters are those regions that are able to adopt technologies invented elsewhere, applying them to production and consumption; they account for 50 percent of the world's population. Finally, the technologically disconnected are those regions that neither innovate nor adopt technologies developed elsewhere; they account for 35 percent of the world's population. In fact, the Organization for Economic Co-operation and Development (OECD 2005b) reports that over half of the patents issued worldwide were concentrated inside just ten regions within the most advanced industrial nations.

Note that Sachs also speaks of regions rather than countries: In today's increasingly borderless world, technology use (or exclusion) does not always respect national frontiers. Technologically disconnected regions such as tropical sub-Saharan Africa or the Ganges valley states of India lack access to markets or major ocean trading routes. They are caught in what Sachs terms a *poverty trap*, plagued by "tropical infectious disease, low agricultural productivity and environmental degradation—all requiring technological solutions beyond their means" (2000).

What can be done to overcome the technological abyss that divides rich and poor countries? Sachs urges the governments of wealthy countries, along with international lending institutions, to provide loans and grants for scientific and technological development. Sachs notes that very little money is available to support research and development in poor countries. The World Bank, a major source of funding for development projects in poor countries, spends only $60 million a year supporting tropical, agricultural, or health research and development. By way of comparison, Pfizer—the world's largest pharmaceutical corporation in terms of market share—spends 108–117 times that much ($6.5–$7.0 billion) for research and development for its own products despite recent downsizing of its R&D (research and development) department (Scientific American 2011). From computers and the Internet to biotechnology, the "wealth of nations" increasingly depends on modern information technology. As long as major regions of the world remain technologically disconnected, it seems unlikely that global poverty will be eradicated.

In the most optimistic view, the republics of the former Soviet Union, as well as the formerly socialist countries of Eastern Europe, will eventually advance into the ranks of the high-income countries. Economic growth will spread to Latin America, Africa, and the rest of the world. Because capitalism requires that workers be mobile, the remaining caste societies around the world will be replaced by class-based societies. These societies will experience enhanced opportunities for upward mobility.

What is the future of global inequality? It is difficult to be entirely optimistic. Global economic growth has slowed, and the economic crisis of 2008 continues to send shock waves around the world. The Russian economy, in its move from socialism to capitalism, has encountered many pitfalls, leaving many Russians poorer than ever. The European Union, once thought to be a pillar of the global economy, is facing many challenges. While many countries have experienced economic growth, many have not; the gap between rich and poor remains large.

The future of global inequality remains an open question—one whose answer will depend, in large part, on whether global economic expansion can be sustained in the face of ecological constraints and a global economy that has proven to be surprisingly fragile. It remains to be seen whether the countries of the world will learn from one another and work together to create better lives for their peoples. Technological advances, including widespread use of the Internet and frequent media reports of tragedy in poorer parts of the world, such as the devastating earthquake in Haiti, may raise awareness of the startling economic and health inequalities in the world today. A well-informed awareness of global inequality may be an essential step toward trying to eradicate the vast gap between the haves and have nots, and developing social programs to eradicate the problems of hunger and disease that plague poorer societies. Although the future is uncertain, there is no question that the past quarter-century has witnessed a global economic transformation of unprecedented magnitude. The effects of this transformation in the next quarter-century will leave few lives on the planet untouched. ✓

CONCEPT CHECKS ✓

1. What is the role of technology in deepening existing global inequalities?

2. According to Sachs, what can be done to reduce the technology gap between rich and poor countries?

EXERCISES:

Thinking Sociologically

1. Concisely review the four theories offered in this chapter that explain why there are gaps between nations' economic developments and resulting global inequality: market-oriented theory, dependency theory, world-systems theory, and state-centered theory. Briefly discuss the distinctive characteristics of each theory and how each differs from the others. Which theory do you feel offers the most explanatory power to addressing economic developmental gaps?

Chapter 8

Global Inequality

2. This chapter states that global economic inequality has personal relevance and importance to people in advanced, affluent economies. Briefly review this argument. Explain carefully whether you were persuaded by it.

p.234 — What Is Global Inequality?

Understand the systematic differences in wealth and power among countries.

p.238 — What Is Daily Life Like in Rich versus Poor Countries?

Recognize the impact of different economic standards of living on people throughout the world.

p.241 — Can Poor Countries Become Rich?

Analyze the success of the emerging economies.

p.243 — How Do Sociological Theories Explain Global Inequality?

Learn several sociological theories explaining why some societies are wealthier than others, as well as how global inequality can be overcome.

p.251 — How Does Global Inequality Affect Your Life?

Understand how global economic inequality affects the daily life of you and your peers.

globalization

global inequality

1. Explain how the World Bank measures global inequality, and discuss some of the problems associated with measuring global inequality.
2. Compare and contrast high-income, middle-income, and low-income countries.

1. Why do people who live in high-income countries have better health than those who live in low-income countries?
2. What factors contribute to famines?

emerging economies

1. What are the five factors that have facilitated the economic success of the East Asian emerging economies?
2. What are potential obstacles to the continued economic success of the emerging economies?

market-oriented theories •
modernization theory •
neoliberalism • dependency
theories • colonialism •
world-systems theory •
core countries • peripheral
countries • semiperipheral
countries • global commodity
chain • state-centered theories

1. Describe the main assumptions of market-oriented theories of global inequality.
2. Why are dependency theories of global inequalities often criticized?
3. Compare and contrast core, peripheral, and semiperipheral nations.
4. How have strong governments of some East Asian nations contributed to the economic development of that region?

1. What is the role of technology in deepening existing global inequalities?
2. According to Sachs, what can be done to reduce the technology gap between rich and poor countries?

9

Gender Inequality

THE BIG QUESTIONS

ARE GENDER DIFFERENCES DUE TO NATURE, NURTURE, OR BOTH?
Evaluate whether differences between women and men are the result of biological differences or social and cultural influences.

HOW DO GENDER INEQUALITIES AFFECT SOCIAL INSTITUTIONS?
Recognize that gender differences are a part of our social structure and create inequalities between women and men. Learn the forms these inequalities take in social institutions such as the workplace, the family, the educational system, and the political system in the United States and globally.

WHY ARE WOMEN THE TARGET OF VIOLENCE?
Learn about the specific ways that women are the target of physical and sexual violence in the United States and globally.

HOW DOES SOCIAL THEORY EXPLAIN GENDER INEQUALITY?
Think about various explanations for gender inequality. Learn some feminist theories about how to achieve gender equality.

WHAT ARE THE GLOBAL CONSEQUENCES OF GENDER INEQUALITY?
Learn how globalization has transformed ideas about women's rights.

Sheryl Sandberg, Chief Operating Officer of Facebook and the author of *Lean In*, which urges women to be more assertive and seek leadership roles in the workplace, gives a talk on contemporary inequality between the sexes. As more and more women enter the realm of corporate America, are they achieving gender parity?

By many indications, it looks like women have made it in the high-pressure, male-dominated fields of business, finance, and technology. Women like Marissa Mayer, president and CEO of Yahoo, Mary Barra, CEO of General Motors, and Sheryl Sandberg, chief operating officer of Facebook, serve as role models for young women hoping to ascend the ranks of corporate America. However, despite the tremendous successes of Mayer, Sandberg, and other high-ranking professional women today, it's still not easy for women to make it to the top. Discrimination, both overt and subtle, still hurts millions of women in the workforce today. Witness the recent case of Merrill Lynch, a venerable brokerage firm that is owned by Bank of America. In September 2013, Bank of America agreed to pay $39 million to nearly 5,000 women who worked at Merrill Lynch as part of a discrimination case filed by the employees (McGeehan 2013).

What was the basis of the lawsuit? The three plaintiffs, Judy Calibuso, a financial adviser at Merrill Lynch, and Julie Moss and Dianne Goedtel, former financial advisers at Bank of America, charged that their employer gave male colleagues bigger annual bonuses and more opportunities to get ahead—such as "plum accounts" and the most high-powered clients. For example, Calibuso had asked her manager to be assigned to the lucrative task of working on "fee-based" accounts and was told that those assignments would instead go to a male colleague. When Calibuso complained to a supervisor, she was reprimanded for making waves. Yet one of the most remarkable aspects of the lawsuit is that there was no dramatic centerpiece; rather, the suit was based on dozens of small slights or injustices that the women faced in their daily work lives. According to the lawsuit's web page, Bank of America and Merrill Lynch engaged in "a pattern and practice of gender discrimination against their female financial advisers with respect to business opportunities, compensation, professional support, and other terms and conditions of employment" (Lieff et al. 2012).

You probably didn't see anything on the nightly news or Twitter about the experiences of Calibuso and her colleagues because we tend to pay attention only to cases where the discrimination is blatant, egregious, or shocking. That's the case with another lawsuit against Merrill Lynch, which attracted media attention in July 2013. Three plaintiffs—Sara Hunter Hudson, Julia Kuo, and Catherine Wharton—alleged that they were fired from their positions as trainees at Merrill Lynch because the firm favored men and promoted a "boys club" work culture. The women claim that their boss ordered them to attend workshops on how to "dress for success" and suggested they read the book *Seducing the Boys Club: Uncensored Tactics from a Woman at the Top* (DiSesa 2008). The book offered the women tips for making it in a man's world; they were advised to flirt with their male colleagues and clients and to use charm, flattery, and sweetness when offering critical feedback to male coworkers (Marsh 2013). In their complaint, Hudson, Kuo, and Wharton protested against a company that "advocated conforming to gender stereotypes to get ahead in the workplace."

As we will see later in the chapter, the demeaning treatment of women at Merrill Lynch and other major financial firms may partly explain why women account for less than one-quarter of all senior officers in finance industries (Catalyst 2012). A casual observer who sees a statistic like this might conclude that women are not cut out for such a cutthroat industry or that they simply prefer to work in other fields. Yet sociology helps us look beyond individual skills and preferences and helps us understand the systematic ways that factors like gender shape one's access to power and resources. Explaining the differences and inequalities between women and men in a society is now one of the most central topics in sociology.

In this chapter, we will take a sociological approach to the exploration of gender differences and gender inequality. Gender is a way for society to divide people into two categories: "men" and "women." Not all persons, however, fit neatly into one of these two categories, as we will see later in this chapter (Heine 2013). According to this socially created division, men and women have different identities and social roles. Men and women are expected to think and act in certain ways across most life domains. Gender also serves as a social status; in almost all societies men's roles are valued more than are women's roles. Men and women are not only different but also unequal in terms of power, prestige, and wealth. Despite the advances that many women have made in the United States and other Western societies, this remains true today. Sociologists are interested in explaining how society differentiates between women and men, and how these differences serve as the basis for social inequalities (Chafetz 1990). Yet sociologists recognize that gender alone does not shape our life experiences. Rather, there are pronounced differences in women's and men's lives on the basis of race, social class, age, birth cohort, religion, nation of origin, sexual orientation, and even one's marital or parental status (Choo and Ferree 2010).

In this chapter, we examine the origins of gender differences, assessing the debate over the role of biological factors versus social influences in the formation of gender roles. We will also look to other cultures for evidence on this debate. Then we will review the various forms of gender inequality that exist in U.S. society and throughout the globe. In this section, we will focus on the prominent social institutions of the educational system, the workplace, the family, and the government. Next, we will examine how and why women are more likely than men to be the targets of sexual violence. We will review the various forms of feminism and assess prospects for future change toward a gender-equal society. We will then analyze some theories of gender inequality and apply them to the lives of women like Judy Calibuso. We conclude the chapter by looking at the role of women around the world in the first two decades of the twenty-first century.

ARE GENDER DIFFERENCES DUE TO NATURE, NURTURE, OR BOTH?

Evaluate whether differences between women and men are the result of biological differences or social and cultural influences.

Are differences between boys and girls, and between men and women, due to nature, nurture, or some combination of the two? As we first noted in Chapter 2, scholars are divided about the degree to which inborn biological characteristics have an enduring impact on our gender identities as "feminine" or "masculine" and the social roles based on those identities. No one would argue that our behavior is purely instinctive or hardwired. Yet scholars disagree as to the extent to which they believe gender differences are the product of learning and socialization.

Before we review the relative influences of nature and nurture, we first need to make an important distinction between sex and gender. **Sex** refers to physical differences of the body, whereas **gender** concerns the psychological, social, and cultural differences between males and females. This distinction is fundamental because many differences between males and females are not biological in origin.

sex • The biological and anatomical differences distinguishing females from males.

gender • Social expectations about behavior regarded as appropriate for the members of each sex. Gender refers not to the physical attributes distinguishing men and women but to socially formed traits of masculinity and femininity.

THE ROLE OF BIOLOGY

How much are differences in the behavior of women and men the result of biological differences? Some researchers hold that innate differences of behavior between women and men appear in some form in all cultures and that the findings of sociobiology point strongly in this direction. Such researchers are likely to draw attention to the fact, for example, that in almost all cultures, men rather than women take part in hunting and warfare. Surely, they argue, this indicates that men possess biologically based tendencies toward aggression that women lack. In looking at the kind of jobs that women and men typically hold, they might point out that women are better suited than men for jobs like store cashier or clerical assistant. Ringing up purchases and assisting with office tasks are more passive occupations than being a stock handler or store security guard, positions that require more physical strength and aggressiveness.

Most sociologists are unconvinced by these arguments. The level of aggressiveness of men, they say, varies widely across cultures, and women are expected to be more passive or gentle in some cultures than in others (Elshtain 1981). Further, some argue that women are just as aggressive as men; however, women use strategies that are consistent with gender role socialization. For instance, women will use "interpersonal aggression," such as malicious gossip or "bad mouthing," rather than engaging in physical fights (Bjorkqvist 1994; Bjorkqvist, Lagerspetz, and Osterman 2006). Theories of "natural difference" are often grounded in data on animal behavior, critics point out, rather than in anthropological or historical evidence about human behavior, which reveals variation over time and place. In the majority of cultures, most women spend a significant part of their lives caring for children and therefore cannot readily take part in hunting or war.

The hypothesis that biological factors wholly determine behavior patterns in men and women is undermined, in part, by a lack of empirical evidence. Nearly a century of research fails to identify the physiological and biological origins of the complex social behaviors exhibited by human males and females (Connell 1987). Theories that see individuals as complying with some kind of innate predisposition neglect the vital role of social interaction and social contexts in shaping human behavior.

What does the research show? Some studies show differences in hormonal makeup between the sexes, with the male sex hormone, testosterone, associated with a propensity to violence (Rutter and Giller 1984). For instance, if male monkeys are castrated at birth, they become less aggressive; conversely, female monkeys given testosterone will become more aggressive than normal females. However, it has also been found that providing monkeys with opportunities to dominate others actually increases the testosterone level. This means that aggressive behavior may affect the production of the hormone, rather than the hormone's causing increased aggression—thus underscoring the importance of social context. In other words, there might be slight biological differences between men and women, but these small differences may be exacerbated and amplified by social contexts that promote behaviors that are consistent with gendered stereotypes and expectations.

Another source of information comes from the experience of identical twins. Identical twins derive from a single egg and have exactly the same genetic makeup. In one particular case, one of a pair of identical male twins was seriously injured while being circumcised, and the decision was made to reconstruct his genitals as a female. He was thereafter raised as a girl. The twins at six years old demonstrated typical male and female traits as found in Western culture. The little girl enjoyed playing with other girls, helped with the housework, and wanted to get married when she grew up. The boy preferred the company of other boys, his favorite toys were cars and trucks, and he wanted to become a firefighter or police officer.

For some time, this case was treated as a conclusive demonstration of the overriding influence of social learning on gender differences. However, when the girl was a teenager she was interviewed during a television program, and the interview showed that she felt some unease about her gender identity, even perhaps that she was "really" a boy after all. She had by then learned of her unusual background, and this knowledge may very well have been responsible for this altered perception of herself (Ryan 1985).

GENDER SOCIALIZATION

gender socialization • The learning of gender roles through social factors such as schooling, the media, and family.

Another explanation for gender differences is **gender socialization**, or ways that individuals learn gender roles from socializing agents such as the family and the media (see also Chapter 4). Through contact with various agents of socialization, children gradually internalize the social norms and expectations that are seen to correspond with their sex. Gender differences are not biologically determined; they are culturally produced. Recall the case of Boo, whom we met in Chapter 3. The social norm that "boys should be boys" is so powerful that the preschool student and his mother were harshly sanctioned when Boo dressed up like a female cartoon character for Halloween. The concept of gender socialization

Almost all team sports are segregated by sex, affirming cultural beliefs in gender difference and inequality.

teaches us that gender inequalities result because men and women are socialized into different roles.

People create gender through social interactions with others, such as family members, friends, and colleagues. This process begins at birth when doctors, nurses, and family members—the first to see an infant—assign the person to a gender category on the basis of physical characteristics. Babies are immediately dressed in a way that marks the sex category: "Parents don't want to be constantly asked if their child is a boy or a girl" (Lorber 1994). Once the child is marked as male or female, everyone who interacts with the child will treat it in accordance with its gender. They do so on the basis of the society's assumptions, which lead people to treat women and men differently, even as opposites (Renzetti and Curran 1995).

THE SOCIAL CONSTRUCTION OF GENDER

In recent years, socialization and gender role theories have been criticized by a growing number of sociologists. Rather than seeing sex as biologically determined and gender as culturally learned, they argue that we should view both sex and gender as socially constructed products. Theorists who believe in the **social construction of gender** reject all biological bases for gender differences. Gender identities emerge, they argue, in relation to perceived sex differences in society and in turn help to shape those differences. For example, a society in which ideas of masculinity are characterized by physical strength and tough attitudes will encourage men to cultivate a specific body image and set of mannerisms (Connell 1987; Butler 1989; Scott and Morgan 1993). Men who fail to comply with what scholars call "hegemonic masculinity," or the beliefs that men should be strong, self-reliant, and unemotional, may be subtly sanctioned for not enacting gender roles in a way that is consistent with prevailing cultural norms (Connell and Messerschmidt 2005). According to this perspective, gender is not something that we are, but something that we "do" (West and Zimmerman 1987) or a role that we perform.

social construction of gender • The learning of gender roles through socialization and interaction with others.

GENDER IDENTITY IN EVERYDAY LIFE

Our conceptions of gender identity are formed so early in life that as adults we mainly take them for granted. Yet gender is more than learning to act like a girl or boy. Gender differences are something we live with every day. Some sociologists argue that we "do gender" in our daily interactions with others (West and Zimmerman 1987); that means that we learn how to present ourselves as "male" or "female" through our choice of behaviors, clothing, hairstyle, stance, body language, and even tone of voice.

These taken-for-granted practices are vividly brought to life by journalist Norah Vincent in her 2006 book *Self-Made Man: One Woman's Year Disguised as a Man*. Vincent spent eighteen months disguised as a man, not only to understand how men behave when women aren't around but to reveal the ways that men (and in Vincent's case, a woman!) "do masculinity" in everyday life.

At 5 feet, 10 inches and 155 pounds, Vincent passed as a man she called Ned. Her transformation began with a very short haircut, baggy men's clothes, and a too-small sports bra to flatten and conceal her breasts. Vincent underwent months of training with a professional voice teacher to learn how to sound like a man. She went undercover in a range of typically male settings, including a bowling league, a strip club, a monastery, and a men's support group. She also observed the importance of gender in even the most ordinary everyday encounters—including shopping for a new car. When she went into the car showroom as Norah, the salesman's pitch quickly turned flirtatious, but when she returned to the same salesman disguised as her alter-ego Ned, the tone was all business and the talk was all about the car's performance.

The subtle ways in which we do gender are so much a part of our lives that we don't notice them until they are missing or radically altered. Because gender is so pervasive in structuring social life, gender statuses must be clearly differentiated if society is to function in an orderly manner (Lorber 1994; West and Fenstermaker 1995).

Journalist Norah Vincent spent eighteen months disguised as a man and chronicled her experiences in her book *Self-Made Man: One Woman's Year Disguised as a Man.*

FINDINGS FROM OTHER CULTURES

If gender differences were mostly the result of biology, then we could expect that gender roles would not vary much from culture to culture. However, one set of findings that helps show how gender roles are in fact socially constructed comes from anthropologists, who have studied gender in other times and cultures.

NEW GUINEA

In her classic New Guinea study, *Sex and Temperament in Three Primitive Societies*, Margaret Mead (1963, orig. 1935) observed wide variability among gender role

Margaret Mead conducts fieldwork with a mother and child in the Admiralty Islands, part of Papua New Guinea, in 1953. Her classic study *Sex and Temperament in Three Primitive Societies* found that gender roles there differed dramatically from the United States.

prescriptions—and such marked differences from those in the United States—that any claims to the universality of gender roles had to be rejected. Mead studied three separate tribes in New Guinea, which varied widely in their gender roles. In Arapesh society, both males and females generally exhibited characteristics and behaviors that would typically be associated with the Western female role. Both sexes among the Arapesh were passive, gentle, unaggressive, and emotionally responsive to the needs of others. In contrast, Mead found that in another New Guinea group, the Mundugumor, both the males and females were characteristically aggressive, suspicious, and, from a Western observer's perspective, excessively cruel, especially toward children. In both cultures, however, men and women were expected to behave very similarly. In a third group, the Tchambuli tribe of New Guinea, gender roles of the males and females were almost exactly reversed from the roles traditionally assigned to males and females in Western society. Women "managed the business affairs of life" while "the men . . . painted, gossiped and had temper tantrums" (Mead 1972).

THE !KUNG

Among the !Kung of the Kalahari desert, who refer to themselves as *zhun/twasi* or "the real people," it is very common for both men and women to engage in child care (Shostak 1981). Due to the nonconfrontational parenting practices of the !Kung, who oppose violent conflict and physical punishment, children learn that aggressive behavior will not be tolerated by either men or women. Although the !Kung abide by the seemingly traditional arrangement where "men hunt and women gather," the vast majority of their food actually comes from the gathering activities of women (see Draper, as cited in Renzetti and Curran 2000). Women return from their gathering expeditions armed not only with food for the community but also with valuable information for hunters.

Mehran Rafaat, with her twin sisters, is regarded as a boy by her family.

THE BACHA POSH IN AFGHANISTAN

In contemporary Afghanistan, boys are so highly prized that families with only daughters often experience shame and pity; as a result, some transform one young daughter into a son. The parents cut the girl's hair short, dress her in boys' clothes, change her name to a boy's name, and encourage her to participate in "boys' activities" like bicycling and playing cricket. These children are called *bacha posh*, which translates into "dressed up as a boy."

Parents of bacha posh believe that boys are afforded so many advantages in Afghan culture that it is helpful, rather than cruel, to transform their girls into boys. A bacha posh can more easily receive an education, work outside the home, even escort her sisters in public, allowing freedoms that are unheard of for girls in a society that strictly segregates men and women. In most cases, a return to womanhood takes place when the child enters puberty, a decision almost always made by her parents (Nordberg 2010).

MULTIPLE GENDERS

The understanding that only two genders (i.e., male and female) exist is not universal. The Spaniards who came to both North and South America in the seventeenth century noticed men in the native tribes who had taken on the mannerisms of women, as well as women who occupied male roles.

A person occupying an opposite gender role is called a *berdache*. Roscoe (1991) has studied berdaches among the Zuni, a Native American tribe. Roscoe documented that berdaches are not necessarily homosexual; rather, some are heterosexual, some homosexual, and others sexually oriented toward other berdaches. Several Native American cultures hold a special honor for persons of "integrated genders." For example, the term *nádleehí* literally means "one who constantly transforms," and refers to a male-bodied person with a feminine nature, a special gift according to Navajo culture. The Navajo believe that to maintain harmony, there must be a balanced interrelationship between the feminine and the masculine within a single individual. Native activists working to renew their cultural heritage adopted the English term *two-spirit* as a useful shorthand to describe the entire spectrum of gender and sexual expression that is better and more completely described in their own languages (Nibley 2011).

The notion that one's sex may transcend the simple male/female dichotomy is not limited to other cultures, however. In recent years, there has been heightened recognition that the anatomical boundaries between the two sexes are not always clear-cut. Some infants, for example, may be born with ambiguous genitalia. These babies, referred to as "intersex," are rare, accounting for far less than 1 percent of the population (Fausto-Sterling 2000). However, they do create a challenge to our traditional notions and practices based on the male-female binary (Weil 2006). In 2013, Germany became the first nation in the world to allow parents three options for denoting their baby's sex on the baby's birth certificate: male, female, or blank. The intention is to allow babies born with biological characteristics of both sexes to make a choice about who they are once they get older. Under this new law, "individuals can . . . opt to remain outside the gender binary altogether" (Heine 2013). ✓

CONCEPT CHECKS

1. What is the difference between sex and gender?

2. How do both biology and gender socialization contribute to differences between men and women?

3. How can studies of gender in other cultures contribute to the argument that gender is socially constructed?

4. What is intersex? How does it challenge the male-female sex dichotomy?

HOW DO GENDER INEQUALITIES AFFECT SOCIAL INSTITUTIONS?

Recognize that gender differences are a part of our social structure and create inequalities between women and men. Learn the forms these inequalities take in social institutions such as the workplace, the family, the educational system, and the political system in the United States and globally.

Anthropologists and historians have found that most groups, collectives, and societies throughout history differentiate between women's and men's roles. Although there are considerable variations in the respective roles of women and men in different cultures, there are few instances of a society in which women are more powerful than men. Women everywhere typically are responsible for child rearing and the maintenance of the home, while political and military activities tend to be resoundingly male. Nowhere in the world do men have primary responsibility for the rearing of children. Conversely, there are few if any cultures in which women are primarily responsible for the herding of large animals, the hunting of large game, deep-sea fishing, or plow agriculture (Brown 1977).

Just because women and men perform different tasks or have different responsibilities in societies does not necessarily mean that women are unequal to men. However, if the work and activities of women and men are valued differently, then the division of labor between them can become the basis for unequal gender relations. In modern societies, the division of labor between the sexes has become less clear-cut than it was in premodern cultures, but men still outnumber women in all spheres of power and influence.

Male dominance in a society is usually referred to as **patriarchy**. Although men are favored in almost all of the world's societies, the degree of patriarchy varies. In the United States, women have made tremendous progress in several realms,

patriarchy • The dominance of men over women. All known societies are patriarchal, although there are variations in the degree and nature of the power men exercise, as compared with women.

especially education and work, but several forms of gender inequality still exist. Yet throughout the world, many cultures exist where women suffer tremendous disadvantages relative to men.

gender inequality • The inequality between men and women in terms of wealth, income, and status.

Sociologists define **gender inequality** as the difference in the status, power, and prestige women and men have in groups, collectives, and societies. In thinking about gender inequality between men and women, we can ask the following questions: Do women and men have equal access to valued societal resources—for example, food, money, power, and time? Second, do women and men have similar life options? Third, are women's and men's roles and activities valued similarly? We will turn to look at the various forms of gender inequality in educational systems, the workplace, the home, and politics. As you read through this section, keep the above questions in mind.

EDUCATION

If you look around your college campus, you might notice roughly equal numbers of men and women, and may think that gender no longer affects whether and how one receives an education. There is some truth to this. College campuses today are roughly 50:50 when it comes to the number of men and women filling undergraduate classrooms; in fact, women slightly outnumber men on college campuses today, and this gender gap is much larger among blacks and Latinos than among whites (Pollard 2011). Yet aggregate numbers are only part of the story. As we will see next, subtle dynamics, starting in primary school, teach boys and girls different skills and direct young men and women into divergent career paths.

UNEQUAL TREATMENT IN THE CLASSROOM

Sociologists have found that schools help foster gender differences in outlook and behavior. Studies document that teachers interact differently—and often inequitably—with their male and female students. These interactions differ in at least two ways: the frequency of teacher-student interactions and the content of those interactions. Both of the patterns are based on—and perpetuate—traditional assumptions about male and female behavior and traits.

One study showed that regardless of the sex of the teacher, male students interacted more with their teachers than female students did. Boys received more teacher attention and instructional time than girls did. This was due in part to the fact that boys were more demanding than girls (American Association of University Women [AAUW] 1992). Another study reported that boys were eight times more likely to call out answers in class, thus grabbing their teachers' attention. This research also showed that even when boys did not voluntarily participate in class, teachers were more likely to solicit information from them than from girls. However, when girls tried to bring attention to themselves by calling out in class without raising their hands, they were reprimanded (Sadker and Sadker 1994). Boys were also disadvantaged in several ways, however. Because of their rowdy behavior, they were more often scolded and punished than the female students.

This differential treatment of boys and girls perpetuates stereotypic gender role behavior. Girls are trained to be quiet and well behaved and to turn to others for answers, while boys are encouraged to be inquisitive, outspoken, active problem solvers.

THE GENDERING OF COLLEGE MAJORS

College is a time of exploration, when students take both general education classes and specialized classes within their chosen major that prepare them for a career after graduation. Men and women differ starkly in the majors they choose, opting for fields that are consistent with gender-typed socialization; women focus on fields associated with caring and nurturing, whereas men tend to pursue fields that emphasize logic and analysis. Yet the majors women tend to choose are precisely those fields that garner the lowest earnings after graduation, whereas men are channeled into majors with high economic returns.

Researchers at Georgetown University documented gender differences in college majors using national data collected by the Census Bureau (Table 9.1). They found that the college majors with the highest proportion of female students were those in the education and health fields. For instance, 97 percent of all persons majoring in early childhood education were women, while more than 90 percent of all majors in nursing, elementary education, library science, and school counseling were female. By contrast, more than 90 percent of engineering majors were men, with the highest concentrations found in electrical, nuclear, and naval architecture and mining engineering.

Feminist scholars note that this stark gender segregation among college majors is one important reason for the persistent gender gap in pay. The Georgetown researchers ranked college majors based on the earnings of graduates and found that the two lowest-earning majors were counseling psychology (with median annual earnings of $29,000) and early childhood education (with median annual earnings of $36,000). Both of these fields are dominated by women. By contrast, of the ten highest-earning majors, eight were engineering fields heavily dominated by men, including petroleum engineering (with median annual earnings of $120,000) and aerospace engineering (with median annual earnings of $87,000). Research on how young people choose their majors consistently shows that subtle forces, including input from parents, friends, and guidance counselors; a lack of same-sex role models; active encouragement (or discouragement) from teachers; and limited exposure to particular fields of study tend to channel women into female-typed majors and men into male-typed majors (Morgan et al. 2013; Porter and Umbach 2006).

Table 9.1 | The Gendering of College Majors

MAJORS WITH HIGHEST CONCENTRATION OF WOMEN

	Median Earnings	Percent Women
Early Childhood Education	$36,000	97
Medical Assisting Services	$56,000	96
Communication Disorders Sciences and Services	$40,000	94
Family and Consumer Sciences	$40,000	93
Nursing	$60,000	92
Elementary Education	$40,000	91
Nutrition Sciences	$46,000	89
Special Needs Education	$42,000	88

MAJORS WITH HIGHEST CONCENTRATION OF MEN

	Median Earnings	Percent Men
Naval Architecture and Marine Engineering	$82,000	97
Mechanical Engineering Related Technologies	$80,000	94
Construction Services	$70,000	92
Electrical and Mechanic Repairs and Technologies	$57,000	91
Industrial Production Technologies	$65,000	91
Mechanical Engineering	$80,000	90
Mining and Mineral Engineering	$80,000	90
Electrical Engineering Technology	$68,000	90

SOURCE: Carnevale, Strohl, and Melton 2011

WOMEN AND THE WORKPLACE

Rates of employment of women outside the home, for all social classes, were quite low until well into the twentieth century in the United States. Even as late as 1910 in the United States, more than a third of gainfully employed women were maids or house servants. The female labor force consisted mainly of young, single women and children. When women or girls worked in factories or offices, employers often sent their wages straight home to their parents. When they married, they withdrew from the labor force.

Since the turn of the twentieth century, women's participation in the paid labor force has risen more or less continuously, especially in the past fifty years (see Figure 9.1). In 2012, 57.2 percent (72.6 million) of women ages sixteen and older were in the labor force (U.S. Bureau of Labor Statistics 2014f). In contrast, 38 percent of working-age women were in the labor force in 1960. An even greater change in the rate of labor force participation has occurred among married mothers of young children. In 1975, only 39 percent of married women with preschool-age children (under six years old) were in the labor force, yet this figure had increased to 64.7 percent by 2012 (U.S. Bureau of Labor Statistics 2014g).

How can we explain this increase? One force behind women's increased entry into the labor force was the increase in demand, since 1940, for clerical and service workers, as the U.S. economy expanded and changed (Oppenheimer 1970). From

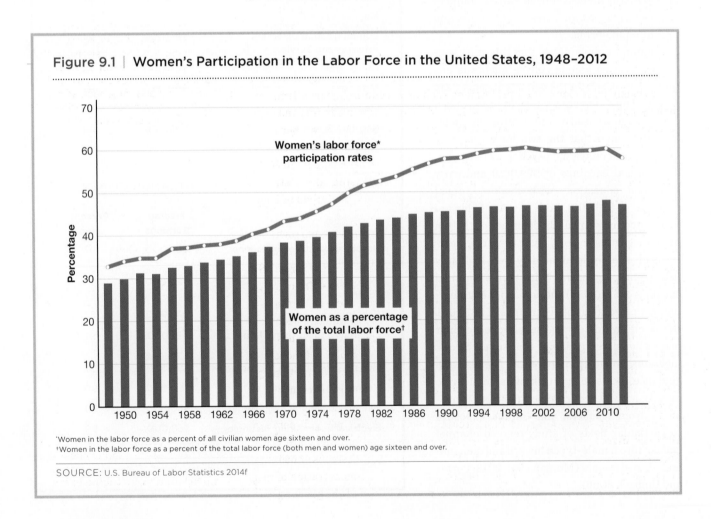

Figure 9.1 | Women's Participation in the Labor Force in the United States, 1948–2012

Women's labor force* participation rates

Women as a percentage of the total labor force†

*Women in the labor force as a percent of all civilian women age sixteen and over.
†Women in the labor force as a percent of the total labor force (both men and women) age sixteen and over.

SOURCE: U.S. Bureau of Labor Statistics 2014f

1940 until the mid- to late 1960s, labor force activity increased among women who were past their prime child-rearing years. During the 1970s and 1980s, as the marriage age rose, birth rates declined, and women's educational attainment increased, the growth in labor force participation spread to younger women. Many women now postpone family formation to complete their education and establish themselves in the labor force. Despite family obligations, today a majority of women of all educational levels now work outside the home during their child-rearing years (Spain and Bianchi 1996).

INEQUALITIES AT WORK

Until recently, women workers were overwhelmingly concentrated in routine, poorly paid occupations. The fate of the occupation of clerk (office worker) provides a good illustration. In 1850 in the United States, clerks held responsible positions, requiring accountancy skills and carrying managerial responsibilities; fewer than 1 percent were women. The twentieth century saw a general mechanization of office work (starting with the introduction of the typewriter in the late nineteenth century), accompanied by a marked downgrading of the status of clerk—together with a related occupation, secretary—into a routine, low-paid occupation. Women filled these occupations as the pay and prestige of such jobs declined. Today, most secretaries and clerks are women. Once an occupation has become **gender typed**—once it is seen as mainly a "man's job" or a "woman's job"—inertia sets in.

Women have recently made some inroads into occupations once defined as "men's jobs" (Figure 9.2). By the 1990s, women constituted a majority of workers in previously male-dominated professions such as accounting, journalism, psychology, public service, and bartending. In fields such as law, medicine, and engineering, their proportion has risen substantially since 1970. While women's employment in professional and managerial occupations has steadily increased to be the largest occupational category for women (27.8 million or 41.6 percent in 2012), a considerable proportion are still employed in sales, office, and administrative support occupations (20.5 million or 30.6 percent in 2012) (U.S. Bureau of Labor Statistics 2014h).

Another important economic trend since the 1970s has been the narrowing of the gender gap in earnings. Between 1979 and 2012, the ratio of women's to men's median weekly earnings among full-time, year-round workers increased from 62.3 to 81 percent. Moreover, this ratio increased among all races and ethnic groups (U.S. Bureau of Labor Statistics 2014j). Some researchers have noted that the narrowing of the gender gap is less a reflection of improvement in women's economic standing than a decline in men's economic standing. The recent recession has been dubbed the "he-cession" or "man-cession" because the types of jobs and industries hardest hit are those in which men are overrepresented, such as construction and finance (Rampell 2009). As men's earnings erode, the female-male earnings ratio starts to inch upward.

Sociologists have identified many reasons why a gender pay gap persists. Although direct discrimination is certainly one explanation, there are other, more subtle reasons why women typically earn less than their male counterparts. Many sociologists point to **sex segregation**, or the concentration of men and women in different occupations, as an important cause of the gender gap in

gender typing • Designation of occupations as male or female, with "women's" occupations, such as secretarial and retail positions, having lower status and pay, and "men's" occupations, such as managerial and professional positions, having higher status and pay.

sex segregation • The concentration of men and women in different jobs. These differences are believed to contribute to the gender pay gap.

Figure 9.2 | Women as a Percent of Total Employed in Selected Occupations

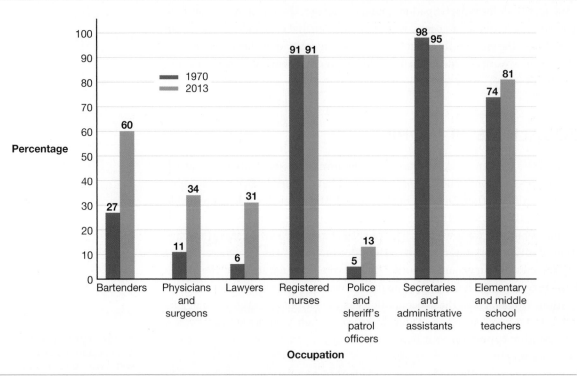

SOURCE: Roberts 1995; U.S. Bureau of Labor Statistics 2014i

earnings. While the Equal Pay Act of 1963 holds that men and women must earn equal pay for performing equal work, women tend to hold different jobs, typically jobs that are dominated by women. These jobs, on average, pay less than occupations dominated by men. For instance, in 2012, occupations with the highest proportion of women included secretary, child-care worker, hairdresser, dental hygienist, occupational therapist, nurse, and preschool and kindergarten teacher. More than 95 percent of secretaries and administrative assistants, nearly 91 percent of registered nurses, and 81 percent of elementary school teachers were women in 2012 (U.S. Bureau of Labor Statistics 2014i). This is not surprising, given what we learned earlier about the concentration of women in health and education-related college majors. Occupations with the highest proportion of male workers included construction worker, truck driver, taxi driver, plumber, electrician, carpenter, firefighter, auto mechanic, and machinist (U.S. Bureau of Labor Statistics 2014i).

Policymakers are aware of the gender pay gap and continue to make efforts to eradicate it. One of the very first things President Barack Obama did after being inaugurated into his second term in January 2009 was sign into law the Lilly Ledbetter Fair Pay Act (Stolberg 2009). The act, named for Lilly Ledbetter, a tire factory supervisor from Alabama, grants workers the right to sue their employer on the grounds of pay discrimination. Although workers previously had this right, they had only a very short time period to file—180 days after the receipt of the first paycheck they deemed as unfair. Now, workers have a six-month period after the receipt of every paycheck they consider unfair.

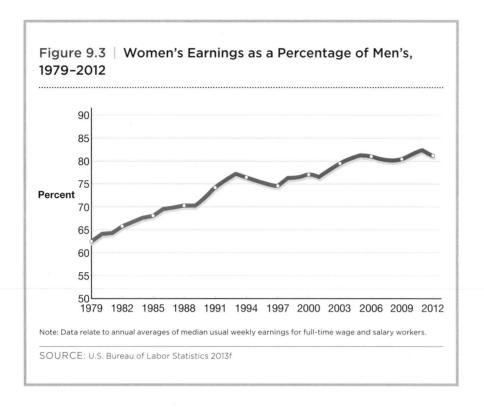

Figure 9.3 | Women's Earnings as a Percentage of Men's, 1979–2012

Percent

Note: Data relate to annual averages of median usual weekly earnings for full-time wage and salary workers.

SOURCE: U.S. Bureau of Labor Statistics 2013f

COMPARABLE WORTH

Comparable worth is a policy that compares pay levels of jobs held disproportionately by women with pay levels of jobs held disproportionately by men and tries to adjust pay so that the women and men who work in female-dominated jobs are not penalized. The policy presumes that jobs can be ranked objectively according to skill, effort, responsibility, and working conditions. After such a ranking, pay is adjusted so that equivalently ranked male- and female-dominated jobs receive equivalent pay (Hartmann et al. 1985).

Although comparable worth policies may help reduce the gender gap in pay, only a handful of states have instituted comparable worth policies for public-sector employees (Blum 1991). One reason for this is that it is very difficult to evaluate and ascertain which particular male- and female-dominated jobs are "comparable" with respect to skill, effort, responsibility, and working conditions (Stryker 1996). Substantial research shows that gender-neutral assessments of jobs and required job skills are very difficult (Steinberg 1990).

Opposition to comparable worth policies has been offered by both economists and feminists. Some economists worry that comparable worth is inflationary and will cause wage losses and unemployment for some (disproportionately women) because of benefits enacted for others. Feminists counter that comparable worth reinforces gender stereotyping rather than breaking down gender barriers at work (Blum 1991). Comparable worth also has faced obstacles in the courts. It suffered its biggest setback in 1985 when the Ninth Circuit Federal Court of Appeals rejected a comparable worth job evaluation as evidence of discrimination. In a case involving the government employees' union (AFSCME) versus the state of Washington, the court upheld the state's right to base pay on market wages rather than on a job evaluation.

comparable worth • Policies that attempt to remedy the gender pay gap by adjusting pay so that those in female-dominated jobs are not paid less for equivalent work.

THE GLASS CEILING

glass ceiling • A promotion barrier that prevents a woman's upward
mobility within an organization.

Although women are increasingly entering "traditionally male" jobs, their entry into such jobs is not necessarily accompanied by increases in pay—and increases in occupational mobility—due to the "glass ceiling." The **glass ceiling** is a promotion barrier that prevents a woman's upward mobility within an organization. The glass ceiling is particularly problematic for women who work in male-dominated occupations and professions. Women's progress is blocked not by virtue of innate inability or lack of basic qualifications, but by not having the sponsorship of well-placed, powerful senior colleagues to articulate their value to the organization or profession (Alvarez et al. 1996). As a result, women tend to progress to mid-level management positions, but they do not, in proportionate numbers, move beyond mid-management ranks. The obstacles women face as they strive to rise through the career ranks are exemplified by the Merrill Lynch cases we read about in the chapter opener. Women like Judy Calibuso, who asked to work with high-profile clients in order to learn about the business and ascend the corporate ladder, were passed over for their male coworkers. Calibuso and her coworkers were forced to watch their male colleagues climb past them in the corporate ranks—a phenomenon that sociologist Christine Williams (1992) calls the "glass elevator."

ECONOMIC INEQUALITY IN GLOBAL PERSPECTIVE

The United States is not alone in having a history of gender inequality in the workplace. Across the globe, men outpace women in most workplace and economic indicators. Most nations, however, like the United States, have witnessed tremendous strides in women's economic progress in recent decades. Some scholars and activists argue that women's economic empowerment has contributed in large part to China's meteoric rise as an economic power. An estimated 80 percent of the factory workers in China's Guangdong province are female; four of the ten richest self-made women in the world are Chinese (Kroll 2011; Kristof and WuDunn 2009).

The International Labor Organization (ILO 2004b) found that while the gap between the number of men and women in the labor force has been decreasing in all regions of the world since 1993, this decrease has varied widely. Women have high labor force participation rates in high-income countries such as most European nations, where over two-thirds of the female adult population participate in the labor market and the male-female gap in labor force participation rates is less than 15 percent on average. This is especially true in nations with extensive social benefits (such as paid maternity leave) and where part-time work is possible. In developing countries, by contrast, women's labor force participation rates are more varied, ranging from a low of 21 percent in the Middle East and North Africa region in 2010, to a high of 71 percent in the East Asia and Pacific region. The gender gaps in labor force participation are also highest in the Middle East and North Africa and South Asia regions, where men's participation rates exceed women's by over 50 percentage points. These gender gaps are due largely to variations in women's labor force participation rates. In contrast, men's participation rates are relatively stable across countries in different income strata (World Bank 2012d).

Women remain in the poorest-paying industrial and service-sector jobs in all countries, and in the less industrialized nations they are concentrated in the declining agricultural sector. Because of persistent discrimination and lower wages, women represent 60 percent of the world's 550 million working poor (ILO 2004b). The feminization of the global workforce has brought with it the increased exploitation of

Female workers watch the launch of a ship into China's Yangtze River. Thanks to the feminization of the global workforce, many women have achieved a degree of economic independence—but often at the price of unsafe labor conditions, low pay, and nonexistent job security.

young, uneducated, largely rural women around the world. These women labor under conditions that are often unsafe and unhealthy, at low pay and with nonexistent job security. For instance, the collapse of the Rana Plaza building in Bangladesh in 2013 was a tragic depiction of the unsafe work conditions facing garment workers, most of whom are women, in parts of the developing world. More than 1,000 workers died in the building collapse, many of whom had been toiling for low wages in a building that had been deemed an unsafe structure.

At the other end of the occupational spectrum, a recent study by the International Labor Organization concludes that women throughout the world still encounter a glass ceiling that restricts their movement into top positions. In 2013, women made up only 17.6 percent of board members of major companies in the European Union (European Parliament 2013). In recognition of these low rates, several national governments have recently passed legislation to increase women's participation in the highest echelons of business. In Japan, for example, women have been particularly likely to face barriers to career advancement, especially in professional and managerial positions. Only 11 percent of such positions are now held by women, due both to discriminatory hiring practices and the fact that fully 70 percent of Japanese women exit the workforce when they have their first child (Cunningham 2013; Simms 2013). However, policymakers in Japan have recently recognized that this is a tremendous loss of worker potential, especially when low birth rates mean that the nation may soon face a dearth of young workers. In 2013, the government issued a mandate that by 2020, women should hold 30 percent of all upper-management positions in major corporations (Cunningham 2013). Similar quota-based policies have already been passed in France, Iceland, the Netherlands, and Spain (ILO 2011). The number of women in leadership roles is growing; female participation in senior management reached over 50 percent in China, 48 percent in Poland, and over 30 percent in Germany, although it remains low (20 percent) in the United States (Thornton 2013).

SEXUAL HARASSMENT IN THE WORKPLACE

Economic disadvantage and daunting work hours are not the only challenges women workers face worldwide. Another pervasive yet poorly documented obstacle is sexual harassment. **Sexual harassment** is unwanted or repeated sexual advances, remarks, or behaviors that are offensive to the recipient and cause discomfort or interfere with job performance. Power imbalances facilitate harassment; even though women can and do sexually harass subordinates; because men usually hold positions of authority, it is more common for men to harass women (Reskin and Padavic 1994).

The U.S. courts have identified two types of sexual harassment. One is the quid pro quo, in which a supervisor demands sexual acts from a worker as a job condition or promises work-related benefits in exchange for sexual acts. The other is the "hostile work environment," in which a pattern of sexual language, lewd posters, or sexual advances makes a worker so uncomfortable that it is difficult to do his or her job (Padavic and Reskin 2002).

Sociologists have observed that "the great majority of women who are abused by behavior that fits legal definitions of sexual harassment—and who are traumatized by the experience—do not label what has happened to them as sexual harassment" (Paludi and Barickman 1991). Women's reluctance to report harassment may be due to the following factors: (1) many still do not recognize that sexual harassment is an actionable offense; (2) victims may be reluctant to come forward with complaints, fearing that they will not be believed, that their charges will not be taken seriously, or that they will be subject to reprisals; and (3) it may be difficult to differentiate between harassment and joking on the job (Giuffre and Williams 1994).

THE FAMILY AND GENDER ISSUES

BALANCING WORK AND CHILD CARE

One key factor affecting women's careers is the perception that for female employees, work comes second to having children. Research by Stanford University sociologist Shelley Correll and colleagues (2007) finds that mothers are 44 percent less likely to be hired than nonmothers who have the same work experience and qualifications, and mothers are offered significantly lower starting pay than equally qualified nonmothers (an average of $11,000 lower in this study) for the same job.

Similar findings emerged in a qualitative study conducted in Great Britain. Homans (1987) investigated the views of managers interviewing female applicants for positions as technical staff in the health services. They found that the interviewers always asked the women about whether they had, or intended to have, children (this is now illegal in the United States). They virtually never followed this practice with male applicants. When asked why, two themes ran through their answers: Women with children may require extra time off for school holidays or if a child falls sick, and responsibility for child care is a mother's problem rather than a parental

sexual harassment • The making of unwanted sexual advances by one individual toward another, in which the first person persists even though it is clear that the other party is resistant.

one. Some managers thought their questions indicated an attitude of "caring" toward female employees. But most saw such a line of questioning as part of their task in assessing how far a female applicant would prove to be a reliable colleague. Women were seen as likely to interrupt their careers to care for young children, no matter how senior a position they might have reached. The few women in this study who held senior management positions were all without children, and several of those who planned to have children in the future said they intended to leave their jobs and would perhaps retrain for other positions subsequently.

How should we interpret these findings? Are women's job opportunities hampered mainly by male prejudices? Some managers expressed the view that women with children should not work, but should occupy themselves with child care and the home. Most, however, accepted the principle that women should have the same career opportunities as men. The bias in their attitudes had less to do with the workplace itself than with the domestic responsibilities of parenting. So long as most of the population take it for granted that parenting cannot be shared on an equal basis by both women and men, the problems facing women employees will persist. It will remain a fact of life, as one of the managers put it, that women are disadvantaged, compared with men, in their career opportunities.

HOUSEWORK AND THE SECOND SHIFT

The struggles facing women workers do not end once they set foot in their homes at the end of the day. Women throughout the world also perform housework and child care at the end of the paid work day, often dubbed the "**second shift**." As a result, women work longer hours than men in most countries.

A recent United Nations report found that women in the United States worked on average 25 minutes each day more than men—a difference that was considerably smaller than that in Austria (45 minutes) or Italy (103 minutes). This gap is considerably worse in developing nations. On average, women worked 165 minutes more than men in Benin, 105 minutes more in Mexico, 66 minutes more in India, 59 in South Africa, 58 in the Republic of Korea, 51 in Madagascar, 44 in Mongolia, and 24 in Mauritius (UNICEF 2006). In an effort to fulfill their often daunting work and domestic demands, women often have no choice but to cut back on their sleep, which in turn may contribute to persistent health problems (Stranges et al. 2012). A recent global study found that women experience more sleep problems, including getting fewer hours of sleep each night, compared with their male counterparts (National Sleep Foundation 2013).

Although there have been revolutionary changes in women's status in recent decades in the United States, including the entry of women into male-dominated professions, one area of work has lagged far behind: **housework**. Because of the increase of married women in the workforce and the resulting change in status, it was presumed that men would contribute more to housework. On the whole, this has not

Making Sociology Work
PARENT

Parenting is often described as the world's toughest job, but also one of the most rewarding. Parents aren't just responsible for feeding, clothing, and protecting their young children; parents know that how they raise their sons and daughters will have powerful consequences for their offspring's experiences as young men and women. Sociologists argue further that parental socialization plays a critical role in one's gender identity; children learn from their parents (as well as from the media and educational system) how to behave in a way that is "male" or "female." Yet strict adherence to typically male or female behavioral expectations may create personal challenges. For instance, boys who are raised to be rowdy and rambunctious often face difficulties as they enter the structured realm of elementary school. Girls who are socialized to be quiet and unassertive may do well at school yet may be disadvantaged as they enter the competitive worlds of work or sports. Given the many ways that gender exposes individuals to inequality in politics, schools, and the workplace, and in terms of crime victimization, what kind of gender role messages would you impart to your children? Drawing on gender socialization literature, what social norms and expectations would you convey to your sons versus your daughters? Why?

second shift • The excessive work hours borne by women relative to men; these hours are typically spent on domestic chores following the end of a day of work outside the home.

housework • Unpaid work carried on in the home, usually by women; domestic chores such as cooking, cleaning, and shopping. Also called *domestic labor*.

been the case. Although men now do more housework than they did three decades ago, a large gender gap persists. In 1965, women ages eighteen to sixty-four performed twenty-eight hours of housework per week, although this number dropped to fifteen hours by 2011. By contrast, men's housework increased from four to nine hours per week between 1965 and 2011. While the gap has decreased, women still put in significantly more time than their male counterparts (Pew Research Center 2013).

Further investigation shows that it is the intersection of gender, marital status, and parental status that most powerfully shapes housework. A recent study showed that whereas women save their husbands an hour of housework a week, husbands create an additional seven hours of housework for their wives every week. Childless women do an average of ten hours of housework a week before marriage and seventeen hours after marriage. Childless men, by contrast, do eight hours before marriage and seven hours afterward. Married women with more than three kids are the most overworked, reporting an average of about twenty-eight hours, while married men with more than three kids logged only ten hours of housework a week (University of Michigan Institute for Social Research 2008).

The United Nations estimates that women in the United States work 6 percent more than men, a majority of which is spent in nonmarket activities such as housework and making clothing and food for their families (United Nations 2003). These figures do not include time spent on child care, which if factored in would increase the gap. The United Nations estimates that women's unpaid care work would account for between 10 and 50 percent of the global GDP if it were assigned a monetary value (United Nations Women 2013).

Some sociologists have suggested that this phenomenon is best explained as a result of economic forces: Household work is exchanged for economic support. Because women typically earn less than men, they are more likely to remain economically dependent on their husbands and thus perform the bulk of the housework. Until the earnings gap is narrowed, women in heterosexual unions will likely remain in their dependent position. Recent evidence suggests same-sex couples maintain a much more egalitarian division of labor in the home, regarding both housework and child care, perhaps reflecting the fact that partners in same-sex relations tend to have less of a pronounced earnings gap than do partners in heterosexual partnerships (Goldberg,

Working women often must multitask in order to keep on top of their work and family demands. Here, a woman blends cleaning tasks with child care.

Smith, Parry-Jenkins 2012). In Chapters 11 and 14, we will discuss more fully the way that relationship dynamics vary based on the sexual orientations of the partners.

GENDER INEQUALITY IN POLITICS

Women are playing an increasingly important role in U.S. politics, although they are still far from achieving full equality. Before 1993, there were only two women in the U.S. Senate (2 of 100 Senate members), and twenty-nine in the U.S. House of Representatives (out of 435). Less than a decade later—in 2001—there were thirteen women in the Senate and fifty-nine in the House. As of May 2014, there are twenty women senators and eighty-two women representatives. In 2013, women held 24.2 percent (1,784) of all seats in state legislatures, five times as many as they held in 1969, but only five governorships (out of fifty) (National Conference of State Legislatures [NCSL] 2013b; Center for American Women and Politics 2013a). The U.S. Supreme Court had its first woman justice appointed in 1981, and its second twelve years later. Three women currently occupy seats on the Supreme Court—Ruth Bader Ginsburg, Elena Kagan, and Sonia Sotomayor, marking an all-time high. It was not until 1984 that a woman was nominated as the vice presidential candidate of either major party, neither of which has ever nominated a woman for the presidency—despite strides made by Hillary Clinton in the 2008 Democratic primaries.

Women politicians are overwhelmingly affiliated with the Democratic Party. In the U.S. Congress, 80 percent of women are Democrats, and in state legislatures, nearly 64 percent of women legislators are Democrats (NCSL 2013; Center for American Women and Politics 2013b). However, the Republican Party and especially the nascent "Tea Party" movement prominently feature women leaders, including former Alaska governor Sarah Palin, former Minnesota congresswoman Michele Bachmann, and South Carolina governor Nikki Haley.

Typically, the more local the political office, the more likely it is to be occupied by a woman. Men outnumber women in politics at all levels, but the gender gap is smaller

The female Democrats of the House of Representatives stand in front of the Capitol Building in Washington, D.C., before the swearing-in of the 113th Congress.

among mayors and elected members of city and county governing boards. In most states, women are more likely to serve as representatives at the local level than the state level and even less likely to serve as senators or members of the House of Representatives. The farther from home the political office, the more likely it is to be regarded as "man's work," providing a living wage, full-time employment, and a lifetime career. The costs of running for local office are typically far lower than a campaign for a higher office, which can require a war chest beyond the reach of many women (Conway 2004).

GENDER AND POLITICS: GLOBAL PERSPECTIVE

Women play an increasing role in politics throughout the world. Yet of the 192 countries that belong to the United Nations, only twenty are presently headed by women. Since World War II, thirty-eight countries have been headed by women; the United States is not among them.

As of 2013, women made up only 20.9 percent of the combined membership of the national legislatures throughout the world (Women in National Parliaments [WNP] 2013a). Only in Rwanda (51.9 percent), Andorra (50.0 percent), Cuba (48.9 percent), Sweden (44.7 percent), Seychelles (43.8 percent), Senegal (42.7 percent), Finland (42.5 percent), South Africa (41.1 percent), and Nicaragua (40.2 percent) do women make up a significant part of parliament; in the Arab states, the figure is only 13.8 percent (WNP 2013a, 2013b).

The United Nations ranks countries according to a measure of "gender empowerment," which is based on such factors as seats in the national legislature held by women, female administrators and managers (as a percentage of total administrators and managers), female professional and technical workers (as a percentage of total professional and technical workers), and the ratio of women's to men's earned income. By this measure, the United States ranks eighteenth—behind the Scandinavian and other northern European countries and Canada and New Zealand.

CONCEPT CHECKS ✓

1. Describe at least three examples of how gender inequalities emerge in the workplace. How would a sociologist explain these inequities?

2. What are the signs of declining economic inequality between men and women from a global perspective?

3. How do inequalities in the home, especially with regard to housework and child care, reflect larger gender inequities in society?

4. What are some important differences between men's and women's political participation in the United States?

5. What are some signs of progress in terms of women's political equality from a global perspective?

Learn about the specific ways that women are the target of physical and sexual violence in the United States and globally.

WHY ARE WOMEN THE TARGET OF VIOLENCE?

Violence directed against women is found in many societies, including the United States. One out of three women has been beaten, coerced into sex, or abused in some other way—most often by someone she knows, including her husband or a male relative (United Nations Population Fund [UNFPA] 2005b). One in five women worldwide will be a victim of rape or attempted rape in her lifetime (UNFPA 2005a). A particularly devastating example was the gang rape of a twenty-three-year-old student in Delhi, India, in December 2012. She had boarded a bus with a male friend after leaving a movie

GENDER INEQUALITY

The Gender Inequality Index (GII), which is used to compare gender inequality across countries, looks at women's educational attainment, labor force participation, and representation in governmental bodies, among other metrics. In the graphic below, the country's GII ranking is displayed in the white circle.

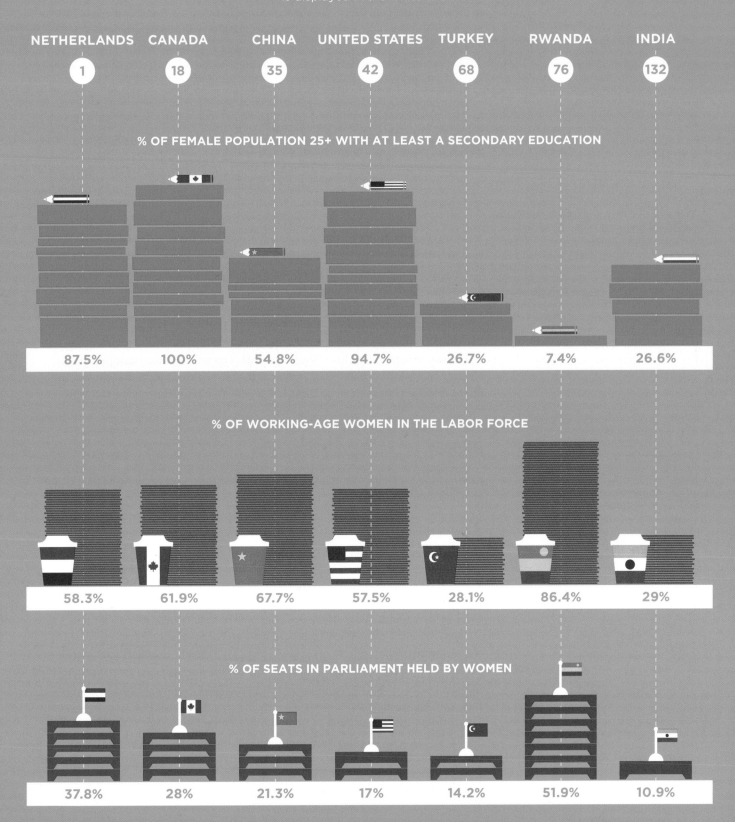

NETHERLANDS	CANADA	CHINA	UNITED STATES	TURKEY	RWANDA	INDIA
1	18	35	42	68	76	132

% OF FEMALE POPULATION 25+ WITH AT LEAST A SECONDARY EDUCATION

87.5%	100%	54.8%	94.7%	26.7%	7.4%	26.6%

% OF WORKING-AGE WOMEN IN THE LABOR FORCE

58.3%	61.9%	67.7%	57.5%	28.1%	86.4%	29%

% OF SEATS IN PARLIAMENT HELD BY WOMEN

37.8%	28%	21.3%	17%	14.2%	51.9%	10.9%

Source: United Nations Development Programme 2013

when she was attacked by five male passengers and the driver. The young woman was beaten and raped so brutally that she died thirteen days later, triggering worldwide protests to stop violence against women (Raina 2013).

Although sexual assault at the hand of strangers triggers moral outrage, statistics show that more women are injured as a result of beatings by spouses than by any other cause, a problem that is ignored by most governments (Human Rights Watch 1995). In India, an estimated 20,000 brides were killed between 1990 and 1995—usually by being burned alive—for bringing an inadequate dowry to their husbands' families (Wagner-Wright 2006). In 2008 alone, there were an estimated 8,172 deaths of women in India at the hands of husbands and relatives because the women brought an insufficient dowry, an increase of 7.3 percent from 2006 (Youthkiawaz.com 2010). Two thousand women committed suicide in dowry disputes in 2006 (Zee News 2007).

Ritualized violence is also a common experience among women throughout the world. For example, between 100 million and 140 million girls and women worldwide have been subjected to "genital mutilation," a practice done to control women's sexuality. Likewise, millions of women and girls throughout the world are "missing," partly as the result of female **infanticide** in cultures where boys are more highly valued than girls (World Health Organization [WHO] 2000).

The trafficking of women for forced prostitution, which has been called "the largest slave trade in history," appears to be a growing problem (UNFPA 2005a). The United Nations Global Initiative to Fight Human Trafficking (UN.GIFT 2008) estimates that at any given time 2.5 million people worldwide are subject to forced labor as a result of human trafficking. Forty-three percent are exploited for forced sexual exploitation and 98 percent of those persons are women or girls.

In the United States, many scholars argue that the increased depiction of violence in movies, on television, and elsewhere in American popular culture contributes to a climate in which women are often victimized. The most common manifestation of violence against women is sexual assault, although stalking and sexual harassment increasingly are seen as a form of psychological (if not physical) violence as well.

RAPE

Rape can be sociologically defined as the forcing of nonconsensual vaginal, oral, or anal intercourse. As one researcher observed, between consensual sex and rape lies "a continuum of pressure, threat, coercion, and force" (Kelly 1987). Common to all forms of rape is the lack of consent: At least in principle, "no" means "no" when it comes to sexual relations in most courts of law in the United States. The vast majority of rapes are committed by men against women, although men rape other men in prisons and other all-male institutional environments. However, recent studies have documented cases where women take sexual advantage of young men who may be insecure, intoxicated, or of a lower status position (Anderson and Struckman-Johnson 1998).

Rape is an act of violence, rather than a purely sexual act. It is often carefully planned rather than performed on the spur of the moment to satisfy some uncontrollable sexual desire. Many rapes involve beatings, knifings, and even murder. In some instances, sexual assault is facilitated by alcohol, or women having their drinks spiked with the sedative Rohypnol (i.e., "roofies") or drugs referred to as "date-rape drugs" (Michigan Department of Community Health 2010). Even when rape leaves no physical wounds, it is a highly traumatic violation of the victim's person that leaves long-lasting psychological scars.

It is difficult to know with accuracy how many rapes actually occur, since most rapes go unreported. One comprehensive study of American sexual behavior found that

infanticide • The intentional killing of a newborn. Female babies are more likely than male babies to be murdered in cultures that devalue women.

rape • The forcing of nonconsensual vaginal, oral, or anal intercourse.

22 percent of the women surveyed reported having been forced into a sexual encounter. Yet the same study found that only 3 percent of the men admitted to having forced a woman into having sex, a discrepancy the study's authors attribute to different perceptions between men and women regarding what constitutes forced sex (Laumann et al. 1994). Based on its semiannual survey of nearly 100,000 Americans, the U.S. Department of Justice estimates that in 2011, there were 83,425 rapes committed on women (U.S. Bureau of Justice Statistics 2013c). The total number of sexual assaults, attempted rapes, and rapes (204,370) was more than 21 percent lower than in 2002—part of an overall decrease in violent crimes since 1994. In fact, criminal victimizations, which include rape and sexual assault, are at their lowest point since 1973 (Catalano 2005).

Most rapes are committed by relatives (fathers or stepfathers, brothers, uncles), partners, or acquaintances. Among college students, most rapes are likely to be committed by boyfriends, former boyfriends, or classmates. The National College Women Sexual Victimization (NCWSV) study, a national survey of 4,446 women attending two- or four-year colleges or universities, presents a chilling picture of violence against women on campuses across the country (Fisher et al. 2000). The study, which was conducted during spring semester 1997, asked college women about their experience with rape, attempted rape, coerced sex, unwanted sexual contact, and stalking during the 1996–1997 school year. Overall, since the beginning of the school year, 1.7 percent had been the victim of a completed rape, and 1.1 percent of an attempted rape.

Moreover, fully a tenth of the female students surveyed had been raped prior to the study period (which began in the fall of 1996), and another tenth had been the victim of attempted rape. The study also found that for both completed and attempted rapes, nine out of ten offenders were known to the victim. Fifty-five percent of rape victims used physical force in an effort to thwart the rape, as did 69 percent of attempted rape victims.

The incidence of other forms of victimization reported in the study was substantially higher than that of rape. Nearly one out of six female students reported being the target of attempted or completed sexual coercion or unwanted sexual contact during the current academic year, half involving the use or threat of physical force. More than a third reported that they had experienced a threatened, attempted, or completed unwanted sexual assault at some time during their lives. And about one out of every eight reported having been stalked at some time during the current year, almost always by someone they knew—typically a former boyfriend or classmate. Stalking, it was reported, was emotionally traumatizing and in 15 percent of the incidents involved actual or threatened physical harm.

SEXUAL VIOLENCE AGAINST WOMEN: EVIDENCE OF "RAPE CULTURE"?

Some radical feminist scholars claim that men are socialized to regard women as sex objects, to feel a sense of sexual entitlement, and to instill fear in women by dominating them (Brownmiller 1986). This socialization context, described as a "**rape culture**" by Susan Brownmiller (1986), may make men insensitive to the difference between consensual and nonconsensual sex and thus contribute to the high levels of victimization women reported to the NCWSV study (Griffin 1979; Dworkin 1981, 1987).

The fact that "acquaintance rapes" occur suggests that at least some men are likely to feel entitled to sexual access if they already know the woman. A survey of nearly 270,000 first-year college students reported that 55 percent of male students agreed with the statement "If two people really like each other, it's all right for them to have sex even if they've known each other only for a very short time." Only

rape culture • Social context where attitudes and norms perpetuate the treatment of women as sexual objects and instill in men a sense of sexual entitlement.

CONCEPT CHECKS ✓

1. How common is violence against women in the United States?

2. What proportion of sexual assaults are believed to go unreported?

3. Why are women more likely than men to be the targets of sexual violence?

31 percent of female students were in agreement, suggesting a rather large gender gap concerning notions of sexual entitlement (American Council on Education [ACE] 2001). When a man goes out on a date with sexual conquest on his mind, he may force his attentions on an unwilling partner, overcoming her resistance through the use of alcohol, persistence, or both. While such an act may not be legally defined as rape, it would be experienced as such by many women. ✓

Think about various explanations for gender inequality. Learn some feminist theories about how to achieve gender equality.

HOW DOES SOCIAL THEORY EXPLAIN GENDER INEQUALITY?

Investigating and accounting for gender inequality has become a central concern of sociologists. Many theoretical perspectives have been advanced to explain men's enduring dominance over women—in the realm of economics, politics, the family, and elsewhere. In this section, we will review the main theoretical approaches to explaining the nature of gender inequality at the level of society.

FUNCTIONALIST APPROACHES

As we saw in Chapter 1, the functionalist approach sees society as a system of interlinked parts that, when in balance, operate smoothly to produce social solidarity. Thus, functionalist and functionalist-inspired perspectives on gender seek to show that gender differences contribute to social stability and integration. Though such views once commanded great support, they have been heavily criticized for neglecting social tensions at the expense of consensus and for promulgating a conservative view of the social world.

Talcott Parsons, a leading functionalist thinker, concerned himself with the role of the family in industrial societies (Parsons and Bales 1955). He was particularly interested in the socialization of children and believed that stable, supportive families are the key to successful socialization. In Parsons's view, the family operates most efficiently with a clear-cut sexual division of labor in which females act in expressive roles, providing care and security to children and offering them emotional support, and men perform instrumental roles—namely, being the breadwinner in the family. This complementary division of labor, springing from a biological distinction between the sexes, would ensure the solidarity of the family according to Parsons.

Feminists have sharply criticized claims of a biological basis to the sexual division of labor, arguing that there is nothing natural or inevitable about the allocation of tasks in society. Women are not prevented from pursuing occupations on the basis of any biological features; rather, humans are socialized into roles that are culturally expected of them. Parsons's notions of the "expressive" female have been attacked by feminists and other sociologists who see his views as condoning the subordination of women in the home. There is no basis to the belief that the "expressive" female is necessary for the smooth operation of the family—rather, it is a role that is promoted largely for the convenience of men.

Why would a functionalist agree that the division of labor between the homemaking wife and breadwinning husband in this Japanese household is ideal?

In addition, cross-cultural and historical studies show that even though most societies distinguish between men's and women's roles, the degree to which they differentiate tasks as exclusively male or female and assign different tasks and responsibilities to women and men can vary greatly across time and place (Coltrane 1992). Thus, gender inequalities do not seem to be fixed or static.

FEMINIST APPROACHES

The feminist movement has given rise to a large body of theory that attempts to explain gender inequalities and set forth agendas for overcoming those inequalities. As we learned in Chapter 1, **feminist theories** related to gender inequality contrast markedly with one another. Feminist writers are all concerned with women's unequal position in society, but their explanations for it vary substantially. Competing schools of feminism have sought to explain gender inequalities through a variety of deeply embedded social processes such as sexism, patriarchy, capitalism, and racism. In the following sections, we will look at the arguments behind three main feminist perspectives—liberal, radical, and black feminism.

feminist theory • A sociological perspective that emphasizes the centrality of gender in analyzing the social world and particularly the experience of women. There are many strands of feminist theory, but they all seek to explain gender inequalities in society and to work to overcome them.

LIBERAL FEMINISM

Liberal feminism looks for explanations of gender inequalities in social and cultural attitudes. Unlike radical feminists, liberal feminists do not see women's subordination as part of a larger system or structure. Instead, they draw attention to many separate factors that contribute to inequalities between men and women. For example, liberal feminists are concerned with sexism and discrimination against women in the workplace, educational institutions, and the media. They tend to focus their energies on establishing and protecting equal opportunities for women through legislation and other democratic means. Legal advances such as the Equal Pay Act of 1963 and the Sex Discrimination Act of 1984 were actively supported by liberal feminists, who argued that enshrining equality in law is important to eliminating discrimination against women. Liberal feminists seek to work through the existing system to bring about reforms in a

liberal feminism • Form of feminist theory that believes that gender inequality is produced by unequal access to civil rights and certain social resources, such as education and employment, based on sex. Liberal feminists tend to seek solutions through changes in legislation that ensure that the rights of individuals are protected.

"His" and "Hers" Apps?

Our face-to-face interactions at school, at work, in the family, and in our everyday lives are powerfully shaped by gender. But how does gender shape our digital lives? Do men and women use the same apps? Researchers are only beginning to document the digital lives of men and women, yet most of the evidence shows that men and women aren't all that different from one another.

A recent study by Pew (Purcell 2011) asked American adults what kinds of apps they had downloaded. Overall, the most popular were apps that provided regular updates on news, weather, sports, or finances (74 percent), that helped people communicate with family and friends (67 percent), and that helped them learn about something they were interested in (64 percent). Not surprisingly, apps with more specific functions were less popular; just 48 percent of people had downloaded apps that helped them with work-related tasks, 46 percent used apps that helped them shop, 43 percent watched movies or TV on their smartphones, and just 29 percent used apps that helped them manage their health.

The study found gender differences on just two dimensions. Men are more likely than women to use apps that help them with work-related tasks (56 percent versus 39 percent) and that advise them in making a purchase (51 percent versus 42 percent). The results of the Pew study suggest that men and women are more similar than different when it comes to their digital lives. Research firm Flurry Analytics similarly found that when it comes to the most popular apps, the breakdown of users is roughly fifty-fifty; women and men are equally likely to use Facebook and Foursquare or to share their thoughts on Twitter (Bonnington 2013, Huffington Post 2012).

If we delve more deeply, however, we see that the specific ways that people use social networking sites and play games online differs by gender in ways that are consistent with gender role socialization. As a 2012 *Time* magazine article proclaimed, "Men are from Google+, women are from Pinterest" (Wagstaff 2012). Men outnumber women on high-tech sites like Google+ and outnumber women four to one on "male-themed" video games that feature themes like gangs, mobsters, and war. By contrast, games such as puzzles and word games (e.g., Words with Friends) or "family-themed" games are downloaded more frequently by women.

Men and women also differ with respect to interest-based social networking apps. Men slightly outpace women on music-streaming and sharing sites like Spotify and Cloud, and far outnumber women on Reddit, a site where people can generate their own news stories. By contrast, women are much more likely to use apps associated with fashion and home design. For example, analysts estimate that anywhere from 75 to 90 percent of all Pinterest users are women (Huffington Post 2012).

What are your favorite apps? Do you think that your identity as male or female has shaped your preferences for particular apps? Why or why not?

Men are more likely than women to visit high-tech websites and play violent video games, whereas women favor puzzles, word games, and fashion-oriented sites and apps.

gradual way. In this respect, they are more moderate in their aims and methods than radical feminists, who call for an overthrow of the existing system.

While liberal feminists have contributed greatly to the advancement of women over the past century, critics charge that they are unsuccessful in dealing with the root cause of gender inequality and do not acknowledge the systemic nature of women's oppression in society. They say that by focusing on the independent deprivations that women suffer—sexism, discrimination, the "glass ceiling," unequal pay—liberal feminists draw only a partial picture of gender inequality. Radical feminists accuse liberal feminists of encouraging women to accept an unequal society and its competitive character.

RADICAL FEMINISM

At the heart of **radical feminism** is the belief that men are responsible for and benefit from the exploitation of women. The analysis of patriarchy—the systematic domination of females by males—is of central concern to this branch of feminism. Patriarchy is viewed as a universal phenomenon that has existed across time and cultures. Radical feminists often concentrate on the family as one of the primary sources of women's oppression in society. They argue that men exploit women by relying on the free domestic labor that women provide in the home, and that as a group, men also deny women access to positions of power and influence in society.

Radical feminists differ in their interpretations of the basis of patriarchy, but most agree that it involves the appropriation of women's bodies and sexuality in some form. Because women are biologically able to give birth to children, they become dependent materially on men for protection and livelihood. As such, the nuclear family is viewed as the site that generates "biological inequality" between women and men. Other radical feminists point to male violence against women as central to male supremacy. According to such a view, domestic violence, rape, and sexual harassment are all part of the systematic oppression of women, rather than isolated cases with their own psychological or criminal roots.

Radical feminists believe that gender equality can be attained only by overthrowing the patriarchal order because patriarchy is a systemic phenomenon. The use of patriarchy as a concept for explaining gender inequality has been popular with many feminist theorists. In asserting that "the personal is political," radical feminists have drawn widespread attention to the many linked dimensions of women's oppression.

radical feminism • Form of feminist theory that believes that gender inequality is the result of male domination in all aspects of social and economic life.

Surrounded by minority women at the Houston Civic Center, Coretta Scott King speaks about the resolution on minority women's rights that won the support of the National Women's Conference in 1977. The minority resolution, proposed by representatives of many races, declared that minority women suffered discrimination based on both race and sex.

Many objections can be raised, however, to radical feminist views. The main one, perhaps, is that the concept of patriarchy as it has been used is inadequate as a general explanation for women's oppression. Radical feminists have tended to claim that patriarchy has existed throughout history and across cultures—that it is a universal phenomenon. Critics argue, however, that such a conception of patriarchy does not leave room for historical or cultural variations. It also ignores the important influence that race, class, or ethnicity may have on the nature of women's subordination. In other words, it is not possible to see patriarchy as a universal phenomenon; doing so risks biological reductionism—attributing all the complexities of gender inequality to a simple distinction between men and women.

BLACK FEMINISM

Do the versions of feminism outlined above apply equally to the experiences of both white and nonwhite women? Many black feminists and feminists from developing countries claim they do not. They argue that ethnic divisions among women are not considered by the main feminist schools of thought, which are oriented to the dilemmas of white, predominantly middle-class women living in industrialized societies. It is not valid, they claim, to generalize theories about women's subordination as a whole from the experience of a specific group of women.

This dissatisfaction has led to the emergence of a **black feminism** that concentrates on the particular problems facing black women. The writings of African American feminists emphasize the influence of the powerful legacy of slavery, segregation, and the civil rights movement on gender inequalities in the black community. They point out that early black **suffragettes** supported the campaign for women's rights but realized that the question of race could not be ignored. Black feminists contend, therefore, that any theory of gender equality that does not take racism into account cannot be expected to explain black women's oppression adequately. Some also argue that black women are multiply disadvantaged on the basis of their color, their sex, and their class position. When these three factors interact, they reinforce and intensify one another (Brewer 1993). ✓

black feminism • A strand of feminist theory that highlights the multiple disadvantages of gender, class, and race that shape the experiences of nonwhite women. Black feminists reject the idea of a single, unified gender oppression that is experienced evenly by all women and argue that early feminist analysis reflected the specific concerns of white, middle-class women.

suffragettes • Members of early women's movements who pressed for equal voting rights for women and men.

CONCEPT CHECKS ✓

1. Contrast functionalist and feminist approaches to understanding gender inequality.

2. What are the key ideas of liberal feminism? What are the critiques of this perspective?

3. What are the key ideas of radical feminism? What are the critiques of this perspective?

4. What are the key ideas of black feminism? What are the critiques of this perspective?

Learn how globalization has transformed ideas about women's rights.

WHAT ARE THE GLOBAL CONSEQUENCES OF GENDER INEQUALITY?

According to a Chinese saying, "Women hold up half the sky." In fact, as we have seen in this chapter, women typically hold up far more than half: Women have become a central part of the world's paid workforce, while at the same time maintaining their traditional responsibilities for home and family. Although global gender inequalities may seem very far removed from your life, they have a direct effect on the daily lives of all the citizens of the globe.

China was the site of the 1995 United Nations' Fourth World Conference on Women, where some 35,000 people, representing 180 governments and 7,000 women's organizations, discussed the problems of women worldwide. The conference, held in the capital city of Beijing, grappled with a central problem women face the world over: What happens when a country's traditional cultural beliefs conflict with modern notions of women's rights? Globalization has not only brought factories and television to nearly every place on the planet but has also exposed people throughout the world to ideas about equality and democracy. The modern women's movement has become a global champion of universal rights for women.

The conference's final action platform was clear: When cultural traditions conflict with women's rights, women's rights should take precedence. The platform called for women's right to control their own reproduction and sexuality, as well as to inherit wealth and property—two rights that women are denied in many countries. It concluded that no society can truly hope to better the lives of its citizens until it fosters gender equality.

The conference in Beijing was a pivotal event; the United Nations anticipates holding its Fifth World Conference on Women in 2015. The goals of the meeting are expected to include examining how effectively the Beijing platform has been implemented and also exploring emerging issues such as trafficking, migration, climate change, and other issues that affect the lives of women, men, and children (Federation of American Women's Clubs Overseas [FAWCO] 2013).

HOW GENDER INEQUALITY AFFECTS OUR LIVES

As we have seen throughout this chapter, women tend to fare worse than men with respect to education, earnings, power, risk of sexual violence, discrimination, and even political representation. Although the severity of the gender gap varies widely across nations, and even across subgroups within a single nation, the evidence and theories we have reviewed clearly reveal that gender inequalities are widespread. However, the processes through which inequalities are perpetuated may be subtle—so subtle, in fact, that we may not easily detect them in our everyday lives.

Women like financial advisers Judy Calibuso, Julie Moss, and Dianne Goedtel might not have noticed the first time they were shut out of the teams that worked on the most lucrative accounts. Similarly, Merrill Lynch trainees Sara Hunter Hudson, Julia Kuo, and Catherine Wharton might have laughed off the first time their male boss encouraged them to behave in a more "perky" and "bubbly" manner in order to get ahead in the male-dominated industry of finance (Sherwell 2013). But when they realized they were being sidelined by their male colleagues, it became clear that they were being discriminated against on the grounds of gender.

The Merrill Lynch lawsuits raise awareness about the subtle ways gender affects us. Can you think of ways that social institutions and forces, such as the media or even peer culture, allow gender biases to "infect, perhaps subconsciously" the ways you evaluate the competence, abilities, and skills of the men and women you meet? If you were going to hire a math tutor, for example, and all you knew about the two candidates was their gender, would you prefer to hire a male or a female tutor? Why? By recognizing the biases we hold and the way these biases may affect our behaviors and by seeking to understand the sources of these biases, we are using our sociological imaginations to fight gender inequalities. ✓

> ## CONCEPT CHECKS ✓
>
> 1. The message emerging from the World Conference on Women was that when cultural traditions conflict with women's rights, women's rights should take precedence. Do you agree with this? Why or why not?
>
> 2. How did gender inequality in the workplace affect the women plaintiffs in the Merrill Lynch lawsuits?

EXERCISES:
Thinking Sociologically

1. What does cross-cultural evidence from tribal societies suggest about the differences in gender roles? Explain.

2. Why are minority women likely to think very differently about gender inequality from how white women think about it? Explain.

3. Do you think Judy Calibosa had a compelling case in the Merrill Lynch lawsuit? Why or why not? What kind of evidence would be needed to make a reasonable judgment in that case?

Chapter 9

Gender Inequality

p.259 — Are Gender Differences Due to Nature, Nurture, or Both?

Evaluate whether differences between women and men are the result of biological differences or social and cultural influences.

p.265 — How Do Gender Inequalities Affect Social Institutions?

Recognize that gender differences are a part of our social structure and create inequalities between women and men. Learn the forms these inequalities take in social institutions including the workplace, the family, the educational system, and the political system in the United States and globally.

p.278 — Why Are Women the Target of Violence?

Learn about the specific ways that women are the target of physical and sexual violence in the United States and globally.

p.282 — How Does Social Theory Explain Gender Inequality?

Think about various explanations for gender inequality. Learn some feminist theories about how to achieve gender equality.

p.286 — What Are the Global Consequences of Gender Inequality?

Learn how globalization has transformed ideas about women's rights.

sex • gender • gender socialization • social construction of gender

1. What is the difference between sex and gender?
2. How do both biology and gender socialization contribute to differences between men and women?
3. How can studies of gender in other cultures contribute to the argument that gender is socially constructed?
4. What is intersex? How does it challenge the male-female sex dichotomy?

patriarchy • gender inequality • gender typing • sex segregation • comparable worth • glass ceiling • sexual harassment • second shift • housework

1. Describe at least three examples of how gender inequalities emerge in the workplace. How would a sociologist explain these inequities?
2. What are the signs of declining economic inequality between men and women from a global perspective?
3. How do inequalities in the home, especially with regard to housework and child care, reflect larger gender inequities in society?
4. What are some important differences between men's and women's political participation in the United States?
5. What are some signs of progress in terms of women's political equality from a global perspective?

infanticide • rape • rape culture

1. How common is violence against women in the United States?
2. What proportion of sexual assaults are believed to go unreported?
3. Why are women more likely than men to be the targets of sexual violence?

feminist theory • liberal feminism • radical feminism • black feminism • suffragettes

1. Contrast functionalist and feminist approaches to understanding gender inequality.
2. What are the key ideas of liberal feminism? What are critiques of this perspective?
3. What are the key ideas of radical feminism? What are critiques of this perspective?
4. What are the key ideas of black feminism? What are critiques of this perspective?

1. The message emerging from the Beijing Women's Conference was that when cultural traditions conflict with women's rights, women's rights should take precedence. Do you agree with this? Why or why not?
2. How did gender inequality in the workplace affect the women plaintiffs in the Merill Lynch lawsuits?

10

Ethnicity and Race

THE BIG QUESTIONS

WHAT ARE RACE AND ETHNICITY?

Learn the cultural bases of race and ethnicity and how racial and ethnic differences create sharp divisions in society. Learn the leading psychological theories and sociological interpretations of prejudice and discrimination.

HOW DO ETHNIC GROUPS COEXIST AND COMPETE?

Recognize the importance of the historical roots, particularly in the expansion of Western colonialism, of ethnic conflict. Understand the different models for a multiethnic society.

WHY DO ETHNIC GROUPS MIGRATE?

Understand global migration patterns and their impact.

HOW DO ETHNIC MINORITIES EXPERIENCE LIFE IN THE UNITED STATES?

Familiarize yourself with the history and social dimensions of ethnic relations in America.

HOW DOES RACIAL AND ETHNIC INEQUALITY AFFECT YOUR LIFE?

Learn the forms of inequality experienced by different racial and ethnic groups in the United States. Understand how the history of prejudice and discrimination against ethnic minorities has created conditions of hardship for many, while others have succeeded despite societal barriers.

The multiracial family of Bill de Blasio, his wife Chirlane McCray, and his children Chiara and Dante became a topic of interest during his campaign for mayor of New York City, and was highlighted even further by the public backlash to a Cheerios commercial featuring the daughter of parents of different races. What do the advertisement, its viewers' responses, and de Blasio's election say about race relations in America today?

When Cheerios unveiled a new television commercial in 2013, ad execs never could have predicted the firestorm that would follow. In the commercial, an adorable young girl, about five years old, asks her mother if Cheerios "are good for your heart." Her mother reads the cereal box and notes that Cheerios' whole-grain oats are "heart healthy." The young girl runs over to her father, who is asleep on the sofa, and sprinkles Cheerios on his heart.

At first blush, the ad shows a little girl who wants her father to stay healthy by eating a low-fat cereal. But some people saw an entirely different scenario. The little girl, with her caramel complexion and bouncy ringlets, was clearly the daughter of a white mother and a black father (Elliott 2013). This simple fact triggered an onslaught of racist comments—so much so that YouTube promptly shut down the "comments" section on the video's web page (Goyette 2013). Angry bloggers noted that the ad was "disgusting" and made them "want to vomit." Others, still, made snide comments about the rarity of an African American man sticking around to raise his children (Goyette 2013).

But the reaction to these mean-spirited and narrow-minded comments was even more powerful. Many wrote poignant responses that this Cheerios ad was the first time they had ever seen a multiracial family—much like their own—on national television. Chirlane McCray, wife of New York City Mayor Bill de Blasio, explained in an e-mail to supporters, "Nineteen years of marriage and two children later, this is the first TV commercial I've seen with a family that looks a little bit like ours." Included in the e-mail was a photo of de Blasio, his wife, McCray, and their teen son, Dante, sitting around their own kitchen table enjoying bowls of Cheerios.

General Mills Foods, the maker of Cheerios, stood by their ad, acknowledging that the family represented millions of American families and noting that the number of multiracial families and children in the United States would continue to rise in the future. They even issued a follow-up ad, which aired during the 2014 Super Bowl. In this new ad, the father breaks the news to his daughter that she will soon have a baby sibling, while his beaming pregnant wife looks on. Despite the outcry following the earlier ad, General Mills remained committed to depicting the new American family. "Cheerios is recognizing the changing face of America," McCray noted, "and celebrating that our differences make us stronger."

Scientific studies similarly document that for growing numbers of Americans, "race" is not a simple or monolithic identity. More than 7 percent of the 3.5 million babies born in 2009 were of two or more races, up from barely 5 percent a decade earlier (Morello 2012). Experts predict that the number of Americans who identify as multiracial will continue to increase steeply in coming decades. Fully 15 percent of all first marriages in 2010 were between spouses of different races; this stands in stark contrast to the rate of 6.7 percent in 1980 (Pew Research Center 2012b). These proportions are expected to climb even higher, as young adults today are far more accepting of interracial dating than were their parents. For example, in 2012, 86 percent of Americans thought it was fine for blacks and whites to date. This statistic varied widely by age, however. Nearly all (93 percent) persons born after 1981 supported interracial dating, while just two-thirds of those born prior to 1946 felt the same.

Yet while the number of Americans of multiracial identity is at an all-time high and rising, these individuals continue to negotiate their identities with observers who cling to the view that "race" is a monolithic construct. For example, Michelle López-Mullins, former president of the University of Maryland's Multiracial and Biracial Student Association (MBSA), gets tired of hearing the question "What are you?" (Saulny 2011). Her father is Chinese and Peruvian, and her mother is white and Native American. López-Mullins recalls that when she was growing up, "I was always having to explain where my parents are from. . . . Saying 'I'm an American' wasn't enough." Although she found this frustrating when she was a child, she now embraces her mixed heritage. "Now when people ask what I am, I say 'How much time do you have?' Race will not automatically tell you my story."

While in past generations mixed-race persons often tolerated negative labels like "mulatto" (that is, a person with one black parent and one white parent), López-Mullins and her friends from MBSA are proud of their backgrounds and embrace all aspects of their ethnicity. As Laura Wood, former vice president of MBSA, says, "It's really important to acknowledge who you are. . . . If someone tries to call me black, I say, 'Yes—and white.'"

The experiences of Laura Wood and Michelle López-Mullins—along with a mounting body of sociological research—illustrate just how difficult it is to pinpoint the conditions of racial and ethnic group membership for some individuals of multiracial heritage. In recent decades, a number of sociologists have turned their attention to this topic of multiracial identity and racial classification schemes. They have argued that a "static measure of race" is not useful for individuals of multiracial heritage who may assert different identities in varied social contexts (Cheng and Lee 2009; Harris 2003; Harris and Sim 2000). As López-Mullins told a *New York Times* reporter, "I'm pretty much checking everything. . . . Hispanic, white, Asian American, Native American" when filling out surveys like the U.S. Census. As we will see throughout this chapter, race and ethnicity are complex identities with powerful implications for our everyday lives.

WHAT ARE RACE AND ETHNICITY?

Learn the cultural bases of race and ethnicity and how racial and ethnic differences create sharp divisions in society. Learn the leading psychological theories and sociological interpretations of prejudice and discrimination.

In your daily life, you have no doubt used the terms *race* and *ethnicity* many times, but do you know what they mean? Defining and differentiating these terms is very difficult.

Ethnicity refers to cultural practices and outlooks of a given community that have emerged historically and tend to set people apart. Members of ethnic groups see themselves as culturally distinct from other groups in a society and are seen by those other groups to be so in return. Different characteristics may serve to distinguish ethnic groups from one another, but the most common are some combination of language, history, religious faith, and ancestry—real or imagined—and styles of dress or adornment. Ethnic differences are learned. Some examples of ethnic groups in the United States are Arab Americans, Jewish Americans, Italian Americans, Cuban Americans, South Asian Americans, and Chinese Americans.

The difference between race and ethnicity is not as clear-cut as some people think. For example, Ian Winchester, Michelle López-Mullins's classmate at Maryland, identifies as black and white. His black ancestors are from Ghana, while his white relatives are of Scottish and Norwegian descent. Winchester recalls that when he was growing up, his Scottish grandfather dressed him in kilts, while his black relatives would dress him in a dashiki. So does this mean that race is really a kind of ethnicity?

In a way it is, but race has certain defining characteristics that make it different from ethnicity. At certain historical moments, ethnic differences take on two additional characteristics. First, some ethnic differences become the basis of stigmas that cannot be removed by conversion or assimilation. Second, these stigmas become the basis of extreme hierarchy.

Race, then, can be understood as a classification system that assigns individuals and groups to categories that are ranked or hierarchical. There really are no clear-cut "races," only a range of physical variations among human beings. Differences in physical type between groups of human beings arise from population inbreeding, which varies according to the degree of contact between different social or cultural groups. Human population groups are a continuum. The genetic diversity within populations that share visible physical traits is as great as the diversity between them. Racial distinctions are more than ways of describing human differences—they are also important factors in the reproduction of patterns of power and inequality within society. In other words, race is much more than physical appearance. Sociological perspectives on race generally cohere with a **theory of racial formation** (Omi and Winant 1994); this is "the process by which social, economic and political forces determine the content and importance of racial categories, and by which they are in turn shaped by racial meanings." Recall our discussion of the social construction of gender in Chapter 9; just as what we think of as "male" and "female" encompasses far more than biology, the social construction of race suggests that our racial identities encompass far more than just our genetic makeup or physical features.

The process by which understandings of race are used to classify individuals or groups of people is called **racialization**. Historically, racialization meant that

ethnicity • Cultural values and norms that distinguish the members of a given group from others. An ethnic group is one whose members share a distinct awareness of a common cultural identity, separating them from other groups.

race • Differences in human physical characteristics used to categorize large numbers of individuals.

theory of racial formation • The process by which social, economic, and political forces determine the content and importance of racial categories.

racialization • The process by which understandings of race are used to classify individuals or groups of people. Racial distinctions are more than ways of describing human differences; they are also important factors in the reproduction of patterns of power and inequality.

certain groups of people came to be labeled as constituting distinct biological groups on the basis of naturally occurring physical features. From the fifteenth century onward, as Europeans came into increased contact with people from different regions of the world, they attempted to "racialize" non-European populations in opposition to the European "white race." In some instances this racialization took on codified institutional forms, as in the case of slavery in the former British, French, and Spanish colonies in the Americas; slavery in the United States; and the establishment of apartheid in South Africa after 1948. More commonly, however, everyday political, educational, legal, and other institutions become racialized through legislation. In the United States, de facto racial segregation and racial hierarchies persisted even after state-sanctioned segregation was dismantled during the civil rights era of the late 1960s. Within a racialized system, an individual's social life and his or her life chances—including education, employment, incarceration, housing, health care, and legal representation—are all shaped and constrained by the racial assignments and racial hierarchies in that system.

Sociologists who study ethnicity in the United States have come to understand that the importance of ethnicity has declined in recent years, at least among whites. As a result, "ethnicity" now includes a choice of whether to be ethnic at all. As we saw earlier in this chapter more and more whites must also make a choice about which ethnicity to be, given high rates of ethnic intermarriage (Passel, Wang, and Taylor 2010; Pew Research Center 2012b; Qian and Lichter 2011). By contrast, race is not always such a choice for nonwhites. One sociologist who has studied the ways in which many Americans think about their ancestry and backgrounds has written that "the social and political consequences of being Asian or Hispanic or black are not symbolic for the most part, or voluntary. They are real and often hurtful" (Waters 1990). Minority group status can have many negative consequences for the members of the group. One such negative consequence is segregation (discussed later in this chapter).

Despite the increase in the number of people in the United States self-identifying as multiracial, many North Americans continue to believe, mistakenly, that race is a natural category and that human beings can be neatly separated into biologically distinct "races." This is a legacy of European colonialism and **scientific racism**, or the misuse of science to support racist assumptions. During the sixteenth century, Europeans began to classify animals, people, and the material culture

scientific racism ● The use of scientific research or data to justify or reify beliefs about the superiority or inferiority of particular racial groups. Much of the "data" used to justify such claims are flawed or biased.

A member of the Tlaxcala tribe of central Mexico dances at Carnaval in New York. Many Latino immigrants and Hispanic Americans are identifying themselves on the U.S. Census as American Indians, a heritage dating back to well before the Spanish conquest.

that they collected as they explored the world. In 1735, Swedish botanist Carolus Linnaeus published what is recognized as the first version of a modern classification scheme of human populations. He grouped human beings into four basic categories—Europaeus, Americanus, Asiaticus, and Africanus. Linnaeus assumed that each subgroup had qualities of behavior or temperament that were innate and could not be altered. He acquired much of his data from the writings, descriptions, commentaries, and beliefs of plantation owners, missionaries, slave traders, explorers, and travelers. Thus, his scientific data were shaped by the prejudices of Europeans and the power that they had over the people whom they conquered (Smedley 1993).

racism • The attribution of characteristics of superiority or inferiority to a population sharing certain physically inherited characteristics.

institutional racism • Patterns of discrimination based on ethnicity that have become structured into existing social institutions.

RACISM

Some see **racism** as a system of domination that operates in social processes and social institutions; others see it as operating in the individual consciousness. Racism can refer to explicit beliefs in racial supremacy such as the systems established in Nazi Germany, before the civil rights movement in the United States, and in South Africa under apartheid.

Yet many have argued that racism is more than simply the ideas held by a small number of bigoted individuals. Rather, racism is embedded in the very structure and operation of society. The idea of **institutional racism** suggests that racism pervades all of society's structures in a systematic manner. According to this view, institutions such as the police, the health care industry, and the educational system all promote policies that favor certain groups while discriminating against others.

The concept of institutional racism was developed in the United States in the late 1960s by black power activists Stokely Carmichael and Charles Hamilton, who believed that white supremacy structured all social relations and that racism was the foundation of the very fabric of U.S. society, rather than merely representing the opinions of a small minority. The term was taken up by civil rights campaigners, and in subsequent years the existence of institutional racism came to be widely accepted and openly acknowledged in many settings, including law enforcement and the media. A 1990s investigation into the practices of the Los Angeles Police Department, in light of the beating of Rodney King, found that institutional racism is pervasive within the police force and the criminal justice system. The recent controversy in New York City regarding the stop-and-frisk policy also heightened awareness of institutional racism. The stop-and-frisk policy was ruled to be unconstitutional in September 2013. Prior to that time, however, police officers could stop and frisk anyone they viewed as suspicious. Although supporters of the policy believed it was effective in saving the lives of New Yorkers, and helped to get guns off the streets, opponents say that police disproportionately targeted "blacks and Hispanics who would not have been stopped if they were white" (Goldstein 2013).

We see instances of institutional racism in Hollywood films, television broadcasting (negative or limited portrayals of racial and ethnic minorities in programming), and the international modeling industry (industry-wide bias against fashion models who appear to be of non-European ancestry and/or mixed race).

Four schoolboys represent the "racial scale" in South Africa— black, Indian, "half-caste" (mixed ethnicity), and white.

PSYCHOLOGICAL INTERPRETATIONS OF PREJUDICE AND DISCRIMINATION

Psychological theories can help us understand the nature of prejudiced and racist attitudes and why ethnic differences matter so much to people.

PREJUDICE, DISCRIMINATION, AND RACISM

prejudice • The holding of preconceived ideas about an individual or group, ideas that are resistant to change even in the face of new information. Prejudice may be either positive or negative.

Prejudice, discrimination, and racism are related but distinctive concepts. **Prejudice** refers to opinions or attitudes—positive or negative—held by members of one group toward another. A prejudiced person's preconceived views are often based on hearsay rather than on direct evidence and are resistant to change even in the face of new information. People may harbor favorable prejudices about groups with which they identify and negative prejudices against others. Someone who is prejudiced against a particular group will refuse to give it a fair hearing.

discrimination • Behavior that denies to the members of a particular group resources or rewards that can be obtained by others. Discrimination must be distinguished from prejudice: Individuals who are prejudiced against others may not engage in discriminatory practices against them; conversely, people may act in a discriminatory fashion toward a group even though they are not prejudiced against that group.

Discrimination refers to actual behavior toward another group. It can be seen in activities that distribute rewards and benefits unequally based on membership in the dominant ethnic groups. It involves excluding or restricting members of specific groups, often defined by "race" or ethnicity, from opportunities that are available to other groups. Discrimination does not necessarily derive directly from prejudice. For example, white home buyers might steer away from purchasing properties in predominantly black neighborhoods, not because of attitudes of hostility they might feel toward African Americans, but because of worries about declining property values. Prejudiced attitudes in this case influence discrimination, but in an indirect fashion.

Perhaps one of the most tragic examples of the dangers of prejudice and discrimination in recent years was the fatal shooting of Trayvon Martin, whom we learned about in Chapter 6. The seventeen-year-old high school junior was shot and killed while walking through a multiethnic gated community in Sanford, Florida, where he was temporarily staying with his father and his fiancée. George Zimmerman, another resident of the community and a neighborhood watch volunteer, claimed he shot Martin in self-defense during an altercation. Martin, however, was found to be unarmed. Zimmerman was put on trial for second-degree murder, but a Florida jury ultimately found him not guilty, ruling that Zimmerman justifiably used deadly force against Martin. In a case that sparked a nationwide debate over racial profiling and civil rights, the jury rejected the prosecution's claims that Zimmerman deliberately pursued and attacked Martin because he assumed the black teenager was a criminal. They determined that Zimmerman believed that shooting Martin was "necessary to prevent imminent death or great bodily harm" to himself—Florida's definition of self-defense (Alvarez and Buckley 2013).

STEREOTYPES AND SCAPEGOATS

stereotype • A fixed and inflexible category.

displacement • The transferring of ideas or emotions from their true source to another object.

scapegoat • An individual or group blamed for wrongs that were not of their doing.

Prejudice operates mainly through the use of **stereotyping**, which means thinking in terms of fixed and inflexible categories. Stereotyping is often closely linked to the psychological mechanism of **displacement**, in which feelings of hostility or anger are directed against objects that are not the real origin of those feelings. People vent their antagonism against **scapegoats**, others who are blamed for problems that are not their fault. Scapegoating is common when two deprived ethnic groups come into competition with each other for economic rewards. People who direct racial attacks against African Americans, for example, are often in a similar economic position to them. They blame blacks for grievances whose real causes lie elsewhere. Scapegoating is normally directed against groups that are distinctive and relatively powerless because they make an easy target.

MINORITY GROUPS

minority group • A group of people who are in a minority in a given society and who, because of their distinct physical or cultural characteristics, find themselves in situations of inequality within that society. Also known as *ethnic minority*.

The term **minority group** as used in everyday life can be quite confusing. This is because the term refers to political power and is not simply a numerical distinction. There are many minorities in a statistical sense, such as people with red hair or people who weigh more than 250 pounds, but these are not minorities according to the sociological concept. In sociology, members of a minority group are disadvantaged as compared with members of the **dominant group** (a group possessing more wealth, power, and prestige) and have some sense of group solidarity, of belonging together. The experience of being subject to prejudice and discrimination usually heightens feelings of common loyalty and interests. For example, several major U.S. cities, including Miami, San Antonio, and El Paso, have majority-Latino populations, while Atlanta; Detroit; Baltimore; Gary, Indiana; and Washington, D.C., have predominantly black populations—yet both ethnic groups still lag behind whites in both groups of cities in terms of outcomes like education and income (Fulwood 2010).

Members of minority groups, such as Spanish speakers in the United States, tend to see themselves as a people separated or distinct from the majority. Minority groups are sometimes, but not always, physically and socially isolated from the larger community. Although they tend to be concentrated in certain neighborhoods, cities, or regions of a country, their children may often intermarry with members of the dominant group. People who belong to minority groups (for example, Jews) sometimes actively promote endogamy (marriage within the group) in order to keep alive their cultural distinctiveness.

The idea of a "minority group" is more confusing today than ever before. Some groups that were once clearly identified as minorities, such as Asians and Jews, now have more resources, intermarry at greater rates, and experience less discrimination than they did when they were originally conceived of as minority groups. This highlights the fact that the concept of a minority group is really about disadvantage, rather than a numerical distinction. Perhaps in the future it would be more meaningful for sociologists to use the terms *dominant* and *disadvantaged* to avoid these misunderstandings; of course, these new terms would be fraught with their own problems. ✓

dominant group • The opposite of a minority group; the dominant group possesses more wealth, power, and prestige in a society.

CONCEPT CHECKS ✓

1. Explain the difference between ethnicity and race.

2. What does the term *racialization* refer to?

3. How does prejudice operate in society?

4. Why are Hispanics and African Americans considered to be minority groups in American society?

HOW DO ETHNIC GROUPS COEXIST AND COMPETE?

Recognize the importance of the historical roots, particularly in the expansion of Western colonialism, of ethnic conflict. Understand the different models for a multiethnic society.

In an age of globalization and rapid social change, the rich benefits and complex challenges of ethnic diversity are confronting a growing number of states. International migration is accelerating with the further integration of the global economy; the movement and mixing of human populations seem sure to intensify in years to come. Meanwhile, ethnic tensions and conflicts continue to flare in societies around the world, threatening to lead to the disintegration of some multiethnic states and hinting at protracted violence in others. How can ethnic diversity be accommodated and the outbreak of ethnic conflict averted? Within multiethnic societies, what should be the relation between ethnic-minority groups and the majority population? There are four primary models of ethnic integration that have been adopted by multiethnic societies in relation to these challenges: assimilation, the "melting pot," pluralism, and multiculturalism. These will be discussed shortly.

To fully analyze ethnic relations in current times, we must first take a historical and comparative perspective. It is impossible to understand ethnic divisions today without giving prime place to the impact of the expansion of Western colonialism on the rest of the world. Global migratory movements resulting from colonialism helped create ethnic divisions by placing different peoples in close proximity. We will now delve into this history in more detail.

ETHNIC ANTAGONISM: A HISTORICAL PERSPECTIVE

From the fifteenth century onward, Europeans began to venture into previously uncharted seas and unexplored landmasses, pursuing the aims of exploration and trade but also conquering and subduing native peoples. They poured out by the millions from Europe to settle in these new areas. In the shape of the slave trade, they also occasioned a large-scale movement of people from Africa to the Americas.

These population flows formed the basis of the current ethnic composition of the United States, Canada, the countries of Central and South America, South Africa, Australia, and New Zealand. In all these societies, the indigenous populations were decimated by disease, war, and genocide and subjected to European rule. They are now impoverished ethnic minorities. Since the Europeans were from diverse national and ethnic origins, they transplanted various ethnic hierarchies and divisions to their new homelands. At the height of the colonial era, in the nineteenth and early twentieth centuries, Europeans also ruled over native populations in many other regions: South Asia, East Asia, the South Pacific, and the Middle East.

For most of the period of European expansion, ethnocentric attitudes were rife among the colonists, many of whom were convinced that, as Christians, they were on a civilizing mission to the rest of the world. Europeans of all political persuasions believed themselves to be superior to the peoples they colonized and conquered. The early period of colonization coincided with the rise of scientific racism, and ever since then, the legacy of European colonization has generated ethnic divisions that have occupied a central place in regional and global conflicts. In particular, racist views distinguishing the descendants of Europeans from those of Africans became central to European racist attitudes.

THE RISE OF RACISM

Why has racism flourished? There are several reasons. The first reason for the rise of modern racism lies in the exploitative relations that Europeans established with the peoples they encountered and conquered. The slave trade could not have carried on had Europeans not constructed a belief system that allowed them to justify their actions by convincing themselves that Africans belonged to an inferior, even subhuman, race. Racism helped justify colonial rule over nonwhite peoples and denied them the rights of political participation that were being won by whites in their European homelands.

Second, an opposition between the colors white and black as cultural symbols was deeply rooted in European culture. White had long been associated with purity, black with evil (there is nothing natural about this symbolism; in some other cultures, it is reversed). The symbol of blackness held negative meanings before the West came into extensive contact with black peoples. These symbolic meanings influenced the Europeans' reactions to blacks when they were first encountered on African shores.

A young girl joins members of the Ku Klux Klan at a demonstration against the Martin Luther King Day holiday in Pulaski, Tennessee.

A third important factor leading to modern racism was simply the invention and diffusion of the concept of race itself. Count Joseph Arthur de Gobineau (1816–1882), who is sometimes called the father of modern racism, proposed ideas that became influential in many circles. According to de Gobineau, three races exist: white, black, and yellow. The white race possesses superior intelligence, morality, and will power, and these inherited qualities underlie the spread of Western influence across the world. The blacks are the least capable, marked by an animal nature, a lack of morality, and emotional instability. The yellows were described as the "exact opposite" of blacks: restrained, discerning, and hardworking, although not particularly creative.

ETHNIC CONFLICT

The most extreme and devastating form of group relations in human history involves **genocide**, the systematic, planned destruction of a particular group on the grounds of group members' ethnicity, religion, culture, or political views. The most horrific recent instance of brutal destructiveness against such a group was the massacre of 6 million Jews in the German concentration camps during World War II. The Holocaust is not the only example of mass genocide in the twentieth century. Between 1915 and 1923 over a million Armenians were killed by the Ottoman Turkish government. In the late 1970s, 2 million Cambodians died in the Khmer Rouge's killing fields. During the 1990s, in the African country of Rwanda, hundreds of thousands of the minority Tutsis were massacred by the dominant Hutu group. And in the former Yugoslavia, Bosnian and Kosovar Muslims were summarily executed by the Serb majority.

genocide • The systematic, planned destruction of a racial, political, or cultural group.

In other areas of the world, exploitation of minority groups has been an ugly part of many countries' histories. The separation of the minority from the majority has been institutionalized in the form of **segregation**, a practice whereby racial and ethnic groups are kept physically separate by law, thereby maintaining the superior position of the dominant group. For instance, in apartheid-era South Africa, laws forced blacks to live separately from whites and forbade sexual relations between races. In the United States, African Americans have also experienced legal forms of segregation. In 1967 the Supreme Court ruled in the case of *Loving v. Virginia* that the prohibition of interracial marriage violated the right to privacy. At that time racial intermarriage was still a crime in most southern states. Interracial marriage had been criminalized for much of the United States' history, in every state except Alaska and Hawaii. Economic and social segregation was enforced by laws, such as those requiring blacks and whites to use separate public bathrooms. Even today, de facto segregated residential areas still exist in many cities, leading some to claim that an American system of apartheid has developed (Massey and Denton 1993).

segregation • The practices of keeping racial and ethnic groups physically separate, thereby maintaining the superior position of the dominant group.

MODELS OF ETHNIC INTEGRATION

For many years, the two most common positive models of political ethnic harmony in the United States were those of assimilation and the melting pot. **Assimilation** meant that new immigrant groups would assume the attitudes and language of the dominant white community. The idea of the **melting pot** was different—it meant merging different cultures and outlooks by stirring them all together. A newer model of ethnic relations is **pluralism**, in which ethnic cultures maintain their unique practices and communities, yet also participate in the larger society's economic and political life. A recent outgrowth of pluralism is **multiculturalism**, in which ethnic groups exist separately and equally. It does seem at least possible to create a society in which ethnic groups are

assimilation • The acceptance of a minority group by a majority population in which the new group takes on the values and norms of the dominant culture.

melting pot • The idea that ethnic differences can be combined to create new patterns of behavior drawing on diverse cultural sources.

pluralism • A model for ethnic relations in which all ethnic groups in a society retain their independent and separate identities, yet share equally in the rights and powers of citizenship.

multiculturalism • The viewpoint according to which ethnic groups can exist separately and share equally in economic and political life.

separate but equal, as is demonstrated by Switzerland, where French, German, and Italian groups coexist in the same society. But this situation is unusual, and it seems unlikely that the United States could come close to mirroring this achievement in the near future.

CONFLICT AND ECONOMIC POWER

Many commentators have argued that the best way to reduce ethnic conflicts such as those discussed earlier is to establish democracy and a free market. They argue that this would promote peace by giving everyone a say in running the country and by giving them access to the prosperity that comes from trading with others. In an influential book, *World on Fire: How Exporting Free Market Democracy Breeds Ethnic Hatred and Global Instability* (2003), Amy Chua, a professor at Yale University, contests this view.

Chua's starting point is that in many developing countries a small ethnic minority enjoys disproportionate economic power. One obvious example is the white minority that exploited the nonwhite ethnic groups in apartheid South Africa. Chua also observes that the massacre of Tutsis by Hutus in Rwanda in 1994 and the hatred felt by Serbs toward Croats in former Yugoslavia were also partly related to the economic advantage enjoyed by the Tutsis and the Croats in their respective countries.

Chua's account shows us that although democracy and the market economy are in principle beneficent forces, they must be grounded in an effective system of law and civil society. Where they are not, as in many parts of the developing world, new and acute ethnic conflicts can emerge. ✓

CONCEPT CHECKS ✓

1. What are three reasons racism has flourished in the United States?

2. Compare and contrast three forms of ethnic conflicts.

3. What is the difference between assimilation and melting pot strategies of ethnic integration?

WHY DO ETHNIC GROUPS MIGRATE?

Understand global migration patterns and their impact.

refugee • A person who has fled his or her home due to a political, economic, or natural crisis.

Today, floods of **refugees** and emigrants move restlessly across different regions of the globe, either trying to escape from conflicts or fleeing poverty in search of a better life. Often they reach a new country only to find they are resented by people who some generations ago were immigrants themselves. Sometimes there are reversals, as has happened in Southern California and other areas of the United States along the Mexican border. Much of what is now California was once part of Mexico. Today, some Mexican Americans might say, the new waves of Mexican immigrants are reclaiming what used to be their heritage.

MIGRATORY MOVEMENTS

Although migration is not a new phenomenon, it is one that seems to be accelerating as part of the process of global integration. Worldwide migration patterns can be seen as one reflection of the rapidly changing economic, political, and cultural ties among countries. It has been estimated that the world's migrant population in 1990 was

RACIAL & ETHNIC POPULATIONS

The racial and ethnic categories that are relevant in a particular nation change over time and vary widely among countries.

ISRAEL

Jewish*
75.1%

Non-Jewish
Mostly Arab
24.9%

*Of which Israel-born 73.6%, Europe/America/Oceania-born 17.9%, Africa-born 5.2%, Asia-born 3.2%

AUSTRALIA

White
92.0%

Asian
7.0%

Aboriginal & Other
1.0%

SOUTH AFRICA

Black African
79.0%

White
9.6%

Colored
8.9%

Indian/Asian
2.5%

BRAZIL

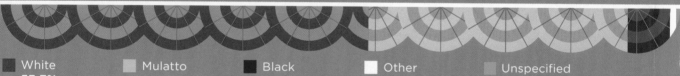

White
53.7%

Mulatto
One white parent and one black parent
38.5%

Black
6.2%

Other
Includes Japanese, Arab, Amerindian
0.9%

Unspecified
0.7%

ROMANIA

Romanian
83.4%

Hungarian
6.1%

Roma
3.1%

Ukrainian
0.3%

German
0.2%

Other
0.7%

Unspecified
6.1%

UNITED STATES

White
63.7%

Hispanic or Latino
16.3%

African American
12.6%

Asian
4.8%

American Indian
Includes Alaska native
0.9%

Native Hawaiian
Includes other Pacific islander
0.2%

Some other race
6.2%

2+ races
2.9%

Source: CIA: The World Factbook 2013

more than 80 million people, 20 million of whom were refugees. By 2010, the number of migrants was estimated at nearly 214 million (United Nations Department of Economic and Social Affairs 2009). This number appears likely to continue increasing in the twenty-first century, prompting some scholars to label this the "age of migration" (Castles and Miller 2009).

immigration • The movement of people into one country from another for the purpose of settlement.

emigration • The movement of people out of one country in order to settle in another.

Immigration, the movement of people into a country to settle, and **emigration**, the process by which people leave a country to settle in another, combine to produce global migration patterns linking countries of origin and countries of destination. Migratory movements add to ethnic and cultural diversity in many societies and help shape demographic, economic, and social dynamics. The intensification of global migration since World War II, and particularly over the last three decades, has transformed immigration into an important political issue in many countries. Rising immigration rates in many Western societies have challenged commonly held notions of national identity and have forced a reexamination of concepts of citizenship.

In examining recent trends in global migration, Stephen Castles and Mark Miller (1993) have identified four tendencies that they claim characterize migration patterns today and that are expected to persist in the coming years:

- **Acceleration:** Migration across borders is occurring in greater numbers than ever before.

Global Map 10.1 | Global Migratory Movements since 1973

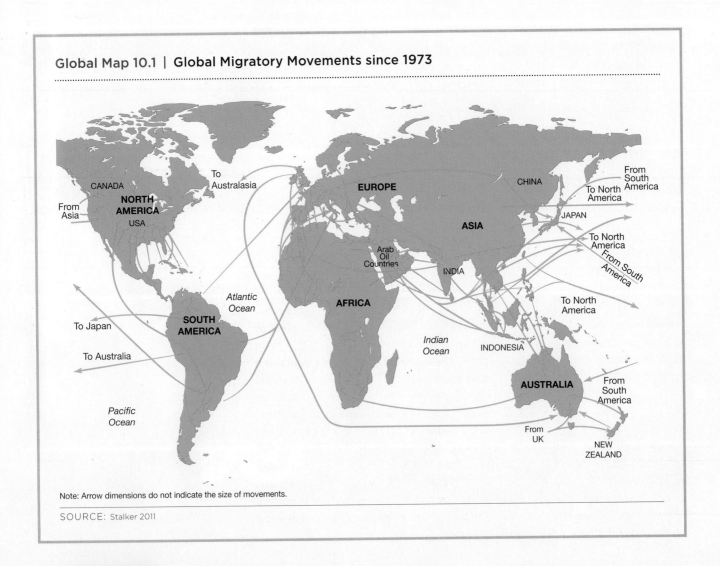

Note: Arrow dimensions do not indicate the size of movements.

SOURCE: Stalker 2011

- **Diversification:** Most countries now receive immigrants of many different types, in contrast with earlier times when particular forms of immigration, such as labor immigration or refugees, were predominant.
- **Globalization:** Migration has become more global in nature, involving a greater number of countries as both senders and recipients (Global Map 10.1).
- **Feminization:** A growing number of migrants are women, making contemporary migration much less male dominated than in previous times. The increase in female migrants is closely related to changes in the global labor market, including the growing demand for domestic workers, the expansion of sex tourism and "trafficking" in women, and the "mail-order brides" phenomenon.

GLOBAL DIASPORAS

diaspora • The dispersal of an ethnic population from an original homeland into foreign areas, often in a forced manner or under traumatic circumstances.

Another way to understand global migration patterns is through the study of diasporas. The term **diaspora** refers to the dispersal of an ethnic population from an original homeland into foreign areas, often in a forced manner or under traumatic circumstances. References are often made to the Jewish and African diasporas to describe the way in which these populations have become redistributed across the globe as a result of slavery and genocide. Although members of a diaspora are by definition scattered apart geographically, they are held together by factors such as shared history, a collective memory of the original homeland, or a common ethnic identity that is nurtured and preserved. ✓

CONCEPT CHECKS ✓

1. According to Castles and Miller, which four trends characterize current and future migration?

2. What is diaspora? Explain the role diasporas play in preserving ethnic culture in contemporary societies.

HOW DO ETHNIC MINORITIES EXPERIENCE LIFE IN THE UNITED STATES?

Familiarize yourself with the history and social dimensions of ethnic relations in America.

We concentrate for the rest of the chapter on the origins and nature of ethnic diversity in the United States—and its consequences, which have often been highly contentious. More than most other societies in the world, the United States is peopled almost entirely by immigrants. Only a tiny minority, less than 1 percent, of the population today are Native Americans, those whom Christopher Columbus, erroneously supposing he had arrived in India, called Indians.

Before the American Revolution, British, French, and Dutch settlers established colonies in what is now the United States. Some descendants of the French colonists are still to be found in parts of Louisiana. Millions of slaves were brought over from Africa to North America. Huge waves of European, Asian, and Latin American immigrants have washed across the country at different periods since then. The United States is one of the most ethnically diverse countries on the face of the globe. In this section we will pay particular attention to the divisions that have separated whites and nonwhite minority groups such as African Americans and Hispanic Americans. The emphasis is on *struggle*. Members of these groups have made repeated efforts to defend the integrity of their cultures and advance their social position in the face of persistent prejudice and discrimination from the wider social environment.

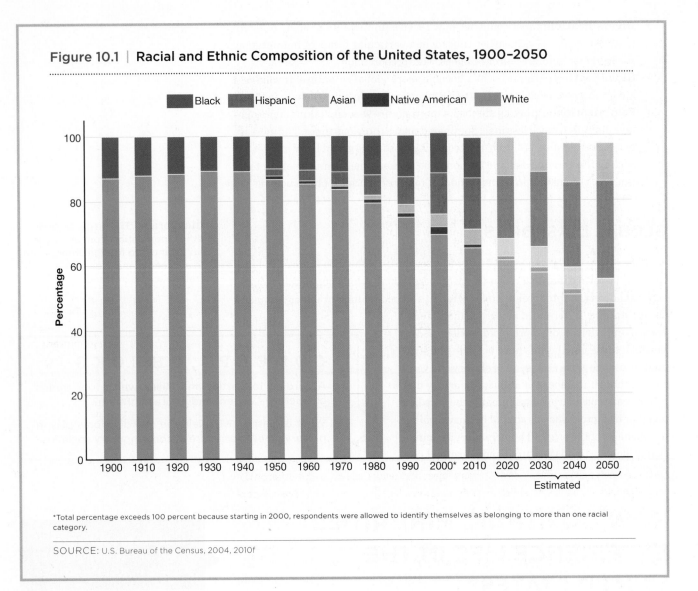

Figure 10.1 | Racial and Ethnic Composition of the United States, 1900–2050

Legend: Black, Hispanic, Asian, Native American, White

*Total percentage exceeds 100 percent because starting in 2000, respondents were allowed to identify themselves as belonging to more than one racial category.

SOURCE: U.S. Bureau of the Census, 2004, 2010f

EARLY COLONIZATION

The first European colonists in what was to become the United States were actually of a quite homogeneous background. At the time of the Declaration of Independence, the majority of the colonial population was of British descent, and almost everyone was Protestant. Settlers from outside the British Isles were at first admitted only with reluctance, but the desire for economic expansion meant having to attract immigrants from other areas. Most came from countries in northwest Europe, such as Holland, Germany, and Sweden; such migration into North America dates initially from around 1820. In the century following, about 33 million immigrants entered the United States. No migrant movement on such a scale had ever been documented, nor has such a migration occurred since.

The early waves of immigrants came mostly from the same countries of origin as the groups already established in the United States. They left Europe to escape economic hardship and religious and political oppression, and for the opportunity to acquire land as the drive westward gained momentum. As a result of successive potato famines that had produced widespread starvation, 1.5 million people migrated from Ireland. The Irish were accustomed to a life of hardship and despair.

The earliest migrants to the United States in the early nineteenth century hailed from northern Europe. By 1920, more than 1.5 million Irish immigrants came to America.

In contrast with other immigrants from rural backgrounds, most Irish settled in urban industrial areas, where they sought work.

A major new influx of immigrants arrived in the 1880s and 1890s, this time mainly from southern and eastern Europe—the Austro-Hungarian Empire, Russia, and Italy. Each successive group of immigrants was subject to considerable discrimination on the part of people previously established in the country. Negative views of the Irish, for example, emphasized their supposedly low level of intelligence and drunken behavior. But as they were concentrated within the cities, the Irish Americans were able to organize to protect their interests and gained a strong influence over political life. The Italians and Polish, when they reached America, were in turn discriminated against by the Irish.

Asian immigrants first arrived in the United States in large numbers in the late nineteenth century, encouraged by employers who needed cheap labor in the developing industries of the West. Some 200,000 Chinese immigrated to the United States during this period. Most were men, who came with the idea of saving money to send back to their families in China, anticipating that they would also later return there. Bitter conflicts broke out between white workers and the Chinese when employment opportunities diminished. The Chinese Exclusion Act, passed in 1882, cut down further immigration to a trickle until after World War II.

Japanese immigrants began to arrive not long after the Chinese Exclusion Act was passed. They were also subject to great hostility from whites. Opposition to Japanese immigration intensified in the early part of the twentieth century, leading to strict limits, or quotas, being placed on the numbers allowed to enter the United States.

Most immigrant groups in the early twentieth century settled in urban areas and engaged in the developing industrial economy. They also tended to cluster in ethnic neighborhoods of their own. Chinatowns, Little Italys, and other clearly defined areas became features of most large cities. The very size of the influx provoked backlash from the Anglo-Saxon segment of the population. One result was the new immigration quotas of the 1920s, which restricted immigration from southern and eastern Europe. Many immigrants found the conditions of life in their new land little better and sometimes worse than in their homelands.

IMMIGRANT AMERICA IN THE TWENTIETH AND TWENTY-FIRST CENTURIES

If globalization is understood as the emergence of new patterns of interconnection among the world's peoples and cultures, then surely one of the most significant aspects of globalization is the changing racial and ethnic composition of Western societies. In the United States, shifting patterns of immigration since the end of World War II have altered the demographic structure of many regions, affecting social and cultural life in ways that can hardly be overstated. Although the United States has always been a nation of immigrants (with the obvious exception of Native Americans), most of those who arrived here prior to the early 1960s were European.

As we just discussed, throughout the nineteenth and early twentieth centuries, vast numbers of people from Ireland, Italy, Germany, Russia, and other European countries flocked to America in search of a new life, giving a distinctive European bent to American culture. (Of course, until 1808, another significant group of immigrants—Africans—came not because America was a land of opportunity but because they had been enslaved.) In part because of changes in immigration policy, however, most of those admitted since 1965 have been Asian or Hispanic. In the years 2000 to 2003, for example, of the approximately 4.5 million immigrants who were legally admitted to the United States, almost 1.2 million came from Asia and nearly 2.6 million were from Latin America (U.S. Bureau of the Census 2003a).

There are also an estimated 7 to 11 million illegal immigrants living in the United States, about 70 percent of whom are Mexican (CNN 2003; National

Nearly 4 million Chinese Americans reside in the United States today. Many participate in cultural events like this Chinese New Year celebration.

Immigration Forum 2006). Thus, as of 2012, 52.6 percent of U.S. residents who were foreign born were from Latin America, and 30 percent were from Asia (U.S. Bureau of the Census 2012f). In contrast, in 1900 almost 85 percent of the foreign born were European (Duignan and Gann 1998).

Most of these new immigrants have settled in six "port of entry" states: California, New York, Texas, Illinois, New Jersey, and Massachusetts. These states are attractive to new immigrants not necessarily because of the job opportunities they afford, but because they house large immigrant communities into which newcomers are welcomed (Frey and Liaw 1998). As the flow of Asian and Hispanic immigration continues, and as some nonimmigrants respond by moving to regions of the country with smaller immigrant populations, the percentage of residents of port-of-entry states who are white will continue to drop. California was approximately 52 percent white in 1996; in 2004 this number had dropped to 44.5 percent. The 2010 U.S. Census reported that 43 percent of Californians were white (Maharidge 1996; Humes et al. 2010). "Other states will follow," Dale Maharidge writes in the book *The Coming White Minority* (1996), "Texas sometime around 2015, and in later years Arizona, New York, Nevada, New Jersey, and Maryland. By 2050 the nation will be almost half nonwhite."

The effect of these demographic changes on everyday social life has been profound. Residents of California's urban centers, for example, fully expect street scenes to be multiethnic in character and would be shocked to visit a state like Wisconsin, where the vast majority of public interactions take place among whites. In some California communities, store and street signs are printed in Spanish or Chinese or Vietnamese, as well as in English. Interracial marriages are on the rise, ethnic restaurants have proliferated, and the schools are filled with nonwhite children. In fact, nonwhites make up two-thirds of the undergraduate population at the University of California at Berkeley, where Asian students are on the verge of predominating.

Unfortunately, these changes have exacerbated social tensions. Many white Californians have retreated into prosperous suburban enclaves and have grown resentful of immigrants and nonwhites. Because rates of voter turnout are higher for whites than for other racial groups in the state and because whites control a significant share of the state's wealth, whites have managed to pass a number of laws that seek to preserve opportunities for the "coming white minority." Proposition 187, for example, passed in 1994, denied vital public services to illegal immigrants. More recently, the regents of the University of California, in a highly controversial move, decided to abolish affirmative action for the entire nine-campus state university system. Were these decisions based on solid economic and philosophical rationales—the perception that California taxpayers were shouldering too much of the economic burden of illegal immigration or the sense that affirmative action constitutes "reverse discrimination" against whites— or were they motivated principally by the fear of immigrants and other persons different from oneself?

Making Sociology Work
AFFIRMATIVE ACTION OFFICER

Affirmative action policies were originally designed as a corrective measure for political, economic, or social injustices against demographic groups that have been subjected to prejudice. In practice, many of these programs aim to increase the numbers of women and racial and ethnic minorities in fields of study and work where they have traditionally been underrepresented. Proponents of affirmative action policies say that college admissions and hiring practices that are purportedly "meritocratic" subtly discriminate against women and minorities because definitions of merit often benefit those with the richest socioeconomic resources or social connections. In recent years, university affirmative action policies have come under fire. The University of California system abolished affirmative action at its nine campuses in 2007. However, the Supreme Court ruled that the University of Michigan Law School could take race into account when admitting applicants because of "the educational benefits that flow from a diverse student body." In May 2011, the Supreme Court extended this policy to include undergraduate admissions at Michigan's College of Literature, Sciences and the Arts. Drawing on your knowledge of racial and ethnic inequality in education, employment, and income, how would you approach your position as a university affirmative action officer? Would you aim your programs toward specific ethnic or racial groups? Why?

Whatever the answer, there can be little doubt that immigration—an important aspect of globalization—is changing the face of American society.

AFRICAN AMERICANS IN THE UNITED STATES

By 1780, there were nearly 4 million slaves in the American South. Because there was little incentive for them to work, white slave owners often resorted to physical punishment. Slaves had virtually no rights in law whatsoever. But they did not passively accept the conditions their masters imposed on them. The struggles of slaves against their oppressive conditions sometimes took the form of direct opposition or disobedience to orders, and occasionally outright rebellion (although collective slave revolts were more common in the Caribbean than in the United States). On a more subtle level, their response took the form of a cultural creativity—a mixing of aspects of African cultures, Christian ideals, and cultural threads woven from their new environments. Some of the art forms their descendants developed, as in music—for example, the invention of jazz—were genuinely new.

Feelings of hostility toward blacks on the part of the white population were in some respects more strongly developed in states where slavery had never been known than in the South itself. Moral rejection of slavery seems to have been confined to a few more educated groups. The main factors underlying the Civil War were political and economic; most northern leaders were more interested in sustaining the Union than in abolishing slavery, although this was the eventual outcome of the conflict. The formal abolition of slavery changed the real conditions of life for African Americans in the South relatively little. The "black codes"—laws limiting the rights of blacks—placed restrictions on the behavior of the former slaves and punished their transgressions in much the same way as under slavery. Acts were also passed legalizing segregation of blacks from whites in public places. One kind of slavery was thus replaced by another, based on social, political, and economic discrimination.

INTERNAL MIGRATION FROM SOUTH TO NORTH

Industrial development in the North, combined with the mechanization of agriculture in the South, produced a progressive movement of African Americans northward from the turn of the century on. In 1900, more than 90 percent of African Americans lived in the South, mostly in rural areas. Today, less than half of the black population remains in the South; three-quarters now live in northern urban areas. African Americans used to be farm laborers and domestic servants, but over a period of little more than two generations, they have become mainly urban, industrial, and service-economy workers. But African Americans have not become assimilated into the wider society in the way in which the successive groups of white immigrants were. They have for the most part been unable to break free from the conditions of neighborhood segregation and poverty that other immigrants faced on arrival. Together with those of Anglo-Saxon origin, African Americans have lived in the United States far longer than most other immigrant groups. What was a transitional experience for most of the later white immigrants has become a seemingly permanent experience for blacks.

In the majority of cities, in both the South and the North, blacks and whites live in separate neighborhoods and are educated in different schools. Demographers have developed a statistic called index of dissimilarity, which tells us the proportion of people who would need to move out of their neighborhood into a new neighborhood in order for the distribution of people in neighborhoods to approximate the overall racial and ethnic breakdown of the United States. According to 2010 Census data, roughly

63 percent of either blacks or whites would have to move in order to desegregate housing fully in the average American city (Nasser 2010).

THE CIVIL RIGHTS MOVEMENT

Struggles by minority groups to achieve equal rights and opportunities have for a long while been a part of the United States. In contrast with other racial and ethnic minorities, blacks and Native Americans have largely been denied opportunities for self-advancement. The National Association for the Advancement of Colored People (NAACP) and the National Urban League, founded in 1909 and 1910, respectively, fought for black civil rights, but only began to have some real effect after World War II, when the NAACP instituted a campaign against segregated public education. This struggle came to a head when the organization sued five school boards, challenging the concept of separate but equal schooling that then prevailed. In 1954, in *Brown v. Board of Education of Topeka, Kansas*, the U.S. Supreme Court unanimously decided that "separate educational facilities are inherently unequal."

Martin Luther King Jr. addresses a large crowd at a civil rights march on Washington in 1963. Born in 1929, King was a Baptist minister, civil rights leader, and winner of the 1964 Nobel Peace Prize. He was assassinated by James Earl Ray in 1968.

This decision became the platform for the struggle for civil rights from the 1950s through the 1970s. The strength of the resistance from many whites persuaded black leaders that mass militancy was necessary to give civil rights any real substance. In 1955, a black woman, Rosa Parks, was arrested in Montgomery, Alabama, for declining to give up her seat on a bus to a white man. As a result, almost the entire African American population of the city, led by a Baptist minister, Martin Luther King Jr., boycotted the transportation system for 381 days. Eventually the city was forced to abolish segregation in public transportation.

Further boycotts and sit-ins followed, with the object of desegregating other public facilities. The marches and demonstrations began to achieve a mass following of blacks and white sympathizers. In 1963, a quarter of a million civil rights supporters staged a march on Washington and cheered as King announced, "We will not be satisfied until justice rolls down like the waters and righteousness like a mighty stream." In 1964, the Civil Rights Act was passed by Congress and signed into law by President Lyndon B. Johnson, comprehensively banning discrimination in public facilities, education, employment, and any agency receiving government funds. Further bills in following years were aimed at ensuring that African Americans became fully registered voters and outlawed discrimination in housing.

How successful has the civil rights movement been? On one hand, a substantial black middle class has emerged over the last three to four decades. And many African Americans—such as President Barack Obama, Senator Cory Booker, the writer Toni Morrison, the literary scholar Henry Louis Gates, media mogul Oprah Winfrey, and rap star Jay-Z—have achieved positions of power and influence in the wider society. On the other hand, a large number of African Americans, making up an underclass, live trapped in the ghettos. Scholars have debated whether the existence of the black underclass has resulted primarily from economic disadvantage or dependency on the welfare system. We will examine the forms of inequality that African Americans and other minority groups continue to experience later in this chapter.

LATINOS IN THE UNITED STATES

The wars of conquest that created the boundaries of the contemporary United States were directed not only against the Native American population but also against Mexico. The territory that later became California, Nevada, Arizona, New Mexico, and Utah—along with a quarter of a million Mexicans—was taken by the United States in 1848 as a result of the American war with Mexico. The terms *Mexican American* and *Chicano* include the descendants of these people, together with subsequent immigrants from Mexico. The term *Latino* refers to anyone from Spanish-speaking regions living in the United States. The words *Latino* and *Hispanic* are often used interchangeably.

The four largest groups of Latinos in the United States today are Mexican Americans (around 34 million), Puerto Ricans (4.9 million), Salvadorans (2 million), and Cubans (2 million). An additional 10.1 million Spanish-speaking residents are from countries in Central and South America (Pew Research Hispanic Trends Project 2014). The Latino population, as mentioned earlier, is increasing at an extraordinary rate—by 53 percent between 1980 and 1990, 58 percent between 1990 and 2000, and almost 10 percent from 2000 to 2010—mainly as a result of the large-scale flow of new immigrants across the Mexican border (U.S. Bureau of the Census 2011g). Latino residents now outnumber African Americans (Pew Research Hispanic Trends Project 2014).

MEXICAN AMERICANS

Mexican Americans reside mainly in California, Texas, and other southwestern states, although there are substantial groups in the Midwest and in northern cities as well. The majority work at low-paying jobs. In the post–World War II period up to the early 1960s, Mexican workers were admitted without much restriction. This was followed by a phase of quotas on legal immigrants and deportations of undocumented immigrants. Today, undocumented immigrants continue to cross the border. Large numbers are intercepted and sent back each year, but most simply try again, and four times as many escape officials as are stopped.

Because Mexico is a relatively poor neighbor of the wealthy United States, this flow of people northward is unlikely to diminish. Undocumented immigrants can be employed more cheaply than other workers, and they perform jobs that most of the rest of the population would not accept. Legislation passed by Congress in 1986 has enabled undocumented immigrants living in the United States for at least five years to claim legal residence.

Mexicans in the United States typically have levels of economic well-being and educational attainment far below that of native-born Americans. As of 2012, 27.8 percent live below the poverty line (Pew Research Hispanic Trends Project 2013). Two-thirds (66 percent) of Mexicans in the United States are proficient in English; however, only around 10 percent hold bachelor's degrees (Pew Research Hispanic Trends Project 2013). Social scientists anticipate that Mexican immigrants and their children may become increasingly assimilated into life in the United States in coming decades, due in part to policies that help them to obtain an affordable college education. As of 2013, fifteen states—including California, Colorado, Connecticut, Illinois, Kansas, Maryland, Minnesota, Nebraska, New Mexico, New York, Oklahoma, Oregon, Texas, Utah, and Washington—have passed laws permitting certain undocumented students who have attended and graduated from their primary and secondary schools to pay in-state tuition at state colleges. In addition, Rhode Island, New Jersey, and Hawaii recently passed legislation that allows certain students, regardless of their immigration status, to pay in-state tuition at the state's public colleges and universities. Given that the majority (58 percent) of undocumented immigrants in the United States hail from Mexico, these policies will have a major impact on the lives of young Mexican immigrants (National Immigration Law Center 2013).

PUERTO RICANS AND CUBANS

Puerto Rico was acquired by the United States through war, and Puerto Ricans have been American citizens since 1917. The island is poor, and many of its inhabitants have migrated to the mainland United States to improve their conditions of life. Puerto Ricans originally settled in New York City, but since the 1960s, they have moved elsewhere. A reverse migration of Puerto Ricans began in the 1970s; more have left the mainland than have arrived over the past three decades. One of the most important issues facing Puerto Rican activists is the political destiny of their homeland. Puerto Rico is at present a commonwealth of the United States. As such, Puerto Ricans residing on the island are U.S. citizens, yet they do not pay federal income tax, nor can they vote for the president of the United States. For years, Puerto Ricans have been divided about whether the island should retain its present status, opt for independence, or attempt to become the fifty-first state of the Union.

A third Latino group in the United States, the Cubans, differs from the two others in key respects. Half a million Cubans fled communism following the rise of Fidel Castro in 1959, and the majority settled in Florida. Unlike other Latino immigrants, they were mainly educated people from white-collar and professional backgrounds. They have managed to thrive within the United States, many finding positions comparable with those they abandoned in Cuba. As a group, Cubans have the highest family income of all Latinos.

A further wave of Cuban immigrants, from less affluent origins, arrived in 1980. Lacking the qualifications held by the first wave, these people tend to live in circumstances closer to those of the rest of the Latino communities in the United States. Both sets of Cuban immigrants are mainly political refugees rather than economic migrants. The later immigrants to a large extent have become the "working class" for the earlier immigrants. They are paid low wages, but Cuban employers tend to take them on in preference to members of other ethnic groups. In Miami, nearly one-third of all businesses are owned by Cubans, and 75 percent of the labor force in construction is Cuban.

THE ASIAN CONNECTION

About 6 percent of the population of the United States is of Asian origin—17.3 million people (Pew Research Center 2012a). Chinese, Filipinos (immigrants from the Philippines), and Asian Indians form the largest groups, but there are also significant numbers of Vietnamese, Koreans, and Japanese living in America. And as a result of the war in Vietnam, some 350,000 refugees from that country entered the United States in the 1970s.

Most of the early Chinese immigrants settled in California, where they were employed mainly in heavy industries such as mining and railroad construction. The retreat of the Chinese into distinct Chinatowns was not primarily their choice, but was made necessary by the hostility they faced.

The early Japanese immigrants also settled in California and the other Pacific states. During World War II, following the attack on Pearl Harbor by Japan, all Japanese Americans in the United States were made to report to "relocation centers," which were effectively concentration camps surrounded by barbed wire and gun turrets. Despite the fact that most of these people were American citizens, they were compelled to live in the hastily established camps for the duration of the war. Paradoxically, this situation eventually led to their greater integration within the wider society, since, following the war, Japanese Americans did not return to the separate neighborhoods in which they had previously lived. They have become extremely successful in reaching high levels of education and income, marginally outstripping whites. The rate of intermarriage of Japanese Americans with whites is now nearly 50 percent.

In this 1942 photo, young Japanese Americans wait for baggage inspection upon arrival at a World War II assembly center in Turlock, California. From here they were transported to one of several internment camps for Japanese Americans.

1. Briefly contrast the migration experiences of African Americans, Latinos, and Asians in the United States.

2. How did the civil rights movement help minority groups achieve equal rights and opportunities?

Following the passage of a new immigration act in 1965, large-scale immigration of Asians into the United States again took place. Foreign-born Chinese Americans today outnumber those brought up in the United States. The newly arrived Chinese have avoided the Chinatowns in which the long-established Chinese have tended to remain, mostly moving into other neighborhoods. ✓

Learn the forms of inequality experienced by different racial and ethnic groups in the United States. Understand how the history of prejudice and discrimination against ethnic minorities has created conditions of hardship for many, while others have succeeded despite societal barriers.

HOW DOES RACIAL AND ETHNIC INEQUALITY AFFECT YOUR LIFE?

Since the civil rights movement of the 1960s, has real progress been made in eliminating racial disparities in life chances? Is racial and ethnic inequality primarily the result of a person's racial or ethnic background or does it reflect a person's class position? In other words, is a black American, for example, more likely to live in poverty because of racial discrimination or because of the lower-class status that many blacks hold? In this section, we will first examine the facts: how racial and ethnic inequality is reflected in terms of educational and occupational attainment, income, health, residential segregation, and political power. We will then look at the divergent social statuses found within the largest racial and ethnic groups. We will conclude by looking at how sociologists have sought to explain racial inequality.

EDUCATIONAL ATTAINMENT

Differences between blacks and whites in levels of educational attainment have decreased, but these seem more the result of long-established trends rather than the direct outcome of the struggles of the 1960s. After steadily improving their levels of educational attainment for the last fifty years, young African Americans are for the first time close to whites in terms of finishing high school. The number of blacks over the age of twenty-five with high school diplomas has increased from about 20 percent in 1960 to 81.9 percent in 2013. By contrast, 90.1 percent of whites have completed high school (U.S. Bureau of the Census 2013f) (Figure 10.2A). Some analysts see this development as a hopeful sign and an indicator that young blacks need not live a life of hopelessness and despair. But not all signs have been positive. While more blacks are attending college now than in the 1960s, a much higher proportion of whites than blacks graduate from college today (Figure 10.2B). The situation is even more dire for black men; throughout the first decade of the twenty-first century, two-thirds of all black college graduates were women (Snyder and Dillow 2010). In today's global economy and job market, which value college degrees, the result is a wide disparity in incomes between whites and blacks.

Another negative trend with potentially far-reaching consequences is the large gap in educational attainment between Latinos and both whites and blacks. Hispanics have by far the highest high school dropout rate of any group in the United States. While rates of college attendance and success in graduation have gradually improved for other groups, the rate for Hispanics has held relatively steady since the mid-1980s. Only 15.1 percent hold a college degree (U.S. Bureau of the Census 2013f).

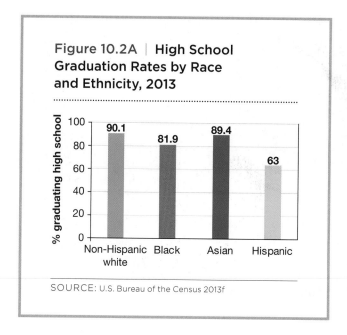

Figure 10.2A | High School Graduation Rates by Race and Ethnicity, 2013

SOURCE: U.S. Bureau of the Census 2013f

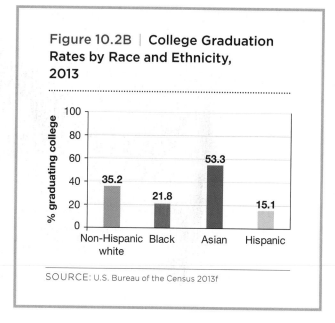

Figure 10.2B | College Graduation Rates by Race and Ethnicity, 2013

SOURCE: U.S. Bureau of the Census 2013f

It is possible that these poor results can be attributed to the large number of poorly educated immigrants from Latin America who have come to the United States in the last two decades. Many of these immigrants have poor English language skills and their children encounter difficulties in schools.

EMPLOYMENT AND INCOME

As a result of the increase in educational attainment, blacks now hold a slightly higher proportion of managerial and professional jobs than in 1960, though still not in proportion to their overall numbers. In 2012, out of the approximately 53.99 million managerial or professional positions in the United States, whites held about 44.42 million (about 82.2 percent); African Americans, about 4.68 million (about 8.7 percent); and Hispanics, about 4.51 million (about 8.4 percent) (U.S. Bureau of Labor Statistics 2013b).

The unemployment rate of black and Hispanic men today outstrips that of whites by the same magnitude as in the early 1960s. The total unemployment rate for blacks and Hispanics is higher than that for whites even in recessionary periods (in 2012, 7.2 percent for whites versus about 13.8 percent for blacks and 10.3 percent for Hispanics) (U.S. Bureau of Labor Statistics 2013d; U.S. Bureau of Labor Statistics 2013e). However, this gap is considerably smaller among more educated persons ages twenty-five and over (the unemployment rates for adults with a bachelor's degree or more are 3.7, 6.3, and 5.1 percent for whites, blacks, and Hispanics, respectively) (U.S. Bureau of Labor Statistics 2013c).

There has also been some debate about whether employment opportunities for minorities have improved or worsened, especially in the wake of the recession that began in 2009. Statistics on unemployment don't adequately measure economic opportunity, since they count only those known to be looking for work. A higher proportion of blacks and Hispanics have simply opted out of the occupational system, neither working nor looking for work. They have become disillusioned by the frustration of searching for employment that is not there. Unemployment figures also do not reflect the increasing numbers of young men from minority groups who have been incarcerated (see also

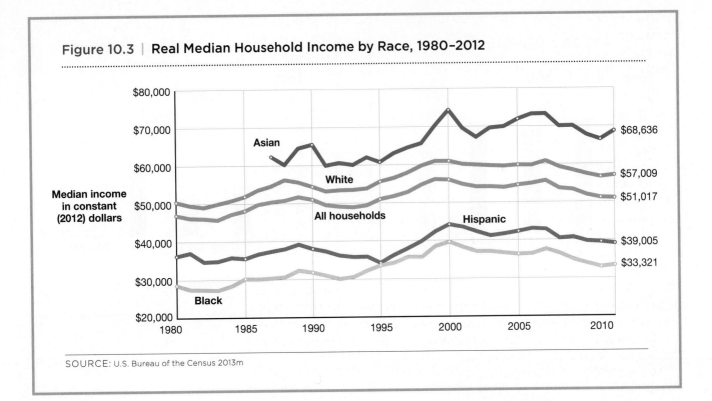

Figure 10.3 | **Real Median Household Income by Race, 1980–2012**

Median income in constant (2012) dollars

$80,000
$70,000 — $68,636
$60,000 — $57,009
$51,017
$50,000
$40,000 — $39,005
$33,321
$30,000
$20,000

Asian

White

All households

Hispanic

Black

1980   1985   1990   1995   2000   2005   2010

SOURCE: U.S. Bureau of the Census 2013m

Chapter 6). Finally, although many new jobs were created during the economic boom of the 1990s, most of them either required a college degree or were in lower-paying service occupations. As we just saw, blacks and Hispanics are underrepresented among college graduates.

Nevertheless, the disparities between the annual earnings of blacks and whites are gradually diminishing. As measured in terms of median weekly income of full-time and salaried workers, black men now earn 75.1 percent of the level of pay of white men (U.S. Bureau of Labor Statistics 2014d). In 1959, the proportion was 49 percent. Black women fare relatively better but still lag behind white women today, earning just 83.9 percent as much. In terms of household family income (adjusted for inflation), blacks are the only social group to have seen an improvement during the 1990s. By 2000, poverty rates for African Americans had fallen to their lowest levels since the government started tracking the figure in 1955, and they continued to improve for much of the decade until the global recession of 2009 when poverty rates began to rise again. In 2011, the poverty rate for all African Americans reached 27.6 percent (U.S. Bureau of the Census 2012n). Even more stark in the recent recessionary era is the black-white gap in wealth; the median household net worth among whites is 17.5 times that of blacks ($110,500 versus $6,314 in 2011) (U.S. Bureau of the Census 2013m).

Though the economic status of blacks appears to have improved, prospects for Hispanics have stagnated or worsened over the same time period (Kochhar, Fry, and Taylor 2011). Between 2000 and 2008, Hispanic household incomes (adjusted for inflation) decreased significantly. Still, Hispanic household poverty remained very similar to that of blacks. In 2012, the poverty rate for Hispanics was 25.6 percent versus 27.2 percent for blacks (U.S. Bureau of the Census 2013m). The large influx of immigrants, who tend to be poor, has caused some of the decline in average income, but even among Hispanics born in the United States, income levels declined as well. As one Latino group leader commented, "Most Hispanic residents are caught in jobs like gardener, nanny, and restaurant worker that will never pay well and from which they will never advance" (quoted in Goldberg 1997). As a result, Hispanic households lag far behind white households; in 2011, the median white household wealth was fourteen times that of Hispanics ($110,500 versus $7,683) (U.S. Bureau of the Census 2013m).

HEALTH

A team of social scientists surveyed the evidence linking health to racial and economic inequalities. After studying data for a number of different countries, including the United States, they concluded that for people in the poorest 20 percent of the income distribution, death rates were 1.5–2.5 times those of the highest 20 percent of income earners (Najman 1993). In the United States, the rate of infant mortality for the poorest 20 percent was four times higher than for the wealthiest 20 percent (Najman 1993). When differences were measured between the wealthiest whites and the poorest African Americans, the contrast in infant mortality rates was even higher—five times higher for blacks than for whites. The race gap in infant mortality has been increasing rather than decreasing in recent years. The same is true of life expectancy—the average age to which individuals at birth can expect to live. In 2007, whites on average could expect to live 3.8 years longer than African Americans (National Center for Health Statistics 2013).

How might the influence of poverty and ethnicity on health be countered? Extensive programs of health education and disease prevention are one possibility. Michelle Obama's Let's Move program, for example, recognizes that high rates of obesity among poor ethnic minorities are harmful, and seeks to bring exercise and healthy food programs to poorer communities. However, some skeptics argue that such "healthy living" programs tend to work better among more prosperous, well-educated groups and in any case usually produce only small changes in behavior. Increased accessibility to health services would help, but probably to a limited degree. The only really effective policy option, it is argued, would be to attack poverty itself, so as to reduce the income gap between rich and poor (Najman 1993).

RESIDENTIAL SEGREGATION

Neighborhood segregation seems to have declined little over the past quarter-century. Studies show that discriminatory practices toward black and white clients in the housing market continue (Pager and Shepard 2008). Black and white children now attend the same schools in most rural areas of the South and in many of the smaller- and medium-size cities throughout the country. Most black college students now also go to the same colleges and universities as whites, instead of the traditional all-black institutions (Journal of Blacks in Higher Education 2007). Yet in the larger cities a high level of educational segregation persists as a result of the continuing movement of whites to suburbs or rural environs.

In *American Apartheid* (1993), Douglas Massey and Nancy A. Denton argue that the history of racial segregation and its specific urban form, the black ghetto, are responsible for the perpetuation of black poverty and the continued polarization of black and white. The persistence of segregation, they say, is not a result of impersonal market forces. Even many middle-class blacks still find themselves segregated from white society. For them, as for poor blacks, this becomes a self-perpetuating cycle. Affluent blacks who can afford to live in comfortable, predominantly white neighborhoods may deliberately choose not to because of the struggle for acceptance

What *Are* You, Anyway?

The number of Americans who identify as multiracial has increased dramatically over the past decade and will continue to increase in the future as more and more young adults marry and have children with partners of a race different from their own. As we learned earlier in this chapter, multiracial individuals and families challenge us to reexamine the ways we think about race. What does a "black" person look like? What does a "Latino" person look like? Is it even possible to determine one's racial identity based on his or her physical features?

Developed by the Race Awareness Project, the Guess My Race app was designed to help users better understand and question the complexities of race. Guess My Race is a game where a user is presented with ten photos of peoples' faces. For each photo, users are asked to click the one answer (of six possible options) that they believe best describes the person in the picture. The app then reveals the "correct" answer, which is accompanied by a quote from the person explaining why the person identifies as he or she does. For example, one user explained, "I consider myself African American, . . . but most people think I'm Asian because of the shape of my eyes." Readers are then directed to more information about the history of race identity in the United States and throughout the world, as well as demographic information based on the 2010 Census. According to the app's website, the program was developed to challenge users' assumptions about individuals, and about race (Cambridge Diversity Consulting 2013). The app's creators, cultural anthropologist Michael Baran and children's game designer Michael Handelman, believe that the app will demonstrate how "something that is considered natural and biological is actually a result of complex historical and cultural constructions" (Cambridge Diversity Consulting 2013).

Baran also believes it is important for app users to interrogate the concept of whiteness. Although many people who are light-complexioned may believe they are simply "white," and that the issue of race does not apply to them, Guess My Race gives users six different options for people who appear to be white—often capturing different ways that whiteness is discussed, such as "elite" or "redneck" (Latour 2011).

Both consumer reviews of the game and assessments by race scholars have been largely positive, noting that the game forces users to think about the complexities of race, to challenge their own assumptions about what different races "look like," and to learn about the history of racial stratification in the United States. One user criticized the app on the grounds that it conflated race with ethnicity; for example, one of the options included along with a photo of a white person was the adjective *Polish*, which is technically an ethnicity rather than a race (Matthews 2011). However, most believe that the app is a clever way to reveal how race is socially constructed. What do you think? What race or races do you identify with, and why? Do you think that app users looking at your photograph would correctly identify your self-perceived racial identity? Why or why not?

Apps like What Race Am I? show the fluidity and complexity of racial identity.

they know they would face. The black ghetto, the authors conclude, was constructed through a series of well-defined institutional practices of racial discrimination—private behavior and public policies by which whites sought to contain growing urban black populations. Until policymakers, social scientists, and private citizens recognize the crucial role of such institutional discrimination in perpetuating urban poverty and racial injustice, the United States will remain a deeply divided and troubled society.

POLITICAL POWER

Barack Obama made history when he was elected the first black president of the United States in 2008. His election is part of a larger trend of blacks making tremendous gains in holding elective offices; the number of black public officials increased from 40 in 1960 to 9,101 in 2000 and more than 10,500 in 2010 (Bositis 2001; Joint Center for Political and Economic Studies 2011). The numbers of black mayors and judges have increased appreciably. Blacks have been voted into every major political office, including in districts where white voters predominate. In 1992, after congressional districts were reshaped to give minority candidates more opportunity, a record number of African Americans and Latinos were elected to Congress. Yet these changes are still relatively small scale; in all of its history, the United States has elected only nine black senators. The share of representation that Latinos and African Americans have in Congress is not proportional to their overall numbers in American society. Currently there are forty-four black members of Congress; following the defeat of Senator Carol Moseley-Braun in 1998, the U.S. Senate had no black members until Barack Obama was elected to represent Illinois in 2004. Currently, Tim Scott of South Carolina and Cory Booker of New Jersey are the only black members of the U.S. Senate (U.S. House of Representatives 2013a). In addition, thirty-five Latinos currently serve in the U.S. House and Senate (U.S. House of Representatives 2013b).

Barack Obama became the first African American president of the United States in the historic election of 2008.

GENDER AND RACE

The status of minority women in the United States is especially plagued by inequalities. Gender and race discrimination combined make it particularly difficult for these women to escape conditions of poverty. They share the legacy of past discrimination against members of minority groups and women in general. Until about twenty-five years ago, most minority women worked in low-paying occupations such as household work, farm work, or low-wage manufacturing jobs. Changes in the law and gains in education have allowed for more minority women to enter white-collar professions, and their economic and occupational status has improved.

Between 1979 and 2009, inflation-adjusted earnings of black women grew by 25 percent, but this increase lagged behind that of white women, who experienced a 32 percent increase in earnings during the same period (U.S. Bureau of Labor Statistics 2011a). Although women have made strides in earnings in the past three decades, stark race and gender earnings disparities persist. In 2013, among full-time workers, white women earned about 81.7 percent as much as their male counterparts, Hispanic women about 91.1 percent, and black

Figure 10.4 | Median Weekly Earnings by Race and Sex, 2013*

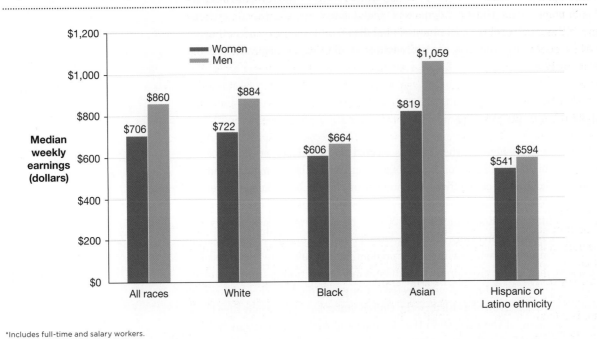

*Includes full-time and salary workers.

SOURCE: U.S. Bureau of Labor Statistics 2014d

women had earnings that were about 91.3 percent of their male counterparts'. In actual dollars, black women who worked full time earned just $606 per week in 2013, compared with $722 for white women, $664 for black men, and $884 for white men (Figure 10.4) (U.S. Bureau of Labor Statistics 2014d).

However unequal their status and pay, minority women play a critical role in their communities. They are often the major or sole wage earners in their families. As we saw earlier, black women are much more likely than their male counterparts to graduate from college. Yet their incomes are not always sufficient to maintain a family. About half of all families headed by African American or Latino women live at poverty levels.

DIVERGENT FORTUNES

When we survey the development and current position of the major ethnic groups in America, one conclusion that emerges is that they have achieved varying levels of success. Whereas successive waves of European immigrants managed to overcome most of the prejudice and discrimination they originally faced and become assimilated into the wider society, other groups have not. These latter groups include two minorities who have lived in North America for centuries, Native Americans and African Americans, as well as Mexicans and Puerto Ricans.

THE ECONOMIC DIVIDE WITHIN THE
AFRICAN AMERICAN COMMUNITY

The situation of blacks is the most conspicuous case of divergent fortunes. A division has opened up between the minority of blacks who have obtained white-collar, managerial, or professional jobs—who form a small black middle class—and the majority, whose living conditions have not improved. In 1960, most of the nonmanual-labor jobs open to blacks were those serving the black community—a small proportion of blacks could work as teachers, social workers, or, less often, lawyers or doctors. No more than about 13 percent of blacks held white-collar jobs, compared with 44 percent of whites. Although there has been significant progress in the fortunes of blacks over the past five decades, pronounced racial differences persist. For example, in 2013, African Americans were still underrepresented in white-collar jobs. Although blacks accounted for roughly 12.9 percent of the U.S. population, they held 8.5 percent of all managerial, professional, or related occupations and 11.8 percent of all sales and office occupations (U.S. Bureau of Labor Statistics 2014c).

THE ASIAN SUCCESS STORY

Unlike African Americans, other minority groups have outlasted the open prejudice and discrimination they once faced. The changing fate of Asians in the United States is especially remarkable. Until about half a century ago, the level of prejudice and discrimination experienced by the Chinese and Japanese in North America was greater than for any other group of nonblack immigrants. Since that time, Asian Americans have achieved a steadily increasing prosperity and no longer face the same levels of antagonism from the white community. The median income of Asian Americans is now actually higher than that of whites.

This statistic conceals some big discrepancies between and within different Asian groups; there are still many Asian Americans, including those whose families have resided in the United States for generations, who live in poverty. For example, in 2012, the overall poverty rate among Asians was 11.7 percent. Rates varied widely, though, from just under 10 percent among Japanese to 38 percent among Hmong, an ethnic group from Laos and surrounding areas (U.S. Bureau of the Census 2013o). However, the turnaround in the fortunes of Asian Americans is on the whole so impressive that some have referred to the Asian American "success story" as a prime example of what minorities can achieve in the United States.

LATINOS: A TALE OF TWO CITIES

Miami and Los Angeles both have substantial Latino populations. In Los Angeles, the large majority of Latinos are well down the ladder of privilege and power. But even though both cities experience ethnic tensions, in Miami, Latinos have achieved a position of economic and political prominence not found elsewhere.

In Miami, those of Cuban origin have often moved into positions of considerable influence. Some Cubans have become very successful in business and have become wealthier than the "old" white families that once ran the city. They haven't been assimilated into the white community but maintain their own customs, institutions, and language. Miami is now a place of "parallel structures" existing alongside one another, each including powerful and wealthy people, not integrated into one unified group. There is much tension, but some Anglo and Cuban politicians now speak of Miami as the capital of the Caribbean—a city not only part of the United States but also looking to the other societies, mostly developing countries, surrounding it.

Los Angeles has been referred to as "the capital of the Third World" because of its large Latino and Asian populations. The city already contained the largest group of Mexicans in the United States in the 1920s. Then, as now, it was Mexicans who

Hundreds of thousands of people marched in Los Angeles on May 1, 2006, to demand basic rights for immigrants.

performed most of the menial jobs. Then, as now, most Anglos "were at once aware that this was the case," and "yet they would act as if these people, once they had finished working, went home not to the Old Plaza or, as now, to East L.A., but to another planet" (Rieff 1991).

UNDERSTANDING RACIAL INEQUALITY

What distinguishes less fortunate groups such as African Americans and Mexican Americans is not just that they are nonwhite, but that they were originally present in America as colonized peoples rather than willing immigrants. In a classic analysis, Robert Blauner (1972) suggested that a sharp distinction should be drawn between groups that journeyed voluntarily to settle in the new land and those that were incorporated into the society through force or violence. Native Americans are part of American society as a result of military conquest; African Americans were transported in the slave trade; Puerto Rico was colonized as a result of war; and Mexicans were originally incorporated as a result of the conquest of the Southwest by the United States in the nineteenth century. These groups have consistently been the target of racism, which both reflects and perpetuates their separation from other ethnic communities.

But, given that this has been the case for most of American history, what explains the growth of the black middle class? William Julius Wilson (1978; see also Wilson et al. 1987) has argued that race is of diminishing importance in explaining inequalities between whites and blacks. In his view, these inequalities are now based on class rather than skin color. The old racist barriers are crumbling. What remain are inequalities similar to those affecting all lower-class groups.

Are racial inequalities to be explained primarily in terms of class? It is true that racial divisions provide a means of social closure, whereby economic resources can be monopolized by privileged class groups. But the argument that racial inequality should be explained primarily in terms of class domination has never been a satisfactory one. Ethnic discrimination, particularly of a racial kind, is partly independent of class differences: The one cannot be separated from the other.

As we look to the future, scholars continue to debate whether racial inequalities and boundaries will persist or diminish. Most agree that the trend we saw earlier in this chapter, the steady increase in the multiracial population, will have powerful implications for race relations in America. However, whether the implications will be positive or negative remains to be seen. Despite the vitriol triggered by the images of a multiracial family in the Cheerios ad campaign discussed in the chapter opener, optimists believe that intermarriage is an essential step toward transcending race, erasing prejudice and bigotry. Pessimists, however, say that the growth in number and political power of multiracial Americans may lead to even more race stratification and will hurt minority groups, especially African Americans (Saulny 2011).

These questions have no easy answers, as we can see from the words of Laura Wood and Michelle López-Mullins, the University of Maryland students whom we met earlier in this chapter. When asked about their views on race in the United States, Wood said, "I don't want a color-blind society at all. I just want both my races to be acknowledged." López-Mullins, however, said, "I want mine not to matter." ✓

> ## CONCEPT CHECKS ✓
>
> 1. What are some of the main reasons there is a large gap in educational attainment between Hispanics and blacks in the United States?
>
> 2. How do Massey and Denton explain the persistence of residential segregation?
>
> 3. Some sociologists argue that racial inequalities should be explained in terms of class rather than race. What are some of the problems associated with social class–based explanations of racial inequalities?

THE BIG PICTURE

KEY CONCEPTS

EXERCISES:
Thinking Sociologically

1. Review the discussion of the assimilation of different American minorities, and then write a short essay comparing the different assimilation experiences of Asians and Latinos. In your essay identify the criteria for assimilation and discuss which group has assimilated most readily. Then explain the sociological reasons for the difference in assimilation between these two groups.

2. Does affirmative action still have a future in the United States? On the one hand, increasing numbers of African Americans have joined the middle class by earning college degrees, professional jobs, and new homes. Yet blacks are still far more likely than

Chapter 10

Ethnicity and Race

whites to live in poverty, to attend poor schools, and to lack economic opportunity. Given these differences and other contrasts mentioned in the text, do we still need affirmative action?

3. How would you explain the rise in intermarriage witnessed in the United States in recent years? What do you think the implications are of the growing mixed-race population in the United States? Will it lead to more or less racial stratification and prejudice?

p.293 — **What Are Race and Ethnicity?**

Learn the cultural bases of race and ethnicity and how racial and ethnic differences create sharp divisions in society. Learn the leading psychological theories and sociological interpretations of prejudice and discrimination.

p.297 — **How Do Ethnic Groups Coexist and Compete?**

Recognize the importance of the historical roots, particularly in the expansion of Western colonialism, of ethnic conflict. Understand the different models for a multiethnic society.

p.300 — **Why Do Ethnic Groups Migrate?**

Understand global migration patterns and their impact.

p.303 — **How Do Ethnic Minorities Experience Life in the United States?**

Familiarize yourself with the history and social dimensions of ethnic relations in America.

p.312 — **How Does Racial and Ethnic Inequality Affect Your Life?**

Learn the forms of inequality experienced by different racial and ethnic groups in the United States. Understand how the history of prejudice and discrimination against ethnic minorities has created conditions of hardship for many, while others have succeeded despite societal barriers.

ethnicity • race • theory of racial formation • racialization • scientific racism• racism • institutional racism • prejudice • discrimination • stereotype • displacement • scapegoat • minority group • dominant group

1. Explain the difference between ethnicity and race.
2. What does the term *racialization* refer to?
3. How does prejudice operate in society?
4. Why are Hispanics and African Americans considered to be minority groups in American society?

genocide • segregation • assimilation • melting pot • pluralism • multiculturalism

1. What are three reasons racism has flourished in the United States?
2. Compare and contrast three forms of ethnic conflicts.
3. What is the difference between assimilation and melting pot strategies of ethnic integration?

1. According to Castles and Miller, which four trends characterize current and future migration?
2. What is diaspora? Explain the role diasporas play in preserving ethnic culture in contemporary societies.

refugee • immigration • emigration • diaspora

1. Briefly contrast the migration experiences of African Americans, Latinos, and Asians in the United States.
2. How did the civil rights movement help minority groups achieve equal rights and opportunities?

1. What are some of the main reasons there is a large gap in educational attainment between Hispanics and blacks in the United States?
2. How do Massey and Denton explain the persistence of residential segregation?
3. Some sociologists argue that racial inequalities should be explained in terms of class rather than race. What are some of the problems associated with social class-based explanations of racial inequalities?

11

Families and Intimate Relationships

THE BIG QUESTIONS

HOW DO SOCIOLOGICAL THEORIES CHARACTERIZE FAMILIES?
Review the development of sociological thinking about families and family life.

HOW HAVE FAMILIES CHANGED OVER TIME?
Understand how families have changed over the last 300 years. See that although a diversity of family forms exists in different societies today, widespread changes are occurring that relate to the spread of globalization.

WHAT DO MARRIAGE AND FAMILY IN THE UNITED STATES LOOK LIKE TODAY?
Learn about patterns of marriage, childbearing, and divorce. Analyze how different these patterns are today compared with other periods.

WHY DOES FAMILY VIOLENCE HAPPEN?
Learn about sexual abuse and violence within families.

HOW DO NEW FAMILY FORMS AFFECT YOUR LIFE?
Learn some alternatives to traditional marriage and family patterns that are becoming more widespread.

Edith Windsor, plaintiff in the *United States v. Windsor* case, celebrates the Supreme Court's decision to overturn the Defense of Marriage Act.

In the early 1960s, Edith Windsor was a young woman living and working in New York. With her master's degree in math from New York University, she was the rare woman working at IBM as a computer programmer. Edith was also a woman in love. She had met Thea Spyer, a clinical psychologist, at Portofino, a restaurant in New York's Greenwich Village that was a popular hangout for gay women. After several years of dating, Thea proposed to Edith in 1967, offering her a brooch, rather than an engagement ring, to symbolize their commitment. Even though Thea and Edith couldn't legally marry at that time, they went on to live together as a loving couple for more than four decades.

In 2007, Thea's health declined, and doctors told the couple that Thea had only a short time to live. The couple wanted to formalize their union before Thea died, so they promptly flew to Toronto, Canada—one of relatively few places where a same-sex couple could marry—and tied the knot. Just two years later, Thea died (Gabbatt 2013).

Edith, then eighty years old and widowed with health problems of her own, soon learned that the IRS was ordering her to pay $363,053 in federal estate taxes on her inheritance from Thea. Edith—knowing full well that heterosexual couples who were legally married did not have to pay a comparable tax—was angry at the injustice.

family • A group of individuals related to one another by blood ties, marriage, or adoption, who form an economic unit, the adult members of which are often responsible for the upbringing of children. All known societies involve some form of family system, although the nature of family relationships varies widely.

kinship • A relation that links individuals through blood ties, marriage, or adoption.

Married couples, according to the federal tax code, are allowed to transfer money or property from spouse to spouse upon death without having to pay estate taxes—a rule referred to as "unlimited marital deduction" (Coplan 2011). Although the state of New York, where Edith lived, recognized her marriage to Thea, the federal government refused to treat them the same way as other married couples because of a federal law called the Defense of Marriage Act (DOMA), which defines marriage as "a legal union between one man and one woman." This injustice impelled Edith to challenge the constitutionality of DOMA and seek a refund of the estate tax she had been forced to pay. In 2010, Edith sued the national government.

In June 2013, after more than two years of appeals and legal red tape, the U.S. Supreme Court declared DOMA to be unconstitutional in the landmark *United States v. Windsor*. The ruling means that married same-sex couples must receive the same federal benefits, rights, and privileges afforded to all other Americans. Gay marriage celebrated another big victory that day when the Supreme Court cleared the way for same-sex marriage in California. Until same-sex marriage is legal in every state in the nation, however, uncertainty remains about the extent to which such couples will receive federal marital-based protections nationwide (Reilly and Siddiqui 2013). However, the overturning of DOMA marked a critical turning point in U.S. history, and will have vast implications for same-sex couples.

Our choices about dating, marriage, cohabitation, childbearing, and divorce may seem highly personal and based on our desire for love and companionship, or adventure and freedom. Yet sociologists recognize that our choices are powerfully shaped by social structures like laws. Whether, when, and under what conditions Edith and Thea could marry were dictated by law. Yet cultural factors, including social norms and subcultural or religious beliefs, also shape our decisions regarding our family lives, as well as our attitudes toward others' families. For example, while the majority of Americans today support gay marriage, these attitudes vary widely by one's generation, religious views, and even geographic region. Two-thirds of those born after 1981 support the legalization of gay marriage, whereas just 35 percent of those born between 1928 and 1945 do so. While just 23 percent of evangelical Christians support gay marriage, three-quarters of persons who are unaffiliated with religious organizations support same-sex marriage (Pew Research Center for the People and the Press 2013a). Understanding families in contemporary society requires a sociological imagination that takes into account both personal preferences as well as the powerful impact of social structures and cultural beliefs.

Sociological research on the family typically involves descriptive or scientific studies that aim to solve some of the most interesting puzzles about marriage and family in the contemporary world. Taken together, the work of these researchers is fascinating and demonstrates that sociology can give us insights that are by no means obvious.

BASIC CONCEPTS

Before delving into questions about why and how people form their families, some basic concepts require review. A **family** is a group of persons directly linked by kin connections, the adult members of which assume responsibility for caring for children. **Kinship**

Edith Windsor holds a photo of Thea Spyer: "If Thea had been Theo, I would have had to pay no estate tax whatsoever."

(a) An extended Kazak family in Mongolia. Kazaks usually live in extended families and collectively herd their livestock. The youngest son will inherit the father's house, and the elder sons will build their own houses close by when they get married. (b) Parents wait for the train with their daughter. How is a nuclear family different from an extended family?

refers to connections among individuals, typically established either through marriage or through the lines of descent that connect blood relatives (mothers, fathers, offspring, grandparents, etc.). **Marriage** can be defined as a socially and legally acknowledged and approved sexual union between two adult individuals. When two people marry, they become kin to each other; the marriage bond also, however, connects together a wider range of kinspeople. Parents, brothers, sisters, and other blood relatives become relatives of the partner through marriage.

In virtually all societies, sociologists and anthropologists have documented the presence of the **nuclear family**, two adults living together in a household with biological or adopted children. In most traditional societies, the nuclear family was part of a larger kinship network of some type. When close relatives in addition to a married couple and children live either in the same household or in a close and continuous relationship with one another, we speak of an **extended family**. An extended family might, for example, include grandparents, brothers and their wives, sisters and their husbands, aunts, and nephews.

Families also can be divided into **families of orientation** and **families of procreation**. The first is the family into which a person is born or adopted; the second is the family into which one enters as an adult and within which a new generation of children is brought up. A further important distinction concerns place of residence. In the United States, when a couple forms a permanent union, they are usually expected to set up an independent household, separate from either partner's family of orientation. This can be in the same region in which one of the partner's parents live, but may be in some different town or city altogether. In some other societies, however, everyone who marries or forms a permanent partnership is expected to live close to or within the same dwelling as the parents of one of the two partners. When the couple lives near or with the bride's parents, the arrangement is called **matrilocal**. In a **patrilocal** pattern, the couple lives near or with the parents of the groom.

In Western societies, marriage, and therefore family, is associated with **monogamy**. It is illegal for a man or woman to be married to more than one individual at any one time. But in many parts of the world, monogamy is far less common than it is in Western nations. In his classic research, George Murdock (1967, 1981) compared several hundred societies from 1960 through 1980 and found that

marriage • A socially and legally approved sexual relationship between two individuals.

nuclear family • A family group consisting of an adult or adult couple and their dependent children.

extended family • A family group consisting of more than two generations of relatives.

family of orientation • The family into which an individual is born or adopted.

family of procreation • The family an individual initiates through marriage or by having children.

matrilocal family • A family system in which the husband is expected to live near the wife's parents.

patrilocal family • A family system in which the wife is expected to live near the husband's parents.

monogamy • A form of marriage in which each married partner is allowed only one spouse at any given time.

polygamy • A form of marriage in which a person may have two or more spouses simultaneously.

polygyny • A form of marriage in which a man may have two or more wives simultaneously.

polyandry • A form of marriage in which a woman may have two or more husbands simultaneously.

polygamy, a marriage that allows a husband or wife to have more than one spouse, was permitted in over 80 percent (see also Gray 1998). There are two types of polygamy: **polygyny**, in which a man may be married to more than one woman at the same time, and **polyandry**, much less common, in which a woman may have two or more husbands simultaneously. Of the 1,231 societies tracked, Murdock found that just 15 percent of societies were monogamous, 37 percent had occasional polygyny, 48 percent had more frequent polygyny, and less than 1 percent had polyandry (Murdock 1981).

Review the development of sociological thinking about families and family life.

HOW DO SOCIOLOGICAL THEORIES CHARACTERIZE FAMILIES?

Sociologists with diverse theoretical orientations have studied family life. Many of the perspectives that prevailed just a few decades ago now seem much less convincing in the light of recent research and important changes in the social world. Nevertheless it is valuable to trace briefly the evolution of sociological thinking before turning to contemporary approaches to studying families.

FUNCTIONALISM

The functionalist perspective sees society as a set of social institutions that perform specific functions to ensure continuity and consensus. According to this perspective, families perform important tasks that contribute to society's basic needs and help to perpetuate the existence of major social institutions and practices. Sociologists working in the functionalist tradition have regarded the nuclear family as fulfilling certain specialized roles in modern societies. With the advent of industrialization, families became less important as a unit of economic production and more focused on reproduction, child rearing, and socialization.

According to the American sociologist Talcott Parsons, the family's two main functions are *primary socialization* and *personality stabilization* (Parsons and Bales 1955). **Primary socialization** is the process by which young children learn the cultural norms of the society into which they are born. **Personality stabilization** refers to the role that families play in assisting adult family members emotionally. Marriage is the arrangement through which adult personalities are supported and kept healthy. In industrial society, the role of the family in stabilizing adult personalities is said to be critical. This is because the nuclear family is often distanced from its extended kin and is unable to draw on larger kinship ties as families could before industrialization.

Parsons regarded the nuclear family as the unit best equipped to handle the demands of industrial society. In the "conventional family," one adult can work outside the home while the second adult cares for the home and children. In practical terms, this specialization of roles within the nuclear family involved the husband adopting the "instrumental" role as breadwinner and the wife assuming the "affective," emotional role in domestic settings.

Parsons's view of the family is now widely regarded by sociologists as inadequate and outdated. Functionalist theories of families have come under heavy

primary socialization • The process by which children learn the cultural norms of the society into which they are born. Primary socialization occurs largely in the family.

personality stabilization • According to the theory of functionalism, the family plays a crucial role in assisting its adult members emotionally. Marriage between adults is the arrangement through which adult personalities are supported and kept healthy.

criticism for justifying the domestic division of labor between men and women as something natural and unproblematic. Moreover, functionalist perspectives presume that a male-female married couple is essential for the successful rearing of children and for the efficient operation of households; Parsons failed to consider that same-sex and single-parent families may run efficiently and effectively parent and socialize their children. Yet Parsons's views reflect the historical period in which he was living and working. The immediate post–World War II years were a period when same-sex relationships were hidden if not outright illegal in some parts of the United States. Divorce and single parenthood were relatively rare, and often stigmatized. This era also saw women returning to their traditional domestic roles and men reassuming positions as sole breadwinners. We can criticize functionalist views of the family on other grounds, however. In emphasizing the importance of families in performing certain functions, Parsons and other functionalist theorists neglect the role that other social institutions—such as government, media, and schools—play in socializing children. Functionalist theories also neglect variations in family forms that do not correspond to the model of the nuclear family. Families that did not conform to the white, suburban, middle-class "ideal" were seen as deviant.

FEMINIST APPROACHES

For many people, families provide a vital source of solace and comfort, love and companionship. Yet the family can also be a locus for exploitation, loneliness, and profound inequality. Feminism has had a great impact on sociology by challenging the vision of the family as a harmonious and egalitarian realm. In the 1960s, one of the first dissenting voices was that of the American feminist Betty Friedan, who wrote of "the problem with no name"—the isolation and boredom that gripped many suburban American housewives, who felt relegated to an endless cycle of child care and housework.

During the 1970s and 1980s, feminist perspectives dominated most debates and research on families. If previously the sociology of family had focused on family structures, the historical development of the nuclear and extended family, and the importance of kinship ties, feminism succeeded in directing attention inside families to examine the experiences of women in the domestic sphere. Many feminist writers have questioned the vision of the family as a cooperative unit based on common interests and mutual support. They have sought to show that the presence of unequal power relationships within families means that certain family members tend to benefit more than others.

Feminist writings have emphasized a broad spectrum of topics, but three main themes are of particular importance. One of the central concerns is the *domestic division of labor*—the way in which tasks are allocated among members of a household. Feminist sociologists have undertaken studies on the way domestic tasks, such as child care and housework, are shared between men and women. Findings have shown that women continue to bear the main responsibility for domestic tasks and enjoy less leisure time than men, despite the fact that more women are working in paid employment outside the home than ever before (Bianchi et al. 2007; Hochschild and Machung 1989). However, in same-sex couples, partners tend to share housework more equally than do heterosexual couples, showing the complex ways that gender shapes household arrangements (Goldberg, Smith, and Perry-Jenkin 2012).

Pursuing a related theme, some sociologists have examined the contrasting realms of paid and unpaid work, focusing on the contribution that women's unpaid domestic labor makes to the overall economy (Oakley 1974). Others have investigated the way in which resources are distributed among family members and the patterns of access to and control over household finances (Pahl 1989; United Nations 2009).

Second, feminists have drawn attention to the *unequal power relationships* that exist within many families. One topic that has received increased attention as a result of this is the phenomenon of domestic violence. Wife battering, marital rape, incest, and the sexual abuse of children have all received more public attention as a result of feminists' claims that the violent and abusive sides of family life have long been ignored in both academic contexts and legal and policy circles. Feminist sociologists have sought to understand how families serve as an arena for gender oppression and even physical abuse. For example, through much of U.S. history, a husband had the legal right to engage his wife in coerced or forced sex. As recently as 1970, marital rape was legal in the United States. Due in large part to efforts of feminist activists and scholars, marital rape became illegal in all fifty states in 1993 (Hines, Malley-Morrison, and Dutton 2012).

The study of *caring activities* is a third area in which feminists have made important contributions. This is a broad realm that encompasses a variety of processes, from child care to elder care. Sometimes caring means simply being attuned to someone else's psychological well-being—several feminist writers have been interested in "emotion work" within relationships. Not only do women tend to shoulder concrete tasks such as cleaning and child care, but they also invest large amounts of emotional labor in maintaining personal relationships (Duncombe and Marsden 1993). While caring activities are grounded in love and deep emotion, they are also a form of work that demands an ability to listen, perceive, negotiate, and act creatively. Caring work also happens outside of the family; thousands of women find work in jobs that require giving care to others. Ironically, jobs that involve caring, such as child-care worker, nanny, or elderly companion, are among the lowest paid of all occupations, and such jobs are typically held by women of color and immigrants in the United States (Macdonald 2011; Rodriquez 2011).

NEW PERSPECTIVES IN THE SOCIOLOGY OF FAMILY

In the past decade, an important body of sociological literature on families has emerged that draws on feminist perspectives but is not strictly informed by them. Of primary concern are the larger transformations that are taking place in family forms—the formation and dissolution of families and households and the evolving expectations within individuals' personal relationships. The rise in divorce and single parenting, the emergence of "reconstituted families" and gay families, and the popularity of cohabitation are all subjects of concern among conservative political and religious groups. Yet these transformations cannot be understood apart from the larger changes occurring in our society. Attention must be paid to the shifts occurring at the societal, and even global, level if we are to grasp the link between personal transformations and larger patterns of change. ✓

CONCEPT CHECKS ✓

1. According to the functionalist perspective, what are two main functions of families?

2. According to feminist perspectives, what three aspects of family life are sources of concern? Why are these three aspects troubling to feminists?

HOW HAVE FAMILIES CHANGED OVER TIME?

Understand how families have changed over the last 300 years. See that although a diversity of family forms exist in different societies today, widespread changes are occurring that relate to the spread of globalization.

Sociologists once thought that prior to the modern period, the extended or multigenerational family was the predominant family form in Western Europe. Research has shown this view to be mistaken. The nuclear family seems long to have been preeminent. Premodern household size was larger than it is today, but the difference is not especially great. In the United States, for example, throughout the seventeenth, eighteenth, and nineteenth centuries, the average household size was 4.75 persons. The current average is 2.6 (U.S. Bureau of the Census 2013i). This low number is partly due to the high proportion of Americans who live alone today, especially older widowed women and young professionals who maintain their own homes. Since the earlier figure includes domestic servants, the difference in family size is small.

Further, more Americans are living in multigenerational households today than ever before. In 2008, a record 49 million Americans, or 16.1 percent of the total population, lived in a family household that contained at least two adult generations or a grandparent and at least one other generation, according to a Pew Research Center analysis of Census data (Pew Social & Demographic Trends 2010). This pattern is caused partly by the economic recession and home foreclosures that force families to live together. The large and growing immigrant population and the rising number of single or divorced parents who reside with their own parents also have contributed to the growing trend of extended family residence. Finally, the number of grandparents living with and raising their grandchildren has increased steadily since the 1990s. These households are often referred to as "skip-generation" households because the "middle" generation (parents) is not present. Social problems like the HIV/AIDS epidemic and "three strikes" policies, which put a disproportionate number of young African American men in jail, created a context where the young children of the deceased or imprisoned would go to live with their grandmothers (Baker, Silverstein, and Putney 2008).

"THE WAY WE NEVER WERE": MYTHS OF THE TRADITIONAL FAMILY

Was the family of the past as peaceful and harmonious as many people recall it, or is this simply an idealized fiction? As Stephanie Coontz points out in her book *The Way We Never Were* (1992), as with other visions of a golden age of the past, the rosy light shed on the "traditional family" dissolves when we look back to previous times to see what things were really like.

Popular lore depicts the family of colonial America as disciplined and stable, the ideal arrangement. However, colonial families suffered from the same disintegrative forces as their counterparts in Europe. Especially high death rates meant that the average length of marriages was less than twelve years, and more than half of all children saw the death of at least one parent by the time they were twenty-one. The admired discipline of the colonial family was rooted in the strict authority of parents over their children. The way in which this authority was exercised would be considered exceedingly harsh by today's standards.

The classic television show *Father Knows Best* ran from 1954 to 1963. The show featured a stay-at-home mother, breadwinner father, and three children.

In the Victorian period, wives were more or less forcibly confined to the home. According to Victorian morality, women were supposed to be strictly virtuous, while men were sexually licentious: Many visited prostitutes and paid regular visits to brothels. Spouses often had little to do with each other, communicating only through their children. Moreover, domesticity wasn't even an option for poorer groups of this period. African American slaves in the South lived and worked in what were frequently appalling conditions. In the factories and workshops of the North, families worked long hours with little time for home life. Child labor was also rampant in these groups.

Our most recent memory draws us to the 1950s as the time of the ideal American family. This was a period when large numbers of white middle-class women worked only in the home, while men were responsible for earning a family wage. Yet large numbers of women didn't actually want to retreat to a purely domestic role and felt unfulfilled and trapped. Women had held paid jobs during World War II as part of the war effort. They lost these jobs when men returned from the war. Moreover, men were still emotionally removed from their wives and often exercised a strong sexual double standard, seeking sexual adventures for themselves but setting strict codes for their spouses.

Betty Friedan's best-selling book *The Feminine Mystique* first appeared in 1963, but its research referred to the 1950s. Friedan struck a chord in the hearts of thousands of women when she spoke of the "problem with no name": the oppressive nature of a domestic life bound up with child care, domestic drudgery, and a husband who only occasionally put in an appearance and with whom little emotional communication was possible.

CHANGES IN FAMILY PATTERNS WORLDWIDE

Just as family structure and family life in the United States have shifted over the past three centuries, family life has also been transformed across the globe.

In some areas, such as more remote regions in Asia, Africa, and the Pacific Rim, traditional family systems are little altered. In most developing countries, however, widespread changes are occurring. The origins of these changes are complex, but several factors can be picked out as especially important. One is the spread of Western culture. Western ideals of romantic love, for example, have spread to societies in which they were previously unknown. One study found evidence of romantic love in nearly 147 of the 166 traditional societies they studied in sub-Saharan Africa, East Eurasia, and elsewhere (Jankowiak and Fisher 1992). Another factor is the development of centralized government in areas previously composed of autonomous smaller societies. People's lives are influenced by their involvement in a national political system; moreover, governments make active attempts to alter traditional ways of behaving.

Because of the problem of rapidly expanding population growth, states frequently introduce programs advocating smaller families, for example, by promoting the use of contraception. One of the world's most effective population control programs is the one-child policy in China, implemented in 1978. After the policy was implemented, births dropped from 5 per woman in the 1970s, to 3 in 1980, to an estimated 1.55 in 2013 (CIA 2013a). However, in November 2013, the Chinese government relaxed this policy. Married couples are now allowed to have a second child if both spouses are only children themselves (Buckley 2013). There are many reasons behind the government's decision to relax the policy, including public anger about a policy viewed as highly restrictive, widespread use of abortion when women become pregnant with a second child, and fears that the small cohorts of young people will not be sufficient to support much larger cohorts of older adults in China.

A further influence on family life is the large-scale migration from rural to urban areas. Often men go to work in towns or cities, leaving family members in the home village. Alternatively, a nuclear-family group will move as a unit to the city. In both cases, traditional family forms and kinship systems may become weakened. Finally, and perhaps most important, employment opportunities away from the land and in such organizations as government bureaucracies, mines,

From 1978 to 2013, China maintained a very strict one-child policy. The government promoted the benefits of one-child families through billboards and other national media.

plantations, and—where they exist—industrial firms tend to have disruptive consequences for family systems previously centered on agricultural production in the local community.

DIRECTIONS OF CHANGE

Families are being transformed throughout the globe today, with extended family systems giving way to the predominance of the nuclear family. This was first documented by William J. Goode in his book *World Revolution in Family Patterns* (1963), and subsequent research has shown that these changes continue. Building on Goode's work, sociologists have identified seven important changes that have characterized global family change over the past half-century:

1. Clans, or small family groups based on shared heredity, and other types of kin groups are declining in their influence.
2. There is a general trend toward the free choice of a spouse.
3. The rights of women are becoming more widely recognized, in respect to both the initiation of marriage and decision making within families.
4. Kin marriages are becoming less common.
5. Higher levels of sexual freedom are developing in societies that were very restrictive.
6. Birth rates are declining, meaning that women are giving birth to fewer babies.
7. There is a general trend toward the extension of children's rights.

In many countries, especially Western industrial societies, five additional trends have occurred within the past three decades:

1. An increase in the number of births that occur outside of marriage.
2. A liberalization of laws and norms regarding divorce.
3. An increase in nonmarital cohabitation among romantic partners.
4. An increasing age at first marriage.
5. A growing number of and acceptance for same-sex couples and their families.

Taken together, most Westernized and an increasing number of non-Western nations have witnessed a slow yet gradual decline of the nuclear family as the preeminent family form. Given the ethnically diverse character of the United States, there are considerable variations in family and marriage within the country, some of the most striking of which are the differences between white and African American family patterns. We will consider the reasons for these differences, and then move on to examine divorce, remarriage, stepparenting, and cohabitation in relation to contemporary patterns of family life. ✓

CONCEPT CHECKS ✓

1. Briefly describe changes in family size over the past three centuries.

2. How has Stephanie Coontz dispelled the myth of the peaceful and harmonious family believed to exist in past decades?

3. Give two examples of problems facing families in past centuries.

4. What are four conditions that have contributed to changing family forms throughout the world?

5. How has migration from rural to urban areas affected family life?

6. What are the seven most important changes occurring in families worldwide?

GLOBALIZATION BY THE NUMBERS

MATERNITY LEAVE BENEFITS

Working moms are guaranteed paid leave in at least 178 countries around the world, with some countries offering as much as a year off. The U.S. is the only industrialized nation that doesn't offer any paid maternity leave.

52 weeks — SERBIA

36 weeks — NORWAY

20 weeks — RUSSIAN FEDERATION

18 weeks — CUBA

17 weeks — GREECE

15 weeks — CONGO

13 weeks — CHINA

12 weeks — HAITI

7 weeks — LEBANON

6 weeks — PHILIPPINES

0 weeks — UNITED STATES

Note: All the countries featured in this graphic pay 100% of wages for the entire period of leave.

Source: International Labour Organization 2010

WHAT DO MARRIAGE AND FAMILY IN THE UNITED STATES LOOK LIKE TODAY?

The United States has long been characterized by high marriage rates. Just under 96 percent of adults sixty-five years or older are or have been married (U.S. Bureau of the Census 2013c). The age at which people first marry has risen steeply over the past half-century, however. In 1960, the average age of first marriages was 22.8 for men and 20.3 for women. The comparable ages in 2011 were 28.7 for men and 26.5 for women (National Marriage Project 2012). Another way of measuring the relation between age and first marriage is to look at the proportion of people who remain unmarried before a certain age (Figure 11.1). Thus, in 1960, just 28 percent of women ages twenty-four or younger had never married. In 2010, that proportion was more than 86 percent (U.S. Bureau of the Census 2013c).

There are several explanations for this trend in the last several decades toward later marriage. First, increases in cohabitation among younger people contribute to the decreases (or delays) in marriage among this group. Young people are cohabiting, or living with a romantic partner, before or instead of marrying. Second, increases in postsecondary school enrollment, especially among women, are partially responsible for delays in marriage. Third, women's increased participation in the labor force often leads to delays in marriage as women work to establish their careers before marrying and starting a family (Oppenheimer 1988). Labor force participation also increases economic independence among women. By earning their own income, many women no longer need a male breadwinner in their home. The flip side of the economic independence argument is the idea that the deterioration of men's economic position since the late 1980s has made them less attractive mates and less ready to marry. Sociologist William Julius Wilson proposed the "marriageable men" hypothesis to explain the especially low marriage

Figure 11.1 | Percentage of Twenty- to Twenty-Four-Year-Olds Who Have Never Married

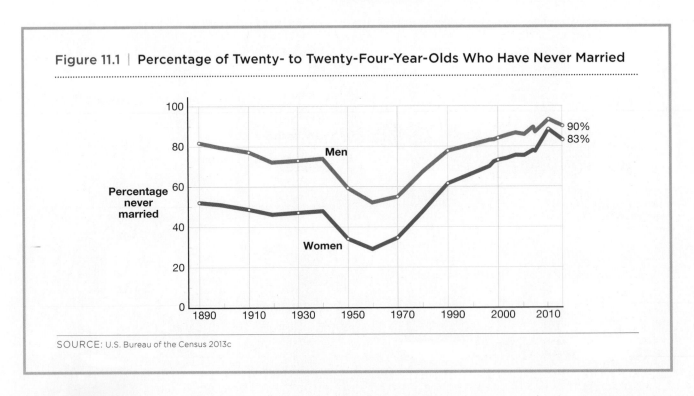

SOURCE: U.S. Bureau of the Census 2013c

rates among blacks: Because black men have suffered the worst economic conditions in the last few decades, they might be viewed by black women as particularly poor marriage candidates (Wilson 1996). As such, African American women may have few prospects for marriage and instead may remain single or have children on their own. Finally, some researchers believe that modernization, changing gender roles, and a shift in attitudes that promote individualism make marriage less important than it once was.

As noted earlier, an extraordinary increase in the proportion of people living alone in the United States has also taken place over recent years—a phenomenon that partly reflects the high levels of marital separation and divorce. A record 28 percent of households now consist of only one person, and the percentage of Americans who live alone has doubled over the last fifty years (Klinenberg 2012). There has been a particularly sharp rise in the proportion of individuals living alone in the forty-five-to-sixty-four age bracket.

Some people still suppose that the average American family is made up of a married couple and their children. This is very different from the real situation: Just one-fifth of U.S. households today are the "traditional" family, down from a quarter a decade ago and 43 percent in 1950 (Tavernise 2011). One reason is the rising rate of divorce: A substantial proportion of the population lives either in single-parent households or in stepfamilies. The expectation that the "traditional" family includes a working husband and stay-at-home wife is also a thing of the past. Dual-career marriages and single-parent families are now the norm. The majority of married women working outside the home also care for a child or children. Although many working women are concentrated in jobs with poor or nonexistent promotion prospects, the standard of living of many American couples is dependent on the income contributed by the wife, as well as on the unpaid work she undertakes in the home.

Family structures and patterns are powerfully shaped by both structural and cultural factors. Structural factors—including shifts in educational attainment, economic prospects of young adults, and whether one has the legal right to marry—have a

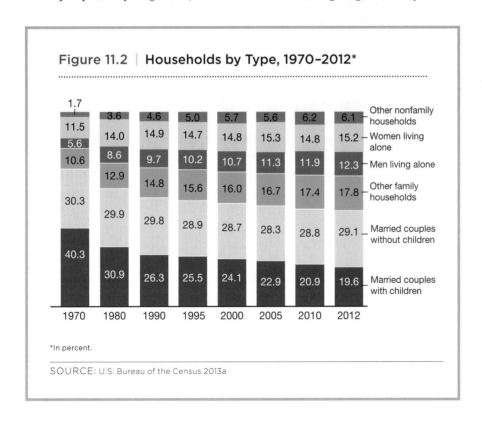

Figure 11.2 | Households by Type, 1970–2012*

*In percent.

SOURCE: U.S. Bureau of the Census 2013a

powerful influence on the ways families are formed. At the same time, cultural factors, ranging from attitudes toward marriage, sexuality, and cohabitation to beliefs about the appropriate context for raising children, shape family lives. For these reasons, American families vary widely based on factors such as social class, race, ethnicity, religion, and even the geographic region where one lives. We briefly focus on the ways that race and social class shape family life in the contemporary United States.

ASIAN AMERICAN FAMILIES

Family forms vary widely by race and ethnicity, as well as immigrant status, in the United States. One of the primary features of the Asian American family is that of dependence on the extended family, a practice that some sociologists attribute to cultural beliefs related to filial piety, or respect for and a sense of responsibility for caring for one's elders (Bengtson et al. 2000). In 2010, 25 percent of Asians in the United States resided in multigenerational households, compared with just 12 percent of whites (Pew Social & Demographic Trends 2010). In many Asian cultures, family concerns are often a priority over individual concerns. Family members' interdependence also helps Asian Americans prosper financially. Asian American family and friend networks often pool money to help their members start a business or buy a house. This help is reciprocated as more of the recipients who prosper as a result then contribute to other family members. The result is a median family income for Asian Americans that is higher than the median family income for non-Hispanic whites.

Asian Americans are a heterogeneous group, however, and vary widely in terms of other family patterns. Chinese American and Japanese American women have much lower fertility rates than do any other racial/ethnic group, due in part to their higher levels of educational attainment. As women remain in school and delay marriage and childbearing, they typically go on to have fewer children. Chinese, Japanese, and Filipino families have lower levels of nonmarital fertility than all other racial/ethnic groups, including non-Hispanic whites. Low levels of nonmarital fertility combined with low levels of divorce for most Asian American groups demonstrate the cultural emphasis on marriage as the appropriate forum for family formation and maintenance.

NATIVE AMERICAN FAMILIES

Kinship ties are also very important in Native American families. As noted family demographer Andrew Cherlin (2005) observes, "Kinship networks constitute tribal organization; kinship ties confer identity" for Native Americans. However, fewer than half of all Native Americans currently live on or near tribal lands, so for those who live in cities or away from reservations, kin ties may be less significant. Furthermore, Native Americans have higher rates of intermarriage than any other racial/ethnic group. In 2009, less than half of all married Native Americans were married to other Native Americans (Park 2011).

The Native American fertility experience is similar to that of African Americans. Native American women have a high fertility rate and a high percentage of nonmarital fertility; 64.0 percent of all Native American women giving birth between January 2010 and December 2011 were not married (U.S. Bureau of the Census 2013p). Sandefur and Liebler (1997) also report a high divorce rate for Native Americans. These patterns of high rates of divorce and nonmarital childbearing are powerfully shaped by structural factors, including limited access to higher education, high unemployment rates, and high levels of poverty, as we saw in Chapter 10.

LATINO FAMILIES

Hispanics, like Asian Americans, are much more likely to reside in multigenerational families than are whites. More than one in five Latinos resides in such a household. This pattern reflects both structural influences, including relatively low income levels, as well as cultural influences, such as an emphasis on filial piety. Another similarity between Hispanics and Asian Americans is that both broad ethnic groups are very heterogeneous when it comes to family patterns—with particular difference documented among Mexican, Cuban, and Puerto Rican American families. Statistically, Mexican American families are characterized by multigenerational households and a high birthrate. Mexican American families are typically better off financially than Puerto Rican families but less well off than Cuban families. Although Latino women had lower rates of labor force participation in 2010 than did white women, fully 41 percent still worked for pay (U.S. Department of Labor 2012). Ethnographic research indicates that this is due to necessity rather than desire. Many Mexican American families say that the breadwinner-homemaker model would be their preference but that they are constrained by finances (Hurtado 1995).

Although Puerto Rico is a U.S. commonwealth, Puerto Ricans are still considered part of the umbrella category of Hispanics. However, because of their status as U.S. citizens, Puerto Ricans can and do move about freely between Puerto Rico and the mainland without the difficulties often encountered by immigrants. Researchers have shown that when barriers to immigration are high, only the most able (physically, financially, and so on) members of a society will be able to leave their homeland and move to another country. Because Puerto Ricans do not face as many barriers, even the least able can manage the migration process. The economic upshot of unrestricted migration for Puerto Ricans is that they are the most economically disadvantaged of all the major Hispanic groups living in the United States. Puerto Rican American families are also characterized by a higher rate of children born to unmarried mothers than any other Hispanic group—65.1 percent in 2012. This percentage is lower than among African Americans (72.1 percent) and higher than among whites (29.3 percent) (Centers for Disease Control and Prevention 2013a). However, consensual unions—cohabiting relationships in which couples consider themselves married but are not legally married—are often the context for births to unmarried mothers. Many Puerto Ricans respond to tough economic times by forming consensual unions as the next best option to what is often a much more expensive legal marriage (Landale and Fennelly 1992).

Cuban American families are the most prosperous of all the Hispanic groups, but are still less prosperous than whites. Most Cuban Americans have settled in the Miami area and have formed immigrant enclaves in which they rely on other Cubans for their business and social needs (for example, banking, schools, and shopping). The relative wealth of Cuban Americans is driven largely by family business ownership. In terms of childbearing, Cuban Americans have lower levels of fertility than non-Hispanic whites and equally low levels of nonmarital fertility.

AFRICAN AMERICAN FAMILIES

White and black family patterns differ dramatically. Blacks have higher rates of childbearing outside of marriage, they are less likely to ever marry, and they are also less likely to marry after having a nonmarital birth. These patterns are shaped by economic factors, including the shortage of "marriageable men" (Wilson 1996) that we discussed earlier in this chapter. That does not necessarily mean that black children have no father figure, however. A growing body of research shows that even children born to single mothers may still have a "social father" or a man who cares for them, such as an uncle, a cousin, or a new romantic partner of their mother. However, these social and psychological ties do not necessarily provide economic stability to children (Berger et al. 2008). As a result, racial differences in family structure are of particular interest to sociologists because single parenthood is associated with high rates of poverty in the United States (Harknett and McLanahan 2004).

In 2012, 52.3 percent of all white people fifteen years and older were married and had a spouse present in the home but the same could be said of only 29.6 percent of blacks (U.S. Bureau of the Census 2013c). Throughout most of the twentieth century, black families were more likely than white families to be headed by a female. In 1960, 21 percent of African American families were headed by females; among white families, the proportion was 8 percent. By 2011, the proportion of black families with children under eighteen headed by single mothers had risen to 55 percent, while the proportion for white families was 22 percent (U.S. Bureau of the Census 2013q). Female-headed families are more prominently represented among poorer blacks—another social condition exacerbated by a shortage of marriageable men. Research shows persuasively that women are most likely to marry—even after the birth of a child—when they live in a geographic area that provides suitable employment opportunities for men (Harknett and McLanahan 2004).

But we should not see the situation of African American families purely in a negative light. When white anthropologist Carol Stack (1975) was a young doctoral student, she entered a black ghetto community in Illinois to study the support systems that poor black families form. Living in the community and getting to know the kinship system from the inside, she found that families adapted to poverty by forming large, complex support networks. Thus a mother heading a one-parent family is likely to have a close and supportive network of relatives to depend on. A far higher proportion of female-headed families among African Americans have other relatives living with them than do white families headed by females. Social scientists disagree about the implications of this family arrangement, however. Stack suggests that extended family provides important support and assistance to single mothers. Yet more recent data suggest that multigenerational families may pose strains and demands on their members, especially among the economically disadvantaged (Cain and Combs-Orme 2005).

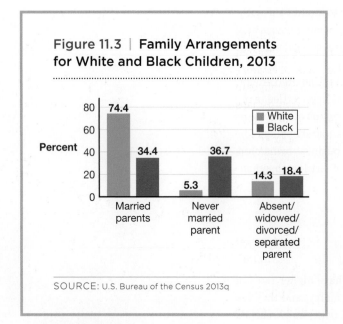

Figure 11.3 | Family Arrangements for White and Black Children, 2013

SOURCE: U.S. Bureau of the Census 2013q

CLASS AND THE AMERICAN FAMILY

While Stack's arguments were specifically geared toward explaining racial differences in the organization of the extended family, contemporary researchers examining similar questions have concluded that "the differences between black and white extended family relationships are mainly due to contemporary differences in social and economic class positions of group members. Cultural differences are less significant" (Sarkisian and Gerstel 2004).

This leads to an interesting question: Are racial differences in family formation primarily due to economic or

Roughly 40 percent of all births in the United States today are to unmarried women. Yet that does not mean that babies are growing up fatherless: Fully half of nonmarital births take place in cohabiting unions, many of which end in marriage.

cultural factors? One of the problems with the culture versus class debate is that there is little research on middle-class black families or low-income white families, which makes it difficult to think about whether cultural factors or structural factors are driving racial differences in terms of family formation.

In their book *Promises I Can Keep: Why Poor Women Put Motherhood Before Marriage*, sociologists Kathryn Edin and Maria Kefalas (2005) offer insightful glimpses into the ways that social class affects the family lives of low-income women. Specifically, the authors conducted interviews with 165 low-income single mothers in black and white neighborhoods to uncover why low-income women continue to have children out of wedlock when they can hardly afford to do so. The women of all races whom they interviewed valued and revered marriage, but they believed that if they married their current partners, they might end up divorced or in an unhappy marriage. As one woman told them in an interview, "I'd rather say I had a child out of wedlock than that I married this idiot."

Edin and Kefalas offer three additional explanations for why poor women often have children out of wedlock. First, young women in poor communities feel confident about their ability to raise children, because most were themselves raised in social environments where young people are typically involved in raising the other kids in a family or in one's neighborhood. Second, the poor place an extremely high value on children, perhaps even higher than that of middle-class families, at least in part because they have fewer things to make their lives meaningful. Finally, many women in the study reported that having a child actually saved their lives, bringing order to an otherwise chaotic life.

DIVORCE AND SEPARATION

Divorce rates increased steadily through the latter half of the twentieth century, yet they have plateaued in recent years. Attitudes have changed in tandem, with a stark decline in the proportion of Americans who disapprove of divorce.

Divorce rates, calculated by looking at the number of divorces per 1,000 married men or women per year, have fluctuated in the United States in different periods

(Figure 11.4). They rose, for example, following World War II, then dropped off before climbing to much higher levels. The divorce rate increased steeply from the 1960s to the late 1970s, reaching a peak in 1980 (thereafter declining somewhat).

Divorce exerts a powerful impact on the lives of children, although most children of divorce fare well in the years after their parents' divorce (Carr and Springer 2010). About one-half of children born in 1980 became members of a one-parent family at some stage in their lives. Since two-thirds of women and three-fourths of men who are divorced eventually remarry, most of these children nonetheless grew up in a two-parent family. In 2013, just 3.7 percent of children under eighteen in the United States were not living with either parent (U.S. Bureau of the Census 2013b).

The economic well-being of women and children declines in the immediate aftermath of divorce. According to a 1996 study, the living standards of divorced women and their children on average fell by 27 percent in the first year following the divorce settlement. The average standard of living of divorced men, by contrast, rose by 10 percent. Most court judgments left the former husband with a high proportion of his income intact; therefore, he had more to spend on his own needs than while he was married (Peterson 1996). The main reason for the gender gap is that women typically earn less than men and take time out of the labor market to raise children. Many cannot return to work, or cannot easily secure high-paying jobs upon divorcing.

Of special interest to family demographers is the fact that the women with the most resources—especially education—are increasingly following trajectories that provide their children with greater resources, primarily by delaying fertility and being more involved in the labor market. In contrast, women who have the fewest resources—low levels of educational attainment or few economic resources—are increasingly following a trajectory of early fertility and infrequent employment. These different trajectories are problematic because they lead to even higher levels of inequality in the future educational, economic, and health experiences of children (McLanahan 2004). Much research demonstrates that young

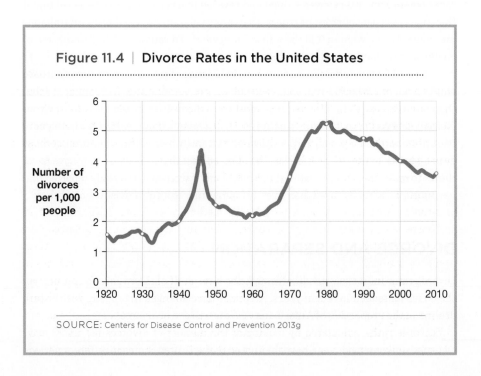

Figure 11.4 | Divorce Rates in the United States

Number of divorces per 1,000 people

SOURCE: Centers for Disease Control and Prevention 2013g

adults from financially disadvantaged homes are less likely to attend college, and thus are more likely to marry younger—often right after high school. As a result, they tend to hold lower-paying jobs than their counterparts who graduate college. Marrying young, before one is emotionally and financially ready, is considered one of the most powerful predictors of divorce (Elliott and Simmons 2011). In this way, early marriage and subsequent divorce play a role in perpetuating social class disadvantage across generations.

REASONS FOR DIVORCE

Why did divorce rates increase so steeply in the 1960s and 1970s? First, changes in the law have made divorce easier. Second, except for a small proportion of wealthy people, marriage today no longer has much connection with the desire to perpetuate property and status from generation to generation. Third, as women become more economically independent, marriage is less of a necessary economic partnership. Greater overall prosperity means that it is easier to establish a separate household in case of marital disaffection (Lee 1982). Fourth, the stigma of divorce has declined, thus removing a psychological obstacle to marital dissolution. Fifth, adults now place a great value on personal satisfaction in marriage; few are willing to remain in a relationship that provides few emotional rewards (Cherlin 1990). Sixth, adults now recognize that staying in an unhappy marriage "for the sake of the kids" is not always the best strategy; children tend to do better when they are spared frequent parental conflicts (Musick and Meier 2010).

Making Sociology Work
FAMILY THERAPIST

Family therapists and counselors find that one of their toughest jobs is counseling husbands and wives who constantly bicker but who want to stay together for the sake of the kids. Some therapists believe that children whose parents have chaotic or unhappy marriages learn bad parenting techniques and that these kids would benefit in the long run by their parents' divorcing. Others disagree and feel that keeping the family intact is so important that parents—even if unhappy or lonely—who are able to remain civil do provide a better option than divorce. Yet others say that the very problems that plague the couple, such as financial troubles or emotional difficulties, may ultimately affect their kids, too, regardless of whether the couple divorces. What useful information can sociology provide to family therapists? What are the consequences of divorce for kids? What are the harmful consequences of divorcing versus staying together for the sake of the kids?

DIVORCE AND CHILDREN

The effects of divorce on children are difficult to gauge. How contentious the relationship is between the parents prior to separation, the age of a child at the time, whether there are siblings, the availability of grandparents and other relatives, the child's relationship with his or her individual parents, and how frequently the child continues to see both parents can all affect the process of adjustment. Since children whose parents are unhappy with each other but stay together may also be affected, assessing the consequences of divorce for children is doubly problematic.

Some of the earliest studies of divorce consequences were based on clinical samples, that is, populations of people seeking counseling; these found that children often suffer a period of marked emotional anxiety following the separation of their parents. Judith Wallerstein and Joan Kelly studied 131 children of sixty families in Marin County, California, following the separation of the parents. They found evidence of both short- and long-term deleterious consequences of parental divorce. Almost all the children experienced intense emotional disturbance at the time of the divorce. Yet even ten or fifteen years later, nearly half the then-young adult children reported difficulties in their romantic relationships, compromised self-esteem, and a sense of underachievement. However, these harmful effects partly reflect the fact that

Divorce—There's an App for That

Divorce rates in the United States have plateaued in the last decade, after having reached their peak in the late 1970s and early 1980s. Still, roughly 40 percent of first marriages will end in divorce, and the proportion of second and third marriages ending in dissolution is even higher. Although most divorced adults and their children will bounce back after the initial periods of sadness, distress, and financial strain, the act of ending a marriage requires multiple adjustments, including setting up separate homes for the two spouses, orchestrating custody arrangements, arranging sleeping arrangements for the children when they're staying at two different parents' houses throughout the week, and coordinating financial issues such as child support.

Technology entrepreneurs recognize that many Americans are facing divorce, and have designed an array of apps to help divorced partners and their children negotiate their new lives (Borreson 2012). Some apps help married persons who are preparing to divorce. For example, nearly all states have apps that provide information on their own particular laws and rules for deciding financial support and custody. Other apps like iSplit Divorce and Divorce Log can help the two bickering spouses create an inventory of their assets—including "his," "hers," and "ours" categories—to help prepare for the formal division of assets when the marriage officially ends. Using the Child Support Calculator app, divorcing parents can determine the estimated cost of monthly child support.

After marital partners have separated, they can rely on apps to help them communicate and make arrangements for the joint care of their children. For example, 2houses helps parents organize custody arrangements and share reports on their children's health and school performance. The app includes a shared digital calendar to help coordinate drop-offs and pickups, and also helps track expenses related to the children.

Divorcing parents who are still struggling with sticky emotional issues, such as how to tell the kids, how to help the kids remain impartial, and when to start dating again, may turn to apps like Parenting Apart, where a therapist will answer parents' tough questions.

The proliferation of these kinds of apps, which help make divorce as easy and painless as possible, represents one of many cultural signs that divorce is a commonly accepted aspect of everyday life in the United States. This is a far cry from just five decades ago, when the word *divorcée* was whispered behind closed doors, and unhappy couples would remain married "for the sake of the kids."

What do you think about these apps? Do you believe they are a necessity during an era when nearly half of all

Apps can make the logistics of divorce, like splitting assets and child custody, easier for separating spouses.

marriages end in divorce? Do you think they focus too much on the logistical and financial aspects of divorce rather than deeper emotional concerns? What kind of apps do you believe would be most helpful for divorcing parents and their children?

the study was based on a clinical sample; by definition, all had already been seeking professional help for their troubles prior to the start of the study.

In sharp contrast, a recent review of studies on divorce and children found that the majority of persons whose parents had divorced did not have serious mental health problems (Carr and Springer 2010). Most studies detect small differences in mental health between those whose parents divorced and those whose parents stayed together (favoring those whose parents stayed together), but much of this difference in mental health reflects family strains that preceded the divorce. In other words, the purportedly harmful effects of divorce could reflect the harmful experiences for children of living with fighting parents. One of the most prominent family sociologists in the United States, Andrew Cherlin, has argued that these are the general effects of divorce on children:

- Almost all children experience an initial period of intense emotional upset after their parents separate.
- Most resume normal development without serious problems within about two years after the separation.
- A minority of children experience some long-term problems as a result of the breakup that may persist into adulthood (Cherlin 1999).

REMARRIAGE AND STEPPARENTING

Odd though it might seem, the best way to maximize the chances of marriage, for both sexes, is to have been married previously. People who have been married and divorced are more likely to marry again than single people in similar age groups are to marry for the first time. At all age levels, divorced men are more likely to remarry than divorced women. Two in every three divorced women remarry, but three in every four divorced men eventually marry again. Many divorced individuals also choose to cohabit instead of remarry.

A **stepfamily** is a family in which at least one of the adults is a stepparent. Official statistics usually define stepfamilies more specifically as those in which the children *reside* with at least one stepparent; there are many more families in which children regularly visit stepparents. Stepfamilies bring into being kinship ties that resemble those of some traditional societies but that are new in Western countries. Children may now have two "mothers" and two "fathers"—one biological parent and one stepparent—contributing to the complexity of their family lives.

Members of stepfamilies are finding their own ways of adjusting to the relatively uncharted circumstances in which they find themselves. Perhaps the most appropriate conclusion to be drawn is that while marriages are broken up by divorce, families on the whole are not. Especially where children are involved, ties persist.

stepfamily • A family in which at least one partner has children from a previous marriage.

SINGLE-PARENT HOUSEHOLDS

Single-parent households have become increasingly common (Figure 11.5). There are two main pathways to single-parent households: divorce, as we discussed earlier, and nonmarital childbearing. In 1950, only 4 percent of all children in the United States were born to unmarried parents; by 2011, nearly 41 percent of all children were born outside of marriage (Hamilton, Martin, and Ventura 2012). Although we often think of nonmarital births as births to teenagers—often abandoned by their male

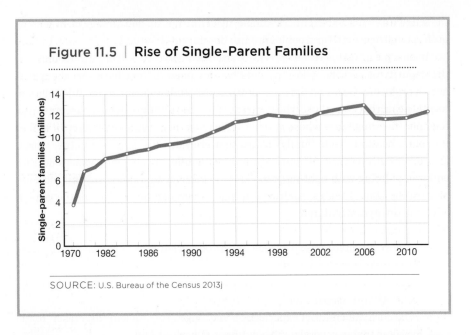

Figure 11.5 | Rise of Single-Parent Families

SOURCE: U.S. Bureau of the Census 2013j

partners—the data show otherwise. An increasingly large number of nonmarital births are to men and women in their twenties who are delaying marriage but not delaying childbearing (Cherlin 2010). In fact, an estimated half of all nonmarital births today occur within cohabiting relationships. Although the mother may be legally "unmarried," both she and her child may very well have a dedicated and involved male figure in their lives and in their home (Kennedy and Bumpass 2008).

Just as single-parent households vary based on the mother's relationship status, they also vary widely by race and ethnicity. Recent research shows that roughly one-quarter of white births and three-quarters of black births occur outside of a marital union. When we expand the definition of "union" to include cohabiting unions, we continue to see pronounced race differences. Roughly half of black women experience a birth outside of any kind of co-residential union, compared with just one-quarter of U.S.-born Hispanics and 9 percent of whites (Manlove, Ryan, Wildsmith, and Franzetta 2010).

In 2013, 20.5 million children under the age of eighteen lived with one parent, 17.5 million with their mother and 3 million with their father (U.S. Bureau of the Census 2013j). The vast majority of single-parent households are headed by women because unmarried women often do not maintain contact with the birth father of the child and may even prefer to raise a child on their own. Moreover, in the case of divorce, the mother usually obtains primary custody of the children. There were 12.3 million single-parent families in the United States in 2012. Of these 12.3 million, 84 percent were headed by women and 16 percent by men. Overall, 14.4 percent of families are single-parent families, while an additional 2.2 percent are cohabiting parents who are not legally married to one another (U.S. Bureau of the Census 2013j).

Most people do not wish to be single parents, but a growing minority choose to become so, setting out to have a child or children without the support of a spouse or partner. "Single mothers by choice" is an apt description of some parents, normally those who possess sufficient resources to manage satisfactorily as a single-parent household. For the majority of unmarried or never-married mothers, however, the reality is different: There is a high correlation between the rate of births outside marriage and indicators of poverty and social deprivation. As we saw earlier, these influences are very important in explaining the high proportion of single-parent households among families of African American background in the United States.

A debate exists among sociologists about the impact on children of growing up with a single parent. The most exhaustive set of studies carried out to date, by Sara McLanahan and Gary Sandefur, rejects the claim that children raised by only one parent do just as well as children raised by both parents. A large part of the reason is economic—the sudden drop in income associated with divorce. But about half of the disadvantage comes from inadequate parental attention and lack of social ties. Separation or divorce weakens the connection between child and father, as well as the link between the child and the father's network of friends and acquaintances. On the basis of wide empirical research, the authors conclude that it is a myth that there are usually strong support networks or extended family ties available to single mothers (McLanahan and Sandefur 1994).

Others have been quick to point out that although children who grow up in a single-parent home are on average disadvantaged, it is better for children's mental health if parents in extremely high-conflict marriages divorce than if they stay together (Amato et al. 1995; Musick and Meier 2010). This suggests that divorce may benefit children growing up in high-conflict marriages but may harm children whose parents have relatively low levels of marital conflict before divorcing. ✓

CONCEPT CHECKS ✓

1. Briefly describe changes in family structure in the United States since 1960.

2. Contrast both general and nonmarital fertility rates among whites, blacks, Hispanics, Asians, and Native Americans in the United States.

3. According to Edin and Kefalas, why do many low-income women have babies out of wedlock?

4. What are the main reasons divorce rates increased sharply during the latter half of the twentieth century?

5. How does divorce affect the well-being of children?

WHY DOES FAMILY VIOLENCE HAPPEN?

Learn about sexual abuse and violence within families.

Family relationships—between wife and husband, parents and children, brothers and sisters, or more distant relatives—can be warm and fulfilling. But they can also be full of extreme tension, driving people to despair or imbuing them with a deep sense of anxiety and guilt. Family discord can take many forms. Among the most devastating in their consequences, however, are the incestuous abuse of children and domestic violence.

FAMILY VIOLENCE

Violence within families is perpetrated primarily by men. The two broad categories of family violence are *child abuse* and *spousal abuse*. Because of the sensitive and private nature of violence within families, it is difficult to obtain national data on levels of domestic violence. Data on child abuse are particularly sparse because of the issues of cognitive development and ethical concerns involved in studying child subjects.

CHILD ABUSE

Definitions of child abuse vary widely, but experts agree that it encompasses serious physical harm (such as physical beatings or severe physical punishment, sexual abuse with injury, or willful malnutrition) with intent to injure. One national study of married or cohabiting adults found that in 1993 about 3 percent of respondent adults abused their children; cohabiting adults are no more or less likely to abuse their children than married couples (Brown 2004; Sedlak and Broadhurst 1996). In 2009, parents—acting alone or with another person—were responsible for 75.8 percent of child abuse or neglect fatalities (Child Welfare 2011).

Studies based on parents' self-report may underreport the frequency of abuse, as parents may be reluctant to report such problematic behaviors. As a result, most studies of abuse are based on national surveys of child welfare professionals. These surveys may fail to include abused children who are not seen by professionals and thus are not reported to state agencies. Researchers estimate that as many as 50 to 60 percent of child deaths from abuse or neglect are not recorded (U.S. Department of Health and Human Services [DHHS] 2004). However, studies based on the reports of child welfare professionals remain the most widely used sources of information on child abuse.

The most recent statistics based on the National Child Abuse and Neglect Reporting System, a data resource of the U.S. Department of Health and Human Services, estimate that in 2011 there were about 676,569 reported child victims of abuse or neglect. Of these, 78.5 percent suffered neglect, 17.6 percent suffered physical abuse, 9.0 percent suffered from psychological maltreatment, and 9.6 percent were sexually abused (DHHS 2012a); 81.2 percent of child abuse or neglect cases are perpetrated by the child's parents, another 4.4 percent by other relatives of the victim.

The highest child victimization rates were for children up to one year old. Researchers concur that child abuse occurs more frequently in low-income families and single-parent families, due in part to high levels of parental stress. Moreover, because economically disadvantaged persons are more likely to live in apartments and densely populated neighborhoods, incidences of abuse also are more likely to be noticed and reported by neighbors or social workers.

SPOUSAL ABUSE

The classic 1988 study by Richard Gelles and Murray Straus found that 16 percent of married persons reported at least one incidence of spousal violence in the prior year, and 28 percent reported that they had at some time in their lives experienced spousal violence. These aggregate statistics do not, however, distinguish between severe acts, such as beating up and threatening with or using a gun or knife, and less severe acts of violence, such as slapping, pushing, grabbing, or shoving one's spouse. When the authors disaggregated this number, they found that approximately 3 percent of all husbands admitted to perpetrating at least one act of severe violence on their spouse in the last year, and this is likely to be an underestimate of actual occurrence.

Straus and his colleagues also reported a finding that has been widely discussed and debated: that equal proportions of women and men reported that they perpetrated spousal abuse. This lies in stark contrast to much of the literature based on crime statistics, hospital records, and shelter administrative records—sources that all indicate that spousal violence is almost exclusively man-on-woman violence.

Michael Johnson (1995) was able to untangle these inconsistencies. Johnson recognized that the data that were generating such conflicting findings were collected from two very different samples. In the shelter samples, respondents are generally women who were severely beaten by their husbands or partners. The severity of their situation drew them to a shelter. On the other hand, those responding to a national survey are generally living in their homes and have the time, energy, or wherewithal to complete a survey. It is unlikely that individuals who are experiencing extreme violence in the home would respond to a national survey. Furthermore, it is unlikely that those who experience less severe kinds of violence (for example, slapping) will end up in a domestic violence shelter. Therefore, these are two very different groups of people.

Johnson argued that the spousal abuse in the two samples was accordingly different in character. He referred to the extreme abuse experienced by many in the shelter samples as "patriarchal terrorism." This type of violence is perpetuated by feelings of power and control. The type of violence reported in national surveys is referred to as "common couple violence." This type of violence is generally reactive to a specific incident and is not rooted in power or control. ✓

CONCEPT CHECKS ✓

1. How do social scientists measure and track patterns of child abuse?

2. Describe gender differences in patterns of spousal abuse.

HOW DO NEW FAMILY FORMS AFFECT YOUR LIFE?

> Learn some alternatives to traditional marriage and family patterns that are becoming more widespread.

COHABITATION

If current statistics are any indicator, at least half of all students reading this textbook will live with their romantic partner before marrying. **Cohabitation**—in which a couple lives together in a sexual relationship without being married—has become increasingly widespread in most Western societies. The proportion of young couples who cohabit has risen steeply, from 11 percent in the early 1970s to 44 percent in the early 1980s and probably about 50 percent today (National Center for Health Statistics 2010). By age thirty about 50 percent of women will have cohabited outside marriage (Bramlett and Mosher 2002). From 1987 to 2002, the percentage of women between the ages of thirty-five and thirty-nine who had ever cohabited doubled, from 30 percent to 61 percent (National Center for Health Statistics 2010).

Cohabitation has become widespread among college and university students, although they were not the initiators of this trend, as many people believe. Bumpass et al. (1991) found that the cohabitation phenomenon started with lower-educated groups in the 1950s because they did not have the economic resources to marry.

While for some cohabitation may be a substitute for marriage, for many it is viewed as a stage in the process of relationship building that precedes marriage. Young people come to live together usually by drifting into it, rather than through calculated planning. A couple that are already having a sexual relationship spend more and more time together, eventually giving up one of their individual homes.

Most cohabiting couples either marry or stop living together, although the chances of a cohabiting union transitioning to a first marriage is related to a number of socioeconomic factors. For instance, the probability that the first cohabitation will become a marriage within five years is 73 percent for white women, but only 53 percent for Hispanic women and 46 percent for black women. Comparable rates for men are 73 percent for white men, 52 percent for black men, and 50 percent for Hispanic men (National Center for Health Statistics 2010). Similarly, the likelihood of a first marriage resulting from cohabitation is positively associated with higher education, the absence of children during cohabitation, and higher family income. It is also more likely in communities with low male unemployment rates (Bramlett and Mosher 2002).

Although many view cohabitation as a precursor to marriage, for a large number of people, it does not end in marriage. Only about 35 percent of cohabitors married their partners within three years of starting to live together. Increasingly, we are

cohabitation • Two people living together in a sexual relationship of some permanence without being married to each other.

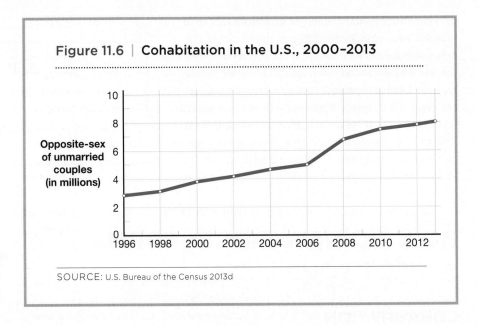

Figure 11.6 | Cohabitation in the U.S., 2000–2013

Opposite-sex of unmarried couples (in millions)

SOURCE: U.S. Bureau of the Census 2013d

seeing evidence that cohabitation is not necessarily a "stage in the process" between dating and marriage, but rather it may be an end in itself for an increasing number of cohabitors.

The United States is certainly not alone in the increasing prevalence of cohabitation. Many European countries are experiencing similar, and in some cases much greater, proportions of unions beginning with cohabitation rather than marriage. The northern European countries of Denmark, Sweden, and Finland, along with France, show particularly high rates of cohabitation. However, unions in the southern European countries of Spain, Greece, and Italy—along with Ireland and Portugal—still largely begin with marriage.

Just as young adults are more likely than ever before to cohabit prior to marriage, young children are more likely than ever before to live with parents who are cohabiting but who are not legally married to each other. As we noted earlier, a recent Pew survey finds that about half of all nonmarital births are to cohabiting couples (Taylor et al. 2007), although this pattern varies widely by race and ethnicity. Sociologists Larry Bumpass and Hsien-Hen Lu (2000) find that about two-fifths of all children spend some time living with their mother and a cohabiting partner and that approximately one-third of the time children spend with unmarried mothers is actually spent in cohabitation. Clearly, the lives of children are increasingly embedded in families formed by cohabitation. The effects of this alternative family form on children will become apparent only as these children age.

DOES LIVING TOGETHER HELP REDUCE THE CHANCES FOR DIVORCE?

As we noted earlier, most readers of this textbook will cohabit before marrying. How will this experience of cohabitation affect their marriages? Many college students believe that by living with a boyfriend or girlfriend, they will learn whether they're right for each other and thus have more successful marriages. As early as the 1960s, anthropologist Margaret Mead (1966) predicted that living together would allow people to make better decisions about marriage. Yet some studies suggest that those who live with their partners before marrying them are slightly more likely to divorce than are individuals who do not cohabit with their partners before marriage (Goodwin et al. 2010). How could this be so?

Sociologists offer two explanations: the *selection explanation* and the *experience of living together explanation*. The selection explanation proposes that people who live together would be more likely to divorce even if they hadn't ever lived together before marriage. That is, the very people who would choose to cohabit differ from those who don't, and the traits that distinguish the two groups are associated with their chances of divorcing. For example, people who cohabit are less religious than those people who refuse to cohabit (Kamp Dush et al. 2003). People who are less religious would be less likely to stay married in any event, whereas people who are more religious would be more likely to stay married.

Although the selection explanation suggests that there is nothing inherent about cohabitation that promotes divorce, there is a competing explanation that suggests that living together is the kind of experience that erodes belief in the permanence of marriage. As people go through their twenties living with various partners, they develop a sense that relationships can be started and ended easily and that they have many options for intimate relations outside of marriage (Teachman 2003).

Which explanation is right? The best evidence seems to indicate that both are correct. While people are selected into cohabitation and divorce based in part on their attitudes, the experience of cohabitation may also slightly alter one's beliefs about marriage.

GAY-PARENT FAMILIES

Gay and lesbian college students today can look forward to a much more accepting social world than the one that greeted generations before them. Many gays and lesbians now live in stable relationships as couples, and there is a swiftly developing movement to legally recognize these unions as marriages. According to estimates from the U.S. Census Bureau, there are currently more than 600,000 same-sex families in the United States, roughly 168,000 of whom report themselves as married (U.S. Bureau of the Census 2013g). Recent decisions in the United States, Canada, Mexico, and several European nations demonstrate the current pulse of this movement.

In 2001 the Netherlands became the first nation to legalize same-sex marriage. Since that time, Belgium, Spain, Canada, South Africa, Norway, Sweden, Portugal, Iceland, Argentina, Denmark, France, Uruguay, New Zealand, Brazil, and the United Kingdom have also legalized such unions. In 2007, Coahuila became the second state in Mexico to legalize civil unions. In 2008, Uruguay became the first nation in Latin America to do so. Countries that do not have same-sex marriage but have laws granting civil unions and other rights include Ecuador, Finland, Germany, Greenland, and Hungary.

Policies are rapidly changing and are hotly contested in the United States. Vermont was the first state to legalize civil unions: In July 2000, the Vermont legislature voted to allow same-sex partners to register their "civil unions" with town clerks. The move gave same-sex couples access to all the state-granted rights, privileges, and responsibilities of marriage. Though this was a big victory for gay and lesbian marriage advocates, the measure falls short of calling the partnerships "marriage" and instead opts for "civil unions." Marriage is seen as a more desirable arrangement by gay and lesbian couples because marriages are respected in all fifty states for all purposes, but civil unions are not necessarily recognized as legally binding when a couple leave the state in which they formed the union.

The most recent victories for same-sex couples came in May 2014 when Oregon and Pennsylvania legalized gay marriage, joining Massachusetts, Connecticut,

Iowa, Vermont, New Hampshire, New York, Maine, Maryland, Washington, Delaware, Rhode Island, Minnesota, New Jersey, Hawaii, New Mexico, Illinois, and the District of Columbia (National Conference of State Legislatures 2013a). In 2013, the U.S. Supreme Court also overturned Proposition 8, which banned same-sex marriage in California. As we saw in the chapter's opener, the court also ruled that Section 3 of the Defense of Marriage Act (DOMA)—which denied same-sex couples federal health, tax, Social Security, and other benefits—was unconstitutional. That section prevented the recognition of same-sex marriages as legal unions under federal law. Whether more states will follow the lead of the states that currently recognize same-sex marriage remains to be seen.

Beyond civil unions or marriages, same-sex couples are forming families with children in unprecedented numbers. According to the Williams Institute, an estimated 37 percent of lesbian, gay, bisexual, and transgendered (LGBT)-identified persons have been a parent, and an estimated 6 million children in the United States have lived with a gay parent at some point in their lives (Gates 2013). Although lesbian couples may have a child by donor insemination and gay men may rely on a surrogate to carry a biological child, LGBT-identified persons are far more likely than heterosexuals to have a child through adoption. Same-sex couples raising children are four times more likely than their heterosexual counterparts to be raising an adopted child, and more than six times as likely to be raising foster children (Gates 2013).

Relaxation of previously intolerant attitudes toward homosexuality has been accompanied by a growing tendency for courts to allocate custody of children to parents living in gay relationships. Although gay adoption had historically been banned in several states, as recently as 2010, Florida was the only remaining state to block such

The number of U.S. states allowing gay marriage increased steadily in the 2010s, with 19 states and the District of Columbia allowing same-sex marriage as of May 2014. Attitudes followed; more than half of all Americans support these changes.

adoption. In September 2010, this ban was struck down, allowing a gay man named Frank Martin Gill to adopt two boys—half-brothers he had been raising as foster children since 2004. While LGBT-identified individuals are allowed to adopt children in all fifty states, a same-sex couple's joint adoption of a child still remains illegal in a handful of states.

One reason for this growing acceptance of gay adoption is that widespread consensus has emerged among scholars that the ability to parent effectively is not related to sexual orientation. For example, in 2013 the American Academy of Pediatrics issued a seminal report, summarizing more than sixty academic studies, where the authors concluded "that children growing up in households headed by gay men or lesbians are not disadvantaged in any significant respect relative to children of heterosexual parents" (Perrin et al. 2013). The sixty studies considered a range of outcomes, including school performance, social adjustment, and emotional well-being, concluding that a child's well-being is much more closely tied to their parents' "sense of competence and security"—and the "social and economic support" they provided their children—than sexual orientation.

STAYING SINGLE

The broad category of "single" encompasses both people who have never married and those who have married but are now single due to divorce, separation, or widowhood. More people are now "never married" today—and remain in this state for a longer period of time—than in the past due to the delayed age of first marriage. A larger proportion of people in their twenties are unmarried than used to be the case. By their mid-thirties, however, only a small minority of men and women have never been married. The majority of single people ages thirty to fifty are divorced and "in between" marriages. Most single people over fifty are widowed (Federal Interagency Forum on Aging-Related Statistics 2008).

More than ever before, young people are leaving their parents' home simply to start an independent life rather than to get married (which had been one of the most common paths out of their parents' home in the past). Hence, it seems that the trend of "staying single" or living on one's own may be part of the societal trend toward valuing independence at the expense of family life. Still, most people (over 90 percent) ultimately marry, including a large majority of those people who originally left home to live independently (Goldscheider and Goldscheider 1999).

In sum, the decisions we make about our family lives are among the most important choices we make. As we have seen in this chapter, marrying (or staying single), having children—whether with a partner or on our own—and staying married (versus divorcing) are personal choices we make. Yet they are also powerfully shaped by other social factors, including our birth cohort, race, ethnicity, and social class. Although our personal preferences and values may shape our choices, the relationship between values and personal decision making is complex. Our personal decisions are also shaped by social institutions, including the law and the economy. When Edith Windsor, whom we met in the chapter opener, was a young woman in the 1960s, she was unable to marry her longtime love, Thea Speyer. Edith and Thea lived together as a loving couple for more than forty years, but were not allowed to legally get married until 2007. Their relationship ultimately changed history by leading to the repeal of the Defense of Marriage Act (DOMA) in 2013. For future generations of same-sex couples, the law may no longer prohibit loving partners from legalizing their relationship, should they choose to do so. ✓

> ### CONCEPT CHECKS ✓
>
> 1. Why has cohabitation become so common in the United States and worldwide?
>
> 2. Does cohabitation lead to divorce? Why or why not?

EXERCISES:

Thinking Sociologically

1. Using this textbook's presentation, compare the characteristics of contemporary white non-Hispanic, Asian American, Latino, and African American families.

2. Increases in cohabitation and single-parent households suggest that marriage may be beginning to fall by the wayside in our contemporary society. However, this chapter claims that marriage and family remain firmly established institutions in our society. Explain the rising patterns of cohabitation and single-parent households and show how these seemingly paradoxical trends can be reconciled with the claims offered by this textbook.

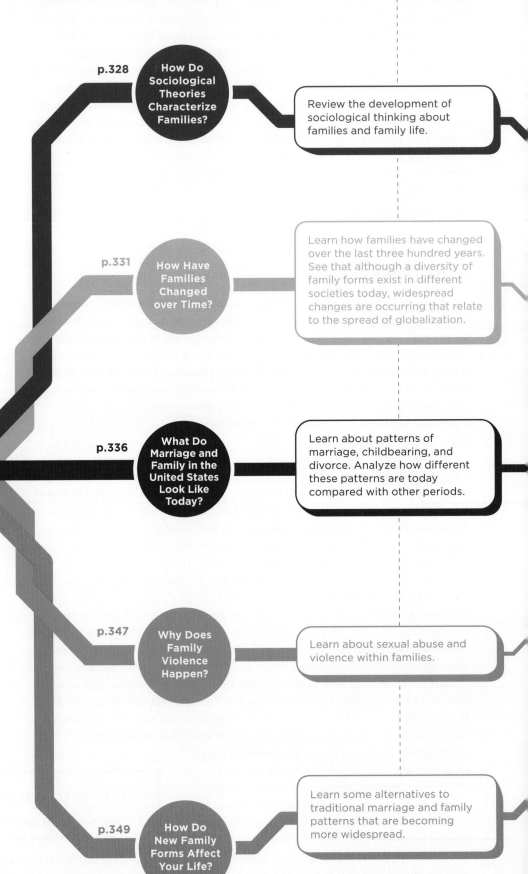

Chapter 11

Families and Intimate Relationships

p.328 How Do Sociological Theories Characterize Families?

Review the development of sociological thinking about families and family life.

p.331 How Have Families Changed over Time?

Learn how families have changed over the last three hundred years. See that although a diversity of family forms exist in different societies today, widespread changes are occurring that relate to the spread of globalization.

p.336 What Do Marriage and Family in the United States Look Like Today?

Learn about patterns of marriage, childbearing, and divorce. Analyze how different these patterns are today compared with other periods.

p.347 Why Does Family Violence Happen?

Learn about sexual abuse and violence within families.

p.349 How Do New Family Forms Affect Your Life?

Learn some alternatives to traditional marriage and family patterns that are becoming more widespread.

family • kinship • marriage •
nuclear family • extended
family • family of orientation •
family of procreation •
matrilocal family • patrilocal
family • monogamy • polygamy •
polygyny • polyandry

primary socialization •
personality stabilization

1. According to the functionalist perspective, what are two main functions of families?
2. According to feminist perspectives, what three aspects of family life are sources of concern? Why are these three aspects troubling to feminists?

1. Briefly describe changes in family size over the past three centuries.
2. How has Stephanie Coontz dispelled the myth of the peaceful and harmonious family believed to exist in past decades?
3. Give two examples of problems facing families in past centuries.
4. What are four conditions that have contributed to changing family forms throughout the world?
5. How has migration from rural to urban areas affected family life?
6. What are the seven most important changes occurring in families worldwide?

stepfamily

1. Briefly describe changes in family structure in the United States since 1960.
2. Contrast both general and nonmarital fertility rates among whites, blacks, Hispanics, Asians, and Native Americans in the United States.
3. According to Edin and Kefalas, why do many low-income women have babies out of wedlock?
4. What are the main reasons divorce rates increased sharply during the latter half of the twentieth century?
5. How does divorce affect the well-being of children?

1. How do social scientists measure and track patterns of child abuse?
2. Describe gender differences in patterns of spousal abuse.

cohabitation

1. Why has cohabitation become so common in the United States and worldwide?
2. Does cohabitation lead to divorce? Why or why not?

12

Education and Religion

THE BIG QUESTIONS

WHY ARE EDUCATION AND LITERACY SO IMPORTANT?
Know how and why systems of mass education emerged in the United States. Know some basic facts about the education system and literacy rates of developing countries.

WHAT IS THE LINKAGE BETWEEN EDUCATION AND INEQUALITY?
Become familiar with the most important research on whether education reduces or perpetuates inequality. Learn the social and cultural influences on educational achievement.

HOW DO SOCIOLOGISTS THINK ABOUT RELIGION?
Learn the elements that make up religion. Know the sociological approaches to religion developed by Marx, Durkheim, and Weber, as well as the religious economy approach.

HOW DOES RELIGION AFFECT LIFE THROUGHOUT THE WORLD?
Understand the various ways religious communities are organized and how they have become institutionalized. Recognize how the globalization of religion is reflected in religious activism in poor countries and the rise of religious nationalist movements.

HOW DOES RELIGION AFFECT YOUR LIFE IN THE UNITED STATES?
Learn about the sociological dimensions of religion in the United States.

Malala Yousafzai has become an internationally recognized advocate for girls' education. At age fifteen in 2012, Malala was shot and gravely wounded by members of the Taliban. Malala survived the injury and was later nominated for the 2013 Nobel Peace Prize.

Most young American men and women take for granted that they will graduate high school, and even go on to college or graduate school. Yet in some parts of the world, young women have to fight to receive even a middle school education. For the remarkable Malala Yousafzai, her desire to receive an education nearly cost the teenager her life.

In October 2012, when Malala was just fifteen years old, she was shot in the head and neck as she rode the bus home from her school in Mingora in the Swat district of Pakistan's Khyber Pakhtunkhwa province. The gunmen were members of the Taliban, an Islamic fundamentalist group that has long oppressed women. The Taliban had set an edict that girls in Mingora could not attend school after the age of fifteen. They had reportedly blown up more than one hundred schools, and threatened to blow up others. But why would they single out Malala for attack?

Several years earlier, Malala had maintained a blog and had spoken out publicly against the Taliban's mistreatment of girls and women. In one of her early public speeches, the bold teenager asked, "How dare the Taliban take away my basic right to education?" By challenging the religious beliefs of the Taliban and advocating for the education of girls and women, Malala had made herself a target (Peer 2012; Yousafzai and Lamb 2013).

The shooting of Malala sent shockwaves throughout the world. In the days after her attack, she lay unconscious at a local hospital in critical condition. As her condition improved, she was sent to a hospital in England for continued care. Her health improved, but she remained at risk; members of the Taliban publicly stated that they still intended to kill Malala and her father, a poet and social activist.

Malala ultimately triumphed, however. She made a full recovery, wrote a book documenting her ordeal (Yousafzai and Lamb 2013), and became an internationally recognized heroine—an advocate for women's education worldwide. She received a litany of awards, including a nomination for the 2013 Nobel Peace Prize. Malala also graced the cover of *Time* magazine in 2013 and was named one of the "100 most influential people in the world" by the publication. Her ordeal also called attention to the state of girls' education in Pakistan, as well as other parts of the world where a high school diploma is not a taken-for-granted part of teenagers' lives. Just 2.4 percent of Pakistan's gross domestic product is dedicated to education. According to United Nations data, 5.1 million children in Pakistan are not attending school, and two-thirds of them are female. Due in part to this gender gap in education, a stark gender gap in literacy rates persists; 38 percent of young women ages fifteen to twenty-four (versus just 21 percent of their male peers) are illiterate, meaning that they cannot read or write (UNICEF 2013).

Malala's story highlights many important themes that are at the core of the sociology of education and the sociology of religion. Education is a social institution that teaches individuals how to be active, engaged members of society. Through education, we become aware of the common characteristics we share with other members of the same society and gain at least some sort of knowledge about our society's geographical and political position in the world and its past history. The educational system both directly and indirectly exposes young people to the lessons that they will need to learn to become players in other major social institutions such as the economy and the family. Yet education also gives us power; it provides us with the intellectual resources to scrutinize and critique the world around us. As we saw in Chapter 7, formal education also provides the tools and credentials needed to seek gainful employment and, in some cases, to become upwardly mobile economically. It's mainly for these reasons that the Taliban so opposed Malala and other girls receiving an education: it would give them freedom, independence, and knowledge of a world beyond the confines of their insular Muslim community in Pakistan.

Like education, religion is an institution that exercises a socializing influence. However, while education is intended to be universalistic and to expose all young people to similar messages, religious institutions vary widely in the values, beliefs, and practices that they impart. Some religions, for example, teach that all persons are created equal, whereas others are based on a foundation of oppression, where some groups are viewed as morally superior to and more worthy than others. Sociologists of religion try to assess under what conditions religion unites communities and under what conditions it divides them. The study of religion is a challenging enterprise that places special demands on the sociological imagination, as we must be sensitive to individual beliefs that may be rooted in faith more so than science.

This chapter focuses on the socializing processes of education and religion. To study these issues, we look at how present-day education developed and analyze its socializing influence. We also look at education in relation to social inequality and consider how far the educational system exacerbates or reduces such inequality. Then we move to studying religion and the different forms that religious beliefs and practices take. We also analyze the various types of religious organizations and the effect of social change on the position of religion in the wider world.

WHY ARE EDUCATION AND LITERACY SO IMPORTANT?

Know how and why systems of mass education emerged in the United States. Know some basic facts about the education system and literacy rates of developing countries.

The term *school* has its origins in a Greek word meaning "leisure," or "recreation." In premodern societies, schooling existed for the few who had the time and resources available to pursue the cultivation of the arts and philosophy. For some, their engagement with schooling was like taking up a hobby. For others, like religious leaders or priests, schooling was a way of gaining skills and thus increasing their ability to interpret sacred texts. But for the vast majority of people, growing up meant learning by example the same social habits and work skills as their elders. Learning was a family affair—there were no schools at all for the mass of the population. Since children often started to help with domestic duties and farming work at very young ages, they rapidly became full-fledged members of the community.

Education in its modern form, the instruction of pupils within specially constructed school premises, gradually emerged in the first few years of the nineteenth century, when primary schools began to be constructed in Europe and the United States. One main reason for the rise of large educational systems was the process of industrialization, with its ensuing expansion of cities.

EDUCATION AND INDUSTRIALIZATION

Until the first few decades of the nineteenth century, most of the world's population had no schooling whatsoever. But as the industrial economy rapidly expanded, there was a great demand for specialized schooling that could produce an educated, capable workforce. As occupations became more differentiated and were increasingly located away from the home, it was impossible for work skills to be passed on directly from parents to children.

As educational systems became universal, more and more people were exposed to abstract learning (of subjects like math, science, history, and literature), rather than to the practical transmission of specific skills. In a modern society, people have to be furnished with basic skills—such as reading, writing, and calculating—and a general knowledge of their physical, social, and economic environment, but it is also important that they know how to learn, so that they are able to master new, sometimes very technical, forms of information. An advanced society also needs pure research and insights with no immediate practical value, in order to push out the boundaries of knowledge. For example, developing complex reasoning skills, the ability to debate the merits of competing theories, and an understanding of philosophical and religious debates are three skills essential to a cultured and well-educated society.

In the modern age, education and other qualifications became an important stepping-stone into job opportunities and careers. For example, colleges and universities not only broaden people's minds and perspectives but are expected

With the spread of industrialization, the demand for educated workers increased. The newly expanded education systems emphasized basic skills like reading, writing, and mathematics instead of specific skills for work.

to prepare new generations of citizens for participation in economic life. Think about your own college education. Perhaps you're required to take certain general-education courses to provide you with a broad base of knowledge; you might also take very specific courses in your major that help prepare you for your future career. It can be difficult to achieve the right balance between receiving a generalist education and learning concepts and skills related to one's chosen profession. Specialized forms of technical, vocational, and professional training often supplement pupils' liberal arts education and facilitate the transition from school to work. Internships, for example, allow young people to develop specific knowledge applicable to their future careers.

Although schools and universities seek above all to provide students with a well-rounded education, policymakers and employers are concerned with ensuring that education and training programs produce a stream of graduates who can meet a country's employment demands. Yet in times of rapid economic and technical change, the priorities of the educational system don't always match up with the availability of professional opportunities. The rapid expansion of a country's health care system, for example, would dramatically increase the demand for trained health professionals, laboratory technicians, capable administrators, and computer systems analysts familiar with public health issues. Industry-wide changes in factory-floor production technology would require a workforce with a set of skills that might be in short supply.

The complex relationship between the educational system and the country's employment demands may be further complicated by an emerging trend: home schooling. Between 2000 and 2010, the number of students who were home schooled increased steadily; an estimated 1.5 to 2 million (or 2.9 percent of all) children are currently home schooled (U.S. Department of Education 2011). **Home schooling** means that a child is taught by his or her parents, guardians, or a team of adults who oversee the child's educational development. The curriculum studied by home-schooled children varies widely from state to state; some states mandate quite strict curricula while others are much more lax and provide the parent with great leeway.

home schooling • A growing trend (but a longtime practice) of parents or guardians educating their children at home, for religious, philosophical, or safety reasons.

A survey conducted by the U.S. Department of Education in 2008 queried parents about their motivation for home schooling their children. The most frequently cited reasons were a concern about the school environment (85 percent), a desire to provide religious or moral instruction (72 percent), and dissatisfaction with the academic instruction at other schools (68 percent). It remains to be seen how well home schooling prepares young adults for the future challenges of college or employment in the United States. Only one study to date has examined how college students who were home schooled compare with their classmates who attended regular high schools. The researchers found that home-schooled young adults enjoyed higher ACT scores, grade point averages, and graduation rates compared with other college students (Cogan 2010). However, many sociologists would like to see these findings confirmed in other samples before concluding that home schooling provides the same benefits as traditional schools.

SOCIOLOGICAL THEORIES

Sociologists have debated why formal systems of schooling developed in modern societies by studying the social functions that schools provide. For example, some have argued that mass education promotes feelings of nationalism and aided the development of national societies comprising citizens from different regions who would know the same history and speak a common language (Ramirez and Boli 1987). Marxist sociologists have argued that the expansion of education was brought about by employers' need for certain personality characteristics in their workers— self-discipline, dependability, punctuality, obedience, and the like—which are all taught in schools (Bowles and Gintis 1976). Another influential perspective comes from the sociologist Randall Collins, who has argued that the primary social function of mass education derives from the need for diplomas and degrees to determine one's credentials for a job, even if the work involved has nothing to do with the education one has received. Over time, the practice of credentialism results in demands for higher credentials, which require higher levels of educational attainment. Jobs that thirty years ago would have required a high school diploma, such as sales representative, now require a college degree. Since educational attainment is closely related to class position, credentialism reinforces the class structure within a society (Collins 1971, 1979).

EDUCATION AND LITERACY IN THE DEVELOPING WORLD

Literacy is the "baseline" of education. Without it, schooling cannot proceed. We take it for granted in the West that the majority of people are literate, but this is only a recent development in Western history. The rise of literacy in Europe was closely tied to sweeping social transformations, particularly the Protestant Reformation, which brought individual study of the Bible, and the rise of modern science. Literacy spread during the Reformation and Renaissance eras due largely to the development of printing from movable type. Compulsory schooling, established in Europe and the United States in the nineteenth century, was perhaps the most important influence on the high rates of literacy in the world today (Barton 2006).

literacy • The ability to read and write.

Today, 20.2 percent of the population ages fifteen years and older in developing countries are illiterate (UNESCO 2013). Although countries have instituted literacy programs, they have made only modest strides in raising the literacy rate. Television, radio, and other electronic media can be used, where they are available, to skip the stage of learning literacy skills and convey educational programs directly to adults. Although these programs may be more appealing to the general public than formal educational programs, they are typically less effective.

During the period of colonialism, colonial governments regarded education with some trepidation. Until the twentieth century, most believed indigenous populations were too primitive to be worth educating. Later, education was seen as a way of making local elites acclimate to European ways of life. To some extent, this backfired: The majority of those who led anticolonial and nationalist movements were educated elites who had attended schools in Europe. They were able to compare firsthand the democratic institutions of the European countries with the absence of democracy in their lands of origin.

The education that the colonizers introduced usually focused on issues relevant to Europe, not the colonial areas themselves. Educated Africans in the British colonies knew about the kings and queens of England and read Shakespeare, but knew next to nothing about their own countries' histories or cultural achievements. Policies of educational reform since the end of colonialism have not completely altered the situation even today. Partly as a result of the legacy of colonial education, which was not directed toward the majority of the population, the educational system in many developing countries is top-heavy: Higher education is disproportionately developed, relative to primary and secondary education. The result is a correspondingly overqualified group that, having attended colleges and universities, cannot find white-collar or professional jobs. Given the low level of industrial development, most of the better-paid positions are in government, and there are not enough of those to go around.

In recent years, some developing countries, recognizing the shortcomings of the curricula inherited from colonialism, have tried to redirect their educational programs toward the rural poor. They have had limited success because usually there is insufficient funding to pay for the scale of the necessary innovations. As a result, countries such as India have begun programs of self-help education. Communities draw on existing resources without creating demands for high levels of financing. Those who can read and write and who perhaps possess job skills are encouraged to take others on as apprentices. ✓

CONCEPT CHECKS ✓

1. Why did schooling become widespread only after the Industrial Revolution?

2. What are some of the functions of formal schooling?

3. What are the three main motivations for home schooling?

4. What are some of the reasons there are many illiterate people in the developing world?

Become familiar with the most important research on whether education reduces or perpetuates inequality. Learn the social and cultural influences on educational achievement.

WHAT IS THE LINKAGE BETWEEN EDUCATION AND INEQUALITY?

The expansion of education in both developing and wealthy nations has always been closely linked to the ideals of democracy. Reformers value education for its own sake—for the opportunity it provides for individuals to develop their capabilities.

EDUCATIONAL ATTAINMENT

Educational attainment is a key indicator of human development. The level and distribution of educational attainment has a strong impact on social outcomes, such as child mortality, fertility, and income distribution.

POPULATION WITH AT LEAST A SECONDARY EDUCATION

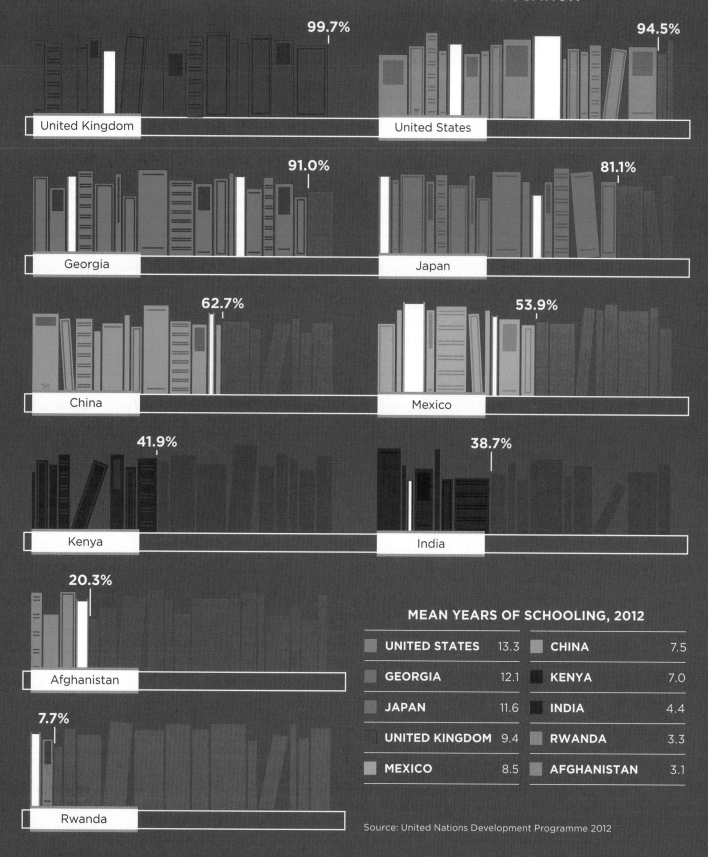

United Kingdom — 99.7%

United States — 94.5%

Georgia — 91.0%

Japan — 81.1%

China — 62.7%

Mexico — 53.9%

Kenya — 41.9%

India — 38.7%

Afghanistan — 20.3%

Rwanda — 7.7%

MEAN YEARS OF SCHOOLING, 2012

UNITED STATES	13.3	CHINA	7.5
GEORGIA	12.1	KENYA	7.0
JAPAN	11.6	INDIA	4.4
UNITED KINGDOM	9.4	RWANDA	3.3
MEXICO	8.5	AFGHANISTAN	3.1

Source: United Nations Development Programme 2012

Yet education has also consistently been seen as a means of promoting equality. Access to universal education, it has been argued, could help reduce disparities of wealth and power. It is for this reason, in part, that the Taliban went to such great lengths to prevent Malala, and other young women like her, from receiving an education; this education would empower her and other girls in her village in Pakistan. Are educational opportunities truly equal for everyone? Has education in fact proved to be a great equalizer? Much research has been devoted to answering these questions.

"FIRE IN THE ASHES"

Over the past three decades, the journalist Jonathan Kozol has studied schools in about thirty neighborhoods around the United States. Through this work, he has vividly shown how unequal schools are in the United States, and has also shown that these inequalities contribute powerfully to students' lives as they enter adulthood. Beginning with his earliest research, conducted between 1988 and 1990, Kozol didn't follow a special logic when he chose the schools in his study. He simply went where he happened to know teachers, principals, or ministers. What startled him most was the segregation within these schools and the inequalities among them. Kozol brought these terrible conditions to the attention of the American people in his best-selling book *Savage Inequalities* (Kozol 1991).

In his passionate opening chapter, he first took readers to East St. Louis, Illinois, a city that has been roughly 98 percent black for the past several decades. At the time of Kozol's research, the city had no regular trash collection and few jobs. Three-quarters of its residents were living on welfare at the time. City residents were forced to use their backyards as garbage dumps, which attracted a plague of flies and rats during the hot summer months. East St. Louis also had some of the sickest children in the United States, with extremely high rates of infant death, asthma, and poor nutrition and extremely low rates of immunization. Only 55 percent of the children had been fully immunized for polio, diphtheria, measles, and whooping cough. Among the city's other social problems were crime, dilapidated housing, poor health care, and lack of education.

Kozol showed how the problems of the city affected the school on a daily basis. Teachers often had to hold classes without chalk or paper. One teacher commented on these conditions affecting her teaching: "I have no materials with the exception of a single textbook given to each child. If I bring in anything else—books or tapes or magazines—I bring it in myself. The high school has no VCRs. . . . The AV equipment in the school is so old that we are pressured not to use it." Comments from students reflected the same concerns. "I don't go to physics class because my lab has no equipment," said one student. Only 55 percent of the students in this high school ultimately graduated, about one-third of whom went on to college.

Kozol also wrote about the other end of the economic spectrum, describing the experiences of students in a wealthy suburban school in Westchester County outside New York City. Two-thirds of the senior class were enrolled in an advanced placement (AP) class. Kozol visited an AP class and asked students about their views on inequalities within the educational system. Students at this school were aware of the economic advantages that they enjoyed at both home and school. They were also aware of the disadvantages experienced by students in inner-city school districts. Although many believed that equalizing resources across schools was a laudable goal,

Journalist Jonathan Kozol documented devastating inequalities in public schools in his 1991 book *Savage Inequalities*. Run-down public schools in East St. Louis, Illinois, had crumbling buildings, leaky ceilings, and few if any school supplies.

they thought it would make little difference in the long run because the poor students lacked motivation and would fail because of the many other problems in their lives. These students also realized that equalizing spending could have adverse effects on their school. As one student observed, "If you equalize the money, someone's got to be shortchanged. I don't doubt that [poor] children are getting a bad deal. But do we want everyone to get a mediocre education?"

More than two decades later, Kozol went back and revisited the neighborhoods and children he studied to find out what happened to them. His portraits are often depressing, with many of the children from the poorer districts growing up to be troubled adults. Their lives often were derailed by alcohol abuse, unwanted pregnancies, murders, prison time, and even death by suicide. Yet Kozol did find that a handful of the students succeeded even though the odds were stacked against them. Most of these resilient children had been fortunate to have especially devoted parents, the support from their religious community, or a serendipitous scholarship opportunity. As Kozol notes in his 2012 book *Fire in the Ashes: Twenty-Five Years among the Poorest Children in America,* "These children had unusual advantages: Someone intervened in every case." For example, one young girl named Pineapple, whom Kozol met when she was a kindergartner, went on to graduate college and become a social worker. Pineapple attended a school that Kozol described as "almost always in a state of chaos because so many teachers did not stay for long." A local minister helped her get scholarships to private schools. The daughter of Spanish-speaking immigrants, Pineapple had to work hard to overcome deficits in reading, writing, and basic study skills, but she and her older sister both were the first in their family to finish high school and go to college (Kozol 2012).

While the personal tales of Pineapple and her sister are inspiring, Kozol's analyses reveal that very little has improved in the past two decades. For example, there remain vast disparities in educational spending in largely black and Latino central cities versus largely white well-to-do suburbs. He reported that in 2002–2003, New York City spent $11,627 on each public school child, while in Nassau County, the towns of Manhasset and Great Neck spent $22,311 and $19,705, respectively. These patterns weren't limited to the New York area but rather were found throughout the United States. Because school funding tends to come from local property taxes, wealthier places have more funding for schools, while poorer neighborhoods with few lavish private homes generate far less money for schools. As with his earlier studies of St. Louis, Kozol visited schools that were just a few miles apart geographically but that offered vastly different educational opportunities. While suburban white schools would offer advanced math, literature, and an array of arts electives, the nearby primarily black school would offer classes like hairdressing, typing, and auto shop.

Kozol's poignant journalistic account of educational inequality has become part of our nation's conventional wisdom on the subject of educational inequality. But many sociologists have argued that although Kozol's book is a moving portrait, it provides an inaccurate and incomplete view of educational inequality. Why would Kozol's research not be compelling? There are several reasons, including the unsystematic way that he chose the schools that he studied. Sociologists, however, have proposed a variety of theories and identified myriad factors that contribute to the inequality and differential outcomes that Kozol witnessed in the schools he visited.

COLEMAN'S STUDY OF "BETWEEN SCHOOL EFFECTS" IN AMERICAN EDUCATION

Studies comparing how schools differ from one another (or "between school effects" studies) have been the focus of sociological research on the educational system for the past three decades. One of the classic investigations of educational inequality was undertaken in the United States in the 1960s. As part of the Civil Rights Act of 1964, the commissioner of education was required to prepare a report on educational inequalities resulting from differences of ethnic background, religion, and national origin. James Coleman, a sociologist, was director of the research program. The outcome was a study, published in 1966, based on one of the most extensive research projects ever carried out in sociology.

Information was collected on more than half a million pupils who were given a range of achievement tests assessing verbal and nonverbal abilities, reading levels, and mathematical skills. Sixty thousand teachers also completed forms providing data for about 4,000 schools. The report found that a large majority of children went to schools that effectively segregated black from white. Almost 80 percent of schools attended by white students contained only 10 percent or fewer African American students. White and Asian American students scored higher on achievement tests than did blacks and other ethnic-minority students. Coleman had supposed his results would also show schools that were mainly African American to have worse facilities, larger classes, and inferior buildings than schools that were predominantly white. But surprisingly, the results showed far fewer differences of this type than had been anticipated.

Coleman therefore concluded that the material resources provided in schools made little difference to educational performance; the decisive influence was the children's backgrounds. In Coleman's words, "Inequalities imposed on children by their home, neighborhood, and peer environment are carried along to become the inequalities with which they confront adult life at the end of school" (Coleman et al. 1966). There was, however, some evidence that students from deprived backgrounds who formed close friendships with those from more favorable circumstances were likely to be more successful educationally. The findings of Coleman's study have been replicated many times over the past decades, most notably by Christopher Jencks and colleagues (Jencks et al. 1972; Schofield 1995).

TRACKING AND "WITHIN-SCHOOL EFFECTS"

The practice of **tracking**—dividing students into groups that receive different instruction on the basis of assumed similarities in ability or attainment—is common in American schools. In some schools, students are tracked only for certain subjects; in others, for all subjects. Sociologists have long believed that tracking partly explains why schooling seems to have little effect on existing social inequalities, since being placed in a particular track labels a student as either able or otherwise. Children from more privileged backgrounds, in which academic work is encouraged, are likely to find themselves in the higher tracks early on—and by and large stay there.

In a classic study of school tracking, Jeannie Oakes (1985) studied twenty-five junior and senior high schools, both large and small and in both urban and rural areas, and concentrated on differences within schools rather than among them. She found that although several schools claimed they did not track students, virtually all of them had mechanisms for sorting students into groups on the basis of purported ability and achievement to make teaching easier. In other words, they employed tracking but did not choose to use the term *tracking* itself. Oakes found that tracking made both teachers and students label students based on their track—high ability, low achieving, slow, average, and so on. Individual students in these groups came to be defined by teachers, other students, and themselves in terms of such labels. A student in a "high-achieving" group was considered a high-achieving person—smart and quick. Pupils in a "low-achieving" group came to be seen as slow, below average—or, in more colloquial terms, as "dummies." What is the impact of tracking on students in the "low" group? A subsequent study by Oakes found that these students received a poorer education in terms of the quality of courses, teachers, and textbooks made available to them (Oakes 1990). Moreover, tracking had a negative impact primarily on students who were poor, and particularly on African American or Latino students.

Despite these negative consequences, school systems typically track students because of the assumption that bright children learn more quickly and effectively in a group of others who are equally able, and that clever students are held back if placed in mixed groups. This assumption is partially supported by a pathbreaking study by the sociologist Adam Gamoran. Gamoran and his colleagues agreed with Oakes's conclusions that tracking reinforces previously existing inequalities for average or poor students. However, they also found that tracking has positive benefits for "advanced" students (Gamoran et al. 1995). The debate about the effects of tracking is sure to continue as scholars analyze more

tracking • Dividing students into groups according to ability.

Making Sociology Work
SCHOOL ADMINISTRATOR

School administrators often must make difficult decisions. Two of the biggest controversies facing educators today are school tracking and social promotion. Tracking is a practice whereby students are assigned to specific groups or classes based on their abilities, talents, or previous achievement. An estimated 60 percent of primary and 80 percent of secondary schools do tracking today. Social promotion is the practice of promoting students to the next grade level, despite their poor grades, to keep them with social peers. A number of cities, including Baltimore, Chicago, New York, and Philadelphia, have stopped social promotions. Decisions about school policy require a strong knowledge of sociological research. Drawing on the research of sociologists like Jeannie Oakes, would you maintain the practices of tracking and social promotion in your school? Why or why not?

data. Nearly two decades after Gamoran's study was published, tracking was still considered "one of the most divisive issues" facing educators and school administrators (*Education Week* 2004).

THE SOCIAL REPRODUCTION OF INEQUALITY

The educational system provides more than formal instruction: It socializes children to get along with one another, teaches basic skills, and transmits elements of culture such as language and values. Sociologists have looked at education as a form of social reproduction, a concept discussed in Chapter 1 and elsewhere. In the context of education, *social reproduction* refers to the ways in which schools help perpetuate social and economic inequalities across the generations. It also directs our attention to the means whereby schools influence the learning of values, attitudes, and habits via the hidden curriculum.

The concept of the **hidden curriculum** addresses the fact that much of what is learned in school has nothing directly to do with the formal content of lessons. The hidden curriculum teaches children that their role in life is "to know their place and to sit still with it" (Illich 1983). Children spend long hours in school, and get an early taste of what the world of work will be like, learning that they are expected to be punctual and apply themselves diligently to the tasks that those in authority set for them.

Another influential theory on the question of how schools reproduce social inequality was introduced by Samuel Bowles and Herbert Gintis. Modern education, they propose, is a response to the economic needs of industrial capitalism. Schools help provide the technical and social skills required by industrial enterprise, and they instill discipline and respect for authority in the future labor force. Authority relations in school, which are hierarchical and place strong emphasis on obedience, directly parallel those dominating the workplace.

Schooling has not become the "great equalizer"; rather, schools merely produce for many the feelings of powerlessness that continue throughout their experience in industrial settings. Under the current system, schools "are destined to legitimize inequality, limit personal development to forms compatible with submission to arbitrary authority, and aid in the process whereby youth are resigned to their fate" (Bowles and Gintis 1976). If there were greater democracy in the workplace and more equality in society at large, Bowles and Gintis argue, a system of education could be developed that would provide for greater individual fulfillment.

INTELLIGENCE AND INEQUALITY

Suppose differences in educational attainment, and in subsequent occupations and incomes, directly reflected differential intelligence. In such circumstances, it might be argued, there is in fact equality of opportunity in the school system for people to find a level equivalent to their innate potential.

WHAT IS INTELLIGENCE?

For years, psychologists, geneticists, statisticians, and others have debated whether there exists a single human capability that can be called **intelligence** and, if so, whether it rests on innately determined differences. Intelligence is difficult to define

hidden curriculum • Traits of behavior or attitudes that are learned at school but not included within the formal curriculum—for example, gender differences.

intelligence • Level of intellectual ability, particularly as measured by IQ (intelligence quotient) tests.

because, as the term is usually employed, it covers qualities that may be unrelated to one another. We might suppose, for example, that the "purest" form of intelligence is the ability to solve abstract mathematical puzzles. However, people who are very good at such puzzles sometimes show low capabilities in other areas, such as history or art. Since the concept has proved so resistant to definition, some psychologists have proposed (and many educators have by default accepted) that intelligence should simply be regarded as "what **IQ (intelligence quotient)** tests measure." Most IQ tests consist of a mixture of conceptual and computational problems. The tests are constructed so that the average score is 100 points: Anyone scoring below is thus labeled "below-average intelligence," and anyone scoring above is "above-average intelligence." In spite of the fundamental difficulty in measuring intelligence, IQ tests are widely used in research studies, as well as in schools and businesses.

IQ (intelligence quotient) •
A score attained on tests of symbolic or reasoning abilities.

Scores on IQ tests do in fact correlate highly with academic performance (which is not surprising, since IQ tests were originally developed to predict success at school). They therefore also correlate closely with social, economic, and ethnic differences, since these are associated with variations in levels of educational attainment. White students score better, on average, than African Americans or members of other disadvantaged minorities.

The relationship between race and intelligence is best explained by social rather than biological causes, according to a team of Berkeley sociologists in their 1996 book *Inequality by Design: Cracking the Bell Curve Myth* (Fischer et al. 1996). The authors conducted this research as a way to rigorously evaluate the controversial claims made by Richard J. Herrnstein and Charles Murray in their book *The Bell Curve* (1994), which argued that the black-white gap in IQ was due in part to genetic differences in intelligence. All societies have oppressed ethnic groups. Low status, often coupled with discrimination and mistreatment, leads to socioeconomic deprivation, group segregation, and a stigma of inferiority. The combination of these forces often prevents racial minorities from obtaining education, and consequently, their scores on standardized intelligence tests are lower.

The average lower IQ score of African Americans in the United States is remarkably similar to that of deprived ethnic minorities in other countries—such as the "untouchables" in India (who are at the very bottom of the caste system), the Maori in New Zealand, and the *burakumin* of Japan. Children in these groups score an average of ten to fifteen IQ points below children belonging to the ethnic majority. Such observations strongly suggest that the IQ variations between African Americans and whites in the United States result from social, cultural, and economic—rather than genetic—factors.

EDUCATIONAL REFORM IN THE UNITED STATES

Research done by sociologists has played a major role in reforming the educational system. The object of James Coleman's research, commissioned as part of the 1964 Civil Rights Act, was not solely academic; it was undertaken to influence policy. Education has long been a political battleground. In the 1960s, partly in response to Coleman's work, some politicians, educators, and community activists pushed for universal access to high-quality education through such initiatives as busing programs to mitigate racial segregation, bilingual education programs, multicultural education, open admissions to college, the establishment of ethnic studies programs on campuses, and more equitable funding schemes. Such initiatives were seen as supporting civil rights and equality. Educational policies in the twenty-first century have similarly intended

In 1970 a U.S. judge in North Carolina ordered that black students be bused to white schools and that white students be bused to black schools in an attempt to end the de facto segregation of public schools caused by white students living in predominantly white neighborhoods and black students living in predominantly black neighborhoods.

to provide quality education to all children and close the achievement gap. However, scholars disagree about how successful recent policies have been in meeting this goal.

One important target of educational policy today is improving levels of **functional literacy** in the United States. Literacy is more than the ability to read and write; literacy is also the ability to process complex information in our increasingly technology-focused society. The National Center for Education Statistics breaks literacy into three components: prose literacy, document literacy, and quantitative literacy. Prose literacy means that a person can look at a short piece of text to get a small piece of uncomplicated information. Document literacy refers to a person's ability to locate and use information in forms, schedules, charts, graphs, and other informational tables. Quantitative literacy is the ability to do simple addition. In the United States today, an estimated 14 percent of the adult population lack prose literacy, 12 percent are at the "below basic" level for document literacy, and 22 percent have quantitative literacy skills that are "basic" or better. Only 13 percent of the population is proficient in these three areas (Kutner et al. 2007). Of course, the United States is a country of immigrants, who, when they arrive, may not be able to read and write, and who may also have trouble with English. However, this doesn't explain why America lags behind most other industrial countries in terms of its level of functional literacy.

Some policymakers believe that one of the most effective ways to enhance literacy and other academic outcomes is through formal testing and benchmarking of student progress. The most significant piece of federal legislation influencing education in the past two decades is the No Child Left Behind (NCLB) Act, signed into law by President George W. Bush in 2002. NCLB implemented a host of policies meant to improve academic outcomes for all children and close achievement gaps. As we saw in Chapter 7, rates of high school graduation and college attendance vary dramatically by race, ethnicity, and one's socioeconomic background.

The most expansive and comprehensive piece of legislation passed since 1965, NCLB addresses virtually every aspect of education, including testing, school choice, teacher quality, the education of English-language learners, military recruitment in schools, and school discipline. At the top of its agenda is instituting **standardized testing**, where all students in a state take the same test under the same conditions, as a means of measuring students' academic performance. The act also provides a strong push for school choice; that is, in the spirit of competition, parents are to be given choices as to where they send their children to school. Low-performing schools, at risk of losing students, may jeopardize their funding and eventually be closed. Another significant implication of NCLB is that for the first time since 1968, states are not required to offer non–English-speaking students bilingual education. Instead, the act emphasizes learning English over using students' native language to support learning objectives and favors English-only program models. NCLB also provides support for a "zero tolerance" approach to school discipline that was first mandated in the 1990 Gun-Free School Act.

The NCLB has been widely criticized, as teachers must "teach to the test." Critics have argued that the emphasis on standardized testing as the means of assessment encourages teachers to teach a narrow set of skills that will increase students' test performance, rather than helping them to acquire an in-depth understanding of important concepts and skills (Hursh 2007). Others have described the program as a punitive model of school reform (i.e., teachers and principals at underperforming schools risk job loss), and note that achievement gaps have not changed, and that the policy neglects the important fact that the broader socioeconomic context affects school functioning.

functional literacy • Having reading and writing skills that are beyond a basic level and are sufficient to manage one's everyday activities and employment tasks.

standardized testing • A procedure whereby all students in a state take the same test under the same conditions.

In 2012, recognizing that the NCLB may not be effective for all school systems, President Barack Obama granted waivers from NCLB requirements to thirty-two states, instead allowing them to develop their own standards and exempting them from the 2014 targets set by NCLB. In exchange for that flexibility, those states "have agreed to raise standards, improve accountability, and undertake essential reforms to improve teacher effectiveness," the White House said in a statement. The Obama administration also implemented its own program, called Race to the Top, a contest where states compete for up to $700 million in funding. The program is meant to spur innovation and reform by rewarding those states that work to develop and retain effective teachers, adopt common standards and assessments, promote charter schools, and turn around low-performing schools. Like NCLB, however, Race to the Top has been roundly criticized for relying too heavily on high-stakes testing and also failing to address the true causes of low student achievement, namely poverty and lack of opportunity. Teachers' unions and educators have also complained that basing teacher evaluations on students' standardized test scores is ineffective (Dillon 2010).

The crisis in American schools won't be solved in the short term, and it won't be solved by educational reforms alone, no matter how well intended. In fact, a 2006 study by the U.S. Department of Education found that schools identified as most in need of improvement were disproportionately urban, high-poverty schools, and that school poverty and district size were more powerful predictors of school success than any policies actually implemented by the schools (U.S. Department of Education 2006). A further unintended consequence of the current emphasis on testing is that schools

Some policymakers favor charter schools, which receive public funding yet operate independently. Many charter schools provide innovative education programs to low-income children. Critics counter that charter schools siphon funding from the public schools that serve a much larger number of children.

have narrowed their course offerings to focus much more heavily on tested subject areas while cutting time in science, social studies, music, art, and physical education (Center on Education Policy 2007).

The lesson of sociological research is that inequalities and barriers in educational opportunity reflect wider social divisions and tensions. While the United States remains wracked by racial tensions, and the polarization between decaying cities and affluent suburbs persists, the crisis in the school system is likely to prove difficult to turn around.

What is to be done? Some have proposed giving schools more control over their budgets (a reform that has been carried out in Britain). The idea is that more responsibility for and control over budgeting decisions will create a greater drive to improve the school. Further proposals include the re-funding of federal programs such as Head Start to ensure healthy early-childhood development and thus save millions of dollars in later costs. Others have called for the privatization of public education, a proposal that has gained numerous supporters in recent years. Yet others call for more vast reforms. Jean Anyon's (2005) analysis of how political and economic forces influence schooling concludes that economic reforms, such as job creation and training programs and corporate tax reform, are necessary for schools to improve.

PRIVATIZATION

Widespread concern about the crisis in education has opened the door for public-private partnerships aimed at injecting private-sector know-how into failing public schools. Local school districts can choose to contract out specific educational services—or the entire school administration—to private companies without losing federal funding. In the past decade, a number of U.S. school districts—including large urban systems such as those in Hartford, Connecticut; Baltimore, Maryland; and Minneapolis, Minnesota—have invited for-profit educational companies to run their school systems.

Supporters of school privatization argue that state and federal education authorities have shown that they are unable to improve the nation's schools. The educational system, they argue, is wasteful and bureaucratic; it spends a disproportionate amount of its funding on noninstructional administrative costs. Because of their top-heavy nature, it is nearly impossible for school systems to be flexible and innovative. Incompetent teachers are difficult to remove because of the strength of teacher unions (Ravitch 2013).

What backers of school privatization claim can solve these problems is a strong dose of private-sector ideology: competition, experimentation, and incentive. For-profit companies can run school systems more efficiently and produce better outcomes by applying private-sector logic. Good teachers would be attracted to teaching—and retained—by performance-based pay schemes, while underperforming teachers could be removed more easily. Competition within and among schools would lead to higher levels of innovation; privatized schools would have more liberty to institutionalize the results of successful experiments.

CONCEPT CHECKS ✓

1. According to Kozol, has education become an equalizer in American society? Why or why not?

2. How do Coleman's findings differ from the results of Kozol's research? Whose theory, in your opinion, can better explain the racial gap in educational achievement?

3. What effect does tracking have on academic achievement?

4. How do schools perpetuate existing inequalities across generations?

5. Explain the relationship between race and intelligence. Do you find the evidence compelling?

6. Describe the components and critiques of the No Child Left Behind Act and Race to the Top.

HOW DO SOCIOLOGISTS THINK ABOUT RELIGION?

Learn the elements that make up religion. Know the sociological approaches to religion developed by Marx, Durkheim, and Weber, as well as the religious economy approach.

While modern education emerged in the nineteenth century, religion is one of the oldest human institutions. Cave drawings suggest that religious beliefs and practices existed more than 40,000 years ago. According to anthropologists, there have probably been about 100,000 religions throughout human history (Hadden 1997a). Sociologists define **religion** as a cultural system of commonly shared beliefs and rituals that provides a sense of meaning and purpose by creating an idea of reality that is sacred, all-encompassing, and supernatural (Durkheim 1965, orig. 1912; Berger 1967; Wuthnow 1988). There are three key elements in this definition:

1. **Religion is a form of culture.** You will recall from Chapter 2 that culture consists of the shared beliefs, values, norms, and material conditions that create a common identity among a group of people. Religion shares all of these characteristics.

2. **Religion involves beliefs that take the form of ritualized practices.** All religions have a behavioral aspect—special activities that identify believers as members of the religious community.

3. **Perhaps most important, religion provides a sense of purpose—a feeling that life is meaningful.** It does so by explaining what transcends or overshadows everyday life in ways that other aspects of culture (such as an educational system or a belief in democracy) typically cannot (Geertz 1973; Wuthnow 1988).

What is absent from the sociological definition of religion is as important as what is included: Nowhere is there mention of God. We often think of **theism**—a belief in one or more supernatural deities (the term originates from the Greek word for God)—as basic to religion, but this is not necessarily the case. Some religions, such as Buddhism, believe in the existence of spiritual forces rather than a particular God.

religion • A set of beliefs adhered to by the members of a community, incorporating symbols regarded with a sense of awe or wonder together with ritual practices. Religions do not universally involve a belief in supernatural entities.

theism • A belief in one or more supernatural deities.

(a) Surrounded by his parents and rabbi, a thirteen-year-old Jewish boy reads from the Torah during his Bar Mitzvah, effectively becoming a man in the eyes of his synagogue. (b) In a Catholic church in Brooklyn, an infant is baptized into the Christian faith when a priest ceremonially anoints him or her with holy water. What are some similarities and differences among the rituals of various religions?

Four broad conditions set the stage for the sociological study of religion:

1. **Sociologists are not concerned with whether religious beliefs are true or false.** From a sociological perspective, religions are regarded not as being decreed by God but as being socially constructed by human beings. As a result, sociologists put aside their personal beliefs when they study religion. They are concerned with the human rather than the divine aspects of religion. Sociologists ask: How is the religion organized? How is it related to the larger society? What explains its success or failure in recruiting and retaining believers? The question of whether a particular belief is "good" or "true," however important it may be to the believers of the religion under study, is not something that sociologists are able to address as sociologists. (As individuals, they may have strong opinions, but one hopes that they can keep these opinions from biasing their research.)

2. **Sociologists are especially concerned with the social organization of religion.** Religions are among the most important institutions in society. They are a primary source of the deepest-seated norms and values. At the same time, religions are typically practiced through an enormous variety of social forms. The sociology of religion is concerned with how different religious institutions and organizations actually function. The earliest European religions were often indistinguishable from the larger society, as religious beliefs and practices were incorporated into daily life. This is still true in many parts of the world today. In modern industrial society, however, religions have become established in separate, often bureaucratic, organizations, and so sociologists focus on the organizations through which religions must operate in order to survive (Hammond 1992).

3. **Sociologists often view religions as a major source of social solidarity because religions often provide their believers with a common set of norms and values.** Religious beliefs, rituals, and bonds help to create a "moral community" in which all members know how to behave toward one another (Wuthnow 1988). If a single religion dominates a society, the religion may be an important source of social stability. However, religion can also be oppressive if, like the Taliban, it requires absolute conformity to a particular set of beliefs and punishes those who deviate from these beliefs. For example, the attempted murder of Malala Yousafzai, whom we met in the chapter's opener, was an effort by some Taliban leaders to punish a young girl who defied their beliefs.

4. **Sociologists tend to explain the appeal of religion in terms of social forces rather than purely personal, spiritual, or psychological factors.** For many people, religious beliefs are a deeply personal experience, involving a powerful sense of connection with forces that transcend everyday reality. Sociologists do not question the depth of such feelings and experiences, but they are unlikely to limit themselves to a purely spiritual explanation of religious commitment. Some researchers argue that people often "get religion" when their fundamental sense of a social order is threatened by economic hardship, loneliness, loss or grief, physical suffering, or poor health (Berger 1967; Schwartz 1970; Glock 1976; Stark and Bainbridge 1980). In explaining the appeal of religious movements, sociologists are more likely to focus on the problems of the social order than on the psychological response of the individual.

THEORIES OF RELIGION

Sociological approaches to religion are strongly influenced by the classical theories of Marx, Durkheim, and Weber. None of the three was religious himself, and they all believed that religion would become less and less significant in modern times. Each argued that religion was fundamentally an illusion: The very diversity of religions and their obvious connection to different societies and regions of the world made the claims by their advocates inherently implausible. An individual born into an Australian society of hunters and gatherers would hold different religious beliefs from someone born into the caste system of India or the Catholic Church of medieval Europe.

MARX: RELIGION AND INEQUALITY

In spite of the influence of his views on the subject, Karl Marx never studied religion in any detail. His thinking on religion was derived mostly from the writings of Ludwig Feuerbach, who believed that through a process he called **alienation**, human beings tend to attribute their own culturally created values and norms to divine forces or gods because they do not understand their own history. Thus, the story of the Ten Commandments given to Moses by God is a mythical version of the origins of the moral precepts that govern the lives of Jewish and Christian believers.

Marx accepted the view that religion represents human self-alienation. In a famous phrase, Marx declared that religion was the "opium of the people." Religion defers happiness and rewards to the afterlife, he said, teaching the resigned acceptance of existing conditions in the earthly life. Attention is thus diverted from injustices in this world by the promise of what is to come in the next. Religious belief also can provide justifications for those in power. For example, "The meek shall inherit the earth" suggests attitudes of humility and nonresistance to oppression.

alienation • The sense that our own abilities as human beings are taken over by other entities. The term was originally used by Karl Marx to refer to the projection of human powers onto gods. Subsequently he used the term to refer to the loss of workers' control over the nature and products of their labor.

DURKHEIM: RELIGION AND FUNCTIONALISM

In contrast to Marx, Émile Durkheim spent a good part of his intellectual career studying religion, concentrating particularly on totemism, an ancient form of religion practiced by aboriginal Australians and Native Americans. *The Elementary Forms of the Religious Life*, first published in 1912, is perhaps the most influential single study in the sociology of religion (1965). Durkheim connected religion not with social inequalities or power but with the overall nature of the institutions of a society. His argument was that totemism represented religion in its most "elementary" form—hence the title of his book.

Durkheim defined religion in terms of a distinction between the sacred and the profane. **Sacred** objects and symbols, he held, are treated as apart from the routine aspects of day-to-day existence—the realm of the **profane**. A totem (an animal or plant believed to have particular symbolic significance), Durkheim argued, is a sacred object, regarded with veneration and surrounded by ritual activities. These ceremonies and rituals, in Durkheim's view, are essential to unifying the members of groups.

Durkheim's theory of religion is a good example of the functionalist tradition in sociology. To analyze the function of a social behavior or social institution like religion is to study the contribution it makes to the continuation of a group, community, or society. According to Durkheim, religion has the function of uniting a society by ensuring that people meet regularly to affirm common beliefs and values.

sacred • Describing something that inspires awe or reverence among those who believe in a given set of religious ideas.

profane • That which belongs to the mundane, everyday world.

WEBER: THE WORLD RELIGIONS AND SOCIAL CHANGE

Whereas Durkheim based his arguments on a restricted range of examples, Max Weber embarked on a massive study of religions worldwide. No scholar before or since has undertaken a task of this scope.

In his research on the social and economic influence of religions around the world, Max Weber categorized Eastern religions as "other-worldly" and Christianity as a "salvation religion." Weber believed that Hinduism stressed escaping material existence to locate a higher plane of being, which cultivated an attitude of passivity. In contrast, he argued that Christianity and its emphasis on salvation and constant struggle could stimulate revolt against the existing order.

Weber's writings on religion differ from those of Durkheim because they concentrate on the connection between religion and social change, something to which Durkheim gave little direct attention. They also contrast with those of Marx because Weber argued that religion was not necessarily a conservative force; on the contrary, religiously inspired movements have often produced dramatic social transformations. Thus, Protestantism, particularly Puritanism, according to Weber, was the source of the capitalistic outlook found in the modern West. The early entrepreneurs were mostly Calvinists. Their drive to succeed, which helped initiate Western economic development, was originally prompted by a desire to serve God. Material success was a sign of divine favor.

Weber conceived of his research on the world religions as a single project. His discussion of the impact of Protestantism on the development of the West was connected to a comprehensive attempt to understand the influence of religion on social and economic life in various cultures. After analyzing Eastern religions, Weber concluded that they provided barriers to the development of industrial capitalism such as that which took place in the West. Eastern civilizations, he observed, were oriented toward different values, such as escape from the toils of the material world.

Weber regarded Christianity as a salvation religion. According to such religions, human beings can be "saved" if they are converted to the beliefs of the religion and follow its moral tenets. The notions of "sin" and of being rescued from sinfulness by God's grace are important. They generate a tension and an emotional dynamism essentially absent from the Eastern religions. Salvation religions have a "revolutionary" aspect. Whereas the religions of the East cultivate an attitude of passivity or acceptance within the believer, Christianity demands a constant struggle against sin and so can stimulate revolt against the existing order. Religious leaders—such as Luther or Calvin—have arisen who reinterpret existing doctrines in such a way as to challenge the extant power structure.

CRITICAL ASSESSMENT OF THE CLASSICAL VIEW

Marx, Durkheim, and Weber each identified some important general characteristics of religion, and in some ways their views complement one another. Marx was correct to claim that religion often has ideological implications, serving to justify the interests of ruling groups at the expense of others. There are innumerable instances of this in history. For example, the European missionaries who sought to convert "heathen" peoples to Christian beliefs were no doubt sincere in their efforts. Yet their teachings contributed to the destruction of traditional cultures and the imposition of white domination. Almost all Christian denominations tolerated, or endorsed, slavery in the United States and other parts of the world into the nineteenth century. Doctrines were developed proclaiming slavery to be based on divine law, disobedient slaves being guilty of an offense against God as well as their masters (Stampp 1956).

Yet Weber was certainly correct to emphasize the unsettling and often revolutionary impact of religious ideals on the established social order. In spite of many churches' early support for slavery in the United States, church leaders later played a key role in fighting to abolish the institution. Religious beliefs have prompted social movements seeking to overthrow unjust systems of authority; for instance, religious sentiments played a prominent part in the civil rights movements of the 1960s.

These divisive influences of religion, so prominent in history, find little mention in Durkheim's work. Durkheim emphasized the role of religion in promoting social cohesion. Yet it is not difficult to redirect his ideas toward explaining religious division, conflict, and change as well as solidarity. After all, much of the strength of feeling that may be generated against other religious groups derives from the commitment to religious values generated within each community of believers.

Among the most valuable points of Durkheim's writings is his stress on ritual and ceremony. All religions comprise regular assemblies of believers, at which ritual prescriptions are observed. As Durkheim rightly points out, ritual activities also mark the major life stages—birth, the transition to adulthood (rituals associated with puberty are found in many cultures), marriage, and death (van Gennep 1977).

Finally, the theories of Marx, Durkheim, and Weber on religion were based on their studies of societies in which a single religion predominated. As a consequence, it seemed reasonable for them to examine the relationship between a predominant religion and the society as a whole. However, in the past fifty years this classical view has been challenged by some U.S. sociologists. Because of their own experience in a society that is highly tolerant of religious diversity, these theorists have focused on religious pluralism rather than on religious domination. Not surprisingly, their conclusions differ substantially from the views of Marx, Durkheim, and Weber, each of whom regarded religion as closely bound up with the larger society. Religion was believed to reflect and reinforce society's values, or at least the values of those who were most powerful; to provide an important source of solidarity and social stability; and to drive social change. According to this view, religion is threatened by the rise of **secular thinking**, particularly as seen in the rise of science, technology, and rational thought in general.

secular thinking • Worldly thinking, particularly as seen in the rise of science, technology, and rational thought in general.

secularization • A process of decline in the influence of religion. Although modern societies have become increasingly secularized, tracing the extent of secularization is a complex matter. Secularization can refer to levels of involvement with religious organizations (such as rates of church attendance), the social and material influence wielded by religious organizations, and the degree to which people hold religious beliefs.

The classical theorists argued that the key problem facing religions in the modern world is **secularization**, or the process by which religious belief and involvement decline and thus result in a weakening of the social and political power of religious organizations. Peter Berger (1967) has described religion in premodern societies as a "sacred canopy" that covers all aspects of life and is therefore seldom questioned. In modern society, however, the sacred canopy is more like a quilt, a patchwork of different religious and secular belief systems. When multiple belief systems coexist, it becomes increasingly difficult to sustain the idea that there is any single true faith. According to this view, secularization is the likely result.

CONTEMPORARY APPROACHES: "RELIGIOUS ECONOMY"

religious economy • A theoretical framework within the sociology of religion that argues that religions can be fruitfully understood as organizations in competition with one another for followers.

One of the most influential contemporary approaches to the sociology of religion is tailored to societies such as the United States that offer many different faiths from which to pick and choose. Sociologists who favor the **religious economy** approach argue that religions can be thought of as organizations in competition with one another for followers (Stark and Bainbridge 1987; Finke and Stark 1988, 1992; Roof and McKinney 1990; Hammond 1992; Warner 1993; Moore 1994).

Like contemporary economists who study businesses, these sociologists argue that competition is preferable to monopoly when it comes to ensuring religious vitality. This position is exactly opposite to that of the classical theorists. Marx, Durkheim, and Weber assumed that religion weakens when challenged by different religious or secular viewpoints, whereas the religious economists argue that competition increases the overall level of religious involvement in modern society. Religious economists believe this is true for two reasons. First, competition makes each religious group try harder to win followers. Second, the presence of numerous religions means that there is likely to be something for just about everyone. In a culturally diverse society such as the United States, a single religion will probably appeal to only a limited range of followers, whereas the presence of Indian gurus and fundamentalist preachers, in addition to mainline churches, is likely to encourage a high level of religious participation.

A criticism of the religious economy approach is that it overestimates the extent to which people rationally pick and choose among different religions, as if they were shopping for a new car or a pair of shoes. Among deeply committed believers, particularly in societies that lack religious pluralism, it is not obvious that religion is a matter of rational choice. Even when people are allowed to choose among different religions, most are likely to practice their childhood religion without ever questioning whether there are more appealing alternatives. Moreover, the spiritual aspects of religion may be overlooked if sociologists simply assume that religious buyers are always on spiritual shopping sprees. Wade Clark Roof's study (1993) of 1,400 baby boomers found that a third had remained loyal to their childhood faith, while another third had continued to profess their childhood beliefs although they no longer belonged to a religious organization. Only a third were actively searching for a new religion, making the sorts of choices presumed by the religious economy approach (Pew Forum on Religion & Public Life 2008). ✓

CONCEPT CHECKS ✓

1. What are the three main components of religion as a social institution?

2. How do sociologists differ from other scholars in their approach to studying religion?

3. Why did Karl Marx call religion the "opium of the people"?

4. What are the differences between classical and contemporary approaches to understanding religion?

HOW DOES RELIGION AFFECT LIFE THROUGHOUT THE WORLD?

Understand the various ways religious communities are organized and how they have become institutionalized. Recognize how the globalization of religion is reflected in religious activism in poor countries and the rise of religious nationalist movements.

Religion is one of the most truly global of all social institutions, affecting almost all aspects of social life. In this section, we describe the way religion shapes life throughout the globe. We will begin, however, by briefly describing the different ways that world religions are organized.

TYPES OF RELIGIOUS ORGANIZATIONS

Early theorists such as Max Weber (1963, orig. 1921), Ernst Troeltsch (1931), and Richard Niebuhr (1929) described religious organizations as falling along a continuum based on the degree to which they are well established and conventional: Churches lie at one end (they are conventional and well established), cults lie at the other (they are neither), and sects fall somewhere in the middle. These distinctions were based on the study of those religions that account for the majority of persons in Europe and the United States. There is much debate over how well they apply to the non-Christian world.

Today, sociologists are aware that the terms *sect* and *cult* have negative connotations, something they wish to avoid. For this reason, contemporary sociologists of religion sometimes use the phrase *new religious movements* to characterize novel religious organizations that have not yet achieved the respectability that comes with being well established for a long period of time (Hexham and Poewe 1997; Hadden 1997b).

CHURCHES AND SECTS

Churches are large, established religious bodies; one example is the Roman Catholic Church. They normally have a formal, bureaucratic structure, with a hierarchy of religious officials. Churches often represent a traditional face of religion, since they are integrated within the existing institutional order. Most of their adherents are born into and grow up within the church.

A **sect** is typically described as a religious subgroup that breaks away from the larger organization and consequently follows its own unique set of rules and principles. Sects are smaller, less highly organized groups of committed believers, usually set up in protest against an established church. Sects aim to discover or follow the "true way" and either try to change the surrounding society or withdraw from it into communities of their own, a process known as *revival*. Many sects have few or no officials, and all members are regarded as equal participants. For the most part, people are not born into sects, but actively join them in order to further commitments in which they believe.

church • A large, established religious body, normally having a formal, bureaucratic structure and a hierarchy of religious officials. The term is also used to refer to the place in which religious ceremonies are carried out.

sect • A religious movement that breaks away from orthodoxy.

DENOMINATIONS AND CULTS

A **denomination** is a sect that has cooled down and become an institutionalized body rather than an activist protest group. Sects that survive over any period of time inevitably become denominations. Denominations are recognized as legitimate by churches and exist alongside them, often cooperating harmoniously with them.

denomination • A religious sect that has lost its revivalist dynamism and become an institutionalized body, commanding the adherence of significant numbers of people.

Members of the Unification Church, also known as "Moonies," named for its founder Reverend Sun Myung Moon, participate in a mass wedding. The Holy Marriage Blessing Ceremony strengthens participants' dedication to the church.

cult • A fragmentary religious grouping to which individuals are loosely affiliated but which lacks any permanent structure.

Cults, by contrast, are the most loosely knit and transient of all religious organizations. They are composed of individuals who reject what they see as the values of the outside society, unlike sects, which try to revive an established church. They are a form of religious innovation, rather than revival. Their focus is on individual experience, bringing like-minded people together. Like sects, cults often form around the influence of an inspirational leader.

Like sects, cults flourish when there is a breakdown in well-established and widespread societal belief systems. This is happening throughout the world today, in places as diverse as Japan, India, and the United States. When such a breakdown occurs, cults may originate within a society, or they may be "imported" from outside. In the United States, examples of homegrown, or indigenous, cults include New Age religions based on such things as spiritualism, astrology, and religious practices adapted from Asian or Native American cultures. One of the largest imported cults is the Reverend Sun Myung Moon's Unification Church ("Moonies"), which originated in South Korea; when the Reverend died in 2012, his wife took over the church.

GLOBALIZATION AND RELIGION

More than half of the world's population follow one of two faiths: Christianity (31.55 percent) or Islam (23.2 percent), religions that have long been unconstrained by national borders (Pew Forum on Religion & Public Life 2012). The current globalization of religion is reflected in political activism among religious groups in poor countries and in the rise of religious nationalist movements in opposition to the modern secular state.

THE GLOBAL RISE OF RELIGIOUS NATIONALISM

One of the most important trends in global religion today is the rise of **religious nationalism**, the linking of strongly held religious convictions with beliefs about a people's social and political destiny. In countries around the world, religious nationalist movements reject the notion that religion, government, and politics should be separate and call instead for a revival of traditional religious beliefs that are directly embodied in the nation and its leadership (Beyer 1994). These nationalist movements represent a strong reaction against the impact of technological and economic modernization on local religious beliefs. In particular, religious nationalists oppose what they see as the destructive aspects of "Western" influence on local culture and religion, ranging from American television to the missionary efforts of foreign evangelicals.

Religious nationalist movements accept many aspects of modern life, including modern technology, politics, and economics. For example, Islamic fundamentalists use video and television to reach millions of Muslims worldwide. However, they also emphasize a strict interpretation of religious values and completely reject the notion of secularization (Juergensmeyer 1994, 2001). Nationalist movements do not simply revive ancient religious beliefs. Rather, nationalist movements partly "invent" the past, selectively drawing on different traditions and reinterpreting past events to serve their current beliefs and interests. Violent conflicts between religious groups sometimes result from their competing interpretations of the same historical event (Anderson 1991; Juergensmeyer 1994, 2001; van der Veer 1994).

Religious nationalism is on the rise throughout the world—perhaps because in times of rapid social change, unshakable ideas have strong appeal. For example, in the early twenty-first century, the aim of the Islamic republic in Iran was to organize government and society so that Islamic teachings would dominate all spheres of life. The Guardian Council of religious leaders determines whether laws, policies, and candidates for Parliament conform to Islamic beliefs, even though Iran has a U.S.-style constitution providing for elected officials and the separation of powers.

Recent years have seen a growing movement to liberalize the country. The reform-minded president Mohammad Khatami and his allies recaptured control of Parliament in the 2000 elections, but that victory proved to be short-lived: The Guardian Council disqualified 2,400 liberal candidates (nearly a third of all candidates) during the 2004 elections, and Mahmoud Ahmadinejad, a conservative candidate close to Iran's religious leaders, won the presidency. The pro-democracy Green Movement mobilized millions of people in peaceful protests against the Ahmadinejad government during the 2009 presidential elections but was brutally repressed as a consequence.

religious nationalism • The linking of strongly held religious convictions with beliefs about a people's social and political destiny.

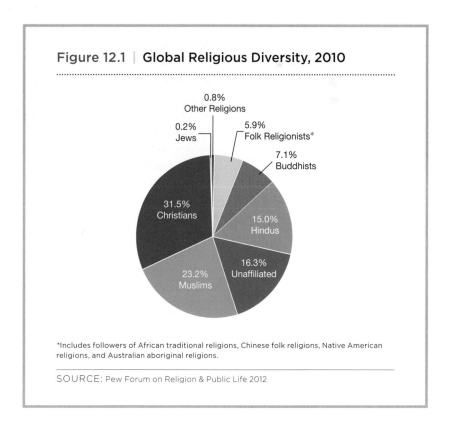

Figure 12.1 | Global Religious Diversity, 2010

0.8% Other Religions
0.2% Jews
5.9% Folk Religionists*
7.1% Buddhists
31.5% Christians
15.0% Hindus
16.3% Unaffiliated
23.2% Muslims

*Includes followers of African traditional religions, Chinese folk religions, Native American religions, and Australian aboriginal religions.

SOURCE: Pew Forum on Religion & Public Life 2012

RELIGIOUS NATIONALISM AND VIOLENCE

How is it that religious views can give rise to a culture of violence? The sociologist Mark Juergensmeyer (2001) has come to a startling conclusion: Even though virtually all major religious traditions call for compassion and understanding, violence and religion nonetheless go hand in hand. Juergensmeyer, who has studied religious violence among Muslims, Sikhs, Jews, Hindus, Christians, and Buddhists, argues that under the right conditions ordinary conflicts can become recast as wars between good and evil that must be won at all costs. He argues that a violent conflict is most likely to seek religious justification as a "sacred war" under three conditions:

- the conflict is regarded as decisive for defending one's basic identity and dignity—for example, when one's culture is seen as threatened; and
- losing the conflict is unthinkable, although
- winning the conflict is unlikely in any realistic sense.

Under these conditions, the proponents of cosmic or sacred warfare may justify the loss of innocent lives as serving God's larger purpose. According to Juergensmeyer, al Qaeda exemplifies such "cosmic warfare." Members of al Qaeda are seeking to defend Islam against the threat of Westernization. Responding to al Qaeda's violence with still greater violence shows the rest of the Islamic world that the conflict is indeed cosmic, particularly if the most powerful nations on earth become embroiled. Based on his interviews with proponents of terrorism around the world, Juergensmeyer concludes that this is just what al Qaeda wants—to be elevated from the status of a minor criminal terrorist organization to a worthy opponent in a global war against the West. This, in the view of some of his interviewees, will increase the appeal of al Qaeda to a wider group of young Islamic men who blame the West for the decline of Islamic influence and the current hardships faced by many Muslims around the world.

ACTIVIST RELIGION AND SOCIAL CHANGE THROUGHOUT THE WORLD

Despite the widespread link between religion and violence, religion has played a critical role in effecting positive social change over the past forty years. In Vietnam in the 1960s, Buddhist priests burned themselves alive to protest the policies of the South Vietnamese government. Their willingness to sacrifice their lives for their beliefs, seen on television sets around the world, contributed to growing U.S. opposition to the war. Buddhist monks in Thailand are currently protesting deforestation and are calling for greater resources for victims of AIDS.

liberation theology • An activist Catholic religious movement that combines Catholic beliefs with a passion for social justice for the poor.

An activist form of Catholicism, termed **liberation theology**, combines Catholic beliefs with a passion for social justice for the poor, particularly in Central and South America and in Africa. Catholic priests and nuns organize farming cooperatives, build health clinics and schools, and challenge government policies that impoverish the peasantry. A similar role is played by Islamic socialists in Pakistan and Buddhist socialists in Sri Lanka (Berryman 1987; Sigmund 1990; Juergensmeyer 1994). Many religious leaders have paid with their lives for their activism, which government and military leaders often regard as subversive.

In some Central and Eastern European countries once dominated by the former Soviet Union, long-suppressed religious organizations provided an important basis for the overturning of socialist regimes during the early 1990s. In Poland, the Catholic Church was closely allied with the Solidarity movement, which toppled the socialist government in 1989. ✓

CONCEPT CHECKS ✓

1. Describe four types of religious organizations.

2. What is religious nationalism? Why can it be viewed as a reaction to economic modernization of local religious beliefs and Westernization?

HOW DOES RELIGION AFFECT YOUR LIFE IN THE UNITED STATES?

Learn about the sociological dimensions of religion in the United States.

In comparison with the citizens of other industrial nations, Americans are highly religious, although levels of religious participation have declined slightly since the mid-twentieth century. Indicators such as belief in God, religious membership, and attendance at religious services found that religiosity reached its highest levels in the 1950s and has been declining ever since—in part because post–World War II baby boomers have been less religious than their predecessors (Roof 1999). In one national survey, overwhelming majorities of Catholics, liberal Protestants, and conservative Protestants reported attending church on a weekly basis while they were children, but their attendance had dropped sharply by the time they reached their early twenties. However, levels of participation remain high among members of conservative Protestant groups.

Another survey of more than 50,000 adults in 2008 and nearly 114,000 adults in 1990 found that religious identification had declined sharply during the eighteen-year period. In 1990, 90 percent of all adults identified with some religious group; in 2008, the figure was less than 80 percent. The principal decline was among self-identified Christians (from 86 percent to 76 percent). This decline was not because a growing proportion of adults identified with other religions; rather, it was because the number of adults reporting no religious identification grew from 8 percent to 15 percent of the population. Membership in religious institutions showed a parallel decline (Kosmin and Keysar 2009).

TRENDS IN RELIGIOUS AFFILIATION

It is difficult to estimate reliably the number of people belonging to churches because the U.S. government does not officially collect such data. Drawing on occasional government surveys, public-opinion polls, and church records, however, sociologists of religion have concluded that church membership has grown steadily in the United States from the eighteenth century to the present. About one in six Americans belonged to a religious organization at the time of the Revolutionary War. That number had grown to about one in three at the time of the Civil War, one in two at the turn of the nineteenth century, and two in three in the 1990s (Finke and Stark 1992).

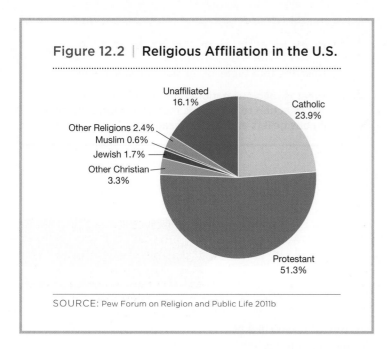

Figure 12.2 | Religious Affiliation in the U.S.

Unaffiliated 16.1%

Other Religions 2.4%
Muslim 0.6%
Jewish 1.7%
Other Christian 3.3%

Catholic 23.9%

Protestant 51.3%

SOURCE: Pew Forum on Religion and Public Life 2011b

One reason so many Americans are religiously affiliated is that religious organizations are an important source of social ties and friendship networks. Churches, synagogues, and mosques are communities of people who share the same beliefs and values, and who support one another during times of need. Religious communities thus often play a family-like role, offering help in times of emergency as well as more routine assistance such as child care.

There are an enormous number of religious organizations one can belong to. The United States is the most religiously diverse country in the world, with more than 1,500 distinct religions (Melton 1989). Yet the vast majority of people belong to a relatively small number of religious denominations (see Figure 12.2). Seventy-eight percent of Americans identify as Christian, with 23.9 percent identifying as Catholic and 51.3 percent as Protestant; 1.7 percent of Americans identify as Jewish, 0.6 percent as Muslim, and 0.4 percent as Hindu. Sixteen percent say they have no religious affiliation at all (Pew Forum on Religion and Public Life 2011).

PROTESTANTS: THE GROWING STRENGTH OF CONSERVATIVE DENOMINATIONS

A more detailed picture of recent trends in American religion can be obtained if we break down the large Protestant category into major subgroups. According to the American Religious Identification Survey (ARIS) of more than 54,000 households in 2008, the largest number of households were Baptist, accounting for 31 percent of all Protestants—over three times the size of the second-largest group, Methodists (9.8 percent). There were far fewer Lutherans (7.5 percent), Presbyterians (4 percent), and Episcopalians (2 percent) (ARIS 2008). More than half of all Protestants today describe themselves as "born again" (The *Economist* 2003). Born-again Christians are those who report that they have experienced a dramatic conversion to faith in Jesus.

These figures are important because they reveal the growing strength of conservative Protestants in the United States. Conservative Protestants, which include denominations such as Baptists and Pentecostals, emphasize a literal interpretation of the Bible, morality in daily life, and conversion through evangelizing. They can be contrasted with the more historically established mainline and liberal Protestants such as Episcopalians and Methodists, who tend to adopt a more flexible, humanistic approach to religious practice.

Although all groups of Protestants showed a growth in membership from the 1920s through the 1960s, a major reversal has since occurred. Both liberal and moderate churches have experienced a decline in membership, whereas the number of conservative Protestants has exploded. Today, twice as many people belong to conservative Protestant groups as liberal ones, and conservative Protestants may soon outnumber moderates as well (though when combined, moderates and liberals still

Evangelical Christians are the most rapidly growing religious denomination in the United States today. Many attend mega-churches, which attract as many as 30,000 congregants on any given Sunday.

outnumber conservatives) (Green 2004; Roof and McKinney 1990). Since the 1960s, the fastest-growing religious group has been self-identified evangelicals. Although all religious groups lose some converts to other denominations or beliefs, the more conservative branches of Protestantism experienced a net gain in converts during the 1990s, whereas the more liberal groups experienced a net loss (Kosmin, Mayer, and Keysar 2001) (Figure 12.3).

CATHOLICISM

Catholics continue to grow in number, yet church attendance declined sharply in the 1960s and 1970s, leveling off in the mid-1970s. One of the main reasons was the papal encyclical of 1968 that reaffirmed the ban on the use of contraceptives by Catholics. The encyclical offered no leeway for people whose conscience allowed for the use of contraceptives. They were faced with disobeying the Church, and many Catholics did just that. According to one study conducted by the Centers for Disease Control and Prevention, 98 percent of all Catholic women who have had sexual relations report having used contraceptives at one time or another (Jones and Dreweke 2011). Similarly, the General Social Survey found that three out of five Catholics say that contraceptives should be available to teens even without parental approval (Catholics for Choice 2004).

The Catholic Church has shown steady increases in membership in recent decades, due largely to the immigration of Catholics from Mexico and Central and South America. Yet the growth in Catholic Church membership has also slowed in recent years, as some followers have drifted away, either ceasing to identify themselves as Catholics or shifting to Protestantism.

OTHER RELIGIOUS GROUPS

Judaism in the United States has historically been divided into three major movements: Orthodox, which believes in the divine origins of the Jewish Bible (called by

Table 12.1 | Changes in Religious Self-Identification in the United States, 1990–2008

RELIGIOUS SELF-IDENTIFICATION	POPULATION, 1990	POPULATION, 2008	NET PERCENTAGE GAINED OR LOST
Catholic	46,004,000	57,199,000	24%
Baptist	33,964,000	36,148,000	6%
No religion/Atheist	14,331,000	34,169,000	138%
Mainline Christian	32,784,000	29,375,000	–10%
Pentecostal/Charismatic	5,647,000	7,948,000	41%
Jewish	3,137,000	2,680,000	–15%
Muslim	527,000	1,349,000	156%
Buddhist	404,000	1,189,000	194%

SOURCE: ARIS 2008

Christians the Old Testament), and follows highly traditional religious practices; Conservative, which is a blend of traditional and more contemporary beliefs and practices; and Reform, which rejects most traditional practices and is progressive in its ritual practices (services, for example, are more likely to be conducted in English than in Hebrew). Both Conservative and Reform Judaism reflect efforts by Jewish immigrants (or their descendants) to develop beliefs and rituals that turned away from "Old World" ones, developing forms more consistent with their new homeland.

Estimates of the number of Jewish Americans in the United States today vary widely. The Census Bureau estimates that in 2010, 2.1 percent of the U.S. population, or 6.5 million persons, were Jews (U.S. Bureau of the Census 2012q). By contrast, survey data from the Pew Organization reports that in 2012, just 1.8 percent of the U.S. population, or 4.2 million persons, were Jews (Pew Research Center 2013). However, these disparities may reflect precisely how Jews are identified and counted. Some Americans identify as Jewish if they have a Jewish mother—even if they have never practiced their religion. Yet other people may self-identify as Jewish only if they participate actively in the religion, whereas others still may identify as "culturally Jewish," meaning they celebrate their heritage and culture but do not actively practice religion.

Among Muslims, growing emigration from Asia and Africa may change the U.S. religious profile. For example, reliable estimates of the number of Muslims in the United States run as high as 2.6 million in 2010 (Pew Forum on Religion and Public Life 2011a), although official government statistics report only roughly half that number (U.S. Bureau of the Census 2011a). The low estimates may be because in the post-9/11 political climate, many Muslims are reluctant to disclose their religious affiliation—only 30 percent of Americans held a favorable view of Islam in 2010 (Pew Research Center for the People and the Press 2010). Two-thirds of U.S. Muslims are foreign-born; many come from Pakistan or are African refugees from countries like Somalia and Ethiopia. A majority of Muslim Americans are first-generation immigrants to the United States (63 percent), with almost half of that number having moved to the United States since 1990. Eighty-one percent of Muslim Americans are citizens of the United States despite the high levels of immigrants, including 70 percent of those born outside the United States (Pew Forum on Religion and Public Life 2008).

RELIGIOUS AFFILIATION AND SOCIOECONOMIC STATUS

The principal religious groupings in the United States vary substantially by region and socioeconomic status. Liberal Protestants tend to be well educated and have jobs and incomes that would classify them as middle or upper class. They are concentrated in the northeastern states, and, to a small extent, in the West as well. Moderate Protestants fall at a somewhat lower level than liberal Protestants in terms of education and income. In fact, they are typical of the national average on these measures. They tend to live in the Midwest, and, to some extent, in the West. Black Protestants are, on average, the least educated and poorest of any of the religious groups. Conservative Protestants have a similar profile, although they fall at a marginally higher level on all these measures (Pew Forum on Religion and Public Life 2011). Catholics strongly resemble moderate Protestants (which is to say, average Americans) in terms of their socioeconomic profile. They are largely concentrated in the Northeast, although many live in the West and the Southwest as well.

Jews historically have had the most successful socioeconomic profile. Jews tend to be college graduates in middle- or upper-income categories. Whereas the large majority of Jews once lived in the northeastern states, today only half do, as many have relocated throughout the United States. One recent study suggests that this high degree of geographical mobility is associated with lowered involvement in Jewish institutions. Jews who move across the country are less likely to belong to synagogues, have Jewish friends, or be married to Jewish spouses (Goldstein and Goldstein 1996).

Although less is known about Hindus, who account for a relatively small proportion (0.4 percent) of all Americans today, national survey data show that Hindus are now the highest-earning religious group in the United States, surpassing Jews for the first time. Nearly three-quarters (65 percent) of Hindus in the United States earned at least $75,000 in 2010, while Jews come in second with 58 percent in the $75,000 or higher earnings category (Pew Forum on Religion and Public Life 2011b). These earnings differences are attributed to the high levels of education and urban residence of many Jews and Hindus in the United States (Leonhardt 2011).

There are political differences across religious groups as well. Jews tend to be the most heavily Democratic of any major religious groups, fundamentalist and evangelical Christians the most Republican. The more moderate Protestant denominations are somewhere in between (Kosmin, Mayer, and Keysar 2001). Religious groups also differ widely regarding their views on major social issues in the United States, including abortion and gay marriage. On average, Jews and persons with no affiliation tend to hold the most liberal political views, meaning that they are likely to say that they

From Pulpits to iPads?

The United States is one of the most religious countries in the world. Yet there are still millions of Americans for whom religion is not an important part of their everyday lives. For example, nearly one in five Americans reports that they have no religious affiliation; this proportion reaches one-third among Americans ages eighteen to twenty-nine (Lipka 2013). And while roughly 40 percent of Americans report that they "usually" attend religious services once a week, recent research based on daily diary data shows that the proportion of Americans who regularly attend services is as low as 24 percent, with rates even lower among young adults (Brenner 2011).

In the past decade, young adults and other Americans have found new ways to incorporate religion and spirituality into their lives, beyond the pews of their local churches and synagogues. The Internet and smartphones have allowed Americans to participate in religious activities on their own grounds and on their own schedules. For example, a spate of new smartphone apps allows users to download full texts of scriptures like the Bible, Book of Mormon, Koran, or Torah. Muslims can use apps to ascertain the time of day for their five daily prayers and to learn what direction to face when praying toward Mecca. Jews and Seventh-Day Adventists can use programs like the Sabbath App to calculate sunset times for Friday evening and Saturday evening each week, so they'll know exactly when the Sabbath begins and ends in their hometowns. Hindus can use their phones to present virtual offerings of incense and coconut to the god Ganesh.

Other apps allow users to type in prayers and send them off to God, the Wailing Wall in Jerusalem, or simply off into cyberspace (Wagner 2011). For those who believe that scriptures can be used to substantiate their political views, there are apps that help users quickly locate a Biblical passage to support arguments for (or against) everything from abortion to same-sex marriage (Vitello 2011). Even those without religious views can use such apps to support their politics; new apps (like BibleThumper) "allow the atheist to keep the most funny and irrational Bible verses right in their pocket" (Vitello 2011).

Technology also keeps us connected to religious communities. Hundreds if not thousands of religious organizations allow people to "attend" religious services virtually. For example, many synagogues throughout the United States live-stream their services over the High Holidays of Rosh Hashanah and Yom Kippur. Advocates say that technology helps to bring worship to people who don't have another way to participate in services and sermons, such as members of the military, the homebound, or Jews who live in areas without a local congregation (Mandel 2010). Similarly, websites like CyberChurch.com give users access to Christian services throughout the world.

Do you believe that technology will help people become more engaged in religion by enabling them to practice their faith where, when, and how they are comfortable? Or do you believe that these apps undermine some of the core aspects of religion, including interacting with a community of like-minded others, or rituals like praying together? Do you think apps will ever replace in-person participation in religious services or activities? Why or why not?

Smartphone apps now allow users to participate virtually in religious services, make offerings to their gods, and read scriptures. Are these apps a reasonable substitute for traditional forms of worship?

believe women should have legal access to abortion and that persons in same-sex relationships should have the legal right to marry. Fundamentalist and evangelical Christians are least likely to support these stances, while liberal Protestants, moderate Protestants, and Catholics sit toward the middle of the political continuum (Pew Forum on Religion and Public Life 2013).

Religion has a subtle yet powerful influence on daily life in the United States and throughout the world. In analyzing religious practices and traditions, we must be sensitive to ideals that inspire profound conviction in believers, yet we must also take a balanced view of them. We must confront ideas that seek the eternal while recognizing that religious groups also promote mundane goals, such as earning money or attracting followers. We need to recognize the diversity of religious beliefs and models of conduct but also the nature of a global phenomenon.

We have also seen that education and religion are two social institutions that are powerful socializing agents. Religion and education teach young people the skills and beliefs that are an essential part of one's culture. However, the two institutions differ in a critical way: Education is intended to be universalistic and to expose all children to similar messages, whereas religious institutions vary widely in the values, beliefs, and practices that they impart. As we saw in our chapter opener, these institutions may occasionally collide; Malala's attempt to obtain an education was at odds with the fundamentalist religious beliefs that reigned in her village. However, both educational systems and religious institutions are dynamic and may change as social contexts and policies change. The efforts of pioneering young women like Malala may be instrumental in helping to create a context where educational and religious institutions meet the needs of all citizens, regardless of their gender, ethnicity, or social background. ✓

CONCEPT CHECKS

1. What are the reasons so many Americans belong to religious organizations?

2. Describe the main differences between conservative and liberal Protestants.

3. Contrast the political views and socioeconomic statuses of major religious groups in the United States.

EXERCISES:
Thinking Sociologically

1. From your reading of this chapter, describe what might be the principal advantages and disadvantages of having children go to private versus public schools in the United States at this time. Assess whether privatization of our public schools would help to improve them.

2. Karl Marx, Émile Durkheim, and Max Weber had different viewpoints on the nature of religion and its social significance. Briefly explain the viewpoints of each. Which theorist's views have the most to offer in explaining the rise of national and international fundamentalism today? Why?

Chapter 12

Education and Religion

p.359 — Why Are Education and Literacy So Important?

Know how and why systems of mass education emerged in the United States. Know some basic facts about the education system and literacy rates of developing countries.

p.362 — What Is the Linkage between Education and Inequality?

Become familiar with the most important research on whether education reduces or perpetuates inequality. Learn the social and cultural influences on educational achievement.

p.373 — How Do Sociologists Think about Religion?

Learn the elements that make up religion. Know the sociological approaches to religion developed by Marx, Durkheim, and Weber, as well as the religious economy approach.

p.379 — How Does Religion Affect Life throughout the World?

Learn the various ways religious communities are organized and how they have become institutionalized. Recognize how the globalization of religion is reflected in religious activism in poor countries and the rise of religious nationalist movements.

p.383 — How Does Religion Affect Your Life in the United States?

Learn about the sociological dimensions of religion in the United States.

home schooling

1. Why did schooling become widespread only after the Industrial Revolution?
2. What are some of the functions of formal schooling?
3. What are the three main motivations for home schooling?
4. What are some of the reasons there are many illiterate people in the developing world?

tracking • hidden curriculum • intelligence • IQ (intelligence quotient) • functional literacy • standardized testing

1. According to Kozol, has education become an equalizer in American society? Why or why not?
2. How do Coleman's findings differ from the results of Kozol's research? Whose theory, in your opinion, can better explain the racial gap in educational achievement?
3. What effect does tracking have on academic achievement?
4. How do schools perpetuate existing inequalities across generations?
5. Explain the relationship between race and intelligence. Do you find the evidence compelling?
6. Describe the components and critiques of the No Child Left Behind Act and Race to the Top.

religion • theism • alienation • sacred • profane • secular thinking • secularization • religious economy

1. What are the three main components of religion as a social institution?
2. How do sociologists differ from other scholars in their approach to studying religion?
3. Why did Karl Marx call religion the "opium of the people"?
4. What are the differences between classical and contemporary approaches to understanding religion?

church • sect • denomination • cult • religious nationalism • liberation theology

1. Describe four types of religious organizations.
2. What is religious nationalism? Why can it be viewed as a reaction to economic modernization of local religious beliefs and Westernization?

1. What are the reasons so many Americans belong to religious organizations?
2. Describe the main differences between conservative and liberal Protestants.
3. Contrast the political news and socioeconomic statuses of major religious groups in the United States.

Politics and Economic Life

THE BIG QUESTIONS

HOW DID THE STATE DEVELOP?
Learn the basic concepts underlying modern nation-states.

HOW DO DEMOCRACIES FUNCTION?
Learn about different types of democracy, how this form of government has spread around the world, key theories about power in a democracy, and some of the problems associated with modern-day democracy.

WHAT IS TERRORISM?
Learn how social scientists define terrorism and the ways that new-style terrorism is different from the old.

WHAT IS THE SOCIAL SIGNIFICANCE OF WORK?
Assess the sociological ramifications of paid and unpaid work. Understand that modern economies are based on the division of labor and economic interdependence. Familiarize yourself with modern systems of economic production.

WHAT ARE KEY ELEMENTS OF THE MODERN ECONOMY?
See the importance of the rise of large corporations; consider particularly the global impact of transnational corporations.

HOW DOES WORK AFFECT EVERYDAY LIFE TODAY?
Learn about the impact of global economic competition on employment. Consider how work will change over the coming years.

In 2014, fast food workers throughout the United States—shown here in Times Square—protested for higher wages and the right to unionize.

F ast food is considered as American as apple pie. Nearly all of us have gone through a McDonald's drive-through to buy a burger, fries, and a soda. Many readers might have even worked briefly in fast food, serving quick, inexpensive burgers, tacos, or shakes during their after-school hours or over summer vacation. Yet how often do we think about what the lives are like for the 4 million American men and women who serve us those burgers? According to a recent study from the University of California at Berkeley, 20 percent of fast-food workers live beneath the poverty line; by contrast, just 5 percent of all American workers overall live in poverty. And while they work hard each day feeding their customers, fully 24 percent of fast-food workers receive food stamps so that they and their families can afford to eat three meals a day (Allegretto et al. 2013).

While food service workers have quietly endured grueling jobs at low pay for years, many are starting to speak up, demanding higher wages and even staging protests and walkouts. The workers and the labor activists who support their cause would like to see their wages increased to $15 per hour—considerably higher than their current median wage of $8.69 per hour. In December 2013, strikes and protests by fast-food workers and their allies erupted in nearly 100 cities throughout the United States (Eidelson 2013a).

Responding to the pickets and protests, the McDonald's Corporation publicly reported that it would likely increase workers' hourly wage (Eidelson 2013b). Yet labor activists and scholars observe that it's not just low pay that hurts fast-food workers. Rather, it's a collection of issues, including the inability to secure full-time work and health benefits (Eidelson 2013a).

The nation's major restaurant associations disagree with these protests, however, and argue that entry-level restaurant work can be a stepping stone to higher-paying jobs with opportunities for upward mobility and access to benefits and full-time work. For example, a spokesperson from the National Restaurant Association, a trade group for the restaurant industry, has argued that nine of ten salaried employees in food service started out as hourly workers. As one representative of the organization noted: "America's restaurant industry provides opportunities for millions of Americans, women and men from all backgrounds, to move up the ladder and succeed" (Linn 2013). Yet sociologists who study work and the economy find that upward mobility can be difficult; during recessionary times especially, the most rapidly growing industries are those offering only part-time and low-wage work in leisure, hospitality, and retail. Some observers have gone so far as to argue that the only way to ensure a reasonable standard of living for fast-food workers and other low-wage workers is for them to unionize and thus gain access to **collective bargaining**, or the rights of employees and workers to negotiate with their employers for basic rights and benefits (Eidelson 2013a).

These protests by fast-food workers—and recent studies showing that millions of Americans are members of the "working poor"—have found a receptive audience. In late 2013, President Barack Obama and congressional Democrats urged their Republican colleagues and business owners to support increasing the minimum wage from $7.25 an hour (in 2014) to $10.10 an hour by 2016 (Martin and Shear 2013).

As these protests reveal, the government, economics, and politics are closely intertwined. **Government** refers to the regular enactment of policies, decisions, and matters of state on the part of the officials within a political apparatus. The government often enacts policies, such as the federal minimum wage, that have sweeping economic consequences, whether for nations, states, cities, or even the individual lives of workers. **Politics** concerns the means whereby power is used to affect the scope and content of governmental activities. But the sphere of the political is not limited only to those who work in government; it also involves the actions of others.

There are many ways in which people outside the political apparatus seek influence. The fast-food workers attempted to exert power both on their employer and on public policies by protesting and threatening workplace walkouts. Major businesses, like McDonald's, responded by saying that they would consider a wage hike for their workers. These actions show how politics are frequently intertwined with economics. The **economy** consists of institutions that provide for the production and distribution of goods and services, including jobs. In this chapter, we study the main factors affecting political and economic life today. We begin with a discussion of politics and then turn to work and the economy. The sphere of government is the sphere of political power. All political life is about power: the people who hold it, how they achieve it, and what they do with it.

POWER AND AUTHORITY

As mentioned in Chapter 1, the study of power is of fundamental importance for sociology. **Power** is the ability of individuals or groups to make their own interests or concerns count, even when others resist. It sometimes involves the direct use of

---

collective bargaining • The rights of employees and workers to negotiate with their employers for basic rights and benefits.

government • The enacting of policies and decisions on the part of officials within a political apparatus. In most modern societies governments are run by officials who do not inherit their positions of power but are elected or appointed on the basis of qualifications.

politics • The means by which power is employed to influence the nature and content of governmental activities.

economy • The system of production and exchange that provides for the material needs of individuals living in a given society. Economic institutions are of key importance in all social orders.

power • The ability of individuals or the members of a group to achieve aims or further the interests they hold. Power is a pervasive element in all human relationships.

physical force, such as when the United States and its coalition forces invaded Iraq in 2003 to overthrow Saddam Hussein and create democracy. At other times, it involves the use of threats, whether a threat to vote out of office a leader who does not meet the needs of the electorate, or a threat to walk off the job, as we saw in the case of the fast-food workers. Power is an element in almost all social relationships, such as that between employer and employee. This chapter focuses on a narrower aspect of power: governmental power. In this form, it is almost always accompanied by ideologies, which are used to justify the actions of the powerful. For example, Democratic congresspersons who support the minimum wage hike tend to embrace ideologies of social justice, whereas their Republican colleagues tend to subscribe to an ideology that emphasizes fiscal conservatism.

Authority is a government's legitimate use of power: Those subject to a government's authority consent to it. Power is thus different from authority. In Iraq, while power is increasingly in the hands of the newly created political institutions, the authority of those institutions remains in doubt. Contrary to what many believe, democracy is not the only type of government people consider legitimate. Dictatorships can have legitimacy as well, as can states governed by religious leaders. But as we shall see later, democracy is presently the most widespread form of government considered legitimate.

authority • A government's legitimate use of power.

HOW DID THE STATE DEVELOP?

Learn the basic concepts underlying modern nation-states.

A **state** exists where there is a political apparatus of government (institutions like a parliament or congress, plus civil service officials) ruling over a given territory whose authority is backed by a legal system and by the capacity to use military force to implement its policies. All modern states lay claim to specific territories, possess formalized codes of law, and are backed by the control of military force. **Nation-states** have come into existence at various times in different parts of the world (for example, the United States in 1776 and the Czech Republic in 1993). Their main characteristics, however, contrast rather sharply with those of states in traditional civilizations.

state • A political apparatus (government institutions plus civil service officials) ruling over a given territorial order whose authority is backed by law and the ability to use force.

nation-state • A particular type of state, characteristic of the modern world, in which a government has sovereign power within a defined territorial area, and the population are citizens who know themselves to be part of a single nation.

CHARACTERISTICS OF THE STATE

SOVEREIGNTY

The territories ruled by traditional states were always poorly defined, the level of control wielded by the central government being quite weak. The notion of **sovereignty**—that a government possesses authority over an area with clear-cut borders, within which it is the supreme power—had little relevance. All nation-states, by contrast, are sovereign states.

sovereignty • The undisputed political rule of a state over a given territorial area.

CITIZENSHIP

In traditional states, most of the population ruled by the king or emperor showed little awareness of, or interest in, those who governed them. Nor did they have any political rights or influence. Normally only the dominant classes or more affluent groups felt a sense of belonging to an overall political community. In modern societies, by contrast, most people living within the borders of the political system are **citizens**, having common rights and duties and knowing themselves to be members of a national community (Brubaker 1992). Although some people are political refugees or are "stateless," almost everyone in the world today is a member of a definite national political order.

NATIONALISM

Nation-states are associated with the rise of **nationalism**, which can be defined as a set of symbols and beliefs providing the sense of being part of a single political community. Thus, individuals feel a sense of pride and belonging in being American, Israeli, or Chinese. Probably people have always felt some kind of identity with social groups of one form or another—their family, village, or religious community. Nationalism, however, made its appearance only with the development of the modern state. It is the main expression of feelings of identity with a distinct sovereign community.

Nationalistic loyalties do not always fit the physical borders marking the territories of states in the world today. Virtually all nation-states were built from communities of diverse backgrounds. As a result, **local nationalisms** have frequently arisen in opposition to those fostered by the states. Thus, in Canada, for instance, nationalist feelings among the French-speaking population in Quebec present a challenge to the feeling of "Canadianness." Yet while the relation between the nation-state and nationalism is a complicated one, the two have come into being as part of the same process. (We will return to nationalism later in the chapter as we look at its impact on international politics in the modern world.)

We can now offer a comprehensive definition of the nation-state: It is possessed of a government apparatus that is recognized to have sovereign rights within the borders of a territorial area, it is able to back its claims to sovereignty by the control of military power, and many of its citizens have positive feelings of commitment to its national identity.

CITIZENSHIP RIGHTS

Most nation-states became centralized and effective political systems through the activities of monarchs who successfully concentrated more and more power in their own hands. Citizenship did not originally carry rights of political participation in these states. Such rights were achieved largely through struggles that limited the power of monarchs, as in Britain, or actively overthrew them—sometimes by a process of revolution, as in the cases of the United States and France, followed by a period of negotiation between the new ruling elites and their subjects (Tilly 1996).

Three types of rights are associated with the growth of citizenship (Marshall 1973). **Civil rights** refer to the rights of the individual by law. These include privileges many of us take for granted today but that took a long time to achieve (and are by no means fully recognized in all countries). Examples are the freedom of individuals to live where they choose, freedom of speech and religion, the right to own property, the right to legally marry, and the right to equal justice before the law. These rights were not fully established in most European countries until the early nineteenth century. Although the U.S. Constitution granted such rights to Americans well before most European states had them, African Americans were excluded. Even after the Civil War, when blacks were formally given these rights,

citizen • A member of a political community, having both rights and duties associated with that membership.

nationalism • A set of beliefs and symbols expressing identification with a national community.

local nationalisms • The beliefs that communities that share a cultural identity should have political autonomy, even within smaller units of a nation-state.

civil rights • Legal rights held by all citizens in a given national community.

they were not able to exercise them. Women also were denied many civil rights; for example, at the turn of the nineteenth century in the United States, women had few rights independent of their husbands. They could not own property, write wills, collect an inheritance, or even earn a salary. Throughout the nineteenth century, states slowly and gradually began affording such rights to women regardless of their marital status (Speth 2011).

The second type of citizenship rights consists of **political rights**, especially the right to participate in elections and to run for public office. Again, these were not won easily or quickly. Except in the United States, the achievement of full voting rights even for all men is relatively recent and was gained only after a struggle in the face of governments reluctant to admit the principle of the universal vote. In most European countries, the vote was at first limited to male citizens owning a certain amount of property, which effectively limited voting rights to an affluent minority. Universal **franchise** for men was won in most Western nations by the early years of the twentieth century. Women had to wait longer; in most Western countries, the vote for women was achieved partly as a result of the efforts of women's movements and partly as a consequence of the mobilization of women into the formal economy during World War I. As recently as September 2011, Saudi Arabia's king Abdullah officially granted women the right to vote and run in 2015 local elections.

The third type is **social rights**, the right of every individual to enjoy a certain minimum standard of economic welfare and security. Social rights include such entitlements as sickness benefits, benefits in case of unemployment, and the guarantee of minimum levels of wages. Although in some countries welfare benefits were introduced before legal and political rights were fully established (for example, in nineteenth-century Germany), in most societies social rights have been the last to develop. This is because the establishment of civil and particularly political rights has usually been the basis of the fight for social rights. Social rights have been won largely as a result of the political strength poorer groups have been able to develop after obtaining the vote.

The broadening of social rights is closely connected with the **welfare state**, which has been firmly established in Western societies only since World War II. A welfare state exists where government organizations provide material benefits for those who are unable to support themselves adequately through paid employment—the unemployed, the sick, the disabled, and the elderly. All Western countries today provide extensive welfare benefits. In many poorer countries, these benefits are virtually nonexistent.

Although an extensive welfare state was seen as the culmination of the development of citizenship rights, in recent years welfare states have come under pressure from increasing global economic competition and the movement of people from poor, underdeveloped societies to richer, developed countries. As a result, the United States and some European countries have sought to reduce benefits to noncitizens and to prevent new immigrants from entering the country. For example, for many years the U.S. government has patrolled its border with Mexico and constructed walls of concrete and barbed wire in an attempt to keep illegal immigrants out of the country. Similarly, one of the most contested issues regarding health care reform in the United States is whether to extend health benefits to immigrants. Although the 600,000 legal permanent residents in the

political rights • Rights of political participation, such as the right to vote in local and national elections, held by citizens of a national community.

franchise • The right to vote.

social rights • Rights of social and welfare provision held by all citizens in a national community, including, for example, the right to claim unemployment benefits and sickness payments provided by the state.

welfare state • A political system that provides a wide range of welfare benefits for its citizens.

A U.S. Border Patrol agent drives along the wall that separates Nogales, Arizona, from Nogales, Sonora, Mexico, on the U.S.–Mexico border. What strategies has the United States used to achieve social closure?

United States pay taxes, as of 2014, they were restricted from receiving health care benefits. In March 2014, Representative Michelle Lujan Grisham introduced the Health Equity and Access under the Law for Immigrant Women and Families Act of 2014, which would give legal immigrants and some undocumented immigrants immediate access to health insurance (Insurance NewsNet 2014). Citizenship, and the bundle of rights and privileges accompanying it, serve as a powerful instrument of social closure, whereby prosperous nation-states have attempted to exclude the migrant poor from the status and the benefits that citizenship confers (Brubaker 1992). Having learned some of the important characteristics of modern states, we now consider the nature of democracy in modern societies. ✓

CONCEPT CHECKS ✓

1. Describe three main characteristics of the state.

2. What is a welfare state? Can the United States be classified as a welfare state? Why?

Learn about different types of democracy, how this form of government has spread around the world, key theories about power in a democracy, and some of the problems associated with modern-day democracy.

HOW DO DEMOCRACIES FUNCTION?

The word *democracy* has its roots in the Greek term *demokratia*, the individual parts of which are *demos* ("people") and *kratos* ("rule"), and its basic meaning is therefore a political system in which the people, not monarchs or aristocracies based on blood lines, rule. What does it mean to be ruled by the people? The answer to that question has taken contrasting forms, at varying periods and in different societies. For example, "the people" have been variously understood as owners of property, white men, educated men, men, and adult men and women. In some societies, the officially accepted version of **democracy** is limited to the political sphere, whereas in others, it is extended to other areas of social life.

democracy • A political system that allows the citizens to participate in political decision making or to elect representatives to government bodies.

PARTICIPATORY DEMOCRACY

In **participatory democracy** decisions are made communally by those affected by them. This was the original type of democracy practiced in ancient Athens. Those who were citizens, a small minority of Athenian society, regularly assembled to consider policies and make major decisions. Participatory democracy is of limited importance in modern societies, where the vast majority of the population has political rights, rendering it impossible for everyone to participate actively in the making of all the decisions that affect them. In modern societies, direct democracy is a much more realistic approach to engaging citizens in decisions. A **direct democracy** is a form of participatory democracy in which citizens vote directly on laws and policies; however, they do not need to convene in one setting to do so. For example, Americans can visit voting booths in their hometowns to vote directly on legislation that affects their lives.

participatory democracy • A system of democracy in which all members of a group or community participate collectively in making major decisions.

direct democracy • A form of participatory democracy that allows citizens to vote directly on laws and policies.

Yet some facets of participatory democracy do play a part in modern societies. The holding of a referendum, for example, whereby the majority express their views on a particular issue, is one form of participatory democracy. Direct consultation of large numbers of people is made possible by simplifying the issue to one or two questions to be answered. Referenda are employed frequently on a state level in the United States to decide controversial issues, such as the legalization of gay marriage.

MONARCHIES AND LIBERAL DEMOCRACIES

Some modern states, including Britain and Belgium, still have monarchs, but these are few and far between. Where traditional rulers of this sort are still found, their real power is usually limited or nonexistent. In a tiny number of countries, such as Saudi Arabia and Jordan, monarchs continue to hold some degree of control over government, but in most cases they are symbols of national identity rather than personages having any direct power in political life. The queen of England, the king of Sweden, and even the emperor of Japan are all **constitutional monarchs**: Their real power is severely restricted by the constitution, which vests authority in the elected representatives of the people. The vast majority of modern states are *republican*—there is no king or queen. Almost every modern state, including constitutional monarchies, professes adherence to democracy.

Countries in which voters can choose between two or more political parties and in which the majority of the adult population has the right to vote are usually called **liberal democracies**. The United States, the Western European countries, Japan, Australia, and New Zealand all fall into this category. Some developing countries, such as India, also have liberal democratic systems.

constitutional monarchs • Kings or queens who are largely figureheads. Real power rests in the hands of other political leaders.

liberal democracies • A type of representative democracy in which elected representatives hold power.

THE SPREAD OF LIBERAL DEMOCRACY

For much of the twentieth century, the political systems of the world were divided primarily between liberal democracy and communism, as found in the former Soviet Union (and which still exists in China, Cuba, and North Korea). As we learned in Chapter 1, the philosophical roots of **communism** can be found in the writings of Karl Marx, who predicted that in the future, capitalism would be supplanted by a society in which there were no classes—no divisions between rich and poor—and the economic system would come under communal ownership. Under these circumstances, Marx believed, a more equal society would be established. Marx's work had a far-reaching effect in the twentieth century. Through most of the century, until the fall of Soviet communism in the early 1990s, more than a third of the world population lived in societies whose governments claimed to derive their inspiration from Marx's ideas. In practice, however, communism often exists as a system of one-party rule. Voters typically were given a choice not between different parties but between different candidates of the same party—the Communist Party; sometimes only one candidate ran. The party controlled the economy as well as the political system.

communism • A set of political ideas associated with Marx, as developed particularly by Lenin and institutionalized in the Soviet Union, Eastern Europe, and some developing countries.

Since 1989, when the hold of the Soviet Union over Eastern Europe was broken, processes of democratization have swept across the world in a sort of chain reaction. The number of democratic nations almost doubled between 1989 and 2012, from 66 to 118 (Freedom House 2005, 2012). Freedom House classifies a nation as democratic if it maintains a competitive multiparty political system, all adults have a right to vote, election procedures are transparent, and major political parties have access to the general public via media and campaigning (Freedom House 2012).

In China, which has about a fifth of the world's population, the communist government is facing strong pressures toward democratization. During the 1990s, thousands of people were held in prison in China for the nonviolent expression of their desire for democracy. Some groups, resisted by the communist government, are still working actively to secure a transition to a democratic system.

The trend toward democracy is hardly irreversible. Electoral democracy does not ensure that liberal democratic governments will be chosen by voters. In post-Arab Spring elections in Egypt, Palestine, and Turkey, the voters chose Islamist parties over more secular, democratic ones.

Why has democracy become so popular? The reasons have to do with the social and economic changes discussed throughout this book. First, democracy tends to be associated with competitive capitalism in the economic system, and capitalism has shown itself to be superior to communism as a wealth-generating system. Second, the more social activity becomes globalized and people's daily lives become influenced by events happening far away, the more they start to push for information about how they are ruled—and therefore for greater democracy (Huntington 1991). Third, with the influence of mass communications, particularly television and the Internet, governments can't maintain control over what their citizens see.

THE INTERNET AND DEMOCRATIZATION

The Internet is a powerful democratizing force. It transcends national and cultural borders, facilitates the spread of ideas around the globe, and allows like-minded people to find one another in the realm of cyberspace. More and more people in countries around the world access the Internet regularly and consider it to be important to their lifestyles.

One prominent example of the political role of the Internet is provided by MoveOn.org, a liberal organization that was originally created in 1998 by the twenty-two-year-old activist Eli Pariser and software entrepreneurs Wes Boyd and Joan Blades to electronically mobilize opposition to the impeachment of President Bill Clinton. The organization now boasts 7 million members. The organization has collected millions of dollars through its website in support of liberal causes and has attracted some big-money contributors, including billionaire George Soros (Neuman 2003, Brownstein 2003, Menn 2003, Avins 2003). Since MoveOn.org was founded, the Internet has flourished as a means of diffusing political information (and rhetoric), especially among young persons. All ends of the political spectrum, from MoveOn.org to the Tea Party, have used the Internet to recruit volunteers, share information on candidate views, and organize rallies and protests (Pilkington 2009). As we will see in Chapter 16, the Internet played an essential role in mobilizing protesters during the Arab Spring, Occupy Wall Street, and Ukrainian Maidan movements.

Yet as we shall also see, political indifference and voter apathy are extremely high in the United States, and winning federal elections requires large sums

Staff members and political strategists of Barack Obama's 2012 bid for president stay glued to their computers for updates on his re-election campaign. In recent years, politicians and pundits have relied more and more heavily on the Internet to communicate with voters and measure the electorate's mood.

of money that are unlikely to be raised through small online contributions. How "Internet democracy" plays itself out in the national political arena will depend not only on technology but on the ability of grassroots efforts to make a real difference in political outcomes.

DEMOCRACY IN THE UNITED STATES

POLITICAL PARTIES

A political party is an organization of individuals with broadly similar political aims, oriented toward achieving legitimate control of government through an electoral process. Two parties tend to dominate the political system where elections are based on the principle of winner take all, as in the United States. Where elections are based on different principles, as in proportional representation (in which seats in a representative assembly are allocated according to the proportions of the vote received), five or six different parties, or even more, may be represented in the assembly. An advantage to this system is that minority political parties have a say. For example, in the United States, the Green Party has almost no presence at the national level. Yet in Germany, which abides by the proportional representation system, new and smaller political parties that are supported by even a small part of the electorate have a chance of being represented in Parliament; these parties are far-ranging and include the Green Party, as well as the Christian Democratic Union/Christian Social Union, Social Democratic Party, and Free Democratic Party (Krennerich 2014). When they lack an overall majority, some of the parties have to form a coalition—an alliance to form a government.

In the United States, the system has become effectively a two-party one between the Republicans and Democrats, although no formal restriction is placed on the number of political parties. The nation's founders made no mention of parties in the Constitution because they thought that party conflict might threaten the unity of the new republic. Two-party systems tend to lead to a concentration on the "middle ground." The parties in these countries often cultivate a moderate image and sometimes come to resemble each other so closely that the choice they offer is relatively slight. Multiparty systems, by contrast, allow divergent interests and points of view to be expressed more directly and provide scope for the representation of radical alternatives. Representatives from the liberal Green Party as well as far right parties, found in some European parliaments, are cases in point. However, under such systems no one party is likely to achieve an overall majority, and the government by coalition that results can lead to indecision and stalemate if compromises can't be worked out.

POLITICS AND VOTING

Building mass support for a party in the United States is difficult because the country is so large and includes so many different regional, cultural, and ethnic groups. The parties have each tried to develop their electoral strength by forging broad regional bases of support and by campaigning for very general political ideals.

As measured by their levels of membership, party identification, and voting support, both of the major American parties are in decline (Wattenberg 1996). In recent years, the proportion of American voters who identify with either the Democratic or Republican party has fallen. The proportion identifying as Democratic dropped from 36 to 32 percent of voters between 2008 and 2012. Similarly, the proportion of voters self-identifying as Republication dropped from 30 percent in 2002 to 25 percent in 2008, falling to just 24 percent in 2012. In contrast, one analysis of polling data showed that the number of voters declaring themselves to be "independent" of either party grew from 21 percent in 1957 to 38 percent in 2012 (Pew Research Center for the People and the Press 2012b).

Moreover, Democrats and Republicans have become increasingly polarized in the past few years. For example, Republicans are much more likely to favor an assertive national security strategy, whereas Democrats are increasingly critical of business and more likely to favor stronger government support for the poor (Pew Research Center for the People and the Press 2009). As we saw earlier in this chapter, for example, Democrats tend to be more supportive of raising the minimum wage to help low-wage workers maintain an adequate standard of living, while their Republican counterparts worry that raising the minimum wage will be hurtful to business owners, especially small independent business owners who may be struggling to make ends meet.

Starting in the early 1960s the proportion of the population that turns out to vote in the United States steadily decreased, to the point where only slightly more than half the electorate voted in presidential elections in the last three decades of the twentieth century. The turnout for congressional elections is lower still—around 40 percent (NES 2003). The presidential election of 2008 bucked this declining trend with voter turnout levels of nearly 64 percent, the highest since the election of 1968. The rate dipped slightly to 62 percent by 2012, however (U.S. Bureau of the Census 2013e).

The recent spike in the number of voters is attributed to campaigns by both parties to mobilize their core constituencies. Inspired by the candidacy of Barack Obama, youthful voters and African Americans also turned out in unprecedented numbers. The 2008 election, in particular, was an anomaly. Political scientists have documented that voter turnout is highest historically among whites and lowest among Hispanics, with blacks and Asian Americans in between. Highly educated persons and those with greater income also are more likely to vote than persons with fewer means. Generally, turnout increases directly with age: Only a little more than a third of all voters in the eighteen-to-twenty-four age group bothered to vote for president in 2000, compared with nearly three-quarters of voters in their sixties. However, in the 2008 presidential election, the number of young voters swelled due to a highly organized voter mobilization campaign. Nearly 52 percent of voters under thirty voted in the 2008 election, although this figure dipped slightly by the 2012 election (United States Election Project 2014).

Voter turnout in the United States is among the world's lowest. Sweden's International Institute for Democracy and Electoral Assistance tracked voter turnout in all countries that held national elections at any time during the period from 2000 to 2009 by comparing the number of voters with the total voting-age population. According to their study, voter turnout in the United States averaged only 58 percent overall, earning it 112th place (of 192 countries). By way of comparison, voter turnout in Europe over the same period averaged 61 percent; Asia, 64 percent; South America, 65 percent; Central America and the Caribbean, 61.5 percent; and Africa, 64.5 percent (IDEA 2009).

Why is voter turnout so low in the United States? Many studies have found that countries with high rates of literacy, high average incomes, and well-established political freedoms and civil liberties are likely to have high voter turnouts. Yet the United States ranks high on all these measures but still fails to motivate people to vote. Compulsory registration is common throughout Europe, and registration is often made easy. In the United States, where voters are required to register well in advance of elections, many fail to do so and are thus disqualified from voting. In addition to compulsory registration, thirty-three countries have compulsory voting. Even though enforcement is often weak or nonexistent, voter turnout tends to be higher where voting is mandated by law (Pintor and Gratschew 2002).

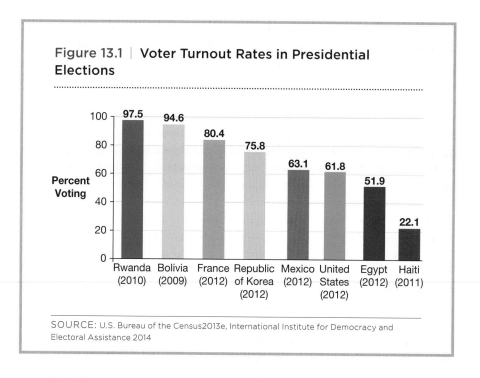

Figure 13.1 | Voter Turnout Rates in Presidential Elections

Percent Voting

- Rwanda (2010): 97.5
- Bolivia (2009): 94.6
- France (2012): 80.4
- Republic of Korea (2012): 75.8
- Mexico (2012): 63.1
- United States (2012): 61.8
- Egypt (2012): 51.9
- Haiti (2011): 22.1

SOURCE: U.S. Bureau of the Census2013e, International Institute for Democracy and Electoral Assistance 2014

Another possible reason is that since "winner-take-all" elections discourage the formation of third parties, voters may sometimes feel that they lack effective choices when it comes time to vote. A staunch environmentalist may decide there is no point in voting if the Green Party candidate has no real chance of winning a seat in Congress. Finally, the range of elections is much more extensive in the United States than in other Western societies. In no other country are such a variety of offices at all levels—including sheriffs, judges, city treasurers, and many other posts—open to election. Americans are entitled to do about three or four times as much electing as citizens elsewhere. Low rates of voter turnout thus have to be balanced against the wider set of opportunities that Americans have to elect candidates for every level of office, from the most local to the highest office.

INTEREST GROUPS

Interest groups and lobbying play a distinctive part in American politics. An **interest group** is any organization that attempts to influence elected officials to consider its aims when deciding on legislation. The American Medical Association, the National Organization for Women, and the National Rifle Association are three examples. Interest groups vary in size; some are national, others statewide. Some are permanently organized; others are short-lived. Lobbying is the act of contacting influential officials to present arguments to convince them to vote in favor of a cause or otherwise lend support to the aims of an interest group. The word *lobby* originated in the British parliamentary system: In days past, members of Parliament did not have offices, so their business was conducted in the lobbies of the Parliament buildings.

To run as a candidate is enormously expensive, and interest groups provide much of the funding at all levels of political office. In the 2012 presidential election, the Obama-Biden campaign spent more than $683 million to win re-election (Center for Responsive Politics 2013a). The Romney-Ryan ticket spent roughly $504 million. Even to run for the House or Senate costs a small fortune. The most expensive congressional race in history, when Elizabeth Warren (Democrat) beat

interest group • A group organized to pursue specific interests in the political arena, operating primarily by lobbying the members of legislative bodies.

Scott Brown (Republican) in the battle to become a senator from Massachusetts in 2012, saw total spending of $82 million (Center for Responsive Politics 2013d). As of May 2014, candidates for House and Senate seats had collectively raised $504 million for the current election cycle (Center for Responsive Politics 2013b).

Incumbents, or those already in office, have an enormous advantage in soliciting money. Incumbents are favored as fund-raisers partly because they can curry favor with special interests and other contributors, since they are in a position to ensure favorable votes on issues of importance to their funders, as well as obtain spending on pet projects and other "pork" for their districts. Incumbency also provides familiarity—a formidable (and costly) obstacle for most challengers to overcome. However, during periods of economic downturn and anxiety, voters often seek a "change" and vote out incumbents. For example, in the 2010 interim elections, fifty-three members of the U.S. House of Representatives were voted out of office. Although this amounts to just 13 percent of incumbents losing their jobs, this proportion was the highest since 1970 (Bowman and Amico 2010). In 2012, 90 percent of incumbent House members and 91 percent of incumbent Senators were re-elected (Center for Responsive Politics 2013c).

About a third of the funding in congressional elections comes from political action committees (PACs), which are set up by interest groups to raise and distribute campaign funds. Paid lobbyists play a significant role in influencing the outcome of votes in Congress and decisions by the president. The Center for Responsive Politics (2011) reported that businesses, unions, and other advocacy groups spent some $3.5 billion in 2009—a third of which ($1.2 billion) went to influence health care reform. The Affordable Care Act, signed into law by President Obama in 2010, overhauled the U.S. health care system. Among other provisions, it extended insurance coverage to an additional 30 million Americans and prohibited insurance companies from denying care for preexisting conditions. When the debate over health care reform began, the White House was seriously considering a "public option," an approach Obama had promoted during his campaign for president. Under this approach, the government would offer its own competing health care insurance program, in hopes of forcing private insurance companies to lower their premiums. Once in the White House, however, it proved impossible to get a public option endorsed by Congress—even though the Democrats held solid majorities in both the House and Senate and public opinion polls showed that a majority of Americans favored this approach (Pew Research Center 2010). Lobbyists for pharmaceutical companies, hospitals, and insurance companies spent millions of dollars in an effort to shape the final outcome in ways they favored (Eggen 2009). A study by the Center for Public Integrity found that nearly 1,800 firms and other organizations hired more than 4,500 lobbyists to influence the outcome of the health care debate—effectively eight lobbyists for each member of Congress (Eaton and Pell 2010).

THE POLITICAL PARTICIPATION OF WOMEN

suffrage • A legal right to vote guaranteed by the Fifteenth Amendment to the U.S. Constitution; guaranteed to women by the Nineteenth Amendment.

Voting has a special meaning for women, given their long struggle to obtain universal **suffrage**. The members of the early women's movements saw the vote both as the symbol of political freedom and as the means of achieving greater economic and social equality.

After what was often a long, hard fight, women now can vote in nearly all of the world's nations; however, this has not greatly altered the nature of politics. Women's voting patterns, like those of men, are shaped by party preferences, policy options,

Hillary Rodham Clinton, former New York Senator and U.S. Secretary of State, shakes hands with current Supreme Court Justices Sonia Sotomayor (middle) and Elena Kagan (right). These three women are part of the small number of females holding federal political office in the United States today.

and the choice of available candidates. The influence of women on politics cannot be assessed solely through voting patterns, however. Feminist groups have made an impact on political life independently of the franchise, particularly in recent decades. Since the early 1960s, the National Organization for Women (NOW) and other women's groups in the United States have played a significant role in the passing of equal opportunity acts and have pressed for a range of issues directly affecting women to be placed on the political agenda. Such issues include equal rights at work, the availability of abortion, changes in family and divorce laws, and lesbian rights. In 1973 women achieved a legal victory when the Supreme Court ruled in *Roe v. Wade* that women had a legal right to abortion. The 1989 Court ruling in *Webster v. Reproductive Health Services*, which placed restrictions on that right, resulted in a resurgence of involvement in the women's movement.

Although women lag far behind men in the ranks of the political elite, they have made important strides in recent decades. Women such as Supreme Court justices Ruth Bader Ginsberg, Elena Kagan, and Sonia Sotomayor, and Nancy Pelosi, minority leader of the U.S. House of Representatives, now play central roles in American politics. Still, women remain underrepresented in government. In 2013, there were only 20 women in the Senate (of 100 members), and only 78 in the House of Representatives (18 percent of total House membership) (Center for American Women and Politics 2014). While these percentages may seem low, from a historical perspective they represent a sea change in women's roles in politics. Just forty years ago, in 1970, there was only a single woman in the Senate, and there were just ten in the House.

Despite the gender gap in Congress and other elected offices, both the Democratic and Republican parties today are nominally committed to securing equal opportunities for women and men. Since 1990, female candidates for political office have been successful *when they have run for office*. The critical factor seems to be that political parties (which are largely run by men) have not recruited as many women to run for office.

We now broaden our scope to look at some basic ideas of political power. First, we take up the issue of who actually holds the reins of power, drawing on comparative materials to help illuminate the discussion. We then consider whether democratic governments around the world are "in crisis."

WHO RULES? THEORIES OF DEMOCRACY

DEMOCRATIC ELITISM

democratic elitism • A theory of the limits of democracy, which holds that in large-scale societies democratic participation is necessarily limited to the regular election of political leaders.

One of the most influential views of the nature and limits of modern democracy was set out by Max Weber and, in rather modified form, by the economist Joseph Schumpeter (1983, orig. 1942). The ideas they developed are sometimes referred to as the theory of **democratic elitism**.

Weber began from the assumption that direct democracy is impossible as a means of regular government in large-scale societies. This is not only for the obvious logistical reason that millions of people cannot meet to make political decisions but because running a complex society demands expertise. Participatory democracy, Weber believed, can only succeed in small organizations in which the work to be carried out is fairly simple and straightforward. Where more complicated decisions have to be made, or policies worked out, even in modest-sized groups—such as a small business firm—specialized knowledge and skills are necessary. Experts have to carry out their jobs on a continuous basis; positions that require expertise cannot be subject to the regular election of people who may only have a vague knowledge of the necessary skills and information. While higher officials, responsible for overall policy decisions, are elected, there must be a large substratum of full-time bureaucratic officials who play a large part in running a country (Weber 1979, orig. 1921).

Weber placed a great deal of emphasis on the importance of leadership in democracy—which is why his view is referred to as "democratic elitism." He argued that rule by elites is inevitable; the best we can hope for is that those elites effectively represent our interests and that they do so in an innovative and insightful fashion. Weber valued multiparty democracy more for the quality of leadership it generates than for the mass participation in politics it makes possible.

Joseph Schumpeter fully agreed with Weber about the limits of mass political participation. For Schumpeter, as for Weber, democracy is more important as a method of generating effective and responsible government than as a means of providing significant power for the majority. Democracy, Schumpeter stated, is the rule of the politician, not the people. Politicians are "dealers in votes" much as brokers are dealers in shares on the stock exchange. To achieve voting support, however, politicians must be at least minimally responsive to the demands and interests of the electorate. Only if there is some degree of competition to secure votes can arbitrary rule effectively be avoided.

PLURALIST THEORIES

pluralist theories of modern democracy • Theories that emphasize the role of diverse and potentially competing interest groups, none of which dominate the political process.

The ideas of Weber and Schumpeter influenced some of the **pluralist theories of modern democracy**, although the pluralists developed their ideas somewhat differently. According to the pluralist view, government policies in a democracy are influenced by the continual processes of bargaining among numerous groups representing different interests—business organizations, trade unions, ethnic groups, environmental organizations, religious groups, and so forth. A democratic political order is one in which there is a balance among competing interests, all having some impact on policy but none dominating the actual mechanisms of government. Elections are also influenced by this situation; to achieve a broad enough base of support to lay claim to government, parties must be responsive to numerous diverse interest groups. The United States, it is held, is the most pluralistic of industrialized societies and, therefore, the most democratic. Competition between diverse interest groups occurs not only at the national level but within the states and in the politics of local communities.

THE POWER ELITE

The view suggested by C. Wright Mills in his celebrated work *The Power Elite* is quite different from pluralist theories (Mills 1956). Mills argues that during the course of the twentieth century a process of institutional centralization occurred in the political order, the economy, and the sphere of the military. Not only did each of these spheres become more centralized, according to Mills, but they became increasingly merged with one another to form a unified system of power. Those who are in the highest positions in all three institutional areas have come from similar social backgrounds, have parallel interests, and often know one another on a personal basis. By the mid-twentieth century they had become a single **power elite** that ran, and continues to run, the country—and, given the international position of the United States, also influences a great deal of the rest of the world.

The power elite, in Mills's portrayal, is composed mainly of white Anglo-Saxon Protestants (WASPs). Many are from wealthy families, have been to the same prestigious universities, belong to the same clubs, and sit on government committees with one another. They have closely connected concerns. Business and political leaders work together, and both have close relationships with the military through weapons contracting and the supply of goods for the armed forces. There is a great deal of movement among top positions in the three spheres. Politicians have business interests; business leaders often run for public office; higher military personnel sit on the boards of the large companies.

Since Mills published his study, numerous other research investigations have analyzed the social background and interconnections of leading figures in the various spheres of American society (Dye 1986). All studies agree on the finding that the social backgrounds of those in leading positions are highly unrepresentative of the population as a whole (Domhoff 1971, 1979, 1983, 1998).

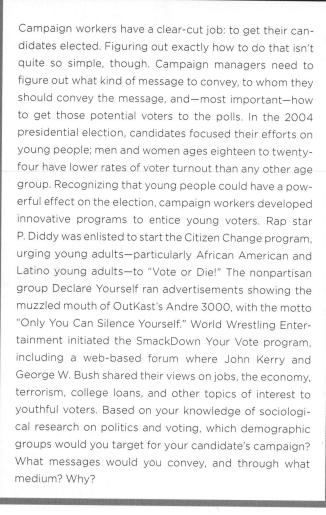

Making Sociology Work
CAMPAIGN WORKER

Campaign workers have a clear-cut job: to get their candidates elected. Figuring out exactly how to do that isn't quite so simple, though. Campaign managers need to figure out what kind of message to convey, to whom they should convey the message, and—most important—how to get those potential voters to the polls. In the 2004 presidential election, candidates focused their efforts on young people; men and women ages eighteen to twenty-four have lower rates of voter turnout than any other age group. Recognizing that young people could have a powerful effect on the election, campaign workers developed innovative programs to entice young voters. Rap star P. Diddy was enlisted to start the Citizen Change program, urging young adults—particularly African American and Latino young adults—to "Vote or Die!" The nonpartisan group Declare Yourself ran advertisements showing the muzzled mouth of OutKast's Andre 3000, with the motto "Only You Can Silence Yourself." World Wrestling Entertainment initiated the SmackDown Your Vote program, including a web-based forum where John Kerry and George W. Bush shared their views on jobs, the economy, terrorism, college loans, and other topics of interest to youthful voters. Based on your knowledge of sociological research on politics and voting, which demographic groups would you target for your candidate's campaign? What messages would you convey, and through what medium? Why?

power elite • Small networks of individuals who, according to C. Wright Mills, hold concentrated power in modern societies.

THE ROLE OF THE MILITARY

Mills's argument that the military plays a central role in the power elite was buttressed by a well-known warning from a former military hero and U.S. president, Dwight David Eisenhower. In his farewell presidential speech in 1961, Eisenhower—who was the supreme commander of the Allied forces in Europe in World War II—warned of the dangers of what he termed the "military-industrial complex." As Eisenhower bluntly put it, "The conjunction of an immense military establishment and a large arms industry is new in the American experience. In the councils of government, we must guard against the acquisition of unwarranted influence, whether sought or unsought, by the military-industrial complex. The potential for the disastrous rise of misplaced power exists and will persist" (Eisenhower Library 1961).

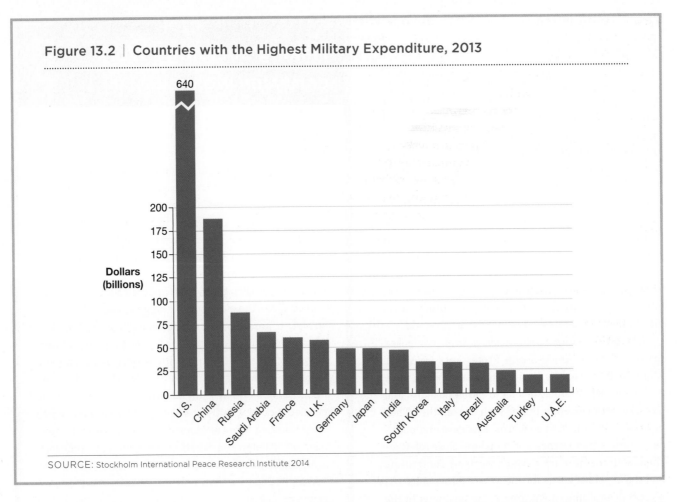

Figure 13.2 | Countries with the Highest Military Expenditure, 2013

SOURCE: Stockholm International Peace Research Institute 2014

With the collapse of the Soviet Union in 1991, the United States has emerged as the world's unrivaled military superpower, accounting for nearly 40 percent of total military spending—more than that of the next eleven countries combined (Figure 13.2) (Stockholm International Peace Research Institute 2012). The global "war on terror," discussed below, has instead triggered yet another cycle of military spending. Eisenhower's dire warning seems no less apt today than when he uttered it some fifty years ago.

DEMOCRACY IN TROUBLE?

Democracy almost everywhere is in some difficulty today. Even in the United States, voter turnout is low, and many people tell pollsters that they don't trust politicians. In 1964, confidence in government was fairly high: Nearly four of five people answered "most of the time" or "just about always" when asked, "How much of the time do you trust the government in Washington to do the right thing?" Americans' confidence in government dropped steadily throughout the late 1960s and 1970s, rising somewhat in the 1980s, then dropping to a low of one in five in 1994. Following the terrorist attacks of September 11, 2001, a solid majority (55 percent) of Americans reported that they trust the government "most of the time" or "just about always." However, as we saw in Chapter 5, confidence in the U.S. government has waned again in the past few years, especially upon the public's discovery in June 2013 that the National Security Agency was collecting and monitoring private citizens' telephone records and Internet use. By mid-2013, just 26 percent of Americans said they could trust the government in Washington almost always or most of the time (Pew Research Center for the People and the Press 2013b).

Of those expressing continuing trust in government, most vote in presidential elections; of those who lack trust, most do not vote. As we have seen, younger people have less interest in electoral politics than older generations have, although the young have a greater interest than their elders in issues like the environment (Nye 1997). Some have argued that trends like these indicate that people are increasingly skeptical of traditional forms of authority. Connected to this has been a shift in political values in democratic nations from "scarcity values" to "post-materialist values" (Inglehart 1997). This means that after a certain level of economic prosperity has been reached, voters become concerned less with economic issues than with the quality of their individual (as opposed to collective) lifestyles, such as whether they have meaningful work. As a result, voters are generally less interested in national politics, except for areas involving personal liberty, such as choices regarding access to legal abortion, and decisions about one's health care providers.

The last few decades have also been a period in which, in several Western countries, the welfare state has come under attack. Rights and benefits, fought for over long periods, have been contested and cut back. One reason for this governmental retrenchment is the decline in revenues available to governments as a result of the general world recession that began in the early 1970s. Yet an increasing skepticism also seems to have developed, shared not only by some governments but by many of their citizens, about the effectiveness of relying on the state for the provision of many essential goods and services. This skepticism is based on the belief that the welfare state is bureaucratic, alienating, and inefficient and that welfare benefits can create perverse consequences that undermine what they were designed to achieve (Giddens 1998).

Why are so many people dissatisfied with the very political system that provides a safety net for its citizens? The answers, curiously, are bound up with the factors that have helped spread democracy—the impact of capitalism and the globalizing of social life. While capitalist economies generate more wealth than any other type of economic system, that wealth is unevenly distributed, as we learned in Chapter 7. And economic inequalities influence who votes, joins parties, and gets elected. Wealthy individuals and corporations back interest groups that lobby for elected officials to support their aims when deciding on legislation. Not being subject to election, interest groups are not accountable to the majority of the electorate. ✓

> ### CONCEPT CHECKS ✓
> 1. Why is it problematic for contemporary states to have participatory democracy?
> 2. Contrast the concepts of democracy and communism.
> 3. Describe the role interest groups play in American politics.
> 4. Compare and contrast pluralist theories of modern democracy and the power elite model.

WHAT IS TERRORISM?

Learn how social scientists define terrorism and the ways that new-style terrorism is different from the old.

Terrorism has seized national headlines in recent decades, yet defining *terrorism* can be a complex and nuanced process (Turk 2004). Terrorism broadly refers to "any action [by a non-state organization] . . . that is intended to cause death or serious bodily harm to civilians or non-combatants, when the purpose of such an act, by its nature or context, is to intimidate a population, or to compel a Government or an international

terrorism • Use of attacks on civilians designed to persuade a government to alter its policies, or to damage its standing in the world.

organization to do or to abstain from doing any act" (Panyarachun et al. 2004). In other words, terrorism concerns attacks on civilians designed to persuade a government to alter its policies, or to damage its standing in the world (Turk 2004).

OLD- AND NEW-STYLE TERRORISM

old-style terrorism • A type of terrorism that is local and linked to particular states and has limited objectives, which means that the violence involved is fairly limited.

A distinction can be drawn between old- and new-style terrorism. **Old-style terrorism** was dominant for most of the twentieth century and still exists today. It is associated primarily with the rise of nationalism and with the establishment of nations as sovereign, territorially bounded entities, which began in Europe in the late eighteenth century. Most forms of old-style terrorism are linked to nations without states. The point of old-style terrorism is to establish states in areas where nations do not have control of the territory's state apparatus. This is true, for example, of Irish nationalists, such as the Irish Republican Army (IRA), and Basque nationalists, such as ETA, in Spain. The main issues are territorial integrity and identity in the formation of a state. Old-style terrorism is found where there are nations without states and where terrorists are prepared to use violence to achieve their ends. Old-style terrorism is fundamentally local because its ambitions are local. It is intended to establish a state in a specific national area.

new-style terrorism • A recent form of terrorism characterized by global ambitions, loose global organizational ties, and a more ruthless attitude toward the violence the terrorists are willing to use.

New-style terrorism, most famously associated with the Islamic fundamentalism of al Qaeda, differs from old-style terrorism in several ways (Tan and Ramakrishna 2002). First, new-style terrorism is different from old-style terrorism in the scope of its claims. One of the distinguishing features of al Qaeda's view of the world, for example, is that it has global geopolitical aims; it seeks to restructure world society. Whereas old-style terrorism is local and linked to particular states, new-style terrorism is global in its ambitions. It seeks to alter the balance of world power (Gray 2003).

Second, new-style terrorism differs from old-style terrorism in its organizational structure. With new-style terrorism, there is a lot of autonomy in local cells, and these can reproduce without necessarily having any strong direction from the center.

An example of an old-style terrorist movement, these Basque Nationalists are mostly concerned with territorial control and the formation of states.

New-style terrorist groups also have some contacts and supports from states as well as a global spread of supporters in many countries.

The third and last way in which old-style and new-style terrorism differ is over means. Old-style terrorism had relatively limited objectives, and as a result the violence involved was fairly limited. New-style terrorism is much more ruthless in the means it is prepared to use. Al Qaeda websites, for example, talk in extremely destructive language of the enemy, which is principally the United States but to some extent the West as a whole. These will often explicitly say that terrorist acts should be carried out that kill as many people as possible. This is very different from the more limited use of violent means characteristic of old-style terrorism.

TERRORISM AND WAR

How should we respond to the threat of new-style terrorism? Terrorism of the kind seen on September 11, 2001, raises difficult questions for political sociologists. Can a "war" on terrorism be fought like a conventional war? The coalition that attacked Afghanistan in 2001 did destroy at least some of the al Qaeda terrorist networks. Yet despite some successes against new-style terrorism through conventional warfare, critics are surely right to argue that in many cases the level of violence, aims, and organizational structure of new-style terrorist groups differentiate them from conventional enemies such as hostile nation-states. The debate about whether terrorism can be tackled through conventional warfare raises further difficult questions regarding the relationship between terrorism and nation-states, like Afghanistan, that have supported it. In turn this leads to questions about global governance. In a global age, what international support and proof are needed to act to prevent a perceived threat? And what are the best institutions to deal with a global terrorist threat? ✓

> ### CONCEPT CHECKS ✓
> 1. How do we define terrorism?
> 2. Compare and contrast old- and new-style terrorism.

WHAT IS THE SOCIAL SIGNIFICANCE OF WORK?

> Assess the sociological ramifications of paid and unpaid work. Understand that modern economies are based on the division of labor and economic interdependence. Familiarize yourself with modern systems of economic production.

Because politics is inextricably linked with economic life, we now turn our attention to the ways that work and the economy have changed. **Work** refers to carrying out tasks that require mental and physical effort, with the objective of the production of goods and services that cater to human needs. An **occupation**, or job, is work that is done in exchange for a regular wage or salary. In all cultures, work is the basis of the economic system.

The study of economic institutions is of major importance in sociology because the economy influences all segments of society and therefore social reproduction in general. Hunting and gathering, pastoralism, agriculture, industrialism—these different ways of gaining a livelihood have a fundamental influence on the lives people lead. The distribution of goods and variations in the economic position of those who produce them also strongly influence social inequalities of all kinds. Wealth and power do not inevitably go together, but in general the privileged in terms of wealth are also among the more powerful groups in a society.

work • The activity by which people produce from the natural world and so ensure their survival. Work should not be thought of exclusively as paid employment. In modern societies, there remain types of work that do not involve direct payment (for example, housework).

occupation • Any form of paid employment in which an individual regularly works.

In the remainder of this chapter, we will analyze the nature of work in modern societies and look at the major changes affecting economic life today. We will investigate the changing nature of industrial production and of work itself. Modern industry differs in a fundamental way from premodern systems of production, which were based above all on agriculture. Most people worked in the fields or cared for livestock. In modern societies, by contrast, only a tiny fraction of the population works in agriculture, and farming itself has become industrialized—it is carried on largely by means of machines rather than by human hands.

Modern industry is itself always changing—technological change is one of its main features. **Technology** involves the use of science and machinery to achieve greater productive efficiency. The nature of industrial production also changes in relation to wider social and economic influences. We focus on both technological and economic change, showing how these are transforming industry today. We will also see that globalization makes a great deal of difference to our working lives; the nature of the work we do is being changed by forces of global economic competition.

technology • The application of knowledge of the material world to production; the creation of material instruments (such as machines) used in human interaction with nature.

THE IMPORTANCE OF PAID AND UNPAID WORK

We often associate the notion of work with drudgery—with a set of tasks that we want to minimize and, if possible, escape from altogether. You may have this very thought in mind as you set out to read this chapter! Is this most people's attitude toward their work, and if so, why?

Work is more than just drudgery, or people would not feel so lost and disoriented when they become unemployed. How would you feel if you thought you would never get a job? In modern societies, having a job is important for maintaining a sense of purpose. Even where work conditions are relatively unpleasant, and the tasks involved are dull, work tends to be a structuring element in people's psychological makeup and the cycle of their daily activities.

Work need not conform to orthodox categories of paid employment. Nonpaid labor (such as repairing one's own car or doing one's own housework) is an important aspect of many people's lives. Much of the work done in the informal economy, for example, is not recorded in official employment statistics. The term **informal economy** refers to transactions outside the sphere of regular employment, sometimes involving the exchange of cash for services provided, but also often involving the direct exchange of goods or services. Your child's baby sitter might be paid in cash "off the books," or without any receipt being given or details of the job recorded; the same may be true of the person who cleans your house or does your gardening, if you use such services.

informal economy • Economic transactions carried on outside the sphere of formal paid employment.

The informal economy includes not only "hidden" cash transactions, but many forms of self-provisioning that people carry on inside and outside the home. Do-it-yourself activities with household appliances and tools, for instance, provide goods and services that would otherwise have to be purchased (Gershuny and Miles 1983). Housework, which has traditionally been carried out mostly by women, is usually unpaid. But it is work, often very hard and exhausting work, nevertheless. Volunteer work, for charities or other organizations, has an important social role. Having a paid job is important—but the category of "work" stretches more widely.

division of labor • The specialization of work tasks, by means of which different occupations are combined within a production system. All societies have at least some rudimentary form of division of labor, especially between the tasks allocated to men and those performed by women.

THE IMPORTANCE OF THE DIVISION OF LABOR

The economic system of modern societies rests on a highly complex **division of labor**. Recall that in Chapter 1 we introduced this concept, which the nineteenth-century scholar Émile Durkheim viewed as the basis for the social cohesion that results when multiple parts of society function as an integrated whole. Under a division of labor, work is divided into an enormous number of different occupations in which people specialize. In traditional societies, nonagricultural work entailed the mastery of a specific skill. A worker typically learned craft skills through a lengthy period of apprenticeship and then carried out all aspects of the production process from beginning to end. For example, a metalworker making a plow would forge the iron, shape it, and assemble the implement itself. With the rise of modern industrial production, most traditional crafts have disappeared altogether, replaced by skills that form part of more large-scale production processes. An electrician working in an industrial setting today, for instance, may inspect and repair only a few parts of one type of machine; different people will deal with the other parts and other machines.

The contrast in the division of labor between traditional and modern societies is truly extraordinary. Even in the largest traditional societies, there usually existed no more than twenty or thirty major craft trades, together with such specialized pursuits as merchant, soldier, and priest. In a modern industrial system, there are literally thousands of distinct occupations. The U.S. Census Bureau lists some 20,000 distinct jobs in the American economy. In traditional communities, most of the population worked on farms and were economically self-sufficient. They produced their own food, clothes, and other necessities of life. One of the main features of modern societies, by contrast, is an enormous expansion of **economic interdependence**. The vast majority of people in modern societies do not produce the food they eat or the material goods they consume.

economic interdependence • The fact that in the division of labor, individuals depend on others to produce many or most of the goods they need to sustain their lives.

INDUSTRIAL WORK

Writing some two centuries ago, Adam Smith, one of the founders of modern economics, identified advantages that the division of labor provides in terms of increasing productivity. His most famous work, *The Wealth of Nations*, opens with a description of the division of labor in a pin factory. A person working alone could perhaps make twenty pins per day. By breaking down that worker's task into a number of simple operations, however, ten workers carrying out specialized jobs in collaboration with one another could collectively produce 48,000 pins per day. The rate of production per

From 1908 to 1927, factory workers at the Ford Motor Company assembled Model T automobiles.

worker, in other words, is increased from 20 to 4,800 pins, each specialist operator producing 240 times more than when working alone.

More than a century later, these ideas reached their most developed expression in the writings of Frederick Winslow Taylor, an American management consultant. Taylor's approach to what he called "scientific management" involved the detailed study of industrial processes in order to break them down into simple operations that could be precisely timed and organized.

Taylor's principles were appropriated by the industrialist Henry Ford. In 1908, Ford designed his first auto plant at Highland Park, Michigan, to manufacture only one product—the Model T Ford—thereby allowing the introduction of specialized tools and machinery designed for speed, precision, and simplicity of operation. One of Ford's most significant innovations was the introduction of the assembly line, said to have been inspired by Chicago slaughterhouses, in which animals were disassembled section by section on a moving conveyor belt. Each worker on Ford's assembly line was assigned a specialized task, such as fitting the left-side door handles as the car bodies moved along the line. By 1929, when production of the Model T ceased, over 15 million cars had been assembled.

WORK AND ALIENATION

Karl Marx was one of the first writers to grasp that the development of modern industry would reduce many people's work to dull, uninteresting tasks. According to Marx, the division of labor alienates human beings from their work. **Alienation** refers to feelings of indifference or hostility not only to work but to the overall framework of industrial production within a capitalist setting.

In traditional societies, Marx pointed out, work was often exhausting; peasant farmers sometimes toiled from dawn to dusk. Yet peasants had control over their work, which required much knowledge and skill. Many industrial workers, by contrast, have little control over their jobs, only contribute a fraction to the creation of the overall product, and have no influence over how or to whom it is eventually sold. Work thus appears as something alien, a task that the worker must carry out in order to earn an income but that is intrinsically unsatisfying.

alienation • The sense that our own abilities as human beings are taken over by other entities. Karl Marx used the term to refer to the loss of workers' control over the nature and products of their labor.

INDUSTRIAL CONFLICT

There have long been conflicts between workers and those with economic and political authority over them. Riots against high taxes and food riots at periods of harvest failure were common in urban areas of Europe in the eighteenth century. These "premodern" forms of labor conflict continued up to the late nineteenth century in some countries. Such traditional forms of confrontation were not just sporadic, irrational outbursts of violence: The threat or use of violence had the effect of lowering the price of grain and other essential foodstuffs (Rudé 1964, Thompson 1971, Booth 1977).

Industrial conflict between workers and employers at first tended to follow these older patterns. In situations of confrontation, workers would quite often leave their places of employment and form crowds in the streets; they would make their grievances known through their unruly behavior or by engaging in acts of violence against the authorities. Workers in some parts of France in the late nineteenth century would threaten disliked employers with hanging (Holton 1978). Use of the strike as a weapon, today commonly associated with organized bargaining between workers and management, developed only slowly and sporadically.

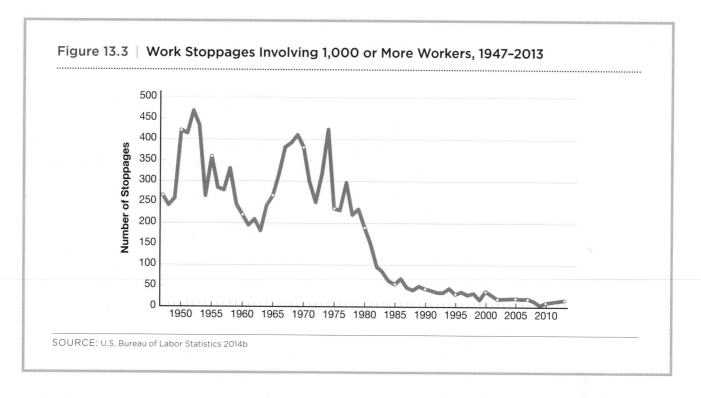

Figure 13.3 | Work Stoppages Involving 1,000 or More Workers, 1947–2013

SOURCE: U.S. Bureau of Labor Statistics 2014b

STRIKES

A **strike** is a temporary stoppage of work by a group of employees in order to express a grievance or enforce a demand (Hyman 1984). As we saw earlier in this chapter, fast-food workers who were dissatisfied with their low wages and working conditions staged work stoppages throughout American cities in late 2013. Workers go on strike for many specific reasons. They may be seeking to gain higher wages, forestall a proposed reduction in their earnings, protest against technological changes that make their work duller or lead to layoffs, or obtain greater job security. However, in all these circumstances the strike is essentially a mechanism of power: a weapon of people who are relatively powerless in the workplace and whose working lives are affected by managerial decisions over which they have little control. Strikes typically occur when other negotiations have failed, because workers on strike either receive no income or depend on union funds, which might be limited. As Figure 13.3 shows, work stoppages in the United States dropped off considerably in the 1980s. This is due in large part to the fact that union membership decreased markedly at this time. In the next section, we will explain the reasons behind this precipitous drop.

strike • A temporary stoppage of work by a group of employees in order to express a grievance or enforce a demand.

LABOR UNIONS

Although their levels of membership and the extent of their power vary widely, union organizations exist in all Western countries, which also all legally recognize the right of workers to strike in pursuit of economic objectives. In the early development of modern industry, workers in most countries had no political rights and little influence over their working conditions. **Unions** developed as a means of redressing the imbalance of power between workers and employers. As we saw earlier in this chapter, one tactic used by unions is collective bargaining. This is the process of negotiations between employers and their workers; these negotiations are used to reach agreements about a broad range of working conditions, including pay scales, working hours, training,

union • An organization that advances and protects the interests of workers with respect to working conditions, wages, and benefits.

health and safety, rights to participate in workplace decision making, and the right to file a grievance if a worker perceives that he or she has been treated unfairly. Whereas workers may have limited power as individuals, through collective organization their influence is considerably increased. An employer can do without the labor of any particular worker but not without that of all or most of the workers in a factory or plant.

After 1980, unions suffered declines across the advanced industrial countries. In the United States, the share of the workforce belonging to unions declined from 23 percent in 1980 to 11.3 percent in 2013 (Hirsch and Macpherson 2004, U.S. Bureau of Labor Statistics 2014e). Americans' perceptions of labor unions also took a hit following the widespread protests by state workers in 2011. In Wisconsin and several other states, state and local workers—ranging from firefighters to teachers—protested because they feared their loss of pensions, a reduction in their health benefits, and their right to collective bargaining. Many Americans, themselves facing higher health insurance costs and reduced pensions in their public-sector jobs, showed little empathy for the protesting state workers. A Gallup poll released in March 2011, the month after the protests, showed that Americans were slightly more likely to describe unions with a negative word or phrase (38 percent) than a positive word or phrase (34 percent). Nearly one-third, however, had no opinion: 17 percent were neutral and 12 percent didn't know. Republicans were much more likely to use a negative descriptive term (58 percent) than Democrats (19 percent), whereas Democrats were much more likely to say a positive term (49 percent) than Republicans (18 percent) (Newport and Said 2011). However, since that time attitudes toward unions have increased slightly; while 52 percent of Americans said they approved of labor unions in 2012, this number crept up to 54 percent by 2013 (Dugan 2013).

There are several widely accepted explanations for the difficulties confronted by unions since 1980. Perhaps the most common explanation is the decline of the older manufacturing industries and the rise of the service sector. Bruce Western (1997) has refined this explanation by documenting that levels of unionization have fallen even within the manufacturing sector. Other explanations include recession in world economic activity associated with high levels of unemployment, which weakens the bargaining position of labor, and the increasing intensity of international competition, particularly from East Asian countries, where wages are often lower than in the West. Unions usually become weakened during periods when unemployment is high, as has been the case for a considerable while in many Western countries. Trends toward more flexible production tend to diminish the force of unionism, which flourishes more extensively where many people are working together in large factories. ✓

capitalism • An economic system based on the private ownership of wealth, which is invested and reinvested in order to produce profit.

CONCEPT CHECKS ✓

1. Why is it important for sociologists to study economic institutions?

2. Define and provide an example of an informal economy.

3. Using the concept of division of labor, describe the key differences in the nature of work in traditional versus modern societies.

4. What is a labor union? Why have unions in the United States suffered from a decline in membership since the 1980s?

See the importance of the rise of large corporations; consider particularly the global impact of transnational corporations.

WHAT ARE KEY ELEMENTS OF THE MODERN ECONOMY?

Modern societies are, in Marx's term, *capitalistic*. As we learned in Chapter 1, **capitalism** is a way of organizing economic life that is distinguished by the following important features: private ownership of the means of production; profit as incentive;

free competition for markets to sell goods, acquire cheap materials, and utilize cheap labor; and expansion and investment to accumulate capital. Capitalism, which began to spread with the growth of the Industrial Revolution in the early nineteenth century, is a vastly more dynamic economic system than any other that preceded it in history. Although the system has had many critics, such as Marx, it is now the most widespread form of economic organization in the world.

So far, we have been looking at industry mostly from the perspective of occupations and employees. But we also have to concern ourselves with the nature of the business firms in which the workforce is employed. (It should be recognized that many people today are employees of government organizations, although we will not consider these here.) What is happening to business corporations today, and how are they run?

CORPORATIONS AND CORPORATE POWER

Since the turn of the twentieth century, modern capitalist economies have been increasingly influenced by the rise of large business **corporations**. The share of total manufacturing assets held by the 200 largest manufacturing firms in the United States has increased by 0.5 percent each year from 1900 to the present day; these corporations now control over half of all manufacturing assets. The 200 largest financial organizations—banks, building societies, and insurance companies—account for more than half of all financial activity.

corporations • Business firms or companies.

Of course, there still exist thousands of smaller firms and enterprises within the American economy. In these companies, the image of the **entrepreneur**—the boss who owns and runs the firm—is by no means obsolete. The large corporations are a different matter. Ever since Adolf Berle and Gardiner Means published their celebrated study *The Modern Corporation and Private Property* more than eighty years ago, it has been accepted that most of the largest firms are not run by those who own them (Berle and Means 1982, orig. 1932). In theory, the large corporations are the property of their shareholders, who have the right to make all important decisions. But Berle and Means argued that since share ownership is so dispersed, actual control has passed into the hands of the managers who run firms on a day-to-day basis.

entrepreneur • The owner or founder of a business firm.

The power of the major corporations is very extensive. Corporations often cooperate in setting prices rather than freely competing with one another. Thus, the giant oil companies normally follow one another's lead in the price charged for gasoline. When one firm occupies a commanding position in a given industry, it is said to be in a **monopoly** position. More common is a situation of **oligopoly**, in which a small group of giant corporations predominate. In situations of oligopoly, firms are able more or less to dictate the terms on which they buy goods and services from the smaller firms that are their suppliers.

monopoly • A situation in which a single firm dominates in a given industry.

oligopoly • The domination of a small number of firms in a given industry.

The emergence of the global economy has contributed to a wave of mergers and acquisitions on an unprecedented scale, which have created oligopolies in industries such as communications and media. In 1999 AT&T acquired the media corporation Media-One for $5 billion to create the world's largest cable company. Also in 1999 CBS purchased Viacom for $35 billion. In 2000 Time Warner and the Internet service provider America Online announced the largest merger in history—worth over $166 billion (Ross and Hansen 2001). By 2004, the value of cross-border mergers and acquisitions had reached $380.6 trillion. About 83 percent of these mergers and acquisitions occurred between companies in the developed world (United Nations Conference on Trade and Development [UNCTAD] 2005). In 2013 alone, the global value of mergers and acquisitions was $2.4 trillion (Thomson-Reuters 2012). As the global market becomes increasingly integrated, we are likely to see even more mergers and acquisitions on an even larger scale. We will explore the complex interplay between globalization and the economy more fully in Chapter 16.

TYPES OF CORPORATE CAPITALISM

There have been three general stages in the development of business corporations, although each overlaps with the others and all continue to coexist today. The first stage, characteristic of the nineteenth and early twentieth centuries, was dominated by **family capitalism**. Large firms were run either by individual entrepreneurs or by members of the same family and then passed on to their descendants. The famous corporate dynasties, such as the Rockefellers and Fords, belong in this category. These individuals and families did not just own a single large corporation, but held a diversity of economic interests and stood at the apex of economic empires.

Most of the big firms founded by entrepreneurial families have since become public companies—that is, shares of their stock are traded on the open market—and have passed into managerial control. In the large corporate sector, family capitalism was increasingly succeeded by **managerial capitalism**. As managers came to have more and more influence through the growth of very large firms, the entrepreneurial families were displaced. The result has been described as the replacement of the family in the company by the company itself (Allen 1981).

Managerial capitalism has left an indelible imprint on modern society. The large corporation drives not only patterns of consumption but also the experience of employment in contemporary society. It is difficult to imagine how different the work lives of many Americans would be in the absence of large factories or corporate bureaucracies. Sociologists have identified another area in which the large corporation has left a mark on modern institutions. **Welfare capitalism** refers to a practice that sought to make the corporation—rather than the state or trade unions—the primary shelter from the uncertainties of the market in modern industrial life. Beginning at the end of the nineteenth century, large firms began to provide certain services to their employees, including child care, recreational facilities, profit-sharing plans, paid vacations, and group life and unemployment insurance. These programs often had a paternalistic bent, such as that sponsoring "home visits" for the "moral education" of employees. Viewed in less benevolent terms, a major objective of welfare capitalism was coercion, as employers deployed all manners of tactics—including violence—to avoid unionization.

Despite the overwhelming importance of managerial capitalism in shaping the modern economy, many scholars now see the contours of a third, different phase in the evolution of the corporation emerging. They argue that managerial capitalism has today partly ceded place to **institutional capitalism**. This term refers to the emergence of a consolidated network of business leadership, concerned not only with decision making within single firms but also with the development of corporate power beyond them. Institutional capitalism is based on the practice of corporations holding shares in other firms. In effect, interlocking boards of directors exercise control over much of the corporate landscape. This reverses the process of increasing managerial control, since the managers' shareholdings are dwarfed by the large blocks of shares owned by other corporations. Rather than investing directly by buying shares in a business, individuals can now invest in money market, trust, insurance, and pension funds that are controlled by large financial organizations, which in turn invest these grouped savings in industrial corporations. However, in coming decades, Americans may be reluctant to put their resources into pension funds because of the economic crisis of the last few years, a time when many people saw their investments decline if not disappear entirely.

family capitalism • Capitalistic enterprise owned and administered by entrepreneurial families.

managerial capitalism • Capitalistic enterprises administered by managerial executives rather than by owners.

welfare capitalism • Practice in which large corporations protect their employees from the vicissitudes of the market.

institutional capitalism • Capitalistic enterprise organized on the basis of institutional shareholding.

Container ships are cargo ships that carry all of their load in truck-sized containers. As this technique greatly accelerates the speed at which goods can be transported to and from ports, these ships now carry the majority of the world's dry cargo.

THE TRANSNATIONAL CORPORATIONS

With the intensifying of globalization, most large corporations now operate in an international economic context. When they establish branches in two or more countries, they are referred to as multinational or **transnational corporations**.

Transnational is the preferred term, indicating that these companies operate across many different national boundaries. Of the 100 transnational companies with the most foreign assets, 17 hold over 90 percent of their assets abroad, including Nestlé and Anheuser-Busch (The *Economist* 2012). The largest transnationals are gigantic; their wealth outstrips that of many countries. The scope of these companies' operations is staggering. In 2011 sales from these corporations reached $28 trillion, and total assets totaled about $82 trillion. An estimated 69 million people worldwide worked for these major entities (The *Economist* 2012).

Of the top 500 transnational corporations in the world in 2013, 132 are based in the United States. The share of American companies has, however, fallen significantly since 1960, during which time Japanese companies have grown dramatically; only five Japanese corporations were included in the top 200 in 1960, as compared with twenty-eight in 2005. Today, sixty-two Japanese companies are in the top 500 (*Fortune* 2013).

The reach of the transnationals over the past thirty years would not have been possible without advances in transport and communications. Air travel now allows people to move around the world at a speed that would have seemed inconceivable even sixty years ago. Telecommunications technologies now permit more or less instantaneous communication from one part of the world to another. Satellites have been used for commercial telecommunications since 1965. The first satellite could carry 240 telephone conversations at once; current satellites can carry 12,000 simultaneous conversations! The larger transnationals now have their own satellite-based communications systems. The Mitsubishi Corporation, for instance, has a massive network across which 5 million words are transmitted to and from its headquarters in Tokyo each day. ✓

transnational corporations •
Business corporations located in two or more countries.

> ## CONCEPT CHECKS ✓
> 1. What are the main features of capitalism?
> 2. Compare and contrast four types of corporate capitalism.

Job Searches Go High Tech

How did you find your last job? If you're like most of your classmates, you probably didn't check the "Help Wanted" section. In fact, you might not even know what that phrase means. Prior to the 1990s, when people wanted to find a job, they typically picked up a copy of the local newspaper, flipped to the back pages called the "Help Wanted" section, and then read through lists of alphabetized job descriptions. They might have placed a phone call, or printed up a copy of their résumé, which they then dropped in the mailbox, hoping to earn an interview for a coveted position.

Today, job searches have been transformed. Since the advent of websites like Craigslist and Monster.com in the late 1990s, job searches have increasingly taken place online. But for some job searchers today, even websites like Craigslist may seem dated. A spate of new apps have been developed to help job hunters seek work using their smartphones. For example, apps like Real-Time Jobs alert users to new job openings in real time. Job seekers using TheLadders app can do targeted searches based on expertise, geography, industry, salary, and target title and can even see a profile of the competition (Locke 2014). Looking for a part-time job? The Snagajob app focuses on hourly employment, connecting users with part-time work in the restaurant, retail, and customer service industries.

Other apps help job hunters prepare for their searches. For example, Interview Questions Pro generates practice questions that an applicant might be asked on an interview. Business Card Reader Pro instantly scans business cards using a smartphone's camera and imports the information to the user's contact list so job seekers can easily store the new contacts they make at a networking event (ResumeGenius 2014).

The research firm IDC predicts that mobile devices will become the most popular way to search for jobs by the year 2015. As a result, employers—and not just potential employees—will need to play an active role in developing and using job search apps. But, early attempts by major employers like Macy's and McDonald's were less than perfect, as designers struggled to create applications that could be completed in the small space of a smartphone screen (Weber 2013).

Do you think that smartphones are an effective way to search for a job? Economists Peter Kuhn and Hani Mansour think so; they did a study concluding that web-based and smartphone-based apps are good for the economy because they help "match" job seekers and employers much more quickly than old search methods. They found that those who searched for jobs virtually were placed 25 percent faster than those using traditional methods (Kuhn and Mansour 2011). Some observers say that the apps are particularly helpful for two groups who typically have higher than average unemployment rates: young

With résumé, portfolio, and cell phone in hand, a woman at a job fair waits to talk with a potential employer. Young people seeking jobs may upload their résumés, find job openings in their neighborhood, and even check out the competition using smartphone apps.

people and economically disadvantaged people who might not have computers and at-home Internet, yet who do have smartphones.

Have you ever used an app to apply for a job? What worked best, and what do you think could be improved? Do you think that these apps are the way of the future? Why or why not?

HOW DOES WORK AFFECT EVERYDAY LIFE TODAY?

Learn about the impact of global economic competition on employment. Consider how work will change over the coming years.

The globalizing of economic production, together with the spread of information technology, is altering the nature of the jobs most people do. As discussed earlier, the proportion of people working in blue-collar jobs in industrial countries has progressively fallen. Fewer and fewer people work in factories. New jobs have been created in offices and in service centers such as superstores like Wal-Mart and airports. Many of these new jobs are filled by women.

WORK AND TECHNOLOGY

The relationship between technology and work has long been of interest to sociologists. How is our experience of work affected by the type of technology that is involved? As industrialization has progressed, technology has assumed an ever-greater role at the workplace—from factory automation to the computerization of office work. The current information technology revolution has attracted renewed interest in this question. Technology can lead to greater efficiency and productivity, but how does it affect the way work is experienced by those who carry it out? For sociologists, one of the main questions is how the move to more complex systems influences the nature of work and the institutions in which it is performed.

AUTOMATION AND THE SKILL DEBATE

The concept of **automation**, or programmable machinery, was introduced in the mid-1800s, when Christopher Spencer, an American, invented the Automat, a programmable lathe that made screws, nuts, and gears. Automation has thus far affected relatively few industries, but with advances in the design of industrial robots, its impact is certain to become greater. A robot is an automatic device that can perform functions ordinarily done by human workers.

automation • Production processes monitored and controlled by machines with only minimal supervision from people.

The majority of the robots used in industry worldwide are found in automobile manufacture. For example, Ford used robots with lasers for eyes and suction cups for hands to manufacture its 2013 Escape (Nishimoto 2012). The usefulness of robots in other forms of production thus far is relatively limited because their capacity to recognize different objects and manipulate awkward shapes is still at a rudimentary level. Yet it is certain that automated production will spread rapidly in coming years; robots are becoming more sophisticated, while their costs are decreasing.

The spread of automation has provoked a heated debate over the impact of the new technology on workers, their skills, and their level of commitment to their work. In his influential *Alienation and Freedom* (1964), Robert Blauner examined the experience of workers in four different industries with varying levels of technology. Blauner measured the extent to which workers in each industry experienced alienation in the form of powerlessness, meaninglessness, isolation, and self-estrangement. He concluded that workers on assembly lines were the most alienated of all, but that levels of alienation were somewhat lower at workplaces using automation. That is, the introduction of automation to factories partly reversed the otherwise steady trend toward increased worker alienation.

A very different thesis was set forth by Harry Braverman in the famous *Labor and Monopoly Capital* (1974). Braverman argued that automation was part of the overall "deskilling" of the industrial labor force. In both industrial settings and modern offices, new technologies have reduced the need for creative human input. Instead, all that is required is an unthinking, unreflective body capable of endlessly carrying out the same unskilled task.

A newer study sheds some more light on this debate. The sociologist Richard Sennett studied the people who worked in a bakery that had been bought by a large food conglomerate and automated with the introduction of high-tech machinery. Instead of using their hands to mix the ingredients and knead the dough and their noses and eyes to judge when the bread was done baking, the bakery's workers had no physical contact with the materials or the loaves of bread. The entire process was controlled and monitored via computer screen. The production process involved little more than pushing buttons on a computer. One time when the computerized machinery broke down, the entire production process was halted because none of the bakery's "skilled" workers was trained or empowered to repair the problem. The workers wanted to be helpful, to make things work again, but they could not because automation had diminished their autonomy (Sennett 1998). The introduction of computerized technology in the workplace has led to a general increase in all workers' skills, but has also led to a two-tiered workforce composed of a small group of highly skilled professionals with a high degree of flexibility and autonomy in their jobs and a larger group of clerical, service, and production workers who lack autonomy in their jobs.

GLOBAL PRODUCTION

For much of the twentieth century, the most important business organizations were large manufacturing firms that controlled both the production and sale of goods. Giant automobile companies such as Ford and General Motors typify this approach, employing tens of thousands of factory workers making everything from components to the final cars, which are then sold in the manufacturers' showrooms. Such manufacture-dominated production processes are organized as large bureaucracies, often controlled by a handful of large firms.

During the past quarter-century, however, another form of production has become important—one that is controlled by giant retailers. In retailer-dominated production, firms such as Wal-Mart and Kmart buy products from manufacturers, who in turn arrange to have their products made by independently owned factories. For example, the sociologists Edna Bonacich and Richard Appelbaum show that in clothing manufacturing, most manufacturers actually employ no garment workers at all. Instead, they rely on thousands of factories around the world to make their apparel, which they then sell in department stores and other retail outlets. Clothing manufacturers do not own any of these factories and therefore are not responsible for the conditions under which the clothing is made.

Two-thirds of all clothing sold in the United States is made in factories in other nations, where workers are paid a fraction of U.S. wages. (In China, workers are lucky to make $40 a month.) Bonacich and Appelbaum argue that such competition has resulted in a global "race to the bottom," in which retailers and manufacturers will go anyplace on earth where they can pay the lowest wages possible. As we saw in Chapter 8, one result of globalization is that much of the clothing we buy today is made in sweatshops by young workers—most likely teenage girls—who get paid pennies for making clothing or pricey athletic shoes (Bonacich and Appelbaum 2000).

The pricey designer jeans sold in U.S. department stores are often made in sweatshops. Young workers, usually women, toil long hours for paltry wages. Xintang, in the Guangdong province of China, alleges that it manufactures 60 percent of jeans sold across the globe.

TRENDS IN THE OCCUPATIONAL STRUCTURE

The occupational structure in all industrialized countries has changed dramatically since the beginning of the twentieth century. In 1900, about three-quarters of the employed population was in manual work, either farming or blue-collar work such as manufacturing. White-collar professional and service jobs were much fewer in number. By 1960, however, more people worked in white-collar professional and service jobs than in manual labor. By 1993, the occupational system had nearly reversed its structure from 1900. Almost three-quarters of the employed population worked in white-collar professional and service jobs, while the rest worked in blue-collar and farming jobs. In the period from May 1999 to May 2009, the United States lost 5.3 million manufacturing jobs (*Business Week* 2009). By 2010, blue-collar work had declined even further, with most of the increase in new jobs occurring in the service industries.

The reasons for the transformation of the occupational structure seem to be several. One is the introduction of labor-saving machinery, culminating in the spread of information technology and computerization in industry in recent decades. Another is the rise of the manufacturing industry in other parts of the world, primarily Asia. The older industries in Western societies have experienced major job cutbacks because of their inability to compete with the more efficient Asian producers, whose labor costs are lower. As we have seen, this global economic transformation has forced American companies to adopt new forms of production, which in turn has impelled employees to learn new skills and new occupations as manufacturing-related jobs move to other countries. A final important trend is the decline of full-time paid employment with the same employer over a long period of time. Not only has the transformation of the global economy affected the nature of day-to-day work, it has also changed the career patterns of many workers.

THE KNOWLEDGE ECONOMY

Taking these trends into account, some observers suggest that what is occurring today is a transition to a new type of society no longer based primarily on industrialism. We are entering, they claim, a phase of development beyond the industrial

knowledge economy • A society no longer based primarily on the production of material goods but based instead on the production of knowledge. Its emergence has been linked to the development of a broad base of consumers who are technologically literate and have made new advances in computing, entertainment, and telecommunications part of their lives.

era altogether. A variety of terms have been coined to describe this new social order, such as the *postindustrial society*, the *information age*, and the *"new" economy*. The term that has come into most common use, however, is the **knowledge economy**.

A precise definition of the knowledge economy is difficult to formulate, but in general terms, it refers to an economy in which ideas, information, and forms of knowledge underpin innovation and economic growth. Knowledge-based industries include high technology, education and training, research and development, and the financial and investment sector. Much of the workforce is involved not in the physical production or distribution of material goods but in their design, development, technology, marketing, sale, and servicing. These employees can be termed *knowledge workers*. The knowledge economy is dominated by the constant flow of information and opinions and by the powerful potentials of science and technology.

The World Bank (2012a) recently developed the Knowledge Economy Index (KEI), which rates 146 countries based on their overall preparedness to compete in the knowledge economy. The factors contributing to this index include technological adoption and innovation, education, and the information and communications infrastructure. Scandinavian nations including Sweden, Finland, and Norway topped the list. For example, Sweden ranked number one because of its high levels of education and high levels of Internet penetration as well as a high number of patents for inventions. Poor developing nations rounded out the bottom of the list, with Angola, Sierra Leone, Myanmar, and Haiti receiving very low scores—due primarily to the fact that poverty is a major obstacle to technological innovation and widespread high-quality education.

THE CONTINGENT WORKFORCE

Another important employment trend of the past decade has been the replacement of full-time workers by part-time workers and contingency workers, or workers who are hired on a contract or "freelance" basis often for a short-term task. Most temporary or contingent workers are hired for the least-skilled, lowest-paying jobs. More generally, part-time jobs do not provide the benefits associated with full-time work, such as medical insurance, paid vacation time, or retirement benefits. Because employers can save on the costs of wages and benefits, the use of part-time and contingent workers has become increasingly common. During economic recessions, in particular, cash-strapped employers may need to rely on this low-cost strategy. Researchers estimate that part-time workers make up between 29 and 33 percent of the American workforce. This is up from 20 to 23 percent just ten years ago. Contingency workers make up approximately 4 percent of the American workforce, or about 5.7 million people (U.S. Bureau of Labor Statistics 2013a).

The temporary employment agency Manpower, Inc., founded in Milwaukee, Wisconsin, in 1948, has become a global leader in the provision of temporary workers. This company employed 3.5 million temps in eighty-two countries in 2010 and was 143rd on *Fortune* magazine's list of the Global 500, with a total revenue of $19 billion in 2010 (Manpower Inc. 2011). Manpower provides labor on a "flexible" basis to 95 percent of Fortune 500 companies.

Scholars have debated the psychological effects of part-time work on the workforce. Many temporary workers fulfill their assignments in a prompt and satisfactory manner, but others rebel against their tenuous positions by shirking their responsibilities or sabotaging their results. Some temporary workers have been observed trying to "look busy" or to work longer than necessary on rather simple tasks.

UNEMPLOYMENT RATES

Almost 202 million people, or 6 percent of the global labor force, are unemployed worldwide, and young people continue to be particularly affected. The highest unemployment rates are seen in North Africa and the Middle East.

GABON 20.3%

UNITED STATES 8.1%

  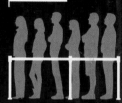

NAMIBIA 16.7%

ISRAEL 6.9%

ICELAND 6.0%

RUSSIAN FED. 5.5%   **MEXICO** 4.9%   **INDIA** 3.4%   **NORWAY** 3.2%   **SINGAPORE** 2.8%   **THAILAND** 0.7%

 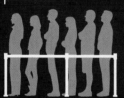

Sources: The World Bank 2013; U.S. Census Bureau, Statistical Abstract of the United States: 2012

UNEMPLOYMENT IN THE UNITED STATES

BY EDUCATIONAL ATTAINMENT

Less than high school — 14.9% unemployed
High school diploma — 10.3% unemployed
Some college — 8.4% unemployed
Bachelor's Degree or more — 4.7% unemployed

BY GENDER

Female — 7.4% unemployed
Male — 8.9% unemployed

BY RACE

White — 7.5% unemployed
Black — 13.4% unemployed
Asian — 6.8% unemployed
Hispanic — 10.8% unemployed

However, some recent surveys of work indicate that part-time workers register higher levels of job satisfaction than those in full-time employment. This may be because most part-time workers are women, who find that part-time work is preferable to full-time employment when trying to juggle work and family demands. Yet men, too, may find that they are able to balance paid part-time work with other activities and enjoy a more varied life. Some people might choose to give full commitment to paid work from their youth to their middle years, then perhaps change to a second part-time career, which would open up new interests. However, workers who desire full-time employment but are able to secure only part-time work are often dissatisfied and anxious about their precarious financial status.

UNEMPLOYMENT

The experience of unemployment—being unable to find a job when one wants it—is a perennially important social problem. Yet some contemporary scholars argue that we should think about the relation between being "in work" and "out of work" in a completely different way from the way we did in the recent past.

Rates of unemployment fluctuated considerably over the course of the twentieth century. In Western countries, unemployment reached a peak in the Depression years of the early 1930s, when some 20 percent of the workforce were out of work in the United States. The economist John Maynard Keynes, who strongly influenced public policy in Europe and the United States during the post–World War II period, believed that unemployment results from consumers' lacking sufficient resources to buy goods. Governments can intervene to increase the level of demand in an economy, leading to the creation of new jobs; the newly employed then have the income with which to buy more goods, thus creating yet more jobs for people who produce them. State management of economic life, most people came to believe, meant that high rates of unemployment belonged to the past. Commitment to full employment became part of government policy in virtually all Western societies. Until the 1970s, these policies seemed successful, and economic growth was more or less continuous.

During the 1970s and 1980s, however, Keynesianism was largely abandoned. In the face of economic globalization, governments lost the capability to control economic life as they once had. One consequence was that unemployment rates shot up in many countries. Several factors explain the increase in unemployment levels in Western countries at that time. First is the rise of international competition in industries on which Western prosperity used to be founded. In 1947, 60 percent of steel production in the world was carried out in the United States. Today, the figure is only about 5.9 percent. China was the largest producer of steel in 2011 at 46.9 percent, followed by the European Union (11.2 percent), Japan (7.1 percent), India (5.1 percent), and Russia (4.7 percent) (Worldsteel.org 2012). Second is the worldwide economic recession of the late 1980s, which has still not fully abated. Third, the increasing use of microelectronics in industry has reduced the need for labor power. Finally, beginning in the 1970s, more women sought paid employment, meaning that more people were chasing a limited number of available jobs.

During this time, rates of unemployment tended to be lower in the United States than in some European nations. This partly reflects the sheer economic strength of the country, giving it more power in world markets than smaller, more fragile economies. Alternatively, it may be that the exceptionally large service sector in the United States provides a greater source of new jobs than in countries where more of the population has traditionally been employed in manufacturing. And within countries, unemployment is not equally distributed. It varies by race or ethnic background, by age, and by industry and geographic region. Ethnic minorities living in central cities in the United States have much higher rates of long-term unemployment than the rest of the population. A substantial proportion of young people are among the long-term unemployed, again especially among minority groups. These disparities were particularly acute during the recent economic recession.

THE FUTURE OF WORK

Over the past twenty years, in all the industrialized countries except the United States, the average length of the working week has become shorter. Workers still undertake long stretches of overtime, but some governments are beginning to introduce new limits on permissible working hours. In France, for example, annual overtime is restricted to a maximum of 130 hours a year. In most countries, there is a general tendency toward shortening the average working career. More people would probably quit the labor force at age sixty or earlier if they could afford to do so.

If the amount of time devoted to paid employment continues to shrink, and the need to have a job becomes less central, the nature of working careers might be substantially reorganized. Job sharing or flexible working hours, which arose primarily as a result of the increasing numbers of working parents trying to balance the commitments of workplace and family, might become more common. Some work analysts have suggested that sabbaticals of the university type should be extended to workers in other spheres: People would be entitled to take a year off in order to study or pursue some form of self-improvement. Some might opt to work part-time throughout their lives, rather than being forced to because of a lack of full-time employment opportunities.

The nature of the work most people do and the role of work in our lives, like so many other aspects of the societies in which we live, are undergoing major changes. As we will see in Chapter 16, the chief reasons are global economic competition, the widespread introduction of information technology and computerization, and the large-scale entry of women into the workforce. As we saw in the case of the fast-food worker protests, the rights of workers may be further eroded during periods of economic downturns. When unemployment rates are high and potential workers outnumber available jobs, workers may be viewed as increasingly dispensable by employers—whether private or public.

How will work change in the future? It appears very likely that people will take a more active look at their lives than in the past, moving in and out of paid work at different points. These are only positive options, however, when they are deliberately chosen. The reality for most is that regular paid work remains the key to day-to-day survival and that unemployment is experienced as a hardship rather than an opportunity. ✓

> ### CONCEPT CHECKS ✓
>
> 1. Why does automation lead to worker alienation?
> 2. What are some of the changes that occurred in the occupational structure in the twentieth century? How can they be explained?
> 3. How did Keynes explain unemployment? What was his solution to high unemployment rates?
> 4. In your opinion, how will globalization change the nature of work?

EXERCISES:
Thinking Sociologically

1. Discuss the differences between the "pluralistic" and the "power elite" theories of democratic political processes. Which theory do you find most appropriate to describe U.S. politics in recent years?

2. Discuss some of the important ways that the nature of work will change for the contemporary worker as companies apply more automation and larger-scale production processes and as oligopolies become more pervasive. Explain each of these trends and how they affect workers, both now and in the future.

Chapter 13

Politics and Economic Life

3. What was the main goal of the fast-food workers who protested their working conditions in 2013 and 2014? What kind of public policies might address their concerns? What does their battle reveal about the sociology of work and the sociology of politics?

p.395 — How Did the State Develop?

Learn the basic concepts underlying modern nation-states.

p.398 — How Do Democracies Function?

Learn about different types of democracy, how this form of government has spread around the world, key theories about power in a democracy, and some of the problems associated with modern-day democracy.

p.409 — What Is Terrorism?

Learn how social scientists define terrorism and the ways that new-style terrorism is different from the old.

p.411 — What Is the Social Significance of Work?

Assess the sociological ramifications of paid and unpaid work. Understand that modern economies are based on the division of labor and economic interdependence. Familiarize yourself with modern systems of economic production.

p.416 — What Are Key Elements of the Modern Economy?

See the importance of the rise of large corporations; consider particularly the global impact of transnational corporations.

p.421 — How Does Work Affect Everyday Life Today?

Learn about the impact of global economic competition on employment. Consider how work will change over the coming years.

collective bargaining • government • politics • economy • power • authority

state • nation-state • sovereignty • citizen • nationalism • local nationalisms • civil rights • political rights • franchise • social rights • welfare state

1. Describe three main characteristics of the state.
2. What is a welfare state? Can the United States be classified as a welfare state? Why?

democracy • participatory democracy • direct democracy • constitutional monarchs • liberal democracies • communism • interest group • suffrage • democratic elitism • pluralist theories of modern democracy • power elite

1. Why is it problematic for contemporary states to have participatory democracy?
2. Contrast the concepts of democracy and communism.
3. Describe the role interest groups play in American politics.
4. Compare and contrast pluralist theories of modern democracy and the power elite model.

terrorism • old-style terrorism • new-style terrorism

1. How do we define terrorism?
2. Compare and contrast old- and new-style terrorism.

work • occupation • technology • informal economy • division of labor • economic interdependence • alienation • strike • unions

1. Why is it important for sociologists to study economic institutions?
2. Define and provide an example of an informal economy.
3. Using the concept of division of labor, describe the key differences in the nature of work in traditional versus modern societies.
4. What is a labor union? Why have unions in the United States suffered from a decline in membership since the 1980s?

capitalism • corporations • entrepreneur • monopoly • oligopoly • family capitalism • managerial capitalism • welfare capitalism • institutional capitalism • transnational corporations

1. What are the main features of capitalism?
2. Compare and contrast four types of corporate capitalism.

automation • knowledge economy

1. Why does automation lead to worker alienation?
2. What are some of the changes that occurred in the occupational structure in the twentieth century? How can they be explained?
3. How did Keynes explain unemployment? What was his solution to high unemployment rates?
4. In your opinion, how will globalization change the nature of work?

14

The Sociology of the Body: Health, Illness, and Sexuality

THE BIG QUESTIONS

HOW DOES SOCIAL CONTEXT AFFECT THE HUMAN BODY?

Understand how social and cultural contexts shape attitudes toward "ideal" body forms and give rise to two body-related social problems in the United States: eating disorders and the obesity crisis.

HOW DO SOCIOLOGISTS UNDERSTAND HEALTH AND ILLNESS?

Learn about functionalist and symbolic interactionist perspectives on health and illness in contemporary society. Understand the relationship between traditional medicine and complementary and alternative medicine (CAM).

HOW DO SOCIAL FACTORS AFFECT HEALTH AND ILLNESS?

Recognize that health and illness are shaped by cultural and social factors. Learn the social and cultural differences in the distribution of disease.

WHAT CAUSES INFECTIOUS DISEASES IN DEVELOPING NATIONS?

Understand the causes underlying high rates of infectious diseases in developing nations. Learn more about HIV/AIDS as a sociological phenomenon.

HOW DOES SOCIAL CONTEXT SHAPE HUMAN SEXUAL BEHAVIOR?

Learn about the debate over the importance of biological versus social and cultural influences on human sexual behavior. Explore the cultural differences in sexual behavior and patterns of sexual behavior today.

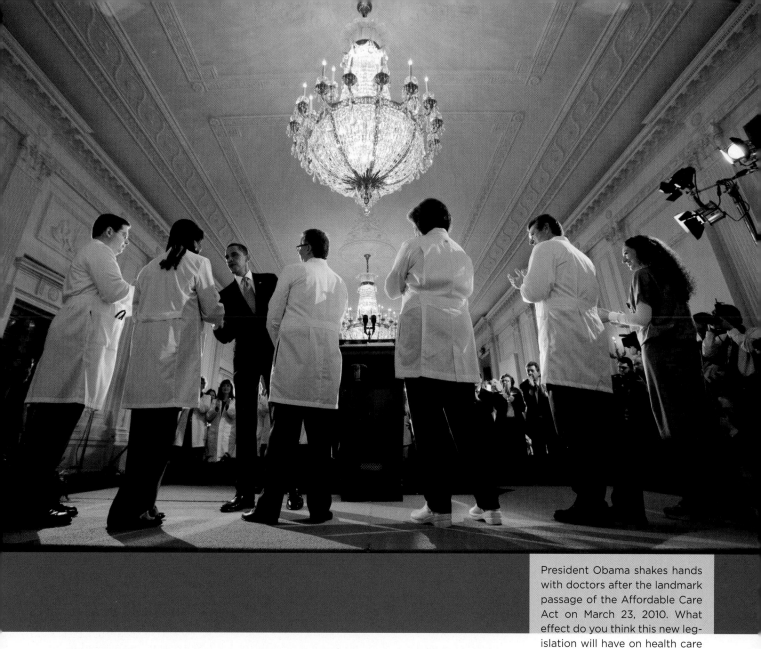

H ealth insurance and access to affordable care may not be issues that you think about every day. Perhaps you think access to medical care is an issue just for older adults or for the very poor. But think for a moment about what you might do if you had no health insurance and got sick or had an accident. Could you afford the hefty costs of X-rays and medications? Without health insurance, even taken-for-granted aspects of health care such as glasses, contact lenses, teeth cleanings, and birth control pills can be prohibitively expensive. For example, in 2013, a single visit to the emergency room averaged more than $2,000 (Kliff 2013), while even a simple inhaler for asthmatics could cost nearly $200 (Rosenthal 2013). Given these prohibitively high costs, many Americans' health problems have gone undetected and untreated.

Seeking to address these deep flaws in the nation's current health care system, President Barack Obama signed into law the controversial Patient Protection and Affordable Care Act (ACA), a comprehensive reform plan designed to help reduce vast inequities in access to health care in the United States.

The ACA is a highly complex program; the original document outlining all components of the policy was more than 12,000 pages long! Two of the most controversial aspects of the act are the "individual mandate," which requires uninsured people to purchase health insurance or else pay a tax penalty, and "low-income subsidies," which are assistance programs to help ensure that all Americans can afford to purchase health insurance. People who don't have access to health insurance through their employers, for instance, and who buy health insurance on their own, are eligible for tax credits that go toward covering their health insurance premiums. These subsidies are based on income level, and assistance is available to people with family income between 100 and 400 percent of the federal poverty level (Kaiser Family Foundation 2013).

These subsidies for low-income individuals are designed to help put affordable health care within the reach of all Americans. Prior to the implementation of ACA, nearly 50 million Americans lacked health insurance. In 2012, 15 percent of all Americans had no health insurance, and these proportions were considerably higher for blacks and Latinos: one in five blacks and one in three Hispanics were uninsured in 2012 (U.S. Bureau of the Census 2013k). Young adults also were likely to lack insurance; fully 27 percent of young adults ages nineteen to twenty-five had no health insurance in 2012 (U.S. Bureau of the Census 2013k).

These figures stand in stark contrast to those in other wealthy nations, including Canada, most European nations, Japan, Israel, New Zealand, Taiwan, and a growing number of nations in Latin America, where each and every individual has some form of health insurance through universal health coverage (World Health Organization 2010). **Universal health coverage** (UHC) is a broad concept whose goal is to ensure that all people can obtain the health services they need without incurring financial hardship. UHC is funded by a variety of sources, which vary across countries. The mix typically includes government funding, taxes, and contributions by employers as well as individuals.

universal health coverage •
Public health care programs motivated by the goal of providing affordable health services to all members of a population.

The ACA is about more than just providing access to health care for people after they get sick. Many components of ACA were designed to promote preventative health care and help people maintain healthy lifestyles and detect health problems early on, rather than seeking medical care only after their conditions have advanced to a dangerous stage. For example, under the program, all Americans have access to free services such as depression screening, substance use disorder screening, blood pressure screening, obesity counseling and screening, assistance with quitting smoking, vaccines, and counseling for domestic abuse victims (Kaiser Family Foundation 2013).

These services are particularly important for low-income Americans, who are at a greater risk for every major health condition than their wealthier counterparts. One of the most consistent patterns documented by sociologists of health and illness is the **social class gradient in health**. This gradient refers to the fact that socioeconomic resources are strongly linked to health, where those with higher levels of education, income, and assets are less likely than their disadvantaged counterparts to suffer from heart disease, diabetes, high blood pressure, early onset of dementia, physical disability, sleep problems, substance use problems, mental illness, and premature death (CDC 2011a). These patterns are so pronounced that one of the four main goals of *Healthy People 2020*, the federal government's health agenda, is to "achieve health equity, eliminate disparities, and improve the health of all groups" (U.S. Department of Health and Human Services 2010).

social class gradient in health •
The strong inverse association between socioeconomic resources and risk of illness or death.

Judging by the chapter title, you might have expected to read about biology, or about the physical ways that our bodies function. You might have been surprised to read about something as seemingly far removed from our everyday lives as federal health care policy. Yet public policies and macro social factors are powerful influences on our health. The field known as **sociology of the body** investigates how and why our bodies are affected by our social experiences and the norms and values of the groups to which we belong. Using this framework, we begin our chapter by analyzing why obesity and an equally problematic phenomenon, eating disorders, have become so common in the Western world. We then describe the ways that sociologists theorize health and medicine; discuss social dimensions of health and illness, with an emphasis on the ways that social class, race, and gender affect our health; and provide an overview of health issues that affect the lives of people in developing nations. We conclude by examining social and cultural influences on our sexual behavior; as we will see, sexual behavior, like health, is a product of biological, cultural, and social forces.

sociology of the body • Field that focuses on how our bodies are affected by social influences. Health and illness, for instance, are shaped by social and cultural influences.

HOW DOES SOCIAL CONTEXT AFFECT THE HUMAN BODY?

Understand how social and cultural contexts shape attitudes toward "ideal" body forms and give rise to two body-related social problems in the United States: eating disorders and the obesity crisis.

Social contexts affect our bodies in myriad ways. The types of jobs we hold, the neighborhoods in which we live, how much money we earn, the cultural practices we partake in, and our relationships all shape how long we live, what types of illnesses we suffer from, and even the shape and size of our bodies. Later in this chapter, we will show how key features of our social lives, including race and social class, affect our physical and mental health. In this section, we will focus on one specific aspect of our bodies to show the power of social and cultural contexts: our body weight. Whether we are slender or heavy is not just a product of our personal choices (such as what foods we eat) or our genes. Rather, body weight is shaped by powerful social structures as well as cultural forces.

Let's take the case of eating disorders, such as anorexia nervosa or bulimia, and **obesity**, or excessive body weight. Both are important social problems in the Western world. Although both are conditions of the body, their causes reflect social factors more than physical or biological factors. If both conditions reflected biology alone, then we would expect that rates would be fairly constant across history—because human physiology has changed little throughout the millennia. However, both are very recent social problems. Both conditions also are highly stratified by social factors such as gender, social class, race, and ethnicity. Women are far more likely than men to have an eating disorder, while economically disadvantaged persons are far more likely than their wealthier counterparts to struggle with obesity today. Both also are shaped by the cultural context. Fashion magazines regularly show images of models who are severely underweight, yet uphold these women as paragons of beauty. The average fashion model today is 23 percent thinner than the average American woman, yet twenty-five years ago that number was 8 percent (Derenne and Beresin 2006). At the same time, our culture also promotes excessive eating; social scientists have observed that we live in an "obesogenic" environment (Brownell and Horgen 2004), where high-fat food and "supersized" meals are plentiful and cheap. A Big Mac is less expensive than a healthy salad in most parts of the country, perpetuating the social class gradient in obesity rates. By contrast, both eating disorders and obesity are virtually unknown in impoverished societies where food is scarce and cherished.

obesity • Excessive body weight indicated by a body mass index (BMI) over 30.

  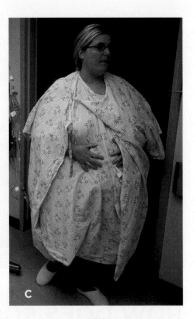

Take a look at the three women above: The first woman (a) is painfully thin as a result of famine and malnutrition, sadly common problems in areas of the world plagued by frequent drought and crop failure. The second (b) has become painfully thin by her own doing; people suffering from anorexia feel compelled by a variety of personal and social pressures to lose weight. The third woman (c) is severely overweight and is preparing for gastric bypass surgery.

Both obesity and eating disorders also illustrate the ways that a "personal trouble" (for example, self-starvation or obesity-related complications such as diabetes) reflects "public issues" (for example, a culture that promotes an unrealistic "thin ideal" for young women), or the ways that poverty makes it difficult for individuals to buy costly healthful foods or to reach public parks and other spaces for regular exercise.

EATING DISORDERS

Anorexia is related to the idea of dieting, and it reflects changing views of physical attractiveness in modern society. In most premodern societies, the ideal female shape was a fleshy one. Thinness was not desirable, partly because it was associated with hunger and poverty. The notion of slimness as the desirable feminine shape originated among some middle-class groups in the late nineteenth century, but it became generalized as an ideal for most women only recently.

Anorexia was identified as a disorder in France in 1874, but it remained obscure until the past thirty or forty years (Brown and Jasper 1993). Since then, it has become increasingly common among young women. So has *bulimia*—bingeing on food, followed by self-induced vomiting. Anorexia and bulimia often occur in the same individual. An estimated 0.9 percent of females have suffered from anorexia at some time during their lives, and an estimated 0.5 percent of women have suffered from bulimia (Hudson et al. 2007). Nearly all (95 percent) of those who have eating disorders are between the ages of 12 and 25.8 (National Association of Anorexia Nervosa and Associated Disorders [ANAD] 2010). Women account for more than 90 percent of all persons with eating disorders, so it is difficult for researchers to estimate rates among men.

However, recent research suggests that gay men have higher rates of eating disorders than heterosexual men (Feldman and Meyer 2007). Rates of eating disorders among all men have risen in recent years as men face mounting pressure for physical perfection, as they are surrounded by unattainable images of muscular physiques, six-pack abs, and lean bodies (Weltzin et al. 2005). Anorexia has the highest mortality rate of any psychological disorder; 20 percent of anorexics will die from it (Eating Disorder Coalition [EDC] 2003).

The occurrence of eating disorders in the United States has doubled since 1960 (EDC 2003). As many as 10 million females and 1 million males are fighting a life-and-death battle with an eating disorder such as anorexia or bulimia (National Eating Disorders Association [NEDA] 2002a). Even those without an eating disorder may still struggle on a daily basis to keep their weight low. On any given day, 25 percent of men and 45 percent of women are dieting; Americans spend over $40 billion each year on dieting and dieting-related products (NEDA 2002b). About 60 percent of girls age thirteen have already begun to diet; this proportion rises to over 80 percent for young women of eighteen. College men also suffer similar experiences, but to a lesser extent. About 50 percent of American male college students want to lose weight, while about 30 percent are on diets (Hesse-Biber 1997). Over 80 percent of ten-year-old children are afraid of being fat (EDC 2003).

Why do eating disorders affect women in particular and young women most acutely? Sociologists note that social norms stress the importance of physical attractiveness more for women than for men and that desirable body images of men differ from those of women. However, men are also less likely to seek treatment for eating disorders because they are considered to be female disorders (ANAD 2010).

Once a young woman starts to diet and exercise compulsively, she can become locked into a pattern of refusing food or vomiting up what she has eaten. As the body loses muscle mass, it loses heart muscle, so the heart gets smaller and weaker, which ultimately leads to heart failure. About half of all anorexics also have low white blood cell counts, and about a third are anemic. Both conditions can lower the immune system's resistance to disease, leaving an anorexic vulnerable to infections. However, these harmful patterns may be broken through psychotherapy and medical treatment.

This unhealthy obsession with slenderness—and the resulting eating disorders—extends beyond the United States and Europe. As Western images of feminine beauty have spread to the rest of the world, so too have associated illnesses. Eating problems also have surfaced among young, primarily affluent women in Hong Kong and Singapore, as well as in urban areas in Taiwan, China, the Philippines, India, and Pakistan (Efron 1997). One famous study showed that in Fiji, a nation where voluptuous bodies were long considered the cultural ideal, rates of eating disorders among young women increased markedly after American television shows like *Beverly Hills 90210* started to air there (Becker 2004).

Making Sociology Work
FASHION MAGAZINE EDITOR

Four months after Christina Kelly was promoted to the position of editor-in-chief of *YM* magazine in 2002, she made a surprising announcement: She was banning dieting stories from the magazine and would feature only "normal" and larger-size models. *YM*, read by more than 2 million tween- and teenage young women, received bagfuls of appreciative letters from readers who always felt that they were ugly or fat when they flipped through images of ultra-skinny women in other fashion magazines. Not everyone agreed with Kelly's decision, though. One magazine photographer refused to shoot photos of models larger than size 6; *YM* promptly stopped working with her. Kelly subsequently took a position as editor-in-chief of *Elle Girl*, and now is a blogger at the web page FallenPrincess. Kelly has continued her commitment to girls' healthy body image at her new ventures. What kind of advice would sociologists of the body give to Kelly in her new editorial role? What kind of effect could Kelly's editorial decisions have on the well-being of young women?

The rise of eating disorders in Western societies coincides with the globalization of food production. Since the 1950s, supermarket shelves have been abundant with foods from all parts of the world. Most foods are available all the time, not just when they are in season locally. When all foods are available all the time, we must decide what to eat. First, we have to decide what to eat in relation to the new medical information that science bombards us with—for instance, that cholesterol levels contribute to heart disease. Second, we worry about calorie content. The fact that we have much more control over our own bodies than before presents us with positive possibilities as well as new anxieties and problems. All this is part of what sociologists call the **socialization of nature**: Phenomena that used to be "natural," or given in nature, have now become social—they depend on our own social decisions.

socialization of nature • The process by which we control phenomena regarded as "natural," such as reproduction.

THE OBESITY EPIDEMIC

Eating disorders are a major social problem that plagues young women in the United States. Yet a very different weight-related health issue, obesity, is considered the top public health problem facing Americans today. As noted earlier in this chapter, obesity is defined as a body mass index (BMI) of 30 or greater (CDC 2008a). Over the past two decades, obesity rates among adults in the United States have risen dramatically. In 1990, ten states had a prevalence of obesity under 10 percent and no states had a prevalence of 15 percent or higher. By 2010, no state had an obesity prevalence under 20 percent; in thirty-six states the rate was 25 percent or higher, and twelve of these states had rates equal to or in excess of 30 percent (CDC 2010c).

Obesity increases an individual's risk for a wide range of health problems, including cardiovascular diseases, diabetes mellitus type 2, sleep apnea, osteoarthritis, and some forms of cancers (Haslam and James 2005). Excessive body weight also may take a severe psychological toll. Overweight and obese Americans are more likely than their thinner peers to experience depression; strained family relationships; poorer-quality sex and dating lives; employment discrimination; discrimination by health care providers; and daily experiences of teasing, insults, and shame (Carr and Friedman 2005, 2006; Carr et al. 2007, 2013). Negative attitudes toward overweight and obese persons develop as early as elementary school (Latner and Stunkard 2003; Richardson et al. 1961).

Sociologists are fascinated with the persistence of negative attitudes toward overweight and obese persons, especially because these individuals currently make up the statistical majority of all Americans. According to the Centers for Disease Control and Prevention, 33 percent of adults are now overweight, 35.7 percent are obese, and more than 6 percent are extremely obese (CDC 2012d). An even more troubling trend is the increase in the proportion of American children and adolescents who are overweight. Nearly 17 percent of children and adolescents are overweight (CDC 2012d).

The reasons behind the obesity crisis are widely debated. Some argue that the apparent increase in the overweight and obese population is a statistical artifact. The proportion of the U.S. population who are middle-aged has increased rapidly during the past two decades, with the aging of the large baby boom cohort. Middle-aged persons, due to slowing metabolism, are at greater risk of excessive body weight. Others attribute the pattern—especially the childhood obesity increase—to shifts in the ethnic makeup of the overall population. The proportion of children today who are black or Hispanic is higher than in earlier decades, and these two ethnic groups are at a much greater risk for becoming overweight than their white peers. Still others argue that the measures used to count and classify obese persons have shifted, thus leading to an excessively high count. Finally, some social observers believe that public concern over obesity is blown out of proportion and reflects more of a "moral panic" than a "public health crisis" (Campos et al. 2006).

Most public health experts believe, however, that obesity is a very real problem caused by what Kelly Brownell calls the "obesogenic environment." Among adults, sedentary jobs have replaced physical jobs, such as farming. Children are more likely to spend their after-school hours sitting in front of a computer or television than playing tag or riding bikes around the neighborhood. Parents are pressed for time given their hectic work and family schedules and turn to unhealthy fast food rather than home-cooked meals. Restaurants, eager to lure bargain-seeking patrons, provide enormous serving sizes at low prices. The social forces that promote high fat and sugar consumption and that restrict the opportunity to exercise are particularly acute for poor persons and ethnic minorities. Small grocery stores in poor neighborhoods rarely sell fresh or low-cost produce. Large grocery stores are scarce in poor neighborhoods and in predominantly African American neighborhoods (Morland et al. 2002). High crime rates and high levels of traffic in inner-city neighborhoods make exercise in public parks or jogging on city streets potentially dangerous (Brownell and Horgen 2004).

Policymakers and public health professionals have proposed a broad range of solutions to the obesity crisis. Some have proposed (unsuccessfully) practices that place the burden directly on the individual. For example, some schools have considered having a "weight report card," where children and parents would be told the child's BMI, in an effort to trigger healthy behaviors at home. Yet most experts endorse solutions that attack the problem at a large-scale level. Such proposed

Fifth-graders in North Carolina dance to a song by Beyoncé and Swizz Beatz as part of Michelle Obama's "Let's Move" campaign, launched in 2010 and aimed at preventing childhood obesity in the United States.

CONCEPT CHECKS ✓

1. Why is anorexia more likely to strike young women than other subgroups?

2. What explanations are offered for the recent increase in obesity rates?

3. What policy solutions have been offered for the obesity crisis?

solutions include making healthy low-cost produce more widely available; providing safe public places for fitness workouts, free exercise classes, and classes in health and nutrition to poor children and their families; and requiring restaurants and food manufacturers to clearly note the fat and calorie content of their products. Only in attacking the "public issue" of the obesogenic environment will the "private trouble" of excessive weight be resolved (Brownell and Horgen 2004). ✓

HOW DO SOCIOLOGISTS UNDERSTAND HEALTH AND ILLNESS?

Learn about functionalist and symbolic interactionist perspectives on health and illness in contemporary society. Understand the relationship between traditional medicine and complementary and alternative medicine (CAM).

Sociologists of health and illness also are concerned with understanding the experience of illness—how being sick, chronically ill, or disabled is experienced by sick persons and by those with whom they interact. If you have ever been ill, even for a short period, you know that patterns of daily life are temporarily modified and your interactions with others change. This is because the normal functioning of the body is a vital, but often taken for granted, part of our daily lives. Our sense of self is predicated on the expectation that our bodies will facilitate, not impede, our social interactions and daily activities.

Illness has both personal and public dimensions. When we fall ill, others are affected as well. Our friends, families, and coworkers may extend sympathy, care, support, and assistance with practical tasks. They may struggle to understand our illness and its cause, or to adjust the patterns of their own lives to accommodate it. Others' reactions to our illness, in turn, shape our own interpretations and can pose challenges to our sense of self. For instance, a longtime smoker who develops lung disease may be made to feel guilty by family members, who provide constant reminders of the link between smoking and lung disease.

Two sociological perspectives on the experience of illness have been particularly influential. The first, associated with the functionalist school, proposes that "being sick" is a social role, just as "worker" or "mother" is a social role. As such, unhealthy persons are expected to comply with a widely agreed-upon set of behavioral expectations. The second view, favored by symbolic interactionists, explores how the meanings of illness are socially constructed and how these meanings influence people's behavior.

THE SICK ROLE

sick role • A term associated with the functionalist Talcott Parsons to describe the patterns of behavior that a sick person adopts in order to minimize the disruptive impact of his or her illness on others.

The functionalist thinker Talcott Parsons (1951) developed the notion of the **sick role** to describe patterns of behavior that a sick person adopts to minimize the disruptive impact of illness. Functionalist thought holds that society usually operates in a smooth and consensual manner. Illness is, therefore, seen as a dysfunction that can disrupt the flow of this normal state. A sick individual, for example, might be unable to perform standard responsibilities or be less reliable and efficient than usual. Because sick people cannot carry out their normal roles, the lives of people around them are disrupted: Assignments at work go unfinished and cause stress for coworkers, responsibilities at home are not fulfilled, and so forth.

According to Parsons, people learn the sick role through socialization and enact it—with the cooperation of others—when they fall ill. Sick persons face societal expectations for how to behave, yet at the same time other members of society abide by a generally agreed-upon set of expectations for how they will treat the sick individual. The sick role is distinguished by three sets of normative expectations:

1. The sick person is not held personally responsible for his or her poor health.
2. The sick person is entitled to certain rights and privileges, including a release from normal responsibilities.
3. The sick person is expected to take sensible steps to regain his or her health, such as consulting a medical expert and agreeing to become a patient.

EVALUATION

Although the sick-role model reveals how the ill person is an integral part of a larger social context, a number of criticisms can be levied against it. Some argue that the sick-role formula does not adequately capture the *lived experience* of illness. Others point out that it cannot be applied across all contexts, cultures, and historical periods. For example, it does not account for instances in which doctors and patients disagree about a diagnosis or have opposing interests. It also fails to explain illnesses that do not necessarily lead to a suspension of normal activity, such as alcoholism, certain disabilities, and some chronic diseases. Furthermore, taking on the sick role is not always a straightforward process. Some individuals who suffer for years from chronic pain or from misdiagnosed symptoms are denied the sick role until they get a clear diagnosis. Other sick people, such as young women with autoimmune diseases, often appear physically healthy despite constant physical pain and exhaustion; because of their "healthy" outward appearance, they may not be readily granted sick-role status. In other cases, social factors such as race, class, and gender can affect whether and how readily the sick role is granted. For example, in the traditional male breadwinner/female homemaker model that prevailed in the United States among middle-class Americans in the mid-twentieth century, men often were reluctant to take time off work as part of their sick role because they had to work to provide for their families. Likewise, single parents or people caring for their ailing relatives may fail to acknowledge or act on their own symptoms because they fear that shirking their social roles will hurt their loved ones. The sick role cannot be divorced from the social, cultural, and economic influences that surround it.

The realities of life and illness are more complex than the sick role suggests. The leading causes of death today are heart disease and cancer, two diseases that are associated with unhealthy behaviors such as smoking, a high-fat diet, and a sedentary lifestyle. Given the emphasis on taking control over one's health and lifestyle in our modern age, individuals bear ever-greater responsibility for their own well-being. This contradicts the first premise of the sick role—that the individual is not to blame for his or her illness. Moreover, in modern societies the shift away from acute infectious disease toward chronic illness has made the sick role less applicable. Whereas it might be useful in understanding acute illness, it is less applicable to chronic illness because there is no single formula for chronically ill or disabled people to follow. Moreover, chronically ill persons often find that their symptoms fluctuate, so that they feel and appear healthy on some days yet experience disabling symptoms on other days. Living with illness is experienced and interpreted in multiple ways.

Can Your Smartphone Keep You Healthy?

Until fairly recently, when a person felt sick, he or she would call the doctor to make an appointment. During this visit, the doctor would likely diagnose the patient's symptoms and perhaps prescribe medication to help treat the patient. Although many Americans, especially those with health insurance and access to providers, still see a health care professional on a regular basis, more and more Americans are trying to diagnose themselves, often with the assistance of websites or new health-related smartphone apps. For the past decade or two, people have been visiting websites like WebMD to determine whether their headache is due to a head cold or is a sign of something more dire. More recently, smartphone owners have relied on apps to do everything from take their pulse, to chart their ovulation cycles, to identify the best medication for depression.

Health-related apps range from the very simple to the very complex. Many apps help us maintain healthy behaviors, like a regular exercise regimen and a healthy diet. For example, RunTracker allows us to track how many miles we've walked, run, biked, or swam in a given day and provides us with information on our speed and how many calories we've burned. MyFitnessPal tracks one's fitness throughout the day, including one's caloric and caffeine intake. Sleep-Cycle not only measures how many hours of sleep you're getting but also how deeply you're sleeping and how much time you're spending in the replenishing REM stage of sleep (Summers 2013). Smartphones are particularly helpful in guiding us to make healthy food choices. For instance, with Fooducate, users swipe the barcodes of food items they're considering buying at the grocery store and are then given detailed information on the product's ingredients and nutritional value (Summers 2013).

Yet smartphones are increasingly being used for more serious health-related issues, like monitoring one's blood pressure, heart rate, and ovulation cycles, and even assessing one's hearing and vision. For example, ECG Check allows patients to analyze their own heart rhythms, while apps like Gluko Logbook and Glucose Buddy help diabetics monitor their blood sugar levels. Fertility Friend helps women who are hoping to conceive by monitoring their menstrual cycles (Edney 2013). PsychDrugs helps people determine which anti-depressant or anti-anxiety medication will best treat their symptoms.

It's not just patients who use apps to enhance their health; health care providers also rely on apps to help them deliver care. Apps like Epocrates help doctors review drug-prescribing and safety information, research potentially harmful drug interactions, and perform calculations like body mass index and glomerular filtration rate (GFR), an indication of how well one's kidneys are functioning (Glenn 2013).

Many health-care providers and patients are enthusiastic about the role of apps in helping to enhance medical care. Doctors believe that symptom-monitoring apps encourage patients to be proactive and knowledgeable

New smartphone apps help users do everything from chart their ovulation to track their blood pressure to keep pace of how fast they run.

about their own health (Edney 2013). However, others counter that even the best app is not a substitute for a regular checkup. What do you think? Are health and wellness apps a cost-effective and efficient way for people to look after one's own health, or do they keep people from receiving potentially valuable professional care?

ILLNESS AS "LIVED EXPERIENCE"

Symbolic interactionists study the ways people interpret the social world and the meanings they ascribe to it. Many sociologists have applied this approach to health and illness and view this perspective as a partial corrective to the limitations of functionalist approaches to health. Symbolic interactionists are not concerned with identifying risk factors for specific illnesses. Rather, they address questions about the personal experience of illness: How do people react and adjust to news about a serious illness? How does illness shape individuals' daily lives? How does living with a chronic illness affect an individual's self-identity?

One theme that sociologists address is how chronically ill individuals cope with the practical and emotional implications of their illness. Certain illnesses require regular treatments or maintenance that can affect daily routines. Undergoing dialysis or insulin injections, or taking large numbers of pills, requires individuals to adjust their schedules. Other illnesses have unpredictable effects, such as sudden loss of bowel or bladder control or violent nausea. People suffering from such conditions often develop strategies for managing their illness in daily life. These include practical considerations—such as noting the location of the restrooms when in an unfamiliar place—as well as skills for managing interpersonal relations, both intimate and commonplace. Although symptoms can be embarrassing and disruptive, people develop coping strategies to live as normally as possible (Kelly 1992).

At the same time, the experience of illness can pose challenges for individuals to manage their illnesses within the overall context of their lives (Jobling 1988; Williams 1993). Corbin and Strauss (1985) identified three types of "work" incorporated in the everyday strategies of the chronically ill. *Illness work* refers to activities involved in managing the condition, such as treating pain, doing diagnostic tests, or undergoing physical therapy. *Everyday work* pertains to the management of daily life—maintaining relationships with others, running household affairs, and pursuing professional or personal interests. *Biographical work* involves the process of incorporating the illness into one's life, making sense of it, and developing ways of explaining it to others. Such a process can help chronically ill people restore meaning and order to their lives.

Each of these processes of adaptation may be particularly difficult for those who suffer from a stigmatized health condition, such as extreme obesity, alcoholism, AIDS, or even lung cancer. Sociologist Erving Goffman (1963) developed the concept of **stigma**, which refers to any personal characteristic that is devalued in a particular social context. Stigmatized individuals and groups often are treated with suspicion, hostility, or discrimination. Stigmas are, however, rarely based on valid understandings or scientific data. They spring from stereotypes or perceptions that may be false or only partially correct. Further, the nature of a stigma varies widely across sociocultural context: The extent to which a trait is devalued depends on the values and beliefs of those who do the stigmatizing. For instance, in the United States, obese persons are much more likely to be stigmatized by white upper-middle-class persons than they are to be stigmatized by African Americans or working-class whites (Carr and Friedman 2005). By contrast, other health conditions, including major mental illness and HIV/AIDS (as we will read about later in this chapter), are much more widely stigmatized. For example, one recent study of sixteen different countries, including the United States and nations in Europe, Africa, and Asia, found that even in the most liberal, tolerant countries, the majority of the public held stigmatizing attitudes and a willingness to exclude people with schizophrenia from close, personal relationships and positions of authority, seeing them as unpredictable and potentially dangerous (Pescosolido et al. 2013).

stigma • Any physical or social characteristic that is labeled by society as undesirable.

CHANGING CONCEPTIONS OF HEALTH AND ILLNESS

A key theme in the sociological study of health is that cultures and societies differ in what they consider healthy and normal. All cultures have known concepts of physical health and illness, but most of what we now recognize as medicine is a consequence of developments in Western society over the past three centuries. In premodern cultures, the family was the main institution for coping with sickness or affliction. There have always been individuals who specialized as healers, using a mixture of physical and spiritual remedies, and many such traditional systems survive today in non-Western cultures. For instance, traditional Chinese medicine aims to restore harmony among aspects of the personality and bodily systems, involving the use of herbs and acupuncture for treatment.

Modern medicine sees the origins and treatment of disease as physical and explicable in scientific terms. The application of science to medical diagnosis and cure underlay the development of modern health care systems. Other features were the acceptance of the hospital as the setting within which to treat serious illnesses and the development of the medical profession as a body with codes of ethics and significant social power. The scientific view of disease was linked to the requirement that medical training be systematic and long term; self-taught healers were excluded. Although professional medical practice is not limited to hospitals, the hospital provided an environment in which doctors could treat and study large numbers of patients in circumstances permitting the concentration of medical technology.

ALTERNATIVE MEDICINE

Alternative therapies, such as herbal remedies, acupuncture, and chiropractic treatments, are being explored by a record high number of adults in the United States today and are slowly gaining acceptance by the mainstream medical community. Physicians increasingly believe that such unorthodox therapies may be an important complement to (although not a substitute for) traditional Western medicine, provided they are upheld to rigorous scientific evaluation. Yet devoted adherents to nontraditional health regimens believe that such practices are effective and that their personal experiences are more meaningful than are the results of controlled trials.

complementary and alternative medicine (CAM) • A diverse set of approaches and therapies for treating different illnesses and promoting well-being that generally falls outside of standard medical practices.

Medical sociologists refer to such unorthodox medical practices as **complementary and alternative medicine (CAM)**. CAM encompasses a diverse set of approaches and therapies for treating illness and promoting well-being that generally fall outside standard medical practices. These approaches are usually not taught in medical schools and not practiced by physicians or other professionals trained in medical programs. However, in recent years a number of medical and nursing schools have started offering courses in alternative medicine (Fenton and Morris 2003; Wetzel et al. 1998). Complementary medicine is distinct from alternative medicine in that the latter is meant to be used in place of standard medical procedures, while the former is meant to be used in conjunction with medical procedures to increase their efficacy or reduce side effects (Saks 1992). Many people use CAM approaches in addition to, rather than in place of, orthodox treatments (although some alternative approaches, such as homeopathy, reject the basis of orthodox medicine entirely).

Industrialized countries have some of the best-developed, best-resourced medical facilities in the world. Why, then, are a growing number of people exploring treatments that have not yet proven effective in controlled clinical trials, such as aromatherapy and hypnotherapy? A survey conducted by the CDC and the National Center for Health Statistics (NCHS) found that 38 percent of all Americans said that they had used some form of CAM in 2007 (CDC 2008b). When CAM is broadly defined to include prayer as well as alternative treatments, a 2002 survey revealed that the proportion of Americans who had used CAM rises to 62 percent (Pagan and Pauly 2005). CAM use is more frequent among women and individuals with higher levels of educational attainment. Furthermore, American Indians and whites are more likely to use CAM than their black and Asian counterparts.

There are many reasons for seeking the services of an alternative medicine practitioner or pursuing CAM regimens on one's own. Some people perceive orthodox medicine to be deficient or ineffective in relieving chronic pain or symptoms of stress and anxiety. Others are dissatisfied with features of modern health care systems such as long waits, referrals through chains of specialists, and financial restrictions. Connected to this are concerns about the harmful side effects of medication and the intrusiveness of surgery, both staples of modern Western medicine. The asymmetrical power relationship between doctors and patients also drives some people to seek alternative medicine. Those people feel that the role of the passive patient does not grant them enough input into their own treatment and healing. Finally, some individuals profess religious or philosophical objections to orthodox medicine, which treats the mind and body separately. They believe that orthodox medicine often overlooks the spiritual and psychological dimensions of health and illness. All these concerns are critiques of the **biomedical model of health** (the foundation of the Western medical establishment), which defines disease in objective terms and believes that scientifically based medical treatment can restore the body to health (Beyerstein 1999).

The growth of alternative medicine is a fascinating reflection of the transformations occurring within modern societies. We are living in an age where much more information is available to draw on in making choices. The proliferation of health-related websites such as WebMD and MedicineNet provides instant access to information on health symptoms and treatments. Thus, individuals are increasingly becoming health consumers, adopting an active stance toward their own health and well-being. Not only are we choosing the type of practitioners to consult, but we are also demanding more involvement in our own care and treatment.

Members of the traditional medical community, once viewed as completely resistant to the notion of alternative medicine, are increasingly taking a more open-minded approach to such therapies. Many now cautiously endorse patients' desires to consult an ever-expanding array of medical information. However, medical leaders believe that CAM should be held to the same level of scientific scrutiny and rigorous scientific evaluation as traditional Western medicine (Angell and Kassirer 1998).

Debates about CAM also shed light on the changing nature of health and illness over the past two centuries. Many conditions and illnesses for which individuals seek

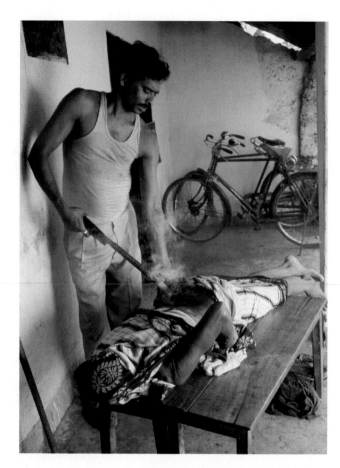

An ayurvedic physician uses a hot iron rod and fabric soaked in herbs to heal an arthritic hip.

biomedical model of health • The set of principles underpinning Western medical systems and practices. The biomedical model of health defines diseases objectively, in accordance with the presence of recognized symptoms, and holds that the healthy body can be restored through scientifically based medical treatment.

1. How do functionalist theorists and symbolic inter-actionists differ in their perspectives on health and illness?

2. What is stigma, and how does it pertain to health and illness?

3. What is the biomedical model of health?

4. Compare complementary medicine with alternative medicine.

alternative medical treatment seem to be products of the modern age itself. Rates of insomnia, anxiety, stress, depression, fatigue, and chronic pain (caused by arthritis, cancer, and other diseases) are increasing in industrialized societies (Kessler and Üstün 2008). Although these conditions have long existed, they are causing greater distress and disruption to people's health than ever before. Ironically, these consequences of modernity are ones that ortho-dox medicine has difficulty addressing. Alternative medicine is unlikely to overtake mainstream health care altogether, but indications are that its role will continue to grow. ✓

Recognize that health and illness are shaped by cultural and social factors. Learn the social and cultural differences in the distribution of disease.

HOW DO SOCIAL FACTORS AFFECT HEALTH AND ILLNESS?

The twentieth century witnessed a significant increase in life expectancy for people living in industrialized countries. Diseases such as polio, scarlet fever, and diphtheria have been all but eradicated. Infant mortality rates have dropped precipitously, leading to an increase in the average life span in the developed world. Compared with other parts of the world, standards of health and well-being are high. Many advances in public health have been attributed to the power of modern medicine. It is commonly assumed that medical research has been—and will continue to be—successful in uncovering the biological causes of disease and in developing effective treatments.

Although this view has been influential, it is somewhat unsatisfactory for sociologists because it ignores the importance of social and environmental influences on patterns of health and illness. The improvements in overall public health over the past century cannot conceal the fact that health and illness occur unevenly throughout the population. As we saw in the chapter opener, certain groups of people enjoy much better health than others. These *health inequalities* appear to reflect larger socioeconomic patterns.

SOCIAL CLASS-BASED INEQUALITIES IN HEALTH

In Chapter 7, we defined social class as a concept that encompasses education, income, occupation, and assets. In American society, people with better educations, higher incomes, and more prestigious occupations have better health. What is fascinating is that each of these dimensions of social class may be related to health and mortality for different reasons.

Income is the most obvious factor. In countries such as the United States, where medical care is expensive and the ACA is still in its infancy, those with more financial resources have better access to physicians and medicine. But inequalities in health also persist in countries like Great Britain that have a long history of national health insurance. Differences in occupational status may lead to inequalities in health and illness even when medical care is fairly evenly distributed. One highly influential study of health inequalities in Great Britain, the *Black Report* (Townsend and Davidson 1982), found that manual workers had substantially higher mortality rates than professional workers, even though Britain's health service had made great strides in equalizing the distribution of health care. Those who work in offices or in domestic settings face less risk of injury and exposure to hazardous materials.

Differences in education, a third dimension of social class, also are correlated with inequalities in health and illness. Numerous studies find a positive correlation between education and a broad array of preventive health behaviors. Better-educated people are significantly more likely to engage in aerobic exercise and to know their blood pressure (Shea et al. 1991) and are less likely to smoke (Kenkel et al. 2006) or be overweight (Himes 1999). Highly educated smokers are also much more likely to quit smoking when faced with a new health threat such as a heart attack (Wray et al. 1998). By contrast, poorly educated people engage in more cigarette smoking; they also have more problems with cholesterol and body weight (Winkleby et al. 1992).

Mental health is similarly affected by social class–based inequalities. In general, persons with lower levels of education and income fare worse along most mental health outcomes, including risk of depression, anxiety, and suicidal ideation. The stressors related to economic adversity, including unsatisfying jobs, strained marriages, and worries about money and one's personal safety, may overwhelm one's ability to cope. Depressive symptoms, or feelings of profound sadness and hopelessness, and anxiety, or nervousness about one's daily experiences, are emotional consequences of living under persistently stressful circumstances (Carr 2014).

RACE-BASED INEQUALITIES IN HEALTH

Blacks fare worse than whites in the United States on nearly all health indicators, ranging from body weight to mortality rates to risk of major illnesses like diabetes and cancer. In the United States, life expectancy at birth in 2010 was slightly less than eighty-four years for Hispanic females and about eighty-one years for white females but seventy-eight years for black females. Likewise, life expectancy at birth in 2010 was over seventy-eight years for Hispanic males and seventy-six years for white males yet seventy-one years for black males (CDC 2013b).

Racial differences in health reveal the complex interrelations among ethnicity, race, social class, and culture. A powerful example of the multiple ways that race affects health is the Hispanic health paradox: Although Hispanics in the United States have poorer socioeconomic resources than whites, on average, their health—and especially the health of their infants—is just as good as if not better than that of whites. Blacks, by contrast, face economic disadvantages that are similar to those of Hispanics, yet blacks do not enjoy the same health benefits. Experts attribute Hispanics' health advantage relative to blacks' to cultural factors such as social cohesion but also to methodological factors. Studies of Hispanic health in the United States focus on those who successfully migrated to the United States; as such, they are believed to be in better health, or more robust, than those Latinos who remained in their native countries (Franzini et al. 2001).

A close inspection of blacks' health and mortality disadvantage further reveals the multiple ways that race matters for health. One of the main reasons for blacks' health disadvantage is that blacks as a group have less money than whites, as noted in Chapter 7. Yet black-white disparities in health go beyond economic causes and reflect other important aspects of the social and cultural landscape. Consider racial gaps in mortality. The homicide rate for young black males ages ten to twenty-four is more than fifteen times higher than for their white peers (CDC 2013f; Flaherty and

Many blacks living in poor inner-city neighborhoods lack access to high-quality grocery stores and instead rely on cheap fast food options.

Sethi 2010). This gap has been attributed to the violent crime that has accompanied the rise of widespread crack cocaine addiction, especially in the late 1980s and 1990s, mainly affecting poor African American neighborhoods plagued by high levels of unemployment (Wilson 1996).

Other race-based inequalities in health status, health behaviors, and health care are also stark. There is a higher prevalence of hypertension among blacks than whites, especially black men; this difference may be partly biological. The pattern also may reflect blacks' tendency to eat high-fat foods, a pattern encouraged by the fast-food industry's targeting of African Americans as a market (Henderson and Kelly 2005). Black women also are far less likely than white women to exercise regularly, a pattern that most social scientists attribute to their hectic schedules of juggling work and family, and the high costs of fitness programs and gym membership (August and Sorkin 2010). However, in 2011, U.S. surgeon general Regina M. Benjamin drew attention by suggesting that one reason why black women avoid exercise is because it may ruin their hair; black women often spend a lot of time and money on treatments such as hair relaxers (O'Connor 2011).

However, researchers have noted one important health-related outcome for which blacks tend to fare better than whites: mental health. Most studies tend to conclude that blacks are less likely than whites to suffer from depressive symptoms. This pattern is paradoxical because blacks tend to have fewer socioeconomic resources than whites. As we saw earlier in this chapter, economic adversity is a risk factor for anxiety, depression, and other mental health. Researchers have not reached a consensus on the reasons behind the so-called race paradox in mental health, although three main explanations are typically offered for blacks' superior mental health (Keyes 2009). First, some believe that strong reliance on religious beliefs and support from members of one's religious community help to protect against stress (Taylor, Chatters, and Levin 2004). Second, blacks may be bolstered by a sense of ethnic pride as they cope with stress (Mandara et al. 2009). Third, some researchers believe that the race paradox is a function of a methodological artifact, where blacks' depressive symptoms are less likely to manifest as sadness, and thus are less likely to be reported on a standard checklist of depressive symptoms. Their depression may instead manifest itself through behaviors such as substance use or through physical health symptoms, such as aches and pains (Keyes, Barnes, and Bates 2011).

Despite the persistence of inequalities in the physical health of blacks and whites, some progress has been made in eradicating them. According to the CDC (2010a), racial differences in cigarette smoking have decreased. In 1965, half of white men and 60 percent of black men age eighteen and older smoked cigarettes. By 2011, 22.5 percent of white men and 24.2 percent of black men smoked (CDC 2012b). Hypertension among blacks has also been greatly reduced. In the early 1970s, half of black adults between the ages of twenty and seventy-four suffered from hypertension. By 2008, however, the proportion of black adults over age eighteen suffering from hypertension had dropped to 42 percent (CDC 2011a).

Patterns of physician visitation, hospitalization, and preventive medicine also have improved, yet racial equity still remains elusive. For example, black women historically have been less likely than white women to receive mammograms. This gap has narrowed in recent years, however. In 2010, roughly equal proportions of white and black women between the ages of fifty and seventy-four had received mammograms within the past two years (73 percent) (CDC 2012a). However, some studies suggest that black women delay receiving mammograms, and thus those with breast cancer have their condition detected at a later—and more dangerous—stage of the disease's progression (Smith-Bindman et al. 2006).

How might the influence of poverty on health be countered? Extensive programs of health education and disease prevention are one possibility. But such programs work better among more prosperous, well-educated groups and in any case usually produce only small changes in behavior. Increased accessibility to health services would help, but probably to a limited degree. Despite the good intentions of programs like "Let's Move!"—a program implemented by First Lady Michelle Obama to bring healthy food and healthy lifestyles to inner-city Americans—the most effective policy option is to attack poverty itself, so as to reduce the income gap between rich and poor (Najman 1993).

GENDER-BASED INEQUALITIES IN HEALTH

Women in the United States generally live longer than men, and this gender gap increased steadily throughout the twentieth century. In the United States, there was only a two-year difference in female and male life expectancies in 1900. By 1940, this gap had increased to 4.4 years; by 1970, to 7.7 years. Since reaching its peak in the 1970s, however, the gender gap in life expectancy has been decreasing. In 2010, the gender gap had fallen to 4.8 years (CDC 2013b; Cleary 1987).

Despite the female advantage in mortality, most large surveys show that women report poor health more often than men. Women have higher rates of illness from acute conditions and nonfatal chronic conditions, including arthritis, osteoporosis, and depressive and anxiety disorders. They are slightly more likely to report their health as fair or poor and spend about 57 percent more days sick in bed each year. Women also report that their physical activities are either restricted or impossible about 50 percent more than men. In addition, they make more physician visits each year and undergo twice the number of surgical procedures as do men (CDC 2013c; NCHS 2003, 2011).

There are two main explanations for women's poorer health yet longer lives: (1) Greater life expectancy and age bring poorer health, and (2) women make greater use of medical services, including preventive care (CDC 2003). Men may experience as many health symptoms as women or more, but may ignore their symptoms, underestimate the extent of their illness, or utilize preventive services less often (Waldron 1986). Further, men who are socialized to believe that men should be "traditionally masculine," strong, and self-sufficient are less likely to seek out annual checkups (Springer and Mouzon 2011), a pattern that may further contribute to men's high rates of mortality relative to women.

A major question for sociologists is whether the gender gap in mortality will continue to decline in coming years. Many researchers believe that it will, yet for an unfortunate reason: Women's life expectancies may erode and thus become more similar to men's. As men's and women's gender roles have converged over the past several decades, women have increasingly taken on unhealthy "male-typed" behaviors such as smoking and alcohol use, as well as emotional and physical stress in the workplace. These patterns are particularly pronounced for women of low socioeconomic status. One recent study found that American women have lost ground with respect to life expectancy compared with women from other nations. In the early 1980s, the life expectancy of women in the United States ranked fourteenth in the world, yet by 2010, American women had fallen to forty-first place (Karas-Montez and Zajacova 2013). These disheartening findings reveal that gender differences in health and mortality are not a function of biology alone but of the social advantages and adversities experienced by men and women in particular sociohistorical contexts. ✓

CONCEPT CHECKS ✓

1. How do social class and race affect health?

2. Name at least two explanations for the gender gap in health.

3. Identify at least two reasons why the gender gap in life expectancy may narrow in the future.

Understand the causes underlying high rates of infectious diseases in developing nations. Learn more about HIV/AIDS as a sociological phenomenon.

WHAT CAUSES INFECTIOUS DISEASES IN DEVELOPING NATIONS?

COLONIALISM AND THE SPREAD OF DISEASE

Thus far we have focused primarily on the United States in the twenty-first century. Yet to understand health and illness, it is also important to take a big-picture view and examine the ways that health and illness have developed over time and throughout the globe. We now provide a brief historical overview of disease, and show how some infectious diseases still persist in many parts of the developing world.

Hunting and gathering communities of the Americas, before the arrival of the Europeans, were not as susceptible to infectious disease as the European societies of the period. Many infectious organisms thrive only when human populations live above the density level that is characteristic of hunting-and-gathering life. Permanently settled communities, particularly large cities, risk the contamination of water supplies by waste products. Hunters and gatherers were less vulnerable in this respect because they moved continuously across the countryside.

During the colonial era, efforts to bring Western ideals to developing societies also brought certain diseases into other parts of the world. Smallpox, measles, and typhus, among other major maladies, were unknown to the indigenous populations of Central and South America before the Spanish conquest in the early sixteenth century. The English and French colonists brought the same diseases to North America (Dubos 1959). Some of these illnesses produced epidemics that ravaged or completely wiped out native populations, which had little or no resistance to them.

In Africa and subtropical parts of Asia, infectious diseases have been rife for a long time. Tropical and subtropical conditions are especially conducive to diseases such as malaria, carried by mosquitoes, and sleeping sickness, carried by the tsetse fly. Historians believe that risks from infectious diseases were lower in Africa and Asia prior to the time that Europeans tried to colonize these regions—as they often brought with them practices that negatively affected the health of local natives. The threat of epidemics, drought, or natural disaster had always loomed, but colonialism led to major unforeseen changes in the relation between populations and their environments, producing harmful effects on health patterns. The Europeans introduced new farming methods, upsetting the ecology of whole regions. For example, before the Europeans' arrival, Africans successfully maintained large herds of cattle in East Africa. Changes introduced by the intruders allowed for the multiplication and uncontrolled spread of the tsetse fly, which carries illnesses that are fatal to both humans and livestock. Today, large areas of East Africa are completely devoid of cattle (Kjekshus 1977).

The most significant consequence of the colonial system was its effect on nutrition and, therefore, on levels of resistance to illness as a result of the changed economic conditions involved in producing for world markets. In many parts of Africa, the nutritional quality of native diets became substantially depressed as cash-crop production supplanted the production of native foods.

This was not a one-way process, however. Indeed, early colonialism also radically changed Western diets, having a paradoxical impact in terms of health. On the one hand, Western diets benefited from the addition of new foods such as bananas, pineapples, and grapefruit. On the other hand, the importation of tobacco and coffee, together with raw sugar (which found uses in all manner of foods), has had harmful consequences.

Insecticide-treated bed nets have served successfully to reduce malaria-related deaths in sub-Saharan Africa.

INFECTIOUS DISEASES TODAY IN THE DEVELOPING WORLD

Although major strides have occurred in reducing, and in some cases eliminating, infectious diseases in the developing world, they remain far more common there than in the West. The most important example of a disease that has almost completely disappeared is smallpox, which as recently as the 1960s was a scourge of Europe as well as many other regions. Campaigns against malaria have been much less successful. When the insecticide DDT was first produced, it was hoped that the mosquito, the prime carrier of malaria, could be eradicated. At first, there was considerable progress, but this has slowed because some strains of mosquito have become resistant to DDT. Malaria is a particularly devastating condition in sub-Saharan Africa, and children are at an especially high risk (Snow et al. 2005). Recognizing the magnitude of this global health concern, in 2005 President George W. Bush initiated the $1.2 billion, five-year President's Malaria Initiative (PMI); its goal was to reduce malaria-related deaths in fifteen African countries by 50 percent. This goal was partly achieved. In its 2013 report to Congress, the PMI reported declines in malaria-related deaths among children under age five for twelve of the fifteen countries for which they had data. Declines ranged from 16 percent in Malawi to 50 percent in Rwanda (President's Malaria Initiative 2013).

HUMAN IMMUNODEFICIENCY VIRUS (HIV) AND ACQUIRED IMMUNE DEFICIENCY SYNDROME (AIDS)

A devastating exception to the trend of eliminating infectious diseases in the developing world is HIV/AIDS, which has become a global epidemic. More than 35 million people were living with HIV at the end of 2012. In 2012 alone, 1.6 million people died from AIDS-related illnesses. Epidemiologists estimate that about 860,000 people are living with HIV/AIDS in Western and Central Europe, 1.3 million in North America, 1.5 million in Latin America and the Caribbean, and 25 million in sub-Saharan Africa (UNAIDS 2013a).

The majority of people affected in the world today are heterosexuals. As of 2012, about half were women. In sub-Saharan Africa, young women are more than one and a half times as likely as men to be infected.

In high-income countries, the rate of new infections has declined, yet the demographics are striking. In the United States, there were 49,273 new HIV infections

Global Map 14.1 | The Number of HIV-Positive People around the World

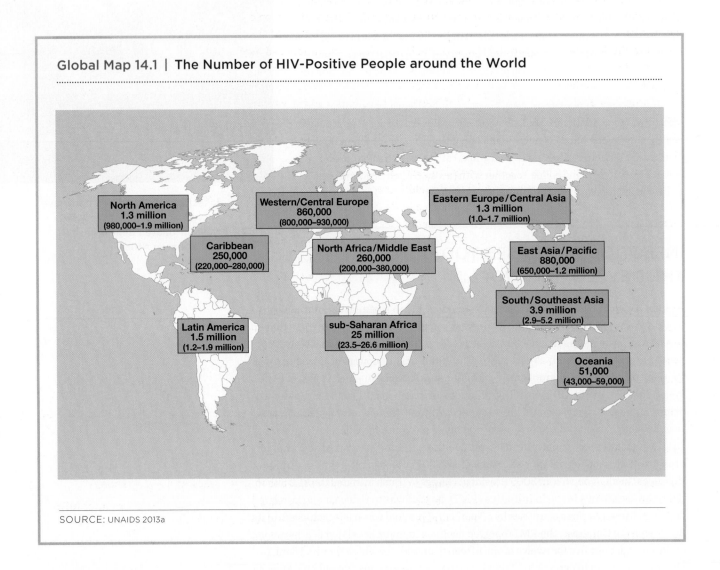

SOURCE: UNAIDS 2013a

among adults and adolescents in 2011 (CDC 2013e). The incidence of infection is not proportionately represented throughout the United States. In 2010, 45 percent of new AIDS diagnoses were made in the South (CDC 2012c). Nearly 44 percent of persons living with HIV in the United States are African Americans and 46 percent of new infections in 2011 are among African Americans (CDC 2011b). By contrast, African Americans comprise just 13 percent of the overall U.S. population. The rate of new HIV infections among African American women was twenty times greater than that of their white counterparts in 2010, and HIV/AIDS is the third leading cause of death among African American men and women ages thirty-five to forty-four in the United States (CDC 2010b, 2013d). Although there was a steep drop in AIDS-related deaths after the introduction of antiretroviral therapy, African Americans are less likely than whites to benefit from such life-prolonging treatments. The United Nations Joint Program on HIV and AIDS reports that African Americans are half as likely as white Americans to be receiving antiretroviral treatment (UNAIDS 2005).

Stigmatization of people with HIV/AIDS remains a major barrier to successful treatment. The stigma that associates HIV-positive status with sexual promiscuity, homosexuality, and IV drug use results in avoidance of HIV/AIDS prevention and treatment programs. In the United States, 15.8 percent of people living with HIV/AIDS do not know they are infected (CDC 2013e). Part of the reason is the high level of fear and denial associated with being diagnosed as HIV positive. The stigma of having HIV/AIDS and the discrimination against people living with these infections are major barriers to the treatment of the epidemic worldwide. A recent study of 1,450 HIV-positive patients seeking care in India found that two-thirds of the patients reported authoritarian behavior from doctors, and 55 percent felt they were not treated in a dignified manner (Mehta 2013).

Although the spread of AIDS has slowed in parts of the developing world, the illness is still a source of crisis. In low- and middle-income countries, the percentage of pregnant women who receive health care services aimed at preventing mother-to-child HIV transmission rose from 9 percent in 2004 to 33 percent in 2007 (UNAIDS 2008). In 2009, 370,000 children, a drop of 24 percent from five years earlier, were infected with HIV through mother-to-child transmission. Besides the devastation to individuals who suffer from it, the AIDS epidemic is creating severe social consequences, including sharply rising numbers of orphaned children. Frail older adults are increasingly called on to provide physical care to their adult children who suffer from AIDS (Knodel 2006). Worldwide, the parents of an estimated 16.6 million children have died as a result of HIV/AIDS; 14.8 million are in sub-Saharan Africa (Global Map 14.1) (UNAIDS 2010). In Uganda alone, 77 percent of the population are under age eighteen; 30 percent of those are orphans (AIDS Orphans Educational Trust 2003). In 2009, there were 1.2 million AIDS orphans in Uganda. The decimated population of working adults combined with the surging population of orphans set the stage for massive social instability; economies break down and governments cannot provide for the social needs of orphans, who become targets for recruitment into gangs and armies. ✓

CONCEPT CHECKS ✓

1. Why are infectious diseases more common in developing nations than in the United States today?

2. What are three social consequences of the AIDS epidemic in developing nations?

HOW DOES SOCIAL CONTEXT SHAPE HUMAN SEXUAL BEHAVIOR?

As with the study of health and illness, scholars disagree as to the importance of biological versus social and cultural influences on human sexual behavior, another important facet of the sociology of the body.

THE DIVERSITY OF HUMAN SEXUALITY

Judith Lorber (1994) distinguishes as many as ten different sexual identities: straight (heterosexual) woman, straight man, lesbian woman, gay man, bisexual woman, bisexual man, transvestite woman (a woman who regularly dresses as a man), transvestite man (a man who regularly dresses as a woman), transsexual woman (a man who becomes a woman), and transsexual man (a woman who becomes a man). Sexual practices themselves are even more diverse. Freud argued that human beings are born with a wide range of sexual tastes that are ordinarily curbed through socialization—although some adults may follow these even when, in a given society, they are regarded as immoral or illegal. Freud began his research during the Victorian period, when many people were sexually prudish; yet his patients still revealed an amazing diversity of sexual pursuits.

Among possible sexual practices are the following: A man or woman can have sexual relations with women, men, or both. This can happen with one partner at a time or with two or more partners participating. One can have sex with oneself (masturbation) or with no one (celibacy). One can have sexual relations with transsexuals or people who erotically cross-dress, use pornography or sexual devices, practice sadomasochism (the erotic use of bondage and the inflicting of pain), and so on (Lorber 1994). In most societies, sexual norms encourage some practices and discourage or condemn others. Such norms, however, vary among cultures. Homosexuality is an example. Among the ancient Greeks, for instance, the love of men for boys was idealized as the highest form of sexual love.

The most extensive cross-cultural study of sexual practices was carried out by Clellan Ford and Frank Beach (1951), using anthropological evidence from more than 200 societies. Striking variations were found in what was regarded as "natural" sexual behavior and in norms of sexual attractiveness. For example, in some cultures, extended foreplay is desirable and even necessary before intercourse; in others, foreplay is nonexistent. In some societies, it is believed that overly frequent intercourse leads to physical debilitation or illness.

In most cultures, norms of sexual attractiveness (held by both females and males) focus more on physical looks for women than for men, a situation that may be changing in the West as women become active in spheres outside the home. The traits seen as most important in female beauty, however, differ greatly. In the modern West, a slim, small physique is admired, while in other cultures a more generous shape is attractive. Sometimes the breasts are not considered a source of sexual stimulus, whereas some societies attach erotic significance to them. Some societies value the shape of the face, whereas others emphasize the shape and color of the eyes or the size and form of the nose and lips.

SEX: A GLOBAL SNAPSHOT

Sexual practices, including when and under what circumstances we engage in
sexual relationships, are powerfully shaped by laws, norms, and cultural practices. In recent decades,
sexual attitudes have become more permissive in most Western countries.

Average lifetime sexual partners

Percent of respondents having sex weekly

GERMANY
5.8 partners
—68%

POLAND
6 partners
—76%

SPAIN
6.1 partners
—72%

SINGAPORE
7.2 partners
—62%

FRANCE
8.1 partners
—70%

UNITED KINGDOM
9.8 partners
—55%

JAPAN
10.4 partners
—34%

UNITED STATES
10.6 partners
—53%

SWITZERLAND
11.1 partners
—72%

ITALY
11.8 partners
—76%

SOUTH AFRICA
12.5 partners
—71%

AUSTRALIA
13.0 partners
—60%

Sources: Durex Sexual Wellbeing Survey (2008); Durex Global Sex Survey (2005)

SEXUALITY IN WESTERN CULTURE

Western attitudes toward sexual behavior were for nearly 2,000 years molded primarily by Christianity, whose dominant view was that all sexual behavior is suspect except that needed for reproduction. During some periods this view produced an extreme prudishness, but at other times many people ignored the church's teachings and engaged in practices such as adultery. The idea that sexual fulfillment can and should be sought through marriage was rare.

In the nineteenth century, religious presumptions about sexuality were partly replaced by medical ones. Most early writings by doctors about sexual behavior, however, were as stern as the views of the church. Some argued that any type of sexual activity unconnected with reproduction would cause serious physical harm. Masturbation was said to cause blindness, insanity, heart disease, and other ailments, while oral sex was claimed to cause cancer. In Victorian times, sexual hypocrisy abounded. Many Victorian men—who appeared to be sober, well-behaved citizens, devoted to their wives—regularly visited prostitutes or kept mistresses. Such behavior was accepted, whereas "respectable" women who took lovers were regarded as scandalous and shunned in polite society. The differing attitudes toward the sexual activities of men and women formed a double standard, which persists today.

Currently, traditional attitudes exist alongside much more permissive attitudes, which developed widely in the 1960s. Some people, particularly those influenced by Christian teachings, believe that premarital sex is wrong; they frown on all forms of sexual behavior except heterosexual activity within marriage—although it is now more commonly accepted that sexual pleasure is an important feature of marriage. Sexual attitudes have undoubtedly become more permissive over recent decades in most Western countries. Movies and plays include scenes that previously would have been unacceptable, and pornographic material is available to most adults who want it. Pornography is reportedly the predominant use for the Internet. An estimated 25 percent of all search engine requests are related to pornography, and an estimated 75 million people visit adult websites each month (The Week 2010).

SEXUAL BEHAVIOR: KINSEY'S STUDY

We can speak more confidently about public values concerning sexuality than we can about private practices, for such practices have gone undocumented for much of history. When Alfred Kinsey began his research in the United States in the 1940s and 1950s, it was the first major investigation of sexual behavior. Kinsey and his co-researchers (1948, 1953) faced condemnation from religious organizations, and his work was denounced as immoral in the newspapers and in Congress. But he persisted, thus making his study the largest rigorous study of sexuality at that time, although his sample was not representative of the overall American population.

Kinsey's results were surprising because they revealed a tremendous discrepancy between prevailing public expectations of sexual behavior and actual sexual conduct. The gap between publicly accepted attitudes and actual behavior was probably especially pronounced just after World War II, the time of Kinsey's study. A phase of sexual liberalization had begun in the 1920s, when many younger people felt freed from the strict moral codes that had governed earlier generations. Sexual behavior probably changed, but issues concerning sexuality were not openly discussed. People participating in sexual activities that were still strongly disapproved of on a public level concealed them, not realizing that others were engaging in similar practices. The more permissive 1960s brought openly declared attitudes more into line with the realities of behavior.

SEXUAL BEHAVIOR SINCE KINSEY

In the 1960s, social movements that challenged the existing order, such as those associated with countercultural lifestyles, also broke with existing sexual norms. These movements preached sexual freedom, and the introduction of the contraceptive pill allowed sexual pleasure to be separated from reproduction. Women's groups also started pressing for greater independence from male sexual values, rejection of the double standard, and the need for women to achieve greater sexual satisfaction in their relationships. Even so, until recently it was unclear to what extent sexual behavior had changed since the time of Kinsey's research.

In the late 1980s, Lillian Rubin (1990) interviewed 1,000 Americans between the ages of thirteen and forty-eight to identify changes in sexual behavior and attitudes over the previous thirty years or so. Her findings indicate significant changes. Sexual activity begins at a younger age; moreover, teenagers' sexual practices are as varied and comprehensive as those of adults. There is still a double standard, but it is not as powerful as before. One of the most important changes is that women now expect, and actively pursue, sexual pleasure in relationships—a phenomenon that Rubin argues has major consequences for both sexes.

Women are more sexually available than before, which most men applaud; but women also have a new assertiveness that men find difficult to accept. The men Rubin talked to often said they "felt inadequate," were afraid they could "never do anything right," and found it "impossible to satisfy women these days." Several recent authors concur that masculinity is a burden as much as a source of reward. Much male sexuality, they add, is compulsive rather than satisfying; that is, men often have sex out of a feeling of obligation rather than desire (Kimmel 2003).

In 1994, a team of researchers led by Edward Laumann published *The Social Organization of Sexuality: Sexual Practices in the United States*, the most comprehensive study of sexual behavior since Kinsey. Their findings reflect an essential sexual conservatism among Americans. For instance, 83 percent of their subjects had had only one partner (or no partner at all) in the preceding year, and among married people the figure was 96 percent. Fidelity to one's spouse was also quite common: Only 10 percent of women and fewer than 25 percent of men reported having an extramarital affair during their lifetime. Despite the apparent ordinariness of sexual behavior, some distinct historical changes were revealed in this study, the most significant being a progressive increase in the level of premarital sexual experience, particularly among women. In fact, more than 95 percent of Americans getting married today are sexually experienced.

In addition, sexual experience among young people is much greater today than it was in the 1970s. According to the Centers for Disease Control and Prevention (2013h), in 2011 nearly half (47 percent) of all high school students reported having had sexual intercourse; 15 percent reported having had four or more partners.

U.S. rates are far higher than those in most Asian nations (Tang and Zuo 2000; Toufexis 1993).

Considering that the General Social Survey in 2012 reported that two-thirds of American adults believed that sex is "always wrong" for teens ages fourteen to sixteen, parental beliefs and adolescent behavior are clearly in conflict (Smith and Son 2013).

SEXUAL ORIENTATION

sexual orientation • The direction of one's sexual or romantic attraction.

Another important aspect of sexuality concerns **sexual orientation**, the direction of one's sexual or romantic attraction. The term *sexual preference*, which is sometimes incorrectly used instead of sexual orientation, is misleading and is to be avoided because it implies that one's sexual or romantic attraction is entirely a matter of personal choice. As you will see below, sexual orientation results from a complex interplay of biological and social factors not yet fully understood.

heterosexuality • Sexual or romantic attraction to persons of the opposite sex.

The most commonly found sexual orientation in all cultures, including the United States, is **heterosexuality**, a sexual or romantic attraction to persons of the opposite sex. Heterosexuals in the United States are also sometimes referred to as "straight." It is important to note that although heterosexuality may be the prevailing norm in most cultures, it is not "normal" in the sense of being dictated by some universal moral or religious standard. Like all behavior, heterosexual behavior is socially learned within a particular culture.

homosexuality • Sexual or romantic attraction to persons of one's own sex.

Homosexuality involves a sexual or romantic attraction to persons of one's own sex. Today, the term *gay* is used to refer to male homosexuals, *lesbian* for female homosexuals, and *bi* as shorthand for *bisexuals*, people who experience sexual or romantic attraction to both men and women. Although it is difficult to know for sure because of the stigma attached to homosexuality, which may result in the underreporting of sexuality in demographic surveys, estimates are that from 2 to 5 percent of all women and 3 to 10 percent of all men in the United States are homosexual or bisexual (Stephens-Davidowitz 2013; Smith 2003).

The term *homosexual* was first used by the medical community in 1869 to characterize what was then regarded as a personality disorder. The American Psychiatric Association did not remove homosexuality from its list of mental illnesses until 1973 or from its influential *Diagnostic and Statistical Manual of Mental Disorders* (DSM) until 1980. These long-overdue steps were taken only after prolonged lobbying and pressure by homosexual rights organizations. The medical community was belatedly forced to acknowledge that no scientific research had ever found homosexuals as a group to be psychologically unhealthier than heterosexuals (Burr 1993). However, the DSM-5 continues to classify other aspects of sexuality as "disorders," including disorders of sexual arousal (e.g., lubrication and erectile problems) and orgasmic disorders (American Psychiatric Association 2013).

In a small number of cultures, same-sex relationships are the norm in certain contexts and do not necessarily signify what today is termed *homosexuality*. For example, the anthropologist Gilbert Herdt (1981, 1984, 1986) reported that among more than twenty tribes in Melanesia and New Guinea, ritually prescribed same-sex encounters among young men and boys were considered necessary for subsequent masculine virility (Herdt and Davidson 1988). Ritualized male-male sexual encounters also occurred among the Azande of Africa's Sudan and Congo (Evans-Pritchard 1970), Japanese samurai warriors in the nineteenth century (Leupp 1995), and highly educated Greek men and boys at the time of Plato (Rousselle 1999).

IS SEXUAL ORIENTATION INBORN OR LEARNED?

Most sociologists believe that sexual orientation—whether homosexual, heterosexual, or bisexual—results from a complex interplay between biological factors and social learning. Since heterosexuality is the norm for most people in U.S. culture, considerable research has focused on why some people are homosexual. Some scholars argue that biological influences predispose certain people to become homosexual from birth (Bell et al. 1981; Green 1987). Biological explanations have included differences in brain characteristics of homosexuals (LeVay 2011) and the effect on fetal development of the mother's in utero hormone production during pregnancy (Blanchard and Bogaert 1996; Manning et al. 1997; McFadden and Champlin 2000). Such studies, which are based on small numbers of cases, give highly inconclusive (and highly controversial) results (Healy 2001). It is virtually impossible to separate biological from early social influences in determining a person's sexual orientation (LeVay 2011).

Studies of twins may shed light on any genetic basis for homosexuality, since identical twins share identical genes. In two related studies, Bailey and Pillard (1991; Bailey 1993) examined 167 pairs of brothers and 143 pairs of sisters, with each pair of siblings raised in the same family, in which at least one sibling defined himself or herself as homosexual. Some of these pairs were identical twins (who share all genes), some were fraternal twins (who share some genes), and some were adoptive brothers or sisters (who share no genes).

The results offer some support that homosexuality, like heterosexuality, results from a combination of biological and social factors. Among the men and women studied, when one twin was homosexual, there was about a 50 percent chance that the other twin was homosexual. In other words, a woman or man is five times as likely to be lesbian or gay if his or her identical twin is lesbian or gay than if his or her sibling is lesbian or gay but related only through adoption. These results offer some support for the importance of biological factors, since the higher the percentage of shared genes, the greater the percentage of cases in which both siblings were homosexual. However, because approximately half of the identical twin brothers and sisters of homosexuals were not themselves homosexual, social learning must also be involved; otherwise one would expect all identical twin siblings of homosexuals to be homosexual as well.

Clearly, even studies of identical twins cannot fully isolate biological from social factors. It is often the case that even in infancy, identical twins are treated more like each other by parents, peers, and teachers than are fraternal twins, who in turn are treated more like each other than are adoptive siblings. Thus, identical twins may have more than genes in common: They may also share a higher proportion of similar socializing experiences. Sociologist Peter Bearman has shown the intricate ways that genetics and social experience are intertwined. Bearman (2002) found that males with a female twin are twice as likely to report same-sex attractions. He theorized that parents of opposite-sex twins are more likely to give them unisex treatment, leading to a less traditionally masculine influence on the males. Having an older brother decreases the rate of homosexuality. Bearman hypothesized that an older brother establishes gender-socializing mechanisms for the younger brother to follow, which allows him to compensate for unisex treatment. Bearman's work is consistent with the statements offered by professional organizations such as the American Academy of Pediatrics, which concludes that "sexual orientation probably is not determined by any one factor but by a combination of genetic, hormonal, and environmental influences" (American Academy of Pediatrics 2004).

HOMOPHOBIA

homophobia • An irrational fear or disdain of homosexuals.

Homophobia, a term coined in the late 1960s, refers to both attitudes and behaviors marked by an aversion to or hatred of homosexuals, their lifestyles, and their practices. It is a form of prejudice reflected not only in overt acts of hostility and violence toward lesbians and gays but also in forms of verbal abuse that are widespread in American culture, for example, using terms like *fag* or *homo* to insult heterosexual males or using female-related offensive terms such as *sissy* or *pansy* to insult gay men.

One recent study of homophobia in U.S. schools concluded that the estimated 2 million lesbian, gay, and bisexual middle and high school students are frequently the targets of humiliating harassment and, sometimes, physical abuse. This harassment may have dire consequences, as evidenced in the case of Tyler Clementi, the Rutgers University freshman who committed suicide in September 2010 after being harassed and humiliated by his roommate Dharun Ravi. Interviews with lesbian, gay, and bisexual students, as well as youth service providers, teachers, administrators, counselors, and parents in seven states, found harassment to be a common and painful experience among lesbian, gay, and bisexual students (Bochenek and Brown 2001).

The Stonewall Inn nightclub raid in 1969 is regarded as the first shot fired in the battle for gay rights in the United States. The twenty-fifth anniversary of the event was commemorated in New York City with a variety of celebrations as well as discussions on the evolution and future of gay rights.

Some studies estimate that as many as 90 percent of gay and lesbian teens have experienced harassment at school (National Youth Association 2010). A 2013 study of cyberbullying found that 42 percent of gay and lesbian teens but just 15 percent of straight teens were harassed or bullied online (Gay, Lesbian, and Straight Education Network 2013).

Homophobia is widespread in U.S. culture, although it is slowly starting to erode. In 2013, a Gallup poll found that 59 percent of Americans viewed same-sex relationships as morally acceptable; this signifies a marked increase from 2001, when just 40 percent of Americans agreed with the sentiment (Gallup Organization 2013a). In May 2011, for the first time in its history, a Gallup poll found that the majority of Americans (53 percent) supported gay marriage (Gallup Organization 2013b). State policies both reflect and shape private attitudes; as we saw in Chapter 11, nineteen states plus Washington, D.C., currently allow legal access to same-sex marriage.

THE MOVEMENT FOR GAY AND LESBIAN CIVIL RIGHTS

Until recently, most gays and lesbians hid their sexual orientation for fear that "coming out of the closet"—publicly revealing one's sexual orientation—would cost them their jobs, families, and friends and leave them open to verbal and physical abuse. Yet, since the late 1960s, many gays and lesbians have acknowledged their homosexuality openly, and in some cities the lives of lesbian and gay Americans have become quite normalized (Seidman et al. 1999). New York City, San Francisco, London, and other large metropolitan areas worldwide have thriving gay and lesbian communities. Coming out may be important not only for the person who does so but also for others in the larger society: Previously closeted lesbians and gays discover they are not alone, while heterosexuals recognize that people whom they admire and respect are homosexual. Although famous actors, singers, and performers such as Ricky Martin, Ellen DeGeneres, and Elton John have been "out" publicly for several years, gays and lesbians in other professions have been more reticent about acknowledging their sexual orientation, perhaps out of fear of persecution. NBA basketball player Jason Collins made national news in April 2013 when he told reporters that he was gay. With his announcement, Collins became the first active player in one of the four major American professional team sports to announce that he is gay (ESPN 2013a). Less than a year later, Michael Sam became the first openly gay player in the NFL when he was drafted by the St. Louis Rams in May 2014.

The current global wave of gay and lesbian civil rights movements began partly as an outgrowth of the U.S. social movements of the 1960s, which emphasized pride in racial and ethnic identity. One pivotal event was the Stonewall riots in June 1969, when New York City's gay community—angered by continual police harassment—fought the New York Police Department for two days (D'Emilio 1983; Weeks 1977). The Stonewall riots became a symbol of gay pride. In May 2005, the International Day Against Homophobia (IDAHO) was first celebrated, with events held in more than forty countries. Clearly, significant strides have been made, although discrimination and homophobia remain serious problems for many lesbian, gay, and bisexual Americans.

Today there is a growing movement worldwide for the civil rights of gays and lesbians. The International Lesbian, Gay, Bisexual, Trans and Intersex Association

Protesters in St. Petersburg stand up against anti-LGBT legislation in Russia. In June 2013 President Vladimir Putin signed into a law a ban on gay media, symbols, and writings.

(ILGA), which was founded in 1978, has 1,044 member organizations from 117 countries (ILGA 2014). It holds international conferences, supports lesbian and gay social movement organizations, and lobbies international organizations. For example, it persuaded the Council of Europe to require all of its member nations to repeal laws banning homosexuality. In general, active lesbian and gay social movements thrive in countries that emphasize individual rights and liberal state policies (Frank and McEneaney 1999).

HOW DOES THE SOCIAL CONTEXT OF BODIES, SEXUALITY, AND HEALTH AFFECT YOUR LIFE?

As we have seen in this section, our bodies, health, health behaviors, and sexual orientations and practices reflect a complex set of biological, social, cultural, and historical influences. For example, although most American young adults believe they have the freedom to choose whomever they like as their romantic partner (and turn up their noses at the idea of arranged marriage), the gender of whom we choose, what we deem attractive, when and under what circumstances we engage in sexual relationships, and even whether we have the legal right to marry our partner are powerfully shaped by laws, norms, and cultural practices.

Similarly, although most people believe that their body size and shape reflect their own personal efforts, such as going to the gym four times a week and counting calories, or biological factors (e.g., "good genes"), sociologists have documented that social factors such as race, class, gender, and region affect one's access to health-enhancing resources like healthy food, safe walking and running paths, and high-quality health care. Solutions to sweeping public health crises, like the obesity epidemic, often require strategies that alter both individual-level choices and behaviors and macrosocial structures. Public programs that target both macro and micro levels, by encouraging healthier food choices and exercise among individuals and by making larger social changes—such as bringing grocery stores and healthy foods to inner-city neighborhoods and ensuring that major corporations that supply foods to public schools abide by healthier food production guidelines—are likely to be more effective. Although it is too soon to tell whether the health care reforms implemented by President Barack Obama will be effective in eradicating persistent race and socio-economic disparities in health, programs such as early screening for high blood pressure, obesity, substance use, and depression may help to ensure that health problems are detected in their earliest stages and that timely treatment is sought. Through the use of these strategies, it is possible that the United States may ultimately reach the goal articulated by the federal government in Healthy People 2020 to "achieve health equity, eliminate disparities, and improve the health of all groups" (U.S. Department of Health and Human Services 2010). ✓

CONCEPT CHECKS ✓

1. Describe several changes in sexual practices over the past two centuries.

2. What are the most important contributions of Alfred Kinsey's research on sexuality?

3. Name at least three important findings about sexual behavior discovered since Kinsey.

4. What is sexual orientation?

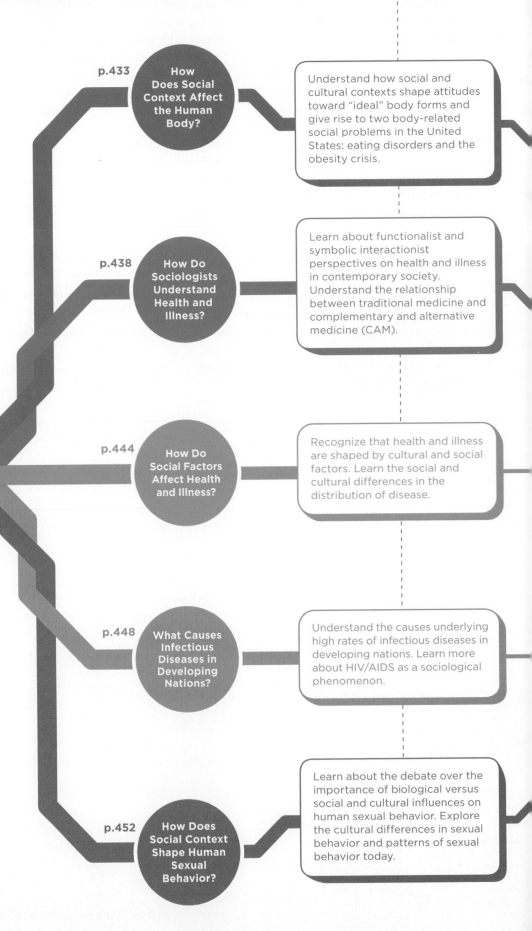

EXERCISES:
Thinking Sociologically

1. Obesity is a major health concern in the United States, especially among poor Americans, blacks, and Latinos. What types of public programs do you believe will be most effective in fighting the obesity epidemic? Why do you think the programs you've proposed are necessary?

2. Statistical studies of our national health show a gap in life expectancies between the rich and the poor. Review all the major factors that would explain why rich people live about eight years longer than poor people.

3. This chapter discusses the biological and sociocultural factors associated with sexual orientation. Why are twin studies the

Chapter 14

The Sociology of the Body: Health, Illness, and Sexuality

most promising type of research on the genetic basis of sexual orientation? Summarize the analysis of these studies, and show whether it presently appears that sexual orientation results from genetic differences, sociocultural practices and experiences, or both.

p.433 **How Does Social Context Affect the Human Body?**

Understand how social and cultural contexts shape attitudes toward "ideal" body forms and give rise to two body-related social problems in the United States: eating disorders and the obesity crisis.

p.438 **How Do Sociologists Understand Health and Illness?**

Learn about functionalist and symbolic interactionist perspectives on health and illness in contemporary society. Understand the relationship between traditional medicine and complementary and alternative medicine (CAM).

p.444 **How Do Social Factors Affect Health and Illness?**

Recognize that health and illness are shaped by cultural and social factors. Learn the social and cultural differences in the distribution of disease.

p.448 **What Causes Infectious Diseases in Developing Nations?**

Understand the causes underlying high rates of infectious diseases in developing nations. Learn more about HIV/AIDS as a sociological phenomenon.

p.452 **How Does Social Context Shape Human Sexual Behavior?**

Learn about the debate over the importance of biological versus social and cultural influences on human sexual behavior. Explore the cultural differences in sexual behavior and patterns of sexual behavior today.

universal health coverage •
social class gradient in health •
sociology of the body

obesity • socialization of nature

1. Why is anorexia more likely to strike young women than other subgroups?
2. What explanations are offered for the recent increase in obesity rates?
3. What policy solutions have been offered for the obesity crisis?

sick role • stigma • complementary and alternative medicine (CAM) • biomedical model of health

1. How do functionalist theorists and symbolic interactionists differ in their perspectives on health and illness?
2. What is stigma, and how does it pertain to health and illness?
3. What is the biomedical model of health?
4. Compare complementary and alternative medicine.

1. How do social class and race affect health?
2. Name at least two explanations for the gender gap in health.
3. Name at least two reasons why the gender gap in life expectancy may narrow in the future.

1. Why are infectious diseases more common in developing nations than in the United States today?
2. What are three social consequences of the AIDS epidemic in developing nations?

sexual orientation •
heterosexuality • homosexuality
• homophobia

1. Describe several changes in sexual practices over the past two centuries.
2. What are the most important contributions of Alfred Kinsey's research on sexuality?
3. Name at least three important findings about sexual behavior discovered since Kinsey.
4. What is sexual orientation?

15 Urbanization, Population, and the Environment

THE BIG QUESTIONS

HOW DO CITIES DEVELOP AND EVOLVE?

Learn how cities have changed as a result of industrialization and urbanization. Learn how theories of urbanism have placed increasing emphasis on the influence of socioeconomic factors on city life.

HOW DO RURAL, SUBURBAN, AND URBAN LIFE DIFFER IN THE UNITED STATES?

Learn about the recent key developments affecting American cities, suburbs, and rural communities in the last several decades: suburbanization, urban decay, gentrification, and population loss in rural areas.

HOW DOES URBANIZATION AFFECT LIFE ACROSS THE GLOBE?

See that global economic competition has a profound impact on urbanization and urban life. Recognize the challenges of urbanization in the developing world.

WHAT ARE THE FORCES BEHIND WORLD POPULATION GROWTH?

Learn why the world population has increased dramatically and understand the main consequences of this growth.

HOW DO URBANIZATION AND ENVIRONMENTAL CHANGES AFFECT YOUR LIFE?

See that the environment is a sociological issue related to urbanization and population growth.

China has undergone rapid economic development over the past three decades, yet this growth has come at great environmental cost. Sixteen of the twenty most polluted cities in the world are in China, and the smog can be heavy enough to compel the closure of highways and schools.

With a population of 1.36 billion, China is the most populous country in the world and accounts for almost one-fifth of the world's total population (U.S. Census Bureau 2014). China's population growth has been accompanied by rapid economic growth; the nation's economy grew at a rate of nearly 10 percent a year from roughly 1980 through 2010. In their rush to re-create the industrial revolution that made Western nations wealthy, Chinese manufacturers—spurred on by strong state support—have become the world's dominant producers of steel, coke, aluminum, cement, chemicals, leather, and paper. China has become the world's factory, but also its smokestack (Landler and Kahn 2007). This rapid industrialization has lifted hundreds of millions of people out of poverty and into the middle class, but at a high environmental cost. Toxic chemical spills have threatened the water supply of millions of people, while the air in major cities has become so polluted that the ultramodern skyscrapers that seemingly go up overnight are often not visible. Sixteen of the twenty most polluted cities in the world are in China (Wagstaff 2013).

The environmental threats are so acute that in February 2011, the nation's environment minister Zhou Shengxian publicly announced that pollution and the nation's high demand for resources—both consequences of prior economic growth—may, ironically, threaten their future economic growth. Making his remarks before the annual session of China's parliament, Zhou noted that manufacturers' heavy reliance on coal and high levels of carbon dioxide (CO_2) emissions could threaten the nation's future. China is the world's leading emitter of greenhouse gases and is highly dependent on coal, which feeds 70 percent of its energy needs (Jacobs 2011). In an uncharacteristically bold proclamation, Zhou warned that "the depletion, deterioration, and exhaustion of resources and the worsening ecological environment have become bottlenecks and grave impediments to the nation's economic and social development" (Jacobs 2011). Two years later, in 2013, Chinese premier Li Keqiang similarly admitted that he was "quite upset" about the nation's smog problem. Even the state-run newspaper *China Daily*, historically known for keeping the nation's problems under wraps, described the nation's major cities as "barely suitable for living," given persistent environmental threats (Wagstaff 2013).

These high levels of discontent were pivotal in triggering several policy initiatives. For instance, in 2011, China's then-prime minister Wen Jiabao lowered the nation's target economic growth rate from 7.5 to 7 percent, recognizing the impact of rapid economic growth on the environment. In 2012, the nation registered a 7.8 percent growth rate, which was slightly higher than its official target of 7 percent yet considerably lower than the nearly 10 percent growth rate of the previous three decades (World Bank 2014a). Defending his call for the lowered growth rate, former Prime Minister Wen warned, "We must no longer sacrifice the environment for the sake of rapid growth and reckless roll-outs, as that would result in unsustainable growth featuring industrial overcapacity and intensive resource consumption." Just two years later, the nation's political leaders are seeing the serious toll that such "reckless roll-outs" have taken on the environment. In 2013, the Chinese government acknowledged that it would need to spend nearly $817 billion each year to fight air pollution (Yongqiang 2013).

A coal miner emerges from a mine after a day's work in Shanxi Province, China.

The potentially dire future facing China reveals in vivid detail the ways that population growth, urbanization, industrialization, and the environment are intertwined. How exactly do these forces mutually influence one another? In the case of China, the rush to develop and meet the demands of its burgeoning population has severely taxed and depleted the nation's natural resources. China has embarked on building a network of highways, like the United States did a half-century ago. The nearly 53,000 miles of new roads will connect all major cities in China, supporting (and generating) automobile use that is projected to outstrip that of the United States by the middle of the century—or earlier. For a country where as recently as twenty-five years ago the bicycle and rickshaw were the principal means of transportation, this is an enormous transformation, and one that will contribute to urban traffic congestion, along with increased levels of energy use and pollution. As China makes the transition from rural to urban in record time, its planners call for relocating some 400 million people—more than the entire U.S. population—to newly built urban centers over the next twenty-five years. If achieved, this will require the construction of half of all the buildings in the world during that time (Economy 2007).

China's booming economy also depends on burning coal. Every week or so a new coal-burning power plant is brought online, most often one using outmoded technology. The sulfur dioxide from these plants is believed to contribute to nearly a half-million deaths a year in China, while causing acid rain that poisons lakes, rivers, and farmlands. Climate-changing smoke and soot from China's power plants have been detected across the Pacific Ocean in California. If China continues on its present course, its demand for energy will double over the next quarter-century, while its increased production of global warming gases will outstrip that of all other industrial countries combined (Bradsher and Barboza 2006). Predictions like these contributed, in part, to the bold moves made by Chinese premier Wen Jiabao and environment minister Zhou Shengxian, when they publicly warned their nation about the threats that development and population growth hold for the country's environmental and economic well-being.

Yet China's environmental and economic threats are not wholly due to internal factors such as population growth. The populous Asian nation also is affected by the acts of nations and governments across the globe. For example, ThyssenKrupp's former steel mill in the Ruhr valley of Germany has since relocated to China. This relocation of a polluting steel plant from Germany to China is just one way in which the environmental costs of a global economy have been transferred from wealthy industrial nations to poorer, less developed ones.

In this chapter we examine the ways in which population growth, urbanization, and environmental change go hand in hand, against the backdrop of rapid industrialization that is transforming many parts of the world. We begin by studying the origins of cities and the vast growth in the numbers of city dwellers that has occurred over the past century. From there, we review the most influential theories of urban life. We then move on to consider patterns of urban development in North America compared with cities in the developing world. Cities in the developing world are growing at an enormous rate. We consider why this is happening and at the same time look at changes now taking place in world population patterns. We conclude by assessing the connections between urbanization, world population growth, and environmental problems.

HOW DO CITIES DEVELOP AND EVOLVE?

CITIES IN TRADITIONAL SOCIETIES

Learn how cities have changed as a result of industrialization and urbanization. Learn how theories of urbanism have placed increasing emphasis on the influence of socioeconomic factors on city life.

The world's first cities appeared about 3500 BCE, in the river valleys of the Nile in Egypt, the Tigris and Euphrates in what is now Iraq, and the Indus in what is today Pakistan. Cities in traditional societies were very small by modern standards. Babylon, for example, one of the largest ancient Middle Eastern cities, extended over an area of only 3.2 square miles, and at its height, around 2000 BCE, probably numbered no more than 15,000 to 20,000 people. Rome under Emperor Augustus in the first century BCE was easily the largest premodern city outside China, with some 300,000 inhabitants—the population of Anchorage, Alaska, Cincinnati, Ohio, or Pittsburgh, Pennsylvania, today.

Most cities of the ancient world shared certain features. They were usually surrounded by walls that served as a military defense and emphasized the separation of the urban community from the countryside. The central area of the city was almost always occupied by a religious temple, a royal palace, government and commercial buildings, and a public square. This ceremonial, commercial, and political center was sometimes enclosed within a second, inner wall and was usually too small to hold more than a minority of the citizens. Although it usually contained a market, the center was different from the business districts found at the core of modern cities because the main buildings were nearly always religious and political rather than commercial (Fox 1964; Sjoberg 1960, 1963; Wheatley 1971).

The dwellings of the ruling class or elite tended to be concentrated in or near the center. Less privileged groups lived toward the perimeter of the city or outside the walls, moving inside if the city came under attack. Different ethnic and religious communities were often segregated in separate neighborhoods, where their members lived and worked. Sometimes these neighborhoods were also surrounded by walls. Communication among city dwellers was erratic. Lacking any form of printing press, and with very low literacy rates, public officials had to shout at the tops of their voices to deliver pronouncements. "Streets" were usually strips of land on which no one had yet built. A few traditional civilizations boasted sophisticated road systems linking particular cities, but these existed mainly for military purposes, and transportation for the most part was slow and limited. Merchants and soldiers were the only people who regularly traveled over long distances.

Although cities were the main centers for science, the arts, and cosmopolitan culture, their influence in surrounding areas was always weak. No more than a tiny proportion of the population lived in the cities, and the division between cities and countryside was pronounced. By far the majority of people lived in small rural communities and rarely came into contact with more than the occasional state official or merchant from the towns.

INDUSTRIALIZATION AND URBANIZATION

The contrast in size between the largest modern cities today and those of premodern civilizations is extraordinary. The most populous cities in the industrialized countries number over 10 million inhabitants. A **conurbation**—a cluster of cities and towns forming a continuous network—may include even larger numbers of people. The peak of urban life today is represented by what is called the **megalopolis**, the "city of cities." The term was originally coined in ancient Greece to refer to a city-state that was planned to be the envy of all civilizations. The current megalopolis, though, bears little relation to that utopia. The term was first applied in modern times to refer to the Northeast Corridor of the United States, an area covering some 450 miles from north of Boston to south of Washington, D.C. In this region, about 44 million people live at a density of over 700 persons per square mile. An urban population almost as large and dense is concentrated in the lower Great Lakes region surrounding Chicago.

Britain was the first society to undergo industrialization, beginning in the mid-eighteenth century. The process of industrialization generated increasing **urbanization**—the movement of the population into towns and cities, away from the land. In 1800, fewer than 20 percent of the British population lived in towns or cities with more than 10,000 inhabitants. By 1900, this proportion had risen to 74 percent. London held about 1.1 million people in 1800; by the beginning of the twentieth century, it had increased in size to a population of over 7.83 million, at that date the largest city ever seen in the world. It was a

conurbation • An agglomeration of towns or cities into an unbroken urban environment.

megalopolis • The "city of all cities" in ancient Greece—used in modern times to refer to very large conurbations.

urbanization • The development of towns and cities.

Traffic outside of the Bank of England in the financial district of London in 1896. In only a century, the population of London grew from just over 1 million people to over 7 million.

vast manufacturing, commercial, and financial center at the heart of the still-expanding British Empire.

The urbanization of most other European countries and the United States took place somewhat later. In 1800, the United States was more of a rural society than were the leading European countries. Fewer than 10 percent of Americans lived in communities with populations of more than 2,500 people. Between 1800 and 1900, as industrialization grew in the United States, the population of New York City leaped from 60,000 people to 8.1 million. Today, slightly more than 80 percent of Americans reside in metropolitan areas.

Urbanization in the twenty-first century is a global process into which the developing world is being drawn more and more (Kasarda and Crenshaw 1991). From 1900 to 1950, world urbanization increased by 239 percent, compared with a global population growth of 49 percent. The six decades since have seen an even greater acceleration in urbanization. From 1950 to 1986, urban population growth worldwide was 320 percent, while the total population grew by 54 percent. Most of this growth occurred in cities in developing world societies. In 1975, 39 percent of the world's population lived in urban areas; the figure was just over 50 percent in 2012 and is predicted to be 70 percent in 2050 (World Bank 2010). East and South Asia will be home to nearly half of the world's people in 2050. By that date, the urban populations of the developing countries will exceed those of Europe or the United States (United Nations 2007).

THEORIES OF URBANISM

THE CHICAGO SCHOOL

Scholars associated with the University of Chicago from the 1920s to the 1940s—especially Robert Park, Ernest Burgess, and Louis Wirth—developed ideas that were for many years the chief basis of theory and research in urban sociology. Two concepts developed by the "Chicago School" are worthy of special attention. One is the so-called **ecological approach** to urban analysis; the other, the characterization of urbanism as a *way of life*, developed by Wirth (Park 1952; Wirth 1938). It is important to understand these ideas as they were initially conceived by the Chicago School and to see how they have been revised and even replaced by sociologists in more recent decades.

ecological approach • A perspective on urban analysis emphasizing the "natural" distribution of city neighborhoods into areas having contrasting characteristics.

URBAN ECOLOGY

Ecology—the study of the adaptation of plant and animal organisms to their environment—is a term taken from the physical sciences. In the natural world, organisms tend to be distributed in systematic ways over the terrain, such that a balance or equilibrium between different species is achieved. The Chicago School believed that the locations of major urban settlements and the distribution of different types of neighborhoods within them can be understood in terms of similar principles. Cities do not grow up at random but in response to advantageous features of the environment. For example, large urban areas in modern societies tend to develop along the shores of rivers, in fertile plains, or at the intersection of trading routes or railways.

According to Park, cities become ordered into "natural areas" through processes of competition, invasion, and succession—all of which also occur in biological ecology. Patterns of location, movement, and relocation in cities, according to the ecological view, have a similar form. Different neighborhoods develop through the adjustments made by inhabitants as they struggle to gain their livelihoods. A city can be pictured as a map of areas with distinct and contrasting social characteristics, in concentric rings, broken up into segments. In the center are the **inner-city** areas, a mixture of big-business prosperity and decaying private homes. Beyond these are older established neighborhoods, housing workers employed in stable manual occupations. Farther out still are the suburbs, in which higher-income groups tend to live. Processes of invasion and succession occur within the segments of the concentric rings. Thus, as property decays in a central or near-central area, ethnic-minority groups might start to move into it. As they do so, more of the preexisting population start to leave, precipitating movement to neighborhoods elsewhere in the city or out to the suburbs. However, as we will see later in this chapter, these traditional patterns are starting to change: Wealthy persons and the young are flooding into urban areas, seeking amenities such as arts and entertainment, and suburban areas are becoming more desirable (and affordable) to poor and working-class persons.

inner city • The areas composing the central neighborhoods of a city, as distinct from the suburbs. In many modern urban settings in industrialized nations inner-city areas are subject to dilapidation and decay, the more affluent residents having moved to outlying areas.

Another aspect of the **urban ecology** approach emphasized the *interdependence* of different city areas. Differentiation—the specialization of groups and occupational roles—is the main way human beings adapt to their environment. Groups on which many others depend will have a dominant role, often reflected in their central geographical position. Business groups, for example, such as large banks or insurance companies, provide key services for many in a community and hence are usually to be found in the central areas of settlements (Hawley 1950, 1968).

urban ecology • An approach to the study of urban life based on an analogy with the adjustment of plants and organisms to the physical environment. According to ecological theorists, the various neighborhoods and zones within cities are formed as a result of natural processes of adjustment on the part of populations as they compete for resources.

URBANISM AS A WAY OF LIFE

Wirth's thesis of **urbanism** (1938) outlines the ways that life in cities is different from life elsewhere. In cities, large numbers of people live in close proximity to one

urbanism • A term used by Louis Wirth to denote distinctive characteristics of urban social life, such as its impersonal or alienating nature.

another without knowing most others personally—a fundamental contrast to small, traditional villages. Most contacts between city dwellers are fleeting and partial and are means to other ends rather than satisfying relationships in themselves. Interactions with sales clerks in stores, baristas at coffee shops, or passengers or ticket collectors on trains are passing encounters, entered into not for their own sake but as means to other aims.

Wirth was among the first to address the "urban interaction problem" (Duneier and Molotch 1999), the necessity for city dwellers to respect social boundaries when so many people are in close physical proximity all the time. Many people walk down the street in cities acting unconcerned about others near them, often talking on cell phones or listening to iPods that block out the sounds of urban life. Through such appearance of apathy they can avoid unwanted transgression of social boundaries.

Wirth's ideas have deservedly enjoyed wide currency. However, in assessing Wirth's ideas, we should consider that neighborhoods marked by close kinship and personal ties often are actively created by city life; they are not just remnants of a preexisting way of life that survive for a period within the city. Claude Fischer (1984) has put forward an explanation for why large-scale urbanism helps promote diverse subcultures. Those who live in cities are able to collaborate with others of similar background and interests to develop local connections, and they can join distinctive religious, ethnic, political, and other subcultural groups. A small town or village does not allow for the development of such subcultural diversity. For example, some gay and lesbian young people may find more hospitable communities in cities that have large gay subcultures like San Francisco, compared with the small towns where they may have grown up.

A large city is a world of strangers, yet it ultimately supports and creates personal relationships. It may be difficult to meet people when one first moves to a large city. But anyone moving to a small, established rural community may find the friendliness of the inhabitants largely a matter of public politeness—it may take years to become accepted when one is "new" in town. This is not the case in the city because cities are continually welcoming new, geographically mobile residents. Although one finds a diversity of strangers, each is a potential friend. And once within a group or network, the possibilities for expanding one's personal connections increase considerably.

JANE JACOBS: "EYES AND EARS UPON THE STREET"

Like most sociologists in the twentieth century, the Chicago School researchers were professors who saw their mission as contributing to a scholarly literature and advancing the field of social science. Yet one of the most influential urban scholars of the twentieth century, Jane Jacobs, author of *The Death and Life of Great American Cities* (1961), was an architecture critic with a high school education. Through her own independent reading and research in the 1950s, she transformed herself into one of the most learned figures in the emerging field of urban studies.

Like sociologists such as Wirth of the Chicago School before her, Jacobs noted that "cities are, by definition, full of strangers," some

The Castro district in San Francisco is not only open to but celebratory about its large and vibrant gay and lesbian population.

of whom are dangerous. She argued that cities are most habitable when they feature a diversity of uses, thereby ensuring that many people will be coming and going on the streets at any time. When enough people are out and about, Jacobs wrote, "respectable" eyes and ears dominate the street and are fixed on strangers, who will thus not get out of hand. The more people are out, or looking from their windows at the people who are out, the more their gazes will safeguard the street.

The world has changed a great deal since Jacobs wrote *The Death and Life of Great American Cities*. Most of the people on the sidewalks Jacobs was writing about were more alike in many respects than they are today; now homeless people, drug users, panhandlers, and others representing economic inequalities, cultural differences, and extremes of behavior can make sidewalk life unpredictable (Duneier 1999). Under these conditions, strangers do not necessarily feel the kind of solidarity and mutual assurance she described. Sociologists today must ask, What happens to urban life when "the eyes and ears upon the street" represent vast inequalities and cultural differences? Do the assumptions Jacobs made still hold up? In many cases the answer is yes, but in other cases the answer is no. Nearly five decades after her book was published, Jacobs's ideas remain extremely influential.

URBANISM AND THE CREATED ENVIRONMENT

created environment •
Constructions established by human beings to serve their needs, derived from the use of man-made technology, including roads, railways, factories, offices, homes, and other buildings.

Whereas the earlier Chicago School of sociology emphasized that the distribution of people in cities occurs naturally, more recent theories of the city have stressed that urbanism is not a natural process but rather is shaped by political and economic forces. These theories focus on the **created environment**, or those constructions established by humans to serve their own needs, including roads, railways, factories, offices, private homes, and other buildings. Urbanism is a core aspect of the created environment. Cities and urban areas were "created" by the spread of industrial capitalism.

According to this view, it is not the stranger on the sidewalk who is most threatening to many urban dwellers, especially the poor; instead, it is the stranger far away, working in a bank or real estate development company, who has the power to make decisions that transform whole blocks or neighborhoods (Logan and Molotch 1987). This focus on the political economy of cities, and on different kinds of strangers, represented a new and critical direction for urban sociology. It emphasizes the ways that everyday life in urban areas is shaped by macrosocial forces and institutions, including corporations and public policies.

According to social geographer David Harvey (1973, 1982, 1985), space is continually *restructured* in modern urbanism. The process is determined by where large firms choose to place their factories, research and development centers, and so forth; the controls that governments operate over both land and industrial production; and the activities of private investors, who are buying and selling houses and land. Businesses, for example, are constantly weighing the relative advantages of new locations against existing ones. As production becomes cheaper in one area than another, or as the firm moves from one product to another, offices and factories will be closed down in one place and opened up elsewhere. Thus, at one period, when there are considerable profits to be made, there may be a spate of office-block buildings in the center of large cities. Once the offices have been built and the central area redeveloped, investors look for the potential for further speculative building elsewhere. Often what is profitable in one period will not be so in another, when the financial climate changes.

The activities of private home buyers are strongly influenced by how far, and where, business interests buy up land, as well as by rates of loans and taxes fixed by local and central government. After World War II, for instance, there was vast expansion of suburban development outside major cities in the United States. This was partly due to ethnic discrimination and the tendency of whites to move away from inner-city areas. However, it was made possible, Harvey argues, only because of government decisions to provide tax breaks to home buyers and construction firms and the willingness of financial organizations to set up special credit arrangements. These provided the basis for the building and buying of new homes on the peripheries of cities and at the same time promoted demand for industrial products such as the automobile (Harvey 1973, 1982, 1985).

Like Harvey, Manuel Castells stresses that the spatial form of a society is closely linked to the overall mechanisms of its development. However, the nature of the created environment is not just the result of the activities of wealthy and powerful people. Castells stresses the importance of the struggles of underprivileged groups to alter their living conditions. Urban problems stimulate a range of social movements, concerned with improving housing conditions, protesting against air pollution, defending parks, and combating building development that changes the nature of an area. For example, Castells has studied the gay movement in San Francisco, which succeeded in restructuring neighborhoods around its own cultural values—allowing many gay organizations, clubs, and bars to flourish—and gained a prominent position in local politics (Castells 1977, 1983). ✓

CONCEPT CHECKS ✓

1. What are two characteristics of ancient cities?

2. What is urbanization? How is it related to globalization?

3. How does urban ecology use physical science analogies to explain life in modern cities?

4. What is the urban interaction problem?

5. According to Jane Jacobs, the more people are on the streets, the more likely the street life will be orderly. Do you agree with Jacobs's hypothesis and her explanation for this pattern?

HOW DO RURAL, SUBURBAN, AND URBAN LIFE DIFFER IN THE UNITED STATES?

Learn about the recent key developments affecting American cities, suburbs, and rural communities in the last several decades: suburbanization, urban decay, gentrification, and population loss in rural areas.

What are the main trends that have affected city, suburban, and rural life in the United States over the past several decades? How can we explain patterns such as suburban sprawl, the disappearance of traditional rural life, and population declines in central cities and older suburbs? These are questions we will take up in the following sections. One of the major changes in population distribution in the period since World War II is the movement of large parts of city populations to newly constructed suburbs; this movement outward has been a particularly pronounced feature of American cities and is related directly to central-city decay. At the same time, rural populations have continued to decline as young people seek richer professional and personal opportunities in our nation's large and small cities. We therefore begin with a discussion of rural America and suburbia before moving on to look at the inner city.

THE DECLINE OF RURAL AMERICA?

Rural life has long been the focus of romanticized images among Americans: close-knit communities and families, stretches of picturesque cornfields, and isolation from social problems such as poverty. Yet these stereotypes stand in stark contrast to life in many parts of rural America today.

Rural areas of the United States are defined by the Census Bureau as those areas located outside urbanized areas or urban clusters. Rural areas have fewer than 2,500 people and typically are areas where people live in open country (U.S. Bureau of the Census 2012g, 2013r). Rural America contains approximately 72 percent of the nation's land area, yet holds only about 15 percent of the total U.S. population. For most of the twentieth and twenty-first centuries, rural communities have experienced significant population losses, despite several modest short-term reversals in the 1970s and the 1990s (U.S. Department of Agriculture 2013). Of the 1,346 U.S. counties that shrank in population between 2000 and 2007, 85 percent were located outside metropolitan areas, and 59 percent rely heavily on farming, mining, and manufacturing as their main revenue sources (Mather 2008).

Population losses in rural areas are attributed to declines in farming and other rural industries, high poverty rates, scarce economic opportunities or lifestyle amenities for young people, lack of government services, and—in some regions—a dearth of natural amenities such as forests, lakes, or temperate winters. Population losses are compounded by the fact that most people leaving rural areas are young people, meaning that fewer babies are born to replace the aging population (Johnson 2006). Rural areas now face the difficult challenge of attracting and retaining residents and businesses.

Yet more troubling than the loss of population in rural areas are concerns about social problems, including high levels of child poverty, high rates of motor vehicle fatalities and other accidental deaths, and low levels of health and educational services (Mather 2008).

Young people often flee rural areas to seek employment and social opportunities in cities. Older adults, like the men pictured here in a diner in Booneville, Kentucky, are often left behind in small towns. In 1940 Booneville had a population of 283; in 2010, it was home to 81 people. Just 15 percent of Americans today reside in rural areas.

Child poverty is usually perceived as an urban problem, yet 2010 data from the U.S. Census Bureau reveal that rural America is far more likely to suffer from child poverty. In 2010, 22 percent of American children lived in poverty, yet this rate was 26 percent among children living in rural counties and 12 percent among children living in urban areas. The counties with persistent child poverty tend to cluster in Appalachia, the Mississippi Delta, the northern Great Plains, along the Texas-Mexico border, and in the Southwest. Although Appalachia is a largely white area, most rural counties are "majority-minority," meaning that less than 50 percent of the population is non-Hispanic white (Mattingly, Johnson, and Schaefer 2011). For example, the Mississippi Delta is largely black and the Texas-Mexico border is primarily Hispanic, whereas poor counties in the Midwest and Southwest have large Native American populations, often dwelling on reservations (O'Hare and Mather 2008).

Despite the challenges facing rural America, many rural sociologists are guardedly optimistic about the future of nonmetropolitan life. Technological innovations in transportation and telecommunications afford people flexibility to work away from their urban office. A number of government programs offer young people financial incentives to serve as teachers or health care professionals in remote areas, while not-for-profits like Teach for America place young teachers at schools in rural areas. However, such programs are likely to be effective only in attracting workers and businesses to rural areas that have at least some natural or recreational amenities (Johnson 2006).

SUBURBANIZATION

In the United States, **suburbanization**, the massive development and inhabiting of towns surrounding a city, rapidly increased during the 1950s and 1960s, a time of great economic growth. World War II had absorbed most industrial resources, and any development outside the war effort was restricted. But by the 1950s, war rationing had ended, and the postwar economic boom facilitated moving out of the city. The Federal Housing Administration (FHA) provided assistance in obtaining mortgage loans, making it possible in the early postwar period for families to buy housing in the suburbs for less than they would have paid for rent in the cities. The FHA did not offer financial assistance to improve older homes or to build new homes in the central areas of ethnically mixed cities; its large-scale aid went only to the builders and buyers of suburban housing.

Early in the 1950s, lobbies promoting highway construction launched Project Adequate Roads, aimed at convincing the federal government to support the building of highways. In 1956, the Highway Act was passed, authorizing $32 billion to be used for building such highways. The new highway program led to the establishment of industries and services in suburban areas themselves. Consequently, the movement of businesses from the cities to the suburbs took jobs in the manufacturing and service industries with them. Many suburban towns became essentially separate cities, connected by rapid highways to the other suburbs around them. From the 1960s on, the proportion of people commuting between suburbs increased more steadily than the proportion commuting to cities.

An important change in suburbs today is that more and more members of racial and ethnic minorities are moving there. Blacks accounted for 7 percent of

suburbanization • The development of suburbia, areas of housing outside inner cities.

(a) Suburban Levittown, New York, in the 1950s. (b) A housing development in the exurb Highland, California.

exurban county • A county that lies within a large metropolitan area but has less than 25 percent of its population in an urbanized area. Tends to sit at periphery of metropolitan areas.

the suburban population in 1990, 9 percent in 2000, and 10 percent in 2010. Comparable increases for Latinos were even steeper, climbing from 8 to 12 to 17 percent during the same time period. Whites as a share of the suburban population declined steeply, from 81 percent in 1990 to 72 percent in 2000 to just 65 percent in 2010. The steady increase in minority suburban populations was concentrated in so-called *melting-pot metros*, or the metropolitan regions of New York, Los Angeles, Chicago, San Francisco, Miami, and other immigrant gateway cities (Frey 2001). In 2010, for the first time, Hispanics rather than blacks made up the largest minority group in major U.S. cities (Frey 2011b). Members of minority groups move to the suburbs for reasons similar to those who preceded them: better housing, schools, and amenities.

However, one particular type of suburb has remained steadfastly white in the twenty-first century: the exurb. An **exurban county** is one that lies within the 100 largest metropolitan areas in the United States but has less than 25 percent of its population living in what the Census Bureau defines as "urbanized" areas. These counties tend to have relatively low population densities and sit on the periphery of metropolitan areas. Exurbs grew rapidly in the 2000s, and depended overwhelmingly on whites for growth during that decade. Whites accounted for 73 percent of population growth in exurbs between 2000 and 2010.

While the last several decades saw a movement from the cities to the suburbs, they also witnessed a shift in the regional distribution of the U.S. population from north to south and east to west. As a percentage of the nation's total population, the Northeast dropped from 25 to 18.5 percent and the Midwest from 29 to 22.3 percent. Meanwhile the population of the South increased from 30.7 to 36.2 percent and that of the West from 15.6 to 23 percent (U.S. Bureau of the Census 2005). These trends continue to be evident today. The 2010 census revealed that while population in the Northeast and Midwest grew by only 3.2 and 3.9 percent, respectively, population in the South and West grew by 14.3 and 13.8 percent, respectively (Mackun and Wilson 2011).

URBAN PROBLEMS

Inner-city decay is partially a consequence of the social and economic forces involved in the movement of businesses, jobs, and middle-class residents from major cities to the outlying suburbs, a trend that began in the 1950s. The manufacturing industries that provided employment for the urban blue-collar class largely vanished and were replaced by white-collar service industries. Millions of blue-collar jobs disappeared, and this affected in particular the poorly educated, drawn mostly from minority groups. Although the overall educational levels of minority groups have improved since the mid-twentieth century, the improvement has not been sufficient to keep up with the demands of an information-based economy (Kasarda 1993). William Julius Wilson (1991, 1996) has argued that the problems of the urban underclass have grown out of this economic transformation (see Chapter 8).

These economic changes also contributed to increased residential segregation of different racial and ethnic groups and social classes, as we saw in Chapter 10. Discriminatory practices by home sellers, real estate agents, and mortgage-lending institutions added to this pattern of segregation (Massey and Denton 1993). In the early 2000s, considering all metropolitan areas, African Americans in the United States lived in neighborhoods, both urban and suburban, that were predominantly black (U.S. Bureau of the Census 2005). Residential segregation as measured by the dissimilarity index ranging from 0 (complete integration) to 1 (complete segregation) indicated that in the early 2000s, on average, African Americans lived in neighborhoods with an index value of 0.64, down from 0.73 in 1980. That is, neighborhoods have become more racially integrated over the past few decades. Nevertheless, the country remains heavily segregated by race. Currently, the average white resident lives in a census tract (groupings of neighborhoods of 5,000 to 10,000 persons) that is 79 percent white; the average black resident lives in a tract that is 46 percent black; and while Hispanics constitute only 15 percent of the population, 45 percent of their neighbors are also Hispanic (Frey 2011a). The social isolation of minority groups, particularly those in the underclass or "ghetto poor," can escalate urban problems such as crime, lack of economic opportunities, poor health, and family breakdown (Massey 1996).

Does gentrification of a rundown inner-city area necessarily result in the dispossession of the existing population, or do renewed interest and an infusion of money in such areas promote a revitalization that works to their advantage? Not long ago, Clinton Street was a grim, graffiti-ridden streetscape (a) but it has evolved into a lively restaurant row on New York's Lower East Side (b).

Adding to these difficulties is the fact that city governments today operate against a background of almost continual financial crisis. As businesses and middle-class residents moved to the suburbs, the cities lost major sources of tax revenue. High rates of crime and unemployment in the city require it to spend more on welfare services, schools, police, and overall upkeep. Yet because of budget constraints, cities are forced to cut back many of these services. A cycle of deterioration develops in which the more suburbia expands, the greater the problems faced by city dwellers become. Problems of urban decline reached a pinnacle in July 2013 when the city of Detroit, Michigan, filed for bankruptcy. Over the course of several decades, both businesses and residents left the city for neighboring suburbs, depleting the city's tax base. By the late 2000s, when the auto industry was in serious crisis, most of the major auto companies had already fled the city and moved their factories to the suburbs. After years of paying its bills with borrowed money, the city finally succumbed to bankruptcy in 2013 (Bomey, Snavely, and Priddle 2013).

URBAN RENEWAL AND GENTRIFICATION

Urban decay is not wholly a one-way process; it can stimulate countertrends, such as **urban renewal**, or **gentrification**. Dilapidated areas or buildings may be renovated as more affluent groups move back into cities. Such a renewal process is called gentrification because those areas or buildings become upgraded and return to the control of the urban "gentry"—high-income dwellers—rather than remaining in the hands of the poor.

urban renewal • The process of renovating deteriorating neighborhoods by encouraging the renewal of old buildings and the construction of new ones.

gentrification • A process of urban renewal in which older, deteriorated housing is refurbished by affluent people moving into the area.

In *Streetwise: Race, Class, and Change in an Urban Community* (1990), sociologist Elijah Anderson analyzed the effect of gentrification on cities. Although the renovation of a neighborhood generally increases its value, it rarely improves the living standards of its current low-income residents, who are usually forced to move out. The poor residents who continue to live in the neighborhood receive some benefits in the form of improved schools and police protection, but the resulting increases in taxes and rents often force them to leave for a more affordable neighborhood, most often deeper into the ghetto.

The white newcomers come to the city in search of cheap "antique" housing, closer access to their city-based jobs, and a trendy urban lifestyle. They profess to be "open-minded" about racial and ethnic differences; in reality, however, little fraternizing takes place between the new and old residents unless they are of the same social class. Over time, the neighborhood is gradually transformed into a white middle-class enclave. ✓

CONCEPT CHECKS ✓

1. Describe at least two problems facing rural America today.

2. Why did so many Americans move to suburban areas in the 1950s and 1960s?

3. What are two unintended consequences of urbanization? How do they deepen socioeconomic and racial inequalities?

See that global economic competition has a profound impact on urbanization and urban life. Recognize the challenges of urbanization in the developing world.

HOW DOES URBANIZATION AFFECT LIFE ACROSS THE GLOBE?

In premodern times, cities were self-contained entities that stood apart from the predominantly rural areas in which they were located. Road systems sometimes linked major urban areas, but travel was a specialized affair for merchants, soldiers, and others who needed to cross distances with any regularity. Communication between cities was limited. The picture at the start of the twenty-first century could hardly be more different. Globalization has had a profound effect on cities by making them more interdependent and encouraging the proliferation of horizontal links between cities across national borders. Physical and virtual ties between cities now abound, and global networks of cities are emerging.

GLOBAL CITIES

The role of cities in the new global order has been attracting a great deal of attention from sociologists. Saskia Sassen has been one of the leading contributors to the debate on cities and globalization. She uses the term **global city** to refer to urban centers that are home to the headquarters of large, transnational corporations and a superabundance of financial, technological, and consulting services. In *The Global City* (1991), Sassen bases her work on the study of three such cities: New York, London, and Tokyo. The contemporary development of the world economy, she argues, has created a novel strategic role for major cities. Most such cities have long been centers of international trade, but they now have four new traits:

1. They have developed into command posts—centers of direction and policymaking—for the global economy.

global city • A city—such as London, New York, or Tokyo—that has become an organizing center of the new global economy.

2. They are the key locations for financial and specialized service firms, which have become more important than manufacturing in influencing economic development.
3. They are the sites of production and innovation in these newly expanded industries.
4. They are markets on which the "products" of financial and service industries are bought, sold, or otherwise disposed of.

Within the highly dispersed world economy of today, cities like these provide for central control of crucial operations. Global cities are much more than simply places of coordination, however; they are also contexts of production. What is important here is not the production of material goods, but the production of the specialized services required by business organizations for administering offices and factories scattered across the world and the production of financial innovations and markets. Services and financial goods are the "things" the global city makes.

INEQUALITY AND THE GLOBAL CITY

The new global economy is highly problematic in many ways. This is seen most clearly in the new dynamics of inequality visible within the global city. It is no coincidence that the central business district adjoins impoverished inner-city areas in many global cities; business and poverty should be seen as interrelated phenomena, as Sassen and others remind us. The growth sectors of the new economy—financial services, marketing, high technology—are reaping profits far greater than any found within traditional economic sectors. Those who work in finance and global services receive high salaries, and the areas where they live become gentrified. At the same time, manufacturing jobs are lost, and the very process of gentrification creates a vast supply of low-wage jobs—in restaurants, hotels, and boutiques. Affordable housing is scarce in gentrified areas, forcing an expansion of low-income neighborhoods. As the salaries and bonuses of the very affluent continue to climb, the wages of those employed to clean and guard their offices are dropping. Sassen (1998) argues that we are witnessing the "valorization" of work located at the forefront of the new global economy and the "devalorization" of work that occurs behind the scenes.

Within global cities, a geography of "centrality and marginality" is taking shape. Alongside resplendent affluence there is acute poverty. These two worlds exist side by side, yet actual contact between them can be surprisingly minimal. As Mike Davis (1990) noted in his study of Los Angeles, there has been a "conscious 'hardening' of the city surface against the poor." Accessible public spaces have been replaced by walled compounds, neighborhoods guarded by electronic surveillance. Benches at bus stops are short or barrel-shaped to prevent people from sleeping on them, the number of

Making Sociology Work
URBAN PLANNER

Many Americans believe that bigger is better when it comes to housing. That philosophy is the driving force behind a new and potentially troubling trend known as tearing down. The National Association of Home Builders estimates about 75,000 houses are being razed each year and replaced with bigger homes (Tarm 2006). Most of the homes being knocked down are located in urban or near-urban areas and are at least fifty years old. Home builders and real estate agents say that the process bolsters the tax base and helps keep families in cities and older suburban neighborhoods. Critics counter that the process is often done without thought to the overall design of the neighborhood, and that neighborhood character is lost when modern cookie-cutter homes replace older residences. For example, a study by the National Trust for Historic Preservation (Moe 2006) found that 1920s bungalows in Denver were being replaced with modern homes three times their size. Denver residents opposed to the teardown process are trying to have older neighborhoods designated as historic, and thus protected from razing. However, it takes two to six years to get this designation. It also costs thousands of dollars and requires that the structures actually be historic. Drawing on your sociological knowledge of suburbanization, urban renewal, and gentrification, what policies and practices would you develop if you were an urban planner? How would you defend your choices?

public toilets is fewer than in any other North American city, and sprinkler systems have been installed in many parks to deter the homeless from living in them. Police and city planners have attempted to contain the homeless population within certain regions of the city, but in periodically sweeping through and confiscating makeshift shelters, they have effectively created a population of "urban bedouins."

URBANIZATION IN THE DEVELOPING WORLD

In 2011, roughly 3.6 billion people, or just over half of the world's population, lived in cities (UNDP 2012). In 2011, more than 80 percent of persons in Australia, New Zealand, and Northern America lived in urbanized areas. Africa and Asia, in contrast, remain mostly rural, with 40 and 45 percent, respectively, of their populations living in urban areas.

The global urban population is expected to grow roughly 1.5 percent per year between 2025 and 2030. By the middle of the twenty-first century, the world's urban population will almost double, increasing from approximately 3.6 billion in 2011 to 6.4 billion in 2050. Yet nearly all of this growth will occur in cities of developing countries, with Africa and Asia urbanizing more rapidly than other nations (WHO 2014).

Why will urban growth be limited largely to developing nations in the coming decades? Two factors in particular must be taken into account. First, rates of population growth are higher in developing countries than they are in industrialized nations. Urban growth is fueled by high fertility rates among people already living in cities. Second, there is widespread *internal migration* from rural areas to urban ones. People are drawn to cities in the developing world either because their traditional systems of rural production have disintegrated or because the urban areas offer superior job opportunities. Rural poverty prompts many people to try their hand at city life. They may intend to migrate to the city only for a short time, aiming to return to their villages once they have earned enough money.

ECONOMIC IMPLICATIONS OF URBANIZATION IN THE DEVELOPING WORLD

informal economy • Economic transactions carried on outside the sphere of formal paid employment.

As a growing number of unskilled and agricultural workers migrate to urban centers, the formal economy often struggles to absorb the influx into the workforce. In most cities in the developing world, it is the **informal economy** that allows those who cannot find formal work to make ends meet. From casual work in manufacturing and construction to small-scale trading activities, the unregulated informal sector offers earning opportunities to poor or unskilled workers. For example, some scholars have estimated that as much as 90 percent of all employment in India is part of the "informal" economy, including shopkeepers, farmers, street vendors, rag pickers, tailors, repairmen, and black marketers (Yardley 2011).

Informal economic opportunities are important in helping thousands of families (and women, especially) to survive in urban conditions, but they are also problematic. The informal economy is untaxed and unregulated. It is also less productive than the formal economy. Countries where economic activity is concentrated in this sector fail to collect much-needed revenue through taxation. The low level of productivity also hurts the general economy—the proportion of the GDP generated by informal economic activity is much lower than the percentage of the population involved in the sector.

The OECD projects that a billion new jobs will be needed by 2025 to sustain the estimated population growth in cities in the developing world (OECD 1999). It is unlikely that all of these jobs will be created within the formal economy. Some development

URBANIZATION

Today more than half of the world's population resides in cities. By 2050, nearly 70 percent of the population will live in megacities of more than 10 million people.

CITY POPULATION
Numbers in millions

	2012	2025*
Tokyo, Japan	37.2	38.7
Delhi, India	22.7	32.9
Mexico City, Mexico	20.5	24.6
New York-Newark, USA	20.4	23.6
Shanghai, China	20.2	28.4
São Paulo, Brazil	19.9	23.2
Mumbai, India	19.7	26.6
Beijing, China	15.6	22.6
Dhaka, Bangladesh	15.4	22.9
Calcutta, India	14.4	18.7

*Projected

PERCENTAGE OF WORLD POPULATION LIVING IN CITIES

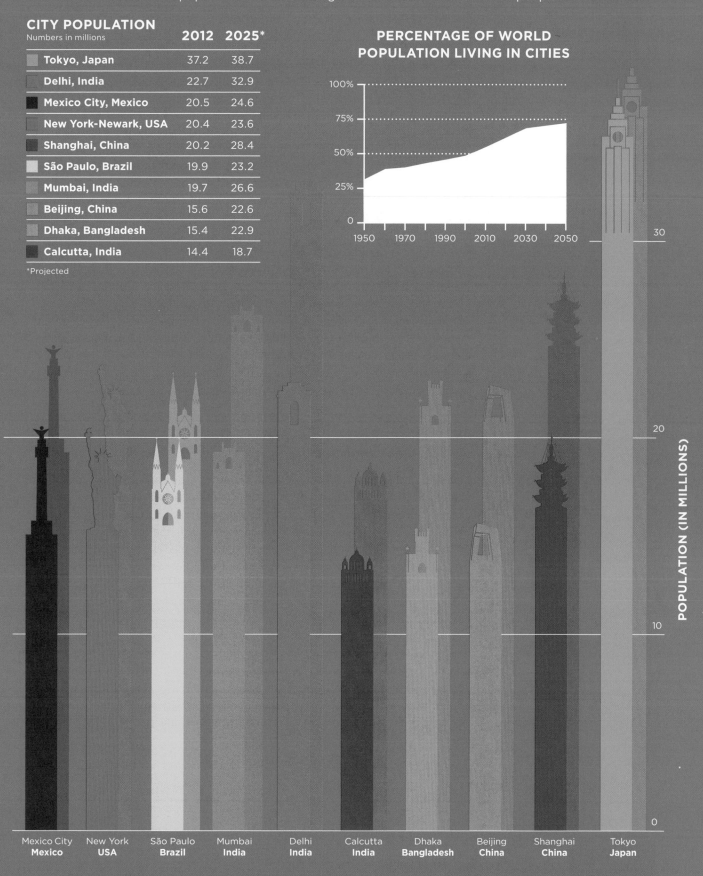

Source: UN Department of Economic and Social Affairs, Population Division 2012

analysts argue that attention should be paid to formalizing or regulating the large informal economy, where much of the excess workforce is likely to cluster in years to come.

ENVIRONMENTAL CHALLENGES OF URBANIZATION IN THE DEVELOPING WORLD

The rapidly expanding urban areas in developing countries differ dramatically from cities in the industrialized world. Although cities everywhere are faced with environmental problems, those in developing countries are confronted by particularly severe risks. As we saw earlier in this chapter, China's leaders have called for a lower economic growth rate, with the explicit goal of capping the nation's energy use and reducing environmental degradation. Pollution, housing shortages, inadequate sanitation, and unsafe water supplies are chronic problems for cities in less developed countries. Housing is one of the most acute problems in many urban areas. Cities such as Calcutta and São Paulo are massively congested. In São Paulo, it is estimated that there was anywhere from a 5.5 million unit to 7.2 million unit shortfall in habitable homes in 2011. Some scholars estimate that in order to adequately satisfy housing needs for the city's population, 1.8 million housing units would need to be built each year between 2011 and 2022 (Fez Ta Pronto 2014).

Congestion and overdevelopment in city centers lead to serious environmental problems in many urban areas. Mexico City is a prime example. About 94 percent of Mexico City consists of built-up areas, with only 6 percent of land being open space. The level of green spaces—parks and open stretches of green land—is far below that found in even the most densely populated U.S. or European cities. Pollution is a major problem, coming mostly from the cars, buses, and trucks that pack the inadequate roads of the city, the rest deriving from industrial pollutants. It has been estimated that living in Mexico City is equivalent to smoking forty cigarettes a day.

SOCIAL EFFECTS OF URBANIZATION IN THE DEVELOPING WORLD

Many urban areas in the developing world are overcrowded, and social programs are underresourced. Poverty is widespread, and existing social services cannot meet the demands for health care, family-planning advice, education, and training. The unbalanced age distribution in developing countries adds to their social and economic difficulties. Compared with industrialized countries, a much larger proportion of the population in the developing world is under age fifteen. For example, in many African nations, nearly half of the population is under age fifteen. In Niger, 52 percent of the national population is under fifteen, while this figure stands at 48 percent in Angola and Uganda, and 47 percent in Mali. By contrast, in Japan and Germany—two of the world's oldest populations—just 13 percent of the national population is under age fifteen (Kaiser Family Foundation 2012). A youthful population needs a good educational system, but many developing countries lack the resources to provide universal education. When their families are poor, many children must work full time, and others have to eke out a living as street children, begging for whatever they can. When the street children mature, most are unemployed, homeless, or both.

THE FUTURE OF URBANIZATION IN THE DEVELOPING WORLD

In considering the scope of the challenges facing urban areas in developing countries, it can be difficult to see prospects for change and development. Conditions of life in

Newspaper salesman Alvarado uses a mask to protect himself from air pollution as he sells papers at a busy crossroad in Mexico City. Behind him a screen indicates the day's pollution levels.

many of the world's largest cities seem likely to decline even further in the years to come. But the picture is not entirely negative.

First, although birthrates remain high in many countries, they are likely to drop in the years to come as urbanization proceeds (United Nations 2013c). Second, globalization is presenting important opportunities for urban areas in developing countries. With economic integration, cities around the world are able to enter international markets, to promote themselves as locations for investment and development, and to create economic links across the borders of nation-states.

Third, migrants to urban areas are often "positively selected" in terms of traits such as higher levels of educational attainment. Thus, migration may be beneficial to those who find better work opportunities, and for their families, who benefit from *remittances*—the money that the migrant workers send back home.

CONCEPT CHECKS ✓

1. Discuss the effects of globalization on cities.

2. What are the four main characteristics of global cities?

3. Urban growth in the developing world is much higher than elsewhere. Discuss several economic, social, and environmental consequences of such rapid expansion of cities in developing nations.

WHAT ARE THE FORCES BEHIND WORLD POPULATION GROWTH?

Learn why the world population has increased dramatically and understand the main consequences of this growth.

In late October 2011, the United Nations Population Fund announced that the world population had reached 7 billion. This announcement invited a flurry of proclamations about where, exactly, "Baby 7 Billion" was born, with India, the Philippines, and other nations claiming this honor (Rauhala 2011). Paul Ehrlich (Fremlin 1964) calculated in the 1960s that if the rate of population growth at that time continued, 900 years from now (not a long period in world history as a whole) there would be

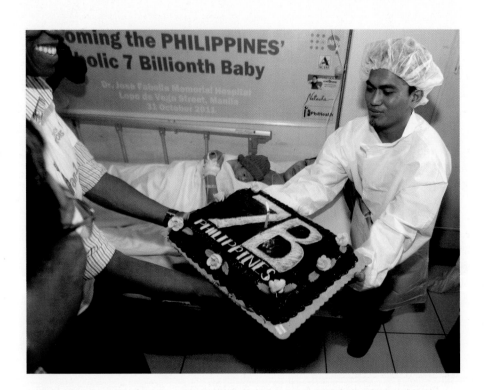

Hospital workers in the Philippines congratulate Camile Dalura on delivering the world's 7 billionth baby on October 31, 2011.

60,000,000,000,000,000 (60 quadrillion) people on the face of the earth. There would be 100 people for every square yard of the earth's surface, including both land and water.

Such a picture, of course, is nothing more than nightmarish fiction designed to drive home how cataclysmic the consequences of continued population growth would be. The real issue is what will happen over the next thirty or forty years, by which time, if current trends are not reversed, the world's population will already have grown to unsustainable levels. Partly because governments and other agencies heeded the warnings of Ehrlich and others forty years ago by introducing population-control programs, there are grounds for supposing that world population growth is beginning to trail off. Estimates calculated in the 1960s of the likely world population by the year 2000 turned out to be inaccurate. Nevertheless, considering that a century ago there were only 1.5 billion people in the world, this still represents growth of staggering proportions. Moreover, the factors underlying population growth are by no means completely predictable, and all estimates have to be interpreted with caution.

POPULATION ANALYSIS: DEMOGRAPHY

demography • The study of the size, distribution, and composition of populations.

The study of population is referred to as **demography**. The term was invented about a century and a half ago, at a time when nations were beginning to keep official statistics on the nature and distribution of their populations. Demography is concerned with measuring the size of populations, explaining their rise or decline, and documenting the distribution of such populations both within and across continents, nations, states, cities, and even neighborhoods. Population patterns are governed by three factors: births, deaths, and migrations. Demography is customarily treated as a branch of sociology because the factors that influence the level of births and deaths in a given group or society, as well as migrations of population, are largely social and cultural.

BASIC DEMOGRAPHIC CONCEPTS

Among the basic concepts used by demographers, the most important are crude birthrates, fertility, fecundity, and crude death rates. **Crude birthrates** are expressed as the number of live births per year per 1,000 persons in the population. They are called "crude" rates because of their very general character. Crude birthrates, for example, do not tell us what proportions of a population are male or female, or what the age distribution of a population is (the relative proportions of young and old people in the population). Where statistics are collected that relate birth or death rates to such categories, demographers speak of "specific" rather than "crude" rates. For instance, an age-specific birthrate might specify the number of births per 1,000 women in the twenty-five- to thirty-four-year-old age group.

If we wish to understand population patterns in any detail, the information provided by specific birthrates is normally necessary. Crude birthrates, however, may be useful for making overall comparisons among different groups, societies, and regions. Thus, the crude birthrate in the United States is almost 14 per 1,000. Other industrialized countries have lower rates: for example, 12 per 1,000 in Russia, and 8 per 1,000 in Germany and in Japan. In many other parts of the world, crude birthrates are much higher. In India, for instance, the crude birthrate is 20 per 1,000. In many African nations, it is more than 40 per 1,000. For example, the crude birthrate in Niger in 2013 was 46.8 (CIA 2013e).

Birthrates are an expression of the fertility of women. **Fertility** refers to how many live-born children the average woman has. A fertility rate is usually calculated as the average number of live births per 1,000 women of childbearing age. Fertility is distinguished from **fecundity**, which refers to the number of children women are biologically capable of bearing. It is physically possible for a normal woman to bear a child every year during the period when she is capable of conception. There are variations in fecundity according to the age at which women reach puberty and menopause, both of which vary among countries as well as among individuals. Although there may be families in which a woman bears twenty or more children, fertility rates in practice are always much lower than fecundity rates because social and cultural factors limit the actual number of children a woman gives birth to.

Crude death rates (also called "mortality rates") are calculated in the same way as birthrates—the number of deaths per 1,000 of population per year. Again, there are major variations among countries, but death rates in many societies in the developing world are falling to levels comparable to those of the West. The death rate in the United States in 2013 was 8 per 1,000. In India it was 7 per 1,000; in Ethiopia it was 9 per 1,000. A few countries have much higher death rates. In Sierra Leone, for example, the death rate was 22 per 1,000 throughout much of the 1990s and 2000s due in part to AIDS, warfare, and high infant mortality rates. However, as these problems subsided, the death rate declined to 11.3 by 2013 (CIA 2013e). Like crude birthrates, crude death rates only provide a very general index of **mortality** (the number of deaths in a population). Specific death rates give more precise information. A particularly important specific death rate is the **infant mortality rate**: the number of babies per 1,000 births in any year who die before reaching age one. One of the key factors underlying the population explosion has been reductions in infant mortality rates.

Declining rates of infant mortality are the most important influence on increasing **life expectancy**—that is, the number of years the average person can expect to live. In 1900, life expectancy at birth in the United States was about forty years. Today it has increased to over seventy-eight years. This does not mean, however, that most people at the turn of the century died when they were about forty years of age.

crude birthrate • A statistical measure representing the number of births within a given population per year, normally calculated as the number of births per 1,000 members. Although the crude birthrate is a useful index, it is only a general measure, because it does not specify numbers of births in relation to age distribution.

fertility • The average number of live-born children produced by women of childbearing age in a particular society.

fecundity • A measure of the number of children that it is biologically possible for a woman to produce.

crude death rate • A statistical measure representing the number of deaths that occur annually in a given population per year, normally calculated as the number of deaths per 1,000 members. Crude death rates give a general indication of the mortality levels of a community or society, but are limited in their usefulness because they do not take into account the age distribution.

mortality • The number of deaths in a population.

infant mortality rate • The number of infants who die during the first year of life, per 1,000 live births.

life expectancy • The number of years the average person can expect to live.

When there is a high infant mortality rate, as there is in many developing nations, the average life expectancy—which is a statistical average—is brought down by deaths that occurred at age 0 or 0.5 years, for example. If we look at the life expectancy of only those people who survive the first year of life, we find that in 1900 the average person could expect to live to age fifty-eight.

Illness, nutrition, and natural disasters are the other factors influencing life expectancy. Life expectancy has to be distinguished from **life span**, which is the maximum number of years that an individual could live. Although life expectancy has increased in most societies in the world over the past century, life span has remained unaltered. Only a small proportion of people live to be 100 or more.

life span • The maximum length of life that is biologically possible for a member of a given species.

DYNAMICS OF POPULATION CHANGE

Rates of population growth or decline are measured by subtracting the number of deaths per 1,000 over a given period from the number of births per 1,000; this is usually calculated annually. Some European countries have negative growth rates—in other words, their populations are declining. Virtually all the industrialized countries have growth rates of less than 0.5 percent. Rates of population growth were high in the eighteenth and nineteenth centuries in Europe and the United States but have since leveled off. Many developing countries today have rates of between 2 and 3 percent (Global Map 15.1). These may not seem very different from the rates of the industrialized countries, but in fact, the difference is enormous.

The reason is that growth in population is **exponential** rather than arithmetic. An ancient Persian myth helps illustrate this concept. A courtier asked a ruler

exponential growth • A geometric, rather than linear, rate of increase. Populations tend to grow exponentially.

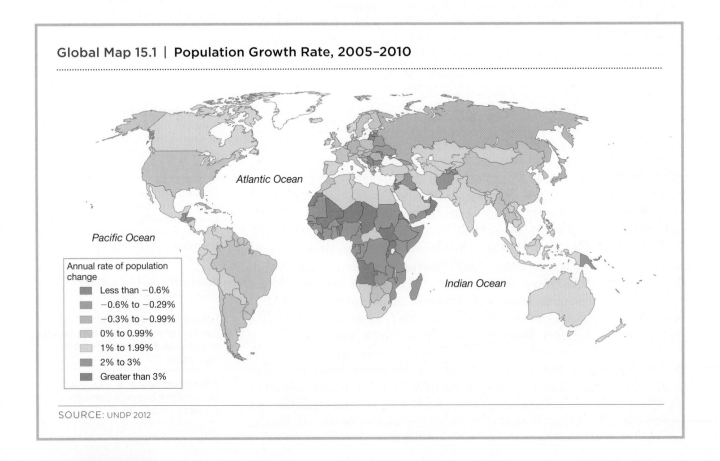

Global Map 15.1 | Population Growth Rate, 2005–2010

Annual rate of population change
- Less than −0.6%
- −0.6% to −0.29%
- −0.3% to −0.99%
- 0% to 0.99%
- 1% to 1.99%
- 2% to 3%
- Greater than 3%

SOURCE: UNDP 2012

to reward him for his services by giving him twice as many grains of rice for each service as he had the time before, starting with a single grain on the first square of a chessboard: that is, one grain on the first square, two on the second, four on the third, and so on. By the twenty-first square, over a million grains were needed, more than a trillion (a million million) on the forty-first square (Meadows et al. 1972). This myth conveys an important mathematical principle: that starting with one item and doubling it, doubling the result, and so on rapidly leads to huge numbers. Exactly the same principle applies to population growth. We can measure this effect by means of the **doubling time**, the period of time it takes for the population to double. The formula used to calculate doubling time is seventy divided by the current growth rate. For example, a population growth of 1 percent will produce a doubling of numbers in seventy years. At 2 percent growth, a population will double in thirty-five years, while at 3 percent it will double in twenty-three years.

doubling time • The time it takes for a particular level of population to double.

MALTHUSIANISM

In premodern societies, birthrates were very high by the standards of the industrialized world today. Nonetheless, population growth remained low until the eighteenth century because there was a rough overall balance between births and deaths. Although there were sometimes periods of marked population increase, these were followed by increases in death rates. In medieval Europe, for example, when harvests were bad, marriages tended to be postponed and the number of conceptions fell while deaths increased. These complementary trends reduced the number of mouths to be fed. No preindustrial society was able to escape from this self-regulating rhythm (Wrigley 1968).

During the rise of industrialism, many looked forward to a new age in which food scarcity would be a phenomenon of the past. The development of modern industry, it was widely supposed, would create a new era of abundance. In his celebrated work *Essay on the Principle of Population* (2003, orig. 1798), Thomas Malthus criticized these ideas and initiated a debate about the connection between population and food resources that continues to this day. At the time Malthus wrote, the population in Europe was growing rapidly. Malthus pointed out that whereas population increase is exponential, food supply depends on fixed resources that can be expanded only by developing new land for cultivation. Population growth, therefore, tends to outstrip the means of support available. The inevitable outcome is famine, which, combined with the influence of war and plagues, acts as a natural limit to population increase. Malthus predicted that human beings would always live in circumstances of misery and starvation, unless they practiced what he called "moral restraint." His cure for excessive population growth was for people to delay marriage and to strictly limit their frequency of sexual intercourse. (The use of contraception he proclaimed to be a "vice.")

For a while, **Malthusianism** was ignored because the population development of the Western countries followed a quite different pattern from that which he had anticipated. Rates of population growth trailed off in the nineteenth and twentieth centuries. In the 1930s there were major worries about population decline in many industrialized countries, including the United States. Malthus also failed to anticipate the technological developments fostering increases in food production that would develop in the modern era. The upsurge in world population growth in the twentieth century has again lent some credence to Malthus's views, although few support them in their original version. Population expansion in developing countries seems to be outstripping the resources that those countries can generate to feed their citizenry.

Malthusianism • A doctrine about population dynamics developed by Thomas Malthus, according to which population increase comes up against "natural limits," represented by famine and war.

THE DEMOGRAPHIC TRANSITION

demographic transition • An interpretation of population change, which holds that a stable ratio of births to deaths is achieved once a certain level of economic prosperity has been reached. According to this notion, in preindustrial societies there is a rough balance between births and deaths, because population increase is kept in check by a lack of available food, by disease, or by war. In modern societies, by contrast, population equilibrium is achieved because families are moved by economic incentives to limit the number of children.

Demographers often refer to the changes in the ratio of births to deaths in the industrialized countries from the nineteenth century onward as the **demographic transition**. This theory was first developed by Warren S. Thompson (1929), who described a three-stage process in which one type of population stability would eventually be replaced by another as a society reached an advanced level of economic development.

Stage 1 refers to the conditions characteristic of most traditional societies, in which both birth and death rates are high and the infant mortality rate is especially large. Population grows little if at all, as the high number of births is more or less balanced by the level of deaths. Stage 2, which began in Europe and the United States in the early part of the nineteenth century—with wide regional variations—occurs when death rates fall while fertility remains high. This is, therefore, a phase of marked population growth. It is subsequently replaced by stage 3, in which, with industrial development, birthrates drop to a level such that population is again fairly stable.

Industrial development was accompanied by a range of social changes that contribute to lower birthrates. As the economy transitioned from agricultural to manufacturing, parents no longer required many children to help maintain their farms. With the advent of compulsory schooling, children cost money rather than earned money for their families. Parents became increasingly concerned with "child quality" and providing resources to ensure the best possible life for their offspring, rather than "child quantity" or having many children. Industrial development also was accompanied by technologies that allowed women to control their own fertility, as well as a cultural change regarding people's views toward childbearing. How many children a woman would have was now viewed as under her own control, rather than a "gift from god." In contemporary society, as women have achieved higher levels of education and higher earnings in the labor market, the incentive to have fewer children has increased. Higher education among both men and women also is linked to delayed marriage and consequently, delayed (and thus diminished) childbearing (Caldwell et al. 2010).

The theories of demographic transition directly oppose the ideas of Malthus. Whereas for Malthus, increasing prosperity would automatically bring about population increase, the thesis of demographic transition emphasizes that economic development, generated by industrialism, would actually lead to a new equilibrium of population stability.

PROSPECTS FOR CHANGE

Fertility remains high in the developing world because traditional attitudes to family size have been maintained. Having large numbers of children is often still regarded as desirable, providing a source of labor on family-run farms. Some religions either are opposed to birth control or affirm the desirability of having many children. Contraception is opposed by Islamic leaders in several countries and by the Catholic Church, whose influence is especially marked in South and Central America.

Yet a decline in fertility levels has at last occurred in some large developing countries. In an effort to slow population growth, in 1979 the Chinese government established one of the most extensive programs of population control that any country has undertaken, with the goal of stabilizing the country's numbers at close to their current level. The government instituted incentives (such as better housing and free health care and education) to promote single-child families, whereas families who have more than one child face special hardships (wages are cut for those who have a third child). China's anti-natal, or population-limiting, policies have effectively transformed the Chinese population. During the 1950s, China had a total fertility rate (TFR) of roughly 6 children per woman. TFR refers to the average number of babies a woman will give birth to in her life, if she conforms to current age-specific fertility rates (ASFRs) through her lifetime. China's TFR fell to about 2.4 by 1990, and demographers pin the current TFR at roughly 1.5 to 1.9.

However, in 2013, the Chinese government abruptly relaxed their one-child policy. Married couples who reside in particular regions as well as couples who are themselves both only children are now allowed to have a second child. This loosening of the one-child policy could increase the number of births in China each year by 1 to 2 million—on top of the approximately 15 million births a year now. This policy shift was triggered by several unintended and undesirable consequences of the one-child policy. Many Chinese couples were angry over the restrictive environment they were living in, while the Chinese public worried that generations of only children (nicknamed "little emperors") were becoming self-absorbed adults. Yet the most serious concern was that there would be insufficient numbers of young people to support China's rapidly aging population (Buckley 2013).

Some claim that the demographic changes that will continue to occur over the next century will be greater than any before in all of human history. It is difficult to predict with any precision the rate at which the world population will rise, but the United Nations has several fertility scenarios. The "high" scenario places the world's population at more than 16.6 billion people by 2100! The "medium" fertility scenario, which the United Nations deems most likely, assumes that fertility levels will stabilize at just over 2 children per woman, resulting in a world population of 10.9 billion people in 2100 (United Nations 2013c).

Passengers travel in an overcrowded train in the eastern Indian city of Patna. The Indian railroad, one of the world's largest rail networks, serves over 13 million people a year and continues to be one of the only forms of affordable transportation available to the majority of Indians.

This overall population increase conceals two distinct trends. First, most developing countries will undergo the process of demographic transition described above. This will result in a substantial surge in the population as death rates fall. China is likely to see its population surpass 1.5 billion people before growth levels off. Areas in Asia, Africa, and Latin America will similarly experience rapid growth before the population eventually stabilizes.

The second trend concerns the developed countries that have already undergone the demographic transition. These societies will undergo very slight population growth, if any at all. Instead, a process of aging will occur in which the number of young people will decline in absolute terms and the older segment of the population will increase markedly (Figure 15.1). This will have widespread economic and social implications for developed countries. First, there will be an increase in the **dependency ratio**, the ratio of the number of economically dependent members of the population to the number of economically productive members. Economically dependent persons are those considered too young or old to work, typically those under age fifteen and over age sixty-five. Productive members of society are those of working age, typically ages fifteen through sixty-four. As the dependency ratio increases, pressure will mount on health and social services. Yet, as their numbers grow, older people will also have more political weight and may be able to push for higher expenditures on programs and services of importance to them.

What will be the consequences of these demographic changes? Some observers see the makings of widespread social upheaval—particularly in the developing countries undergoing demographic transition. Changes in the economy and labor markets may prompt widespread internal migration as people in rural areas search for work. The rapid growth of cities will be likely to lead to environmental damage, new public health risks, overloaded infrastructures, rising crime, and impoverished squatter settlements.

Famine and food shortages are another serious concern. There are already 842 million people in the world who suffer from hunger or undernourishment, and 98 percent of them live in developing nations (U.S. Department of Agriculture 2013). In some parts of the world, more than a third of the population are undernourished (United Nations Food and Agriculture Organization [UN FAO 2013b]). As the

dependency ratio • The ratio of people of dependent ages (children and the elderly) to people of economically active ages.

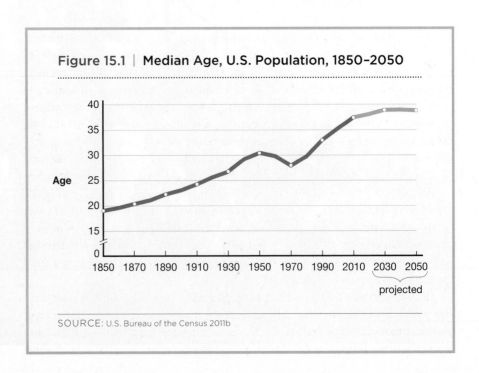

Figure 15.1 | Median Age, U.S. Population, 1850–2050

Age

SOURCE: U.S. Bureau of the Census 2011b

projected

population rises, levels of food output will need to rise accordingly to avoid widespread scarcity. Yet this scenario is unlikely; many of the world's poorest areas are particularly affected by water shortages, shrinking farmland, and soil degradation—processes that reduce, rather than enhance, agricultural productivity. It is almost certain that food production will not occur at a level to ensure self-sufficiency. Large amounts of food and grain will need to be imported from areas where there are surpluses. ✓

CONCEPT CHECKS

1. What is the difference between fertility and fecundity?

2. Explain Malthus's position on the relationship between population growth and the food supply.

3. Describe the stages of the demographic transition.

4. What is life expectancy? How does it differ from life span?

HOW DO URBANIZATION AND ENVIRONMENTAL CHANGES AFFECT YOUR LIFE?

> See that the environment is a sociological issue related to urbanization and population growth.

Today the human onslaught on the environment is so intense that few natural processes are uninfluenced by human activity. Nearly all cultivatable land is under agricultural production. What used to be almost inaccessible wildernesses are now often nature reserves, visited routinely by thousands of tourists. Modern industry, still expanding worldwide, has led to steeply climbing demands for sources of energy and raw materials. Yet the world's supply of such energy sources and raw materials is limited, and some key resources are bound to run out if global consumption is not restricted. Even the world's climate, as we shall see, has probably been affected by the global development of industry. Nearly every aspect of daily life has been affected, either directly or indirectly, by urbanization, population growth, and climate change.

GLOBAL ENVIRONMENTAL THREATS

One problem we all face concerns **environmental ecology**. The spread of industrial production may already have done irreparable damage to the environment. Ecological questions concern not only how we can best cope with and contain environmental damage but also the very ways of life within industrialized societies. According to one popular website, Global Footprint, if all people on earth were to somehow achieve the standard of living of the average American, it would require seven planets to feed, clothe, shelter, and provide the countless consumer items that make up what most of us consider a decent life. If developing countries are to achieve living standards comparable to those currently enjoyed in the West, global readjustments will be necessary.

According to the International Union for Conservation of Nature (IUCN 2013), the most widely accepted authoritative source, more than 20,000 species are currently threatened with extinction. The loss of biodiversity, in turn, means more to humans than merely the loss of natural habitat. Biodiversity also provides humans with new medicines and sources and varieties of food and plays a role in regulating atmospheric and oceanic chemistry.

Global environmental threats are of several basic sorts: pollution, the creation of waste that cannot be disposed of in the short term or recycled, and the depletion of resources that cannot be replenished. The amount of domestic waste—what goes into our garbage cans—produced each day in the industrialized societies is staggering;

environmental ecology •
A concern with preserving the integrity of the physical environment in the face of the impact of modern industry and technology.

A worker at an e-waste recycling company in Bangalore, India, shows shredded pieces of printed circuit boards of obsolete electronic gadgets undergoing the recycling process. E-waste is a growing environmental and public health concern as the world becomes more wired and companies introduce new products at a faster pace.

these countries have sometimes been called the "throwaway societies" because the volume of items discarded as a matter of course is so large. Food is mostly bought in packages that are thrown away at the end of the day. Some of these can be reprocessed and reused, but most cannot. The disposal of electronic waste—computers, mobile phones, MP3 players, and the host of toys and gadgets that contain electronic circuits—is a growing problem. Discarded electronics, which contain toxins that cause cancer and other illnesses, are routinely "recycled" to landfills in China, India, and other poor countries, where there are few if any safeguards against contaminating local watersheds, farmlands, and communities.

Global green movements and political parties (such as Friends of the Earth, Greenpeace, or Conservation International) have developed in response to these new environmental hazards. Although green philosophies are varied, a common thread concerns taking action to protect the world's environment, conserve rather than exhaust its resources, and protect the remaining animal species.

GLOBAL WARMING AND CLIMATE CHANGE

Global warming is thought to happen in the following way. Carbon dioxide and other greenhouse gases are released into the atmosphere by the burning of fuels such as oil and coal in cars and power stations and gases released into the air by the use of such things as aerosol cans, material for insulation, and air-conditioning units. This buildup of greenhouse gases in the earth's atmosphere functions like the glass of a greenhouse. The atmosphere allows the sun's rays to pass through but acts as a barrier to prevent the rays from passing back, causing the earth to heat up. For this reason, global warming is sometimes termed the "greenhouse effect."

In 2007 the Intergovernmental Panel on Climate Change (IPCC), a blue-ribbon group of scientists created by the United Nations Environment Program and its World Meteorological Organization in 1988, took the planet's temperature and found it has risen steadily since the mid-twentieth century. Rising temperatures result in the rapid shrinking of arctic ice caps, along with mountain glaciers; long-term droughts in some regions, with greater rainfall in others; an increase in hurricane activity in the North Atlantic; and in general, more turbulence in global weather. Most significantly, the IPCC report stated unequivocally that human activity is the principal source of global warming, very likely causing most of the temperature increase over the last century.

How does global warming affect our lives? Apart from severe droughts—which will turn once-fertile lands into deserts—global warming will threaten the water supplies of hundreds of millions of people, increase the danger of flooding for others, adversely affect agriculture in parts of the world, and further reduce planetary biodiversity. It will likely have devastating consequences for low-lying areas, as melting polar ice caps—particularly in Greenland and the Antarctic—lead

Kids play on a merry-go-round near an oil refinery at the Carver Terrace housing project playground in west Port Arthur, Texas. Port Arthur sits squarely on a two-state corridor routinely ranked as one of the country's most polluted regions.

to rising sea levels. Cities that lie near the coasts or in low-lying areas will be flooded and become uninhabitable. The IPCC specifically identified many potential impacts:

- *very likely* increase in frequency of hot extremes, heat waves, and heavy precipitation
- *likely* increase in tropical cyclone intensity; less confidence in global decrease of tropical cyclone numbers
- poleward shift of extratropical storm tracks with consequent changes in wind, precipitation, and temperature patterns
- *very likely* precipitation increases in high latitudes and likely decreases in most subtropical land regions, continuing observed recent trends

The IPCC (2007) suggests ways that the worst consequences of global warming can be mitigated. They include national policies that encourage water, land, and energy conservation, the development of alternative energy sources, and in general incorporating scientific thinking about global climate change into our ways of thinking about everything from tourism to transportation. While the IPCC report addresses government policies, it also stands to reason that individual behavior can make a difference, even if that difference is small. Because individuals in the United States and other advanced industrial nations consume far more than the average person in developing nations, their ecological footprint is much larger. Recycling, walking, or riding a bicycle rather than driving whenever possible, buying fuel-efficient cars, turning the heat down and the air-conditioning off—all of these are small steps that can add up, if practiced by a large enough number of people.

ENERGY

At current rates of use, the known oil resources of the world will be completely consumed by the year 2050. New reserves of oil may be discovered, or alternative sources of cheap energy invented, but there plainly is a point at which some key resources will run out if global consumption is not limited. China, with a population of 1.36 billion, is home to five times as many people as the United States. For the first time in 2010, it surpassed the United States as the largest consumer of energy in the world and as the world's largest producer of greenhouse gases, accounting for perhaps a quarter of the world's total. Most of America's energy comes from nonrenewable fossil fuels—mainly petroleum, and to a lesser degree coal and natural gas.

The high level of U.S. consumption is partly due to the fact that, because Americans have an advanced industrial economy and a high standard of living, they consume more energy from all sources (such as natural gas, coal, and electricity) than persons in all other nations (Figure 15.2). There is an emerging consensus among scientists and policymakers around the world that if economic development is to occur, it has to be concerned increasingly with conserving scarce resources, as well as reducing the production of greenhouse gases and other pollutants.

SUSTAINABLE DEVELOPMENT

sustainable development •
The notion that economic growth should proceed only insofar as natural resources are recycled rather than depleted; biodiversity is maintained; and clean air, water, and land are protected.

Rather than calling for a reining in of economic growth, more recent policy recommendations are focused on sustainable development. **Sustainable development** means that growth should, at least minimally, be carried on in such a way as to recycle physical resources rather than deplete them and to keep levels of pollution to a minimum.

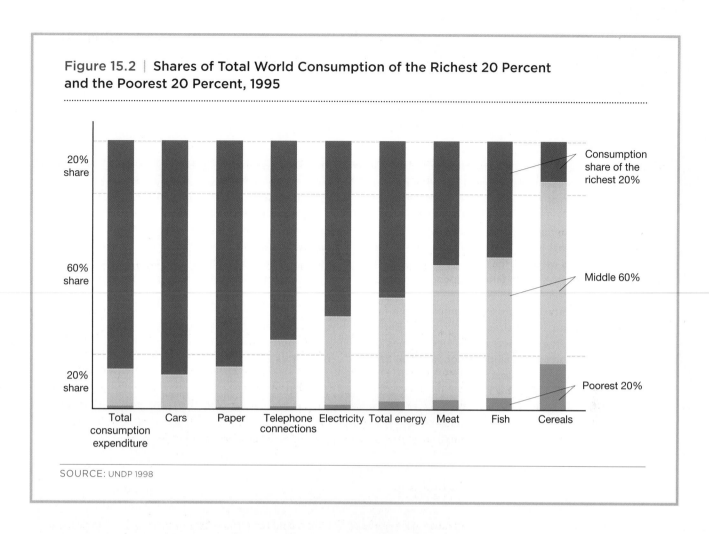

Figure 15.2 | Shares of Total World Consumption of the Richest 20 Percent and the Poorest 20 Percent, 1995

SOURCE: UNDP 1998

Critics see the notion of sustainable development as too vague and as neglecting the specific needs of poorer countries. According to critics, the idea of sustainable development tends to focus attention only on the needs of richer countries; it does not consider the ways in which the high levels of consumption in the more affluent countries are satisfied at the expense of other people. For instance, demands on Indonesia to conserve its rain forests could be seen as unfair because Indonesia has a greater need than the industrialized countries for the revenue it must forgo by accepting conservation.

PROSPECTS FOR CHANGE

Of all the environmental problems discussed in this chapter, global warming is arguably the most pressing. Greenhouse gases released in the atmosphere do not simply affect the climate of the country in which they were produced but alter climatic patterns for the entire world. For this reason, many policymakers and scientists believe that any viable solution to the problem must also be global in scale. Yet the political difficulties in negotiating an international treaty to reduce greenhouse gases are enormous and suggest that although globalization has ushered in a new era of international cooperation, the world is still far from being able to speak decisively with a unified political voice about many of the issues that it confronts.

In December 1997, delegates from 166 nations gathered in Kyoto, Japan, in an effort to hammer out an agreement to reduce global warming. The summit was the culmination of two years of informal discussions among the countries. World leaders,

What's Your Carbon Footprint?

As we saw earlier in this chapter, the United States is among the world's largest consumers of natural resources. According to Worldwatch Institute (2012), the United States makes up less than 5 percent of the global population yet uses about a quarter of the world's fossil fuel resources—burning up nearly 25 percent of the coal, 26 percent of the oil, and 27 percent of the world's natural gas. The many decisions that individuals make each day—including what kind of cars we drive, the size of the homes we purchase, and even how much time we spend in the shower each morning—contribute to the United States' high level of resource consumption. For example, while family sizes are shrinking, home sizes are increasing. Between 2009 and 2012, the average size of new homes grew by 8 percent, reaching an all-time high of 2,306 square feet. To put this in context, the average new home built in 1970 was just 1,400 square feet (Christie 2013).

Many Americans, however, especially young adults, are taking conscious steps to monitor their energy use, by biking rather than driving to school or work, recycling paper, bringing old cell phones to e-waste facilities, and using refillable water bottles. But how do we know whether these efforts are enough, or what their impact is? Many smartphone apps have been developed over the past five years to help us monitor our carbon footprints. For example, the app Carbon Footprint lets users track their fuel usage for all the cars they own. Each time a user fills his or her car with fuel, the app then tracks the miles per gallon and other statistics. It also reports one's estimated carbon dioxide emissions each year based on fuel use and driving habits (Wagner 2012). Similarly, the Extra Mile app calculates how much carbon dioxide one's car trip will produce based on the number of travelers and the car's fuel efficiency.

Moving beyond one's car, Zero Carbon tracks users' emissions linked to their daily routines and activities, compares them to global averages, and offers advice on how to reduce one's footprint. The app also lets users share their personal goals and suggestions on Facebook. These carbon footprint calculators make users much more aware of their daily energy use and suggest ways to reduce it.

A growing number of apps also help us to directly reduce our energy use. The app Trees for Cars helps people lower their greenhouse gas emissions by connecting them with others who would be willing to carpool together. The driver selects a meeting point, and the app then suggests nearby riders. If both the driver and riders accept one another's invitations, they'll be connected and can meet together for a carpool. The app also reports how much carbon dioxide is saved by each ride (Moss 2013).

A student bicycles around West Village on the campus of the University of California, Davis. West Village is the biggest "zero net energy" community in America, meaning that it produces an amount of energy equal to what it consumes thanks to innovations like solar panels and sustainable building design. On a smaller scale, you and your peers can use apps to help make your lifestyle more eco-friendly.

Do you think these apps are an effective way to help preserve natural resources? Would these apps make you more conscious of your own consumption habits? Is placing individual responsibility in the hands of app users enough, or are more sweeping legislative changes needed to reduce the collective carbon footprint of Americans?

faced with mounting scientific evidence that global warming is indeed occurring and under pressure from voters to adopt environmentally friendly policies, clearly recognized that international action of some kind was needed. But faced as well with intense lobbying by industry, which fears it will bear the brunt of the cost for reducing fossil fuel emissions, world leaders felt compelled to balance safeguarding the environment against the threat of economic disruption.

As a result, the pollution reductions agreed to by the countries were meager, and different countries agreed to different specific targets: The United States agreed (upon ratification by the U.S. Congress) to reduce emissions levels by 7 percent from their 1990 levels, during the period 2008–2012. The fifteen countries of the European Union similarly pledged an 8 percent reduction, and Japan promised a 6 percent cut. The nations also tentatively agreed to establish an emissions "trading" system whereby a country that has reduced emissions levels beyond its target will be able to sell emissions "credits" to countries that have been unable to meet their goals. The agreement also includes commitments on behalf of the industrialized countries to assist developing countries by providing technology and funding to help overcome their limited capacity to respond to climate change.

As of January 2014, 192 countries had ratified the agreement. Notably, the United States has refused to ratify the treaty even though, as we have noted, it is responsible for the largest single share of global greenhouse gases of any country after China (United Nations Framework Convention on Climate Change 2014).

While politicians hailed the accord as an important first step in dealing with global warming, there are three serious problems with the Kyoto accord. First, while many newly industrialized countries, such as China, India, and Russia, have now ratified the treaty, the terms of the agreement largely exempt them from making emissions reductions. Second, many environmentalists warn that the reduction in greenhouse gases agreed to at Kyoto is only enough to slow global warming, not reverse it. Third, and most problematic, the Kyoto accord, which must be ratified by the legislative bodies of all the signatory countries, faces stiff political opposition. Industry leaders and conservative politicians in the United States, for example, claim that reaching even the 7 percent reduction agreed to by the U.S. delegation would be tremendously expensive and that the environmental regulations required to achieve even this modest goal would hamstring U.S. business and impede economic growth.

The IPCC's 2007 report has been seen as a wake-up call by many, including the U.S. government, which, as noted above, endorsed the commission's findings. This wake-up call was echoed by China's environment minister Zhou Shengxian and then-prime minister Wen Jiabao in 2011. As Zhou eloquently described the tensions between economic growth and environmental well-being, he observed that "in China's thousands of years of civilization, the conflict between humankind and nature has never been as serious as it is today" (Jacobs 2011). Scholars, policymakers, and citizens ultimately hope that these strong words will lead to actions that will halt and even reverse the worst effects of global climate change. It is clear that modern technology, science, and industry are not exclusively beneficial in their consequences. Sociologists perceive a responsibility to examine closely the social relations and institutions that brought about the current state of affairs because rectifying the situation will require a profound awareness of human responsibility. ✓

CONCEPT CHECKS ✓

1. Describe the basic processes that give rise to global warming.

2. Define sustainable development, and provide at least one critique of the concept.

3. What are the three main problems with the Kyoto accord?

4. In the case of China, how have population growth and economic growth contributed to environmental degradation?

THE BIG PICTURE

KEY CONCEPTS

EXERCISES:
Thinking Sociologically

1. Explain what makes the urbanization now occurring in developing countries, such as Brazil and India, different from and more problematic than the urbanization that took place a century ago in New York, London, Tokyo, and Berlin.

2. Following analysis presented in this chapter, concisely explain how the expanded quest for cheap energy and raw materials and present-day dangers of environmental pollution and resource depletion threaten not only the survival of people in developed countries but also that of people in less developed countries.

Chapter 15

Urbanization, Population, and the Environment

p.467 **How Do Cities Develop and Evolve?**

Learn how cities have changed as a result of industrialization and urbanization. Learn how theories of urbanism have placed increasing emphasis on the influence of socioeconomic factors on city life.

p.473 **How Do Rural, Suburban, and Urban Life Differ in the United States?**

Learn about the recent key developments affecting American cities, suburbs, and rural communities in the last several decades: suburbanization, urban decay, gentrification, and population loss in rural areas.

p.478 **How Does Urbanization Affect Life Across the Globe?**

See that global economic competition has a profound impact on urbanization and urban life. Recognize the challenges of urbanization in the developing world.

p.483 **What Are the Forces Behind World Population Growth?**

Learn why the world population has increased dramatically and understand the main consequences of this growth.

p.491 **How Do Urbanization and Environmental Changes Affect Your Life?**

See that the environment is a sociological issue related to urbanization and population growth.

TERMS TO KNOW	CONCEPT CHECKS

conurbation • megalopolis • urbanization • ecological approach • inner city • urban ecology • urbanism • created environment

1. What are two characteristics of ancient cities?
2. What is urbanization? How is it related to globalization?
3. How does urban ecology use physical science analogies to explain life in modern cities?
4. What is the urban interaction problem?
5. According to Jane Jacobs, the more people are on the streets, the more likely the street life will be orderly. Do you agree with Jacobs's hypothesis and her explanation for this pattern?

suburbanization • exurban county • urban renewal • gentrification

1. Describe at least two problems facing rural America today.
2. Why did so many Americans move to suburban areas in the 1950s and 1960s?
3. What are two unintended consequences of urbanization? How do they deepen socioeconomic and racial inequalities?

global city • informal economy

1. Discuss the effects of globalization on cities.
2. What are the four main characteristics of global cities?
3. Urban growth in the developing world is much higher than elsewhere. Discuss several economic, social, and environmental consequences of such rapid expansion of cities in developing nations.

demography • crude birthrate • fertility • fecundity • crude death rate • mortality • infant mortality rate • life expectancy • life span • exponential growth • doubling time • Malthusianism • demographic transition • dependency ratio

1. What is the difference between fertility and fecundity?
2. Explain Malthus's position on the relationship between population growth and the food supply.
3. Describe the stages of the demographic transition.
4. What is life expectancy? How does it differ from life span?

environmental ecology • sustainable development

1. Describe the basic processes that give rise to global warming.
2. Define sustainable development, and provide at least one critique of the concept.
3. What are the three main problems with the Kyoto accord?
4. In the case of China, how have population growth and economic growth contributed to environmental degradation?

Globalization in a Changing World

THE BIG QUESTIONS

HOW DOES GLOBALIZATION AFFECT SOCIAL CHANGE?
Recognize that a number of factors influence social change, including the physical environment, political organization, culture, and economic factors.

WHAT COMES AFTER MODERN INDUSTRIAL SOCIETY?
Be able to critically evaluate the notion that social change is leading us into a postindustrial or postmodern stage of social organization.

WHAT ARE SOCIAL MOVEMENTS?
Understand what social movements are, why they occur, and how they affect society.

WHAT FACTORS CONTRIBUTE TO GLOBALIZATION?
Recognize the importance of information flows, political changes, and transnational corporations.

HOW DOES GLOBALIZATION AFFECT YOUR LIFE?
Recognize the ways that large global systems affect local contexts and personal experiences.

More than 300,000 young people took to the streets in the Ukraine in 2013 and 2014, protesting former president Viktor Yanukovych's positions on important economic and trade issues.

On December 17, 2010, Tunisian street vendor Mohamed Bouazizi set himself on fire in protest of the local police's confiscation of his wares and the harassment and humiliation that he experienced at the hands of a local government bureaucrat. This act of frustration and defiance, many people believe, was the initial catalyst for the Tunisian Revolution, or the demonstrations and riots that erupted in protest of widespread corruption and inequality in the country. The Tunisian Revolution, in turn, triggered what has been called Arab Spring, or the Arab Awakening. In the following months, protests spread like wildfire throughout Jordan, Egypt, Libya, Yemen, and elsewhere in the Middle East in the spring of 2011. And in the years that followed, protests continued to erupt throughout the Middle East, Europe, and even North America.

The nature and causes of the protests varied across countries and over time, yet most were led by educated but discontented young people who sought to fight against dictatorships, human rights violations, government corruption, economic declines, unemployment, extreme poverty, and persistent inequalities between the "haves and have nots." As of January 2014, these revolutions had led to the overthrow or resignation of four heads of state: Tunisian president Zine El Abidine Ben Ali, Egyptian president Hosni Mubarak, President Ali Abdullah Saleh of Yemen, and Libyan leader Muammar al-Gaddafi. Unlike revolutions and protests at earlier points in history, the Arab Spring was facilitated by the Internet. Through the use of Twitter, Facebook, and Internet chat rooms, protesters could report in "real time" what they did and saw. These messages were transmitted not only to their peers and fellow protesters but to captivated viewers worldwide.

The 2011 Arab Spring protests had far-reaching effects on protests worldwide. The young people's activism—and the political changes it forged—inspired large protests across the globe (Kulish 2011). In India, hundreds of thousands of disillusioned young people supported rural activist Kisan Baburao "Anna" Hazare in his hunger strike. Hazare starved himself for twelve days until the Indian Parliament met some of his demands to implement an anticorruption measure. In Israel, an estimated 430,000 people gathered in Tel Aviv, Jerusalem, and Haifa to protest high unemployment, high costs of living, and other social injustices. In London, violence erupted at a protest march organized by the Trades Union Congress (TUC); an estimated 250,000 to 500,000 people marched from the Thames Embankment to the Houses of Parliament to Hyde Park to show their opposition to planned public spending cuts. Throughout the United States, "Occupy Wall Street" and "We Are the 99%" protests were held at city parks and plazas. In the Ukraine, more than 300,000 young people took to the streets to protest the actions of President Viktor Yanukovych in January 2014. In one of the most violent days of protest in mid-February 2014, twenty-six protesters were killed, more than 200 were seriously injured, and dozens were detained, sending shock waves throughout the nation (Black, Pearson, and Butenko 2014). The rapid spread of these social protests vividly reveals the power of globalization.

Globalization refers to the fact that we all live in one world, so that individuals, groups, and nations become more interdependent. Such interdependence is increasingly at a global scale—that is, what happens halfway across the globe is more likely than ever before to have enormous consequences for our daily lives. A key part of the study of globalization is the emergence of a world system—for some purposes, we need to regard the world as forming a single social order. As we saw in the case of the Arab Spring and protests that have surged throughout the world, we are all global citizens and our lives are interdependent. In this chapter, we examine these global processes and see what leading sociologists and other social scientists have had to say about them.

Some of these ideas will already be familiar to you, since much of this book has been about the consequences of globalization. In this chapter, we go beyond our earlier discussions, considering why the modern period is associated with especially profound and rapid social change. We examine how globalization has contributed to such rapid social change and offer some thoughts on what the future is likely to bring.

globalization • The development of social and economic relationships stretching worldwide. In current times, we are all influenced by organizations and social networks located thousands of miles away.

Recognize that a number of factors influence social change, including the physical environment, political organization, culture, and economic factors.

HOW DOES GLOBALIZATION AFFECT SOCIAL CHANGE?

The ways of living and the social institutions characteristic of the modern world are radically different from those of even the recent past. During a period of only two or three centuries—a small sliver of time in the context of human history—human social life has been wrenched away from the types of social order in which people lived for thousands of years. **Social change** can be defined as the transformation over time of the institutions and culture of a society. Globalization has accelerated the pace of social change, bringing virtually all of humanity into the same turbulent seas. As a result, far more than any generations before us, we face an uncertain future. To be sure, conditions of life for previous generations were always insecure: People were at the mercy of natural disasters, plagues, and famines. Yet, although these problems still trouble much of the world, today we must also deal with the social forces that we ourselves have unleashed.

Social theorists have tried for the past two centuries to develop a single grand theory that explains the nature of social change. Marx, for example, emphasized the importance of economic factors in shaping all aspects of social life, including politics and culture. But no single-factor theory can adequately account for the diversity of human social development from hunting and gathering and pastoral societies to traditional civilizations and finally to the highly complex social systems of today. In analyzing social change, we can at most accomplish two tasks: We can identify major factors that have consistently influenced social change, such as the physical environment, economics, political organization, and culture; and we can also develop theories that account for particular periods of change, such as modern times.

social change • Alteration in basic structures of a social group or society. Social change is an ever-present phenomenon in social life, but has become especially intense in the modern era. The origins of modern sociology can be traced to attempts to understand the dramatic changes shattering the traditional world and promoting new forms of social order.

THE PHYSICAL ENVIRONMENT

The physical environment often has an effect on the development of human social organization. This is clearest in extreme environmental conditions, where people must organize their ways of life in relation to weather conditions. People who live in Alaska, where the winters are long and cold and the days very short, tend to follow different patterns of social life from people who live in the much warmer American South. Most Alaskans spend more of their lives indoors and, except for the summer months, plan outdoor activities carefully, given the frequently inhospitable environment in which they live.

Less extreme physical conditions can also affect society. The native population of Australia has never stopped being hunters and gatherers, since the continent contained hardly any indigenous plants suitable for regular cultivation or animals that could be domesticated to develop pastoral production. The ease of communications across land and the availability of sea routes are also important: Societies cut off from others by mountain ranges, impassable jungles, or deserts often remain relatively unchanged over long periods of time.

A strong case for the importance of environment is made by Jared Diamond (2005) in his widely acclaimed book *Collapse: How Societies Choose to Fail or Succeed*. Diamond, a physiologist, biologist, and geographer, examines more than a dozen past and present societies, some of which collapsed (past examples include Easter Island and the Anasazi of the southwestern United States; more recent candidates include Rwanda and Haiti) and some of which overcame serious challenges to succeed.

Diamond identifies five sets of factors that can contribute to a society's collapse: the presence of hostile neighbors, the absence (or collapse of) trading partners for essential goods, climate change, environmental problems, and an inadequate response to environmental problems. Three of these five factors have to do with environmental conditions. The first four factors are often outside of a society's control and need not always result in collapse. The final factor, however, is always crucial: As the subtitle of his book suggests, success or failure depends on the choices made by a society and its leaders.

Rwandan refugees try to reach the United Nations camp in Tanzania. Over 800,000 Tutsi and moderate Hutu were killed during a period of 100 days in 1994. Hundreds of thousands of Rwandans fled to neighboring countries to escape the bloodshed.

The collapse of Rwanda, for example, is typically attributed to ethnic rivalries between Hutu and Tutsi, fueled by Rwanda's colonial past. According to some explanations of the genocide that left more than 800,000 Tutsi dead in the span of a few horrific months in 1994, a large part of the cause lay in the legacy of colonialism. During the first part of the twentieth century, Belgium ran Rwanda through Tutsi administrators because according to the prevailing European racial theories of the time, the Tutsi—who tended on average to be somewhat taller and lighter skinned than the Hutu and, therefore, closer in resemblance to Europeans—were believed by the Belgians to be more civilized. This led to resentments and hatred, which boiled over in 1994, fueled by Hutu demagogues urging the killing of all Tutsi.

Diamond does not reject this explanation but shows that it is only part of the story and by itself cannot account for the depth of the violence. Instead, through careful analysis of patterns of landholding, population, and killing, he argues that the root causes are found in overpopulation and resulting environmental destruction. Rwanda, he shows, had one of the fastest-growing populations on earth, with disastrous consequences for its land as well as its people, who had become some of the most impoverished on the planet. Faced with starvation and the absence of land to share among the growing number of (male) children, Rwanda was ripe for violence and collapse. Although ethnic rivalries may have fueled the fires of rage, Diamond shows that in some hard-hit provinces Hutu killed other Hutu, as young men sought to acquire scarce farmland by any means.

Some have criticized Diamond for overemphasizing the importance of the environment, at the expense of other factors. The environment alone does not necessarily determine how a society develops. Today especially, when humans can exert a high degree of control over their immediate living conditions, environment would seem to be less important: Modern cities have sprung up in the arctic cold and the harshest deserts.

POLITICAL ORGANIZATION

A second factor strongly influencing social change is the type of political organization that operates in a society. In hunter-gatherer societies, this influence is minimal, since there are no political authorities capable of mobilizing the community. In all other types of society, however, the existence of distinct political agencies—chiefs, lords, monarchs, and governments—strongly affects the course of development a society takes.

How a society and its leaders respond to a crisis can play a decisive role in whether they thrive or fail. A leader capable of pursuing dynamic policies and generating a mass following or radically altering preexisting modes of thought can overturn a previously established order. However, individuals can reach positions of leadership and become effective only if favorable social conditions exist. Mahatma Gandhi, the famous pacifist leader in India, effectively secured his country's independence from Britain because World War II and other events had unsettled the existing colonial institutions in India.

The most important political factor that has helped speed up patterns of change in the modern era is the emergence of the modern state, which has proved a vastly more efficient mechanism of government than the types that existed in premodern societies.

Globalization today may be challenging the ability of national governments to effectively exert leadership. Sociologist William Robinson (2001), for one, claims that as economic power has become increasingly deterritorialized, so too has political power: Just as transnational corporations operate across borders, with little or no national allegiance, transnational political organizations are becoming stronger even as national governments are becoming weaker. The World Trade Organization (WTO), for example, has the power to punish countries that violate its principles of free trade (Conti 2011).

Will the twenty-first century see new forms of political organization better suited to a world in which people, products, knowledge, religious beliefs, and social networking all cross borders with ever-greater ease? As the recent string of protests suggest, it seems likely that the most important forms of political organization of the twenty-first century will bear little resemblance to those of the twentieth.

CULTURE

The third main influence on social change is culture, including communication systems, religious and other belief systems, and popular culture. Communication systems, in particular, affect the character and pace of social change. The invention of writing, for instance, allowed for effective record keeping, making possible the development of large-scale organizations. In addition, writing altered people's perception of the relation between past, present, and future. Societies that write keep a record of past events, which then enables them to develop a sense of their society's overall line of evolution. The existence of a written constitution and laws makes it possible for a country to have a legal system based on the interpretation of specific legal precedents—just as written scripture enables religious leaders to justify their beliefs by citing chapter and verse from religious texts like the Bible or the Qur'an.

We have seen in this and previous chapters how in recent years the Internet and the proliferation of smartphones have transformed our personal relationships, the nature of politics and social movements, our forms of recreation, and the ways in which we learn and work—in fact, almost every aspect of modern life. These changes have been among the most rapid in human history, resulting in what geographer David Harvey (1989) has aptly referred to as "the time-space compression." And they have all occurred within the last three decades—a single generation.

Religion, as we have seen, may be either a conservative or an innovative force in social life. Some forms of religious belief and practice have acted as a brake on change, emphasizing above all the need to adhere to traditional values and rituals. Yet, as Max Weber emphasized, religious convictions frequently play a mobilizing role in pressures for social change. For instance, throughout history many American church leaders have promoted attempts to lessen poverty or diminish inequalities in society. Religious leaders such as Dr. Martin Luther King Jr. were at the forefront of the American civil rights movement.

Yet at the same time, religion today has become one of the driving forces against many of the cultural aspects of globalization. Islamic fundamentalists, fundamentalist Christians, and ultra-Orthodox Jewish *haredim* all reject what they regard as the corrupting influences of modern secular culture, now rapidly spreading throughout the world thanks to mass media and the Internet (Juergensmeyer 1994, 2001). Fundamentalist Islamists call this "westoxification"—literally, getting drunk on the temptations of modern Western culture. Although such religious communities are usually willing to embrace modern technology, which they often use effectively to disseminate their ideas, they reject what they view as the "McWorld" corruptions that go along with it.

Juergensmeyer (1994) predicted that in the twenty-first century, the principal cultural clashes would not be between so-called civilizations but rather between those who believe that truthful understanding is derived from religious faith and those who argue that such understanding is grounded in science, critical thinking, and secular thought. Although it is too early to fully evaluate the accuracy of Juergensmeyer's prediction, we do see compelling evidence already. For example, in the United States, political debates rage between right-wing Republicans who promote teaching creationism (versus evolution) in schools and oppose gay marriage on religious grounds and liberal Democrats whose policies are guided by scientific evidence and preservation of civil rights. Not surprisingly, creationism is much more likely to be taught in public school systems in politically conservative districts in the South than more liberal regions of the North (Kirk 2014).

ECONOMIC FACTORS

Of economic influences, the farthest reaching is industrial capitalism. Capitalism differs in a fundamental way from preexisting production systems because it involves the constant expansion of production and the ever-increasing accumulation of wealth. In traditional production systems, levels of production were fairly stable, since they were geared to habitual, customary needs. Capitalism requires the constant revision of the technology of production, a process into which science is increasingly drawn. The rate of technological innovation fostered in modern industry is vastly greater than in any previous type of economic order. And such technological innovation, as we have seen, has helped create a truly global economy—one whose production lines draw on a worldwide workforce.

Economic changes help shape other changes as well. Science and technology, for example, are driven in part (often in large part) by economic factors. Governments often get into the act, spending far more money than individual businesses can afford in an effort to ensure that their countries don't fall behind technologically, militarily, or economically. For instance, when the Soviet Union launched the world's first satellite (Sputnik) into space in 1957, the United States responded with a massive and costly space program, inspired by fear that the Russians were winning the space race. During the 1960 presidential campaign, John F. Kennedy effectively stoked that fear by repeatedly accusing the Republicans of being lax on Russian missile technology, suggesting that a growing "missile gap" made us vulnerable to a nuclear attack. Even as recently as 2013, President Barack Obama proposed boosting funding for the Energy Department to modernize the United States' existing nuclear weapons with the goal of maintaining "a safe, secure and effective nuclear deterrent" (Guarino 2013). In each of these historical cases, the arms race—fueled by government contracts with corporations—provides major economic support for scientific research as well as more general support for the U.S. economy. ✓

> ## CONCEPT CHECKS
>
> 1. Name three examples of cultural factors that may influence social change.
> 2. What are the most important political factors that influence social change?
> 3. How does industrial capitalism affect social change?

WHAT COMES AFTER MODERN INDUSTRIAL SOCIETY?

> Be able to critically evaluate the notion that social change is leading us into a postindustrial or postmodern stage of social organization.

Where is social change leading us today? In this section, we examine two competing perspectives: the notion that we are a postindustrial society and the idea that we have reached a postmodern period. In the final section of this chapter, we examine theories that have focused on the dimensions, causes, and consequences of globalization.

TOWARD A POSTINDUSTRIAL SOCIETY?

Some observers have suggested that what is occurring today is a transition to a new society no longer primarily based on industrialism. We are entering, they claim, a phase of development beyond the industrial era altogether. A variety of terms have been coined to describe this new social order, such as **information society**, **service society**, and **knowledge society**. The term that has come into most common use, however—first employed by Daniel Bell in the United States and Alain Touraine in France—is **postindustrial society** (Touraine 1974; Bell 1976), the *post* (meaning "after") referring to the sense that we are moving beyond the old forms of industrial development.

The diversity of names is one indication of the many ideas put forward to interpret current social changes. But one theme appears consistently: the significance of information or knowledge in the society of the future. Our way of life throughout the nineteenth and twentieth centuries, based in large part on machine power—the manufacture of material goods in factories—is being gradually displaced by one in which information is the basis of the production system.

One of the earliest comprehensive portrayals of these changes is provided by Daniel Bell in his now-classic *The Coming of the Post-Industrial Society* (1976). The postindustrial order, Bell argues, is distinguished by a growth of service occupations

information society • A society no longer based primarily on the production of material goods but on the production of knowledge. The notion of the information society is closely bound up with the rise of information technology.

service society • A social order distinguished by the growth of service occupations at the expense of industrial jobs that produce material goods.

knowledge society • Another common term for information society—a society based on the production and consumption of knowledge and information.

postindustrial society • A postindustrial society is based on the production of information rather than material goods. According to postindustrialists, we are currently experiencing a series of social changes as profound as those that initiated the industrial era some 200 years ago.

Scholars say that we now live in a postindustrial society, and that knowledge and information—rather than manufactured goods—are the chief output of the U.S. economy.

at the expense of jobs that produce material goods. The blue-collar worker, employed in a factory or workshop, is no longer the most essential type of employee. White-collar (clerical and professional) workers outnumber blue-collar (factory) workers, with professional and technical occupations growing fastest of all.

People working in higher-level white-collar occupations specialize in the production of information and knowledge. The production and control of what Bell calls "codified knowledge"—systematic, coordinated information—are society's main productive resource. Those who create and distribute this knowledge—scientists, computer specialists, economists, engineers, and professionals of all kinds—increasingly become the leading social groups, replacing the industrialists and entrepreneurs of the old system.

POSTMODERNITY

Some scholars have gone as far as saying that the developments now occurring are even more profound than signaling the end of the era of industrialism. They claim that what is happening is nothing short of a movement beyond modernity—the attitudes and ways of life associated with modern societies, such as our belief in progress, the benefits of science, and our ability to control the modern world. An era of **postmodernism** is arriving, or has already arrived.

The advocates of postmodernity claim that modern societies took their inspiration from the idea that history has a shape—it "goes somewhere" and leads to progress—and that now this notion has collapsed. Not only is there no general notion of progress that can be defended, there is no such thing as history. The postmodern world is thus a highly pluralistic and diverse one. In countless films, videos, websites, and TV programs, images circulate around the world. We come into contact with many ideas and values, but these have little connection with the

postmodernism • The belief that society is no longer governed by history or progress. Postmodern society is highly pluralistic and diverse, with no "grand narrative" guiding its development.

history of the areas in which we live, or indeed with our own personal histories. Everything seems constantly in flux.

Most contemporary social theorists accept that information technology and new communications systems, together with other technological changes, are producing major social transformations for all of us. However, the majority disagree with core ideas of the postmodernists, who argue that our attempts to understand general processes in the social world are doomed to fail, as is the notion that we can change the world for the better. Writers such as Ulrich Beck and one of the authors of this textbook, Anthony Giddens, claim that we need as much as ever to develop general theories of the social world and that such theories can help us intervene to shape it in a positive way. Such theories have focused on how contemporary societies are becoming globalized, while everyday life is breaking free from the hold of tradition and custom. But these changes should not spell the end of attempts at social and political reform. Values such as a belief in the importance of social community, equality, and caring for the weak and vulnerable are still very much alive throughout the world. ✓

CONCEPT CHECKS ✓

1. What is "postindustrial society"?

2. What is the "postmodern era"? What is the main critique of this concept?

WHAT ARE SOCIAL MOVEMENTS?

> Understand what social movements are, why they occur, and how they affect society.

In addition to economics, technology, politics, and culture, one of the most common ways social change occurs is through social movements. As we saw earlier in this chapter, *social movements* are collective attempts to further a common interest or secure a common goal (such as forging social change) through action outside the sphere of established institutions. A wide variety of social movements, some enduring, some transient, have existed in modern societies. They are a vital feature of the contemporary world as are the formal, bureaucratic organizations they often oppose. Many contemporary social movements are international in scope and rely heavily on the use of information technology in linking local social movement participants to global issues, as we saw in the case of many of the Arab Spring uprisings and the protests that followed in Israel, India, England, the Ukraine, and elsewhere (Kulish 2011).

WHY DO SOCIAL MOVEMENTS OCCUR?

Sociology arose in the late nineteenth century as part of an effort to come to grips with the massive political and economic transformations that Europe experienced on its way from the preindustrial to the modern world (Moore 1966). Perhaps because sociology was founded in this context, sociologists have never lost their fascination with these transformations.

Since mass social movements have been so important in world history over the past two centuries, it is not surprising that a range of theories exist to try to account for them. Some theories were formulated early in the history of the social sciences; the most important was that of Karl Marx. Marx, who lived well before any of the social movements undertaken in the name of his ideas took place, intended his views to be taken not just as an analysis of the conditions of revolutionary change but as a means of furthering such change. Whatever their intrinsic validity, Marx's ideas had an immense practical impact on twentieth-century social change.

We shall look at four frameworks for the study of social movements, many of which were developed in the context of revolution: economic deprivation, resource mobilization, structural strain, and fields of action.

ECONOMIC DEPRIVATION

Marx's view of social movements is based on his general interpretation of human history (see Chapter 1). According to Marx, the development of societies is marked by periodic class conflicts that, when they become acute, tend to end in a process of revolutionary change. Class struggles derive from the unresolvable tensions in societies. The main sources of tension can be traced to economic changes, or changes in the *forces of production*. In any stable society, there is a balance between the economic structure, social relationships, and the political system. As the forces of production alter, contradiction is intensified, leading to open clashes between classes—and ultimately to revolution.

Contrary to Marx's expectations, revolutions failed to occur in the advanced industrialized societies of the West. Why? The sociologist James Davies, a critic of Marx, pointed to periods of history when people lived in dire poverty but did not rise up in protest. Constant poverty or deprivation does not make people into revolutionaries; rather, they usually endure such conditions with resignation or silent frustration. Social protest, and ultimately revolution, is more likely to occur when there is an improvement in people's living conditions, according to Davies. Once standards of living have started to rise, people's levels of expectation also go up. If improvement in actual conditions subsequently slows down, propensities to revolt are created because rising expectations are frustrated (Davies 1962). Thus, it is not absolute deprivation that leads to protest but *relative deprivation*—the discrepancy between the lives people are forced to lead and what they think could realistically be achieved.

Davies's theory, however, does not show how and why different groups mobilize to seek revolutionary change. Charles Tilly's theory of resource mobilization, by contrast, helps explain how groups become collectively organized to make effective political challenges.

RESOURCE MOBILIZATION

In *From Mobilization to Revolution*, Charles Tilly analyzed processes of revolutionary change in the context of broader forms of protest and violence (Tilly 1978). He distinguished four main components of *collective action*, action taken to contest or overthrow an existing social order:

1. The *organization* of the group or groups involved. Protest movements are organized in many ways, varying from the spontaneous formation of crowds to tightly disciplined revolutionary groups. The Russian Revolution, for example, began as a small group of activists.

2. *Mobilization*, the ways in which a group acquires sufficient resources to make collective action possible. Such resources may include material goods, political support, and weaponry. In the Russian Revolution, Vladimir Lenin was able to acquire material and moral support from a sympathetic peasantry.

Relative deprivation between the peasantry and the elite in France led to the overthrow of the monarchy in the late eighteenth century.

3. **The *common goals and interests* of those engaging in collective action, what they see as the gains and losses likely to be achieved by their policies.** Lenin managed to weld together a broad coalition of support because many people had a common interest in removing the existing government.

4. ***Opportunity.*** Chance events may occur that provide opportunities to pursue revolutionary aims. There was no inevitability to Lenin's success, which depended on a number of contingent factors—including success in battle. If Lenin had been killed, would there have been a revolution?

Collective action itself can simply be defined as people acting together in pursuit of interests they share. For example, nearly a half-million young Israelis disenchanted with the nation's high costs of living and other social injustices gathered in 2011 to form the nation's largest street demonstration in history (Sherwood 2011). Similarly, in December 2013, an estimated 300,000 people, mostly students, protested in the streets in the Ukraine, calling for the resignation of President Viktor Yanukovych after he failed to deliver on his promise to sign political and free-trade agreements with the European Union (Herszenhorn 2014). In many such protests, some activists may be intensely involved; others may lend more passive or sporadic support. Effective collective action, such as action that culminates in revolution, usually moves through a series of gradual stages.

Typical modes of collective action and protest vary with historical and cultural circumstances. In the United States today, for example, most people are familiar with forms of demonstration like mass marches, large assemblies, and street riots, whether or not they have participated in such activities. Other types of collective protest, however, have become less common or have disappeared altogether in most modern societies (such as fights between villages or lynching). Protesters can also build on strategies adopted elsewhere; for instance, guerrilla movements proliferated in various parts of the world once disaffected groups learned how successful guerrilla actions can be against regular armies.

STRUCTURAL STRAIN

Neil Smelser (1963) distinguished six conditions underlying the origins of collective action in general, and social movements in particular:

1. *Structural conduciveness* refers to the general social conditions promoting or inhibiting the formation of social movements of different types.
2. Just because the conditions are conducive to the development of a social movement does not mean those conditions will bring it into being. There must be **structural strain** or tensions that produce conflicting interests within societies. Uncertainties, anxieties, ambiguities, or direct clashes of goals are expressions of such strains.
3. *Generalized beliefs and ideologies* crystallize grievances and suggest courses of action that might be pursued to remedy them.
4. *Precipitating factors* are events or incidents that actually trigger direct action by those who become involved in the movement.
5. The first four conditions combined might precede minor protests, but they do not lead to the development of social movements unless there is a coordinated group that becomes mobilized for action. *Leadership* and some means of regular *communication* among participants, together with funding and material resources, are necessary for a social movement to exist.
6. The development of a social movement is strongly influenced by *social control forces*. A harsh reaction by governing authorities might encourage further protest and help solidify the movement, whereas divisions within the military can be crucial in deciding the outcome of confrontations with revolutionary movements.

structural strain • Tensions that produce conflicting interests within societies.

Smelser's model is useful for analyzing the sequences in the development of social movements, and collective action in general. His theory treats social movements as responses to situations, rather than allowing that their members might spontaneously organize to achieve desired social changes. In this respect his ideas contrast with the approach developed by Alain Touraine. While Smelser maintained that social movements develop in response to situations of structural strain, Touraine examined the historical context of social movements and the "field of action," or the arena within which social movements interact with established organizations. Touraine argued that this process of interaction was central in shaping social movements.

FIELDS OF ACTION

Alain Touraine's (1977, 1981) theory of social movements is based on four main ideas. The first, which he called *historicity*, explains why there are so many more movements in the modern world than there were in earlier times. In modern societies, individuals and groups know that social activism can be used to achieve social goals and reshape society.

Second, social movements typically have *rational objectives*; they develop from specific views and rational strategies as to how injustices can be overcome.

Third, social movements are shaped by *social interaction*. They do not develop in isolation; instead, they develop in deliberate antagonism with established organizations and sometimes with other rival social movements.

Fourth, social movements and change occur in the context of what Touraine called "fields of action," referring to the connections between a social movement and the forces or influences opposing it. The process of mutual negotiation among antagonists in a field of action may lead to the social changes sought by the movement as well as to changes in the social movement itself and in its antagonists. In either circumstance, the movement may evaporate—or become institutionalized as a permanent organization. For example, while the Tea Party began as a grassroots movement of politically conservative Americans concerned with national spending, it became institutionalized when national political figures like former Minnesota representative Michele Bachmann helped to form and ultimately chair an official Tea Party caucus (Lorber 2010).

GLOBALIZATION AND SOCIAL MOVEMENTS

Social movements come in all shapes and sizes. Some are very small, numbering fewer than a dozen members; others include thousands or even millions of people. Some social movements carry on their activities within the laws of the society, such as those carrying out peaceful protests in public squares, while others operate as illegal or underground groups, perhaps by breaking into a nuclear power plant to protest its operations. However, most protest movements operate near the margins of what is defined as legally permissible by governments at any particular time or place.

Social movements often arise with the aim of bringing about a major change, such as expanding civil rights for a segment of the population. In response, countermovements sometimes arise in defense of the status quo. The campaign for women's right to legal abortion, for example, has been vociferously challenged by antiabortion ("pro-life") activists, who believe that abortion should be illegal. Similarly, protests calling for the rights of gays and lesbians to legally marry are often met by counterprotests from religious conservatives who believe that marriage must occur between one man and one woman.

Making Sociology Work
COMMUNITY ORGANIZER/ SOCIAL ACTIVIST

In July 2006, one of the largest student protests since Tiananmen Square erupted in China. An estimated 10,000 students in Zhengzhou clashed with police and ransacked classrooms and administrative offices at Shengda Economic, Trade and Management College, which is affiliated with the prestigious Zhengzhou University. What sparked the protest? After paying expensive tuition fees and completing their years of study, graduating students were angered by the college's decision to award diplomas in its own name, rather than in the name of Zhengzhou University, as promised in its advertisements. This seeming bait-and-switch is due to a 2003 government regulation requiring colleges to issue diplomas in their own names rather than those of their higher-prestige affiliates. A diploma from Zhengzhou University Shengda Economic, Trade and Management College will reveal the second-tier character of the students' qualifications to employers. Concern about the prestige of one's alma mater is particularly acute in China today. Given the nation's intensely competitive labor market, even a degree from a well-known university no longer guarantees a job to a new graduate. A 2012 government survey found that 16 percent of Chinese ages twenty-one to twenty-five who hold college degrees are unemployed (Bradsher and Wong 2013). Drawing on the concepts of economic deprivation, relative deprivation, structural strain, and fields of action, do you believe that student protests like these are an effective way to forge social or organizational change? Why or why not? If you were a community organizer, what conditions would be necessary to ensure a successful protest?

Often, laws or policies are altered as a result of the action of social movements. These changes in legislation can have far-ranging effects. For example, it used to be illegal for groups of workers to call their members out on strike, and striking was punished with varying degrees of severity in different countries. Eventually, however, the laws were amended, making the strike a permissible tactic of industrial conflict.

NEW SOCIAL MOVEMENTS

The last three decades have seen an explosion of social movements in countries around the globe, with a heightened increase in the last two years alone. These movements—epitomized by the civil rights and feminist movements of the 1960s and 1970s, antinuclear and ecological movements of the 1980s, the gay rights campaign of the 1990s, and protests against government corruption, joblessness, and economic inequalities in the 2010s—are often referred to by commentators as *new social movements*. This description seeks to differentiate contemporary social movements from those that preceded them in earlier decades. They are often concerned with the quality of private life as much as with political and economic issues, calling for large-scale changes in the way people think and act.

In other words, what makes new social movements "new" is that—unlike conventional social movements—they are not based on single-issue objectives that typically involve changes in the distribution of economic resources or power. Rather, they involve the creation of collective identities based around entire lifestyles, often calling for sweeping cultural changes. New social movements have emerged in recent years around issues such as ecology, peace, gender and sexual identity, gay and lesbian rights, women's rights, alternative medicine, and opposition to globalization. Although the triggers of the Arab Spring protests differed across nations, the catalysts for many of the uprisings in Northern African and the Persian Gulf countries included discontent over the persistent concentration of wealth in the hands of autocrats in power, insufficient transparency in government policies and practices, corruption, and the refusal of the youth to accept the status quo (Khalidi 2011).

Participation in new social movements often is viewed as a moral obligation (and even a pleasure), rather than a calculated effort to achieve some specific goal. Moreover, the forms of protest chosen by new social movements are a form of "expressive logic" whereby participants make a statement about who they are: Protest is an end in itself, a way of affirming one's identity, as well as a means to achieving concrete objectives (Polletta and Jasper 2001).

The rise of new social movements in recent years is a reflection of the changing risks facing human societies. The conditions are ripe for social movements—increasingly traditional political institutions are unable to cope with the challenges before them. Existing democratic political institutions cannot hope to fix sweeping problems like climate change and the dangers of nuclear energy. As a result, these unfolding challenges are frequently ignored or avoided until it is too late and a full-blown crisis is at hand.

The cumulative effect of these new challenges and risks is a sense that people are losing control of their lives in the midst of rapid change. Individuals feel less secure and more isolated—a combination that leads to a sense of powerlessness. By contrast, corporations, governments, and the media appear to be dominating more and more aspects of people's lives, heightening the sensation of a runaway world. There is a growing sense that, left to its own logic, globalization will present ever-greater risks to citizens' lives.

Although faith in traditional politics seems to be waning, the growth of new social movements is evidence that citizens in late modern societies are not apathetic or uninterested in politics, as is sometimes claimed. Rather, there is a belief that direct action and participation are more useful than reliance on politicians and political systems. New social movements are helping to revitalize democracy in many countries. They are at the heart of a strong civic culture or **civil society**—the sphere between the state and the marketplace occupied by family, community associations, and other noneconomic institutions.

civil society • The realm of activity that lies between the state and the market, including the family, schools, community associations, and other noneconomic institutions. Civil society, or civic culture, is essential to vibrant democratic societies.

TECHNOLOGY AND SOCIAL MOVEMENTS

In recent years, two of the most influential forces in late modern societies—information technology and social movements—have come together with astonishing results. In our current information age, social movements around the globe are able to join together in huge regional and international networks comprising nongovernmental organizations, religious and humanitarian groups, human rights associations, consumer protection advocates, environmental activists, and others who campaign in the public interest. These electronic networks now have the unprecedented ability to respond immediately to events as they occur, gain access to and share sources of information, and put pressure on corporations, governments, and international bodies as part of their campaigning strategies. For example, crowdsourcing websites like Rally and ActBlue allow like-minded individuals to make contributions to the political causes and candidates whom they support (see Digital Life box in Chapter 5). And some political candidates are even accepting contributions through bitcoin. Texas representative Steve Stockman shocked members of the political "old guard" when he announced in 2014 that he would accept donations in bitcoins, a controversial virtual currency (Siner 2014).

The Internet has been the driving force behind these changes, although Twitter, smartphones, and satellite broadcasting have also hastened their evolution. With the click of a finger, local stories are disseminated internationally. The ability of citizens to coordinate international protests is highly worrisome for governments. For example, in response to massive protests against government corruption in January 2011, the Egyptian government blocked social media sites and mobile phone networks, before ultimately pulling the plug on Egypt's access to the Internet. The attempts at censorship were fruitless in the end; millions of Egyptians took to the streets on January 28, 2011, further incensed by the government's attempted censorship. Egyptian president Hosni Mubarak resigned on February 11, 2011, following eighteen days of widespread protests (BBC 2011).

The January 25, 2011, protest in Egypt relied so heavily on social media for its organization that pundits refer to the day as the "Facebook Revolution."

From global protests in favor of canceling developing nations' debt to the international campaign to ban land mines (which culminated in a Nobel Peace Prize), the Internet has the potential to unite campaigners across national and cultural borders. Some observers argue that the information age is witnessing a migration of power away from nation-states into new nongovernmental alliances and coalitions. ✓

Recognize the importance of information flows, political changes, and transnational corporations.

WHAT FACTORS CONTRIBUTE TO GLOBALIZATION?

Globalization is often portrayed solely as an economic phenomenon. Some make much of the role of transnational corporations whose massive operations stretch across national borders, influencing global production processes and the international distribution of labor. Others point to the electronic integration of global financial markets and the enormous volume of global capital flows. Still others focus on the unprecedented scope of world trade, which involves a much broader range of goods and services than ever before.

Although economic forces are an integral part of globalization, it would be wrong to suggest that they alone produce it. Globalization is created by the coming together of technological, political, and economic factors. It has been driven forward above all by the development of information and communications technologies that have intensified the speed and scope of interaction between people all over the world.

INFORMATION FLOWS

The explosion in global communications has been facilitated by some important advances in technology and the world's telecommunications infrastructure. In the post–World War II era, there has been a profound transformation in the scope and intensity of telecommunications flows. Traditional telephone communication, which depended on analog signals sent through wires and cables, has been replaced by integrated systems in which vast amounts of information are compressed and transferred digitally. Cable technology and the spread of communications satellites, beginning in the 1960s, have been integral in expanding international communications. The Union of Concerned Scientists (2013) estimates that 555 satellites are in orbit as of 2011 for communications purposes.

The impact of these communications systems has been staggering. In countries with highly developed telecommunications infrastructures, homes and offices now have multiple links to the outside world, including telephones (both landlines and mobile phones), fax machines, digital and cable television, and the Internet. The Internet has emerged as the fastest-growing communication tool ever developed. Over 2.4 billion people worldwide (slightly more than one-third of the world population) were estimated to be using the Internet at the end of June 2012, a 70 percent increase over the number of users in 2008 and more than six times as many as in 2000 (Internet World Stats 2013).

As we noted earlier, these forms of technology facilitate the compression of time and space: Two individuals located on opposite sides of the planet—in Tokyo and London, for example—not only can hold a conversation in real time but also can send documents and images or tweet their ideas to each other with the help of satellite technology. Widespread use of the Internet and mobile phones is spurring on and accelerating processes of globalization; more and more people are becoming interconnected through the use of these technologies and are doing so in places that have previously been isolated or poorly served by traditional communications. Although the telecommunications infrastructure is not evenly developed around the world, a growing number of countries now have access to international communications networks in a way that was previously impossible.

Globalization is also being driven forward by the electronic integration of the world economy. The global economy is increasingly dominated by activity that is weightless and intangible (Quah 1999). This *weightless economy* is one in which products have their base in information, as is the case with computer software, media and entertainment products, and Internet-based services. The emergence of the knowledge society has been linked to the development of a broad base of consumers who are technologically literate and eagerly integrate new advances in computing, entertainment, and telecommunications into their everyday lives.

The very operation of the global economy reflects the changes that have occurred in the information age. Many aspects of the economy now work through networks that cross national boundaries, rather than stopping at them (Castells 1996). To be competitive in globalizing conditions, businesses and corporations have restructured themselves to be more flexible and less hierarchical in nature. Production practices and organizational patterns have become more flexible, partnering arrangements with other firms have become commonplace, and participation in worldwide distribution networks has become essential for doing business in a rapidly changing global market.

Whether a job is in a factory or a call center, it can be done more cheaply in China, India, or some other developing country than in developed countries like the United States. This is increasingly true for the work of software engineers,

At a call center in Gurgaon, India, employees field questions and concerns from people in the U.S. and elsewhere, representing a global flow of information.

Online Activism Trends Upward

The words *social movement* or *political protest* typically conjure up images of groups of people, mostly young adults, coming together in public squares, carrying homemade signs, and chanting slogans like "Peace Now" or "Hell No, We Won't Go!" But for young adults today, political protests have been reinvented by digital media technologies. As we have seen in this chapter, technology has played a critical role in mobilizing both social movements and public protests. Social networking tools like Facebook and Twitter are changing political protests in ways that the rebellious youth of the 1960s never could have imagined.

For example, Twitter was an essential player in the antigovernment protests in Turkey in 2013. Since the local media did not adequately cover the protests, many Turks would have had little knowledge of what was happening without Twitter. Over the course of three days, an estimated 10 million tweets were sent by protesters and observers using the most popular hashtags, according to researchers from New York University. Unlike other recent protests, however, these tweets came from people on the front-lines, rather than people sharing their views from outside the nation. Researchers have documented that roughly 90 percent of geotagged tweets were coming from inside the country, with half from Istanbul—the epicenter of the protests (Fitzpatrick 2013).

Dissatisfied with the local mainstream media's coverage of the uprisings, young Turkish protesters began live-tweeting about their actions and using their smartphones to live-stream video of the daily events. These tweets and videos, along with articles in the Western news media, became the major source of information about the movement. Protesters even urged their fellow Turks to turn off their televisions in protest of the lack of coverage by the local mainstream media, using the hashtag #BugünTelevizyonlarıKapat (literally, "turn off the TVs today"). Instead, they directed people to turn to the Internet to find out what was really happening (Fitzpatrick 2013).

Electronic media was also a critical player in the January 2014 protests in the Ukraine. For example, early tweets by journalists and activists were considered the primary trigger that brought hundreds of thousands of Ukrainians into the streets on the eve of November 21, 2013. Even before dedicated Twitter feeds and Facebook pages were created, protesters tracked the events using hashtags. Very early on, #Euromaidan emerged as the main hashtag used for protest-related tweets. Shortly thereafter, an official Euromaidan Facebook page was created. Its popularity set a record in Ukraine, attracting 76,000 "likes" in its first week. The page was used to provide real-time updates, as well as information on activists' future plans and advice on how to deal with potentially aggressive police officers. The official Euromaidan Twitter account provided similar information. The speed and reach of such digital messages was remarkable and unprecedented (Arndt 2014).

Young people increasingly use social media and smartphone apps to engage in political protests. Those on the front lines of protest, such as these activists in Kiev, provide reports to followers worldwide via Twitter and Facebook.

Have you ever used a Facebook site, followed tweets, or used digital media to participate in or spread news about a political issue or event? What do you see as the pros and cons? What can digital media achieve that old 1960s-style protests could not?

graphic designers, and financial consultants as well. Of course, to the extent that global competition for labor reduces the cost of goods and services, it also provides for a wealth of cheaper products (Roach 2005). As consumers we all benefit from low-cost flat-panel TVs made in China and inexpensive computer games programmed in India. It is an open question, however, whether the declining cost of consumption will balance out wage and job losses due to globalization.

POLITICAL CHANGES

A number of political changes are driving forces behind contemporary globalization. One of the most significant of these is the collapse of Soviet-style communism, which occurred in a series of dramatic revolutions in Eastern Europe in 1989 and culminated in the dissolution of the Soviet Union itself in 1991. Since the fall of Soviet-style communism, countries in the former Soviet bloc—including Russia, Ukraine, Poland, Hungary, the Czech Republic, the Baltic states, the states of the Caucasus and Central Asia, and many others—are moving toward Western-style political and economic systems. They are no longer isolated from the global community but are becoming integrated within it. The collapse of communism has hastened processes of globalization but should also be seen as a result of globalization itself. The centrally planned communist economies and the ideological and cultural control of communist political authority were ultimately unable to survive in an era of global media and an electronically integrated world economy.

A second important political factor leading to intensifying globalization is the growth of international and regional mechanisms of government. The United Nations and the European Union (EU) are the two most prominent examples of international organizations that bring together nation-states in a common political forum. Whereas the United Nations does this as an association of individual nation-states, the EU is a more pioneering form of transnational governance in which a certain degree of national sovereignty is relinquished by its member states. The governments of individual EU states are bound by directives, regulations, and court judgments from common EU bodies, but they also reap economic, social, and political benefits from their participation in the regional union.

A third important political factor is the growing importance of *international governmental organizations* (IGOs) and *international nongovernmental organizations* (INGOs). An IGO is a body that is established by participating governments and given responsibility for regulating or overseeing a particular domain of activity that is transnational in scope. The first such body, the International Telegraph Union, was founded in 1865. Since that time, a great number of similar bodies have been created to regulate a range of business activities, including civil aviation, broadcasting, and the disposal of hazardous waste. In 1909, there were thirty-seven IGOs in existence to regulate transnational affairs; by 2005, there were estimated to be more than 7,000 (Union of International Organizations 2005). As the name suggests, INGOs differ from IGOs in that INGOs are not affiliated with government institutions. Rather, they are independent organizations that work alongside governmental bodies in making policy decisions and addressing international issues. Some of the best-known INGOs—Greenpeace, Médecins Sans Frontières (Doctors without Borders), the Red Cross, and Amnesty International—are involved in environmental protection and humanitarian relief efforts. But the activities of the nearly 40,000 lesser-known groups also link together countries and communities (United States Institute of Peace 2013).

Finally, the spread of information technology has expanded the possibilities for contact between people around the globe. Every day, the global media bring news, images, and information into people's homes, linking them directly and continuously to the outside world. Some of the most gripping events of the past three decades—such as the fall of the Berlin Wall, the violent crackdown on democratic protesters in Beijing's Tiananmen Square, the terrorist attacks of September 11, 2001, and the Arab Spring protests and subsequent protests that erupted worldwide—have unfolded through the media before a truly global audience. Such events, along with thousands of less dramatic ones, have resulted in a reorientation in people's thinking from the level of the nation-state to the global stage. Individuals are now more aware of their interconnectedness with others and more likely to identify with global issues and processes than in times past.

This shift to a global outlook has two significant dimensions. First, as members of a global community, people increasingly perceive that social responsibility does not stop at national borders but instead extends beyond them. There is a growing assumption that the international community has an obligation to act in crisis situations to protect the physical well-being or human rights of people whose lives are under threat. In the case of natural disasters, such interventions take the form of humanitarian relief and technical assistance. In recent years, earthquakes in Haiti and Japan, floods in Mozambique, famine in Africa, hurricanes in Central America, the tsunami that hit Asia and Africa, and most recently, the 2013 typhoon that struck the Philippines have been rallying points for global assistance.

Second, a global outlook means that people are increasingly looking to sources other than the nation-state in formulating their own sense of identity. Local cultural identities in various parts of the world are experiencing powerful revivals at a time when the traditional hold of the nation-state is undergoing profound transformation. In Europe, for example, inhabitants of Scotland and the Basque region of Spain might be more likely to identify themselves as Scottish or Basque—or simply as Europeans—rather than as British or Spanish. The nation-state as a source of identity is waning in many areas as political shifts at the regional and global levels loosen people's orientations toward the states in which they live.

TRANSNATIONAL CORPORATIONS

transnational corporations •
Business corporations located in
two or more countries.

Among the many economic factors driving globalization, the role of transnational corporations is particularly important. **Transnational corporations** are companies that produce goods or market services in more than one country. These may be relatively small firms with one or two factories outside the country in which they are based, or gigantic international ventures whose operations crisscross the globe.

Transnational corporations account for two-thirds of all world trade, they are instrumental in the diffusion of new technology around the globe, and they are major actors in international financial markets. As one observer has noted, they are "the linchpins of the contemporary world economy" (Held et al. 1999). Nearly 500 transnational corporations had annual sales of more than $23.2 billion in 2012, whereas only 102 countries (over half of all countries in the world) could boast gross domestic products (GDPs) of at least that amount; the world's leading transnational corporations are larger economically than most of the world's countries. Royal Dutch Shell, the world's largest corporation in terms of sales as of 2012, had sales revenues that surpassed the GDPs of all but twenty-five countries. Among the world's largest fifty economies, twelve are transnational corporations (Central Intelligence Agency 2013e, CNN's Money magazine 2013). For example, the fiftieth-largest national economy is

Transnational corporations such as Coca-Cola are eager to tap growing markets in countries like China and India. Corporate leaders break ground on a new plant in the Gansu province of China. The plant is one of thirty-five bottling plants Coca-Cola has opened in mainland China since it re-entered the country in 1979.

Kazakhstan with a GDP of $196.4 billion; by contrast, the twelfth-largest transnational corporation is Glencore Xstrata with revenues of $214.4 billion.

The "electronic economy" is another factor that underpins economic globalization. Banks, corporations, fund managers, and individual investors are able to shift funds internationally with the click of a mouse or the tap of a smartphone. This new ability to move "electronic money" instantaneously carries with it great risks, however. Transfers of vast amounts of capital can destabilize economies, triggering international financial crises such as the ones that spread from the Asian "tiger economies" to Russia and beyond in 1998. As the global economy becomes increasingly integrated, a financial collapse in one part of the world can have an enormous effect on distant economies. This became painfully evident when the once-venerable financial services firm Lehman Brothers filed for bankruptcy in 2008. The collapse of Lehman Brothers, which held an estimated $600 billion in assets, caused financial shockwaves throughout the United States and global economies. The Dow Jones dropped by more than 4 percentage points immediately following Lehman's filing for Chapter 11 bankruptcy, making it the largest single drop since the 9/11 attacks in 2001. Banks and insurers throughout the world, from Scotland to Japan, registered devastating losses as a result (Council on Foreign Relations 2013).

The political, economic, social, and technological factors described above are joining together to produce a phenomenon that lacks any earlier parallel in terms of its intensity and scope. The consequences of globalization are many and far-reaching, as we will see later in this chapter. But first we will turn our attention to the main views about globalization that have been expressed in recent years.

THE GLOBALIZATION DEBATE

In recent years, globalization has become a hotly debated topic. Most people accept that important transformations are occurring around us, but the extent to which it is valid to explain these as "globalization" is contested. As an unpredictable and turbulent process, globalization is seen and understood very differently by observers. David Held and his colleagues (1999) have surveyed the controversy and divided its participants into three schools of thought: *skeptics, hyperglobalizers,* and *transformationalists.* These three tendencies within the globalization debate are summarized in Table 16.1.

THE SKEPTICS

Some thinkers argue that the idea of globalization is overrated—that the debate over globalization is a lot of talk about something that is not new. The skeptics in the globalization controversy believe that present levels of economic interdependence are not unprecedented. Pointing to nineteenth-century statistics on world trade and investment, they contend that modern globalization differs from the past only in the intensity of interaction between nations.

The skeptics agree that there may now be more contact between countries than in previous eras, but in their eyes the current world economy is not sufficiently integrated to constitute a truly globalized economy. This is because the bulk of trade occurs within three regional groups: Europe, Asia-Pacific, and North America (Hirst 1997).

Table 16.1 | Conceptualizing Globalization: Three Tendencies

CHARACTERISTIC	SKEPTICS	TRANSFORMATIONALISTS	HYPERGLOBALIZERS
What's new?	Trading blocs, weaker geogovernance	Historically unprecedented levels of global interconnectedness	A global age
Dominant features	World less interdependent than in 1890s	"Thick" (intensive and extensive) globalization	Global capitalism, global governance, global civil society
Power of national governments	Reinforced or enhanced	Reconstituted, restructured	Declining or eroding
Driving forces of globalization	Governments and markets	Combined forces of modernity	Capitalism and technology
Pattern of stratification	Increased marginalization of global south	New architecture of world order	Erosion of old hierarchies
Dominant motif	National interest	Transformation of political community	McDonald's, Beyonce, etc.
Conceptualization of globalization	As internationalization and regionalization	As the reordering of interregional relations and action at a distance	As a reordering of the framework of human action
Historical trajectory	Regional blocs/clash of civilizations	Indeterminate: global integration and fragmentation	Global civilization
Summary argument	Internationalization depends on government acquiescence and support	Globalization transforming government power and world politics	The end of the nation-state

SOURCE: Adapted from Held et al. 1999

Many skeptics focus on processes of regionalization within the world economy such as the emergence of major financial and trading blocs. To skeptics, the growth of regionalization is evidence that the world economy has become less integrated rather than more (Boyer and Drache 1996; Hirst and Thompson 1999). Compared with the patterns of trade that prevailed a century ago, they argue, the world economy is less global in its geographical scope and more concentrated on intense pockets of activity.

According to the skeptics, national governments continue to be key players because of their involvement in regulating and coordinating economic activity. For example, skeptics point out that national governments are the driving force behind many trade agreements and policies of economic liberalization.

THE HYPERGLOBALIZERS

The hyperglobalizers take an opposing position to that of the skeptics. They argue that globalization is a very real phenomenon whose consequences can be felt almost everywhere. They see globalization as a process that is indifferent to national borders. It is producing a new global order, swept along by powerful flows of cross-border trade and production. One of the best-known popularizers of the idea of hyperglobalization is the Japanese writer Kenichi Ohmae (1990, 1995), who sees globalization as leading to a "borderless world"—a world in which market forces are more powerful than national governments. Another is journalist Thomas Friedman, whose pair of best-selling books—*The Lexus and the Olive Tree* (2000) and *The World Is Flat* (2005)—paint a picture of globalization as a juggernaut that sweeps up everything in its path, sometimes with unfortunate short-term results but ultimately with enormous benefit for everyone.

Much of the analysis of globalization offered by hyperglobalizers focuses on the changing role of the nation-state. It is argued that individual countries no longer control their economies because of the vast growth in world trade. Some hyperglobalizers believe that the power of national governments is also being challenged from above—by new regional and international institutions such as the EU. Taken together, these shifts signal to the hyperglobalizers the dawning of a global age (Albrow 1997) in which national governments decline in importance and influence.

Social scientists endorsing the "strong globalization" position include sociologists such as William Robinson (2001, 2004, 2005a, 2005b), Leslie Sklair (2002a, 2002b, 2003), and Saskia Sassen (1996, 2005). These scholars do not see themselves as hyperglobalists, yet they argue that transnational economic actors and political institutions are challenging the dominance of national ones. Robinson, one of the strongest proponents of this position, has studied these changes throughout the world, with a special focus on Latin America. He argues that the most powerful economic actors on the world scene today are not bound by national boundaries; they are, instead, transnational in nature. For example, he argues that nation-states are being transformed into "component elements" of a transnational state—exemplified by the WTO, whose purpose is to serve the interests of global businesses as a whole by ensuring that individual countries adhere to the principles of free trade. Robinson (2001) concludes that "the nation-state is a historically-specific form of world social organization in the process of becoming transcended by globalization."

THE TRANSFORMATIONALISTS

The transformationalists take more of a middle position. Writers such as David Held (Held et al. 1999) and one of the authors of this textbook, Anthony Giddens (1990), see globalization as the central force behind a broad spectrum of changes that are currently shaping modern societies. In this view, the global order is being transformed, but many of the old patterns remain. Governments, for instance, retain a good deal of power in spite of the advance of global interdependence. These transformations are not restricted to economics alone but are equally prominent within the realms of politics, culture, and personal life. Transformationalists contend that the current level of globalization is breaking down established boundaries between internal and external, international and domestic. In trying to adjust to this new order, societies, institutions, and individuals are being forced to navigate contexts where previous structures have been shaken up.

Unlike hyperglobalizers, transformationalists see globalization as a dynamic and open process that is subject to influence and change. Globalization is not a one-way process, as some claim, but a two-way flow of images, information, and influences. Global migration, media, and telecommunications are contributing to the diffusion of cultural influences. The world's vibrant "global cities" are thoroughly multicultural, with ethnic groups and cultures intersecting and living side by side. According to transformationalists, globalization is a decentered and self-aware process characterized by links and cultural flows that work in a multidirectional way. Because globalization is the product of numerous intertwined global networks, it cannot be seen as being driven from one particular part of the world.

Rather than losing sovereignty, as the hyperglobalizers argue, countries are seen by transformationalists as restructuring in response to new forms of economic and social organization that are nonterritorial in basis (e.g., corporations, social movements, and international bodies). They argue that we are no longer living in a state-centric world; governments are being forced to adopt a more active, outward-looking stance toward governance under the complex conditions of globalization (Rosenau 1997).

Whose view is most nearly correct? There are elements of truth in all three views, although the view of the transformationalists is perhaps the most balanced. The skeptics underestimate how far the world is changing; world finance markets, for example, are organized on a global level much more than they ever were before. Yet, at the same time, the world has undergone periods of intense globalization before, only to withdraw into periods in which countries sought to protect their markets and closed their borders to trade. While the march of globalization today often seems inevitable, it is by no means certain that it will continue unabated: Countries that find themselves losing out may attempt to stem the tide.

The hyperglobalizers are correct in pointing to the current strength of globalization as dissolving many national barriers, changing the nature of state power, and creating new and powerful transnational social classes. On the other hand, they often see globalization too much in economic terms and as too much of a one-way process. In reality, globalization is much more complex. National governments will neither dissolve under the weight of a globalized economy (as some hyperglobalizers argue) nor reassert themselves as the dominant political force (as some skeptics argue) but rather will seek to steer global capitalism to their own advantage. The world economy of the future may be much more globalized than today's, with multinational corporations and global institutions such as the WTO playing increasingly important roles. But some countries in the world economy may still be more powerful than even the most powerful transnational actors. ✓

CONCEPT CHECKS ✓

1. Compare and contrast how skeptics, hyperglobalizers, and transformationalists explain the phenomenon of globalization.

2. How might skeptics, hyperglobalizers, and transformationalists differently interpret the growing global prominence of China?

HOW DOES GLOBALIZATION AFFECT YOUR LIFE?

Recognize the ways that large global systems affect local contexts and personal experiences.

Although globalization is often associated with changes within big systems—such as the world financial markets, production and trade, and telecommunications—the effects of globalization are felt equally strongly in the private realm. We read earlier in this chapter about protests happening across the Atlantic, yet more and more protests are erupting in the United States, inspired in part by young protesters abroad. Many of the uprisings in the United States are led by recent college graduates or current college students who are disenchanted with high tuition costs, bleak job prospects, and high-visibility examples of corruption in major corporations. Some observers believe that the April 2011 college campus protests and September 2011 Occupy Wall Street protests were inspired, in part, by the protests in the Middle East and Europe (Bellafante 2011; Taxin 2011).

Globalization is fundamentally changing the nature of our everyday experiences. As societies undergo profound transformations, the established institutions that used to underpin them have become outmoded. This is forcing a redefinition of intimate and personal aspects of our lives, such as the family, gender roles, sexuality, personal identity, our interactions with others, and our relationships to work.

THE RISE OF INDIVIDUALISM

In our current age, individuals have much more opportunity to shape their own lives than once was the case. At one time, tradition and custom exercised a very strong influence on the path of people's lives. Factors such as social class, gender, ethnicity, and even religious affiliation could close off certain avenues for individuals or open up others. In times past, individuals' personal identities were formed in the context of the community into which they were born. The values, lifestyles, and ethics prevailing in that community provided relatively fixed guidelines according to which people lived their lives.

Under conditions of globalization, however, we are faced with a move toward a new individualism in which people have to actively construct their own identities. The weight of tradition and established values is diminishing as local communities interact with a new global order. We are constantly responding and adjusting to the changing environment around us; as individuals, we evolve with and within the larger context in which we live. Even the small choices we make in our daily lives—what we wear, how we spend our leisure time, and how we take care of our health—are part of an ongoing process of creating and re-creating our self-identities.

WORK PATTERNS

Globalization has unleashed profound transformations within the world of work. New patterns of international trade and the move to a knowledge economy have had a significant impact on long-standing employment patterns. Many traditional industries have been made obsolete by new technological advances or are losing their share of the market to competitors abroad whose labor costs are lower than in industrialized countries. Global trade and new forms of technology have had a strong effect on traditional manufacturing communities, where industrial workers have been left unemployed and without the types of skills needed to enter the new knowledge-based economy. These communities are facing a new set of social problems, including long-term unemployment and rising crime rates, as a result of economic globalization.

If at one time people's working lives were dominated by employment with one employer over the course of several decades—the so-called job-for-life framework—today many more individuals create their own career paths, pursuing individual goals and exercising choice in attaining them. Often this involves changing jobs several times over the course of a career, building up new skills and abilities, and transferring them to diverse work contexts. Standard patterns of full-time work are being dissolved into more flexible arrangements: working from home with the help of information technology, job sharing, short-term consulting projects, flextime, and so forth (Beck 1992). While this affords new opportunities for some, for most it means far greater uncertainty. Job security—and the health and retirement benefits that went with it—have largely become things of the past.

Women have entered the workforce in large numbers, a fact that has strongly affected the personal lives of people of both sexes. Expanded professional and educational opportunities have led many women to delay marriage and children until after they have begun a career. These changes have also meant that many working women return to work shortly after having children, instead of remaining at home with young children as was once the case. These shifts have required important adjustments within families, in the nature of the domestic division of labor, in the role of men in child rearing, and with the emergence of more family-friendly working policies to accommodate the needs of dual-earner couples.

POPULAR CULTURE

The cultural effects of globalization have received much attention. Images, ideas, goods, and styles are now disseminated around the world more rapidly than ever before. Trade, new information technologies, the international media, and global migration have all contributed to the free movement of culture across national borders. Many people believe that we now live in a single information order—a massive global network where information is shared quickly and in great volumes. Films like *Marvel's The Avengers* and *Iron Man 3* have enjoyed worldwide popularity. The film *Avatar*, the most popular film of all time, has grossed nearly $2.8 billion in fifty-five countries since its release in 2009—two-thirds of it outside the United States.

Some people worry that globalization is leading to the creation of a global culture in which the values of the most powerful and affluent—in this instance, Hollywood filmmakers—overwhelm the strength of local customs and tradition. According to this view, globalization is a form of cultural imperialism in which the values, styles, and outlooks of the Western world are being spread so aggressively that they smother individual national cultures.

Others, by contrast, claim that global society is now characterized by an enormous diversity of cultures existing side by side. Local traditions are joined by a host of additional cultural forms from abroad, presenting people with a bewildering array of lifestyle options from which to choose. Rather than a unified global culture, what we are witnessing is the fragmentation of cultural forms (Baudrillard 1988). Established identities and ways of life grounded in local communities and cultures

A movie poster for the film *Avatar* is displayed in China. Box office sales for the movie reached over $180 million in China alone.

are giving way to new forms of hybrid identity composed of elements from contrasting cultural sources (Hall 1992). For example, while *bhangra* melodies hail from the Punjab region of India, U.S. music fans may recognize bhangra harmonies and rhythms from hip-hop artists such as Beyonce and Beenie Man.

GLOBALIZATION AND RISK

The consequences of globalization are far-reaching, affecting virtually all aspects of the social world. Yet because globalization is an open-ended and internally contradictory process, it produces outcomes that are difficult to predict and control. Another way of thinking of this dynamic is in terms of risk. Many of the changes wrought by globalization are presenting us with new forms of risk that differ greatly from those that existed in previous eras. Unlike risks from the past, which had established causes and known effects, today's risks are incalculable in origin and indeterminate in their consequences.

THE SPREAD OF "MANUFACTURED RISK"

external risk • Dangers that spring from the natural world and are unrelated to the actions of humans. Examples of external risk include droughts, earthquakes, famines, and storms.

manufactured risk • Dangers that are created by the impact of human knowledge and technology on the natural world. Examples of manufactured risk include global warming and genetically modified foods.

Humans have always had to face risks of one kind or another, but today's risks are qualitatively different from those of earlier times. Until quite recently, human societies were threatened by **external risk**—dangers such as drought, earthquakes, famines, and storms that spring from the natural world and are unrelated to the actions of humans. Today, however, we are increasingly confronted with various types of **manufactured risk**—risks that are created by the impact of our own knowledge and technology on the natural world. As we shall see, many environmental and health risks facing contemporary societies are instances of manufactured risk; they are the outcomes of our own interventions into nature.

One of the clearest illustrations of manufactured risk can be found in threats currently posed by the natural environment (see Chapter 15). One of the consequences of accelerating industrial and technological development is that few aspects of the natural world remain untouched by humans. Urbanization, industrial production and pollution, large-scale agricultural projects, the construction of dams and hydroelectric plants, and nuclear power are just some of the ways in which human beings have had an impact on their natural surroundings. The collective outcome of such processes has been widespread environmental destruction whose precise cause is indeterminate and whose consequences are similarly difficult to calculate.

In our globalizing world, ecological risk confronts us in many guises. Concern over global warming has been mounting in the scientific community for some years. Most scientists now accept that the earth's temperature has been increasing due to a rising concentration of greenhouse gases—a by-product of man-made processes such as deforestation and the burning of fossil fuels.

The potential consequences of global warming are devastating: If polar ice caps continue to melt at the current rate, sea levels will rise and may threaten low-lying land masses and their human populations. Changes in climate patterns have been cited as possible causes of the severe floods that afflicted Mozambique in 2000; the record number of hurricanes that swept through the Atlantic and the Gulf of Mexico in the fall of 2005 as well as Hurricane Katrina, which devastated New Orleans; and Hurricane Sandy, which leveled entire neighborhoods in New Jersey and New York in 2012.

Climate change has led to an escalation in the frequency of floods, hurricanes, and other natural disasters in the twenty-first century.

In the past decade, the dangers posed to human health by manufactured risks have attracted great attention. For example, in recent years, sun exposure has been linked to a heightened risk of skin cancer in many parts of the world. This is thought to be related to the depletion of the ozone layer—the layer of the earth's atmosphere that normally filters out ultraviolet light. Due to the high volume of chemical emissions that are produced by human activities and industry, the concentration of ozone in the atmosphere has been diminishing and, in some cases, ozone holes have opened up.

There are many examples of manufactured risk that are linked to food. For example, chemical pesticides and herbicides are widely used in commercial agriculture, and many animals (such as chickens and pigs) are pumped full of hormones and antibiotics. Some scientists have suggested that farming techniques such as these, and widespread production of genetically modified foods, could compromise food safety and have an adverse effect on humans.

THE GLOBAL "RISK SOCIETY"

Manufactured risks have presented individuals with new choices and challenges in their everyday lives. Because there is no road map to these new dangers, individuals, countries, and transnational organizations must negotiate risks as they make choices about how lives are to be lived. The German sociologist Ulrich Beck sees these risks contributing to the formation of a global *risk society* (1992). As technological change progresses more and more rapidly and produces new forms of risk, we must constantly respond and adjust to these changes. The risk society, he argues, is not limited to environmental and health risks alone; it includes a whole series of interrelated changes within contemporary social life: shifting employment patterns, heightened job insecurity, the erosion of traditional family patterns, and the democratization of personal relationships. Because personal futures are much less fixed than they were in traditional societies, decisions of all kinds present risks for individuals. According to Beck, an important aspect of the risk society is that its hazards are not restricted spatially, temporally, or socially

(1995). Today's risks affect all countries and all social classes; they have global, not merely personal, consequences.

GLOBALIZATION AND INEQUALITY

Beck and other scholars have drawn attention to risk as one of the main outcomes of globalization and technological advance. New forms of risk present complex challenges for both individuals and whole societies that are forced to navigate unknown terrain. Yet globalization is generating other important challenges as well.

Globalization is proceeding in an uneven way. The impact of globalization is experienced differentially, and some of its consequences are far from benign. Next to mounting ecological problems, the expansion of inequalities within and between societies is one of the most serious challenges facing the world at the start of the twenty-first century.

INEQUALITY AND GLOBAL DIVISIONS

As we learned in our discussions of types of societies (Chapter 2) and of global inequality (Chapter 8), the vast majority of the world's wealth is concentrated in the industrialized or developed countries of the world, whereas the nations of the developing world suffer from widespread poverty, overpopulation, inadequate educational and health care systems, and crippling foreign debt. The disparity between the developed and the developing worlds widened steadily over the course of the twentieth century and is now the largest it has ever been.

According to a 2014 report by Oxfam International, almost half of the world's wealth is currently owned by just 1 percent of the population. The wealth of the richest 1 percent amounts to $110 trillion, which is sixty-five times the total wealth held by the bottom 50 percent of the world's population. To put this in perspective, the bottom half of the world's population owns the same as the richest eighty-five people in the world (Oxfam 2014).

These vast disparities in economic well-being are all the more jarring when daily income is considered. Recent data from the World Bank shows that there are 1.2 billion people living in extreme poverty today; that is, they live on less than $1.25 per day. Although the proportion of persons in developing nations who live under such dire circumstances has decreased markedly over the last three decades—from half in 1981 to 21 percent in 2010—the absolute numbers living in abject poverty remain high, because the populations in these poor nations are so large. Further, extreme poverty is clustered in sub-Saharan Africa, which still accounts for more than one-third of the world's extreme poor (World Bank 2013c).

In much of the developing world, levels of economic growth and output over the past century have not kept up with the rate of population growth, whereas the level of economic development in industrialized countries has far outpaced it. These opposing tendencies have led to a marked divergence between the richest and poorest countries of the world. The world's richest country had a GDP per captia approximately 3 times that of the poorest country in 1820. The gap grew to 11 to 1 in 1913, 35 to 1 in 1950, 72 to 1 in 1992, and 173 to 1 in 2001. The figure for 2012 using GDP per capita is nearly 414 to 1.

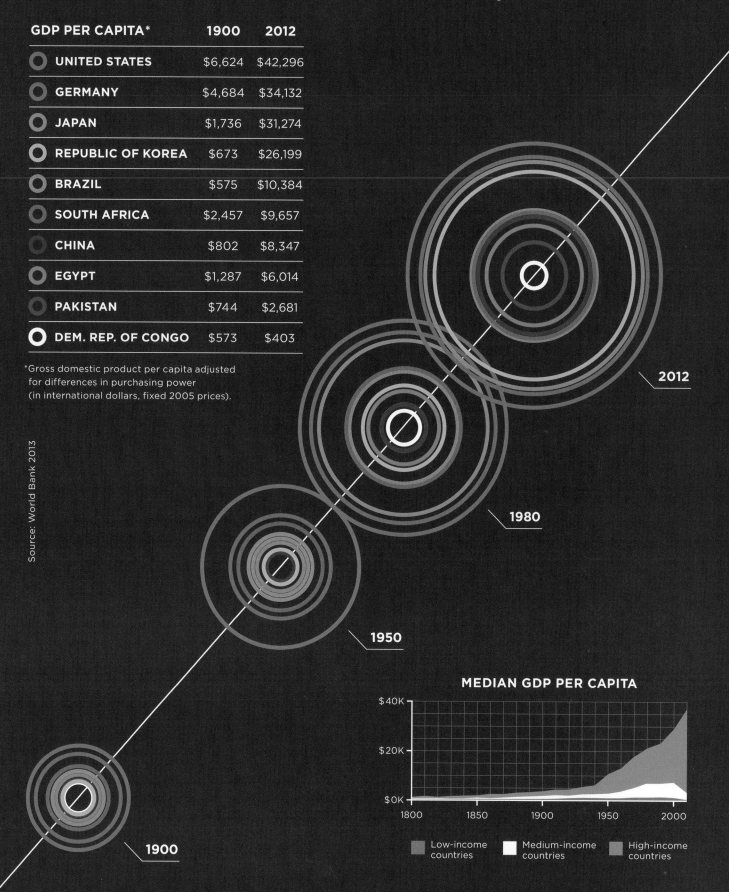

THE WIDENING GAP

The disparity between the developed and the developing worlds widened steadily over the course of the twentieth century and is now the largest it has ever been. While the global economy is growing at a rapid rate, only a small core of countries has managed to benefit from it.

GDP PER CAPITA*	1900	2012
UNITED STATES	$6,624	$42,296
GERMANY	$4,684	$34,132
JAPAN	$1,736	$31,274
REPUBLIC OF KOREA	$673	$26,199
BRAZIL	$575	$10,384
SOUTH AFRICA	$2,457	$9,657
CHINA	$802	$8,347
EGYPT	$1,287	$6,014
PAKISTAN	$744	$2,681
DEM. REP. OF CONGO	$573	$403

*Gross domestic product per capita adjusted for differences in purchasing power (in international dollars, fixed 2005 prices).

Source: World Bank 2013

2012

1980

1950

1900

MEDIAN GDP PER CAPITA

$40K

$20K

$0K

1800   1850   1900   1950   2000

Low-income countries   Medium-income countries   High-income countries

Globalization is exacerbating these trends by further concentrating income, wealth, and resources within a small core of countries. As we have seen in this chapter, the global economy is growing and integrating at an extremely rapid rate. The expansion of global trade has been central to this process. The volume of merchandise exports and imports in 2012 exceeded $18 trillion or 25.6 percent of total global output (World Bank 2013c). Only a handful of developing countries have managed to benefit from that rapid growth, and the process of integration into the global economy has been uneven. Some countries—such as the East Asian economies, Chile, India, and Poland—have fared well, with growth in exports of over 5 percent. Other countries—such as Russia, Venezuela, and Algeria—have seen few benefits from expanding trade and globalization (United Nations Development Programme [UNDP] 1999). There is a danger that many of the countries most in need of economic growth will be left even further behind as globalization progresses (World Bank 2000).

Free trade is seen by many as the key to economic development and poverty relief. Organizations such as the WTO work to liberalize trade regulations and to reduce barriers to trade among the countries of the world. Free trade across borders is viewed as a win-win proposition for developed and developing countries alike. While the industrialized economies are able to export their products to markets around the world, it is claimed that developing countries will also benefit by gaining access to world markets. This, in turn, is supposed to improve their prospects for integration into the global economy.

THE CAMPAIGN FOR GLOBAL JUSTICE

Not everyone agrees that free trade is the solution to poverty and global inequality. In fact, many critics argue that free trade is a rather one-sided affair that benefits those who are already well-off and exacerbates existing patterns of poverty and dependency within the developing world. Recently, much of this criticism has focused on the activities and policies of the WTO, which is at the forefront of efforts to increase global trade.

In December 1999, more than 50,000 people from around the world took to the streets of Seattle, Washington, to protest during the WTO's "Millennium Round" of trade talks. Negotiators from the WTO's 134 member states (the number of members has since risen to 153) had come together to discuss and agree on measures to liberalize conditions for global trade and investment in agriculture and forest products, among other issues. Yet the talks broke off early with no agreements reached. The trade unionists, environmentalists, human rights activists, farmers, and representatives from hundreds of NGOs were triumphant—not only had the demonstrations succeeded in disrupting the talks, but internal disputes among delegates had also risen to the surface. The Seattle protests were heralded as the biggest victory to date for campaigners for "global justice." Since that time, every ministerial meeting of the WTO has been met by massive demonstrations by those excluded from the processes of setting the rules for global trade.

But what is this campaign about, and does it represent the emergence of a powerful anti-globalization movement, as some commentators have suggested? In the months following the Seattle protests, similar demonstrations were held in other cities around the world, such as London and Washington, D.C. These events were much smaller than those that took place in Seattle, but they were organized around similar themes. Protesters argued that free trade and economic globalization succeed in further concentrating wealth in the hands of a few, while increasing poverty for the majority of the world's population. Most of these activists agree that global trade is necessary and potentially beneficial for national economies, but they claim that it needs to be regulated by different rules from those favored by the WTO. They argue that trade rules should be focused, first and foremost, on protecting human rights, the environment, labor rights, and local economies—not on ensuring larger profits for already rich corporations.

The protesters claim that the WTO is an undemocratic organization that is dominated by the interests of the world's richest nations—particularly the United States. Such imbalances have very real consequences. For example, although the WTO has insisted that developing nations open their markets to imports from industrialized countries, it has allowed developed countries to maintain high barriers to agricultural imports and provide vast subsidies for their domestic agriculture production in order to protect their own agricultural sectors. Between 1995 and 2012, the U.S. government spent $292.5 billion to subsidize the income of crop and livestock farmers (Environmental Working Group 2013). For certain crops, like sugar and rice, agricultural subsidies amount to as much as 80 percent of farm income (Stiglitz 2007). In fact, the average European cow gets a subsidy of approximately $2 a day; more than half of the people in the developing world live on less than that (Stiglitz 2007). This has meant that the world's poorest countries, many of which remain predominantly agricultural, do not have access to the large markets for agricultural goods in developed countries.

Protesters against the WTO and other international financial institutions such as the World Bank and the International Monetary Fund argue that exuberance over global economic integration and free trade is forcing people to live in an economy rather than a society. Many are convinced that such moves will further weaken the economic position of poor societies by allowing transnational corporations to operate with few or no safety and environmental regulations. Commercial interests, they claim, are increasingly taking precedence over concern for human well-being. Not only within developing nations but in industrialized ones as well, there needs to be more investment in "human capital"—public health, education, and training—if global divisions are not to deepen even further. The issues raised in the WTO protests, in many ways, were echoed in the protests that sprung up throughout dozens of nations in 2011. The key challenge for the twenty-first century is to ensure that globalization works for people everywhere, not only for those who are already well placed to benefit from it. ✓

CONCEPT CHECKS ✓

1. How has technology facilitated the compression of time and space?

2. What are the three causes of increasing globalization?

3. What effects does globalization have on our everyday lives?

4. Why is globalization associated with new forms of risks? What are they?

THE BIG PICTURE

EXERCISES:
Thinking Sociologically

1. Discuss the many influences on social change: environmental, political, and cultural factors. Summarize how each element can contribute to social change.

2. According to this chapter, we now live in a society where we are increasingly confronted by various types of manufactured risks. Briefly explain what these risks consist of. Do you think the last decade has brought us any closer to or farther away from confronting the challenges of manufactured risks? Explain.

Chapter 16

Globalization in a Changing World

3. Provide an evaluation of how well the four theories of social movements explain Arab Spring uprisings. Which theory is most effective? Why?

p.502 — How Does Globalization Affect Social Change?

Recognize that a number of factors influence social change, including the physical environment, political organization, culture, and economic factors.

p.507 — What Comes after Modern Industrial Society?

Be able to critically evaluate the notion that social change is leading us into a postindustrial or postmodern stage of social organization.

p.509 — What Are Social Movements?

Understand what social movements are, why they occur, and how they affect society.

p.516 — What Factors Contribute to Globalization?

Recognize the importance of information flows, political changes, and transnational corporations.

p.525 — How Does Globalization Affect You Life?

Recognize the ways that large global systems affect local contexts and personal experiences.

globalization

social change

1. Name three examples of cultural factors that may influence social change.
2. What are the most important political factors that influence social change?
3. How does industrial capitalism affect social change?

information society • service society • knowledge society • postindustrial society • postmodernism

1. What is "postindustrial society"?
2. What is the "postmodern era"? What is the main critique of this concept?

structural strain • civil society

1. Compare and contrast four theoretical approaches to the study of social movements.
2. What distinguishes new social movements from their precursors?

transnational corporations

1. Compare and contrast how skeptics, hyperglobalizers, and transformationalists explain the phenomenon of globalization.
2. How might skeptics, hyperglobalizers, and transformationalists differently interpret the growing global prominence of China?

external risk • manufactured risk

1. How has technology facilitated the compression of time and space?
2. What are the three causes of increasing globalization?
3. What effects does globalization have on our everyday lives?
4. Why is globalization associated with new forms of risks? What are they?

535

glossary

absolute poverty • The minimal requirements necessary to sustain a healthy existence.

activity theory • A functionalist theory of aging, which holds that busy, engaged people are more likely to lead fulfilling and productive lives.

age-grades • The system found in small traditional cultures by which people belonging to a similar age group are categorized together and hold similar rights and obligations.

ageism • Discrimination or prejudice against a person on the grounds of age.

agency • The ability to think, act, and make choices independently.

agents of socialization • Groups or social contexts within which processes of socialization take place.

aging • The combination of biological, psychological, and social processes that affect people as they grow older.

agrarian societies • Societies whose means of subsistence are based on agricultural production (crop growing).

alienation • The sense that our own abilities as human beings are taken over by other entities. The term was originally used by Karl Marx to refer to the projection of human powers onto gods. Subsequently he used the term to refer to the loss of workers' control over the nature and products of their labor.

anomie • A concept first brought into wide usage in sociology by Durkheim, referring to a situation in which social norms lose their hold over individual behavior.

assimilation • The acceptance of a minority group by a majority population, in which the new group takes on the values and norms of the dominant culture.

authority • A government's legitimate use of power.

automation • Production processes monitored and controlled by machines with only minimal supervision from people.

biological determinism • The belief that differences we observe between groups of people, such as men and women, are explained wholly by biological causes.

biomedical model of health • The set of principles underpinning Western medical systems and practices. The biomedical model of health defines diseases objectively, in accordance with the presence of recognized symptoms, and holds that the healthy body can be restored through scientifically based medical treatment. The human body is likened to a machine that can be returned to working order with the proper repairs.

black feminism • A strand of feminist theory that highlights the multiple disadvantages of gender, class, and race that shape the experiences of nonwhite women. Black feminists reject the idea of a single, unified gender oppression that is experienced evenly by all women and argue that early feminist analysis reflected the specific concerns of white, middle-class women.

blue- and pink-collar jobs • Jobs that typically pay low wages and often involve manual or low-skill labor. Blue-collar jobs typically are held by men (e.g., factory worker), whereas pink-collar jobs are typically held by women (e.g., clerical assistant).

bourgeoisie • People who own companies, land, or stocks (shares) and use these to generate economic returns, according to Marx.

broken windows theory • A theory proposing that even small acts of crime, disorder, and vandalism can threaten a neighborhood and render it unsafe.

bureaucracy • A type of organization marked by a clear hierarchy of authority and the existence of written rules of procedure and staffed by full-time, salaried officials.

capitalism • An economic system based on the private ownership of wealth, which is invested and reinvested in order to produce profit.

caste society • A society in which different social levels are closed, so that all individuals must remain at the social level of their birth throughout life.

caste system • A social system in which one's social status is determined at birth and set for life.

church • A large, established religious body, normally having a formal, bureaucratic structure and a hierarchy of religious officials. The term is also used to refer to the place in which religious ceremonies are carried out.

citizen • A member of a political community, having both rights and duties associated with that membership.

civil inattention • The process whereby individuals in the same physical setting demonstrate to each another that they are aware of the other's presence.

civil rights • Legal rights held by all citizens in a given national community.

civil society • The realm of activity that lies between the state and the market, including the family, schools, community associations, and other noneconomic institutions. Civil society, or civic culture, is essential to vibrant democratic societies.

class • Although it is one of the most frequently used concepts in sociology, there is no clear agreement about how the term should be defined. Most sociologists use the term to refer to socioeconomic variations among groups of individuals that create variations in their material prosperity and power.

clock time • Time as measured by the clock, in terms of hours, minutes, and seconds. Before the invention of clocks, time reckoning was based on events in the natural world, such as the rising and setting of the sun.

cognition • Human thought processes involving perception, reasoning, and remembering.

cohabitation • Two people living together in a sexual relationship of some permanence without being married to each other.

collective bargaining • The rights of employees and workers to negotiate with their employers for basic rights and benefits.

colonialism • The process whereby Western nations established their rule in parts of the world away from their home territories.

communism • A set of political ideas associated with Marx, as developed particularly by Lenin and institutionalized in the Soviet Union, Eastern Europe, and some developing countries.

community policing • A renewed emphasis on crime prevention rather than law enforcement to reintegrate policing within the community.

comparable worth • Policies that attempt to remedy the gender pay gap by adjusting pay so that those in female-dominated jobs are not paid less for equivalent work.

comparative questions • Questions concerned with drawing comparisons among different human societies for the purposes of sociological theory or research.

comparative research • Research that compares one set of findings on one society with the same type of findings on other societies.

complementary and alternative medicine (CAM) • A diverse set of approaches and therapies for treating different illnesses and promoting well-being that generally falls outside of standard medical practices.

compulsion of proximity • People's need to interact with others in their presence.

concrete operational stage • A stage of human cognitive development, as formulated by Jean Piaget, in which the child's thinking is based primarily on physical perception of the world. In this phase, the child is not yet capable of dealing with abstract concepts or hypothetical situations.

conflict theory • Argument that deviance is deliberately chosen and often political in nature.

constitutional monarchs • Kings or queens who are largely figureheads. Real power rests in the hands of other political leaders.

continuity theory • Theoretical perspective on aging that specifies that older adults fare best when they participate in activities consistent with their personality, preferences, and activities earlier in life.

control theory • A theory that views crime as the outcome of an imbalance between impulses toward criminal activity and controls that deter it. Control theorists hold that criminals are rational beings who will act to maximize their own reward unless they are rendered unable to do so through either social or physical controls.

conurbation • An agglomeration of towns or cities into an unbroken urban environment.

conversation analysis • The empirical study of conversations, employing techniques drawn from ethnomethodology. Conversation analysis examines details of naturally occurring conversations to reveal the organizational principles of talk and its role in the production and reproduction of social order.

core countries • According to world-systems theory, the most advanced industrial countries, which take the lion's share of profits in the world economic system.

corporate crime • Offenses committed by large corporations in society, including pollution, false advertising, and violations of health and safety regulations.

corporate culture • An organizational culture involving rituals, events, or traditions that are unique to a specific company.

corporations • Business firms or companies.

correlation coefficient • A measure of the degree of correlation between variables.

created environment • Constructions established by human beings to serve their needs, derived from the use of man-made technology—including, for example, roads, railways, factories, offices, private homes, and other buildings.

crime • Any action that contravenes the laws established by a political authority. Although we may think of criminals as a distinct subsection of the population, there are few people who have not broken the law in one way or another during their lives. While laws are formulated by state authorities, it is not unknown for those authorities to engage in criminal behavior in certain situations.

crude birthrate • A statistical measure representing the number of births within a given population per year, normally calculated as the number of births per 1,000 members. Although the crude birthrate is a useful index, it is only a general measure, because it does not specify numbers of births in relation to age distribution.

crude death rate • A statistical measure representing the number of deaths that occur annually in a given population per year, normally calculated as the number of deaths per 1,000 members. Crude death rates give a general indication of the mortality levels of a community or society, but are limited in their usefulness because they do not take into account the age distribution.

cult • A fragmentary religious grouping to which individuals are loosely affiliated but which lacks any permanent structure.

cultural capital • Noneconomic or cultural resources that parents pass down to their children, such as language or knowledge. These resources contribute to the process of social reproduction, according to Bourdieu.

cultural relativism • The practice of judging a society by its own standards.

cultural universals • Values or modes of behavior shared by all human cultures.

culture • The values, norms, and material goods characteristic of a given group. Like the concept of society, the notion of culture is widely used in sociology and the other social sciences (particularly anthropology). Culture is one of the most distinctive properties of human social association.

culture of poverty • The thesis, popularized by Oscar Lewis, that poverty is not a result of individual inadequacies but is instead the outcome of a larger social and cultural atmosphere into which successive generations of children are socialized. The culture of poverty refers to the values, beliefs, lifestyles, habits, and traditions that are common among people living under conditions of material deprivation.

data • Factual information used as a basis for reasoning, discussion, or calculation. Social science data often refer to individuals' responses to survey questions.

debriefing • Following a research study, the investigator will inform study participants about the true purpose of the study, and will reveal any deception that happened during the study.

degree of dispersal • The range or distribution of a set of figures.

democracy • A political system that allows the citizens to participate in political decision making or to elect representatives to government bodies.

democratic elitism • A theory of the limits of democracy, which holds that in large-scale societies democratic participation is necessarily limited to the regular election of political leaders.

demographic transition • An interpretation of population change, which holds that a stable ratio of births to deaths is achieved once a certain level of economic prosperity has been reached. According to this notion, in preindustrial societies there is a rough balance between births and deaths, because population increase is kept in check by a lack of available food, by disease, or by war. In modern societies, by contrast, population equilibrium is achieved because families are moved by economic incentives to limit the number of children.

demography • The study of the size, distribution, and composition of populations.

denomination • A religious sect that has lost its revivalist dynamism and become an institutionalized body, commanding the adherence of significant numbers of people.

dependency culture • A term popularized by Charles Murray to describe individuals who rely on state welfare provision rather than entering the labor market. The dependency culture is seen as the outcome of the "paternalistic" welfare state that undermines individual ambition and people's capacity for self-help.

dependency ratio • The ratio of people of dependent ages (children and the elderly) to people of economically active ages.

dependency theories • Marxist theories of economic development arguing that the poverty of low-income countries stems directly from their exploitation by wealthy countries and the multinational corporations that are based in wealthy countries.

developing world • The less-developed societies, in which industrial production is either virtually nonexistent or only developed to a limited degree. The majority of the world's population live in less-developed countries.

developmental questions • Questions that sociologists pose when looking at the origins and path of development of social institutions from the past to the present.

deviance • Modes of action that do not conform to the norms or values held by most members of a group or society. What is regarded as deviant is as variable as the norms and values that distinguish different cultures and subcultures from one another. Forms of behavior that are highly esteemed by one group are regarded negatively by others.

deviant subculture • A subculture whose members hold values that differ substantially from those of the majority.

diaspora • The dispersal of an ethnic population from an original homeland into foreign areas, often in a forced manner or under traumatic circumstances.

differential association • An interpretation of the development of criminal behavior proposed by Edwin H. Sutherland, according to whom criminal behavior is learned through association with others who regularly engage in crime.

direct democracy • A form of participatory democracy that allows citizens to vote directly on laws and policies.

discrimination • Behavior that denies to the members of a particular group resources or rewards that can be obtained by others. Discrimination must be distinguished from prejudice: Individuals who are prejudiced against others may not engage in discriminatory practices against them; conversely, people may act in a discriminatory fashion toward a group even though they are not prejudiced against that group.

disengagement theory • A functionalist theory of aging that holds that it is functional for society to remove people from their traditional roles when they become elderly, thereby freeing up those roles for others.

displacement • The transferring of ideas or emotions from their true source to another object.

division of labor • The specialization of work tasks, by means of which different occupations are combined within a production system. All societies have at least some rudimentary form of division of labor, especially between the tasks allocated to men and those performed by women. With the development of industrialism, the division of labor became vastly more complex than in any prior type of production system. In the modern world, the division of labor is international in scope.

dominant group • The opposite of a minority group; the dominant group possesses more wealth, power, and prestige in a society.

doubling time • The time it takes for a particular level of population to double.

downward mobility • Social mobility in which individuals' wealth, income, or status is lower than what they or their parents once had.

dyad • A group consisting of two persons.

ecological approach • A perspective on urban analysis emphasizing the "natural" distribution of city neighborhoods into areas having contrasting characteristics.

economic interdependence • The fact that in the division of labor, individuals depend on others to produce many or most of the goods they need to sustain their lives.

economy • The system of production and exchange that provides for the material needs of individuals living in a given society. Economic institutions are of key importance in all social orders. What goes on in the economy usually influences other areas in social life. Modern economies differ substantially from traditional ones, because the majority of the population is no longer engaged in agricultural production.

egocentric • According to Jean Piaget, the characteristic quality of a child during the early years of his or her life. Egocentric thinking involves understanding objects and events in the environment solely in terms of the child's own position.

emerging economies • Developing countries that over the past two or three decades have begun to develop a strong industrial base, such as Singapore and Hong Kong.

emigration • The movement of people out of one country in order to settle in another.

empirical investigation • Factual inquiry carried out in any area of sociological study.

encounter • A meeting between two or more people in a situation of face-to-face interaction. Our daily lives can be seen as a series of different encounters strung out across the course of the day. In modern societies, many of these encounters are with strangers rather than people we know.

endogamy • The forbidding of marriage or sexual relations outside one's social group.

entrepreneur • The owner or founder of a business firm.

environmental ecology • A concern with preserving the integrity of the physical environment in the face of the impact of modern industry and technology.

ethnicity • Cultural values and norms that distinguish the members of a given group from others. An ethnic group is one whose members share a distinct awareness of a common cultural identity, separating them from other groups. In virtually all societies, ethnic differences are associated with variations in power and material wealth. Where ethnic differences are also racial, such divisions are sometimes especially pronounced.

ethnocentrism • The tendency to look at other cultures through the eyes of one's own culture, and thereby misrepresent them.

ethnography • The firsthand study of people using participant observation or interviewing.

ethnomethodology • The study of how people make sense of what others say and do in the course of day-to-day social interaction. Ethnomethodology is concerned with the "ethnomethods" by which people sustain meaningful exchanges with one another.

experiment • A research method in which variables can be analyzed in a controlled and systematic way, either in an artificial situation constructed by the researcher or in naturally occurring settings.

exponential growth • A geometric, rather than linear, rate of increase. Populations tend to grow exponentially.

extended family • A family group consisting of more than two generations of relatives.

external risk • Dangers that spring from the natural world and are unrelated to the actions of humans. Examples of external risk include droughts, earthquakes, famines, and storms.

exurban country • A county that lies within a large metropolitan area but has less than 25 percent of its population in an urbanized area. Tends to sit at periphery of metropolitan areas.

factual questions • Questions that raise issues concerning matters of fact (rather than theoretical or moral issues).

family • A group of individuals related to one another by blood ties, marriage, or adoption, who form an economic unit, the adult members of which are often responsible for the upbringing of children. All known societies involve some form of family system, although the nature of family relationships varies widely. While in modern societies the main family form is the nuclear family, extended family relationships are also found.

family capitalism • Capitalistic enterprise owned and administered by entrepreneurial families.

family of orientation • The family into which an individual is born or adopted.

family of procreation • The family an individual initiates through marriage or by having children.

fecundity • A measure of the number of children that it is biologically possible for a woman to produce.

feminism • Advocacy of the rights of women to be equal with men in all spheres of life. Feminism dates from the late eighteenth century in Europe, and feminist movements exist in most countries today.

feminist theory • A sociological perspective that emphasizes the centrality of gender in analyzing the social world and particularly the experiences of women. There are many strands of feminist theory, but they all share the intention to explain gender inequalities in society and to work to overcome them.

feminization of poverty • An increase in the proportion of the poor who are female.

fertility • The average number of live-born children produced by women of childbearing age in a particular society.

focused interaction • Interaction between individuals engaged in a common activity or in direct conversation with each other.

folkways • A subtype of norm; they guide our casual or everyday interactions. Violations are sanctioned subtly or not at all.

formal operational stage • According to Jean Piaget, a stage of human cognitive development at which the growing child becomes capable of handling abstract concepts and hypothetical situations.

formal organization • Means by which a group is rationally designed to achieve its objectives, often using explicit rules, regulations, and procedures.

formal relations • Relations that exist in groups and organizations, laid down by the norms, or rules, of the official system of authority.

franchise • The right to vote.

functional literacy • Having reading and writing skills that are beyond a basic level and are sufficient to manage one's everyday activities and employment tasks.

functionalism • A theoretical perspective based on the notion that social events can best be explained in terms of the functions they perform—that is, the contributions they make to the continuity of a society.

gender • Social expectations about behavior regarded as appropriate for the members of each sex. Gender refers not to the physical attributes distinguishing men and women but to socially formed traits of masculinity and femininity. The study of gender relations has become one of the most important areas of sociology in recent years.

gender inequality • The inequality between men and women in terms of wealth, income, and status.

gender socialization • The learning of gender roles through social factors such as schooling, the media, and family.

gender typing • Designation of occupations as male or female, with "women's" occupations, such as secretarial and retail positions, having lower status and pay, and "men's" occupations, such as managerial and professional positions, having higher status and pay.

generalized other • A concept in the theory of George Herbert Mead, according to which the individual takes over the general values of a given group or society during the socialization process.

genocide • The systematic, planned destruction of a racial, political, or cultural group.

gentrification • A process of urban renewal in which older, deteriorated housing is refurbished by affluent people moving into the area.

glass ceiling • A promotion barrier that prevents a woman's upward mobility within an organization.

global city • A city—such as London, New York, or Tokyo—that has become an organizing center of the new global economy.

global commodity chain • A worldwide network of labor and production processes yielding a finished product.

global inequality • The systematic differences in wealth and power among countries.

globalization • The economic, political, and social interconnectedness of individuals and nations throughout the world.

government • The enacting of policies and decisions on the part of officials within a political apparatus. While in the past virtually all governments were headed by monarchs or emperors, in most modern societies governments are run by officials who do not inherit their positions of power but are elected or appointed on the basis of qualifications.

groupthink • A process by which the members of a group ignore ways of thinking and plans of action that go against the group consensus.

hate crime • A criminal act by an offender who is motivated by some bias, such as racism, sexism, or homophobia.

heterosexuality • Sexual or romantic attraction to persons of the opposite sex.

hidden curriculum • Traits of behavior or attitudes that are learned at school but not included within the formal curriculum—for example, gender differences.

home schooling • A growing trend (but a longtime practice) of parents or guardians educating their children at home, for religious, philosophical, or safety reasons.

homosexuality • Sexual or romantic attraction of persons of one's own sex.

housework • Unpaid work carried on in the home, usually by women; domestic chores such as cooking, cleaning, and shopping. Also called domestic labor.

human resource management • A style of management that regards a company's workforce as vital to its economic competitiveness.

hypothesis • An idea or a guess about a given state of affairs, put forward as a basis for empirical testing.

ideal type • A "pure type," constructed by emphasizing certain traits of a social item that do not necessarily exist in reality. An example is Max Weber's ideal type of bureaucratic organization.

ideology • Shared ideas or beliefs that serve to justify the interests of dominant groups. Ideologies are found in all societies in which there are systematic and ingrained inequalities among groups. The concept of ideology connects closely with that of power, since ideological systems serve to legitimize the power that groups hold.

immigration • The movement of people into one country from another for the purpose of settlement.

impression management • Preparing for the presentation of one's social role.

income • Payment, usually derived from wages, salaries, or investments.

industrialization • The emergence of machine production, based on the use of inanimate power resources (such as steam or electricity).

industrialized societies • Highly developed nation-states in which the majority of the population work in factories or offices rather than in agriculture, and most people live in urban areas.

infant mortality rate • The number of infants who die during the first year of life, per 1,000 live births.

infanticide • The intentional killing of a newborn. Female babies are more likely than male babies to be murdered in cultures that devalue women.

informal economy • Economic transactions carried on outside the sphere of formal paid employment.

informal networks • Relations that exist in groups and organizations developed on the basis of personal connections; ways of doing things that depart from formally recognized modes of procedure.

information society • A society no longer based primarily on the production of material goods but on the production of knowledge. The notion of the information society is closely bound up with the rise of information technology.

information technology • Forms of technology based on information processing and requiring microelectronic circuitry.

informed consent • The process whereby the study investigator informs potential participants about the risks and benefits involved in the research study. Informed consent must be obtained before an individual participates in a study.

in-group • A group toward which one feels particular loyalty and respect—the group to which "we" belong.

inner city • The areas composing the central neighborhoods of a city, as distinct from the suburbs. In many modern urban settings in industrialized nations inner-city areas are subject to dilapidation and decay, the more affluent residents having moved to outlying areas.

instinct • A fixed pattern of behavior that has genetic origins and that appears in all normal animals within a given species.

institutional capitalism • Capitalistic enterprise organized on the basis of institutional shareholding.

institutional racism • Patterns of discrimination based on ethnicity that have become structured into existing social institutions.

intelligence • Level of intellectual ability, particularly as measured by IQ (intelligence quotient) tests.

interactional vandalism • The deliberate subversion of the tacit rules of conversation.

interest group • A group organized to pursue specific interests in the political arena, operating primarily by lobbying the members of legislative bodies.

intergenerational mobility • Movement up or down a social stratification hierarchy from one generation to another.

intragenerational mobility • Movement up or down a social stratification hierarchy within the course of a personal career.

IQ (intelligence quotient) • A score attained on tests of symbolic or reasoning abilities.

iron law of oligarchy • A term coined by Weber's student Robert Michels meaning that large organizations tend toward centralization of power, making democracy difficult.

kinship • A relation that links individuals through blood ties, marriage, or adoption. Kinship relations are by definition part of marriage and the family, but extend much more broadly. While in most modern societies few social obligations are involved in kinship relations extending beyond the immediate family, in other cultures kinship is of vital importance to social life.

knowledge economy • A society no longer based primarily on the production of material goods but based instead on the production of knowledge. Its emergence has been linked to the development of a broad base of consumers who are technologically literate and have made new advances in computing, entertainment, and telecommunications part of their lives.

knowledge society • Another common term for information society—a society based on the production and consumption of knowledge and information.

labeling theory • An approach to the study of deviance that suggests that people become "deviant" because certain labels are attached to their behavior by political authorities and others.

language • The primary vehicle of meaning and communication in a society, language is a system of symbols that represent objects and abstract thoughts.

latent functions • Functional consequences that are not intended or recognized by the members of a social system in which they occur.

law • A rule of behavior established by a political authority and backed by state power.

leader • A person who is able to influence the behavior of other members of a group.

liberal democracies • A type of representative democracy in which elected representatives hold power.

liberal feminism • Form of feminist theory that believes that gender inequality is produced by unequal access to civil rights and certain social resources, such as education and employment, based on sex. Liberal feminists tend to seek solutions through changes in legislation that ensure that the rights of individuals are protected.

liberation theology • An activist Catholic religious movement that combines Catholic beliefs with a passion for social justice for the poor.

life chances • A term introduced by Max Weber to signify a person's opportunities for achieving economic prosperity.

life course • The various transitions and stages people experience during their lives.

life course theory • A perspective based on the assumptions that the aging process is shaped by historical time and place. Individuals make choices that reflect both opportunities and constraints. Aging is a lifelong process, and the relationships, events, and experiences of early life have consequences for later life.

life expectancy • The number of years the average person can expect to live.

life span • The maximum length of life that is biologically possible for a member of a given species.

linguistic relativity hypothesis • A hypothesis, based on the theories of Edward Sapir and Benjamin Lee Whorf, that perceptions are relative to language.

literacy • The ability to read and write.

local nationalisms • The beliefs that communities that share a cultural identity should have political autonomy, even within smaller units of a nation-state.

lower class • A social class composed of those who work part time or not at all and whose household income is typically low.

macrosociology • The study of large-scale groups, organizations, or social systems.

Malthusianism • A doctrine about population dynamics developed by Thomas Malthus, according to which population increase comes up against "natural limits," represented by famine and war.

managerial capitalism • Capitalistic enterprises administered by managerial executives rather than by owners.

manifest functions • The functions of a particular social activity that are known to and intended by the individuals involved in the activity.

manufactured risk • Dangers that are created by the impact of human knowledge and technology on the natural world. Examples of manufactured risk include global warming and genetically modified foods.

market-oriented theories • Theories about economic development that assume that the best possible economic consequences will result if individuals are free to make their own economic decisions, uninhibited by governmental constraint.

marriage • A socially approved sexual relationship between two individuals.

Through much of history, marriage involved two persons of opposite sexes, but in the past decade, same-sex couples have gained legal access to marriage in some parts of the world. Marriage normally forms the basis of a family of procreation—that is, it is expected that the married couple will produce and raise children. Some societies and subcultures permit polygamy, in which an individual may have more than one spouse at the same time.

Marxism • A body of thought deriving its main elements from Karl Marx's ideas.

material goods • The physical objects that a society creates; these influence the ways in which people live.

materialist conception of history • The view developed by Marx, according to which material, or economic, factors have a prime role in determining historical change.

matrilocal family • A family system in which the husband is expected to live near the wife's parents.

mean • A statistical measure of central tendency, or average, based on dividing a total by the number of individual cases.

means of production • The means whereby the production of material goods is carried on in a society, including not just technology but the social relations among producers.

measures of central tendency • The ways of calculating averages.

median • The number that falls halfway in a range of numbers—a way of calculating central tendency that is sometimes more useful than calculating a mean.

Medicare • A program under the U.S. Social Security Administration that reimburses hospitals and physicians for medical care provided to qualifying people over sixty-five years old.

megalopolis • The "city of all cities" in ancient Greece—used in modern times to refer to very large conurbations.

melting pot • The idea that ethnic differences can be combined to create new patterns of behavior drawing on diverse cultural sources.

microsociology • The study of human behavior in contexts of face-to-face interaction.

middle class • A social class composed broadly of those working in white-collar and lower managerial occupations.

minority group • A group of people who are in a minority in a given society and who, because of their distinct physical or cultural characteristics, find themselves in situations of inequality within that society. Also known as ethnic minority.

mode • The number that appears most often in a given set of data. This can sometimes be a helpful way of portraying central tendency.

modernization theory • A version of market-oriented development theory that argues that low-income societies develop economically only if they give up their traditional ways and adopt modern economic institutions, technologies, and cultural values that emphasize savings and productive investment.

monogamy • A form of marriage in which each married partner is allowed only one spouse at any given time.

monopoly • A situation in which a single firm dominates in a given industry.

mores • A subtype of norm; they are widely adhered to and have great moral or social significance. Violations are generally sanctioned strongly.

mortality • The number of deaths in a population.

multiculturalism • The viewpoint according to which ethnic groups can exist separately and share equally in economic and political life.

nationalism • A set of beliefs and symbols expressing identification with a national community.

nation-state • A particular type of state, characteristic of the modern world, in which a government has sovereign power within a defined territorial area, and the population are citizens who know themselves to be part of a single nation. Nation-states are closely associated with the rise of nationalism, although nationalist loyalties do not always conform to the boundaries of specific states. Nation-states developed as part of an emerging nation-state system, originating in Europe; in current times, they span the whole globe.

neoliberalism • The economic belief that free-market forces, achieved by minimizing government restrictions on business, provide the only route to economic growth.

network • A set of informal and formal social ties that links people to one another.

new criminology • A branch of criminological thought, prominent in Great Britain in the 1970s, that regarded deviance as deliberately chosen and often political in nature. The new criminologists argued that crime and deviance could be understood only in the context of power and inequality within society.

new-style terrorism • A recent form of terrorism characterized by global ambitions, loose global organizational ties, and a more ruthless attitude toward the violence the terrorists are willing to use.

nonverbal communication • Communication between individuals based on facial expression or bodily gestures rather than on language.

norms • Rules of conduct that specify appropriate behavior in a given range of social situations. A norm either prescribes a given type of behavior or forbids it. All human groups follow norms, which are always backed by sanctions of one kind or another—varying from informal disapproval to physical punishment.

nuclear family • A family group consisting of an adult or adult couple and their dependent children.

obesity • Excessive body weight indicated by a body mass index (BMI) over 30.

occupation • Any form of paid employment in which an individual regularly works.

old old • Sociological term for persons between the ages of seventy-five and eighty-four.

oldest old • Sociological term for persons age eighty-five and older.

old-style terrorism • A type of terrorism that is local and linked to particular states and has limited objectives, which means that the violence involved is fairly limited.

oligarchy • Rule by a small minority within an organization or society.

oligopoly • The domination of a small number of firms in a given industry.

oral history • Interviews with people about events they witnessed or experienced at some point earlier in their lives.

organic solidarity • According to Émile Durkheim, the social cohesion that results from the various parts of a society functioning as an integrated whole.

organization • A large group of individuals with a definite set of authority relations. Many types of organizations exist in industrialized societies, influencing most aspects of our lives. While not all organizations are bureaucratic, there are close links between the development of organizations and bureaucratic tendencies.

organized crime • Criminal activities carried out by organizations established as businesses.

out-group • A group toward which one feels antagonism and contempt—"those people."

pariah groups • Groups that suffer from negative status discrimination—they are looked down on by most other members of society. The Jews, for example, have been a pariah group throughout much of European history.

participant observation • A method of research widely used in sociology and anthropology in which the researcher takes part in the activities of the group or community being studied. Also called fieldwork.

participatory democracy • A system of democracy in which all members of a group or community participate collectively in making major decisions.

pastoral societies • Societies whose subsistence derives from the rearing of domesticated animals.

patriarchy • The dominance of men over women. All known societies are patriarchal, although there are variations in the degree and nature of the power men exercise, as compared with women. One of the prime objectives of women's movements in modern societies is to combat existing patriarchal institutions.

patrilocal family • A family system in which the wife is expected to live near the husband's parents.

peer group • A friendship group composed of individuals of similar age and social status.

peripheral countries • Countries that have a marginal role in the world economy and are thus dependent on the core producing societies for their trading relationships.

personal space • The physical space individuals maintain between themselves and others.

personal troubles • Difficulties that are located in individual biographies and their immediate milieu, a seemingly private experience.

personality stabilization • According to the theory of functionalism, the family plays a crucial role in assisting its adult members emotionally. Marriage between adults is the arrangement through which adult personalities are supported and kept healthy.

pilot study • A trial run in survey research.

pluralism • A model for ethnic relations in which all ethnic groups in a society retain their independent and separate identities, yet share equally in the rights and powers of citizenship.

pluralist theories of modern democracy • Theories that emphasize the role of diverse and potentially competing interest groups, none of which dominate the political process.

political rights • Rights of political participation, such as the right to vote in local and national elections, held by citizens of a national community.

politics • The means by which power is employed to influence the nature and content of governmental activities. The sphere of the political includes the activities of those in government, but also the actions of others. There are many ways in which people outside the governmental apparatus seek to influence it.

polyandry • A form of marriage in which a woman may have two or more husbands simultaneously.

polygamy • A form of marriage in which a person may have two or more spouses simultaneously.

polygyny • A form of marriage in which a man may have two or more wives simultaneously.

postindustrial society • A postindustrial society is based on the production of information rather than material goods. According to postindustrialists, we are currently experiencing a series of social changes as profound as those that initiated the industrial era some 200 years ago.

postmodernism • The belief that society is no longer governed by history or progress. Postmodern society is highly pluralistic and diverse, with no "grand narrative" guiding its development.

poverty line • An official government measure to define those living in poverty in the United States.

power • The ability of individuals or the members of a group to achieve aims or further the interests they hold. Power is a pervasive element in all human relationships. Many conflicts in society are struggles over power, because how much power an individual or group is able to achieve governs how far they are able to put their wishes into practice.

power elite • Small networks of individuals who, according to C. Wright Mills, hold concentrated power in modern societies.

prejudice • The holding of preconceived ideas about an individual or group, ideas that are resistant to change even in the face of new information. Prejudice may be either positive or negative.

preoperational stage • According to Jean Piaget, a stage of human cognitive development in which the child has advanced sufficiently to master basic modes of logical thought.

primary deviance • According to Edwin Lemert, the actions that cause others to label one as a deviant.

primary group • A group that is characterized by intense emotional ties, face-to-face interaction, intimacy, and a strong, enduring sense of commitment.

primary socialization • The process by which children learn the cultural norms of the society into which they are born. Primary socialization occurs largely in the family.

profane • That which belongs to the mundane, everyday world.

proletariat • People who sell their labor for wages, according to Marx.

psychopath • A specific personality type; such individuals lack the moral sense and concern for others held by most normal people.

public issues • Difficulties or problems that are linked to the institutional and historical possibilities of social structure.

race • Differences in human physical characteristics used to categorize large numbers of individuals.

racialization • The process by which understandings of race are used to classify individuals or groups of people. Racial distinctions are more than ways of describing human differences; they are also important factors in the reproduction of patterns of power and inequality.

racism • The attribution of characteristics of superiority or inferiority to a population sharing certain physically inherited characteristics. Racism is a form of prejudice focusing on physical variations among people. Racist attitudes became entrenched during the period of Western colonial expansion, but also rest on mechanisms of prejudice and discrimination found in human societies today.

radical feminism • Form of feminist theory that believes that gender inequality is the result of male domination in all aspects of social and economic life.

random sampling • Sampling method in which a sample is chosen so that every member of the population has the same probability of being included.

rape • The forcing of non-consensual vaginal, oral, or anal intercourse.

rape culture • Social context where attitudes and norms perpetuate the treatment of women as sexual objects and instill in men a sense of sexual entitlement.

reference group • A group that provides a standard for judging one's attitudes or behaviors.

refugee • A person who has fled his or her home due to a political, economic, or natural crisis.

regionalization • The division of social life into different regional settings or zones.

relative deprivation • The recognition that one has less than his or her peers.

relative poverty • Poverty defined according to the living standards of the majority in any given society.

religion • A set of beliefs adhered to by the members of a community, incorporating symbols regarded with a sense of awe or wonder together with ritual practices. Religions do not universally involve a belief in supernatural entities.

religious economy • A theoretical framework within the sociology of religion that argues that religions can be fruitfully understood as organizations in competition with one another for followers.

religious nationalism • The linking of strongly held religious convictions with beliefs about a people's social and political destiny.

representative sample • A sample from a larger population that is statistically typical of that population.

resocialization • The process of learning new norms, values, and behaviors when one joins a new group or takes on a new social role, or when life circumstances change dramatically.

response cries • Seemingly involuntary exclamations individuals make when, for example, being taken by surprise, dropping something inadvertently, or expressing pleasure.

sacred • Describing something that inspires awe or reverence among those who believe in a given set of religious ideas.

sample • A small proportion of a larger population.

sampling • Studying a proportion of individuals or cases from a larger population as representative of that population as a whole.

sanction • A mode of reward or punishment that reinforces socially expected forms of behavior.

scapegoat • An individual or group blamed for wrongs that were not of their doing.

science • The disciplined marshaling of empirical data, combined with theoretical approaches and theories that illuminate or explain those data. Scientific activity combines the creation of new modes of thought with the careful testing of hypotheses and ideas. One major feature that helps distinguish science from other idea systems (such as religion) is the assumption that all scientific ideas are open to criticism and revision.

scientific racism • The use of scientific research or data to justify or reify beliefs about the superiority or inferiority of particular racial groups. Much of the "data" used to justify such claims is flawed or biased.

second shift • The excessive work hours borne by women relative to men; these hours are typically spent on domestic chores following the end of a day of work outside the home.

secondary deviance • According to Edwin Lemert, following the act of primary deviance, secondary deviation occurs when an individual accepts the label of deviant and acts accordingly.

secondary group • A group characterized by its large size and by impersonal, fleeting relationships.

sect • A religious movement that breaks away from orthodoxy.

secular thinking • Worldly thinking, particularly as seen in the rise of science, technology, and rational thought in general.

secularization • A process of decline in the influence of religion. Although modern societies have become increasingly secularized, tracing the extent of secularization is a complex matter. Secularization can refer to levels of involvement with religious organizations (such as rates of church attendance), the social and material influence wielded by religious organizations, and the degree to which people hold religious beliefs.

segregation • The practices of keeping racial and ethnic groups physically separate, thereby maintaining the superior position of the dominant group.

self-consciousness • Awareness of one's distinct social identity as a person separate from others. Human beings are not born with self-consciousness but acquire an awareness of self as a result of early socialization. The learning of language is of vital importance to the processes by which the child learns to become a self-conscious being.

self-identity • The ongoing process of self-development and definition of our personal identity through which we formulate a unique sense of ourselves and our relationship to the world around us.

semiperipheral countries • Countries that supply sources of labor and raw materials to the core industrial countries and the world economy but are not themselves fully industrialized societies.

sensorimotor stage • According to Jean Piaget, a stage of human cognitive development in which the child's awareness of his or her environment is dominated by perception and touch.

service society • A concept related to postindustrial society, it refers to a social order distinguished by the growth of service occupations at the expense of industrial jobs that produce material goods.

sex • The biological and anatomical differences distinguishing females from males.

sex segregation • The concentration of men and women in different jobs. These differences are believed to contribute to the gender pay gap.

sexual harassment • The making of unwanted sexual advances by one individual toward another, in which the first person persists even though it is clear that the other party is resistant.

sexual orientation • The direction of one's sexual or romantic attraction.

shaming • A way of punishing criminal and deviant behavior based on rituals of public disapproval rather than incarceration. The goal of shaming is to maintain the ties of the offender to the community.

short-range downward mobility • Social mobility that occurs when an individual moves from one position in the class structure to another of nearly equal status.

sick role • A term associated with the functionalist Talcott Parsons to describe the patterns of behavior that a sick person adopts in order to minimize the disruptive impact of his or her illness on others.

signifier • Any vehicle of meaning and communication.

slavery • A form of social stratification in which some people are owned by others as their property.

social aggregate • A collection of people who happen to be together in a particular place but do not significantly interact or identify with one another.

social capital • The social knowledge and connections that enable people to accomplish their goals and extend their influence.

social category • People who share a common characteristic (such as gender or occupation) but do not necessarily interact or identify with one another.

social change • Alteration in basic structures of a social group or society. Social change is an ever-present phenomenon in social life, but has become especially intense in the modern era. The origins of modern sociology can be traced to attempts to understand the dramatic changes shattering the traditional world and promoting new forms of social order.

social class gradient in health • The strong inverse association between socioeconomic resources and risk of illness or death.

social conflict theories of aging • Arguments that emphasize the ways in which the larger social structure helps to shape the opportunities available to the elderly. Unequal opportunities are seen as creating the potential for conflict.

social constraint • The conditioning influence on our behavior by the groups and societies of which we are members. Social constraint was regarded by Émile Durkheim as one of the distinctive properties of social facts.

social construction of gender • The learning of gender roles through socialization and interaction with others.

social exclusion • The outcome of multiple deprivations that prevent individuals or groups from participating fully in the economic, social, and political life of the society in which they live.

social facts • According to Émile Durkheim, the aspects of social life that shape our actions as individuals. Durkheim believed that social facts could be studied scientifically.

social gerontologists • Social scientists who study aging and the elderly.

social group • A collection of people who regularly interact with one another on the basis of shared expectations concerning behavior and who share a sense of common identity.

social interaction • The process by which we act and react to those around us.

social mobility • Movement of individuals or groups among different social positions.

social position • The social identity an individual has in a given group or society. Social positions may be general in nature (those associated with gender roles) or may be more specific (occupational positions).

social reproduction • The process whereby societies have structural continuity over time. Social reproduction is an important pathway through which parents transmit or produce values, norms, and social practices among their children.

social rights • Rights of social and welfare provision held by all citizens in a national community, including, for example, the right to claim unemployment benefits and sickness payments provided by the state.

social roles • Socially defined expectations of an individual in a given status, or occupying a particular social position. In every society, individuals play a number of social roles, such as teenager, parent, worker, or political leader.

Social Security • A government program that provides economic assistance to persons faced with unemployment, disability, or old age.

social self • The basis of self-consciousness in human individuals, according to the theory of George Herbert Mead. The social self is the identity conferred upon an individual by the reactions of others. A person achieves self-consciousness by becoming aware of this social identity.

social stratification • The existence of structured inequalities among groups in society, in terms of their access to material or symbolic rewards. While all societies involve some forms of stratification, only with the development of state-based systems did wide differences in wealth and power arise. The most distinctive form of stratification in modern societies is class divisions.

socialization • The social processes through which we develop an awareness of social norms and values and achieve a distinct sense of self. Although socialization processes are particularly significant in infancy and childhood, they continue to some degree throughout life. None of us are immune from the reactions of others around us, which influence and modify our behavior at all phases of our life course.

socialization of nature • The process by which we control phenomena regarded as "natural," such as reproduction.

society • A group of people who live in a particular territory, are subject to a common system of political authority, and are aware of having a distinct identity from other groups. Some societies, like hunting and gathering societies, are small, numbering no more than a few dozen people. Others are large, numbering millions—modern Chinese society, for instance, has a population of more than a billion people.

sociobiology • An approach that attempts to explain the behavior of both animals and human beings in terms of biological principles.

sociological imagination • The application of imaginative thought to the asking and answering of sociological questions. Someone using the sociological imagination "thinks himself away" from the familiar routines of daily life.

sociology • The study of human groups and societies, giving particular emphasis to analysis of the industrialized world. Sociology is one of a group of social sciences, which include anthropology, economics, political science, and human geography. The divisions among the various social sciences are not clear-cut, and all share a certain range of common interests, concepts, and methods.

sociology of the body • Field that focuses on how our bodies are affected by social influences. Health and illness, for instance, are shaped by social and cultural influences.

sovereignty • The undisputed political rule of a state over a given territorial area.

standard deviation • A way of calculating the spread of a group of figures.

standardized testing • A procedure whereby all students in a state take the same test under the same conditions.

state • A political apparatus (government institutions plus civil service officials) ruling over a given territorial order, whose authority is backed by law and the ability to use force. The emergence of the state marked a distinctive transition in human history, because the centralization of political power involved in state formation introduced new dynamics into processes of social change.

state-centered theories • Development theories that argue that appropriate government policies do not interfere with economic development, but rather can play a key role in bringing it about.

status • The social honor or prestige that a particular group is accorded by other members of a society. Status groups normally display distinct styles of life—patterns of behavior that the members of a group follow. Status privilege may be positive or negative. Pariah status groups are regarded with disdain or treated as outcasts by the majority of the population.

stepfamily • A family in which at least one partner has children from a previous marriage.

stereotype • A fixed and inflexible category.

stigma • Any physical or social characteristic that is labeled by society as undesirable.

strike • A temporary stoppage of work by a group of employees in order to express a grievance or enforce a demand.

structural strain • Tensions that produce conflicting interests within societies.

structuration • The two-way process by which we shape our social world through our individual actions and by which we are reshaped by society.

structure • The recurrent patterned arrangements and hierarchies that influence or limit the choices and opportunities available to us.

subculture • Values and norms distinct from those of the majority, held by a group within a wider society.

suburbanization • The development of suburbia, areas of housing outside inner cities.

suffrage • A legal right to vote guaranteed by the Fifteenth Amendment to the U.S. Constitution; guaranteed to women by the Nineteenth Amendment.

suffragettes • Members of early women's movements who pressed for equal voting rights for women and men.

surplus value • In Marxist theory, the value of a worker's labor power left over when an employer has repaid the cost of hiring the worker.

survey • A method of sociological research in which questionnaires are administered to the population being studied.

sustainable development • The notion that economic growth should proceed only insofar as natural resources are recycled rather than depleted; biodiversity is maintained; and clean air, water, and land are protected.

symbol • One item used to stand for or represent another—as in the case of a flag, which symbolizes a nation.

symbolic interactionism • A theoretical approach in sociology developed by George Herbert Mead that emphasizes the role of symbols and language as core elements of all human interaction.

target hardening • Practical measures used to limit a criminal's ability to commit crime, such as community policing and use of house alarms.

technology • The application of knowledge of the material world to production; the creation of material instruments (such as machines) used in human interaction with nature.

terrorism • Use of attacks on civilians designed to persuade a government to alter its policies, or to damage its standing in the world.

theism • A belief in one or more supernatural deities.

theoretical questions • Questions posed by sociologists when seeking to explain a particular range of observed events. The asking of theoretical questions is crucial to allowing us to generalize about the nature of social life.

theory of racial formation • The process by which social, economic, and political forces determine the content and importance of racial categories.

time-space • When and where events occur.

tracking • Dividing students into groups according to ability.

transactional leader • A leader who is concerned with accomplishing the group's tasks, getting group members to do their jobs, and making certain that the group achieves its goals.

transformational leader • A leader who is able to instill in the members of a group a sense of mission or higher purpose, thereby changing the nature of the group itself.

transnational corporations • Business corporations located in two or more countries.

triad • A group consisting of three persons.

triangulation • The use of multiple research methods as a way of producing more reliable empirical data than are available from any single method.

underclass • A class of individuals situated at the bottom of the class system, often composed of people from ethnic minority backgrounds.

unfocused interaction • Interaction occurring among people present in a particular setting but not engaged in direct face-to-face communication.

Uniform Crime Reports (UCR) • Documents that contain official data on crime that are reported to law enforcement agencies that then provide the data to the FBI.

union • An organization that advances and protects the interests of workers with respect to working conditions, wages, and benefits.

universal health coverage • Public health care programs motivated by the goal of providing affordable health services to all members of a population.

upper class • A social class broadly composed of the more affluent members of society, especially those who have inherited wealth, own businesses, or hold large numbers of stocks (shares).

urban ecology • An approach to the study of urban life based on an analogy with the adjustment of plants and organisms to the physical environment. According to ecological theorists, the various neighborhoods and zones within cities are formed as a result of natural processes of adjustment on the part of populations as they compete for resources.

urban renewal • The process of renovating deteriorating neighborhoods by encouraging the renewal of old buildings and the construction of new ones.

urbanism • A term used by Louis Wirth to denote distinctive characteristics of urban social life, such as its impersonal or alienating nature.

urbanization • The development of towns and cities.

values • Ideas held by individuals or groups about what is desirable, proper, good, and bad. What individuals value is strongly influenced by the specific culture in which they happen to live.

wealth • Money and material possessions held by an individual or group.

welfare capitalism • Practice in which large corporations protect their employees from the vicissitudes of the market.

welfare state • A political system that provides a wide range of welfare benefits for its citizens.

white-collar crime • Criminal activities carried out by those in white-collar, or professional, jobs.

work • The activity by which people produce from the natural world and so ensure their survival. Work should not be thought of exclusively as paid employment. In traditional cultures, there was only a rudimentary monetary system, and few people worked for money. In modern societies, there remain types of work that do not involve direct payment (for example, housework).

working class • A social class broadly composed of people working in blue-collar, or manual, occupations.

working poor • People who work, but whose earnings are not enough to lift them above the poverty line.

world-systems theory • Pioneered by Immanuel Wallerstein, this theory emphasizes the interconnections among countries based on the expansion of a capitalist world economy. This economy is made up of core countries, semiperipheral countries, and peripheral countries.

young old • Sociological term for persons between the ages of sixty-five and seventy-four.

bibliography

AARP. (2012). Loneliness among older adults: a national survey of adults 45+. http://www.aarp.org/content/dam/aarp/research/surveys_statistics/general/2012/loneliness_2010.pdf, accessed 7/13/13.

ABC News. (2013). Lulu' App Allows Women to Dish Dirt on Exes. ABC Nightly News (July 12, 2013). http://abcnews.go.com/blogs/lifestyle/2013/07/lulu-app-allows-women-to-dish-dirt-on-exes/, accessed 7/27/13.

Abeles, R. P. and M. W. Riley. (1987). Longevity, social structure, and cognitive aging. In C. Schooler and K. Warner Schaie (Eds.), *Cognitive functioning and social structure over the life course.* Norwood, NJ: Ablex.

Accad, E. (1991). Contradictions for contemporary women in the Middle East. In C. Talpade Mohanty, A. Russo, and L. Torres (Eds.), *Third world women and the politics of feminism.* Bloomington: Indiana University Press.

Acs, G. (2011). *Downward Mobility from the Middle Class: Waking up from the American Dream.* Washington, DC: Pew Charitable Trusts. http://www.pewstates.org/uploadedFiles/PCS_Assets/2011/MiddleClassReport.pdf, accessed 10/12/13.

AIDS.gov. (2013). Global AIDS overview. http://aids.gov/federal-resources/around-the-world/global-aids-overview, accessed 5/27/14.

AIDS Orphans Educational Trust. (2003). *AIDS Orphans Educational Trust– Uganda.* www.orphanseducation.org, accessed 12/28/04.

Akashi H, A. Senju, H. Uibo, Y. Kikuchi, T. Hasegawa, et al. (2013). Attention to Eye Contact in the West and East: Autonomic Responses and Evaluative Ratings. PLoS ONE 8(3): e59312. doi:10.1371/journal.pone.0059312.

Albrow, M. (1997). *The global age: State and society beyond modernity.* Stanford, CA: Stanford University Press.

Aldrich, H. E. and P. Marsden. (1988). Environments and organizations. In N. J. Smelser (Ed.), *Handbook of sociology.* Newbury Park, CA: Sage.

Al-Haqhaq, L. (2011). Social media megaphone reaches to more people. *Kuwait Times* (August 9, 2011). http:// www.kuwaittimes.net/read_news.php?newsid=OTMzMDA5MDQ1NA==, accessed 8/13/11.

Allegretto, S. M. Doussard, D. Graham-Squire, K. Jacobs, D. Thompson and J. Thompson. (2013). Fast food, poverty wages: The public cost of low-wage jobs in the fast-food industry. University of California-Berkeley Labor. http://laborcenter.berkeley.edu/publiccosts/fast_food_poverty_wages.pdfCenter, accessed 3/17/14.

Allen, M. P. (1981). Managerial power and tenure in the large corporation. *Social Forces*, 60.

Alvarez, L. (2013). A University Band, Chastened by Hazing, Makes Its Return. *New York Times* (September 6, 2013). http://www.nytimes.com/2013/09/07/us/a-university-band-chastened-by-hazing-makes-its-return.html?pagewanted=all, accessed 9/22/13.

Alvarez, L. and C. Buckley. (2013). Zimmerman Is Acquitted in Killing of Trayvon Martin. *New York Times* (July 14, 2013). http://www.nytimes.com/2013/07/15/us/george-zimmerman-verdict-trayvon-martin.html, accessed 10/19/13.

Alvarez et al. (1996). Women in the professions: Assessing progress. In P. J. Dubeck and K. Borman (Eds.), *Women and work: A handbook*. New York: Garland.

Amato et al. (1995). Parental divorce, marital conflict, and offspring well-being during early Adulthood. *Social Forces, 73*, 895–915.

American Academy of Pediatrics. (2004). Sexual orientation and adolescents. *Pediatrics, 113*(6), 1827–1832.

American Association of University Women (AAUW). (1992). *How schools shortchange girls*. Washington, DC: American Association of University Women Educational Foundation.

American Council on Education (ACE). (2001). The American freshman: National norms for fall 2000. Los Angeles, CA: UCLA Higher Education Research Institute and ACE. Results also published in This year's freshmen at 4-year colleges: Their opinions, activities, and goals. *Chronicle of Higher Education* (January 26, 2001).

American Psychiatric Association (2013). *Diagnostic and Statistical Manual of Mental Disorders* (Fifth ed.). Arlington, VA: APA.

American Religious Identification Survey (ARIS). (2008). Part 1A: Belonging. http://b27.cc.trincoll.edu/weblogs/AmericanReligionSurvey-ARIS/reports/p1a_belong.html, accessed August 2009.

Amin, S. (1974). *Accumulation on a world scale*. New York: Monthly Review Press.

Ammons, S. and W. Markham. (2004). Working at home: Experiences of skilled white collar workers. *Sociological Spectrum, 24*(2), 191–238.

Amromin, G. and A. L. Paulson. (2010). Default rates on prime and subprime mortgages: differences and similarities. Chicago: Federal Reserve Bank. http://www.chicagofed.org/digital_assets/publications/profitwise_news_and_views/2010/PNV_Aug2010_ReEd_FINAL_web.pdf, accessed 10/18/13.

Amsden, A. H. (1989). *Asia's next giant: South Korea and late industrialization*. New York: Oxford University Press.

Amsden, A., J. Kochanowicz, and L. Taylor. (1994). *The market meets its match: Restructuring the economies of Eastern Europe*. Cambridge, MA: Harvard University Press.

Anderson, B. (1991). *Imagined communities: Reflections on the origin and spread of nationalism*. Rev. ed. New York: Routledge.

Anderson, E. (1990). *Streetwise: Race, class, and change in an urban community*. Chicago: University of Chicago Press.

Anderson, P. B., and C. Struckman-Johnson (Eds.). (1998). *Sexually aggressive women: Current perspectives and controversies*. New York: Guilford Press.

Angell, M. and J. P. Kassirer. (1998). Alternative medicine—the risks of untested and unregulated remedies. *New England Journal of Medicine, 339*, 839.

Angier, N. (1995). If you're really ancient, you may be better off. *New York Times* (June 11, 1995). http://www.nytimes.com/1995/06/11/weekinreview/the-nation-if-you-re-really-ancient-you-may-be-better-off.html.

Annie E. Casey Foundation. (2011). Kids Count Data Center. http://datacenter.kidscount.org/, accessed 8/31/11.

Anyon, J. (2005). *Radical Possibilities: Public Policy, Urban Education, and a New Social Movement*. New York: Taylor & Francis.

Anzaldua, G. (1990). *Making face, making soul: Haciendo caras: Creative and cultural perspectives by feminists of color*. San Francisco: Aunt Lute Foundation.

Appadurai, A. (1986). Introduction: Commodities and the politics of value. In A. Appadurai (Ed.), *The social life of things*. Cambridge: Cambridge University Press.

Appelbaum, R. P. (1990). Counting the homeless. In J. A. Momeni (Ed.), *Homeless in the United States* (Vol. 2). New York: Praeger.

Appelbaum, R. P. and B. Christerson. (1997). Cheap labor strategies and export-oriented industrialization: Some lessons from the East Asia/Los Angeles apparel connection. *International Journal of Urban and Regional Research, 21*(2).

Ariès, P. (1965). *Centuries of childhood*. New York: Random House.

Arndt, F. (2014). Social Media in Ukraine's #Euromaidan Protests. *Epoch Times* (January 9, 2014), http://www.theepochtimes.com/n3/blog/social-media-in-ukraines-euromaidan-protests/, accessed 2/9/14.

Asch, S. (1952). *Social psychology*. Englewood Cliffs, NJ: Prentice-Hall.

Ashworth, A. E. (1980). *Trench warfare: 1914–1918*. London: Macmillan.

Atchley, R. (1989). A continuity theory of normal aging. *Gerontologist, 29*, 183–190.

Atchley, R. C. (2000). *Social forces and aging: An introduction to social gerontology* (9th ed.). Belmont, CA: Wadsworth.

Attaran, M. (2004). Exploring the relationship between information technology and business process reengineering. *Information & Management, 41*(5), 585–596.

August, K. J. and D. H. Sorkin. (2010). Racial and ethnic disparities in indicators of physical health status: Do they still exist throughout late life? *Journal of the American Geriatrics Society, 58*, 2009–2015.

Avert.org. (2013). Worldwide HIV & AIDS statistics. http://avert.org/worldstats.htm, accessed 8/26/13.

Avery, R. and G. Canner. (2005). New information reported under HMDA and its application in fair lending enforcement. *Federal Reserve Bulletin*. www.federalreserve.gov/pubs/bulletin/2005/3-05hmda.pdf, accessed spring 2006.

Avins, M. (2003). MoveOn redefines party politics. *Los Angeles Times*, p. A1 (December 9, 2003).

Bachmann, H. (2012). The Swiss Difference: A Gun Culture that Works. *TIME Magazine* (December 20, 2012). http://world.time.com/2012/12/20/the-swiss-difference-a-gun-culture-that-works/, accessed 9/22/13.

Bailey, J. M. (1993). Heritable factors influence sexual orientation in women. *Archives of General Psychiatry, 50*.

Bailey, J. and R. Pillard. (1991). A genetic study of male sexual orientation. *Archives of General Psychiatry, 48*.

Baker, L. A., M. Silverstein, and N. M. Putney. (2008). Grandparents raising grandchildren in the United States: changing family forms, stagnant social policies. *Journal of Societal & Social Policy, 7*, 53.

Bales, R. F. (1953). The egalitarian problem in small groups. In T. Parsons (Ed.), *Working papers in the theory of action*. Glencoe, IL: Free Press.

Bales, R. F. (1970). *Personality and interpersonal behavior*. New York: Holt, Rinehart, and Winston.

Baltic 21 Secretariat. (2006). *Passenger car density*. www.baltic21.org/reports/indicators/re08.atm, accessed spring 2009.

Baranowski T., D. Abdelsamad, J. Baranowski, T. M. O'Connor, D. Thompson, A. Barnett, E. Cerin, and T. A. Chen. (2012). Impact of an active video game on healthy children's physical activity. *Pediatrics*. 129(3): 636–42.

Barton, D. (2006). *Literacy: An introduction to the ecology of written language* (2nd ed.). Malden, MA: Wiley Blackwell.

Baudrillard, J. (1988). *Jean Baudrillard: Selected writings*. Stanford, CA: Stanford University Press.

Baxter, S. (2011). New Santa Cruz police smartphone application includes police scanner, alerts, tip submissions. *San Jose Mercury News* (March 29, 2011). http://www.mercurynews.com/ci_17728800, accessed 9/23/13.

BBC. (2011). Internet role in Egypt's protest. http://www.bbc.co.uk/news/world-middle-east-12400319, accessed 8/30/11.

Bearman, P. (2002). Opposite-sex twins and adolescent same-sex attraction. *American Journal of Sociology, 107*, 1179–1205.

Beck, U. (1992). *Risk society*. London: Sage.

Beck, U. (1995). *Ecological politics in an age of risk*. Cambridge: Polity Press.

Becker A. (2004). Television, Disordered Eating, and Young Women in Fiji: Negotiating Body Image and Identity during Rapid Social Change. *Culture, Medicine and Psychiatry* 28:533–559.

Becker, H. S. (1963). *Outsiders: Studies in the sociology of deviance.* New York: Macmillan.

Bell, A., M. S. Weinberg, and S. K. Hammersmith. (1981). *Sexual preference: Its development in men and women.* Bloomington: Indiana University Press.

Bell, D. (1976). *The coming of post-industrial society: A venture in social forecasting.* New York: Basic Books.

Bellafante, G. (2011). Gunning for Wall Street, with faulty aim. *New York Times* (September 25, 2011). http://www.nytimes.com/2011/09/25/nyregion/protesters-are-gunning-for-wall-street-with-faulty-aim.html, accessed 9/27/11.

Bellah, et al. (1985). *Habits of the heart: Individualism and commitment in American life.* New York: Harper & Row.

Bengtson, V., K-D Kim, G. C. Myers, and K-S Eun. (2000). *Aging East and West: Families, States and the Elderly.* New York: Springer.

Bennett, J. W. (1976). *The ecological transition: Cultural anthropology and human adaptation.* New York: Pergamon Press.

Berger, P. L. (1967). *The sacred canopy: Elements of a sociological theory of religion.* Garden City, NY: Anchor Books.

Berger, P. L. (1986). *The capitalist revolution: Fifty propositions about prosperity, equality, and liberty.* New York: Basic Books.

Berger, P. L. and H. Hsiao. (1988). *In search of an East Asian development model.* New Brunswick, NJ: Transaction.

Berger, P. L. et al. (2008). Predictors of father involvement in social father and biological father families. *Journal of Marriage and Family, 70*(3).

Berlan, E. D., et al. (2010). Sexual orientation and bullying among adolescents in the Growing Up Today Study. *Journal of Adolescent Health, 46*(4), 366–371.

Berle, A. and G. Means. (1982; orig. 1932). *The modern corporation and private property.* Buffalo, NY: Heim.

Berryman, P. (1987). *Liberation theology: Essential facts about the revolutionary movement in Central America and beyond.* Philadelphia: Temple University Press.

Beyer, P. (1994). *Religion and globalization.* Thousand Oaks, CA: Sage.

Beyerstein, B. L. (1999, Fall/Winter). Psychology and "alternative medicine": Social and judgmental biases that make inert treatments seem to work. *Scientific Review of Alternative Medicine, 3*(2).

Bianchi, S. M., et al. (2007). *Changing rhythms of American family life.* New York: Russell Sage.

Birren, J. and V. Bengston (Eds.). (1988). *Emerging theories of aging.* New York: Springer.

Bjorkqvist, K. (1994). Sex differences in physical, verbal, and indirect aggression: A review of recent research. *Sex Roles, 30*(3–4), 177–188.

Bjorkqvist, K., K. Lagerspetz, and K. Osterman. (2006). Sex differences in covert aggression. *Aggressive Behavior* (December 6, 2006), *202,* 27–33.

Black, P. M. Pearson and V. Butenko, (2014). Ukraine protesters stand ground as European, U.S. leaders ramp up pressure. *CNN* (February 19, 2014). http://www.cnn.com/2014/02/19/world/europe/ukraine-protests/, accessed 2/19/14.

Black, R., and L. Goldwert. (2010). 'Ugly Meter' iPhone app may be hurtful to kids and fodder for bullies. *Daily News* (October 20, 2010). http://www.nydailynews.com/life-style/alibi-iphone-app-tells-user-ugly-article-1.190668#ixzz2ZFJKLMA6, accessed 7/16/13.

Blanchard, R., and A. Bogaert. (1996). Homosexuality in men and number of older brothers. *American Journal of Psychiatry, 153.*

Blau, P. M. and O. D. Duncan. (1967). *The American occupational structure.* New York: Wiley.

Blauner, R. (1964). *Alienation and freedom.* Chicago: University of Chicago Press.

Blauner, R. (1972). *Racial oppression in America.* New York: Harper and Row.

Blum, L. M. (1991). *Between feminism and labor: The significance of the comparable worth movement.* Berkeley: University of California Press.

Bochenek, M. and A. W. Brown. (2001). *Hatred in the hallways: Violence and discrimination against lesbian, gay, bisexual, and transgender students in U.S. schools.* New York: Human Rights Watch, www.hrw.org/reports/2001/uslgbt/toc.htm, accessed 12/28/04.

Boden, D. and H. L. Molotch. (1994). The compulsion of proximity. In D. Boden and R. Friedland (Eds.), *Nowhere: Space, time, and modernity.* Berkeley: University of California Press.

Bomey, N. B. Snavely, and A. Priddle. (2013). Judge rules Detroit eligible for historic Chapter 9 bankruptcy, says pensions can be cut. *Detroit Free Press* (December 3, 2013). http://www.freep.com/article/20131203/NEWS01/312030084/Detroit-bankruptcy-eligibility-Steven-Rhodes-Chapter-9-Kevyn-Orr, accessed 1/3/14.

Bonacich, E. and R. Appelbaum. (2000). *Behind the label: Inequality in the Los Angeles garment industry.* Berkeley: University of California Press.

Bonnington, C. (2012). Are Men and Women Using Mobile Apps Differently? *Wired* (April 12, 2013). http://www.wired.com/gadgetlab/2013/04/men-women-app-usage/, accessed 6/9/13.

Booth, A. (1977). Food riots in the northwest of England, 1770–1801. *Past and Present,* no. 77.

Borreson, K. (2012). Divorce Help; 5 Apps to Make Your Split Less Stressful. *The Huffington Post* (October 22, 2012). http://www.huffingtonpost.com/2012/10/22/divorce-help-5-apps-to-ma_n_2003780.html?view=print&comm_ref=false, accessed 12/1/13.

Bositis, D. (2001). Black elected officials: A statistical summary, 2001. Joint Center for Political and Economic Studies. http://www.jointcenter.org/sites/default/files/upload/research/files/Black%20Elected%20Officials%20A%20Statistical%20Summary%202001.pdf, accessed 1/27/06.

Botelho, G. E. Payne, and A. Watts. (2013). 1 teen arrested, 1 at large in beating death of WWII vet. *CNN* (August 23, 2013). http://www.cnn.com/2013/08/23/us/world-war-vet-beating-death/index.html, accessed 9/24/13.

Bouma et al. (2004). CHI '04 extended abstracts on Human factors in computing systems. Conference on Human Factors in Computing Systems. New York: ACM Press.

Bourdieu, P. (1984). *Distinction: A social critique of judgement of taste.* Cambridge, MA: Harvard University Press.

Bourdieu, P. (1988). *Language and symbolic power.* Cambridge, UK: Polity Press.

Bourdieu, P. (1990). *The logic of practice.* Palo Alto, CA: Stanford University Press.

Bowles, S. and H. Gintis. (1976). *Schooling in capitalist America.* New York: Basic Books.

Bowman, Q. and C. Amico. (2010). Congress loses hundreds of years of experience—but majority of incumbents stick around. *PBS Newshour* (November 5, 2010). http://www.pbs.org/newshour/rundown/congress-loses-hundreds-of-years-of-experience-but-vast-majority-of-incumbents-stick-around/, accessed 9/27/11.

Boyer, R. and D. Drache (Eds.). (1996). *States against markets: The limits of globalization.* New York: Routledge.

Bradsher, K. and D. Barboza. (2006). Pollution from Chinese coal casts shadow around globe. *New York Times* (June 11, 2006). http://www.nytimes.com/2006/06/11/business/worldbusiness/11chinacoal.html?pagewanted=all, accessed 12/7/11.

Bradsher, K., and S-L. Wong. (2013). Faltering Economy in China Dims Job Prospects for Graduations. *The New York Times*

(June 16, 2013). http://www.nytimes.com/2013/06/17/business/global/faltering-economy-in-china-dims-job-prospects-for-graduates.html?pagewanted=all&_r=0, accessed 3/7/14.

Braithwaite, J. (1996). Crime, shame, and reintegration. In P. Cordella and L. Siegal (Eds.), *Readings in contemporary criminological theory*. Boston: Northeastern University Press.

Bramlett, M. and W. Mosher. (2002). Cohabitation, marriage, divorce, and remarriage in the United States. *Vital Health Statistics* vol. 23, no. 22. Washington, DC: National Center for Health Statistics. www.cdc.gov/nchs/data/series/sr_23/sr23_022.pdf, accessed 1/9/07.

Brass, D. J. (1985). Men's and women's networks: A study of interaction patterns and influence in an organization. *Academy of Management Journal, 28*.

Braverman, H. (1974). *Labor and monopoly capital*. New York: Monthly Review Press.

Brenner, P. S. (2011). Exceptional Behavior or Exceptional Identity? Overreporting of Church Attendance in the U.S. *Public Opinion Quarterly* 75(1):19–41.

Bresnahan, T. F., E. Brynjolfsson, and Lorin M. Hitt. (2002). Information technology, workplace organization, and the demand for skilled labor: firm-level evidence. *Quarterly Journal of Economics, 117*(1), 33976.

Brewer, R. M. (1993). Theorizing race, class and gender: The new scholarship of black feminist intellectuals and black women's labor. In S. M. James and A. P. A. Busia (Eds.), *Theorizing black feminisms: The visionary pragmatism of black women*. New York: Routledge.

Bricker, J., A. B. Kennickell, K. B. Moore, and J. Sabelhaus. (2012). Changes in U.S. family finances from 2007 to 2010: Evidence from the survey of consumer finances. *Federal Reserve Bulletin* 98(2): 1–80. http://www.federalreserve.gov/pubs/bulletin/2012/pdf/scf12.pdf, accessed 7/25/13.

Bricout, J. C. (2004). Using telework to enhance return to work outcomes for individuals with spinal cord injuries. *Neurorehabilitation, 19*(2), 147–159.

Brown, C. and K. Jasper (Eds.). (1993). *Consuming passions: Feminist approaches to eating disorders and weight preoccupations*. Toronto: Second Story Press.

Brown, D. E. (1991). *Human universals*. New York: McGraw-Hill.

Brown, J. K. (1977). A note on the division of labor by sex. In N. Glazer and H. Y. Waehrer (Eds.), *Woman in a man-made world*. 2nd ed. Chicago: Rand McNally.

Brown, S. L. (2004). Family structure and child well-being: The significance of parental cohabitation. *Journal of Marriage and Family, 66* (May), 351–367.

Brownmiller, S. (1986). *Against our will: Men, women, and rape* (Rev. ed.). New York: Bantam.

Brownell, K. and K. Horgen. (2004). *Food fight: The inside story of the food industry, America's obesity crisis, and what we can do about it*. New York: McGraw-Hill.

Brownstein, R. (2003). Liberal group flexes online muscle in its very own primary. *Los Angeles Times* (June 23, 2003), p. A9.

Brubaker, R. (1992). *The politics of citizenship*. Cambridge, MA: Harvard University Press.

Buckley, Chris. (2013). China to Ease Long-time Policy of 1-Child Limit. *New York Times* (November 15, 2013). http://www.nytimes.com/2013/11/16/world/asia/china-to-loosen-its-one-child-policy.html?_r=0, accessed 1/4/14.

Bull, P. (1983). *Body movement and interpersonal communication*. New York: Wiley.

Bumpass, L. and H-H Lu. (2000). Trends in cohabitation and implications for children's family context in the United States. *Population Studies, 54, 29–41*.

Bumpass, L., et al. (1991, November). The role of cohabitation in declining rates of marriage. *Journal of Marriage and the Family, 53*.

Burns, J. M. (1978). *Leadership*. New York: Harper & Row.

Burr, C. (1993, March). Homosexuality and biology. *Atlantic Monthly*.

Burris, B. H. (1993). *Technocracy at work*. Albany, NY: State University of New York Press.

Burris, B. H. (1998). Computerization of the workplace. In *Annual Review of Sociology, 24*. Palo Alto, CA: Annual Reviews.

Business Week. (December 15, 1998). Good news on wage inequality.

Business Week. (2009). A lost decade for jobs. (June 23, 2009) http://www.businessweek.com/the_thread/economicsunbound/archives/2009/06/a_lost_decade_f.html, accessed September 2009.

Butler, J. (1989). *Gender trouble: Feminism and the subversion of identity*. New York: Routledge.

Cain D. S. and T. Combs-Orme. (2005). Family structure effects on parenting stress and practices in the African-American family. *Journal of Sociology and Social Welfare, 32*(2), 19–40.

Caldwell, J., B. K. Caldwell, P. Caldwell, P. F. McDonald, and T. Schindlmayr. (2010). *Demographic transition theory*. New York: Springer.

Cambridge Diversity Consulting. (2013). The Race Awareness Project. http://www.raceawarenessproject.com, accessed 2/19/2014.

Campos, P., et al. (2006). The epidemiology of overweight and obesity: Public health crisis or moral panic? *International Journal of Epidemiology, 35, 55–60*.

Carnevale, A. P., J. Strohl, and M. Melton. (2011). What's it worth: The economic value of college majors. Washington, DC: Georgetown University Center on Education and the Workforce. http://www9.georgetown.edu/grad/gppi/hpi/cew/pdfs/whatsitworth-complete.pdf.

Carr, D. (2010). Golden years? Poverty among older adults. *Contexts, 9*(1), 62–63.

Carr, D. (2014). *Worried sick: Why stress hurts and what to do about it*. (Pinpoint Series) New Brunswick, NJ: Rutgers University Press.

Carr, D. and M. Friedman. (2005). Is obesity stigmatizing? Body weight, perceived discrimination and psychological well-being in the United States. *Journal of Health and Social Behavior, 46, 244–259*.

Carr, D. and M. Friedman. (2006). Body weight and interpersonal relationships. *Social Psychology Quarterly, 69, 127–149*.

Carr, D., et al. (2007). Understanding the relationship between obesity and positive and negative affect: The role of psychosocial mechanisms. *Body Image, 4*(2), 165–177.

Carr, D., et al. (2013). Bigger isn't always better: The effect of obesity on the sexual well-being of adult men in the U.S. *Men and Masculinities, 16, 452–477*.

Carr, D. and K. Springer. (2010). Advances in families and health research in the 21st century. *Journal of Marriage and Family, 72*(3), 743–761.

Castells, M. (1977). *The urban question: A Marxist approach*. Cambridge, MA: MIT Press.

Castells, M. (1983). *The city and the grass roots: A cross-cultural theory of urban social movements*. Berkeley: University of California Press.

Castells, M. (1992). Four Asian tigers with a dragon head: A comparative analysis of the state, economy, and society in the Asian Pacific Rim. In R. P. Appelbaum and J. Henderson (Eds.), *States and development in the Asian Pacific Rim*. Newbury Park, CA: Sage.

Castells, M. (1996). *The rise of the network society*. Malden, MA: Blackwell.

Castells, M. (1998). *End of millennium*. Malden, MA: Blackwell.

Castells, M. (2000). *The rise of the network society*. Oxford: Oxford University Press.

Castells, M. (2001). *The internet galaxy*. Oxford: Oxford University Press.

Castles, S. and M. J. Miller. (1993). *The age of migration: International population movements in the modern world*. London: Macmillan.

Castles, S. and M. J. Miller. (2009). *The age of migration, fourth edition: International population movements in the modern world*. London: The Guilford Press.

Catalano, S. M. (2005). Criminal victimization, 2004. *National crime victimization survey*, Table 2. http://www.bjs.gov/content/pub/pdf/cv04.pdf, accessed 10/5/05.

Catalyst (2012). Women in Financial Services. Catalyst Knowledge Center (March 14, 2013). http://catalyst.org/knowledge/women-financial-services, accessed 10/12/13.

Catholics for Choice. (2004). Catholic attitudes on sexual behavior & reproductive health. Washington, DC. http://www.catholicsforchoice.org/topics/international/documents/2004worldview.pdf, accessed fall 2009.

Center for American Women and Politics. (2013a). Statewide elective executive women, 2013. www.cawp.rutgers.edu/fast_facts/levels_of_office/documents/stwide.pdf, accessed 9/15/13.

Center for American Women and Politics. (2013b). Women in the U.S. Congress, 2013. www.cawp.rutgers.edu/fast_facts/levels_of_office/documents/cong.pdf, accessed 9/5/13.

Center for American Women and Politics. (2014). Facts on Women in Congress, 2014. Eagleton Institute. http://www.cawp.rutgers.edu/fast_facts/levels_of_office/Congress-CurrentFacts.php, accessed 3/17/14.

Center for Responsive Politics (CRP). (2011). Lobbying database. http://www.opensecrets.org/lobby/index.php, accessed 11/29/11.

Center for Responsive Politics. (2013a). *2012 Presidential race*. http://www.opensecrets.org/pres12/index.php, accessed 9/22/13.

Center for Responsive Politics. (2013b). *2014 overview: Stats as a glance*. http://www.opensecrets.org/overview/index.php, accessed 9/22/13.

Center for Responsive Politics. (2013c). *Historical elections: Reelection rates over the years*. http://www.opensecrets.org/bigpicture/reelect.php, accessed 9/22/13.

Center for Responsive Politics. (2013d). Most expensive races. http://www.opensecrets.org/bigpicture/topraces.php?cycle=2010&display=currcands, accessed 9/22/13.

Center on Education Policy. (2007). Choices, Changes, and Challenges: Curriculum and Instruction in the NCLB Era. http://www.cep-dc.org/publications/index.cfm?selectedYear=2007, accessed 2/19/2014.

Centers for Disease Control and Prevention (CDC). (2003). National ambulatory care survey, 2001 summary. Advanced data from vital and health statistics, Number 337 (August 11, 2003). www.cdc.gov/nchs/data/ad/ad337.pdf, accessed 12/29/04.

Centers for Disease Control and Prevention (CDC). (2008a). Childhood overweight and obesity. http://www.cdc.gov/obesity/childhood, accessed August 2009.

Centers for Disease Control and Prevention (CDC). (2008b). *Complementary and alternative medicine use among adults and children: United States, 2007.* http://www.cdc.gov/nchs/data/nhsr/nhsr012.pdf, accessed 8/4/13.

Centers for Disease Control and Prevention (CDC). (2010a). Cigarette smoking: United States, 1965–2008. http://www.cdc.gov/mmwr/preview/mmwrhtml/su6001a24.htm#tab2. accessed 8/23/11.

Centers for Disease Control and Prevention (CDC). (2010b). HIV in the United States. http://www.cdc.gov/hiv/resources/factsheets/us.htm, accessed 8/23/11.

Centers for Disease Control and Prevention (CDC). (2010c). Prevalence of overweight, obesity, and extreme obesity among adults: United States, trends 1960–1962 through 2007–2008. http://www.cdc.gov/NCHS/data/hestat/obesity_adult_07_08/obesity_adult_07-08.pdf, accessed 8/23/11.

Centers for Disease Control and Prevention (CDC). (2011a). *CDC Health Disparities and Inequalities Report — United States, 2011.* http://origin.glb.cdc.gov/mmwr/pdf/other/su6001.pdf, accessed 12/8/13.

Centers for Disease Control and Prevention (CDC). (2011b). Rates of diagnoses of HIV infection among adults and adolescents, by area of residence, 2011—United States and 6 dependent areas. *HIV Surveillance Report* 23:5–84. http://www.cdc.gov/hiv/pdf/statistics_2011_HIV_Surveillance_Report_vol_23.pdf, accessed 11/1/13.

Centers for Disease Control and Prevention (CDC). (2012a). Cancer screening—United States, 2010. *Morbidity and Mortality Weekly Report (MMWR)* 61(3):41–45. http://www.cdc.gov/mmwr/preview/mmwrhtml/mm6103a1.htm, accessed 8/4/13.

Centers for Disease Control and Prevention (CDC). (2012b). "Current Cigarette Smoking Among Adults—United States, 2011." *Morbidity and Mortality Weekly Report* 61(44):889–94. http://www.cdc.gov/mmwr/preview/mmwrhtml/mm6144a2.htm?s_cid=%20mm6144a2.htm_w, accessed 7/18/13.

Centers for Disease Control and Prevention (CDC). (2012c). *HIV and AIDS in the United States by Geographic Distribution.* http://www.cdc.gov/hiv/statistics/basics/geographicdistribution.html, accessed 11/1/13.

Centers for Disease Control and Prevention (CDC). (2012d). *Prevalence of obesity in the United States, 2009–2010.* http://www.cdc.gov/nchs/data/hestat/obesity_adult_09_10/obesity_adult_09_10.pdf, accessed 8/4/13.

Centers for Disease Control and Prevention (CDC). (2013a). Births: Final data for 2011. *National Vital Statistics Report* 62(1). http://www.cdc.gov/nchs/data/nvsr/nvsr62/nvsr62_01.pdf, accessed 10/17/13.

Centers for Disease Control and Prevention (CDC). (2013b). Deaths: Final data for 2010. *National Vital Statistics Reports* 61(4):1–118. http://www.cdc.gov/nchs/data/nvsr/nvsr61/nvsr61_04.pdf, accessed 11/1/13.

Centers for Disease Control and Prevention (CDC). (2013c). Health, United States, 2012: with special feature on emergency care. http://www.cdc.gov/nchs/data/hus/hus12.pdf, Table 98, accessed 8/4/13.

Centers for Disease Control and Prevention (CDC). (2013d). *HIV among women.* http://www.cdc.gov/hiv/pdf/risk_women.pdf, accessed 11/3/13.

Centers for Disease Control and Prevention (CDC). (2013e). HIV in the United States: At a Glance. http://www.cdc.gov/hiv/statistics/basics/ataglance.html#ref1, accessed 1/13/14.

Centers for Disease Control and Prevention (CDC). (2013f). *Homicide rates among persons ages 10–24 years, by race/ethnicity and sex, United States, 2010.* http://www.cdc.gov/violenceprevention/youthviolence/stats_at-a_glance/hr_age-race.html, accessed 8/4/13.

Centers for Disease Control and Prevention (CDC). (2013g). National Marriage and Divorce Rate Trends, 2010–2011. http://www.cdc.gov/nchs/nvss/marriage_divorce_tables.htm, accessed 5/22/14.

Centers for Disease Control and Prevention (CDC). (2013h). Sexual risk behavior: HIV, STD, & teen pregnancy prevention. http://www.cdc.gov/HealthyYouth/sexualbehaviors/,accessed 11/2/13.

Central Intelligence Agency (CIA). (2000). *CIA world fact book.* www.cia.gov/cia/publications/factbook/geos/rs.html#Econ, accessed 12/29/04.

Central Intelligence Agency (CIA). (2013a). *CIA world fact book.* China. https://www.cia.gov/library/publications/the-world-factbook/geos/ch.html, accessed 8/27/13.

Central Intelligence Agency (CIA). (2013b). *CIA world fact book.* Haiti. https://www.cia.gov/library/publications/the-world-factbook/geos/ha.html, accessed 8/20/13.

Central Intelligence Agency (CIA). (2013c). *CIA world fact book.* Japan. https://www.cia.gov/library/publications/the-world-factbook/geos/ja.html, accessed 8/20/13.

Central Intelligence Agency (CIA). (2013d). Country Comparison: Exports. https://www.cia.gov/library/publications/the-world-factbook/rankorder/2078rank.html, accessed 6/20/13.

Central Intelligence Agency (CIA). (2013e). The World Factbook. https://www.cia.gov/library/publications/the-world-factbook/rankorder/2066rank.html, accessed 1/4/14.

Chafetz, J. S. (1990). *Gender equity: An integrated theory of stability and change.* Newbury Park, CA: Sage.

Chambliss, W. J. (1988). *On the take: From petty crooks to presidents.* Bloomington: Indiana University Press.

Charles River Editors. (2013). *Legends of the frontier: Daniel Boone, Davy Crockett and Jim Bowie.* CreateSpace Independent Publishing Platform.

Chase-Dunn, C. (1989). *Global formation: Structures of the world economy.* Cambridge, MA: Basil Blackwell.

Cheng, C-Y., and F. Lee. (2009). Multiracial identity integration: Perceptions of conflict and distance among multiracial individuals. *Journal of Social Issues, 65*(1): 51–68.

Cherlin, A. (1990). Recent changes in American fertility, marriage, and divorce. *Annals of the American Academy of Political and Social Science, 510* (July).

Cherlin, A. (1999). *Public and private families: An introduction* (2nd ed.). New York: McGraw-Hill.

Cherlin, A. (2005). American marriage in the early twenty-first century. *The Future of Children, 15*(2), 33–55.

Cherlin, A. (2010). Demographic Trends in the United States: A Review of Research in the 2000s. *Journal of Marriage and Family, 72*: 1–17.

Child Welfare. (2011). Child abuse and neglect fatalities 2009: Statistics and interventions. http://www.childwelfare.gov/pubs/factsheets/fatality.pdf, accessed 8/16/11.

Choo, H. Y. and M. M. Ferree. (2010). Practicing intersectionality in sociological research: A critical analysis of inclusions, interactions, and institutions in the study of inequalities. *Sociological Theory, 28*, 129–149.

Christie, L. (2013). McMansions are making a comeback. *CNN* (June 4, 2013). http://money.cnn.com/2013/06/04/real_estate/home-size/, accessed 1/4/14.

Chua, A. (2003). *World on fire: How exporting free market democracy breeds ethnic hatred and global instability.* New York: Doubleday.

Cleary, P. D. (1987). Gender differences in stress-related disorders. In R. C. Barnett (Ed.), *Gender and stress.* New York: Free Press.

Cloward, R. and Ohlin, L. E. (1960). *Delinquency and opportunity.* New York: Free Press.

CNN. (2003). INS: 7 million Illegal Immigrants in United States. (February 1, 2003). www.cnn.com/2003/US/01/31/illegal.immigration, accessed 1/27/06.

CNN. (2013). The CNN Freedom Project: Ending Modern-Day Slavery (May 30, 2014). http://thecnnfreedomproject.blogs.cnn.com/, accessed 10/12/13.

CNN's Money. (2013). Fortune Global 500. http://money.cnn.com/magazines/fortune/global500/2013/full_list/, accessed 3/9/14.

Coate, J. (1994). Cyberspace innkeeping: Building online community. Online paper, www.well.com:70/0/Community/innkeeping, accessed 12/29/04.

Cogan, M. F. (2010). Exploring Academic Outcomes of Homeschooled Students, *Journal of College Admission 208*: 18–25.

Cohen, A. (1955). *Delinquent boys: The culture of the gang.* Glencoe, IL: Free Press.

Cohen, L., J. P. Broschak, and H. A. Haveman. (1998). And then there were more? The effect of organizational sex composition on the hiring and promotion of managers. *American Sociological Review, 63*(5).

Cohen, P. (2012). *In our prime: The invention of middle age,* New York: Scribner.

Coleman, J. S. (1988). Social capital in the creation of human capital. *American Journal of Sociology,* supplement, *94.*

Coleman, J. S. (1990). *The foundations of social theory.* Cambridge, MA: Harvard University Press.

Coleman, J. S., et al. (1966). *Equality of educational opportunity.* Washington, DC: U.S. Government Printing Office.

Collins, R. (1971). Functional and conflict theories of educational stratification. *American Sociological Review, 36.*

Collins, R. (1979). *The credential society: An historical sociology of education.* New York: Academic Press.

Coltrane, S. (1992). The micropolitics of gender in non-industrial societies. *Gender & Society, 6.*

Congressional Research Service. (2012). An Analysis of the Distribution of Wealth Across Households, 1989-2010 (7–5700). Washington, DC: Congressional Research Service. http://www.fas.org/sgp/crs/misc/RL33433.pdf, accessed 10/12/13.

Conley, D. (1999). *Being black, living in the red: Race, wealth, and social policy in America.* Berkeley: University of California Press.

Connell, R. W. (1987). *Gender and power: Society, the person, and sexual politics.* Boston: Allen and Unwin.

Connell, R. and J. W. Messerschmidt. (2005). Hegemonic Masculinity: Rethinking the Concept. *Gender and Society 19*: 829–859.

Conti, J. (2011). *Between law and diplomacy: The social contexts of disputing at the World Trade Organization.* Palo Alto, CA: Stanford University Press.

Conway, M. (2004). Women's Political Participation at the State and Local Level in the United States. *Political Science & Politics*: 60–61.

Cooley, C. H. (1964; orig. 1902). *Human nature and the social order.* New York: Schocken Books.

Coontz, S. (1992). *The way we never were: American families and the nostalgia trap.* New York: Basic Books.

Coplan, J. H. (2011). In the fight for marriage equality, it's Edith Windsor vs. the United States of America. *New York University Alumni Magazine* (Fall 2011). http://www.nyu.edu/alumni.magazine/issue17/17_FEA_DOMA.html, accessed 12/1/13.

Corbin, J. and A. Strauss. (1985). Managing chronic illness at home: Three lines of work. *Qualitative Sociology, 8.*

Correll, S. J., S. Benard, and I. Paik. (2007). Getting a job: Is there a motherhood penalty? *American Journal of Sociology, 112*, 1297–1338.

Corsaro, W. (1997). *The sociology of childhood.* Thousand Oaks, CA: Pine Forge Press.

Cosmides, L., and J. Tooby. (1997). Evolutionary psychology: A primer. University of California at Santa Barbara: Institute for Social, Behavioral, and Economic Research Center for Evolutionary Psychology, available at http://www.cep.ucsb.edu/primer.html, accessed 1/11/05.

Council on Foreign Relations. (2013). Reflecting on Lehman's Global Legacy (September 13, 2013). http://www.cfr.org/economics/reflecting-lehmans-global-legacy/p31391, accessed 2/8/14.

Creswell, J., and L. Thomas. (2009).The talented Mr. Madoff. *New York Times* (January 24). http://www.nytimes.com/2009/01/25/business/25bernie.html?pagewanted=1, accessed fall 2009.

Crowdsourcing. (2013). Crowdfunding Market Grew 81% in 2012, finds Massolution Industry Report. http://www.crowdsourcing.org/editorial/crowdfunding-market-grew-81-in-2012-finds-massolution-industry-report/25049, accessed 9/22/13.

Cumings, B. (1987). The origins and development of the northeast Asian political economy: Industrial sectors, product cycles, and political consequences. In F. C. Deyo (Ed.), *The political economy of the new Asian industrialism.* Ithaca, NY: Cornell University Press.

Cumings, B. (1997). *Korea's place in the sun: A modern history.* New York: Norton.

Cumming, E. (1963). Further thoughts on the theory of disengagement. *International Social Science Journal, 15.*

Cumming, E. (1975). Engagement with an old theory. *International Journal of Aging and Human Development, 6.*

Cumming, E., and W. E. Henry. (1961). *Growing old: The process of disengagement.* New York: Basic.

Cunningham, L. (2013). Hiring more women seen as answer to economic malaise: 'Womenomics' pushed as fix for population woes. *The Washington Post* (September 18, 2013). http://www.japantimes.co.jp/news/2013/09/18/national/hiring-more-women-seen-as-answer-to-economic-malaise/#.UwYsoYU2XO0, accessed 2/20/14.

Danziger, S., and P. Gottschalk. (1995). *America unequal.* Cambridge, MA: Harvard University Press.

David, R. (2007). Indian middle class slowly changing its ways. *Forbes* (November 11, 2007). http://www.forbes.com/2007/11/10/india-middleclass-survey-face-markets-cx_rd_1108autofacescan01.html, accessed fall 2007.

Davies, B. (1991). *Frogs and snails and feminist tales.* Sydney: Allen and Unwin.

Davies, J. (1962). Towards a theory of revolution. *American Sociological Review, 27.*

Davis, D. D., and K. A. Polonko. (2001). Telework in the United States: Telework American Research Study 2001. Washington, DC: International Telework Association & Council.

Davis, K. (1937). The sociology of prostitution. *American Sociological Review, 11,* 744–755.

Davis, K. and W. E. Moore. (1945). Some principles of stratification. *American Sociological Review, 10.*

Davis, L. and S. D. James. (2011). Canadian Mother Raising 'Genderless' Baby, Storm, Defends Her Family's Decision. *ABC News.* http://abcnews.go.com/Health/genderless-baby-controversy-mom-defends-choice-reveal-sex/story?id=13718047, accessed 7/29/13.

Davis, M. (1990). *City of quartz: Excavating the future in Los Angeles.* New York: Verso.

Davis, S. (1987). *Future perfect.* Reading, MA: Addison-Wesley.

Deacon, T. (1998). *The symbolic species: The co-evolution of language and the brain.* New York: Norton.

Death Penalty Information Center (2013). The Death Penalty in 2013: A Year End Report. http://deathpenaltyinfo.org/documents/YearEnd2013.pdf, accessed 1/28/14.

de Jong Gierveld, J. and B. Havens. (2004). Cross-national comparisons of social isolation and loneliness: Introduction and overview. *Canadian Journal on Aging, 23,* 109–113.

de Jong Gierveld, J. et al. (2009). Quality of marriages in later life and emotional and social loneliness. *Journals of Gerontology, 64B,* 497–506.

D'Emilio., J. (1983). *Sexual politics, sexual communities: The making of a homosexual minority in the United States, 1940–1970.* Chicago: University of Chicago Press.

Demos. (2010). At What Cost? How Student Debt Reduces Lifetime Wealth. http://www.demos.org/sites/default/files/imce/AtWhatCostFinal.pdf, accessed 1/28/14.

DeNavas-Walt, C., B. D. Proctor and C. H. Lee. (2005). *Income, poverty, and health insurance coverage in the United States: 2004.* U.S. Bureau of the Census, Current Population Reports, P60-229. Washington, DC.: U.S. Government Printing Office. www.census.gov/prod/2005pubs/p60-229.pdf, accessed spring 2006.

DeNavas-Walt, C., B. D. Proctor and C. H. Lee. (2010). Income, poverty, and health insurance coverage in the United States: 2009. http://www.census.gov/prod/2010pubs/p60-238.pdf, accessed 7/3/11.

Derenne, J. L., and E. V. Beresin. (2006). Body image, media, and eating disorders. *Academic Psychiatry, 30,* 257–261.

Deutsche Bank Research. (2010). The middle class in India: Issues and opportunities. http://www.dbresearch.de/PROD/DBR_INTERNET_DE-PROD/PROD0000000000253735.pdf, accessed 8/26/13.

Deyo, F. (1987). *The political economy of the new Asian industrialism.* Ithaca, NY: Cornell University Press.

Diamond, J. (2005). *Collapse: How societies choose to fail or succeed.* New York: Penguin.

Dillon, S. (2010). Formula to Grade Teachers' Skill Gains Acceptance, and Critics. *New York Times* (August 31, 2010). http://www.nytimes.com/2010/09/01/education/01teacher.html, accessed 10/19/13.

Dimitrova, D. (2003). Controlling teleworkers: Supervision and flexibility revisited. *New Technology Work and Employment, 18*(3), 181–195.

DiSesa, N. (2008). *Seducing the boys club: Uncensored tactics from a woman at the top.* New York: Ballantine.

Dolbeare, C. (1995). *Out of reach: Why everyday people can't find affordable housing.* Washington, DC: Low Income Housing Information.

Domhoff, W. (1971). *The higher circles: The governing class in America.* New York: Vintage Books.

Domhoff, W. (1979). *The powers that be: Processes of ruling class domination in America.* New York: Vintage Books

Domhoff, W. (1983). *Who rules America now? A view for the '80s.* New York: Prentice-Hall.

Domhoff, W. (1998). *Who rules America?: Power and politics in the year 2000.* Belmont, CA: Mayfield.

Donadio, R. (2013). When Italians Chat, Hands and Fingers Do the Talking. *New York Times* (June 30, 2013). http://www.nytimes.com/2013/07/01/world/europe/when-italians-chat-hands-and-fingers-do-the-talking.html?_r=0, accessed 7/26/13.

Douglas, S. and M. Michaels. (2005). *The mommy myth: The idealization of motherhood and how it has undermined women.* New York: Free Press.

Dreier, P., and R. Appelbaum. (1992, Spring/Summer). The housing crisis enters the 1990s. *New England Journal of Public Policy* (8)1.

Du Bois, W. E. B. (1903). *The souls of black folk.* Chicago: A. C. McClurg.

Dubos, R. (1959). *Mirage of health.* New York: Doubleday/Anchor.

Dugan, A. (2012). Americans Most Likely to Say They Belong to the Middle Class. Washington, DC: Gallup Politics (November 30, 2012). http://www.gallup.com/poll/159029/americans-likely-say-belong-middle-class.aspx, accessed 10/12/13.

Dugan, A. (2013). In U.S., Majority Approves of Unions, but Say They'll Weaken. Gallup Polls (August 30, 2013). http://www.gallup.com/poll/164186/majority-approves-unions-say-weaken.aspx, accessed 6/4/13.

Duignan, P., and L. H. Gann (Eds.). (1998). *The debate in the United States over immigration.* Stanford, CA: Hoover Institution Press.

Duncan, G. J., J. Brooks-Gunn, W. J. Yeung, and J. R. Smith. (1998, June). How much does childhood poverty affect the life chances of children? *American Sociological Review, 63*(3), 406–423.

Duncombe, J., and D. Marsden. (1993). Love and intimacy: The gender division of emotion and emotion work: A neglected aspect of sociological discussion of heterosexual relationships. *Sociology, 27.*

Duneier, M. (1999). *Sidewalk.* New York: Farrar, Straus and Giroux.

Duneier, M., and H. Molotch. (1999). Talking city trouble: Interactional vandalism, social inequality, and the urban interaction problem. *American Journal of Sociology, 104.*

Durkheim, É. (1964; orig. 1893). *The division of labor in society.* New York: Free Press.

Durkheim, É. (1965; orig. 1912). *The elementary forms of the religious life.* New York: Free Press.

Durkheim, É. (1966; orig. 1897). *Suicide.* New York: Free Press.

Dworkin, A. (1981). *Pornography: Men possessing women.* New York: Pedigree.

Dworkin, A. (1987). *Intercourse.* New York: Free Press.

Dye, T. (1986). *Who's running America?* (4th ed.). Englewood Cliffs, NJ: Prentice Hall.

Eating Disorder Coalition (EDC). (2003). Statistics. www.eatingdisorderscoalition.org/reports/statistics.html, accessed 12/29/04.

Eaton, J., and M. B. Pell. (2010). Lobbyists swarm Capitol to influence health care reform. Center for Public Integrity (February 24, 2010). www.publicintegrity.org/articles/entry/1953/, accessed spring 2011.

Ebomoyi, E. (1987). The prevalence of female circumcision in two Nigerian communities. *Sex Roles, 17*(3–4).

The Economist. (1996). *Pocket world in figures.* London: Profile Books.

The Economist. (2003). A nation apart (May 6, 2003). http://www.economist.com/node/2172066, accessed 12/29/04.

The Economist. (2012). Biggest transnational corporations (July 10, 2012). http://www.economist.com/blogs/graphicdetail/2012/07/focus-1, accessed 3/30/14.

Economy, E. (2007, September/October). The Great Leap Backward? *Foreign Affairs, 86*(5). http://www.foreignaffairs.com/articles/62827/elizabeth-c-economy/the-great-leap-backward , accessed 11/3/07.

Edin, K., and M. J. Kefalas. (2005). *Promises I can keep: Why poor women put motherhood before marriage.* Berkeley: University of California Press.

Edney, A. (2013). Medical Advice Just a Touch Away With Smartphone Apps. *Bloomberg News* (November 1, 2013). http://www.bloomberg.com/news/2013-11-01/medical-advice-just-a-touch-away-with-smartphone-apps.html, accessed 12/9/13.

Education Week. (2004). Tracking. http://www.edweek.org/ew/issues/tracking/, accessed 10/11/12.

Efron, S. (1997). Eating disorders go global. *Los Angeles Times* (October 18, 1997), p. A1.

Eggen, D. (2009). Lobbyists spend millions to influence health care reform. *Washington Post* (July 21, 2009). http://voices.washingtonpost.com/health-care-reform/2009/07/health_care_continues_its_inte.html, accessed fall 2010.

Eibl-Eibesfeldt, I. (1972). Similarities and differences between cultures in expressive movements. In R. A. Hinde (Ed.), *Nonverbal communication.* New York: Cambridge University Press.

Eidelson, J. (2013a). Biggest-ever fast food strike today! Thousands to walk out across 100 cities. *Salon* (December 5, 2013). http://www.salon.com/2013/12/05/biggest_ever_fast_food_strike_today_thousands_walk_out_across_100_cities/, accessed 3/17/14.

Eidelson, J. (2013b). McDonald's to SEC: Strikes hurt, and we might have to hike pay. *Salon* (March 4, 2014). http://www.salon.com/2014/03/04/mcdonalds_to_sec_strikes_hurt_and_we_might_have_hike_pay/, accessed 3/17/14.

Eisenhower Library. (1961). Farewell address, Abilene, Kansas: The Dwight D. Eisenhower Presidential Library. http://www.eisenhower.archives.gov/research/online_documents/farewell_address.html, accessed 12/29/04.

Ekman, P., and W. V. Friesen. (1978). *Facial action coding system.* New York: Consulting Psychologists Press.

El Dareer, A. (1982). *Woman, why do you weep? Circumcision and its consequences.* Westport, CT: Zed.

Elias, N. (1987). *Involvement and detachment.* Oxford: Oxford University Press.

Elias, N., and E. Dunning. (1987). *Quest for excitement: Sport and leisure in the civilizing process.* Oxford: Blackwell.

Elliott, S. (2013). Vitriol Online for Cheerios Ad With Interracial Family. *New York Times* (May 31, 2013). http://www.nytimes.com/2013/06/01/business/media/cheerios-ad-with-interracial-family-brings-out-internet-hate.html?_r=0, accessed 10/16/13.

Elliott, D. B., and T. Simmons. (2011). Marital events of Americans: 2009. Washington, DC: U.S. Census. http://www.census.gov/prod/2011pubs/acs-13.pdf, accessed 8/29/11.

Elshtain, J. (1981). *Public man: Private woman.* Princeton, NJ: Princeton University Press.

Emerson, M. (2013). How Crowdfunding Worked for One Timely Start-Up. *New York Times* (June 21, 2013). http://boss.blogs.nytimes.com/2013/06/21/how-crowdfunding-worked-for-one-timely-start-up/, accessed 8/27/13.

Emirbayer, M., and A. Mische. (1998). What is Agency? *American Journal of Sociology, 103*, 962–023.

Emmanuel, A. (1972). *Unequal exchange: A study of the imperialism of trade.* New York: Monthly Review Press.

Environmental Working Group. (2013). The United States summary information. http://farm.ewg.org/region.php?fips=00000, accessed 3/7/2014.

Ericson, R. V., and K. D. Haggerty. (1997). *Policing the risk society.* Toronto: University of Toronto Press.

Erlanger, S. (2011). France enforces ban on full-face veils in public. *New York Times* (April 11, 2011). http://www.nytimes.com/2011/04/12/world/europe/12france.html, accessed 8/13/11.

ESPN. (2013a). Jason Collins Says He's Gay. ESPN (April 30, 2013). http://espn.go.com/nba/story/_/id/9223657/jason-collins-first-openly-gay-active-player, accessed 12/9/13.

ESPN. (2013b). Story of Manti Te'o girlfriend a hoax. ESPN (January 17, 2013). http://espn.go.com/college-football/story/_/id/8851033/story-manti-teo-girlfriend-death-apparently-hoax, accessed 9/21/13.

Estes, C. (1986). The politics of aging in America. *Aging and Society, 6.*

Estes, C. (1991). The Reagan legacy: Privatization, the welfare state, and aging. In J. Myles and J. Quadagno (Eds.), *States, labor markets, and the future of old age policy.* Philadelphia: Temple University Press.

Estes, C., E. A. Binney, and R. A. Culbertson. (1992). The gerontological imagination: Social influences on the development of gerontology, 1945–present. *Aging and Human Development, 35.*

European Parliament. (2013). 40% of seats on company boards for women. http://www.europarl.europa.eu/news/en/news-room/content/20131118IPR25532/html/40-of-seats-on-company-boards-for-women, accessed 2/20/14.

Evans, P. (1987). Class, state, and dependence in East Asia: Some lessons for Latin Americanists. In F. C. Deyo (Ed.), *The political economy of the new Asian industrialism.* Ithaca, NY: Cornell University Press.

Evans, P. (1995). *Embedded autonomy: States and industrial transformation.* Princeton, NJ: Princeton University Press.

Evans-Pritchard, E. (1970). Sexual inversion among the Azande. *American Anthropologist, 72.*

Fausto-Sterling, A. (2000). *Sexing the body: Gender politics and the construction of sexuality.* New York: Basic Books.

Federal Bureau of Investigation (FBI). (2011). Hate Crime Statistics, 2011. http://www.fbi.gov/news/stories/2012/december/annual-hate-crimes-report-released/annual-hate-crimes-report-released, accessed 1/28/14.

Federal Bureau of Investigation (FBI). (2012a). Crime in the United States. http://www.fbi.gov/about-us/cjis/ucr/crime-in-the-u.s/2011/crime-in-the-u.s.-2011/persons-arrested, accessed 8/19/13.

Federal Bureau of Investigation (FBI). (2012b). Crime in the U.S., 2012, Expanded homicide data tables. http://www.fbi.gov/about-us/cjis/ucr/crime-in-the-u.s/2012/crime-in-the-u.s.-2012/offenses-known-to-law-enforcement/expanded-homicide/expanded_homicide_data_table_6_murder_race_and_sex_of_vicitm_by_race_and_sex_of_offender_2012.xls, accessed 5/27/14.

Federal Bureau of Investigation (FBI). (2012c). Crime in the United States by volume and rate per 100,000 inhabitants, 1992–2011. http://www.fbi.gov/about-us/cjis/ucr/crime-in-the-u.s/2011/crime-in-the-u.s.-2011/tables/table-1, accessed 8/19/13.

Federal Bureau of Investigation (FBI). (2013a). Crime in the United States by volume and rate per 100,000 inhabitants, 1992–2012. http://www.fbi.gov/about-us/cjis/ucr/crime-in-the-u.s/2012/crime-in-the-u.s.-2012/tables/1tabledatadecoverviewpdf/table_1_crime_in_the_united_states_by_volume_and_rate_per_100000_inhabitants_1993-2012.xls, accessed 3/19/14.

Federal Bureau of Investigation (FBI). (2013b). Crime in the United States, Persons Arrested. http://www.fbi.gov/about-us/cjis/ucr/crime-in-the-u.s/2012/crime-in-the-u.s.-2012/persons-arrested/persons-arrested, accessed 8/19/13.

Federal Interagency Forum on Aging-Related Statistics. (2008). Key indicators of well-being. www.agingstats.gov/Agingstatsdotnet/Main_Site/Data/2008_Documents/OA_2008.pdf, accessed June 2009.

Federal Interagency Forum on Aging-Related Statistics. (2010). Older Americans 2010: Key indicators of well-being. Washington, DC: U.S. Government Printing Office. www.agingstats.gov/agingstatsdotnet/main_site/default.aspx, accessed 8/23/11, accessed 7/30/10.

Federal Interagency Forum on Aging-Related Statistics. (2013). Older Americans 2012: Key Indicators of Well-Being, Federal Interagency Forum on Aging-Related Statistics. http://www.agingstats.gov/Main_Site/Data/2012_Documents/docs/EntireChartbook.pdf, accessed 7/30/13.

Federation of American Women's Clubs Overseas (FAWCO). (2013). 5th World Conference on Women Announced. http://www.fawco.org/index.php?option=com_content&view=article&id=1976:5th-world-conference-on-women-2015-announced&Itemid=100584, accessed 11/8/13.

Feldman, M. B., and I. H. Meyer. (2007). Eating disorders in diverse lesbian, gay, and bisexual populations. *International Journal of Eating Disorders, 40*(3), 218–226.

Fenner, L. (2012). Apps4Africa Announces Winners, More to Come. *IIP Digital* (January 27, 2012). http://iipdigital.usembassy.gov/st/english/article/2012/01/20120127173716esiuol0.3623316.html#axzz2iNapYA39, accessed 10/20/13.

Fenton, M. V. and D. L. Morris. (2003). The integration of holistic nursing practices and complementary and alternative modalities into curricula of schools of nursing. *Alternative Therapies in Health and Medicine, 9*(4), 62–67.

Feuer, A. (2013). Transgender Woman Dies in Possible Hate Crime. *New York Times* (August 23, 2013). http://www.nytimes.com/2013/08/24/nyregion/beating-death-of-transgender-woman-is-investigated-as-hate-crime.html, accessed 9/24/13.

Fez Tá Pronto. (2014). How large is the Brazilian housing deficit? http://www.feztapronto.com/resources/en/general-resources/how-large-is-the-brazilian-housing-deficit.pdf, accessed 1/3/14.

Finke, R. and R. Stark. (1988). Religious economies and sacred canopies: Religious mobilization in American cities, 1906. *American Sociological Review, 53*.

Finke, R. and R. Stark. (1992). *The churching of America, 1776–1990: Winners and losers in our religious economy.* New Brunswick, NJ: Rutgers University Press.

Finley, N. J., M. D. Roberts, and B. F. Banahan. (1988). Motivators and inhibitors of attitudes of filial obligation toward aging parents. *The Gerontologist, 28*, 73–78.

Fischer, C. (1984). *The urban experience* (2nd ed.). New York: Harcourt Brace Jovanovich.

Fischer, C., et al. (1996). *Inequality by design: Cracking the bell curve myth.* Princeton, NJ: Princeton University Press.

Fisher, B. S., F. T. Cullen, and M. G. Turner. (2000, December). The sexual victimization of college women. Washington, DC: U.S. Department of Justice, National Institute of Justice, Bureau of Justice Statistics, NJJ 182369, https://www.ncjrs.gov/pdffiles1/nij/182369.pdf, accessed 12/29/04.

Fitzpatrick, A. (2013). Turkey Protesters Take to Twitter as Local Media Turns a Blind Eye. Mashable.com (June 3, 2013). http://mashable.com/2013/06/03/twitter-turkey-protests/accessed 2/9/14.

Flaherty, B. and R. Sethi. (2010). Homicide in black and white, *Journal of Urban Economics*, Elsevier, vol. 68(3): 215–230.

Forbes. (2009). The World's Billionaires. www.forbes.com/2009/03/11/worlds-richest-people-billionaires-2009-billionaires-intro.html, accessed July 2009.

Forbes. (2012). The Forbes 400: The richest people in America. http://www.forbes.com/sites/luisakroll/2012/09/19/the-forbes-400-the-richest-people-in-america/, accessed 8/22/13.

Forbes. (2013a). The Forbes 400: The richest people in America. http://www.forbes.com/forbes-400/, accessed 10/12/13.

Forbes. (2013b). Inside the 2013 billionaires list: Facts and figures. http://www.forbes.com/sites/luisakroll/2013/03/04/inside-the-2013-billionaires-list-facts-and-figures/, accessed 8/25/13.

Forbes. (2013c). Inside the 2013 Forbes 400: Facts and Figures on America's richest. http://www.forbes.com/sites/luisakroll/2013/09/16/inside-the-2013-forbes-400-facts-and-figures-on-americas-richest/, accessed 6/12/14.

Forbes. (2014). Inside the 2014 Forbes Billionaires List: Facts and Figures. http://www.forbes.com/sites/luisakroll/2014/03/03/inside-the-2014-forbes-billionaires-list-facts-and-figures/, accessed 6/12/14.

Ford, C. S. and F. A. Beach. (1951). *Patterns of sexual behavior.* New York: Harper and Row.

Fortune. (2013). Fortune Global 500. http://money.cnn.com/magazines/fortune/global500/2013/full_list/, accessed 11/1/2013.

Foucault, M. (1979). *Discipline and punish: The birth of the prison.* New York: Random House.

Foucault, M. (1988). Technologies of the self. In L. H. Martin et al. (Eds.), *Technologies of the self: A seminar with Michel Foucault.* Amherst: University of Massachusetts Press.

Fox, O. (1964). The pre-industrial city reconsidered. *Sociological Quarterly, 5*.

Frank, A. (1966). The development of underdevelopment. *Monthly Review, 18*.

Frank, A. (1969a). *Latin America: Underdevelopment or revolution.* New York: Monthly Review Press.

Frank, A. (1969b). *Capitalism and underdevelopment in Latin America: Historical studies of Chile and Brazil.* New York: Monthly Review Press.

Frank, A. (1979). *Dependent accumulation and underdevelopment.* London: Macmillan.

Frank, D. J. and E. H. McEneaney. (1999). The individualization of society and the liberalization of state policies on same-sex sexual relations, 1984–1995. *Social Forces, 7*(3).

Franzini, L., J. C. Ribble, and A. M. Keddie. (2001). Understanding the Hispanic paradox. *Ethnicity & Disease, 11*(3), 496–518.

Freed, B. R. 2012. Pussy Riot and a Protest Legacy. *The New Republic* (August 17, 2012). http://www.newrepublic.com/blog/plank/106288/pussy-riot-and-protest-legacy, accessed 7/8/13.

Freedom House. (2005). Electoral democracies, 2005. www.freedomhouse.org/template.cfm?page=205&year=2005, accessed 1/9/06.

Freedom House. (2012). Freedom in the World, 2012. http://www.freedomhouse.org/report/freedom-world-2012/methodology, accessed 12/17/13.

Freeman, R. (1999). *The new inequality: Creating solutions for poor America.* Boston: Beacon Press.

Fremlin, J. (1964). How many people can the world support? *New Scientist* (October 19, 1964).

French, H. (2001 January 1). Diploma at hand, Japanese women find glass ceiling reinforced with iron. *New York Times*, p. A1.

Frey, W. H. and K-L Liaw. (1998). The impact of recent immigration on population redistribution in the United States. In J. Smith and B. Edmonston (Eds.), *The immigration debate*. Washington, DC: National Academy Press.

Frey, W. H. (2001). Melting pot suburbs: A Census 2000 study of suburban diversity. Washington, DC: The Brookings Institution, Census 2000 Series, 2001.

Frey, W. H. (2011a). Census data: Blacks and Hispanics take different segregation paths. www.brookings.edu/opinions/2010/1216_census_frey.aspx, accessed 8/23/11.

Frey, W. H. (2011b). Melting pot cities and suburbs: Racial and ethnic change in metro America in the 2000s. *Brookings* Institution. http://www.brookings.edu/~/media/research/files/papers/2011/5/04%20census%20ethnicity%20frey/0504_census_ethnicity_frey.pdf, accessed 2/8/2014.

Friedan, B. (1963). *The feminine mystique.* New York: Norton.

Friedman, R. A. and S. C. Currall. (2003). Conflict escalation: Dispute exacerbating elements of e-mail communication. *Human Relations, 56*(11), 1325–1347.

Friedman, T. (2000). *The Lexus and the olive tree: Understanding globalization.* New York: Anchor.

Friedman, T. (2005). *The world is flat: A brief history of the twenty-first century.* New York: Farrar, Straus and Giroux.

Fulwood, S., III. (2010). Race and beyond: Majority-minority conflicts: Nationwide lessons from the D.C. mayoral election. Center for American Politics (September 21, 2010). www.americanprogress .org/issues/2010/09/rab_092110 .html.

Furstenburg, F. et al. (2004). Growing up is Harder to Do. *Contexts 3*: 33–41.

Furstenburg, F. and S. Kennedy. (2013). The Changing Transition to Adulthood in the U.S.: Trends in Demographic Role Transitions and Age Norms since 2000. *Paper presented at annual meetings of Population Association of America.*

Gabbatt, A. (2013). Edith Windsor and Thea Spyer: 'A Love Affair that Just Kept On and On and On. *The Guardian* (June 26, 2013). http://www.theguardian.com/world/2013/jun/26/edith-windsor-thea-spyer-doma, accessed 11/1/13.

Gallagher, J. (2013). Optician's clinic that fits a pocket. *BBC News* (August 14, 2013). http://www.bbc.co.uk/news/health-22553730, accessed 10/21/13.

Gallup Organization. (1998). *Have and have-nots: Perceptions of fairness and opportunity—1998.* www.gallup.com/poll/9877/havenots-perceptions-fairness-opportunity-1998.aspx, accessed 2/3/10.

Gallup Organization. (2012). U.S. Death Penalty Support Stable at 63%. http://www.gallup.com/poll/159770/death-penalty-support-stable.aspx, accessed 1/28/14.

Gallup Organization. (2013a). *In U.S., record-high say gay, lesbian relations morally OK.* http://www.gallup.com/poll/162689/record-high-say-gay-lesbian-relations-morally.aspx, accessed 11/1/13.

Gallup Organization. (2013b). *Same-Sex marriage support solidifies above 50% in U.S.* http://www.gallup.com/poll/162398/sex-marriage-support-solidifies-above.aspx, accessed 11/1/13.

Gamoran, A., et al. (1995). An organizational analysis of the effects of ability grouping. *American Educational Research Journal, 32*(4).

Gans, D. and M. Silverstein. (2006). Norms of filial responsibility for aging parents across time and generations. *Journal of Marriage and the Family, 68*(4), 961–976.

Gardner, C. (1995). *Passing by: Gender and public harassment.* Berkeley: University of California Press.

Garfinkel, H. (1963). A conception of, and experiments with, "trust" as a condition of stable concerted actions. In O. J. Harvey (Ed.), *Motivation and social interaction.* New York: Ronald Press.

Gates, G. J. (2013). LGBT Parenting in the United States. Los Angeles: The Williams Institute (February 2013). http://williamsinstitute.law.ucla.edu/wp-content/uploads/LGBT-Parenting.pdf, accessed 10/30/13.

Gay, Lesbian, and Straight Education Network. (2013). "Out Online: The Experiences of Lesbian, Gay, Bisexual and Transgender Youth": First National Report to Look In-Depth at LGBT Youth Experience Online (July 10, 2013). http://www.glsen.org/press/study-finds-lgbt-youth-face-greater-harassment-online, accessed 1/13/14.

Gayomali, C. (2013). Ghetto Tracker: A website that helps rich people avoid poor people. *The Week* (September 3, 2013). http://theweek.com/article/index/249056/ghetto-tracker-a-website-that-helps-rich-people-avoid-poor-people, accessed 10/14/13.

Geertz, C. (1973). *The interpretation of cultures.* New York: Basic Books.

Gelb, I. (1952). *A study of writing.* Chicago: University of Chicago Press.

Gelles, R.J., and M. A. Straus. (1988). *Intimate violence.* New York: Simon & Schuster.

Genworth. (2011). Executive Summary: Genworth 2011 Cost of Care Survey. www .genworth.com/content/etc/medialib/genworth_v2/pdf/ltc_cost_of_care .Par.85518.File.dat/Executive%20 Summary_gnw.pdf, accessed 7/4/11.

Gerbner, G. and M. Morgan, Eds. (2002). *Against the mainstream: The selected works of George Gerbner.* New York: Peter Lang.

Gereffi, G. (1995). Contending paradigms for cross-regional comparison: Development strategies and commodity chains in East Asia and Latin America. In P. H. Smith (Ed.), *Latin America in comparative perspective: New approaches to methods and analysis.* Boulder, CO: Westview Press.

Gereffi, G. (1996). Commodity chains and regional divisions of labor in East Asia. *Journal of Asian Business, 12*(1).

Gershuny, J. and I. Miles. (1983). *The new service economy: The transformation of employment in industrial societies.* London: Francis Pinter.

Giddens, A. (1984). *The constitution of society.* Cambridge, UK: Polity Press.

Giddens, A. (1990). *The consequences of modernity.* Cambridge, UK: Polity Press.

Giddens, A. (1998). *The third way: The renewal of social democracy.* Cambridge, UK: Polity Press.

Giuffre, P. A. and C. L. Williams. (1994). Boundary lines: Labeling sexual harassment in restaurants. *Gender & Society, 8,* 378–401.

Glenn, B. (2013). Physicians' top 5 most-used medical apps for smartphones and tablets. *Medical Economics* (June 13, 2013). http://medicaleconomics.modern-medicine.com/medical-economics/news/physicians-top-5-most-used-medical-apps-smartphones-and-tablets#sthash.O7srHRzZ.dpuf, accessed 12/9/13.

Global Issues. (2006). Poverty facts and stats. www.globalissues.org/article/26/poverty-facts-and-stats, accessed 2/4/10.

Glock, C. (1976). On the origin and evolution of religious groups. In C. Y. Glock and R. N. Bellah (Eds.), *The new religious consciousness.* Berkeley: University of California Press.

Glueck, S. S. and E. T. Glueck. (1956). *Physique and delinquency.* New York: Harper and Row.

Goffman, E. (1963). *Stigma: Notes on the management of spoiled identity.* Englewood Cliffs, NJ: Prentice-Hall.

Goffman, E. (1967). *Interaction ritual.* New York: Doubleday/Anchor.

Goffman, E. (1971). *Relations in public: Microstudies of the public order.* New York: Basic Books.

Goffman, E. (1973). *The presentation of self in everyday life.* New York: Overlook Press.

Goffman, E. (1981). *Forms of talk*. Philadelphia: University of Pennsylvania Press.

Gold, T. (1986). *State and society in the Taiwan miracle*. Armonk, NY: M. E. Sharpe.

Goldberg, C. (1997). Hispanic households struggle amid broad decline in income. *New York Times* (January 30, 1997), pp. A1, A16.

Goldberg, A. E., J. Z. Smith, and M. Perry-Jenkins. (2012). The division of labor in lesbian, gay, and heterosexual new adoptive parents. *Journal of Marriage and Family, 74*, 812–828.

Goldscheider, F. (1990). The aging of the gender revolution: What do we know and what do we need to know? *Research on Aging, 12.*

Goldscheider, F. and C. Goldscheider. (1999). *The changing transition to adulthood: Leaving and returning home*. Thousand Oaks, CA: Sage.

Goldstein, J. (2013). Judge Rejects New York's Stop-and-Frisk Policy. *New York Times* (August 12, 2013). http://www.nytimes.com/2013/08/13/nyregion/stop-and-frisk-practice-violated-rights-judge-rules.html?pagewanted=all&_r=0, accessed 10/14/13.

Goldstein, S. and A. Goldstein. (1996). *Jews on the move: Implications for Jewish identity*. Albany: State University of New York Press.

Goode, W. (1963). *World revolution in family patterns*. New York: Free Press.

Goodwin , P. Y., et al. (2010). Marriage and cohabitation in the United States: A statistical portrait based on Cycle 6 (2002) of the National Survey of Family Growth. National Center for Health Statistics. *Vital Health Stat, 23*(28). www.cdc.gov/nchs/data/series/sr_23/sr23_028.pdf, accessed 8/29/11.

Gottfredson, M. R. and T. Hirschi. (1990). *A general theory of crime*. Stanford, CA: Stanford University Press.

Goyette, B. (2013). Cheerios Commercial Featuring Mixed Race Family Gets Racist Backlash. Huffington Post. http://www.huffingtonpost.com/2013/05/31/cheerios-commercial-racist-backlash_n_3363507.html, accessed 10/17/13.

Grabe, S., L. M. Ward, and J. S. Hyde. (2008). The Role of the Media in Body Image Concerns among Women: A Meta-Analysis of Experimental and Correlational Studies. *Psychological Bulletin, 134*, 460–476.

Granovetter, M. (1973). The strength of weak ties. *American Journal of Sociology, 78.*

Gray, J. (1998). Ethnographic atlas codebook. *World Cultures, 10*(1), 86–136.

Gray, J. (2003). *Al Qaeda and what it means to be modern*. Chatham, UK: Faber and Faber.

Green, F. (1987). *The "sissy boy" syndrome and the development of homosexuality*. New Haven, CT: Yale University Press.

Green, J. (2004). The American religious landscape and political attitudes: A baseline for 2004. *Pew Forum on Religion & Public Life*. Table 1. http://pewforum.org/publications/surveys/green-full.pdf, accessed 1/23/06.

Greenfield, P. (1993). Representational competence in shared symbol systems. In R. R. Cocking & K. A. Renninger (Eds.), *The development and meaning of psychological distance*. Hillsdale, NJ: Erlbaum.

Griffin, S. (1979). *Rape, the power of consciousness*. New York: Harper & Row.

Guarino, D. P. (2013). Obama Seeks Boost in DOE Nuclear Weapons Spending, Cut to Nonproliferation. *Global Security Newswire* (April 10, 2013). http://www.nti.org/gsn/article/obama-seeks-boost-doe-nuclear-weapons-spending-cut-nonproliferation/, accessed 2/8/14.

Hadden, J. (1997a). The concepts "cult" and "sect" in scholarly research and public discourse. *New religious movements*. http://religiousmovements.lib.virginia.edu/cultsect/concult.htm, accessed 1/10/05.

Hadden, J. (1997b). New religious movements mission statement. *New religious movements*. http://religiousmovements.lib.virginia.edu/welcome/mission.htm, accessed 1/10/05.

Hagan, J. and B. McCarthy. (1992). Mean streets: The theoretical significance of situational delinquency among homeless youth. *American Sociological Review, 98.*

Haggard, S. (1990). *Pathways from the periphery: The politics of growth in newly industrializing countries*. Ithaca, NY: Cornell University Press.

Haig, M. (2011). *Brand failures: The truth about the 100 biggest branding mistakes of all times* (2nd ed.). London: Kogan.

Hall, E. (1969). *The hidden dimension*. New York: Doubleday.

Hall, E. (1973). *The silent language*. New York: Doubleday.

Hall, S. (1992). The question of cultural identity. In S. Hall, D. Held, and A. McGrew (Eds.), *Modernity and its futures*. Cambridge, UK: Polity Press.

Hamamura, T. (2012). Are Cultures Becoming Individualistic? A Cross-Temporal Comparison of Individualism–Collectivism in the United States and Japan. *Personality and Social Psychology Review* 16(1):3–24.

Hamilton, B. E., J. A. Martin, and S. J. Ventura. (2012). National Vital Statistics Reports: Births: Preliminary Data for 2011. http://www.cdc.gov/nchs/data/nvsr/nvsr61/nvsr61_05.pdf, accessed 6/30/14.

Hammond, P. (1992). *Religion and personal autonomy: The third disestablishment in America*. Columbia: University of South Carolina Press.

Hampton, K. N., L. Sessions Goulet, L. Rainie, and K. Purcell. (2011). Social networking sites and our lives. Washington, DC: Pew Internet and American Life Project. http://pewinternet.org/~/media//Files/Reports/2011/PIP%20-%20Social%20networking%20sites%20and%20our%20lives.pdf, accessed 8/19/11.

Hare, A. P., E. F. Borgatta, and R. F. Bales. (1965). *Small groups: Studies in social interaction*. New York: Knopf.

Harknett, K. and S. S. McLanahan. (2004). Racial and ethnic differences in marriage after the birth of a child. *American Sociological Review, 69*, 790–811.

Harris, D. (2003). Racial classification and the 2000 census. Commissioned paper, Panel to Review the 2000 Census. *Committee on National Statistics*. University of Michigan, Ann Arbor.

Harris, D. and J. Sim. (2000). An empirical look at the social construction of race: The case of mixed-race adolescents. Population Studies Center Research Report 00-452, University of Michigan.

Harris, J. (1998). *The nurture assumption: Why children turn out the way they do*. New York: Free Press.

Harris, M. (1975). *Cows, pigs, wars, and riches: The riddles of culture*. New York: Random House.

Harris, M. (1978). *Cannibals and kings: The origins of cultures*. New York: Random House.

Harris, M. (1980). *Cultural materialism: The struggle for a science of culture*. New York: Vintage Books.

Hartig, T., G. Johansson, and C. Kylin. (2003). Residence in the social ecology of stress and restoration. *Journal of Social Issues, 59*(3), 611–636.

Hartmann, H. I., et al. (1985). An agenda for basic research on comparable worth. In H. I. Hartmann et al. (Eds.), *Comparable worth: New directions for research*. Washington, DC: National Academy Press.

Harvey, D. (1973). *Social justice and the city*. Oxford: Blackwell.

Harvey, D. (1982). *The limits to capital*. Oxford: Blackwell.

Harvey, D. (1985). *Consciousness and the urban experience: Studies in the history and theory of capitalist urbanization*. Oxford: Blackwell.

Harvey, D. (1989). *The condition of postmodernity: An enquiry into the origins of cultural change*. Cambridge, MA: Blackwell.

Haslam, D.W., and W. P. James. (2005). *Obesity. Lancet, 366*(9492), 1197–1209.

Hathaway, A. D. (1997). Marijuana and tolerance: Revisiting Becker's sources of control. *Deviant Behavior, 18*(2).

Haugen, E. (1977). Linguistic relativity: Myths and methods. In W. C. McCormack and S. A. Wurm (Eds.), *Language and thought: Anthropological issues*. The Hague: Mouton.

Hawkes, T. (1977). *Structuralism and semiotics*. Berkeley: University of California Press.

Hawley, A. (1950). *Human ecology: A theory of community structure*. New York: Ronald Press Company.

Hawley, A. (1968). Human ecology. In *International encyclopedia of social science* (Vol. 4). New York: Free Press.

Healy, M. (2001). Pieces of the Puzzle. *Los Angeles Times*, http://pqasb. pqarchiver .com/latimes/results.html?RQT=511&sid=1&firstIndex=460&PQACnt=1, accessed 1/10/05.

Heine, F. (2013). M, F or blank: 'Third gender' official in Germany from November. *Der Spiegel* (August 13, 2013). http://www. spiegel.de/international/germany/third-gender-option-to-become-available-on-german-birth-certificates-a-916940. html, accessed 8/26/13.

Held, D., et al. (1999). *Global transformations: Politics, economics, and culture*. Cambridge, UK: Polity Press.

Helm, L. (1992, November 21). Debt puts squeeze on Japanese. *Los Angeles Times*.

Henderson, J. (1989). *The globalization of high technology production: Society, space, and semiconductors in the restructuring of the modern world*. London: Routledge.

Henderson, J. and R. P. Appelbaum. (1992). Situating the state in the Asian development process. In R. P. Appelbaum and J. Henderson (Eds.), *States and development in the Asian Pacific rim*. Newbury Park, CA: Sage.

Henderson, V. and B. Kelly. (2005). Food advertising in the age of obesity: content analysis of food advertising on general market and African American television. *Journal of Nutrition Education and Behavior, 37*, 191–196.

Hendricks, J. (1992). Generation and the generation of theory in social gerontology. *Aging and Human Development, 35*.

Hendricks, J. and L. R. Hatch. (1993). Federal policy and family life of older Americans. In J. Hendricks and C. J. Rosenthal (Eds.), *The remainder of their days: Impact of public policy on older families*. New York: Greenwood.

Hendricks, J. and C. D. Hendricks. (1986). *Aging in mass society: Myths and realities*. Boston: Little, Brown.

Henry, W. (1965). *Growing older: The process of disengagement*. New York: Basic Books.

Herdt, G. (1981). *Guardians of the flutes: Idioms of masculinity*. New York: McGraw-Hill.

Herdt, G. (1984). *Ritualized homosexuality in Melanesia*. Berkeley: University of California Press.

Herdt, G. (1986). *The Sambia: Ritual and gender in New Guinea*. New York: Holt, Rinehart and Winston.

Herdt, G. H. and J. Davidson. (1988). The Sambia 'urnim-man': Sociocultural and clinical aspects of gender formation in Papua, New Guinea. *Archives of Sexual Behavior, 17*.

Heritage, J. (1985). *Garfinkel and ethnomethodology*. New York: Basil Blackwell.

Herrnstein, R. J. and C. Murray. (1994). *The bell curve: Intelligence and class structure in American Life*. New York: Free Press.

Herszenhorn, David. (2014). Unrest Deepens in Ukraine as Protests Turn Deadly. *New York Times* (January 22, 2014). http://www.nytimes.com/2014/01/23/world/europe/ukraine-protests.html, accessed 2/8/14.

Hesse-Biber, S. (1997). *Am I thin enough yet?: The cult of thinness and the commercialization of identity*. New York: Oxford University Press.

Hexham, I. and K. Poewe. (1997). *New religions as global cultures*. Boulder, CO: Westview Press.

Higher Education Research Institute. (2009). Financial concerns of first-year college students have wide impact. www. heri.ucla.edu/pr-display .php?prQry= 42 and http://www.heri .ucla.edu/pr-display.php?prQry=28, accessed 7/23/11.

Higher Education Research Institute. (2012). *The American Freshman: National Norms Fall 2012*. Los Angeles: Higher Education Research Institute, UCLA. http://www. heri.ucla.edu/monographs/TheAmerican Freshman2012.pdf, accessed 7/16/13.

Himes, C. (1999). Racial differences in education, obesity, and health in later life. In N. E. Adler et al. (Eds.), Socioeconomic status and health in industrial nations: Social, psychological, and biological pathways. *Annals of the New York Academy of Sciences, 896*, 370–372.

Hines, D. A., K. Malley-Morrison, and L. B. Dutton. (2012). *Family violence in the United States: Defining, understanding, and combating abuse*. New York: Sage.

Hirsch, B. T. and D. A. Macpherson. (2004, January). Wages, sorting on skill, and the racial composition of jobs. *Journal of Labor Economics, 22*(1), 189–210.

Hirschi, T. (1969). *Causes of delinquency*. Berkeley: University of California Press.

Hirst, P. (1997). The global economy: Myths and realities. *International Affairs, 73*.

Hirst, P. and G. Thompson. (1992). The problem of "globalization": International economic relations, national economic management, and the formation of trading blocs. *Economy and Society, 24*.

Hirst, P. and G. Thompson. (1999). *Globalization in question: The international economy and the possibilities of governance* (Rev. ed.). Cambridge, UK: Polity Press.

Hochschild, A. (1975). Disengagement theory: A critique and proposal. *American Sociological Review, 40*.

Hochschild, A. and A. Machung. (1989). *The second shift: Working parents and the revolution at home*. New York: Viking.

Hoffman, J. (2010). As bullies go digital, parents play catch up. *New York Times* (December 4, 2010). http://www. nytimes.com/2010/12/05/us/05bully. html?pagewanted=all, accessed 7/16/10.

Hofstede, G. (1997). *Cultures and organizations: Software of the mind*. New York: McGraw Hill.

Holton, R. (1978). The crowds in history: Some problems of theory and method. *Social History, 3*.

Homans, G. (1950). *The human group*. New York: Harcourt, Brace.

Homans, H. (1987). Man-made myth: The reality of being a woman scientist in the NHS. In A. Spencer and D. Podmore (Eds.), *In a man's world: Essays on women in male-dominated professions*. London: Tavistock.

Hopkins, T. K. and I. M. Wallerstein. (1996). *The age of transition: Trajectory of the world-system, 1945–2025*. London: Zed Books.

Howard, P. (2011, February 23). The Arab Spring's cascading effects. *Miller-McCune*. www.miller-mccune.com/politics/the-cascading-effects-of-the-arab-spring-28575/, accessed 8/13/11.

Hudson, J. I., E. Hiripi, H. G. Pope, and R. C. Kessler. (2007). The prevalence and correlates of eating disorders in the National Comorbidity Survey Replication. *Biological Psychiatry, 61*:348–58.

Huffington Post. (2012). Social Media By Gender: Women Dominate Pinterest, Twitter, Men Dominate Reddit, YouTube (Infographic). *The Huffington Post* (June 21, 2012). http://www.huffingtonpost. com/2012/06/20/social-media-by-gender-women-pinterest-men-reddit-infographic_ n_1613812.html, accessed 10/13/13.

Human Rights Watch. (1995). The Global Report on Women's Human Rights. www. hrw.org/about/projects/womrep/, accessed 1/3/05.

Humes, K. R., N. A. Jones, and R. R.Ramirez. (2010). Overview of race and Hispanic origin: 2010. U.S. Bureau of the Census (March 2011). www.census.gov/prod/ cen2010/ briefs/c2010br-02.pdf, accessed 11/15/11.

Humphreys, L. (1970). *Tearoom trade: Impersonal sex in public places*. Chicago: Aldine.

Huntington, S. (1991). *The third wave: Democratization in the late twentieth century*. Norman, UK: University of Oklahoma Press.

Hursh, D. (2007). Assessing No Child Left Behind and the Rise of Neoliberal Education Policies. American Educational Research Journal 44: 493–518.

Hurtado, A. (1995). Variation, combinations, and evolutions: Latino families in the United States. In R. Zambrana (Ed.), *Understanding Latino families*. Thousand Oaks, CA: Sage.

Hyman, R. (1984). *Strikes* (2nd ed.). London: Fontana.

Hyman, H. H. and E. Singer. (1968). *Readings in reference group theory and research*. New York: Free Press.

Illegems, V. and A. Verbeke. (2004). Telework: What does it mean for management? *Long Range Planning, 37*(4), 319–334.

Illich, I. (1983). *Deschooling society*. New York: Harper & Row.

Inglehart, R. (1997). *Modernization and postmodernization: Cultural, economic and political change in 43 societies*. Princeton, NJ: Princeton University Press.

Institute for Women's Policy Research (IWPR). (2010). *The gender wage gap by occupation*. IWPR Fact Sheet #C350a. Washington, DC: IWPR. http://www.iwpr.org/pdf/C350a.pdf, accessed 8/13/10.

Insurance NewsNet. (2014). New Mexico Dems: Congresswoman Lujan Grisham Introduces HEAL Immigrant Women and Families Act of 2014. *Insurance NewsNet.com* (March 15, 2014). http://insurancenewsnet.com/oarticle/2014/03/15/new-mexico-dems-congresswoman-lujan-grisham-introduces-heal-immigrant-women-and-a-474885.html#.UydMsPldU0Q, accessed 3/17/14.

Institute for Democracy and Electoral Assistance (IDEA). (2009). Voter Turnout 2009. www.idea.int/vt/view_data.cfm, accessed September 2009.

International Institute for Democracy and Electoral Assistance (IDEA). (2014). Voter Turnout Database. www.idea.int/vt, accessed 5/19/14.

International Labor Organization (ILO). (2004a). Breaking the glass ceiling: Women in management. www.ilo.org/dyn/gender/docs/RES/292/F267981337/Breaking%20Glass%20PDF%20English.pdf, accessed 12/4/05.

International Labor Organization (ILO). (2004b). More women are entering the global labor force than ever before, but job equality, poverty reduction remain elusive. http://www.ilo.org/global/about-the-ilo/newsroom/news/WCMS_005243/lang—en/index.htm, accessed 12/4/05.

International Labor Organization (ILO). (2008). Global employment trends for women. http://www.ilo.org/wcmsp5/groups/public/@dgreports/@dcomm/documents/publication/wcms_091225.pdf, accessed 8/8/11.

International Labor Organization (ILO). (2010). *Global child labour developments: Measuring trends from 2004 to 2008*. Geneva: International Labor Office. http://www.ilo.org/ipecinfo/product/download.do?type=document&id=13313, accessed 8/26/13.

International Labor Organization (ILO). (2011). *Female Future: Turning the Tide*. http://www.ilo.org/global/publications/magazines-and-journals/world-of-work-magazine/articles/WCMS_165993/lang—en/index.htm, accessed 2/20/2014.

International Lesbian, Gay, Bisexual, Trans and Intersex Association (ILGA). (2009). About ILGA. www.ilga.org/aboutilga.asp, accessed August 2009.

International Lesbian, Gay, Bisexual, Trans and Intersex Association (ILGA). (2011). *2011 annual report*. http://old.ilga.org/documents/ILGA_Annual_Report_2011.pdf, accessed 11/1/13.

International Lesbian, Gay, Bisexual, Trans and Intersex Association (ILGA). (2014). About ILGA. www.ilga.org/ilga/en/article/about_ilga, accessed 6/27/14.

International Monetary Fund (IMF). (2005). Chapter IV: Will the World Oil Market Continue to be Tight? *World economic lookout*. www.imf.org/external/pubs/ft/weo/2005/01/pdf/chapter4.pdf, accessed spring 2006.

International Monetary Fund (IMF). (2013). World Economic Outlook Database. http://www.imf.org/external/pubs/ft/weo/2013/02/weodata/index.aspx, accessed 1/28/14.

International Panel on Climate Change (IPCC). (2007). Climate change 2007: Synthesis report, summary for policymakers. Intergovernmental Panel on Climate Change Fourth Assessment Report. www.ipcc.ch/pdf/assessment-report/ar4/syr/ar4_syr_spm.pdf, accessed fall 2010.

International Road Federation. (1987). United Nations annual bulletin of transport statistics, cited in *Social Trends*. London: HMSO.

International Telework Association and Council (ITAC). (2004). Telework Facts and Figures. www.telecommute.org/resources/abouttelework.htm, accessed 1/20/05.

International Telecommunication Union (ITU). (2011). Key Global Telecom Indicators for the World Telecommunication Service Sector. www.itu.int/ITU-D/ict/statistics/at_glance/KeyTelecom.html, accessed spring 2011.

Internet Society (ISOC). (1997). Web Languages Hit Parade. http://alis.isoc.org/palmares.en.html, accessed 1/11/05.

International Union for Conservation of Nature (IUCN) (2013). *The IUCN Red List of Threatened Species 2013.2*, http://www.iucnredlist.org/, accessed 2/8/14.

Internet World Stats. (2012a). Internet Users—Top 20 Countries. http://www.internetworldstats.com/top20.htm, accessed 6/23/13.

Internet World Stats. (2012b). North American internet usage statistics, population and telecommunications reports. www.internetworldstats.com/stats14.htm, accessed 7/19/13.

Internet World Stats. (2013). Internet Usage Statistics. http://www.internetworld-stats.com/stats.htm, accessed 3/7/14.

Ipsos. (2011). Global telecommuting section. http://www.ipsos-na.com/download/pr.aspx?id=11326, accessed 7/19/23.

Jackson, J. K. (2013). CRS Report for Congress Prepared for Members and Committees of Congress Outsourcing and Insourcing Jobs in the U.S. Economy: Evidence Based on Foreign Investment Data. Congressional Research Service. https://www.fas.org/sgp/crs/misc/RL32461.pdf, accessed 6/2/14.

Jacobs, A. (2011). China issues warning on climate and growth. *New York Times* (February 28, 2011). www.nytimes.com/2011/03/01/world/asia/01beijing.html, accessed 12/7/11.

Jacobs, J. (1961). *The death and life of great American cities*. New York: Random House.

Jaher, F. C. (Ed.). (1973). *The rich, the well born, and the powerful*. Urbana, IL: University of Illinois Press.

Janis, I. (1972). *Victims of groupthink*. Boston: Houghton Mifflin.

Janis, I. (1989). *Crucial decisions: Leadership in policy making and crisis management*. New York: Free Press.

Janis, I. and Leon Mann. (1977). *Decision making: A psychological analysis of conflict, choice, and commitment*. New York: Free Press.

Jankowiak, W. and E. Fisher (1992). Romantic Love: A Cross-Cultural Perspective. *Ethnology*: 149–156.

Jencks, C., et al. (1972). *Inequality: A reassessment of the effects of family and school in America*. New York: Basic Books.

Jobling, R. (1988). The experience of psoriasis under treatment. In M. Bury and R. Anderson (Eds.), *Living with chronic illness: The experience of patients and their families*. London: Unwin Hyman.

Johnson, K. (2006). *Demographic trends in rural and small town America*. Carsey Institute Reports on Rural America: 1.

Johnson, M. (1995). Patriarchal terrorism and common couple violence: Two forms of violence against women in U.S. families. *Journal of Marriage and the Family, 57*.

Johnson, M. and J. Morton. (1991). *Biology and cognitive development: The case of face recognition*. Oxford: Blackwell.

Johnson-Odim, C. (1991). Common themes, different contexts: Third World women and feminism. In C. Mohanty et al. (Eds.), *Third World women and the politics of feminism*. Bloomington, IN: Indiana University Press.

Joint Center for Housing Studies of Harvard University. (2005). The state of the nation's housing, 2005. www.jchs.harvard.edu/publications/markets/son2005/son2005.pdf, accessed spring 2006.

Joint Center for Housing Studies of Harvard University. ((2011). Rental market stresses: Impacts of the Great Recession on affordability and multifamily lending. www.jchs.harvard.edu/publications/rental/jchs_what_works_rental_market_stresses.pdf, accessed 8/23/11.

Joint Center for Political and Economic Studies. (2011). National roster of black elected officials. http://www.jointcenter.org/research/national-roster-of-black-elected-officials, accessed 8/22/13.

Jones, S. (1995). Understanding community in the information age. In S. G. Jones (Ed.), *CyberSociety: Computer-mediated communication and community*. Thousand Oaks, CA: Sage.

Jones, R. K. and J. Dreweke. (2011). Countering conventional wisdom: New evidence on religion and contraceptive use. Guttmacher Institue. www.guttmacher.org/pubs/Religion-and-Contraceptive-Use.pdf, accessed 8/9/11.

Jones, L. M., K. J. Mitchell, and D. Finkelhor. (2012). Trends in Youth Internet Victimization: Findings from Three Youth Internet Safety Surveys 2000–2010. *Journal of Adolescent Health 50*(2):179–186. http://dx.doi.org/10.1016/j.jadohealth.2011.09.015, accessed 7/16/13.

Journal of Blacks in Higher Education. (2007). Black student college graduation rates inch higher but a large racial gap persists. www.jbhe.com/preview/winter07preview.html.

Juergensmeyer, M. (1994). *The new cold war? Religious nationalism confronts the secular state (Comparative studies in religion and society)*. Berkeley: University of California Press.

Juergensmeyer, M. (2001). *Terror in the mind of God: The global rise of religious violence*. Berkeley: University of California Press.

Kaiser Family Foundation. (2010). *Generation M²: media in the lives of 8- to 18-year-olds*. http://kaiserfamilyfoundation.files.wordpress.com/2013/01/8010.pdf, accessed 7/1/13.

Kaiser Family Foundation. (2012). Global Health Facts: Population Under Age 15 (percentage). http://kff.org/global-indicator/population-under-age-15/#, accessed 1/4/14.

Kaiser Family Foundation. (2013). Focus on Health Reform: Summary of the Affordable Care Act. http://kaiserfamilyfoundation.files.wordpress.com/2011/04/8061-021.pdf, accessed 6/27/14.

Kamp Dush, C. M., C. L. Cohan, and P. R. Amato. (2003). The relationship between cohabitation and marital quality and stability: Change across cohorts? *Journal of Marriage and Family, 65*, 539–549.

Kanter, R. (1977). *Men and women of the corporation*. New York: Basic Books.

Kanter, R. (1983). *The change masters: Innovation for productivity in the American corporation*. New York: Simon & Schuster.

Kanter, R. (1991). The future of bureaucracy and hierarchy in organizational theory. In P. Bourdieu and J. Coleman (Eds.), *Social theory for a changing society*. Boulder, CO: Westview.

Karas, D. (2012). Petition objecting to 'whistling' Princeton MarketFair billboard leads to its removal. *The Times* (June 22, 2012). http://www.nj.com/mercer/index.ssf/2012/06/online_chain_reaction_gets_pri.html, accessed 9/21/13.

Karas-Montez, J. and A. Zajacova. (2013). Explaining the Widening Education Gap in Mortality Risk among U.S. White Women. *Journal of Health and Social Behavior 54*(2): 165–181.

Kasarda, J. (1993). Urban industrial transition and the underclass. In W. J. Wilson (Ed.), *The ghetto underclass*. Newbury Park, CA: Sage.

Kasarda, J. D. and E. N. Crenshaw. (1991). Third World urbanization: Dimensions, theories, and determinants. *Annual Review of Sociology, 17*. Palo Alto, CA: Annual Reviews.

Kautsky, J. (1982). *The politics of aristocratic empires*. Chapel Hill: University of North Carolina Press.

Kelling, G. L. and C. M. Coles. (1997). *Fixing broken windows: Restoring order and reducing crime in our communities*. New York: Free Press.

Kelley, J. and M. D. R. Evans. (1995). Class and class conflict in six western nations. *American Review of Sociology, 60*(2).

Kelly, L. (1987). The continuum of sexual violence. In J. Hanmer and M. Maynard (Eds.), *Women, violence, and social control*. Atlantic Highlands, NJ: Humanities Press.

Kelly, M. (1992). *Colitis: The experience of illness*. London: Routledge.

Kenkel, D. S., D. R. Lillard, and A. D. Mathios. (2006). The roles of high school completion and GED receipt in smoking and obesity. *Journal of Labor Economics, 24*(3), 635–660.

Kennedy, S. and L. Bumpass. (2008). Cohabitation and children's living arrangements: New estimates from the United States. *Demographic Research*, 19 (47), http://www.demographic-research.org/volumes/vol19/47/19-47.pdf, accessed 2/19/2014.

Kernaghan, Charles. (2012). *Chinese Sweatshop in Bangladesh*. Institute for Global Labour and Human Rights, http://www.globallabourrights.org/admin/reports/files/1203-Chinese-Sweatshop-in-Bangladesh.pdf, accessed 10/12/13.

Kessler, R. C. and T. B. Üstün (Eds.). (2008). *The WHO world mental health surveys: Global perspectives on the epidemiology of mental disorders*. New York: Cambridge University Press.

Keyes, C. L. M. (2009). The Black-White Paradox in Health: Flourishing in the Face of Social Inequality and Discrimination. *Journal of Personality*, 77(6).

Keyes K. M., D. Barnes, and L. Bates. (2011). Stress, coping, and depression: testing a new hypothesis in a prospectively studied general population sample of U.S. born Whites and Blacks. *Social Science and Medicine*, 72(5): 650–659.

Khalidi, R. (2011). The Arab Spring. *The Nation* (March 3, 2011). http://www.thenation.com/article/158991/arab-spring, accessed 9/27/11.

Kimmel, M. (2003). *The gender of desire: Essays on male sexuality*. Albany, NY: State University of New York Press.

King, N. (1984). Exploitation and abuse of older family members: An overview of the problem. In J. J. Cosa (Ed.), *Abuse of the elderly*. Lexington, MA: Lexington Books.

Kingston, Paul. (2001). *The Classless Society*. Palo Alto, CA: Stanford University Press.

Kinsey, A., et al. (1948). *Sexual behavior in the human male*. Philadelphia: Saunders.

Kinsey, A., et al. (1953). *Sexual behavior in the human female*. Philadelphia: Saunders.

Kirk, C. (2014). Map: Publicly Funded Schools That Are Allowed to Teach Creationism. *Slate* (January 26, 2014). http://www.slate.com/articles/health_and_science/science/2014/01/creationism_in_public_schools_mapped_where_tax_money_supports_alternatives.html, accessed 6/11/14.

Kjekshus, H. (1977). *Ecology, control, and economic development in East African History*. Berkeley: University of California Press.

Kliff, S. (2013). An average ER visit costs more than an average month's rent. *Washington Post* (March 2, 2013). http://www.washingtonpost.com/blogs/wonkblog/wp/2013/03/02/an-average-er-visit-costs-more-than-an-average-months-rent/, accessed 1/13/14.

Klinenberg, E. (2012). *Going solo: The extraordinary rise and surprising appeal of living alone.* New York: Penguin Press.

Kling, R. (1996). Computerization at work. In R. Kling (Ed.), *Computers and controversy* (2nd ed.). New York: Academic Press.

Kluckhohn, C. (1949). *Mirror for man.* Tucson: University of Arizona Press.

Knodel, J. (2006, August). Parents of persons with AIDS: Unrecognized contributions and unmet needs. *Journal of Global Ageing, 4,* 46–55.

Knoke, D. (1990). *Political networks: The structural perspective.* New York: Cambridge University Press.

Knorr-Cetina, K. and A. V. Cicourel (Eds.). (1981). *Advances in social theory and methodology: Towards an integration of micro- and macro-sociologies.* Boston: Routledge and Kegan Paul.

Kobrin, S. (1997, Summer). Electronic cash and the end of national markets. *Foreign Policy, 107,* 65–77.

Kochhar, R., R. Fry, and P. Taylor. (2011). Twenty-to-one wealth gaps rise to record highs between whites, blacks and Hispanics. Washington, DC: Pew Research Center. http://pewsocialtrends.org/files/2011/07/SDT-Wealth-Report_7-26-11_FINAL.pdf, accessed 8/17/11.

Kohn, M. (1977). *Class and conformity* (2nd ed.). Homewood, IL: Dorsey Press.

Kollock, P. and M. Smith. (1996). Managing the virtual commons: Cooperation and conflict in computer communities. In S. Herring (Ed.), *Computer-mediated communication.* Amsterdam: John Benjamins.

Kosmin, B. and A. Keysar. (2009). American Religious Identification Survey (ARIS). www.americanreligionsurvey-aris.org/reports/ARIS_Report_2008.pdf, accessed 8/9/11.

Kosmin, B., E. Mayer, and A. Keysar. (2001). American Religious Identification Survey (ARIS). New York: *CUNY Graduate Center* (December 19). http://www.gc.cuny.edu/CUNY_GC/media/CUNY-Graduate-Center/PDF/ARIS/ARIS-PDF-version.pdf, accessed 1/3/05.

Kozol, J. (1991). *Savage inequalities: Children in America's schools.* New York: Crown.

Kozol, J. (2012). *Fire in the ashes: Twenty-five years among the poorest children in America.* New York: Crown.

Kravitz, D. (2011). Foreclosures made up 31 pct. of home sales in 2nd Quarter. MSN-BC (August 25, 2011). www.msnbc.msn.com/id/44267325/ns/business-stocks_and_economy/t/foreclosures-made-pct-home-sales-q/, accessed 8/31/11.

Krennerich, M. (2014). Germany: The Original Mixed Member Proportional System. The Electoral Project Network. http://aceproject.org/regions-en/countries-and-territories/DE/case-studies/germany-the-original-mixed-member-proportional-system/view, accessed 3/30/14.

Kristof, N. and S. WuDunn. (2009). *Half the sky: Turning oppression into opportunity for women worldwide.* New York: Knopf.

Kroll, Louisa. (2011). The world's richest self-made women. *Forbes* (May 4, 2011). http://www.forbes.com/forbes/2011/0523/focus-winfrey-fisher-hendricks-whitman-wynn-self-made.html, accessed 2/20/14.

Kuhn, P. J. and H. Mansour. (2011). Is Internet Job Search Still Ineffective? Institute for the Study of Labor Working Paper Series (No. 5955). http://econpapers.repec.org/paper/izaizadps/dp5955.htm, accessed 3/17/14.

Kulish, N. (2011). As scorn for vote grows, protests surge around the globe. *New York Times* (September 27, 2011). www.nytimes.com/2011/09/28/world/as-scorn-for-vote-grows-protests-surge-around-globe.html?pagewanted=all, accessed 12/12/11.

Kutner, M., et al. (2007). *Literacy in everyday life: Results from the 2003 National Assessment of Adult Literacy* (NCES 2007–480). U.S. Department of Education.Washington, DC: National Center for Education Statistics. http://eric.ed.gov/PDFS/ED495996.pdf, accessed 8/28/11.

Lacayo, R. (1994). Lock 'em up! *Time* (February 7, 1994).

Lachman, M. (2001). *Handbook of Midlife Development.* Wiley: New York.

Landale, N. S. and K. Fennelly. (1992). Informal unions among mainland Puerto Ricans: Cohabitation or an alternative to legal marriage? *Journal of Marriage and the Family, 54.*

Landler, M. and J. Kahn. (2007). China grabs West's smoke spewing factories. *New York Times* (December 21, 2007). www.nytimes.com/2007/12/21/world/asia/21transfer.html?_r=1&oref=slogin.

Landler, M. and M. Barbaro. (2006). No, not always. Wal-Mart discovers that its formula doesn't fit every culture. *New York Times* (August 2, 2006), C1, 4.

LaPorte, N. (2013). Medical Care: Aided by the Crowed. *New York Times* (April 13, 2013). http://www.nytimes.com/2013/04/14/business/watsi-a-crowdfunding-site-offers-help-with-medical-care.html?pagewanted%253Dall&_r=0, accessed 9/22/13.

Latner, J. D. and A. J. Stunkard. (2003). Getting worse: The stigmatization of obese children. *Obesity Research, 11,* 452–456.

Latour, F. (2011). Ready. Set. Race. Boston.com (December 9, 2011). http://www.boston.com/community/blogs/hyphenated_life/2011/12/bake_me_a_race_as_fast_as_you.html, accessed 10/20/13.

Laumann, E. O., et al. (1994). *The social organization of sexuality: Sexual practices in the United States.* Chicago: University of Chicago Press.

Laumann, E. O., et al. (2008). Elder mistreatment in the United States: Prevalence estimates from a nationally representative study. *Journal of Gerontology: Social Sciences, 63,* 248–254.

Leach, E. (1976). *Culture and communication: The logic by which symbols are connected.* New York: Cambridge University Press.

Lee, G. (1982). *Family structure and interaction: A comparative analysis* (2nd ed.). Minneapolis: University of Minnesota Press.

Lemert, E. (1972). *Human deviance, social problems, and social control.* Englewood Cliffs, NJ: Prentice-Hall.

Lenhart, A. (2007). Cyberbullying. Pew Internet & American Life Project. www.pewinternet.org/Reports/2007/Cyberbullying.aspx, accessed 8/19/11.

Lenhart, A., M. Madden, A. Smith, K. Purcell, K. Zickuhr, and L. Rainie. (2011). Teens, kindness and cruelty on social network sites. Pew Research Internet Project (November 9, 2011). www.pewinternet.org/2011/11/09/teens-kindness-and-cruelty-on-social-network-sites/.

Leonhardt, D. (2011). Is your religion your financial destiny? *New York Times* (May 11, 2011). www.nytimes.com/2011/05/15/magazine/is-your-religion-your-financial-destiny.html, accessed 8/28/11.

Leupp, G. (1995). *Male colors: the construction of homosexuality in Tokugawa Japan.* Berkeley: University of California Press.

LeVay, Simon. (2011). *Gay, straight, and the reason why: The science of sexual orientation.* New York: Oxford.

Levitt, S. (2004). Understanding why crime fell in the 1990s: Four factors that explain the decline and six that do not. *Journal of Economic Perspectives, 18,* 163–190.

Lewin, T. (2012). College of Future Could Be Come One, Come All. *New York Times* (November 19, 2012). http://www.nytimes.com/2012/11/20/education/colleges-turn-to-crowd-sourcing-courses.html?pagewanted=all, accessed 8/26/13.

Lewis, O. (1968). The culture of poverty. In D. P. Moyhihan (Ed.), *On understanding poverty: Perspectives from the social sciences.* New York: Basic Books.

Lieff, Cabraser, Heimann, and Bernstein, LLP and Outten and Golden, LLP. (2013). Bank of America and Merrill Lynch Sex Discrimination Lawsuit. http://www.bofa-genderlawsuit.com/, accessed 10/12/13.

Lightfoot-Klein, H. (1989). *Prisoners of ritual: An odyssey into female genital circumcision in Africa.* New York: Haworth.

Lin, G. and P. A. Rogerson. (1995). Elderly parents and the geographic availability of their adult children. *Research on Aging, 17*, 303–331.

Linn, A. (2013). Many fast-food workers living in poverty, analysis finds. *NBC News.* http://www.nbcnews.com/news/us-news/many-fast-food-workers-living-poverty-analysis-finds-v20975132, accessed 3/17/14.

Lipka, M. (2013). What surveys say about worship attendance–and why some stay home? *Pew Research Center* (September 13, 2013). http://www.pewresearch.org/fact-tank/2013/09/13/what-surveys-say-about-worship-attendance-and-why-some-stay-home/, accessed 11/10/13.

Locke, B. (2014). 6 Free Smartphone Apps for the Post-Grad Job Seeker. *Grad Guard.* http://blog.gradguard.com/2014/01/free-smartphone-apps-post-grad-job-seeker/, accessed 3/17/14.

Loder, A. and E. Deprez. (2013). Boston Bomb Victim in Photo Helped Identify Suspects. *Bloomberg* (April 19, 2013). http://www.bloomberg.com/news/2013-04-19/boston-bombing-victim-in-iconic-photo-helped-identify-attackers.html, accessed 9/25/13.

Logan, J. R. and H. Molotch. (1987). *Urban fortunes: The political economy of place.* Berkeley: University of California Press.

Lorber, J. (1994). *Paradoxes of gender.* New Haven, CT: Yale University Press.

Lorber, J. (2010). Republicans Form Caucus for Tea Party in the House. *The New York Times* (July 21, 2010). http://www.nytimes.com/2010/07/22/us/politics/22tea.html?_r=0, accessed 2/19/14.

Loury, G. (1987). Why should we care about group inequality? *Social Philosophy and Policy, 5.*

Luzar, C. (2013). *Star Citizen* Hits $18 Million, RSI Aims For Much More Than Money. *Crowdfund Insider* (September 6, 2013). http://www.crowdfundinsider.com/2013/09/22151-star-citizen-18-million-rsi-pr-strategy/, accessed 5/26/14.

Lyotard, J. (1985). *The post-modern condition: A report on knowledge.* Minneapolis: University of Minnesota Press.

Macdonald, C. (2011). *Shadow mothers: Nannies, au pairs, and the micropolitics of mothering,* Berkeley: University of California Press.

Mackun, P. and S. Wilson. (2011). Population distribution and change: 2000 to 2010, 2010 Census briefs. www.census.gov/prod/cen2010/briefs/c2010br-01.pdf, accessed 12/7/11.

Maddox, G. (1965). Fact and artifact: Evidence bearing on disengagement from the Duke Geriatrics Project. *Human Development, 8.*

Maddox, G. (1970). Themes and issues in sociological theories of human aging. *Human Development, 13.*

Maharidge, D. (1996). *The coming white minority.* New York: Times Books.

Malotki, E. (1983). *Hopi time: A linguistic analysis of the temporal concepts in the Hopi language.* Berlin: Mouton.

Malthus, T. (2003; orig. 1798). *Essay on the principle of population: A Norton critical edition* (Rev. ed.). Ed. P. Appleman. New York: Norton.

Mandara, J., N. K. Gaylord-Harden, M. H. Richards, and B. L. Ragsdale. (2009). The effects of changes in racial identity and self-esteem on changes in African American Adolescents' mental health. *Child Development, 6*: 1660–1675.

Mandel, J. (2010). Rosh Hashanah online: Yom Kippur services go mobile. *Jerusalem Post* (September 7, 2010). http://www.jpost.com/Arts-and-Culture/Entertainment/Rosh-Hashana-online-Yom-Kippur-services-go-mobile, accessed 11/8/13.

Manik, J. A. and J. Yardley. (2013). Building Collapse in Bangladesh Leaves Scores Dead. *New York Times* (April 24, 2013). http://www.nytimes.com/2013/04/25/world/asia/bangladesh-building-collapse.html?pagewanted=all, accessed 9/25/13.

Manlove J., S. Ryan, E. Wildsmith, and K. Franzetta. (2010). The relationship context of nonmarital childbearing in the U.S. *Demographic Research, 23*(22), 615–654.

Manning, J. T., K. Koukourakis, and D. A. Brodie. (1997). Fluctuating asymmetry, metabolic rate and sexual selection in human males. *Evolution and Human Behavior, 18*(1).

Manpower Inc. (2011). About ManPower Group. www.manpowergroup.com/about/about.cfm, accessed 8/23/11.

Mare, R. (1991). Five decades of educational assortative mating. *American Sociological Review, 56*(1).

Marsden, P. V. and N. Lin. (1982). *Social structure and network analysis.* Beverly Hills, CA: Sage.

Marsh, Julia. (2013). Merrill bias suit: Women employees claim they were given book urging them to 'stroke men's egos' to advance. *New York Post* (July 25, 2013). http://nypost.com/2013/07/25/merrill-bias-suit-women-employees-claim-they-were-given-book-urging-them-to-stroke-mens-egos-to-advance/, accessed 10/12/13.

Marshall, T. (1973). *Class, citizenship, and social development: Essays by T. H. Marshall.* Westport, CT: Greenwood Press.

Martin, J. and M. Shear. (2013). Democrats Turn to Minimum Wage as 2014 Strategy. *The New York Times* (December 29. 2013), http://www.nytimes.com/2013/12/30/us/politics/democrats-turn-to-minimum-wage-as-2014-strategy.html?pagewanted=all, accessed 3/17/14.

Martineau, H. (2009; orig. 1837) *Society in America.* 3 vols. Saunders & Otley; Reissued by Cambridge University Press.

Marx, K. (1977; orig. 1864). *Capital: A critique of political economy.* Vol. 1. New York: Random House.

Massey, D. (1996). The age of extremes: Concentrated affluence and poverty in the twenty-first century. *Demography, 33*(4).

Massey, D. and N. A. Denton. (1993). *American apartheid: Segregation and the making of the underclass.* Cambridge, MA: Harvard University Press.

Mather, M. (2008). *Population losses mount in U.S. rural areas.* Washington, DC: Population Reference Bureau.

Matsueda, R. (1992). Reflected appraisals, parental labeling, and delinquency: Specifying a symbolic interactionist theory. *American Journal of Sociology, 97.*

Matthews, D. (2011). Racial identity becomes a guessing game—literally. *CNN* (December 22, 2011). http://inamerica.blogs.cnn.com/2011/12/22/racial-identity-becomes-a-guessing-game-literally/, accessed 10/20/13.

Mattingly, M. J., K. M. Johnson, and Andrew Schaefer. (2011). More poor kids in more poor places: Children increasingly live where poverty persists. Durham, NH: Carsey Institute. http://www.carseyinstitute.unh.edu/publications/IB-Mattingly-Persistent-Child-Poverty.pdf, accessed 1/3/14.

McCabe, J., et al. (2011). Gender in twentieth-century children's books: Patterns of disparity in titles and central characters. *Gender & Society, 25*(2), 197.

McFadden, D. and C. A. Champlin. (2000). Comparison of auditory evoked potentials in heterosexual, homosexual, and bisexual males and females. *Journal of the Association for Research in Otolaryngology, 1.*

McGeehan, P. (2013). Bank of America to Pay $39 Million in Gender Bias Case. *New York Times* (September 6, 2013). http://dealbook.nytimes.com/2013/09/06/bank-of-america-to-pay-39-million-in-gender-bias-case/?_r=0, accessed 10/13/13.

McLanahan, S. (2004). Diverging destinies: How children are faring under the second demographic transition. *Demography, 41,* 607–627.

McLanahan, S. and G. Sandefur. (1994). *Growing up with a single parent: What hurts, what helps.* Cambridge, MA: Harvard University Press.

Mead, M. (1966). Marriage in two steps. *Redbook Magazine 127* (3), 48–49, 84–86.

Mead, M. (1963; orig. 1935). *Sex and temperament in three primitive societies.* New York: William Morrow.

Mead, M. (1972). *Blackberry Winter: My earlier years.* New York: William Morrow.

Meadows, D. L., et al. (1972). *The limits to growth.* New York: Universe Books.

Mehta, S. (2013). Treatment of HIV-AIDS still poses socio-psychological issues: Study. *Times of India* (November 30, 2013). http://articles.timesofindia. indiatimes.com/2013-11-30/ visakhapatnam/44595899_1_hiv-aids-patients-treatment-study, accessed 1/13/14.

Melton, J. (1989). *The encyclopedia of American religions* (3rd ed.). Detroit, MI: Gale Research Co.

Menn, J. (2003, August 11). The "geeks" who once shunned activism amid the digital revolution are using their money and savvy to influence public policy. *Los Angeles Times*, p. A1.

Merton, R. (1957). *Social theory and social structure* (Rev. ed.). New York: Free Press.

Merton, R. (1968; orig. 1938). Social structure and anomie. *American Sociological Review, 3.*

Meyer, J. W. and B. Rowan. (1977). Institutionalized organizations: Formal structure as myth and ceremony. *American Journal of Sociology, 83.*

Michels, R. (1967; orig. 1911). *Political parties.* New York: Free Press.

Michigan Department of Community Health. (2010). Watch out for date rape drugs. www.michigan.gov/documents/ publications_date_rape_drugs_8886_7. pdf, accessed 9/20/10.

Milgram, S. (1963). Behavioral studies in obedience. *Journal of Abnormal Psychology, 67.*

Mills, C. (1956). *The power elite.* New York: Oxford University Press.

Mills, C. (1959). *The sociological imagination.* New York: Oxford University Press.

Mills, T. (1967). *The sociology of small groups.* Englewood Cliffs, NJ: Prentice-Hall.

Mirza, H. (1986). *Multinationals and the growth of the Singapore economy.* New York: St. Martin's Press.

Mitnick, K. and W. L. Simon. (2011). *Ghost in the wires: My adventures as the world's most wanted hacker.* New York: Little, Brown.

Moe, R. (2006, June 28). Presidential address. National Trust for Historic Preservation. Commonwealth Club, San Francisco, CA. www.nationaltrust.org/ news/2006/20060628_speech_sf.html, accessed 1/8/07.

Moffitt, T. (1996). The neuropsychology of conduct disorder. In P. Cordella and L. Siegel (Eds.), *Readings in contemporary criminological theory.* Boston: Northeastern University Press.

Mohanty, C. (1991). Under Western eyes: Feminist scholarship and colonial discourse. In C. Talpade Mohanty et al. (Eds.), *Third World women and the politics of feminism.* Bloomington, IN: Indiana University Press.

Moore Jr., B. (1966). *Social origins of dictatorship and democracy: Lord and peasant in the making of the modern world.* Boston: Beacon Press.

Moore, L. (1994). *Selling God: American religion in the marketplace of culture.* New York: Oxford University Press.

Morello, C. (2012). Number of biracial babies soars over past decade. *The Washington Post* (April 26, 2012). http://www. mixedracestudies.org/wordpress/?tag= carol-morello, accessed 2/19/2014.

Morgan, S. L., D. Gelbgiser, and K. A. Weeden. (2013). Feeding the Pipeline: Gender, Occupational Plans, and College Major Selection. *Social Science Research* 42: 989–1005.

Morland, K., et al. (2002). Neighborhood characteristics associated with the location of food stores and food service places. *American Journal of Preventive Medicine, 22*(1), 23–29.

Moss, C. (2013). Leo the homeless coder finished his app, and you can download it right now. *Business Insider* (December 10, 2013). http://www.businessinsider. com/homeless-coders-trees-for-cars-app-2013-12#ixzz2pYN5Tc7x.

Mumford, L. (1973). *Interpretations and forecasts.* New York: Harcourt Brace Jovanovich.

Muncie, J. (1999). *Youth and crime: A critical introduction.* London: Sage.

Murdock, G. (1967). *Ethnographic atlas.* Pittsburgh, PA: Pittsburgh University Press.

Murdock, G. P. (1981). *Atlas of world cultures.* Pittsburgh, PA: University of Pittsburgh Press.

Murray, C. (1984). *Losing ground: American social policy, 1950–1980.* New York: Basic Books.

Murray, L. (2010). *Breaking night: A memoir of forgiveness, survival, and my journey from homeless to Harvard.* New York: Hyperion.

Musick, K. and A. Meier. (2010). Are both parents always better than one? Parental conflict and young adult well-being. *Social Science Research. 39,* 814–830.

Mwizabi, G. (2013). Using cell-phones to fight HIV/AIDS. *Zambia Times* (May 7, 2013). http://www.times.co.zm/?p=9537, accessed 10/20/13.

Myrdal, G. (1963). *Challenge to affluence.* New York: Random House.

Najman, J. (1993). Health and poverty: past, present, and prospects for the future. *Social Science and Medicine, 36*(2).

Narayan, D. (1999, December). *Can anyone hear us? Voices from 47 countries.*

Washington, DC: World Bank Poverty Group, PREM.

Nasser, Haya-El. (2010). Census Data Show 'Surprising' Segregation. *USA Today* (December 20, 2012). http:// usatoday30.usatoday.com/news/ nation/census/2010-12-14-segregation_ N.ht, accessed 10/19/13.

National Alliance to End Homelessness. (2011).State of Homelessness in America 2011. http://www.endhomelessness.org/ library/entry/state-of-homelessness-in-america-2011, accessed 1/28/14.

National Assessment Center. (2008). There's safety in numbers. http://isafe.org/imgs/ pdf/nac/NAC_One_Sheet.pdf, accessed 7/9/11.

National Association of Anorexia Nervosa and Associated Disorders (ANAD). (2010). Eating Disorder Statistics. http://www.anad.org/get-information/ about-eating-disorders/eating-disorders-statistics/, accessed 8/23/11.

National Association of State Budget Officers. (2012). Examining fiscal 2010-2012 state spending. http://www.nasbo.org/ sites/default/files/State%20Expenditure%20Report_1.pdf, accessed 7/23/13.

National Center for Family and Marriage Research. (2013). Divorce Rate in the U.S., 2011. Bowling Green, OH: National Center for Family & Marriage Research. http://ncfmr.bgsu.edu/pdf/family_ profiles/file131530.pdf, accessed 7/16/13.

National Center for Health Statistics (NCHS). (2003). Women's health. www. cdc.gov/nchs/fastats/womens_health. htm, accessed 1/11/05.

National Center for Health Statistics (NCHS). (2010). Marriage and cohabitation in the United States. www.cdc.gov/ nchs/data/series/sr_23/sr23_028.pdf, accessed 8/14/11.

National Center for Health Statistics (NCHS). (2011). Summary health statistics for U.S. adults: national health interview survey, 2011. http://www.cdc. gov/nchs/data/series/sr_10/sr10_256.pdf, accessed 8/4/13.

National Center for Health Statistics (NCHS). (2013). *Health, United States 2012: With special feature on emergency care.* http://www.cdc.gov/nchs/data/ hus/hus12.pdf, accessed 8/23/13.

National Center on Elder Abuse (NCEA). (1999). Types of elder abuse in domestic settings. Elder Abuse Information Series No. 1. www.elderabusecenter.org/pdf/ basics/fact1.pdf, accessed 12/7/05.

National Center on Family Homelessness. (2011). The characteristics and needs of families experiencing homelessness. http://www.familyhomelessness.org/ media/306.pdf, accessed 8/25/13.

National Coalition for the Homeless. (2011). Who is homeless? http://www.nationalhomeless.org/factsheets/who.html, accessed 8/25/13.

National Coalition of Homeless Veterans. (2011). FAQ about homeless veterans. www.nchv.org/background.cfm, accessed 8/23/11.

National Conference of State Legislatures (NCSL). (2013a). Defining marriage: Defense of marriage acts and same-sex marriage laws. http://www.ncsl.org/issues-research/human-services/same-sex-marriage-overview.aspx, accessed 10/18/13.

National Conference of State Legislatures (NCSL). (2013b). Women in state legislatures 2013. www.ncsl.org/legislatures-elections/win/women-in-state-legislatures-for-2013.aspx, accessed 9/5/13.

National Eating Disorders Association (NEDA). (2002a). Facts and stats. www.nationaleatingdisorders.org/infor mation-resources/general-information.php#facts-statistics, accessed 8/23/11.

National Eating Disorders Association (NEDA). (2002b). Statistics: Eating disorders and their precursors. www.nationaleatingdisorders.org/p.asp?WebPage_ID=286&Profile_ID=41138, accessed 1/29/06.

National Election Studies. (NES). (2003). *The NES guide to public opinion and electoral behavior, The national election studies,* graph 5A.1.2, Center for Political Studies, University of Michigan. Ann Arbor, MI: University of Michigan, *Center for Political Studies.* www.umich.edu/nes/nesguide/graphs/g5a_1_2.htm, accessed 1/3/05.

National Immigration Forum. (2006, January 26). Facts on immigration. www.immigrationforum.org/DesktopDefault .aspx?tabid=790, accessed 1/27/06.

National Immigration Law Center. (2013). Basic Facts about In-State Tuition for Undocumented Immigrant Students (May 2013). http://www.nilc.org/Basic-Facts-Instate.Html, accessed 10/19/13.

National Low Income Housing Coalition (NLIHC). (2000, September). Out of reach: The growing gap between housing costs and income of poor people in the United States. Washington, DC: National Low Income Housing Coalition/Low Income Housing Information Service. www.nlihc.org/oor2000/index.htm, accessed 1/3/05.

National Marriage Project. (2012). The state of our unions 2012. http://nationalmarriage-project.org/wp-content/uploads/2012/12/SOOU2012.pdf, accessed 8/27/13.

National Opinion Research Center (NORC). (2001). The Paycheck Fairness Act: The Next Step in the Fight for Fair Pay. www.now.org/issues/economic/022709pfa.html, accessed 9/20/10.

National Poverty Center. (2013). Poverty in the United States: Frequently asked questions. http://www.npc.umich.edu/poverty/#3, accessed 8/25/13.

National Sleep Foundation. (2013). 2013 International Bedroom Poll: Summary of Findings. http://www.sleepfoundation.org/sites/default/files/RPT495a.pdf, accessed 11/8/13.

National Youth Association. (2010). Gay Bullying. (November 7, 2010). http://www.nyaamerica.org/2010/11/07/gay-bullyin/, accessed 1/13/14.

Neate, R. (2013 July 29). Apple investigates new claims of China factory staff mis-treatment. *The Guardian.* http://www.theguardian.com/technology/2013/jul/29/apple-investugates-claims-china-factory, accessed 8/26/13.

Neuman, J. (2003). Liberals take a cue from Republicans and turn to big donors to set up think tanks and media outlets to counter the conservative message. *Los Angeles Times* (November 30, 2003), p. A20.

Nerdy Apple Bottom. (2010). My son is gay (November 2, 2010). http://nerdyapplebottom.com/2010/11/02/my-son-is-gay/#comments, accessed summer 2011.

Newman, K. (2000). *No shame in my game: The working poor in the inner city.* New York: Vintage.

Newport, F. and L. Said. (2011). Republicans negative, Democrats positive in describing unions. Gallup Poll (March 11, 2011). www.gallup.com/poll/146588/Republicans-Negative-Democrats-Positive-Describing-Unions.aspx, accessed 9/27/11.

Nibley, L. (2011). Two spirits PBS. www.pbs.org/independentlens/two-spirits/resources/two-spirits-discussion.pdf, accessed 8/25/11.

Nie, N., et al. (2004). Ten years after the birth of the Internet, how do Americans use the Internet in their daily lives? Draft Report. Stanford University. www.stanford.edu/group/siqss/SIQSS_Time_Study_04.pdf, accessed 9/23/05.

Niebuhr, R. (1929). *The social sources of denominationalism.* New York: Holt.7

Nielsen, F. (1994). Income inequality and industrial development: Dualism revisited. *American Sociological Review, 59* (October).

Nielsen Media Research. (2001a). Internet access for blue collar workers spikes 52 percent, according to Nielsen/NetRatings, http://209.249.142.22/press_releases/PDF/pr_010412.pdf, accessed 5/3/01.

Nielsen Media Research. (2001b). Lower income surfers are the fastest growing group on the web, according to Nielsen/NetRatings. http://209.249.142.22/press_releases/PDF/pr_010313.pdf, accessed 5/3/01.

Nishimoto, A. (2012). Robots with Laser Eyes Help Manufacture 2013 Ford Escape. *Motor Trends* (April 12, 2012). http://wot.motortrend.com/robots-with-laser-eyes-help-manufacture-2013-ford-escape-191735.html#ixzz2wFvdD26i, accessed 3/17/14.

Nonprofit Voter Engagement Network. (2013). *America goes to the polls 2012: a report on voter turnout in the 2012 election.* http://www.nonprofitvote.org/download-document/america-goes-to-the-polls-2012.html, accessed 7/19/13.

Nordberg, J. (2010). Afghan boys are prized, so girls live the part. *New York Times* (September 21, 2010). www.nytimes.com/2010/09/21/world/asia/21gender.html, accessed 9/22/10.

NPD. (2009). Total game console sales, May 2009. www.digital-digest.com/blog/DVDGuy/2009/06/13/game-consoles-may-2009-npd-sales-figure-analysis/, accessed 06/09.

Nuasoft. (2000). Irish Internet usage statistics. www.nua.ie/surveys/how_many_online/index.html, accessed 1/3/05.

Nuwer, H. (2013). Chronology of deaths among U.S. college students as a result of hazing, initiation, and pledging-related accidents. http://hazing.hanknuwer.com/listoflists.html, accessed 8/27/13.

Nye, J. (1997). In government we don't trust. *Foreign Policy,* fall, 99–111.

Oakes, J. (1985). *Keeping track: How schools structure inequality.* New Haven, CT: Yale University Press.

Oakes, J. (1990). *Multiplying inequalities: The effects of race, social class, and tracking on opportunities to learn mathematics and science.* Santa Monica, CA: Rand.

Oakley, A. (1974). *The sociology of housework.* New York: Pantheon.

O'Connor, A. (2011). Surgeon General calls for health over hair. *New York Times* (August 25, 2011). http://well.blogs.nytimes.com/2011/08/25/surgeon-general-calls-for-health-over-hair/, accessed 8/31/11.

O'Connor, L. (2013). 'Ghetto Tracker,' App That Helps Rich Avoid Poor, Is As Bad As It Sounds. *The Huffington Post* (September 4, 2013). http://www.huffingtonpost.com/2013/09/04/ghetto-tracker-n_3869051.htmlaccessed 10/14/13.

O'Hare, W. and M. Mather. (2008). Child poverty is highest in rural counties in U.S. Population Reference Bureau. http://www.prb.org/Publications/Articles/2008/childpoverty.aspx, accessed 2/15/08.

Ohmae, K. (1990). *The borderless world: Power and strategy in the industrial economy.* New York: HarperCollins.

Ohmae, K. (1995). *The end of the nation state: How region states harness the prosperity of the global economy.* New York: Free Press.

Oliver, O. and T. M. Shapiro. (1995). *Black wealth/white wealth: A new perspective on racial inequality.* New York: Routledge.

Omi, M. and H. Winant. (1994). *Racial formation in the United States: From the 1960s to the 1990s,* 2nd ed. New York: Routledge.

Oppenheimer, V. (1970). *The female labor force in the United States.* Westport, CT: Greenwood Press.

Oppenheimer, V. (1988). A theory of marriage timing. *American Journal of Sociology, 94.*

Organization for Economic Co-operation and Development (OECD). (1999). The city in the global village. *OECD Observer.* http://www.oecdobserver.org/news/archivestory.php/aid/41/The_city_in_the_global_village.html, accessed 3/16/14.

Organization for Economic Co-operation and Development (OECD). (2005a). Fact book: Economic, environmental, and social statistics. www.oecd.org/site/0,2865, en_21571361_34374092_1_1_1_1_1,00/html, accessed spring 2006.

Organization for Economic Co-operation and Development (OECD). (2005b). OECD science, technology, and industry scoreboard 2005—Towards a knowledge-based economy. Section C.11. http://lysander.sourceoecd.org/vl=11306884/cl=28/nw=1/rpsv/scoreboard/c11.htm, accessed 12/1/05.

Organization for Economic Co-Operation and Development (OECD). (2010). *OECD factbook 2010: Economic, environmental and social statistics.* Paris: OECD Publishing. http://www.oecd-ilibrary.org/economics/oecd-factbook-2010/prison-population-rate-table_factbook-2010-table271-en;jsessionid=317c5gbm9urwo.x-oecd-live-02, accessed 8/19/13.

Organization for Economic Co-operation and Development (OECD). (2013). Education at a glance: OECD indicators 2012. Japan. http://www.oecd.org/education/EAG2012%20-%20Country%20note%20-%20Japan.pdf, accessed 8/20/13.

Ortiz, V. (1995). Families. In R. Zambrana (Ed.), *Understanding Latino families.* Thousand Oaks, CA: Sage.

Oxfam. (2014). *Working for the Few.* Oxfam Briefing Paper (January 20, 2014). http://www.oxfam.org/sites/www.oxfam.org/files/bp-working-for-few-political-capture-economic-inequality-200114-summ-en.pdf, accessed 2/9/14.

Padavic, I. and B. F. Reskin. (2002). *Women and men at work* (2nd ed.). Thousand Oaks, CA: Pine Forge Press.

Pagan, J. A. and M. V. Pauly. (2005). Access to conventional medical care and the use of complementary and alternative medicine. *Health Affairs, 24,* 255–263.

Pager, D. (2003). The mark of a criminal record, *American Journal of Psychology, 108*(5), 937–975.

Pager, D. and H. Shepard. (2008). The sociology of discrimination: Racial discrimination in employment, housing, credit and consumer markets. *Annual Review of Sociology, 34,* 181–209.

Pahl, J. (1989). *Money and Marriage.* London: Macmillan.

Paludi and Barickman. (1991). *Academic and workplace sexual harassment: A resource manual.* Albany, NY: State University of New York Press.

Panyarachun, M. A., et al. (2004). A more secure world: Our shared responsibility: Report of the high-level panel on threats, challenges and change. New York: United Nations. www.un.org/secureworld, accessed spring 2006.

Paoletti, J. (2012). *Pink and blue: Telling the girls from the boys in America.* Bloomington, IN: Indiana University Press.

Parents Television Council. (2007). The alarming family hour . . . No place for children: A content analysis of sex, foul language and violence during network television's family hour. www.parentstv.org/ptc/publications/reports/familyhour/exsummary.asp, accessed 7/3/11.

Park, K. (2011). Who is Marrying Whom? *New York Times* (January 29, 2011). http://www.nytimes.com/interactive/2011/01/29/us/20110130mixedrace.html?ref=us&_r=0, accessed 11/1/13.

Park, R. (1952). *Human communities: The city and human ecology.* New York: Free Press.

Parker-Pope, T. (2010). When boys dress like girls for Halloween. *New York Times* (November 5, 2010). http://well.blogs.nytimes.com/2010/11/05/when-boys-dress-like-girls-for-halloween/.

Parsons, T. (1951). *The social system.* Glencoe, IL: Free Press.

Parsons, T. (1960). Towards a healthy maturity. *Journal of Health and Social Behavior, 1.*

Parsons., T (1964). *The social system.* New York: Free Press.

Parsons, T. and R. F. Bales. (1955). *Family, socialization, and interaction process.* Glencoe, IL: Free Press.

Pascoe, E. (2000). Can a sense of community flourish in cyberspace? *The Guardian* (March 11, 2000).

Passel, J. S., W. Wang, and P. Taylor. (2010, June 4). Marrying out. Pew Research Center. http://pewresearch.org/pubs/1616/american-marriage-interracial-interethnic, accessed 11/14/11.

Pearce, F. (1976). *Crimes of the powerful: Marxism, crime, and deviance.* London: Pluto Press.

Peer, B. (2012). The Girl Who Wanted To Go To School. *The New Yorker* (October 10, 2012), www.newyorker.com/online/bbgs/newdesk/2012/10/the-girl-who-wanted-to-go-to-school.html, accessed 11/8/13.

Penenberg, A. L. (2004). Calling the election: a primer. *Wired* (November 2, 2004). http://www.wired.com/politics/law/news/2004/11/65557?currentPage=all, accessed 1/16/14.

Perrin, E. C., B. S. Siegel, and the Committee on Psychosocial Aspects of Child and Family Health. (2013). Promoting the Well-Being of Children Whose Parents are Gay or Lesbian. *Pediatrics 131:* 1374–83.

Pescosolido, B. A., T. R. Medina, J. K. Martin, and J. S. Long. (2013). The "Backbone" of Stigma: Identifying the Global Core of Public Prejudice Associated With Mental Illness. *American Journal of Public Health 103:* 853–860.

Peterson, R. (1996). A re-evaluation of the economic consequences of divorce. *American Sociological Review, 61.*

Pew Center on the States. (2008). *One in 100: Behind bars in America 2008.* Washington, DC: Pew Charitable Trusts.

Pew Forum on Religion & Public Life. (2008). U.S. Religious Landscape Survey: Religious Affiliation: Diverse and Dynamic. http://religions.pewforum.org/pdf/report-religious-landscape-study-full.pdf, accessed 2/19/14.

Pew Forum on Religion & Public Life. (2009). Mapping the Global Muslim Population: A report on the Size and Distribution of the World's Muslim Population. http://www.pewforum.org/files/2009/10/Muslimpopulation.pdf, accessed 2/19/14.

Pew Forum on Religion & Public Life. (2011a). The Future of the Global Muslim Population, features. http://www.pewforum.org/2011/01/27/the-future-of-the-global-muslim-population/, accessed 4/8/14.

Pew Forum on Religion & Public Life. (2011b). U.S. religious landscape survey. http://religions.pewforum.org/pdf/report-religious-landscape-study-full.pdf#page=61, accessed 11/23/11.

Pew Forum on Religion & Public Life. (2012). Global religious landscape: Religious composition by country, in numbers. http://features.pewforum.org/grl/population-number.php, accessed 11/2/13.

Pew Forum on Religion & Public Life. (2013). U.S. Religious Landscape Survey. http://religions.pewforum.org/. accessed 11/27/13.

Pew Forum on Religion & Public Life. (2014). The Global Religious Landscape. http://www.pewforum.org/2012/12/18/global-religious-landscape-exec/, accessed 4/8/14.

Pew Internet & American Life Project. (2005). Internet: The mainstreaming of on-line life. www.pewinternet.org/pdfs/Internet_Status_2005.pdf, accessed 9/25/05.

Pew Internet & American Life Project. (2010). Use of the internet in higher income households. Figure 2. http://www.pewinternet.org/~/media//Files/Reports/2010/PIP-Better-off-households-final.pdf, accessed 7/19/13.

Pew Internet & American Life Project. (2011). 65% of online adults use social networking sites. http://www.pewinternet.org/~/media//Files/Reports/2011/PIP-SNS-Update-2011.pdf accessed 7/13/13.

Pew Internet & American Life Project. (2012). Older adults and internet use. http://www.pewinternet.org/~/media//Files/Reports/2012/PIP_Older_adults_and_internet_use.pdf, accessed 7/13/13.

Pew Internet & American Life Project. (2013). Coming and going on Facebook. http://pewinternet.org/Reports/2013/Coming-and-going-on-facebook.aspx, accessed 7/13/13.

Pew Research Center. (2010). Distrust, discontent, anger and partisan rancor. http://pewresearch .org/pubs/1569/trust-in-government-distrust-discontent-anger-partisan-rancor, accessed 7/11/11.

Pew Research Center. (2012a). The rise of Asian Americans. http://www.pewsocialtrends.org/files/2013/04/Asian-Americans-new-full-report-04-2013.pdf, accessed 8/22/13.

Pew Research Center. (2012b). *The Rise of Intermarriage: Rates, Characteristics Vary by Race and Gender*. Washington, DC: Pew Research Center. http://www.pewsocialtrends.org/files/2012/02/SDT-Intermarriage-II.pdf, accessed 10/12/13.

Pew Research Center. (2013). *Modern parenthood: Roles of moms and dads converge as they balance work and family*. Washington, DC: Pew Research Center. http://www.pewsocialtrends.org/files/2013/03/FINAL_modern_parenthood_03-2013.pdf, accessed 8/20/13.

Pew Research Center for the People and the Press. (2002, March 7). Public opinion six months later. http://people-press.org/commentary/display .php3?AnalysisID=44, accessed 9/25/05.

Pew Research Center for the People and the Press. (2009). Independents take center stage in Obama era. http://people-press.org/2009/05/21/independents-take-center-stage-in-obama-era/, accessed 8/23/11.

Pew Research Center for the People and the Press. (2010). Public Remains Conflicted Over Islam. http://www.people-press.org/2010/08/24/public-remains-conflicted-over-islam/, accessed 2/19/14.

Pew Research Center for the People and the Press. (2012a). Pew Research Center for the People & the Press values survey, April 2012. http://www.people-press.org/question-search/?qid=1811708&pid=51&ccid=51#top, accessed 8/25/13.

Pew Research Center for the People and the Press. (2012b). Trend in party identification: 1939–2012. http://www.people-press.org/2012/06/01/trend-in-party-identification-1939-2012/, accessed 9/22/13.

Pew Research Center for the People and the Press. (2013a). In Gay Marriage Debate, Both Supporters and Opponents See Legal Recognition as 'Inevitable' (June 6, 2013). http://www.people-press.org/files/legacy-pdf/06-13%20LGBT%20General%20Public%20Release.pdf, accessed 11/2/13.

Pew Research Center for the People and the Press. (2013b). Majority says the federal government threatens their personal rights. http://www.people-press.org/2013/01/31/majority-says-the-federal-government-threatens-their-personal-rights/, accessed 9/22/13.

Pew Research Center for the People and the Press. (2013c). Trust in Government Nears Record Low, But Most Federal Agencies Are Viewed Favorably (October 18, 2013). http://www.people-press.org/files/legacy-pdf/10-18-13%20Trust%20in%20Govt%20Update.pdf, accessed 1/28/14.

Pew Research Center Religion & Public Life Project. (2013). A Portrait of Jewish Americans: Findings from a Pew Research Center Survey of U.S. Jews. http://www.pewforum.org/files/2013/10/jewish-american-full-report-for-web.pdf, accessed 6/30/14.

Pew Research Hispanic Trends Project. (2013). A Demographic Portrait of Mexican-Origin Hispanics in the United States. www.pewhispanic.org/2013/05/01/a-demographic-portrait-of-mexican-origin-hispanics-in-the-united-states, accessed 6/25/14.

Pew Research Hispanic Trends Project. (2014). Statistical Portrait of Hispanics in the United States, 2012. www.pewhispanic.org/2014/04/29/statistical-portrait-of-hispanics-in-the-united-states-2012/, accessed 6/25/14.

Pew Social & Demographic Trends. (2010). The return of the multi-generational family household. http://pewsocialtrends .org/files/2010/10/752-multi-generational-families.pdf, accessed 8/29/11.

Pew Social & Demographic Trends. (2011). Is college worth it? http:// pewsocialtrends.org/files/2011/05/ Is-College-Worth-It.pdf, accessed 8/16/11.

Pilkington, E. (2009). Republicans steal Barack Obama's Internet campaigning tricks: Since their election disaster, the right has used new media to gather strength, culminating in last weekend's huge protest. *The Guardian* (September 18, 2009). www.guardian.co.uk/world/2009/sep/18/republicans-internet-barack-obama/print, accessed 9/27/11.

Pillemer, K. (1985). The dangers of dependency: New findings in domestic violence against the elderly. *Social Problems, 33*.

Pintor, R. L. and M. Gratschew. (2002). Voter turnout since 1945: A global report. Stockholm, Sweden: International Institute for Democracy and Electoral Assistance (International IDEA). www.idea.int/publications/turnout/ VT_screenopt_2002.pdf, accessed 1/3/05.

Pollak, O. (1950). *The criminality of women*. Philadelphia: University of Pennsylvania Press.

Pollard, K. (2011). *The Gender Gap in College Enrollment and Graduation*. Washington, DC: Population Reference Bureau. http://www.prb.org/Publications/Articles/2011/gender-gap-in-education.aspx, accessed 10/12/13.

Polletta, F. and J. M. Jasper. (2001). Collective identity and social movements. *Annual Review of Sociology, 27*, 283–305.

Porter, S. R. and P. D. Umbach. (2006). College major choice: An analysis of student-environment fit. Research in Higher Education, 47(4), 429–449.

Prebisch, R. (1967). *Hacia una dinamica del desarollo Latinoamericano*. Montevideo, Uruguay: Ediciones de la Banda Oriental.

Prebisch, R. (1971). *Change and development—Latin America's great task: Report submitted to the Inter-American Bank*. New York: Praeger.

President's Commission on Organized Crime. (1986). Records of hearings, June 24–26, 1985. Washington, DC: U.S. Government Printing Office.

President's Malaria Initiative. (2013). Seventh annual report to Congress: April 2013. http://www.fightingmalaria.gov/resources/reports/pmi_annual_report13.pdf, accessed 11/1/13.

Provenzo Jr., E. (1991). *Video kids: Making sense of Nintendo*. Cambridge, MA: Harvard University Press.

Purcell, K. (2011). Half of adult cell phone owners have apps on their phones. Pew Research Internet Project. http://www.pewinternet.org/2011/11/02/half-of-adult-cell-phone-owners-have-apps-on-their-phones/, accessed 2/20/14.

Putnam, R. (1993). The prosperous community: Social capital and public life. *American Prospect, 13*.

Putnam, R. (1995). Bowling alone: America's declining social capital. *Journal of Democracy, 6.*

Putnam, R. (2000). *Bowling alone: The collapse and revival of American community.* New York: Simon & Schuster.

Qian, Z-C. and D. T. Lichter. (2011). Changing Patterns of Interracial Marriage in a Multiracial Society. *Journal of Marriage and Family,* 73: 1065–84.

Quah, D. (1999). *The weightless economy in economic development.* London: Centre for Economic Performance.

Quinnipiac University Poll. (2013). iPOLL Databank, The Roper Center for Public Opinion Research, University of Connecticut. http://www.ropercenter.uconn.edu/data_access/ipoll/ipoll.html, accessed 07/22/13.

Radford, B. (2012). On Children Whose Murders Don't Make The News. *Discovery News* (December 26, 2012). http://news.discovery.com/human/psychology/when-killing-children-doesnt-make-the-news-121226.htm, accessed 0/23/13.

Raghuram, S. and B. Wiesenfeld. (2004). Work-nonwork conflict and job stress among virtual workers, *Human Resource Management, 43*(2–3), 259–277.

Raina, P. (2013). Delhi Gang Rape Accused Gets Three Years. *The New York Times* (August 31, 2013). http://india.blogs.nytimes.com/2013/08/31/delhi-gang-rape-accused-gets-three-years/, accessed 10/12/13.

Ramirez, F. O. and J. Boli. (1987). The political construction of mass schooling: European origins and worldwide institutionalism. *Sociology of Education, 60.*

Rampell, C. (2009). As Layoffs Surge, Women May Pass Men in Job Force. *The New York Times.* (February 5, 2009). http://www.nytimes.com/2009/02/06/business/06women.html?, accessed 10/13/13.

Ranis, G. (1996). *Will Latin America now put a stop to "stop-and-go"?* New Haven, CT: Yale University, Economic Growth Center.

Ranis, G. and S. Mahmood. (1992). *The political economy of development policy change.* Cambridge, MA: Blackwell.

Rauhala, E. (2011). The World Welcomes 'Baby 7 Billion,' but What Does Her Future Hold? *Time.* http://world.time.com/2011/10/31/the-world-welcomes-baby-7-billion%E2%80%94what-does-her-future-hold/, accessed 3/17/14.

Ravitch, D. (2013). *Reign of Error: The Hoax of the Privatization Movement and the Danger to America's Public Schools.* New York: Knopf.

Redding, S. (1990). *The spirit of Chinese capitalism.* Berlin: De Gruyter.

Reilly, R. J., and S. Siddiqui. (2013). Supreme Court DOMA Decision Rules Federal Same-Sex Marriage Ban Unconstitutional. *The Huffington Post* (June 26, 2013). http://www.huffingtonpost.com/2013/06/26/supreme-court-doma-decision_n_3454811.html, accessed 12/1/13.

Renzetti, C. M. and D. J. Curran. (1995). *Women, men, and society* (3rd ed.). Needham Heights, MA: Allyn and Bacon.

Renzetti, C. M. and D. J. Curran. (2000). *Social problems: Society in crisis* (5th ed.). Needham Heights, MA: Allyn & Bacon.

Reskin, B. F. and I. Padavic. 1994. *Women and Men at Work.* Thousand Oaks, CA: Pine Forge Press.

ResumeGenius. (2014). 12 Job Hunting Apps Every Job Seeker Should Have For 2014. http://resumegenius.com/blog/job-hunting-apps-every-job-seeker-should-have-for-2014, accessed 3/17/14.

Richardson, S. A., et al. (1961). Cultural uniformity in reaction to physical disabilities. *American Sociological Review, 26,* 241–247.

Rieff, D. (1991). *Los Angeles: Capital of the Third World.* New York: Simon & Schuster.

The Right Stuff. (2013). http://www.rightstuffdating.com/v_index.cfm, accessed 10/14/13.

Riley, M. W., A. Foner, and J. Waring. (1988). Sociology of age. In Neil J. Smelser (Ed.), *Handbook of Sociology.* Newbury Park, CA: Sage.

Ritzer, G. (1993). *The McDonaldization of society.* Newbury Park, CA: Pine Forge Press.

Roach, S. (2005, June 6). The new macro of globalization. *Global: Daily Economic Comment.*

Roberts, S. (2010). Listening to (and Saving) the World's Languages. *The New York Times* (April 28, 2010). http://www.nytimes.com/2010/04/29/nyregion/29lost.html?hpw&_r=0, accessed 6/28/13.

Robinson, W. (2001, April). Social theory and globalization: The rise of a transnational state. *Theory and Society, 30*(2), 157–200.

Robinson, W. ((2004). *A theory of global capitalism: Production, class and state in a transnational world.* Baltimore, MD: Johns Hopkins University Press.

Robinson, W. (2005a, July). Global capitalism: The new transnationalism and the folly of conventional thinking. *Science and Society, 69*(3), 316–328.

Robinson, W. (2005b, December). Gramsci and globalisation: From nation-state to transnational hegemony, *Critical Review of International Social and Political Philosophy, 8*(4), 1–16.

Rocheleau, M. (2010). Senior citizens carve their own niche with laptops and Facebook. *Christian Science Monitor* (July 24, 2010). www.csmonitor.com/Innovation/Tech/2010/0724/Senior-citizens-carve-their-own-niche-with-laptops-and-Facebook, accessed 8/1/10.

Rodriquez, J. (2011). "It's a dignity thing": Nursing home care workers' use of emotions. *Sociological Forum, 26*(2), 265–286.

Roof, W. (1993). *A generation of seekers: The spiritual journeys of the baby boom generation.* San Francisco: Harper San Francisco.

Roof, W. (1999). *Spiritual marketplace: Baby boomers and the remaking of American religion.* Princeton, NJ: Princeton University Press.

Roof, W. and W. McKinney. (1990). *American mainline religion: Its changing shape and future prospects.* New Brunswick, NJ: Rutgers University Press.

Roscoe, W. (1991). *The Zuni Man-Woman.* Albuquerque, NM: University of New Mexico Press.

Rosenau, J. (1997). *Along the domestic-foreign frontier: Exploring governance in a turbulent world.* Cambridge, UK: Cambridge University Press.

Rosenthal, E. (2013). The soaring cost of a simple breath. *The New York Times* (October 12, 2013). http://www.nytimes.com/2013/10/13/us/the-soaring-cost-of-a-simple-breath.html, accessed 1/13/14.

Ross, P. and E. Hansen (2001). AOL, Time Warner complete merger with FCC blessing. *CNET News.com.* http://news.cnet.com/2100-1023-250781.html, accessed 12/16/09.

Rossi, A. (1973). The first woman sociologist: Harriett Martineau. In *The feminist papers: From Adams to de Beauvoir.* New York: Columbia University Press.

Rostow, W. (1961). *The stages of economic growth.* Cambridge, UK: Cambridge University Press.

Rousselle, R. (1999). Defining ancient Greek sexuality. *Digital Archives of Psychohistory, 26*(4), http://www.geocities.ws/kidhistory/ja/defining.htm, accessed 1/11/05.

Rowe, J. W. and R. L. Kahn. (1987). Human aging: Usual and successful. *Science* (July 10, 1987).

Rubin, L. (1990). *Erotic wars: What happened to the sexual revolution?* New York: Farrar, Straus and Giroux.

Rubinstein, W. (1986). *Wealth and inequality in Britain.* Winchester, MA: Faber and Faber.

Rudé, G. (1964). *The crowd in history: A study of popular disturbances in France and England, 1730–1848.* New York: Wiley.

Rugh, J. S. and D. S. Massey. (2010). Racial Segregation and the American Foreclosure Crisis. *American Sociological Review 75*: 629–651.

Rutter, M. and H. Giller. (1984). *Juvenile delinquency: Trends and perspectives.* New York: Guilford Press.

Ryan, T. (1985). The roots of masculinity. In A. Metcalf and M. Humphries (Eds.), *Sexuality of men.* London: Pluto.

Ryzik, M. (2013). Pussy Riot Releases First Song and Video Since Members' Jailing. *The New York Times* (July 17, 2013). http://artsbeat.blogs.nytimes.com/2013/07/17/pussy-riot-releases-its-first-song-and-video-since-the-jailing-of-its-three-members/, accessed 7/18/13.

Sacco, D. T., K. Silbaugh, F. Corredor, J. Casey, and D. Doherty. (2013). *Kinder & Braver World Project*: Research Series: An Overview of State Anti-Bullying Legislation and Other Related Laws. Research Publication No. 2013–4, The Berkman Center for Internet & Society at Harvard University, Cambridge, MA.

Sachs, J. (2000, June 22). A new map of the world. *The Economist.*

Sadker, M. and D. Sadker. (1994). *Failing at fairness.* New York: Scribner.

Saez, E. (2013). *Striking it richer: The evolution of top incomes in the United States* (updated with 2012 preliminary estimates) (September 3, 2013). Unpublished manuscript, University of California-Berkeley. http://elsa.berkeley.edu/~saez/saez-UStopincomes-2012.pdf, accessed 10/12/13.

Sagan, A. (2013). Anti-bullying apps will fail unless society takes action, critics say. *CBC News* (April 25, 2013). www.cbc.ca/news/canada/story/2013/04/18/f-anti-bullying-apps.html, accessed 7/16/13.

Saks, M. (Ed.) (1992). *Alternative medicine in Britain.* Oxford: Clarendon.

Sampson, R. J. and J. Cohen. (1988). Deterrent effects of the police on crime: A replication and theoretical extension. *Law and Society Review, 22*(1).

Sandefur, G. D. and C. A. Liebler. (1997). The demography of American Indian families. *Population Research and Policy Review, 16.*

Sarkisian, N. and N. Gerstel. (2004). Kin support among blacks and whites: Race and family organization. *American Sociological Review, 69,* 812–837.

Sartre, J. (1965; orig. 1948). *Anti-Semite and Jew.* New York: Schocken Books.

Sassen, S. (1991). *The global city: New York, London, Tokyo.* Princeton, NJ: Princeton University Press.

Sassen, S. (1996). *Losing control: Sovereignty in the age of globalization.* New York: Columbia University Press.

Sassen, S. (1998). *Globalization and its discontents.* New York: New Press.

Sassen, S. (2005). *Denationalization: Territory, authority and rights.* Princeton, NJ: Princeton University Press.

Saulny, S. (2011, January 29). Black? White? Asian? More young Americans choose all of the above. *The New York Times* (January 29, 2011). www.nytimes.com/2011/01/30/us/30mixed.html.

Schaie, K. (1983). *Longitudinal studies of adult psychological development.* New York: Guilford Press.

Scheff, T. (1966). *Being mentally ill.* Chicago: Aldine.

Schofield, J. (1995). Review for research on school desegregation's impact on elementary and secondary school students. In J. A. Banks and C. A. M. Banks (Eds.), *Handbook on research on multicultural education.* New York: Simon & Schuster.

Schrock, Karen. (2011). Why Penn State Students Rioted—They Deify Joe Paterno. *Scientific American* (November 10, 2011). http://www.scientificamerican.com/article.cfm?id=penn-state-students-rioted-defied-joe-paterno, accessed 8/26/13.

Schumpeter, J. (1983; orig. 1942). *Capitalism, socialism, and democracy.* Magnolia, MA: Peter Smith.

Schwartz, G. (1970). *Sect ideologies and social status.* Chicago: University of Chicago Press.

Scientific American. (2011). Pfizer slashed R&D. www.scientificamerican.com/article.cfm?id=pfizer-slashes-r-and-d, accessed 8/23/11.

Scott, S. and D. Morgan. (1993). Bodies in a social landscape. In S. Scott and D. Morgan (Eds.), *Body matters: Essays on the sociology of the body.* Washington, DC: Falmer Press.

Secret, M. and W. K. Rashbaum. (2013). U.S. Seizes 14 7-Eleven Stores in Immigration Raids. *The New York Times* (June 17, 2013). http://www.nytimes.com/2013/06/18/nyregion/us-seizes-14-7-eleven-stores-in-immigration-raids.html?_r=0, accessed 10/12/13.

Sedlak, A. and D. D. Broadhurst. (1996). *Third national incidence study of child abuse and neglect.* Washington, DC: U.S. Department of Health and Human Services.

Seidenberg, P. et al. (2012). Early infant diagnosis of HIV infection in Zambia through mobile phone texting of blood test results. *Bulletin of the World Health Organization* 90: 348–356. http://www.who.int/bulletin/volumes/90/5/11-100032/en/index.html, accessed 10/20/13.

Seidman, S., C. Meeks, and F. Traschen. (1999). Beyond the closet? The changing social meaning of homosexuality in the United States. *Sexualities, 2*(1).

Sennett, R. (1998). *The corrosion of character: The personal consequences of work in the new capitalism.* New York: Norton.

The Sentencing Project. (2013). The changing racial dynamics of women's incarceration. http://www.scribd.com/doc/127583695/Changing-Racial-Dynamics-2013, accessed 7/19/13.

Sepulveda, Ana R. and Maria Calado. (2012). Westernization: The Role of Mass Media on Body Image and Eating Disorders. School of Psychology, Autonomous University of Madrid. http://cdn.intechopen.com/pdfs/29049/InTech Westernization_the_role_of_mass_media_on_body_image_and_eating_disorders.pdf, accessed 7/18/13.

Seville Statement on Violence. (1990). *American Psychologist, 45*(10). www.lrainc.com/swtaboo/taboos/seville1.html, accessed 1/3/05.

Sewell, W. and R. Hauser. (1980). The Wisconsin longitudinal study of social and psychological factors in aspirations and achievements. *Research in Sociology of Education and Socialization, 1.*

Sharp, G. (2012). Working-Class Masculinity and Street Harassment. *Sociological Images* (June 26, 2012). http://thesocietypages.org/socimages/2012/06/, accessed 1/15/14.

Shaver, K. (2011). Donations to Japan lag behind those for Katrina, Haiti. *Washington Post* (March 18, 2011). www.washingtonpost.com/wp-dyn/content/article/2011/03/18/AR2011031806162_pf.html, accessed 8/29/11.

Shea, S., et al. (1991). Independent associations of educational attainment and ethnicity with behavioral risk factors for cardiovascular disease. *American Journal of Epidemiology, 134*(6).

Sheldon, W. H., et al. (1949). *Varieties of delinquent youth.* New York: Harper & Row.

Sherwell, Philip. (2013). Merrill Lynch female trainees 'given Seducing the Boys Club book.' *Telegraph* (July 25, 2013). http://www.telegraph.co.uk/news/worldnews/northamerica/usa/10203266/Merrill-Lynch-female-trainees-given-Seducing-the-Boys-Club-book.html, accessed 10/12/13.

Sherwood, H. (2011). Israeli protests: 430,000 take to streets to demand social justice. *The Guardian* (September 4, 2011). www.guardian.co.uk/world/2011/sep/04/israel-protests-social-justice, accessed 9/27/11.

Shostak, M. (1981). *Nisa: The Life and Words of a !Kung Woman.* Cambridge, MA: Harvard University Press.

Sigmund, P. (1990). *Liberation theology at the crossroads: Democracy or revolution?* New York: Oxford University Press.

Simmel, G. (1955). *Conflict and the web of group affiliations.* Trans. K. Wolff. Glencoe, IL: Free Press.

Simms, J. (2013). Asia's Women In the Mix: Sakie Fukushima On Gender Adversity In Japan. *Forbes Asia* (February 27, 2013). http://www.forbes.com/sites/forbesasia/2013/02/27/asias-women-in-the-mix-sakie-fukushima-on-gender-adversity-in-japan/, accessed 6/11/14.

Simpson, I.H., D. Stark, and R. A. Jackson. (1988). Class identification processes of Married, Working Men an Women. *American Sociological Review, 53.*

Siner, E. (2014). Bitcoin Takes Stage In Texas Senate Campaign. National Public Radio (January 10, 2014). http://www.npr.org/blogs/itsallpolitics/2014/01/10/260572933/bitcoin-takes-stage-in-texas-campaign, accessed 2/8/14.

Sjoberg, G. (1960). *The pre-industrial city: Past and present.* New York: Free Press.

Sjoberg, G. (1963). The rise and fall of cities: A theoretical perspective. *International Journal of Comparative Sociology, 4.*

Sklair, L. (2002a). Democracy and the transnational capitalist class. *Annals of the American Academy of Political and Social Science, 581,* 144–157.

Sklair, L. (2002b). *Globalization: Capitalism and its alternatives* (3rd ed.). New York: Oxford University Press.

Sklair, L. (2003). Transnational practices and the analysis of the global system. In A. Hulsemeyer (Ed.), *Globalization in the twenty-first century: Convergence or divergence?,* pp. 15–32. New York: Palgrave Macmillan.

Slapper, G. and S. Tombs. (1999). *Corporate crime.* Essex, UK: Longman.

Smedley, A. (1993). *Race in North America: Origin and evolution of a world view.* Boulder, CO: Westview Press.

Smeeding, T. (2000). Changing income inequality in OECD countries: Updated results from the Luxembourg income study (LIS). *Luxembourg Income Study Working Paper #252,* March. Syracuse, NY: Maxwell School of Citizenship and Public Affairs, Syracuse University. www.lisproject.org/publications/liswps/252.pdf, accessed 1/11/05.

Smeeding, T., L. Rainwater, and G. Burtles. (2000). United States poverty in a cross-national context. *Luxembourg Income Study Working Paper #244,* September. Syracuse, NY: Maxwell School of Citizenship and Public Affairs, Syracuse University, www.lisproject.org/publications/liswps/244.pdf, accessed 1/11/05.

Smelser, N. (1963). *Theory of collective behavior.* New York: Free Press.

Smith, D. (2003). The older population in the United States: March 2002. U.S. Bureau of the Census Current Population Reports, PP.20-546. Washington, DC. www.census.gov/prod/2003pubs/p20-546.pdf, accessed spring 2006.

Smith, T. and J. Son. (2013). Trends in Public Attitudes toward Sexual Morality. National Opinion Research Center (April 2013). http://www.norc.org/PDFs/sexmoralfinal_06-21_FINAL.PDF, accessed 1/13/14.

Smith-Bindman, R., et. al. (2006). Does utilization of screening mammography explain racial and ethnic differences in breast cancer? *Annals of Internal Medicine, 144*(8), 541–553.

Snow, R., et al. (2005). The global distribution of clinical episodes of Plasmodium falciparum malaria. *Nature, 434*(7030): 214–217.

Snyder, T. D. and S. A. Dillow. (2010). *Digest of education statistics 2009* (NCES 2010-013). National Center for Education Statistics, Institute of Education Sciences. Washington, DC: U.S. Department of Education.

So, A. (1990). *Social change and development: Modernization, dependency, and world-systems theories.* Newbury Park, CA: Sage.

Social Security Administration. (2012). Income of the population 55 or older, 2010. http://www.ssa.gov/policy/docs/statcomps/income_pop55/2010/incpop10.pdf, accessed 8/25/13.

Southwick, S. (1996). Liszt: Searchable Directory of E-Mail Discussion Groups. www.liszt.com, accessed 1/3/05.

Spain, D. and S. Bianchi. (1996). *Balancing act: Motherhood, marriage, and employment among American women.* New York: Russell Sage Foundation.

Spectrem Group (2009). Affluent market insights 2009. www.luxist.com/2009/03/11/number-of-u-s-millionaires-falls-steeply/, accessed July 2009.

Spectrem Group. (2013). The number of UHNW households climb on stock market rally. http://www.spectrem.com/news/number-uhnw-households-climb-stock-market-rally-624, accessed 8/25/13.

Spectrem Group. (2014). Number of millionaire households reaches record high. http://spectrem.com/Content/Affluent-Market-Size-2014.aspx, accessed 6/12/14.

Speth, Linda E. (2011). The Married Women's Property Acts, 1839-1865: Reform, Reaction, or revolution? In J. Ralph Lindgren, et al (Eds.), *The law of sex discrimination,* 4th ed. New York: Wadsworth, pp. 12–15.

Spinks, W. A. and J. Wood. (1996). Office-based telecommuting: An international comparison of satellite offices in Japan and North America. In *Proceedings of SIGCPR/SIGMIS '96.* Denver, CO: ACM.

Springer, K. W. and D. M. Mouzon. (2011). "Macho men" and preventive health care: implications for older men in different social classes. *Journal of Health and Social Behavior, 52,* 212–227,

Stack, C. (1975). *All our kin: Strategies for survival in a black community.* New York: Harper Calophon.

Stampp, K. (1956). *The peculiar institution.* New York: Knopf.

Stalker, P. (2011). *Stalker's guide to international migration—map of migration flows.* www.pstalker.com/migration/mg_map.htm, accessed 5/27/11.

Stark, R. and W. S. Bainbridge. (1980). Towards a theory of religious commitment. *Journal for the Scientific Study of Religion, 19.*

Stark, R. and W. S. Bainbridge. (1987). *A theory of religion.* New Brunswick, NJ: Rutgers University Press.

Statistical Office of the European Communities. (1991). *Basic statistics of the community.* Luxembourg: European Union.

Steinberg, R. (1990). Social construction of skill: Gender, power, and comparable worth. *Work and Occupations, 17.*

Steinmetz, S. (1983). Family violence toward elders. In S. Saunders et al. (Eds.), *Violent individuals and families: A practitioner's handbook.* Springfield, IL: Charles C. Thomas.

Stephens-Davidowitz, S. (2013). How Many American Men are Gay? *The New York Times* (December 8, 2013). http://www.nytimes.com/2013/12/08/opinion/sunday/how-many-american-men-are-gay.html?ref=opinion, accessed 12/9/13.

Sterbenz, C. (2013.) Your smartphone can make you a crime-fighting hero. *Business Insider* (July 1, 2013). http://www.businessinsider.com/crime-fighting-apps-2013-6#ixzz2dM2bXFF0, accessed 8/29/13.

Stewart, J. B. (2013). Looking for a Lesson in Google's Perks. *The New York Times* (March 15, 2013). http://www.nytimes.com/2013/03/16/business/at-google-a-place-to-work-and-play.html?pagewanted=all&_r=1&, accessed 5/26/14.

Stiglitz, J. (2007). *Making globalization work.* New York: Norton.

Stillwagon, E. (2001, May 21). AIDS and poverty in Africa. *The Nation.* http://www.thenation.com/article/aids-and-poverty-africa

Stockholm International Peace Research Institute. (2012). *The 15 countries with the highest military expenditure in 2012.* http://www.sipri.org/research/armaments/milex/Top%2015%20table%202012.pdf, accessed 9/22/13.

Stockholm International Peace Research Institute. (2014). Trends in Military Expenditure, 2013. www.sipri.org/publications, accessed 5/19/14.

Stolberg, S. G. (2009). Obama Signs Equal-Pay Legislation. *The New York Times* (January 29, 2009). http://www.nytimes.com/2009/01/30/us/politics/30ledbetter-web.html, accessed 10/12/13.

Stone, C., C. Van Horn, and C. Zukin. (2012). Chasing the American dream: Recent college graduates and the great recession. http://www.heldrichpodcasts.com/Chasing_American_Dream_Report.pdf, accessed 8/25/13.

Stranges, S., W. Tigbe, F. Z. Gomez-Olive, M. Thorogood, and N.-B. Kaldala. (2012). Sleep Problems: Am Emerging Global Epidemic? Findings from the INDEPTH WHO-SAGE Study among more than 40,000 Older Adults from 8 Countries. *Sleep*. 35(8):1173–81.

Stryker, R. (1996). Comparable worth and the labor market. In P. J. Dubeck and K. Borman (Eds.), *Women and work: A handbook*. New York: Garland.

Summers, N. (2013). The future of health apps: Personalized advice combining your diet, sleep pattern and fitness regime. The Next Web.com. http://thenextweb.com/apps/2013/08/07/the-future-of-health-apps-smart-recommendations-for-your-diet-sleep-pattern-and-fitness-regime/#!pn9Hz, accessed 12/9/13.

Survey of Consumer Finances. (2009). Changes in U.S. family finances from 2004 to 2007: Evidence from the Survey of Consumer Finances. www.federalreserve.gov/pubs/bulletin/2009/pdf/scf09.pdf, accessed July 2009.

Sutherland, E. (1949). *Principles of criminology*. Chicago: Lippincott.

Swidler, A. (1986). Culture in action: Symbols and strategies. *American Sociological Review*, 51.

Symantec Corporation. (2013). Internet Security Threat Report 2013: Volume 18. http://www.symantec.com/content/en/us/enterprise/other_resources/b-istr_main_report_v18_2012_21291018.en-us.pdf, accessed 8/28/13.

Tan, A. and K. Ramakrishna (Eds.). (2002). *The new terrorism*. Singapore: Eastern Universities Press.

Tang , S. and J. Zuo. (2000). Dating attitudes and behaviors of American and Chinese college students. *Social Science Journal*, 37(1).

Tarm, M. (2006). Old houses spared by slow market: Decade-long teardown tide turns as preservationists gain influence. *Chicago Sun-Times* (December 22, 2006). www.suntimes.com/classifieds/homes/homelife/181875,HOF-News-oldhouses22.article, accessed 1/8/07.

Tavernise, S. (2011). More unwed parents live together, report finds. *New York Times* (August 16, 2011). http://www.nytimes.com/2011/08/17/us/17cohabitation.html, accessed 6/27/14.

Taxin, A. (2011). College students to protest higher ed budget cuts across the country. *The Huffington Post* (April 13, 2011). www.huffingtonpost.com/2011/04/13/college-students-to-prote_n_848625.html#s264549, accessed 12/12/11.

Taylor, R. J., L. M. Chatters,, and J. S. Levin. (2004). *Religion in the lives of African Americans: Social, psychological and health perspectives*. Thousand Oaks, CA: Sage.

Taylor, P., C. Funk, and A. Clark. (2007). As marriage and parenthood drift apart, public is concerned about social impact. *Pew Research Center* http://pewresearch.org/assets/social/pdf/Marriage.pdf, accessed January 2008.

Teach for America. (2012). Teach For America announces the schools contributing the most graduates to its 2012 teaching Corps. (September 5, 2012). http://www.teachforamerica.org/press-room/press-releases/2012/teach-america-announces-schools-contributing-most-graduates-its-2012, accessed 8/21/13.

Teachman, J. (2003). Premarital sex, premarital cohabitation, and the risk of subsequent marital dissolution among women. *Journal of Marriage and the Family, 65*, 444–455.

Television Bureau of Advertising. (2010). *TVB 2010 Media comparisons study*. New York: Television Bureau of Advertising. http://www.tvb.org/media/file/TVB_PB_Media_Comparisons_2010_PERSONS.pdf, accessed 7/19/13.

Telework Coalition. (2004). Telework facts. www.telcoa.org/id33.htm, accessed 9/23/05.

Thompson, E. (1971). The moral economy of the English crowd in the eighteenth century. *Past and Present, 50*.

Thompson, W. (1929). Population. *American Journal of Sociology, 34*.

Thomson Reuters. (2012). Mergers and Acquisitions Review. http://dmi.thomsonreuters.com/Content/Files/4Q2012_MA_Financial_Advisory_Review.pdf, accessed 3/30/14.

Thomson Reuters. (2014). Mergers and Acquisitions Review: Full Year 2013. http://www.pwc.es/es/servicios/trans-acciones/assets/thomson-reuters-mergers-and-acquisitions-review-2013.pdf, accessed 6/27/14.

Thornton, G. (2013). Women in senior management: Setting the stage for growth. http://www.gti.org/files/ibr2013_wib_report_final.pdf, accessed 2/20/2014.

Tilly, C. (1978). *From mobilization to revolution*. Reading, MA: Addison-Wesley.

Tilly, C. (1996). The emergence of citizenship in France and elsewhere. In C. Tilly (Ed.), *Citizenship, identity, and social history*. Cambridge: Cambridge University Press.

Totti, X. (1987, Fall). The making of a Latino ethnic identity. *Dissent, 34*.

Toufexis, A. (1993, May 24). Sex has many accents. *Time*.

Touraine, A. (1974). *The post-industrial society*. London: Wildwood.

Touraine, A. (1977). *The self-production of society*. Chicago: University of Chicago Press.

Touraine, A. (1981). *The voice and the eye: An analysis of social movements*. New York: Cambridge University Press.

Townsend, P. and N. Davidson (Eds.) (1982). *Inequalities in health: The Black report*. Harmondsworth, UK: Penguin.

Toyota Corporation. (2003). 2001 Number and diffusion rate for motor vehicles in major countries. www.toyota.co.jp/IRweb/corp_info/and_the_word/pdf/2003_c07.pdf, accessed spring 2006.

Treas, J. (1995). Older Americans in the 1990s and beyond. *Population bulletin 50*. Washington, DC: Population Reference Bureau.

Treiman, D. (1977). *Occupational prestige in comparative perspective*. New York: Academic Press.

Troeltsch, E. (1931). *The social teaching of the Christian churches* (2 vols.). New York: Macmillan.

Turk, Austin. (2004). Sociology of terrorism, *Annual Review of Sociology* 30(1): 271–286.

Turnbull, C. (1983). *The human cycle*. New York: Simon & Schuster.

Union of Concerned Scientists. (2013). Nuclear Weapons and Global Security. http://www.ucsusa.org/nuclear_weapons_and_global_security/space_weapons/technical_issues/ucs-satellite-database.html, accessed 3/16/14.

Union of International Organizations. (2005). *Yearbook of international organizations—Guide to global civil society* (42nd ed.). Vol. 1B, appendix 3, table 1. Munich: K.G. Saur.

United Nations. (1995). Human Development Report. Gender and human development—overview. http://hdr.undp.org/reports/global/1995/en/pdf/hdr_1995_overview.pdf, accessed 1/3/05.

United Nations. (2003). Table 26. United Nations Human Development Report, 2003. www.undp.org/hdr2003/pdf/hdr03_HDI.pdf, accessed 1/3/05.

United Nations. (2004). The Impact of AIDS. http://www.un.org/esa/population/publications/AIDSimpact/1CoverNotePrefaceContents.pdf, accessed 1/28/14.

United Nations. (2007). World urbanization prospects. http://esa.un.org/unup/, accessed August 2009.

United Nations. (2009). 2009 World survey on the role of women in development: Women's control over economic resources and access to financial resources, including microfinance. New York: Department of Economic and Social Affairs.

United Nations. (2012). World Urbanization Prospects: The 2011 Revision. New York: United Nations. http://esa.un.org/unup/pdf/WUP2011_Highlights.pdf, accessed 7/16.13.

United Nations. (2013a). Haiti country profile: Human development indicators. http://hdrstats.undp.org/en/countries/profiles/HTI.html, accessed 8/20/13.

United Nations. (2013b).The millennium development goals report 2013. http://www.un.org/millenniumgoals/pdf/report-2013/mdg-report-2013-english.pdf, accessed 8/26/13.

United Nations. (2013c). World Population Prospects : The 2012 Revision. http://esa.un.org/unpd/wpp/Documentation/pdf/WPP2012_HIGHLIGHTS.pdf, accessed 2/8/14.

United Nations Children's Fund (UNICEF). (2006). Equality in employment. www.unicef.org/sowc07/docs/sowc07_chap3.pdf, accessed 8/16/11.

United Nations Children's Fund (UNICEF). (2009). *The state of the world's children 2009.* New York: United Nations Children's Fund. www.unicef.org/sowc09/docs/SOWC09-FullReport-EN.pdf, accessed 2/4/2010.

United Nations Children's Fund (UNICEF). (2013). Pakistan. http://www.unicef.org/pakistan/, accessed 12/8/13.

United Nations Conference on Trade and Development (UNCTAD). (2005). World Investment Report, 2005, p. 325, annex table B4.

United Nations Department of Economic and Social Affairs, Population Division. (2009). Trends in international migrant stock: The 2008 revision. http://esa.un.org/migration/p2k0data.asp, accessed 5/27/11.

United Nations Development Programme (UNDP). (1998). Human Development Report 1998. New York: Oxford University Press.

United Nations Development Programme (UNDP). (1999). Human Development Report 1999. New York: Oxford University Press.

United Nations Development Programme (UNDP). (2012). World Urbanization Prospects: The 2011 Revision. http://esa.un.org/unup/pdf/WUP2011_Highlights.pdf, accessed 2/8/14.

United Nations Economic Commission for Europe. (2003). Ireland. www.unece.org/stats/trend/irl.pdf, accessed spring 2006.

United Nations Economic and Social Commission for Western Asia (UNESCWA). (2011). The Demographic Profile of Kuwait. http://www.escwa.un.org/popin/members/kuwait.pdf, accessed 6/22/13.

United Nations Educational, Scientific, and Cultural Organization (UNESCO). (2013). Adult and youth literacy: national, regional and global trends, 1985–2015. http://www.uis.unesco.org/Education/Documents/literacy-statistics-trends-1985-2015.pdf, accessed 8/19/13.

United Nations Food and Agriculture Organization (UN FAO). (2001). The impact of HIV/AIDS on food security. United Nations Food and Agriculture Organization, Conference on World Food Security, May 28–June 1.

United Nations Food and Agriculture Organization (UN FAO). (2004). The state of food insecurity, 2004. United Nations Food and Agriculture Organization. www.fao.org/documents/show_cdr.asp?url_file=/docrep/007/y5650e/y5650e00.htm, accessed 11/30/05.

United Nations Food and Agriculture Organization (UN FAO). (2005). Armed conflicts leading cause of world hunger emergencies. United Nations Food and Agriculture Organization. www.fao.org/newsroom/en/news/2005/102562/index.html, accessed 12/1/05.

United Nations Food and Agriculture Organization (UN FAO). (2011). Global hunger declining but still unacceptably high. www.fao.org/hunger/en/, accessed 8/23/11.

United Nations Food and Agriculture Organization (UN FAO). (2013a). FAO statistical yearbook 2013. Rome: Food and Agriculture Organization of the United Nations. http://www.fao.org/docrep/018/i3107e/i3107e00.htm, accessed 8/26/13.

United Nations Food and Agriculture Organization (UN FAO). (2013b). The state of food insecurity in the world: The multiple dimensions of food security. http://www.fao.org/docrep/018/i3434e/i3434e.pdf, accessed 11/29/13.

United Nations Framework Convention on Climate Change. (2014). Status of Ratification of Kyoto Accord. http://unfccc.int/kyoto_protocol/status_of_ratification/items/2613.php, accessed 1/3/14.

United Nations Global Initiative to Fight Human Trafficking (UN.GIFT). (2008). Human trafficking: The facts. http://www.unglobalcompact.org/docs/issues_doc/labour/Forced_labour/human_trafficking_-_the_facts_-_final.pdf, accessed 9/6/13.

United Nations Joint Programme on HIV/AIDS (UNAIDS). (2005). AIDS epidemic update, December 2005: North America, Western and Central Europe. www.unaids.org/epi/2005/doc/EPIupdate2005_pdf_en/Epi05_10_en.pdf, accessed spring 2006.

United Nations Joint Programme on HIV/AIDS (UNAIDS). (2008). Report on the Global AIDS Epidemic: Executive Summary. http://data.unaids.org/pub/GlobalReport/ 2008/JC1511_GR08_ExecutiveSummary_en.pdf, accessed August 2009.

United Nations Joint Programme on HIV/AIDS (UNAIDS). (2010). Global Report. http://www.unaids.org/globalreport/documents/20101123_GlobalReport_full_en.pdf, accessed 8/25/11.

United Nations Joint Programme on HIV/AIDS (UNAIDS). (2012). Global report: UNAIDS report on the global AIDS epidemic 2012. http://www.unaids.org/en/media/unaids/contentassets/documents/epidemiology/2012/gr2012/20121120_UNAIDS_Global_Report_2012_with_annexes_en.pdf, accessed 8/4/13.

United Nations Joint Programme on HIV/AIDS (UNAIDS). (2013a). Global Report: UNAIDS report on the global AIDS epidemic 2013. http://www.unaids.org/en/media/unaids/contentassets/documents/epidemiology/2013/gr2013/unaids_global_report_2013_en.pdf, accessed 6/8/13.

United Nations Joint Programme on HIV/AIDS (UNAIDS). (2013b). Haiti. http://www.unaids.org/en/regionscountries/countries/haiti/, accessed 8/20/13.

United Nations Office on Drugs and Crime. (2013). 2013 World Drug Report. http://www.unodc.org/unodc/secured/wdr/wdr2013/World_Drug_Report_2013.pdf, accessed 8/28/13.

United Nations Population Fund (UNFPA). (2005a). Gender-based violence: A price too high. *State of the world population, 2005.* www.unfpa.org/ swp/ 2005/english/ch7/index.htm, accessed 12/4/05.

United Nations Population Fund (UNFPA). (2005b). Violence against women fact sheet. www.unfpa.org/swp/2005/presskit/factsheets/facts_vaw.htm, accessed 12/4/05.

United Nations Women. (2013). Special Rapporteur positions unpaid care work as major human rights issue. United Nations Women. http://www.unwomen.org/ru/news/stories/2013/10/special-rapporteur-positions-unpaid-care-work-as-major-human-rights-issue#sthash.UVtO6Vfv.dpuf, accessed 2/20/14.

United Nations World Food Programme (UN WFP). (2004). *Paying the price of hunger: The impact of malnutrition on women and children.* United Nations World Food Program. http://documents.wfp .org/stellent/groups/public/documents/newsroom/wfp076313.pdf, accessed 12/1/05.

United States Conference of Mayors. (2008). Hunger and homelessness survey: A status report on hunger and homelessness in America's cities. http://usmayors.

org/pressreleases/documents/ hungerhomelessnessreport_121208.pdf, accessed 8/22/13.

United States Institute of Peace. (2013). Guide for participants in peace, stability, and relief operations. http://www.usip. org/node/5599, accessed 11/28/13.

Urban Institute. (2005, August 25). *Low-income working families: Facts and figures.* www.urban.org/UploadedPDF/ 900832.pdf, accessed spring 2006.

U.S. Bureau of Justice Statistics. (2012a). Correctional populations in the United States, 2011. http://www.bjs.gov/ content/pub/pdf/cpus11.pdf, accessed 7/23/13.

U.S. Bureau of Justice Statistics. (2012b). Prisoners in 2011. http://www.bjs.gov/ content/pub/pdf/p11.pdf, accessed 7/19/13.

U.S. Bureau of Justice Statistics. (2012c). State corrections expenditures, FY 1982–2010. http://www.bjs.gov/ content/pub/pdf/scefy8210.pdf, accessed 7/23/13.

U.S. Bureau of Justice Statistics. (2013a). Criminal Victimization, 2012. http:// www.bjs.gov/content/pub/pdf/cv12.pdf, accessed 3/19/14.

U.S. Bureau of Justice Statistics. (2013b). Correctional populations in the United States, 2012. http://www.bjs.gov/ content/pub/pdf/cpus12.pdf, accessed 7/23/13.

U.S. Bureau of Justice Statistics. (2013c). Female Victims of Sexual Violence, 1994–2010. http://www.bjs.gov/index. cfm?ty=pbdetail&iid=4594, accessed 2/20/14.

U.S. Bureau of Labor Statistics. (2011a). Employment status of the Hispanic or Latino population by sex, age, and detailed ethnic group. ftp://ftp .bls.gov/pub/special. requests/lf/aat6.txt, accessed 5/27/11.

U.S. Bureau of Labor Statistics. (2011b). Highlights of women's earnings in 2009. www.bls.gov/cps/cpswom2009.pdf, accessed 5/27/11.

U.S. Bureau of Labor Statistics. (2011c). A profile of the working poor 2009. www. bls.gov/cps/cpswp2009.pdf, accessed 8/23/11.

U.S. Bureau of Labor Statistics. (2013a). Employed and unemployed full- and part-time workers by age, sex, race, and Hispanic or Latino ethnicity. http:// www.bls.gov/cps/cpsaat08.pdf, accessed 11/2/13.

U.S. Bureau of Labor Statistics. (2013b). Employed persons by occupation, race, Hispanic or Latino ethnicity, and sex. http://www.bls.gov/cps/cpsaat10.pdf, accessed 8/23/13.

U.S. Bureau of Labor Statistics. (2013c). Employment status of the civilian nonin-stitutionalized population 25 years and over by educational attainment, sex, race, and Hispanic or Latino ethnicity. http:// www.bls.gov/cps/cpsaat07.pdf, accessed 8/23/13.

U.S. Bureau of Labor Statistics. (2013d). Employment status of the civilian noninsti-tutionalized population by sex, age, and race. http://www.bls.gov/cps/cpsaat05. pdf, accessed 8/23/13.

U.S. Bureau of Labor Statistics. (2013e). Employment status of the Hispanic or Latino population by sex, age, and detailed ethnic group. http://www.bls.gov/cps/ cpsaat06.pdf, accessed 8/23/13.

U.S. Bureau of Labor Statistics. (2013f). Highlights of women's earnings, 2012. http://www.bls.gov/cps/cpswom2012. pdf, accessed 4/3/14.

U.S. Bureau of Labor Statistics. (2013g). Highlights of women's earnings in 2013. http://www.bls.gov/cps/cpswom2012. pdf, accessed 4/3/14.

U.S. Bureau of Labor Statistics. (2013h). Median weekly earnings of full-time wage and salary workers by selected characteristics. http://www.bls.gov/cps/ cpsaat37.pdf, accessed 8/23/13.

U.S. Bureau of Labor Statistics. (2013i). A profile of the working poor, 2011. http:// www.bls.gov/cps/cpswp2011.pdf, accessed 8/25/13.

U.S. Bureau of Labor Statistics. (2014a). The Editor's Desk, Major work stop-pages in 2013. http://www.bls.gov/opub/ ted/2014/ted_20140226.htm, accessed 3/27/14.

U.S. Bureau of Labor Statistics. (2014c). Employed persons by detailed occupa-tion, sex, race, and Hispanic or Latino ethnicity. http://www.bls.gov/cps/ cpsaat11.htm, accessed 4/2/14.

U.S. Bureau of Labor Statistics. (2014d). Median weekly earnings of full-time wage and salary workers by selected characteristics. http://www.bls.gov/cps/ cpsaat37.htm, accessed 4/2/14.

U.S. Bureau of Labor Statistics. (2014e). Union members–2013. http://www.bls. gov/news.release/pdf/union2.pdf, accessed 3/27/14.

U.S Bureau of Labor Statistics. (2014f). Women in the labor force: A databook. Table 1. http://www.bls.gov/cps/wlf-databook-2013.pdf, accessed 5/30/14.

U.S Bureau of Labor Statistics. (2014g). Women in the labor force: A databook. Table 6. http://www.bls.gov/cps/wlf-databook-2013.pdf, accessed 5/30/14.

U.S Bureau of Labor Statistics. (2014h). Women in the labor force: A databook. Table 10. http://www.bls.gov/cps/wlf-databook-2013.pdf, accessed 5/20/14.

U.S Bureau of Labor Statistics. (2014i). Women in the labor force: A databook. Table 11. http://www.bls.gov/cps/wlf-databook-2013.pdf, accessed 5/30/14.

U.S Bureau of Labor Statistics. (2014j). Women in the labor force: A databook. Table 16. http://www.bls.gov/cps/wlf-databook-2013.pdf, accessed 5/30/14.

U. S. Bureau of Prisons. (2013). Annual de-termination of average cost of incarcera-tion. *Federal Register* 78:52 (March 18, 2013), p. 16711.

U.S. Bureau of the Census. (2000). *The chang-ing shape of the nation's income distribu-tion.* www.census .gov/prod/2000pubs/ p60-204.pdf, accessed 1/4/05.

U.S. Bureau of the Census. (2001). *Asset own-ership of households: 1995.* www.census. gov/hhes/ www/wealth/ 1995/wlth95-1. html, accessed 1/4/05.

U.S. Bureau of the Census. (2003a). *Char-acteristics of the foreign born by world region of birth.* Table 3.1. www.census. gov/population/www/socdemo/foreign/ ppl-174.html#reg, accessed spring 2006.

U.S. Bureau of the Census. (2003b). Sta-tistical Abstract of the United States 2000. Washington, DC: U.S. Govern-ment Printing Office. www .census. gov/prod/2004pubs/03statab/pop.pdf, accessed 1/4/05.

U.S. Bureau of the Census. (2004). Interim Projections of the U.S. Population by Age, Race, Sex, and Hispanic Origin. *2004 Interim National Population Projections.* http://www.census.gov/population/ projections/files/methodology/ idbsummeth.pdf, accessed 6/17/14.

U.S. Bureau of the Census. (2005). *America's families living arrangements: 2004.* Cur-rent Population Survey. www.census. gov/population/www/socdemo/hh-fam/ cps2004.html, accessed 1/12/06.

U.S. Bureau of the Census. (2009). *Foreign-born population of the United States.* Current Population Survey. www.census. gov/population/www/socdemo/foreign/ cps2009.html (table 2.13), accessed 7/3/11.

U.S. Bureau of the Census. (2010a). *Children by presence and type of parent(s), race, and Hispanic origin: 2010.* www.census. gov/population/www/socdemo/hh-fam/ cps2010.html, accessed 8/14/11.

U.S. Bureau of the Census. (2010b). *House-hold relationship and living arrange-ments of children under 18 years, by age and sex: 2010.* www .census.gov/ population/www/socdemo/hh-fam/ cps2010.html, accessed 8/14/11.

U.S. Bureau of the Census. (2010c). Income Tables. www.census .gov/hhes/www/ income/data/historical/people/index. html, accessed 8/23/11.

U.S. Bureau of the Census. (2010d). *Marital status of people 15 years and over, by age, sex, personal earnings, race, and Hispanic origin, 2010.* www.census.gov/population/ www/ socdemo/hh-fam/cps2010.html, accessed 8/10/11.

U.S. Bureau of the Census. (2010e). Projections: Population under age 18 and 65 and older: 2000, 2010, and 2030, table 5. www.census.gov/population/ www/ projections/projectionsagesex.html, accessed 7/3/11.

U.S. Bureau of the Census. (2010f). Selected Social Characteristics in the United States. *American Community Survey: 2010.* http://www.culvercity.org/~/ media/Files/Planning/Census2010/ US%20Census%20DP-02%20Selected% 20Social%20Char.%202010.ashx, accessed 6/17/13.

U.S. Bureau of the Census. (2011a). 2011 Statistical Abstract of the United States. Table 1156, www.census.gov/compendia/ statab/2011/tables/11s1156.pdf, accessed 7/19/13.

U.S. Bureau of the Census. (2011b). *Age and sex composition: 2010.* www.census.gov/ prod/cen2010/briefs/c2010br-03.pdf, accessed 7/3/11.

U.S. Bureau of the Census. 2011c). *Families below poverty level and below 125 percent of poverty by race and Hispanic origin: 1980 to 2008.* www.census.gov/compendia/ statab/2011/tables/11s0714.pdf, accessed 5/27/11.

U.S. Bureau of the Census. (2011d). Historical Income Tables: Households. www. census.gov/hhes/www/income/data/ historical/household/index.html, accessed 11/1/11.

U.S. Bureau of the Census. (2011e). Median value of assets for households, by type of asset owned and selected characteristics: 2010. http://www.census.gov/ people/wealth/files/Wealth_ Tables_2010.xls, accessed 7/25/13.

U.S. Bureau of the Census. (2011f). The older population: 2010. www.census.gov/ prod/cen2010/briefs/c2010br-09.pdf, accessed 7/1/13.

U.S. Bureau of the Census. (2011g). *Overview of race and Hispanic origin: 2010.* www. census.gov/prod/cen2010/briefs/ c2010br-02.pdf, accessed 11/7/11.

U.S. Bureau of the Census. (2012a). 2012 national population projections: summary tables, table 2. www.census.gov/ population/projections/data/national/ 2012/summarytables.html, accessed 7/1/13.

U.S. Bureau of the Census. (2012b). Age and sex of all people, family Members and unrelated individuals iterated by income-to-poverty ratio and race: 2011. http://www.census.gov/hhes/www/ cpstables/032012/pov/POV01_100_3. xls, accessed 8/24/13.

U.S. Bureau of the Census. (2012c). America's families and living arrangements: 2012, table A1. http://www.census.gov/hhes/ families/data/cps2012.html, accessed 8/27/13.

U.S. Bureau of the Census. (2012d). Educational attainment in the United States: 2012—detailed tables, table 3. http://www.census.gov/hhes/socdemo/ education/data/cps/2012/tables.html, accessed 8/23/13.

U.S. Bureau of the Census. (2012e). Educational attainment of the population 18 years and over, by age, sex, race, and Hispanic origin: 2012. http://www. census.gov/hhes/socdemo/education/ data/cps/2012/tables.html, accessed 7/25/13.

U.S. Bureau of the Census. (2012f). The Foreign Born Population in the United States: 2010. http://www.census.gov/ prod/2012pubs/acs-19.pdf, accessed 4/2/14.

U.S. Bureau of the Census. (2012g). Growth in urban population outpaces rest of nation, census bureau reports. http:// www.census.gov/newsroom/releases/ archives/2010_census/cb12-50.html, accessed 11/14/13.

U.S. Bureau of the Census. (2012h). Historical income tables: households, table H-2. http://www.census.gov/hhes/www/ income/data/historical/household/, accessed 7/25/13.

U.S. Bureau of the Census. (2012i). Historical income tables: households, table H-3. http://www.census.gov/hhes/www/ income/data/historical/household/, accessed 7/25/13.

U.S. Bureau of the Census. (2012j). Historical income tables: income inequality. http://www.census.gov/hhes/www/ income/data/historical/inequality/, accessed 7/25/13.

U.S. Bureau of the Census. (2012k). Households and families: 2010. http:// www.census.gov/prod/cen2010/briefs/ c2010br-14.pdf, accessed 8/27/13.

U.S. Bureau of the Census. (2012l). *Income, Poverty, and Health Insurance Coverage in the United States: 2011.* Washington, DC: U.S. Government Printing Office. www.census.gov/prod/2012pubs/ p60-243.pdf, accessed 8/25/13.

U.S. Bureau of the Census. (2012m). Poverty status, by type of family, presence of related children, race and Hispanic origin. http://www.census.gov/hhes/www/ poverty/data/historical/hstpov4.xls, accessed 8/25/13.

U.S. Bureau of the Census. (2012n). Poverty status of people by family relationship, race, and Hispanic origin: 1959 to 2011. http://www.census.gov/hhes/www/ poverty/data/historical/hstpov2.xls, accessed 8/23/13.

U.S. Bureau of the Census. (2012o). Poverty Status of the Foreign-Born Population by Sex, Age, and Year of Entry: 2011. http:// www.census.gov/population/foreign/ data/cps2012.html, accessed 6/5/2014.

U.S. Bureau of the Census. (2012p). *The Statistical Abstract of the United States.* http://www.census.gov/compendia/ statab/2012/tables/12s0064.pdf (table 64), accessed 7/13/13.

U.S. Bureau of the Census. (2012q). Statistical Abstract 2012, Table 77. Christian Church Adherents, 2000, and Jewish Population, 2010—States. http://www. census.gov/compendia/statab/2012/ tables/12s0077.pdf, accessed 7/1/14.

U.S. Bureau of the Census. (2013a). America's Families and Living Arrangements: 2012. http://www.census.gov/ prod/2013pubs/p20-570.pdf, accessed 4/3/14.

U.S. Bureau of the Census. (2013b). America's Families and Living Arrangements: 2013: Children, table C3. http:// www.census.gov/hhes/families/data/ cps2013C.html, accessed 4/4/14.

U.S. Bureau of the Census. (2013c). America's families and living arrangements: 2013, table A1. https://www.census.gov/hhes/ families/data/cps2013A.html, accessed 9/3/13.

U.S. Bureau of the Census. (2013d). Current Population Survey Data on Families and Living Arrangements. http://www. census.gov/hhes/families/data/cps. html, accessed 4/15/14.

U.S. Bureau of the Census. (2013e). *The diversifying electorate—voting rates by race and Hispanic origin in 2012 (and other recent elections).* http://www.census.gov/ prod/2013pubs/p20-568.pdf, accessed 11/3/13.

U.S. Bureau of the Census. (2013f). Educational attainment in the United States. http://www.census.gov/hhes/socdemo/ education/data/cps/2012/tables.html, accessed 7/25/13.

U.S. Bureau of the Census. (2013g). *Frequently Asked Questions About Same-Sex Couple Households.* Fertility and Family Statistics Branch. http://www.census. gov/hhes/samesex/files/SScplfactsheet_ final.pdf, accessed November 1, 2013.

U.S. Bureau of the Census. (2013h). Historical Income Tables: Households. http:// www.census.gov/hhes/www/income/ data/historical/household/, accessed 3/25/14.

U.S. Bureau of the Census. (2013i). Households and Families: 2010. http://www. census.gov/prod/cen2010/briefs/ c2010br-14.pdf, accessed 8/27/13.

U.S. Bureau of the Census. (2013j). Household relationship and living arrangements of children under 18 years, by age and sex, 2013. http://www.census.gov/ hhes/families/data/cps2013C.html, accessed 4/4/14.

U.S. Bureau of the Census. (2013k). *Income, Poverty, and Health Insurance in the United States: 2012.* http://www.census.

gov/prod/2013pubs/p60-245.pdf, accessed 4/2/14.

U.S. Bureau of the Census. (2013l). Mean earnings of workers 18 years and over, by educational attainment, race, Hispanic origin, and sex: 1975 to 2011. http://www.census.gov/hhes/socdemo/education/data/cps/historical/tabA-3.xls, accessed 8/25/13.

U.S. Bureau of the Census. (2013m). Median value of assets for households, by type of asset owned and selected characteristics: 2011. http://www.census.gov/people/wealth/files/Wealth_Tables_2011.xlsx, accessed 8/23/13.

U.S. Bureau of the Census. (2013n). Percent of People 25 years and over who have completed high school or college, table A-2. http://www.census.gov/hhes/socdemo/education/data/cps/historical/index.html, accessed 5/22/14.

U.S. Bureau of the Census. (2013o). Poverty status of people by family relationship, race, and Hispanic origin: 1959 to 2012. http://census.gov/hhes/www/poverty/data/historical/hstpov2.xls, accessed 4/2/14.

U.S. Bureau of the Census. (2013p). Social and economic characteristics of currently unmarried women with a recent birth: 2011. http://www.census.gov/prod/2013pubs/acs-21.pdf, accessed 8/27/13.

U.S. Bureau of the Census. (2013q). The statistical abstract of the United States. Table 67, family groups with children under 18 years old by race and Hispanic origin: 2000 to 2011. Washington, DC: U.S. Bureau of the Census.

U.S. Bureau of the Census. (2013r). Urban, urbanized area, urban cluster, and rural population, 2010 and 2000: United States. http://www.census.gov/geo/reference/ua/urban-rural-2010.html, accessed 11/14/13.

U.S. Bureau of the Census. (2013s). Years of school completed by people 25 years and over, by age and sex: Selected years 1940 to 2012. http://www.census.gov/hhes/socdemo/education/data/cps/historical/tabA-1.xls

U.S. Bureau of the Census. (2014). U.S. and World Population Clock. https://www.census.gov/popclock/, accessed 3/7/14.

U.S. Courts. (2008). Costs of imprisonment far exceed supervision costs. www.uscourts.gov/newsroom/2009/costsOfImprisonment.cfm, accessed July 2009.

U.S. Department of Agriculture. (2013). How is rural America changing? http://www.census.gov/newsroom/cspan/rural_america/20130524_rural_america_slides.pdf, accessed 11/14/13.

U.S. Department of Education. (2006). The Condition of Education. http://nces.ed.gov/pubs2006/2006071.pdf, accessed 2/19/14.

U.S. Department of Education. (2008). *1.5 million homeschooled students in the United States in 2007.* Washington, DC: Institute of Education Sciences (December 2008). http://nces.ed.gov/pubs2009/2009030.pdf, accessed 8/28/11.

U.S. Department of Education. (2011). *Digest of education statistics 2011.* Washington, DC: National Center for Education Statistics. http://nces.ed.gov/pubs2012/2012001_0.pdf, accessed 8/13/13.

U. S. Department of Health and Human Services. (2004). *Child abuse and neglect fatalities: Statistics and interventions.* National Clearinghouse on Child Abuse and Neglect Information. http://nccanch.acf.hhs.gov/pubs/factsheets/fatality.cfm, accessed spring 2006.

U.S. Department of Health and Human Services. (2010). Healthy People 2020. http://www.healthypeople.gov/2020/Consortium/HP2020Framework.pdf, accessed 12/8/13.

U.S. Department of Health and Human Services. (2012a). Child maltreatment 2011. Washington, DC: Administration on Children, Youth and Families Children's Bureau. http://www.acf.hhs.gov/sites/default/files/cb/cm11.pdf, accessed 9/3/13.

U.S. Department of Health and Human Services. (2012b). Profile of older Americans. http://www.aoa.gov/AoARoot/Aging_Statistics/Profile/2012/10.aspx, accessed 8/25/13.

U.S. Department of Health and Human Services. (2012c). Results from the 2011 National Survey on Drug Use and Health: Mental health findings. Rockville, MD: Substance Abuse and Mental Health Services Administration. http://www.samhsa.gov/data/NSDUH/2k11MH_FindingsandDetTables/2K11MHFR/NSDUHmhfr2011.pdf, accessed 8/19/13.

U.S. Department of Health and Human Services. (2013). Annual update of the HHS poverty guidelines. *Federal Register* 78(16): 5182–5183. http://www.gpo.gov/fdsys/pkg/FR-2013-01-24/pdf/2013-01422.pdf, accessed 8/25/13.

U.S. Department of Housing and Urban Development. (2012). The 2011 annual homeless assessment report to Congress. https://www.onecpd.info/resources/documents/2011AHAR_FinalReport.pdf, accessed 8/25/13.

U.S. Department of Labor. (2012). *The Latino Labor Force at a Glance.* http://www.dol.gov/_sec/media/reports/HispanicLaborForce/HispanicLaborForce.pdf, accessed 2/20/14.

U.S. Department of Labor. (2013). Minimum wage laws in the states—January 1, 2013. http://www.dol.gov/whd/minwage/america.htm, accessed 8/25/13.

U.S. House of Representatives. (2013a). Black Americans in congress: Member profiles. http://history.house.gov/Exhibitions-and-Publications/BAIC/Black-Americans-in-Congress/, accessed 8/23/13.

U.S. House of Representatives. (2013b). House press gallery: Hispanic Americans. http://housepressgallery.house.gov/member-data/demographics/hispanic-americans, accessed 8/23/13.

United States Election Project. (2014). United States Election Project, George Mason University. http://elections.gmu.edu/voter_turnout.htm, accessed 3/30/14.

University of Michigan Institute for Social Research. (2008). www.nsf.gov/discoveries/disc_summ.jsp?cntn_id=111458, accessed 8/16/11.

van der Veer, P. (1994). *Religious nationalism: Hindus and Muslims in India.* Berkeley: University of California Press.

van Gennep, A. (1977; orig. 1908). *The rites of passage.* London: Routledge and Kegan Paul.

Vanneman, R. and L. W. Cannon. (1987). *The American perception of class.* Philadelphia: Temple University Press.

Vedantam, S. and D. Schultz. (2013). 'Stand Your Ground' Linked To Increase In Homicides. *National Public Radio* (January 2, 2013). http://www.npr.org/2013/01/02/167984117/-stand-your-ground-linked-to-increase-in-homicide, accessed 9/24/13.

Venkatesh, S. (2008). *Gang leader for a day: A rogue sociologist takes to the streets.* New York: Penguin.

Vincent, N. (2006). *Self-made man: One woman's year disguised as a man.* New York: Penguin.

Vitello, P. (2011). You Say God Is Dead? There's an App for That. *The New York Times* (July 2, 2010). http://www.nytimes.com/2010/07/03/technology/03atheist.html?_r=0, accessed 2/19/2014.

Vocativ. (2013). Peace Corps Applications Lowest in a Decade: Doing Good is Great but Young People Want Jobs. *Vocative* (March 21, 213). http://www.vocativ.com/03-2013/peace-corps-applications-lowest-in-a-decade-doing-good-is-great-but-young-people-want-jobs/, accessed 8/21/13.

Wacquant, L. (1993). Redrawing the urban color line: The state of the ghetto in the 1980s. In Craig Calhoun and George Ritzer (Eds.), *Social problems.* New York: McGraw-Hill.

Wacquant, L. (1996). The rise of advanced marginality: Notes on its nature and implications. *Acta Sociologica, 39*(2).

Wacquant, L. and W. J. Wilson. (1993). The cost of racial and class exclusion in the inner city. In W. J. Wilson (Ed.), *The ghetto underclass: Social science perspectives*. Newbury Park, CA: Sage.

Wagar, W. (1992). *A short history of the future*. Chicago: University of Chicago Press.

Wagner, Rachel. (2011). *Godwired: Religion, ritual and virtual reality*. New York: Routledge.

Wagner-Wright, S. (2006). *Birth, marriage, honor & poverty: Ramifications of traditional Hindu culture & custom on modern Indian women*. Oxford, UK: Forum on Public Policy.

Wagstaff, K. (2012). Men Are from Google+, Women Are from Pinterest. *Time* (February 15, 2012). http://techland.time.com/2012/02/15/men-are-from-google-women-are-from-pinterest/#ixzz2hiZG4YA7, accessed 10/14/13.

Wagstaff, K. (2013). China's massive pollution problem. *The Week*. http://theweek.com/article/index/252440/chinas-massive-pollution-problem, accessed 3/7/14.

Waldron, I. (1986). Why do women live longer than men? In P. Conrad and R. Kern (Eds.), *The sociology of health and illness*. New York: St. Martin's.

Wallace, N. (2011, March 16). Response to Japan disaster lags donor response to other recent catastrophes. *Chronicle of Philanthropy*. http://philanthropy.com/article/Response-to-Japan-Disaster/126760/, accessed 8/29/11.

Wallerstein, I. (1974a). *Capitalist agriculture and the origins of the European world-economy in the sixteenth century*. New York: Academic Press.

Wallerstein, I. (1974b). *The modern world-system*. New York: Academic Press.

Wallerstein, I. (1979). *The capitalist world economy*. Cambridge, UK: Cambridge University Press.

Wallerstein, I. (1990). *The modern world-system II*. New York: Academic Press.

Wallerstein, I. (1996a). *Historical capitalism with capitalist civilization*. New York: Norton.

Wallerstein, I. (Ed.). (1996b). *World inequality*. St. Paul, MN: Consortium Books.

Wallerstein, J. and J. Kelly. (1980). *Surviving the breakup: How children and parents cope with divorce*. New York: Basic Books.

Wallraff, B. (2000). What global language? *Atlantic Monthly* (November). http://www.theatlantic.com/past/docs/issues/2000/11/wallraff.htm

Walmsley, R. (2009). *World prison population list*. (8th ed.). International Centre for Prison Studies, Kings College London. www.kcl.ac.uk/depsta/law/research/icps/downloads/wppl-8th_41.pdf, accessed 10/25/11.

Warikoo, Hiraj. (2013). Washington Township man held without bond after death of girlfriend's son, 2. *Detroit Free Press* (August 27, 2013). http://www.freep.com/article/20130827/NEWS04/308270054/child-abuse-boy-beaten-court-washington-twp, accessed 9/24/13.

Warner, St. (1993). Work in progress toward a new paradigm for the sociological study of religion in the United States. *American Journal of Sociology, 98*.

Warren, B. (1980). *Imperialism: Pioneer of capitalism*. London: Verso.

Waters, M. (1990). *Ethnic options: Choosing identities in America*. Berkeley: University of California Press.

Wattenberg, Martin P. (1996). *The decline of American political parties, 1952–1994* (Rev. ed.). Cambridge, MA: Harvard University Press.

Waxman, L. and S. Hinderliter. (1996). *A status report on hunger and homelessness in America's cities*. Washington, DC: U.S. Conference of Mayors.

Weber, Lauren. (2013). How Your Smartphone Could Get You a Job. *Wall Street Journal* (April 24, 2013). http://online.wsj.com/news/articles/SB10001424127887323551004578441130657837720, accessed 3/17/14.

Weber, M. (1947). *The theory of social and economic organization*. New York: Free Press.

Weber, M. (1963; orig. 1921). *The sociology of religion*. Boston: Beacon Press.

Weber, M. (1977; orig. 1904). *The Protestant ethic and the spirit of capitalism*. New York: Macmillan.

Weber, M. (1979; orig. 1921). *Economy and society: An outline of interpretive sociology* (2 vols.). Berkeley: University of California Press.

The Week. (2010). The internet porn 'epidemic': By the numbers. *The Week* (June 17, 2010). http://theweek.com/article/index/204156/the-internet-porn-epidemic-by-the-numbers, accessed 12/9/13.

Weeks, J. (1977). *Coming out: Homosexual politics in Britain, from the nineteenth century to the present*. New York: Quartet.

Weil, E. (2006). What if It's (Sort of) a Boy and (Sort of) a Girl? *New York Times* (September 24, 2006). http://www.nytimes.com/2006/09/24/magazine/24intersexkids.html?pagewanted=all, accessed 10/12/13.

Weitzman, L., et al. (1972). Sexual socialization in picture books for preschool children. *American Journal of Sociology, 77*.

Wellman, B. (2008). What is the Internet doing to community—and vice-versa? In T. Haas (Ed.), *New urbanism and beyond*, pp. 239–242. Milan: Rizzoli.

Wellman, B., P. Carrington, and A. Hall. (1988). Networks as personal communities. In B. Wellman and S. D. Berkowitz (Eds.), *Social structures: A network approach*. New York: Cambridge University Press.

Wellman, B., et al. (1996). Computer networks as social networks: Collaborative work, telework, and virtual community. *Annual Review of Sociology, 22*.

Weltzin, T. E., et al. (2005). Eating disorders in men: Update. *Journal of Men's Health & Gender, 2*(2), 186–191.

West, C. and S. Fenstermaker. (1995). Doing difference. *Gender & Society, 9*(1).

West, C. and D. H. Zimmerman. (1987). Doing gender. *Gender & Society, 1*(2), 125–151.

Western, B. (1997). *Between class and market: Postwar unionization in the capitalist democracies*. Princeton, NJ: Princeton University Press.

Western, B. and K. Beckett. (1999). How unregulated is the U.S. labor market?: The penal system as a labor market institution. *American Journal of Sociology, 104*(4).

Wetzel, M. S., D. M. Eisenberg and T. J. Kaptchuk. (1998). Courses involving complementary and alternative medicine at US medical schools. *Journal of the American Medical Association, 280*(9), 784–787.

Wheary, J., et al. (2010). *By a thread: The new experience of America's middle class*. New York: Demos and Institute on Assets and Social Policy at Brandeis University. http://iasp.brandeis.edu/pdfs/byathread_web.pdf, accessed 8/31/11.

Wheatley, P. (1971). *The pivot of the four quarters*. Edinburgh: Edinburgh University Press.

Wheeler, D. L., T. M. Harrison, and T. Stephen. (2006). *The Internet in the Middle East: Global Expectations and Local Imaginations in Kuwait*. Albany: SUNY Press.

Widom, C. and J. Newman. (1985). Characteristics of non-institutionalized psychopaths. In D. P. Farrington and J. Gunn (Eds.), *Aggression and dangerousness*. Chichester, UK: Wiley.

Will, J. and N. Datan. (1976). Maternal behavior and perceived sex of infant. *American Journal of Orthopsychiatry, 46*.

Williams, C. (1992). The glass escalator: Hidden advantages for men in the "female" professions. *Social Problems, 39*.

Williams, S. (1993). *Chronic respiratory illness*. London: Routledge.

Wilson, E. (1975). *Sociobiology: The new synthesis*. Cambridge, MA: Harvard University Press.

Wilson, J. Q. and G. Kelling. (1982). Broken windows. *Atlantic Monthly* (March 1, 1982).

Wilson, W. (1978). *The declining significance of race: Blacks and changing American institutions.* Chicago: University of Chicago Press.

Wilson, W. (1991, February). Studying inner-city social dislocations: The challenge of public agenda research. *American Sociological Review, 56.*

Wilson, W. (1996). *When work disappears: The world of the new urban poor.* New York: Knopf.

Wilson, W., et al. (1987). The changing structure of urban poverty. Paper presented at the annual meeting of the American Sociological Association.

Winkleby, M., et al. (1992). Socioeconomic status and health: How education, income, and occupation contribute to risk factors for cardiovascular disease. *American Journal of Public Health, 82.*

Wirth, L. (1938, July). Urbanism as a way of life. *American Sociological Review, 44.*

Witkowski, S. and C. Brown. (1982). Whorf and universals of number nomenclature. *Journal of Anthropological Research, 38.*

Women in National Parliaments (WNP). (2013a). Women in parliaments: World and regional averages. http://www.ipu.org/wmn-e/world.htm, accessed 9/6/2013.

Women in National Parliaments (WNP). (2013b). Women in parliaments: World classification. www.ipu.org/wmn-e/classif.htm, accessed 9/6/13.

Wong, S. (1986). Modernization and Chinese culture in Hong Kong. *Chinese Quarterly, 106.*

WorldatWork. (2011). Telework 2011: A WorldatWork Special Report. www .worldatwork.org/waw/adimLink?id= 53034, accessed 7/10/11.

World Bank. (1997). *World development report 1997: The state in a changing world.* New York: Oxford University Press.

World Bank. (1999). *International Bank for Reconstruction and Development.* World Development Indicators 1999. Washington, DC: World Bank.

World Bank. (2000). World Development Report. New York: Oxford University Press.

World Bank. (2000–2001). World Development Indicators. In *World Development Report 2000–2001: Attacking Poverty.* http://poverty.worldbank.org/library/topic/3389/, accessed 1/4/05.

World Bank. (2001). PovertyNet: Topics relevant to social capital.

World Bank. (2005). World Development Indicators 2005. http://devdata.worldbank.org/wdi2005/cover.htm, accessed spring 2006.

World Bank. (2010). Urban population (% of total). http://data.worldbank.org/indicator/SP.URB.TOTL.IN.ZS?display=graph, accessed 8/23/11.

World Bank. (2012a). Knowledge Economy Index (KEI) 2012 Rankings. http://siteresources.worldbank.org/

INTUNIKAM/Resources/2012.pdf, accessed 3/30/14.

World Bank (2012b). Mortality Rate, Infant (Per 1,000 Live Births). http://data.worldbank.org/indicator/SP.DYN.IMRT.IN, accessed 1/28/14.

World Bank. (2012c). An Update to the World Bank's Estimates of Consumption Poverty in the Developing World. Washington, DC: The World Bank. http://siteresources.worldbank.org/INTPOVCALNET/Resources/Global_Poverty_Update_2012_02-29-12.pdf, accessed 6/21/13.

World Bank. (2012d). Women are less likely than men to participate in the labor market in most countries. http://data.worldbank.org/news/women-less-likely-than-men-to-participate-in-labor-market, accessed 2/20/14.

World Bank (2012e). The World Bank: GDP. http://data.worldbank.org/indicator/NY.GDP.MKTP.CD?order=wbapi_data_value_2012+wbapi_data_value+wbapi_data_value-last&sort=desc, accessed 1/28/14.

World Bank. (2013a). How we classify countries. http://data.worldbank.org/about/country-classifications, accessed 8/20/13.

World Bank. (2013b). Income Share Held by Highest 10%. data.worldbank.org/indicator, accessed 6/12/14.

World Bank. (2013c). Remarkable Declines in Global Poverty, But Major Challenges Remain (April 17, 2013). http://www.worldbank.org/en/news/press-release/2013/04/17/remarkable-declines-in-global-poverty-but-major-challenges-remain, accessed 2/9/14.

World Bank. (2013d). World Development Indicators. http://data.worldbank.org/indicator, accessed 3/26/14.

World Bank. (2013e). World Development Indicators, "Passenger Cars (per 1,000 People)." http://data.worldbank.org/indicator/IS.VEH.PCAR.P3, accessed 6/20/13.

World Bank. (2014a). GDP Growth (Annual %). http://data.worldbank.org/indicator/NY.GDP.MKTP.KD.ZG, accessed 1/3/14.

World Bank. (2014b). GNI Per Capita, Atlas Method (Current US$). http://databank.worldbank.org/data/views/reports/tableview.aspx, accessed 4/4/14.

World Bank. (2014c). Poverty Overview. www.worldbank.org/en/topic/poverty/overview, accessed 05/23/14.

World Health Organization (WHO). (2000). What is female genital mutilation? www.who.int/mediacentre/factsheets/fs241/en/print.html, accessed 12/4/05.

World Health Organization (WHO). (2010). The world health report: Health systems financing: The path to universal coverage. Geneva: World Health

Organization. http://whqlibdoc.who.int/whr/2010/9789241564021_eng.pdf, accessed 12/10/13.

World Health Organization (WHO). (2014). Urban population growth. http://www.who.int/gho/urban_health/situation_trends/urban_population_growth_text/en/, accessed 2/8/14.

Worldsteel.org. (2012). Steel production 2012. http://www.worldsteel.org/statistics/statistics-archive/2012-steel-production.html, accessed 11/2/13.

World Trade Organization (WTO). (2011). World Trade Report 2011. http://www.wto.org/english/res_e/booksp_e/anrep_e/world_trade_report11_e.pdf, accessed 1/28/14.

Worldwatch Institute. 2012. *Vital Signs.* http://www.worldwatch.org/vitalsigns2012, accessed 1/4/14.

Worrall, A. (1990). *Offending women: Female lawbreakers and the criminal justice system.* London: Routledge.

Wortham, Jenny. (2013). Tinder: A Dating App with a Difference. *The New York Times* (February 26, 2013). http://bits.blogs.nytimes.com/2013/02/26/tinder-a-dating-app-with-a-difference/?_r=0, accessed 5/26/13.

Wray, L., et al. (1998). The impact of education and heart attack on smoking cessation among middle-aged adults. *Journal of Health and Social Behavior, 39(4),* 271–294.

Wrigley, E. (1968). *Population and history.* New York: McGraw-Hill.

Wuthnow, R. (1988). Sociology of religion. In N. J. Smelser (Ed.), *Handbook of sociology.* Newbury Park, CA: Sage.

Yardley, Jim. (2011). In One Slum, Misery, Work, Politics and Hope. *The New York Times* (December 28, 2011). http://www.nytimes.com/2011/12/29/world/asia/in-indian-slum-misery-work-politics-and-hope.html?pagewanted=all&_r=0, accessed 1/3/14.

Yongqiang, Gu. (2013). The cost of cleaning China's filthy air? About $817 billion, one official says. *Time* (September 25, 2013). http://world.time.com/2013/09/25/the-cost-of-cleaning-chinas-filthy-air-about-817-billion-one-official-says/#ixzz2pMUvXP3t, accessed 1/3/14.

Yousafzai, Malala and Christina Lamb. (2013). *I am malala: The girl who stood up for education and was shot by the Taliban.* New York: Little, Brown & Company.

Youthkiawaz.com. (2010). Dowry in India: Putting the Institution of Marriage at Stake. www.youthkiawaaz.com/2010/08/dowry-in-india-putting-the-institution-of-marriage-at-stake/, accessed 8/8/11.

Zammuner, V. L. (1986). Children's sex-role stereotypes: A cross-cultural analysis. In P. Shaver and C. Hendrick (Eds.), *Sex and gender*. Beverly Hills, CA: Sage.

Zee News. (2007). 1 Dowry death every 4 hrs in India. www.zeenews.com/news414869.html, accessed July 2009.

Zerubavel, E. (1979). *Patterns of time in hospital life*. Chicago: University of Chicago Press.

Zerubavel, E. (1982). The standardization of time: A sociohistorical perspective. *American Journal of Sociology, 88*.

Zickuhr, Kathryn. (2013). *Who's Not Online and Why?* Pew Research Center (September 25, 2013). http://www.pewinternet.org/~/media//Files/Reports/2013/PIP_Offline%20adults_092513_PDF.pdf, accessed 10/12/13.

Zimbardo, P. (1969). The human choice: Individuation, reason, and order versus deindividuation, impulse, and chaos. In W. J. Arnold and D. Levine (Eds.), *Nebraska symposium on motivation* (Vol. 17.). Lincoln: University of Nebraska Press.

Zimbardo, P. (1972). *The psychology of imprisonment: Privation, power and pathology*. Stanford, CA: Stanford University.

Zimbardo, P., E. B. Ebbesen, and C. Maslach. (1977). *Influencing attitudes and changing behavior*. Reading, MA: Addison-Wesley.

Zuboff, S. (1988). *In the age of the smart machine: The future of work and power*. New York: Basic Books.

credits

index

assimilation, 51, 299
atheism, 386
Athens, ancient, 194
attachment (control theory), 167
audience segregation, 110–12
authority, obedience to, 136–37

B

bacha posh tradition, 264
Bachmann, Michele, 277
background expectancies, 114
Back Off Bully, 10
Baptists, 384
Barnes, T. Hayden, 111–12
Baudrillard, Jean, 18–19
Bay of Pigs invasion, 138
beauty, cultural definitions of, 49
Becker, Howard S., 168
belief (control theory), 167
Bell, Daniel, 17
Bell Curve, The (Herrnstein and
    Murray), 369
berdaches, 264–65
between-school effects, 366–67
Bhopal disaster, 177
BibleThumper, 388
biology
    deviance and, 161–62
    gender and, 259–60
    human nature and, 48–49
birth control, 385
black feminism, 286
"blame the victim" and "blame the
    system" theories, 223–24
Blau, Peter M.
    The American Occupational Structure
        (with Duncan), 17
    on intergenerational mobility, 214–15
blue-collar workers, 210
Blumer, Herbert, 104
body type, crime and, 162
Bono (musician and philanthropist), 99, 207
Booker, Cory, 309
Boo (schoolchild), 72–74, 260
Borochoff, Daniel, 233
Bourdieu, Pierre
    on cultural capital, 215
    Distinction, 17
bourgeoisie, 198–99
Bowles, Samuel, 368
Bowling Alone (Putnam), 150
Braithwaite, John, 187
Breaking Night (Murray), 194
breast implants, 177–78
broken windows theory, 185
Brown, Devin, 4, 5
Brown, Jill, 10
Brownmiller, Susan, 281
*Brown v. Board of Education of Topeka,
    Kansas,* 309

Buddhism, 382
Buffett, Warren, 240
bullying
    Internet and, 10, 28
    teenage suicide and, 3, 4–5
Bumpass, Larry, 350
bureaucracies
    alternatives to bureaucracy model:
        McDonaldization of society,
        148–49; recent management
        trends, 145–46
    democracy and, 143
    formal and informal relations in, 142–43
    overview, 141–42
Bush, George W., 370
busing, 369
Byrnes, Doyle, 112

C

Calibuso, Judy, 257–58, 272, 287
Calvinism, 376
Cambodian genocide, 299
capitalism
    ethnic conflict and, 300
    market-oriented theories of global
        inequality and, 244–45, 249, 251
    Marx on, 12, 13
capitalists (bourgeoisie), 198–99
capital punishment, 180–81
Carmichael, Stokely, 295
Castells, Manuel
    End of Millennium, 179
    *The Information Age: Economy, Society,
        and Culture,* 17
caste systems, 197
Castles, Stephen, 302
Castro, Fidel, 138
Catholics
    contraception and, 385
    political views of, 389
    social justice movements and, 382–83
    socioeconomic status of, 387
Causes of Delinquency (Hirschi), 167
cell phone subscriptions, 113
Challenger disaster, 138
Champion, Robert, 129–30
charitable giving, 232–33
charter schools, 371
Cheerios commercial, 291–92
Cherlin, Andrew, 338, 345
Chicano, as term, 310
child care. *See* parenting
childhood
    as life course stage, 85–86
    socialization and development: agents
        of socialization, 77–80; overview,
        72–75
    theories of development: Mead and
        self-awareness, 75–76; Piaget
        and cognitive stages, 76–77

children
    abuse of, 347–48
    divorce and, 343–45
    labor of, in developing world, 246
    poverty and, 221–22
Child Support Calculator, 344
China, population control programs in, 333
Chinese Americans, 305, 306, 311, 312
Chinese Empire, 59
Chua, Amy, 300
churches, 379
civil inattention, 104–5
class, social. *See also* poverty; stratification,
    social
    family patterns and, 340–41
    inequality and: conclusion, 226–27; drug
        use, 176; gap between rich and poor,
        212–14; new criminology, 167–68;
        social mobility, 214–16
    introduction, 192–94
    levels: lower class, 211; middle class,
        209–10; underclass, 211–12; upper
        class, 207, 209; working class, 211
    religious affiliation and, 387, 389
    as type of stratification system, 197–98
    ways of defining: education, 205–7;
        income, 202–4; occupation, 207,
        208; wealth, 204–5
class conflict (in Marxism), 16, 18
class inequality. *See* social inequality
Clementi, Tyler, 4, 5, 10, 32
Clinton, Chelsea, 215
Clinton, Hillary, 277
clitoridectomy, 52, 280
clock time, 119–20
Cloward, Richard A., 165, 166
coalitions, 133
coffee drinking, 6–7
cognition (definition of term), 75
cognitive development, 76–77
cohabitation, 336, 349–51
Cohen, Albert, 165, 166
Coleman, James, 366–67, 369
college majors, 267
Collins, Randall, 361
colonialism
    dependency theory and, 245–46
    education and, 362
    ethnic diversity and, 303
    racism and, 298–99
    as shaping force, 61
Columbus, Christopher, 303
*Coming of Post-Industrial Society,
    The* (Bell), 17
Coming White Minority, The
    (Maharidge), 307
commitment (control theory), 167
Communist Manifesto (Marx and
    Engels), 17
community policing, 185, 187

index of infographics

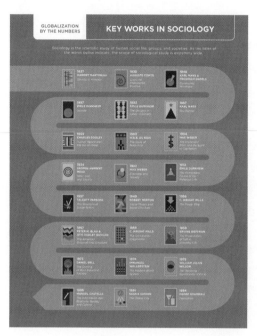

Key Works in Sociology
Chapter 1, Page 17

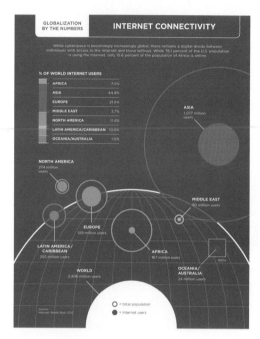

Internet Connectivity
Chapter 2, Page 67

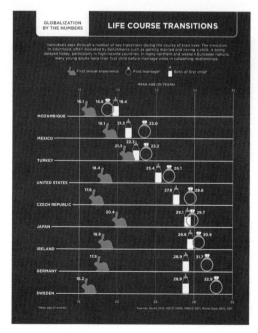

Life Course Transitions
Chapter 3, Page 87

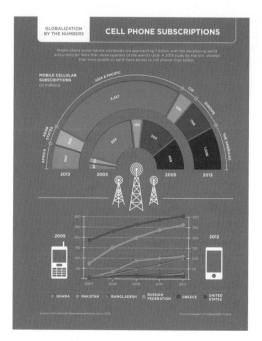

Cell Phone Subscriptions
Chapter 4, Page 113

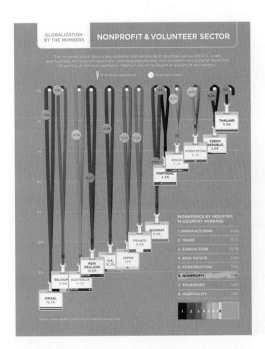

Nonprofit and Volunteer Sector
Chapter 5, Page 151

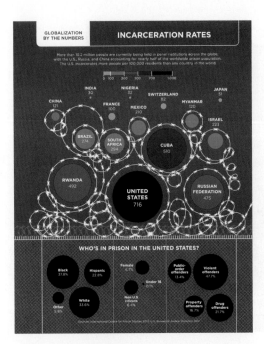

Incarceration Rates
Chapter 6, Page 183

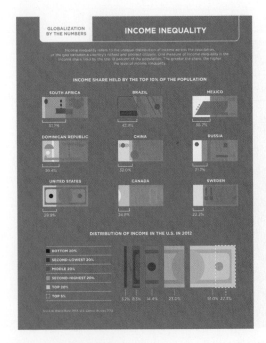

Income Inequality
Chapter 7, Page 203

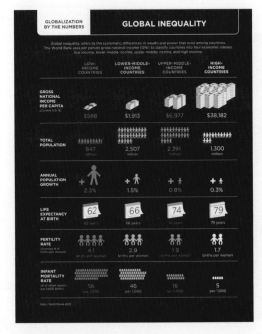

Global Inequality
Chapter 8, Page 235

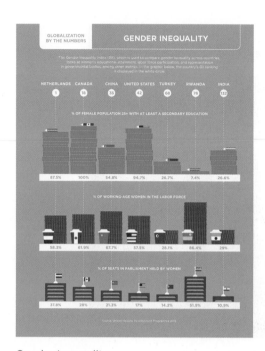

Gender Inequality
Chapter 9, Page 279

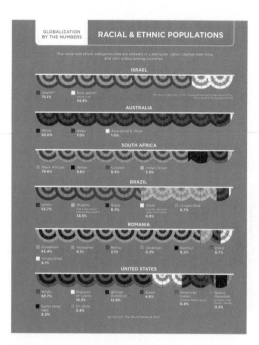

Racial & Ethnic Populations
Chapter 10, Page 301

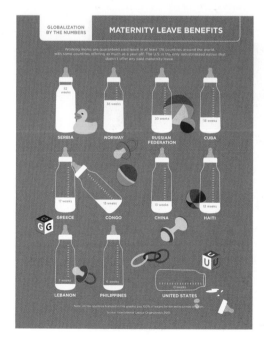

Maternity Leave Benefits
Chapter 11, Page 335

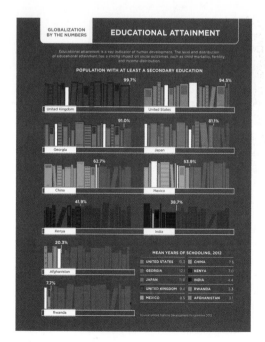

Educational Attainment
Chapter 12, Page 363

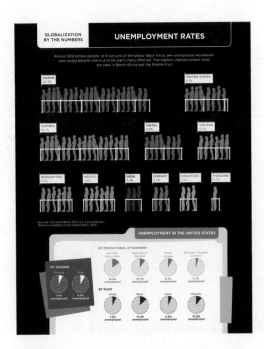

Unemployment Rates
Chapter 13, Page 425

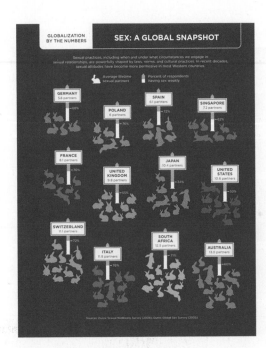

Sex: A Global Snapshot
Chapter 14, Page 453

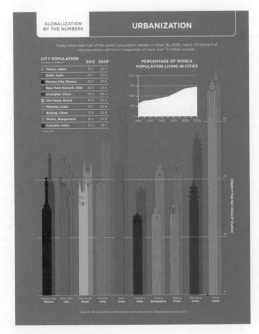

Urbanization
Chapter 15, Page 481

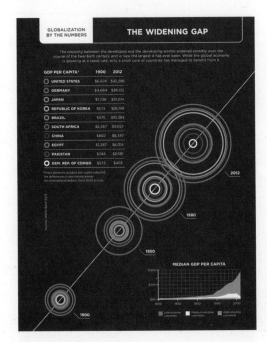

The Widening Gap
Chapter 16, Page 531